**Essential Papers on Jewish Culture
in Renaissance and Baroque Italy**

ESSENTIAL PAPERS ON JEWISH CULTURE IN RENAISSANCE AND BAROQUE ITALY

Edited by
David B. Ruderman

New York University Press
New York and London

NEW YORK UNIVERSITY PRESS
New York and London

Library of Congress Cataloging-in-Publication Data
Essential papers on Jewish culture in Renaissance and baroque Italy /
edited by David B. Ruderman.
p. cm. — (Essential papers on Jewish studies)
Includes bibliographical references and index.
ISBN 0–8147–7419–9 (cloth : acid-free paper) : —ISBN
0–8147–7420–2 (paper : acid-free paper)
1. Judaism—Italy—History. 2. Jews—Italy—Intellectual life.
3. Renaissance—Italy. 4. Italy—Ethnic relations. I. Ruderman,
David B. II. Series.
BM322.E87 1992
296'.0945—dc20 91–33352
CIP

10 0 0 0 2 2 6 0 1 5

New York University Press books are printed on acid-free paper,
and their binding materials are chosen for strength and durability.

Manufactured in the United States of America

c 10 9 8 7 6 5 4 3 2 1
p 10 9 8 7 6 5 4 3 2 1

For my son, Noah, with affection

Contents

Acknowledgments   ix

Introduction   1
David B. Ruderman

I JEWISH CULTURE AND THE RENAISSANCE

A. New Forms of Hebrew Literary Execution: Rhetoric, Humanism, and the Jewish Sermon

1. Jewish Adaptation of Humanist Concepts in Fifteenth- and Sixteenth-Century Italy   45
   Arthur M. Lesley

2. *Ars Rhetorica* as Reflected in Some Jewish Figures of the Italian Renaissance   63
   Alexander Altmann

3. Italian Jewish Preaching: An Overview   85
   Marc Saperstein

B. The Jewish Encounter with Magic, Ancient Theology, and Neoplatonism

4. The Magical and Neoplatonic Interpretations of the Kabbalah in the Renaissance   107
   Moshe Idel

5. The Place of the *Dialoghi d'amore* in Contemporaneous Jewish Thought   170
   Arthur M. Lesley

C. Jewish Historical Writing in the Sixteenth Century

6. Clio and the Jews: Reflections on Jewish Historiography in
   the Sixteenth Century   191
   Yosef Hayim Yerushalmi

7. How Golden Was the Age of the Renaissance in Jewish
   Historiography?   219
   Robert Bonfil

8. Azariah de' Rossi and the Forgeries of Annius of Viterbo   252
   Joanna Weinberg

D. Sixteenth-Century Messianism and Kabbalah and Their
Transformations in Italy

9. Messianic Expectations and Spiritualization of Religious Life in
   the Sixteenth Century   283
   Rachel Elior

10. Hope against Hope: Jewish and Christian Messianic Expectations
    in the Late Middle Ages   299
    David B. Ruderman

11. Particularism and Universalism in Kabbalah, 1480–1650   324
    Moshe Idel

12. Major Currents in Italian Kabbalah between 1560 and 1660   345
    Moshe Idel

II JEWISH CULTURE IN THE SETTING OF THE GHETTO

A. The Significance of the Ghetto in Shaping Jewish Society
and Culture

13. From Geographical Realia to Historiographical Symbol: The
    Odyssey of the Word *Ghetto*   373
    Benjamin C. I. Ravid

14. The Consciousness of Closure: Roman Jewry and Its *Ghet*   386
    Kenneth R. Stow

15. Change in the Cultural Patterns of a Jewish Society in Crisis: Italian Jewry at the Close of the Sixteenth Century   401
Robert Bonfil

B. Cultural Trends in the Age of the Ghetto

16. Leone da Modena's *Riti:* A Seventeenth-Century Plea for Social Toleration of Jews   429
Mark R. Cohen

17. Tradition and Innovation in Jewish Music of the Later Renaissance   474
Don Harrán

18. Baroque Trends in Italian Hebrew Poetry as Reflected in an Unknown Genre   502
Dan Pagis

19. The Impact of Science on Jewish Culture and Society in Venice   519
David B. Ruderman

20. The Eve of the Circumcision: A Chapter in the History of Jewish Nightlife   554
Elliott Horowitz

Index   589

About the Editor   598

Acknowledgments

I wish to thank my colleagues Robert Bonfil, Moshe Idel, Benjamin Ravid, and Yosef Kaplan for reading a draft of my Introduction and for offering their wise and constructive criticisms. My discussions with Robert Bonfil over the Introduction and the shape of this volume were especially intense. While I have not accepted all of his provocative suggestions, I have profited immensely from this and earlier dialogues with him over the past twenty years. His significant impact on this and my earlier writing on the subject of Jewish culture in Renaissance and Baroque Italy is sincerely noted and deeply appreciated. My debts to other illustrious members of the scholarly community from which this volume emerges are duly acknowledged in the notes to my Introduction below.

In editing this volume, I have preserved each contributor's method of transliteration and other stylistic preferences. For certain chapters, I have also eliminated unnecessary appendixes and, where technically problematic, the Hebrew material.

Introduction

David B. Ruderman

To an earlier generation of students of Renaissance and baroque Italy, even as recently as some fifteen or twenty years ago, an entire book of essays devoted exclusively to the culture of its small Jewish minority might have appeared somewhat odd and anomalous. Renaissance studies had always been concerned with almost exclusively Christian, Latin, and eventually Italian cultural phenomena, grounded in the political realities of despotic or republican city-states, and produced by an elite political or clerical order. Still drawn primarily in the image of the nineteenth-century historian Jacob Burkhardt and his twentieth-century followers,[1] the central subjects of the Renaissance and the less studied baroque period were still the *condottieri*, the courtier culture as described by Baldassare Castiglione, the polymaths like Leon Battista Alberti and Leonardo da Vinci, the politics of Machiavelli and the Medici, and the painting, sculpture, architecture, music, and literature emanating from a predominantly male cultural elite patronized lavishly by princes and popes. The world of Jews in this same period seemed, at worst, totally irrelevant, and, at best, marginally represented by an occasional Jewish moneylender masking his Shylockian image, or by the even more mysterious presence of a Jewish astrologer satisfying sycophantically every whim and wish of his courtly benefactor. The overwhelming majority of Jews living in small communities throughout the northern and central regions of Italy during the Renaissance, and eventually concentrated in segregated ghettos from the mid-sixteenth century on, hardly appeared to inhabit a significant cultural space of their own, let alone to contribute to or interact with the Christian majority. Living under the

1

continuous threat of degradation and harassment that had marked their alien status within medieval civilization, and experiencing an even greater decline and marginalization by the erection of the ghetto walls, Italian Jews could hardly have been expected to produce a culture of inherent interest to any but a few Jewish antiquarians.

That this portrait of Italian Jewish culture in early modern Europe has been radically altered in recent years is the result of at least two factors patently related to each other. In the first place, a new preoccupation with popular culture, with the history of nonelite, seemingly marginal and powerless groups such as rural peasants, the urban poor, and women has revolutionized the ways we have come to think about the past in general and this period in particular, especially the manner in which "low" has influenced "high" culture, and the channels by which the two continuously interact with each other.[2] In the second place, the study of Jewish culture in this era has been dramatically enhanced by the extraordinary growth of Judaic studies first in Israel, and then throughout American and European universities, during the last twenty-five years. The emergence of a significant community of scholars, of scholarly books and journals in Hebrew and in Western languages, of conferences and graduate studies in the field of Italian Jewish culture and society is both an exciting by-product of the newly acquired status of Judaic studies within the academy of learning, as well as a part of the process of reevaluation within the humanities of what is worthy of study about the past.

Of course, the academic study of Jewish culture in Italy had evolved long before this most recent phase of Judaic studies. Jewish historians had long appreciated that Jewish cultural life in this region was considerably less sterile and less hermetically sealed off from the rest of Italy than one might initially assume. On the contrary, it constituted a historical subject of intrinsic interest and real fascination to such towering scholars of Jewish history and literature in the nineteenth and early twentieth centuries as Heinrich Graetz, Simon Dubnov, and Israel Zinberg, who shared Burkhardt's sense of enthusiasm for the Renaissance with its celebration of individualism and its emphasis on artistic creativity. They also discovered within the communities of Renaissance Italy a refreshing paradigm of Jewish enlightenment and cultural symbiosis with the outside world, traits they strongly perceived as lacking among their own co-religionists in Germany and especially in Eastern Europe.

Italian Jewish culture in the Renaissance and even into the seventeenth century provided them a model worthy of emulation for contemporary Jews still fettered, so they thought, by the bonds of obscurantism and medieval fanaticism.[3]

Their successors, like the polished Oxford historian Cecil Roth, and like the more modest student of Hebraic culture, Moses Avigdor Shulvass, were similarly attracted to the study of Italian Jewish culture for roughly the same reasons. Sharing a perspective of traditional Judaism that was predominantly Ashkenazic, often narrow, and generally intolerant of cultural change or pluralism, these more secularly inclined scholars were clearly enamored of the Italian Jewish environment that offered them a refreshingly different case study of a traditional Jewish society more open and more receptive to cultural change than that which they had intimately known. In holding up a single monolithic concept of Jewish traditional society and by generally approaching Renaissance culture from a superficial and overly romantic Burkhardtian perspective (Shulvass even patterned his own chapters after those of Burkhardt), their idealized portrait of Jewish culture in the Renaissance was imprecise, unbalanced, and highly apologetic. Equally inaccurate was their depiction of the decline of Jewish culture in the age of the ghetto, the supposed lessening of cultural liaisons with the outside world engendered by the harsh policies of Counter-Reformation popes, and the apparent denouement of Italian Jewish life as one of cultural stagnation and impoverishment roughly comparable to that of its Ashkenazic counterparts. By maintaining a fundamental opposition between a traditional Jewish culture, antirationalistic and unreceptive to external culture, and an open, rational, tolerant Renaissance culture, they tended to distort the nature of Jewish culture in both its medieval and early modern settings, as well as the complex and heterogeneous character of Renaissance and baroque civilizations. The history of Jewish culture was often reduced to a treatment of the supposed tension between the core and shell, the original essence and its external borrowings, legalistic talmudists versus enlightened philosophers, obscurantist kabbalists versus creative artists and musicians, a conservative rabbinic establishment versus a free-spirited class of private Jewish literati, or the *volksgeist* of Judaism versus the *zeitgeist* of the Renaissance era.[4]

This same perspective still dominated the histories of Italian Jewish culture produced as late as the 1960s. Shlomo Simonsohn, in his massive study of Jewish society in the Duchy of Mantua, and Isaac Barzilay in his treatment of antirationalistic tendencies among certain Italian thinkers, both assumed that Jewish traditional values stood in continuing tension with external culture, and that the Renaissance ambiance ultimately accelerated centrifugal assimilatory forces eroding the traditional values and life-styles of Italian Jews. Only with the institution of ghetto segregation were these forces curtailed and eventually arrested.[5]

More recently, a group of younger scholars has begun to view the emergence of Jewish culture in the Renaissance and the ghetto periods from a more nuanced perspective.[6] Some have examined more closely the relationship between Jewish and various strands of Renaissance culture, especially humanism and Neoplatonism. Others have described more precisely the transformation of the *kabbalah*, the traditions of Jewish esoterism, within the Italian ambiance, its critical mediating function between Jews and Christians, and its merger with ancient pagan philosophies and magic. Others have reexamined the place of historical writing within sixteenth-century Jewish culture. Still others have rethought the causes and significance of messianic currents within the Jewish community. Most significant of all, an entire reevaluation of the effect of ghetto segregation in transforming Jewish cultural activity has recently begun. Rather than viewing the ghetto era in Jewish history as merely a belated expression of "Renaissance" trends, or as marking a serious decline and closure, some scholars have considered the period of the late sixteenth and seventeenth centuries as a watershed, releasing, rather than stifling, new cultural energies and incipiently modern attitudes, or, at the very least, further stimulating those already set in motion during the Renaissance. All of this new work has forced these new researchers to reexamine the issue of periodization: What precisely do the terms *Renaissance, ghetto, baroque* or *early modern* mean when applied to Jewish history? In what ways did the Renaissance and the ghetto era initiate a process of restructuring a medieval and traditional Jewish mentality?

Building on the substantial findings of their predecessors, availing themselves of the extraordinary amount of archival and manuscript sources of Italian Jewish history published in recent years, and integrating the plethora of new work on Renaissance and early modern Italian society within their own historical reconstructions, these scholars have produced a substantial body of new work, of interest both to the student of Jewish as well as Renaissance and baroque culture. As we shall soon discover, their conclusions are hardly unanimous; their understandings of the meaning of the Renaissance or of the ghetto for Jewish cultural history are still inconclusive, and vary considerably. Nevertheless, they have raised fascinating questions about their material and provide some insightful, albeit tentative, responses. Conditioned by the cultural worlds they themselves inhabit, whether in Israel or in the Diaspora, their interpretations are surely not fully dispassionate nor unbiased. Like all historians, they may have corrected some of the ideological distortions of their predecessors only to replace them unwittingly with some of their own, and surely they will be criticized by future students of Jewish history. What remains for this generation, however, is a fresh and engaging examination of a proud Jewish minority, the heir of a richly endowed medieval legacy, attempting to assert and to reformulate its own specific identity within the context of an ongoing dialogue and negotiation with the cultural concepts, tastes, and values of the larger Christian landscape.

The essays that comprise this volume are conveniently divided into two distinct eras of Jewish communal life: at the height of Jewish settlement during the Renaissance (generally c. 1450–c. 1550), and during their enclosure in ghettos, roughly coterminous with the baroque period and beyond it (c. 1550 through the seventeenth and much of the eighteenth century), even though there is some unavoidable overlap between the two. To appreciate fully their appropriate contexts and specific contributions, I have attempted to provide a succinct orientation for the general reader on the development of Jewish culture and society in both periods. Consequently, I first consider the Renaissance period in general, introduce each of the essays relating to that period, and then proceed in a similar manner with respect to the age of the ghetto.

The focus of this collection is, as I have stated, the history of culture, as reflected primarily in learned society. The concerns of the nonlearned, women, and the family are minimally represented (see especially the essays of Bonfil and Horowitz). This emphasis accurately reflects the state of present studies and, in part, my own primary interests. I have omitted a sizable and significant scholarly literature on the history of individual Jewish communities like Florence, Venice, Padua, Perugia, Assisi, Verona, Rome, Milan, Piedmont, and Mantua.[7] I have also not included chapters on Jewish moneylenders and merchants,[8] on papal

Jewry policy,[9] on the political and legal status of Jews in Italy,[10] on internal communal organization, and on intracommunal relations.[11] There exists a rich literature on all of these subjects, some of which is mentioned in my notes and those of the other chapters. I also have not addressed comprehensively the interesting topic of the contemporaneous Jewish impact on Renaissance and baroque cultures.[12] Although I will refer to this impact below, and some of the chapters treat it indirectly (see especially those of Moshe Idel), the book deals primarily with Jewish culture, with the shaping of a collective Jewish identity within the context of the political, social, and intellectual realities of Christian civilization during the Renaissance and baroque periods. Finally, I have restricted myself to essays in the English language, limiting my choice among authors, and even among the scholarly writings of authors I have included here. No doubt all of this has placed obvious restraints on what I have included and what I have left out. My choices thus constitute only a sampling of recent work, as my supplementary bibliographical references amply indicate. They also offer sufficient testimony to the still open nature of the field, to the manifold challenges offered for future research. In the final analysis, however, I do believe that this imperfect collection illustrates clearly the vitality and creativity of some recent work in this relatively young field, and that the general reader both in Judaic studies and in European history will profit immensely from the community of learning this collection represents. Surely the issues of integration and segregation, of cross-cultural dialogue and ghettoization raised in these essays are not mere questions confined solely to the past but impinge upon contemporary realities as well. And the mixed fortunes of a Jewish minority bearing its ancient legacy while attempting to steer its own dignified course against the background of open but tenuous dialogue with, or outright sequestration and closure from its Christian majority is of no small interest to either contemporary Jews or Christians and the present realities of their old-new relationship.[13]

I

While the origins of Jewish life in Italy can be traced back to Hellenistic times, the Jewish communities emerging in the northern and central regions of the peninsula by the middle of the fifteenth century are of more recent origin.[14] Before the thirteenth century only a handful of

Jews were allowed to live north of Rome; Jewish merchants and artisans
had been prohibited from settling in northern neighborhoods out of fear
of economic competition. This situation gradually changed in the thirteenth and fourteenth centuries by the simultaneous rise to prominence
of Jewish moneylending, spurred by the church's campaign against
Christian usury, and by the burgeoning populations and economies of
the northern Italian communes, which created an increasing need for
capital. With the concomitant political and economic decline of Jewish
communities that had existed in the South for centuries, increasing
numbers of Jews emigrated from the southern regions and invested in
pawnbroking banks in cities throughout northern and central Italy.[15]

Subject to the vagaries of an agrarian economy and constantly in need
of cash to support their standing militia and public projects, the petty
city-states of this region were predisposed to invite individual Jewish
bankers to settle in their communities. Usually such Jews were offered a
condotta (charter) by the civic authorities for a limited number of years
with the possibility of extensions. The arrival of relatively affluent Jews
in cities such as Ancona, Urbino, Perugia, Forlì, Padua, Bologna, Milan,
and Ferrara eventually paved the way for the entrance of their co-
religionists. Jewish moneylenders thus became the economic mainstay of
the small Jewish settlements sprouting up north of Rome and the chief
source of communal leadership. When their economic power and position were threatened, the welfare of every member of the Jewish community was adversely affected.

The concentration of economic power in the hands of a small number
of relatively affluent banking families left its impact on Jewish cultural
life. Not surprisingly the major luminaries of Jewish culture—rabbinic
scholars, poets, physicians, astrologers, or philosophers (quite often the
same individual)—usually aligned themselves with these families. Their
intellectual activities were supported by those privileged patrons of higher
culture in a manner not unlike that of their counterparts in the Christian
world of letters. This system of Jewish patronage, which continued to
expand during the Renaissance, could not help but broaden the range of
cultural interests pursued by an intellectual class dependent on the good-
will and economic support of economic magnates and their families.[16]

By the fifteenth century, Jewish loan bankers were a noticeable element in the major urban centers of northern and central Italy and in
many of the smaller towns as well. In a few instances Jewish families

such as the Da Pisa or Norsa had succeeded in amassing a considerable fortune and had established a rather intricate network of loan banks in several communities. Jewish loan banking was well entrenched in such cities as Florence, Siena, Ferrara, Mantua, Pesaro, Reggio, Modena, Padua, and Bologna.

With the gradual increase of Jewish residents in these cities, encouraged by economic opportunities engendered by the loan bankers, recurrent signs of organized Jewish communal activity became more visible by the second half of the fifteenth century. One notes the appearance of cemeteries, synagogues, community schools, and later, voluntary associations to maintain basic social services for the community. In the same era immigrants from Germany and southern France joined the original native Italian element in settling these regions. The expulsion of the Jews from Spain resulted in a new influx of Sephardic Jews, who arrived in Italy as early as 1493. They were later joined by a steady stream of New Christian (=Marrano) immigrants throughout the sixteenth and seventeenth centuries, fleeing the Iberian peninsula in search of more tolerant surroundings. The new Italian communities became more international in flavor, and understandably the process of political and social self-definition and differentiation that these increasingly heterogeneous communities underwent was sometimes accompanied by considerable stress, internal conflict, and even bitter struggles over religious and political authority.[17]

The infusion of larger numbers of Jews into these regions evoked hostile reactions from elements of the local populace as well. The concentrated and conspicuous presence of Jewish moneylenders was particularly offensive to certain churchmen, especially members of the Franciscan order. The most vigorous attacks against Jewish usury in the fifteenth century came from such preachers as Bernardino of Siena and Antonino of Florence, who openly deplored the economic basis of the Jewish community and its supposed cancerous effect upon the local Christian populace. Others, like Bernardino of Feltre, launched the drive to establish *Monti di Pietà*, public free-loan associations with the avowed purpose of eliminating Jewish usury in Italy altogether. Such campaigns often had painful consequences for Jewish victims: riots, physical harassment, even loss of life. In some cases Jews were expelled from various cities, although these measures were usually temporary. Sometimes the results of such provocations were disastrous. Bernardino of Feltre's charge of ritual murder in the city of Trent in 1475 had serious repercussions for Jews not only in that city but throughout northern Italy.[18]

If there was a shelter from such disasters, it was to be found in the fragmented political nature of the Italian city-states. The Jewish victims of persecution often sought refuge in neighboring communities and on occasion even succeeded in returning to their original neighborhoods when the hostilities had subsided. An outburst in one locality, however, could easily trigger a similar explosion in another contiguous with it. The friars' inflammatory sermons, accompanied by severe public pressure against the local Jewish citizenry, usually traveled from town to town with the same predictable results. Yet such disruptions, no matter how harmful, lacked the finality and drastic consequences associated with anti-Jewish hostility elsewhere in western Europe. Because of the localized and circumscribed nature of the outbursts, Jewish life in Italy was never fully suppressed and continued to flourish through the modern era.

Incessant hostility was also counterbalanced by the relatively benign relations that existed between certain Jewish and Christian intellectuals in Italy at the height of the Renaissance and long after. The new cultural intimacy could not dissipate the recurrent animosities between Jews and Christians, but it did allow some Jews greater access to Christian society than before, and accordingly their impact on certain sectors of the majority culture was more profound. This intense interaction between intellectuals of different faiths would have a significant impact on the cultural concerns of both communities.

II

These cultural liaisons between Jewish and Christian savants have been the focus of much of the earlier scholarly writing on Jewish cultural life in the Renaissance, especially the synthetic histories of Roth and Shulvass. That a small community of enlightened Jews by the second half of the fifteenth century had established close contacts with Renaissance courts and scholars has never been in doubt, but the precise ways in which the majority culture symbiotically affected the entire Jewish community and its intellectual life has not been thoroughly elucidated. To what extent were Jews earnestly preoccupied with the concerns of Renaissance culture? Was there a Jewish humanist movement comparable to that of Italian culture in this period? Can one legitimately speak of a Jewish Renaissance in Italy coterminous with the Italian Renaissance? Was there something unique about the development of Jewish thought in the Italian Renaissance to distinguish it from that of other enlightened civilizations in Spain, Provence, or Turkey? Did Italian Renaissance culture actually exert a decisive influence on Jewish thought or did its impact constitute no more than a passing fad or superficial encounter? Was, for example, the traditional core of rabbinic studies of the Jewish school noticeably affected at all by such external intellectual developments? When weighed against other factors affecting the Jewish community throughout western and eastern Europe and the Mediterranean regions—such as the expulsion from Spain, the emergence of new Jewish settlements in the Ottoman Empire and eastern Europe, dramatic developments in Jewish political organization, in religious law and ethics, and in mystical and messianic speculation—was the Renaissance relatively less important to Jews, even those living in Italy, than to Christians living in the same era? [19] These are the kind of questions the chapters in the first part of our book address. Their responses are hardly complete or unanimous, and their assessments are surely complicated by the disagreements of general historians regarding the specific character of the Renaissance and of humanism. [20]

Recent scholarship has pointed out that all three of the major intellectual traditions of Renaissance culture—Aristotelianism, humanism, and Neoplatonism—affected certain Jewish thinkers in various ways, and should be evaluated both separately and collectively as overlapping cultural influences in attempting to formulate responses to the above questions. Our essays discuss comprehensively the last two. Before turning to their analyses, we should briefly mention the first.

Due to the recent work of Charles Schmitt and others, the dominant role of Aristotelian philosophy and the scholastic tradition in Renaissance culture has been fully appreciated. [21] The Peripatetic tradition not only survived during the Renaissance and well beyond it, but even flourished in all the major Italian universities, utilizing newly discovered materials and fresh translations of Aristotle and his commentators, and absorbing some of the new linguistic-humanistic methodology for the study of ancient texts. For fifteenth-century Italian Jews, the scholastic tradition remained a dominant aspect of their intellectual life, the rich legacy of Judeo-Arabic philosophy, as exemplified by Moses Maimonides, being amplified and refined by Christian scholastic influences from the Middle Ages.[22]

Italian scholasticism molded the intellectual interests of at least three important Jewish thinkers living in the late fifteenth and early sixteenth centuries: Elijah Delmedigo, Judah Messer Leon, and his son David. Of the three, Delmedigo was the most prominent and outspoken student of Aristotelianism. Born and raised in Crete, where he died, Delmedigo spent considerable time among scholastic academic circles in Venice and Padua, where he acquired his fame as an authority on the writings of Aristotle's Arabic commentator, Averroes. The influence of Averroes is especially apparent in his *Beḥinat ha-Dat* (Examination of the Faith), his major work of Jewish philosophy, written in Hebrew in 1490, where he delineates the boundaries of philosophical speculation and religious faith.[23] As Arthur Lesley discusses below in his essay on Leone Ebreo, Delmedigo opposed the syncretistic tendencies of some of his Jewish colleagues, particularly their public promotion of rhetoric and kabbalah, and was clearly uneasy with the kind of speculations stimulated by one of his Christian patrons, Giovanni Pico della Mirandola, the illustrious Florentine Neoplatonist, in discussions he initiated between Jews and Christians.[24]

Judah and David Messer Leon acquired similar training in scholastic studies. Judah even earned a doctorate in philosophy and medicine, acquired the unique privilege of conferring medical degrees on his own students, and wrote scholastic commentaries on grammar, logic, and rhetoric.[25] In contrast to the more restricted commentaries of his father, David composed several original philosophical works, expounded the philosophy of Moses Maimonides, and elucidated his own theology of Judaism, based on an interesting merger of Averroist and Thomist sources, among others.[26] For all three Jewish thinkers, it was necessary to formulate their Jewish faith by reference to Aristotelian texts or through scholastic modes of investigation.

Judah Messer Leon along with David, his son, parted company, however, with Elijah Delmedigo in widening their intellectual horizons beyond scholasticism. Messer Leon's intellectual interests were broader than his contemporary's in absorbing the influence of the humanistic studies of his day. In composing his Hebrew work, *Sefer Nofet Ẓufim* (The Book of the Honeycomb's Flow), Messer Leon introduced for the first time to his Italian Jewish readers a new genre of rhetorical writing, placing himself squarely in the center of a new and dominant expression of Renaissance culture, that of Italian humanism. With the revival and imitation of classical antiquity beginning as early as the fourteenth century, the humanists had reclaimed rhetoric as a significant and independent part of the new *studia humanitatis,* which also included grammar, poetry, history, and moral philosophy. Reacting to the excessively technical philosophical interests of Aristotelian scholars, the humanists revived the ideal of the ancient Latinists Cicero and Quintilian. They maintained that the integration of rhetoric with philosophy would shape a new breed of educated persons endowed with both wisdom and eloquence.

As the late Alexander Altmann carefully demonstrates in his essay, Messer Leon's compendium likewise projected to its Hebrew readers the ideal of a good and righteous man, gifted in the oratorical art, who thus combined his knowledge and noble character to produce a new and effective leadership for the Jewish community. Furthermore, in grafting the Ciceronian ideal onto Judaism, he boldly attempted to portray his new image of leadership as an intrinsic part of Jewish tradition in the first place. He designated his new Jewish leader the *ḥakham kolel* (a direct Hebrew translation of the Latin *homo universalis*), a person obliged to lead his community by virtue of a unique combination of broad and substantive learning together with good character. As Messer Leon Judaized the civic orator, so too did he treat the entire field of rhetoric. The model of classical oratory initially was conceived not in Greece or Rome but in ancient Israel itself, he claimed. If indeed the entire Hebrew Bible, especially its prophetic orations, was the font and exemplar of the rhetorical art, it followed not only that rhetoric was a subject worthy for Jews, but that it was incumbent upon them to appreciate and to master a discipline that had been theirs in the first place, and that their sacred scriptures might now be examined in the light of literary criticism. Moreover, the idea that rhetoric had been perfected first by the Hebrews offered Jewish readers of *Nofet Ẓufim* a satisfying reassurance regarding the intrinsic worth of their own cultural legacy.[27]

Were Messer Leon's pedagogical goals shared by other contemporary Jews? Arthur Lesley, in his first essay, addresses this question affirmatively by describing the emergence of an entire humanist program among certain members of the Jewish leadership in Italy who not only subjected the Bible to rhetorical analysis, but reflected on Hebrew poetics, on drama, biography, and historiography, all components of the new *studia humanitatis*.[28] Alexander Altmann points to a continuous Jewish interest in rhetoric well into the sixteenth century in his discussions of Azariah de' Rossi's analysis of rabbinic homily, and in Judah Moscato's polished Hebrew orations.[29] Lesley adds the critical point that the new Hebrew literary products of Italian Jews were never a mere unreflective imitation of a foreign fashion. On the contrary, their authors were pursuing a resolutely independent religious and learned program, adapting it to their own heritage, "opening themselves up to the world without being assimilated by it."[30]

One of the major questions of current research concerns the precise relationship between humanist rhetorical theory and the actual sermons of rabbis preached from their Italian pulpits during the Renaissance and especially in the period of ghetto. Did the typical Italian Jewish preacher, in contrast to Jewish preachers elsewhere, imbibe directly the Ciceronian ideal? Besides the sermons of the sixteenth-century Mantuan preacher Judah Moscato, the subject of Altmann's remarks, are there other examples of direct humanist influences on other preachers in either their oral sermons usually delivered in Italian, or in their later written versions usually written in Hebrew? The answer is not so clear, given the vast variety of sermons and preachers among Italian Jews, the present incomplete state of research, and the formidable problem of reconstructing the actual preaching situation. Marc Saperstein, in his survey of the entire field, illustrates the gap between theory and practice, points out the still untapped possibilities of studying Italian Jewish sermons, and surely suggests that the lines of continuity between the Jewish humanists of Lesley's and Altmann's portraits and the actual practitioners of the rhetorical art are not as direct as they might seem.[31]

III

Even more decisive than the impact of humanism on Italian Jewish culture was that of the encounter of the aforementioned Neoplatonist Giovanni Pico della Mirandola and his colleagues with a number of contemporary Jewish scholars. Out of a mutually stimulating interaction between Pico and his Jewish associates and a prolonged study of Jewish texts emerged one of the most unusual and exotic currents in the intellectual history of the Renaissance, the Christian kabbalah. While in the case of humanism the encounter between Renaissance and Jewish culture was generally one-sided, wherein Jews were primarily recipients of cultural forms that they absorbed from the outside, the interaction with Pico's circle was substantially different since it was mutual. In an unprecedented manner a very select but influential group of Christian scholars actively desired to understand the Jewish religion and its sacred texts in order to penetrate their own spiritual roots more deeply. Such a major reevaluation of contemporary Jewish culture by Christians would leave a noticeable mark on both Christian and Jewish self-understanding in this and in later periods.[32]

Pico and his intellectual circle were drawn to Jewish study partially out of a sincere devotion to missionary activity, as were earlier Christians before them, especially in Spain. But Pico's attraction to Jewish texts in general, and to the corpus of Jewish mystical texts known as the *kabbalah* in particular, had more to do with the philosophical and theological currents among his Florentine contemporaries. From Marsilio Ficino (1433–1499), the leading Neoplatonist in Florence, Pico derived the vital concept of "ancient theology," the notion that a single truth pervades all periods and all cultures, and that among the ancient writers—pagan, Jewish, or Christian—a unity and harmony of religious insight can be discerned. By universalizing all religious knowledge, Ficino and Pico fashioned a more open and tolerant Christian theology. In searching for truth in cultural and religious settings distant from their own, they ultimately came to appreciate the centrality and priority of Hebraic wisdom in Western civilization.[33]

While ancient theology led Pico back to the biblical beginnings of Western culture, his employment of the concept of "poetic theology" led him to he kabbalah. Pico believed that the ancient pagan religions had concealed their sacred truths through a kind of "hieroglyphic" imagery of myths and fables. Moses had similarly addressed the Israelite nation in a veiled manner called the kabbalah. The kabbalah then constituted that part of the Jewish tradition where the essential divine truths could be located; it was the key to lay bare the secrets of Judaism, to reconcile them with the mysteries of other religions and cultures, and thus to universalize them. Kabbalah also represented a higher power for Pico, a means of enhancing man's ability to control his destiny. In fusing the kabbalah with the cultures of pagan antiquity, Pico also juxtaposed it with the magical traditions associated with the ancient Hermes Trisme-

gistus, whose writings had been recently brought to prominence by
Marsilio Ficino. Kabbalah thus became more than a spiritual tradition
of passive piety or meditation; it was conceived to be a superior form of
licit magic, superior to the magical practices taught by the ancient pagans, establishing a direct link between heaven and earth. It enabled man
to assert his true nobility and dignity as a true "magus" with divine
power.[34]

In order to study Jewish sources systematically, Pico engaged three
notable Jewish scholars, among others: the aforementioned Elijah Delmedigo, who elucidated certain kabbalistic concepts for him and supplied him with an initial bibliography of kabbalistic works; a Sicilian
convert called Flavius Mithridates, who translated some forty works of
Hebrew exegetical, philosophical, and kabbalistic works into Latin for
Pico;[35] and an erudite and prolific Jewish writer and physician, a disciple
of Judah Messer Leon, named Yohanan Alemanno. Through the instruction he received from these teachers and through his own synthetic
powers, Pico became the pioneering figure in the gradual penetration of
contemporary Jewish thought into European culture. His Christianization of kabbalistic techniques and his fusion of magic and Jewish mysticism, while officially condemned by the church, were enthusiastically
endorsed by a significant number of Christian thinkers in Italy, France,
Germany, and England well into the eighteenth century. Christian kabbalah through Pico left its mark on Renaissance culture through its
integration with Neoplatonism. It also influenced both the Protestant
and Catholic Reformations through its impact on such thinkers as Egidio
of Viterbo, Francesco Giorgio, Cornelius Agrippa, Johann Reuchlin, and
Guillaume Postel, to name only a few. Its remarkable persistence as a
thread in post-Renaissance culture—in art, in literature, and even in
scientific thought—has also been well observed.[36]

Pico's syncretistic theology also noticeably affected contemporary Jewish
thought. Yohanan Alemanno, the subject of Moshe Idel's pioneering
essay in chapter 4, had been asked by Pico to explain the allegorical
sense of the Song of Songs to which he agreed, initiating a wider and
more intensive contact between the two for several years. Alemanno, the
older of the two, and an accomplished master of the rich traditions of
Jewish kabbalistic and philosophic learning, especially those cultivated
in medieval Spain, had much to offer his enthusiastic Christian pupil.
On the other hand, Alemanno betrays the profound influence of the

Florentine ambiance in his own Hebrew writings. His references to Neoplatonic and magical sources and their fusion with Jewish kabbalistic concepts clearly mirror similar efforts on the part of Pico. Because of the similarity of their intellectual systems, it is difficult to determine who was the primary influence on the other. What seems clear, as Idel put it, is that a mutual openness existed between them, beginning with a Christian desire to learn from Jews and continuing with a Jewish willingness to absorb ideas developed by Christian Renaissance culture.[37]

Under the influence of Pico and his contemporaries, Alemanno and his Jewish disciples in Italy well into the seventeenth century denuded the kabbalah of its mythical sensibility and its emphasis on the performance of the commandments of Jewish law in influencing God, and instead recast it in a magical and Neoplatonic framework. This new speculative framework, in turn, facilitated even greater Christian acceptance and appropriation of the concepts and exegetical methods of the kabbalah. In his comprehensive treatment of Alemanno's extensive but complex literary corpus, Idel shows how Alemanno reinterpreted the traditional notions of the temple, the oral law, and prophecy to bring out their magical potency, and how he correlated kabbalistic descriptions of the Godhead with notions found in Plato and Proclus.[38]

As in the case of Alemanno, Florentine Neoplatonism left its impression on the most illustrious Jew of the Italian Renaissance, Judah ben Isaac Abravanel, better known as Leone Ebreo (c. 1460–1523). Unlike the case of his older Jewish contemporary, however, there is no firm evidence that Leone ever visited Florence or that he ever met Pico before the latter's death in 1494. Yet without assuming that Leone knew intimately the cultural ambiance of Pico's circle, it becomes most difficult to comprehend the genesis of his well-known work, the *Dialoghi d'amore*. More than any other Jewish work written during the Renaissance, Leone's composition has been linked to the same literary and intellectual currents associated with the Florentine school of Ficino and Pico. Exhaustively studied by numerous scholars and passionately hailed as the most truly representative Jewish work of Renaissance thought, Leone and his treatise on love still remain somewhat of a mystery to contemporary scholarship, especially the peculiar background of the author and the extraordinary literary and philosophical sophistication of his final printed work.[39]

Most studies of the *Dialoghi* have focused on its relationship with the Neoplatonic discussions of love initiated in Florence by Ficino and with the contemporary literary genre of the *trattati d'amore,* of which the *Dialoghi* has been considered to be the most distinguished masterpiece. Arthur Lesley argues instead that the *Dialoghi*'s primary context is the Jewish cultural milieu of Italy at the beginning of the sixteenth century. Reviving a theory first propounded by Isaiah Sonne some fifty years ago,[40] Lesley maintains that Leone originally wrote his treatise in Hebrew some thirty years before its first printed Italian edition. What is particularly relevant for understanding the objective of Leone's work, according to Lesley, is the earlier debate between Leone's older contemporaries, Elijah Delmedigo and his putative adversary, Yohanan Alemanno, regarding the challenge Neoplatonism, especially combined with Christian kabbalah, posed to a weak and vulnerable Jewish community. Delmedigo's answer was his Averroistic one, to demarcate the boundaries of philosophical speculation and religious truth accessible to the masses, and to reject the encroachment of kabbalah tinged with Neoplatonism into the heart of Judaism. In contrast, Alemanno adapted "a strategy of inclusiveness" by combining wisdom and eloquence, logic and rhetoric, philosophy and kabbalah to demonstrate the unity of truth. Leone Ebreo followed the same path but went beyond Alemanno in taking up the apologetic task of defending Judaism through underscoring the affinity between Jewish and pagan truths. As Lesley puts it, "if the Florentines could christen pagan myths, Abravanel [i.e., Leone] could circumcise them." And Saul Cohen Ashkenazi, Delmedigo's faithful student, brought the debate full circle by opposing Leone's syncretistic effort. For him, Judaism was violated by its fusion with rhetorical discourse, pagan myths, and Neoplatonic concepts.[41]

IV

According to Lesley, the same humanist impetus that stimulated a literature of Jewish rhetoric and poetics also aroused a new interest in writing history, for historiography was intimately wedded to rhetoric in the new *studia humanitatis.* The great classical historians lionized by their Renaissance imitators had been the great masters of rhetorical style. The resurgence of Jewish historiography in the sixteenth century then, the conscious choice of some ten individual authors to write historical narratives, following a hiatus of hundreds of years, perhaps since the time of the first-century Josephus, was, above all, a literary choice engendered by humanist educational values.[42]

Such a suggestion about the genesis of Jewish historical writing in the sixteenth century, however, has been previously rejected by Yosef Yerushalmi. According to him, the primary stimulus for this historiographical outpouring was the expulsion of Hispanic Jewry in 1492. The majority of the authors of these works were exiles themselves or were deeply affected by this catastrophic event. Their interest in postbiblical history and in events unrelated to Jews was spurred by their messianic yearnings and their existential need to understand the present and future by searching for signs of divine providence in the past. Medieval Jews had never nurtured a significant historiographical tradition, and even this sixteenth-century aberration would soon abort—"a sudden flowering and withering away"—to be overtaken by an ideology transcending history, that of the Lurianic kabbalah. Yerushalmi notes one exception, which for him, proves the rule: the *Me'or Einayim* of Azariah de' Rossi, a collection of critical essays evaluating rabbinic homilies by the standards of profane history, written in Mantua in 1575. This work, and this work alone, was "the fruit of a creative encounter between Jewish tradition and Italian Renaissance culture."[43]

The difference of interpretation between Lesley and Yerushalmi returns us to our basic set of questions about the actual import of the Renaissance in determining Jewish cultural priorities, particularly when weighed against such momentous historical events as the expulsion. As Robert Bonfil mentions in his chapter 7 on Jewish historiography, Yerushalmi understands the origin of historical trends in the same way the late Gershom Scholem understood the origin of mystical trends in the sixteenth century: as a novel and dramatic response to the central historical event of the period, the eviction from Spain.[44] As we shall see, the assumption of 1492's central role in transforming Jewish intellectual and spiritual life has recently been challenged, if not totally dislodged.[45] The issue is significant, at least with respect to Italy, for in de-emphasizing the Spanish factor, we are obliged to consider Lesley's suggestion in favor of a Renaissance influence, even beyond that on de' Rossi's unique work.

Robert Bonfil's revisionist essay, while strongly taking issue with Yerushalmi's position that 1492 was decisive in shaping Jewish historical writing, does not adopt Lesley's suggestion either. Bonfil begins by questioning Yerushalmi's assumption that medieval Jews produced no significant historiographical literature. Judged by the standards of their time, these works, Bonfil contends, compare most favorably with those of their Christian counterparts. On the other hand, judged by the standards of the sixteenth century, the later Jewish historiography is hardly impressive. Since humanist histories, in the traditions of Machiavelli and Guicciardini, were primarily concerned with political and military events, with the *narratio rerum gestarum,* the Jews had nothing to write about and the humanist historiographical model became hopelessly irrelevant to them. The only Jewish historian to produce a general history in the Ciceronian mode was Elijah Capsali, but he remained virtually unread. In contrast, most Jews of the sixteenth century continued to read with great fascination the medieval classics: the *Sefer Yossiphon,* a chronicle of ancient Jewish history based on Josephus, the adventures of the messianic adventurer, Eldad the Danite, and various fanciful medieval homilies. Despite the pretensions of such authors as Capsali, Joseph Ha-Cohen, and David Ganz, they, in fact, made little impression on their contemporaries and their efforts were no more than "the swan song of medieval Jewish historiography." Their failure was the result of an essential incompatibility of the subject matter of history as conceived in the Renaissance with the destiny of the Jewish people.[46]

Bonfil's startling and original approach requires us to reconsider entirely Yerushalmi's position, which has become a standard account of the subject. Surely a proper assessment of the medieval historiographical legacy is critical in evaluating that of the sixteenth century, one that requires a comparative Christian (and Moslem) perspective. *Yosipphon*'s popularity in the sixteenth century in comparison with Ha-Cohen's or Capsali's obscurity also requires explanation. We might quibble with Bonfil's definition of what constitutes genuine Renaissance history as perhaps being too constrictive in focusing exclusively on great political and military events. And, even assuming it was, were Jews fully incapable of rediscovering their own political and military legacy? Certainly Abraham Portaleone, the author of a sixteenth-century Hebrew excursus on the wars of ancient Israel, identified fully with this subject.[47] Even the popular *Yosipphon* recalled in striking detail the great Jewish war with Rome. One might also be uneasy with Bonfil's hasty exclusion of two of the most creative works generally classified as works of history but considered by him as unhistorical: Samuel Usque's Portuguese *Consola-*

tions for the Tribulations of Israel and Solomon ibn Verga's Hebrew *Shevet Yehudah,* one of the most widely read books of the sixteenth century.[48] Surely, despite Usque's use of the dialogical form and Ibn Verga's "fanciful presentation of the persecution of the Jews," as Bonfil calls it, both authors purport to present a continuous history of the Jewish past to their readers. At the very least, by reintroducing these two works into the Jewish historiographical corpus, the weight of the Spanish expulsion as a factor in sixteenth-century Jewish historiography is somewhat strengthened. Nevertheless, Bonfil's conclusion that Jewish historiographical production in the sixteenth and seventeenth century was neither rich, nor exceptional, nor popular in comparison with the extraordinary products of the Christian world is compelling and obliges us to rethink entirely the basic assumptions shared by both Yerushalmi, Lesley, and most others who have previously considered the subject.

Bonfil also notes the exceptional status of de' Rossi among other Jewish historical works. But unlike the goal of integrating Jewish and non-Jewish history, the elusive goal of Capsali, de' Rossi's objective was more modest. His main tool, according to Bonfil, was philological criticism; his format consisted of erudite and highly unreadable essays; his primary motivation was to defend Judaism and its sacred traditions within the particular religious and cultural context of Jewish life in sixteenth-century Italy. But, Bonfil contends, sheer erudition was not enough; the *Me'or Einayim* had no immediate successors and few readers until its rediscovery in the nineteenth century.[49]

Concentrating exclusively on de' Rossi's exceptional work, Joanna Weinberg offers a portrait of this important Italian scholar that differs from that of Bonfil or Yerushalmi. Bonfil, in both his chapter 7 below and in a separate study,[50] emphasizes the goal of self-differentiation, of defending Judaism against Christians and Jewish apostates, as a primary motivation of de' Rossi. Weinberg accepts this conclusion but emphasizes more the Christian scholarly community with whom de' Rossi was associated as a potent factor informing his work. By demonstrating how de' Rossi uncritically accepted the notorious forgeries of Annius of Viterbo, Weinberg convincingly shows how de' Rossi was as good a scholar as some of his contemporaries but certainly not any better than them. Like his Christian colleagues, he continued to use these fictions since they shed light on his religious history. In contrast to Yerushalmi's interpretation of this work as the fruit of an encounter with the Italian

Renaissance, Weinberg correctly points to the historical scholarship of Counter-Reformation Italy, not Renaissance humanism, as the proper context of the work. According to Weinberg, by eschewing universal history for concentrated essays on historical chronology, de' Rossi revealed himself primarily a practitioner of esoteric scholarship rather than public polemics, and fully comfortable with the intellectual tastes of a highly elite community of Jews and Catholics living in a post-Renaissance age.[51]

V

Like the subject of historiography, Jewish messianism and mysticism are themes that transcend both the chronological limits of the Renaissance and the geographical limits of Italy. Nevertheless, given Italy's geographical and cultural centrality in Jewish life, especially after the Spanish expulsion, neither of these broad themes can be ignored since they impinge directly on the particular character of Italian Jewish culture. Accordingly, the essays selected for this section offer a variety of interpretations on the place of messianism and the kabbalah in the culture of Mediterranean Jewry in general, as well as their peculiar fate within the Italian setting. The question of the Renaissance impact on Jewish cultural development is again relevant in this context in exploring how messianic and mystical ideologies emanating in Spain and later in Safed were transformed by the special ambiance of Italian Jewry, While placed in the first section of the book, it is obvious that this subject overlaps with the second and should provide a good transition to considering the age of the ghetto.

Rachel Elior's chapter 9 with slight modifications, represents quite well the dominant way in which sixteenth-century messianic and mystical activity have been interpreted in the last fifty years, following the highly influential reconstruction of Gershom Scholem.[52] Like Scholem, Elior considers the expulsion from Spain as the primary catalyst in unleashing a popular yearning for spiritual and physical redemption among the generation of the exiles. Focusing on the fate of the kabbalah after 1492, she argues, also following Scholem, that it was transformed into a popular doctrine and fused with contemporary messianic agitation. Its new status within sixteenth-century Jewish culture was due to the preference of Jews for a spiritual reality of hopeful revelation over a

disappointing and arbitrary historical one. The new kabbalists challenged the norms of rabbinic authority by proposing their own spiritualized ideals based on their visionary pneumatic authority. In viewing the
Lurianic kabbalah as a culmination of these spiritual tendencies already
emerging after 1492, rather than their initiation, Elior modifies Scholem's position somewhat. Nevertheless, in underscoring the power of a
historical event to alter mystical sensibilities, in viewing post-expulsion
kabbalah as messianic and popular, and in considering sixteenth-century
kabbalah as a prelude and necessary condition for the messsianic explosion of the seventeenth century surrounding the figure of Shabbetai Ẓevi,
Elior reiterates all the major features of Scholem's regnant interpretation.[53]

Elior's essay, of course, does not focus on Italy. When I wrote chapter
10 on sixteenth-century messianism in 1981, several years before Moshe
Idel's assault on the still dominant view of Scholem (see chapter
11 below), I was approaching the subject from the perspective I knew
best, that of the Italian ambiance. My suggestion that Jewish messianism
need not be understood only as a direct internal response to 1492, but
should be linked to the wider landscape of Jewish-Christian interactions
in this era, was offered modestly and hesitantly, without any interest in
negating the prevailing understanding. My essay summarizes the "ecumenical" atmosphere generating messianic behavior on the part of Jews
and Christians alike; the mutual influences of Christian and Jewish
messianisms on each other; and the role of the conduits of Christian
kabbalah and converso (Marrano) messianic enthusiasts in cross-fertil-
izing the messianic anticipations of both faith communities. I concluded
with a highly speculative comparison of Lurianic kabbalah (which I
assumed then to be thoroughly messianic), with Loyolan spirituality on
the one hand, and Protestant radical dissent, on the other. I suggested
that the ideology of Luria was unlike either of the two, but rather a
unique expression of gradualistic reform grounded in a cosmic myth of
renewal.[54]

Several years later, Moshe Idel presented his highly revisionist perspective on the development of Jewish mystical and messianic trends in
the sixteenth century. I have included one of his earliest essays on the
subject (previously unpublished) in which he first stated his highly controversial view regarding the expulsion from Spain. In that essay, and in
its sequel, which traces the evolution of Italian kabbalah well into the

seventeenth century, the Italian Renaissance's encounter with the kabbalah and the latter's ultimate transformation, in contrast to its evolution in Spain, North Africa, and the Ottoman Empire, are carefully delineated. They place the Italian experience within a comparative context, and allow the reader to trace the evolution of a unique strain of kabbalist thought in Italy from Alemanno until the middle of the seventeenth century.[55]

Idel's first essay (chapter 11) initially provides a quick overview of the development of the kabbalah in Spain, and then describes the emergence of a southern and a northern route when the kabbalah migrates from Spain in the wake of the expulsion. The kabbalah which traveled through North Africa and finally reached Safed was primarily anti-Christian, antiphilosophical, esoteric and revelatory, and preoccupied with mythologies and mystical praxis. In contrast, the kabbalah that reached Italy was open to Jewish-Christian cultural dialogue, was pro-philosophical, exoteric, and encouraged hermeneutical freedom. Because of its contact with the Renaissance, the highly mythological and messianic kabbalah was metamorphosed into a speculative and syncretistic occult philosophy. This comparison leads Idel to conclude that the kabbalah of the South, undiluted by external influences, was intensely creative and original. But due to its close interaction with European culture, the unique structures of the kabbalah were effaced in the North. Idel concludes this essay by denying any connection between the stimulus of 1492 and the evolution of Lurianic kabbalah. Concluding, as Elior does, that Luria was not an innovator but merely constructed a comprehensive system of earlier ideas, he proceeds to argue that historical events hardly ever affected doctrinal matters in the history of the kabbalah. Luria, an Ashkenazic Jew, never mentioned an event that occurred some seventy years earlier, and was generally oblivious to mere external events which could never shape his internalized and spiritualized understanding of reality.[56]

In his second essay (chapter 12), Idel traces the subsequent journey of the kabbalah in Italy well beyond the era of the expulsion and the Renaissance. What is important in his analysis is the stress on continuity from Alemanno until the late seventeenth century. During this entire span, Alemanno's blueprint persisted: kabbalah was viewed as a kind of ancient lore to be compared and correlated with other ancient philosophies; it was fused with magic, it was explained philosophically and exoterically; and it served as a cultural bridge with the Christian world.

Lurianic ideas were marginal within the Italian context. When they were finally introduced into Italy, they were demythologized and philosophized, and eventually translated into the occult philosophical language of European culture. As a bridge to our consideration of Jewish culture in the ghetto age, Idel's discussion is important in arguing for the persistence of Renaissance trends well beyond the initial encounter of Jewish thought with the Renaissance in the time of Pico and Alemanno.[57]

VI

The Jewish communities of the papal states as well as the rest of Italy experienced a radical deterioration in their legal status and physical state in the middle of the sixteenth century due to a new oppressive policy instituted by Pope Paul IV and his successors. Italian Jews suddenly faced a major offensive against their community and its religious heritage, culminating in the public incineration of the Talmud in 1553 and in restrictive legislation leading to increased impoverishment, ghettoization, and even expulsion. Jews had previously been expelled from the areas under the jurisdiction of Naples in 1541. In 1569, they were removed from most of the papal states, excluding the cities of Ancona and Rome. Those who sought refuge in Tuscany, Venice, or Milan faced oppressive conditions as well. The only relatively tolerable havens were in the territories controlled by the Gonzaga of Mantua or the Estensi of Ferrara.

The situation was aggravated further by increasing conversionary pressures, including compulsory appearances at Christian preaching in synagogues and the establishment of transition houses for new converts, which were designed to facilitate large-scale conversion to Christianity. Whether motivated primarily by the need to fortify Catholic hegemony against all dissidence, Christian and non-Christian alike, or driven by a renewed missionary zeal for immediate and mass conversion, spurred in part by apocalyptic frenzy, the papacy acted resolutely to undermine the status of these small Jewish communities in the heart of western Christendom.[58]

The most conspicuous phenomenon associated with these changes was the erection of the ghetto itself, "a compulsory segregated Jewish quarter in which all Jews were required to live and in which no Christians were allowed to live," as Benjamin Ravid defines it.[59] The word was probably first used to describe an area in Venice supposedly once the site of a foundry (*getto*), selected as early as 1516 as the compulsory residential quarter for Jews. With the passage of Paul IV's infamous bull *Cum Nimis Absurdum* in 1555, a ghetto was erected in Rome. The phenomenon gradually spread to most Italian cities through the next century.

As Kenneth Stow makes perfectly clear, the notion of the ghetto fit well into the overall policy of the new Counter-Reformation papacy. Through enclosure and segregation, the Catholic community could be shielded more effectively from Jewish contamination. Since Jews could be more easily controlled within a restricted neighborhood, the mass conversionary program of the papacy would prove to be more effective, and canon law could be rigidly enforced. When in 1589 the ghetto of Rome was enlarged, making it an even more permanent feature of Jewish life, Jews even began to refer to it as their *ghet*, possibly ascribing a Hebrew etymology (the Hebrew *get*, meaning divorce) to the Italian term. As Stow suggests, the Jews now innately felt that their "divorce" was final, that they were fated to live in a permanent state of subservience and separation from the rest of Christian society.[60]

Yet the ghetto always constituted a kind of paradox in defining the relationships between Jews and Christians in Italy. No doubt Jews confined to a heavily congested area surrounded by a wall shutting them off from the rest of the city, except for entrances bolted at night, were subjected to considerably more misery, impoverishment, and humiliation than before. And clearly the result of ghettoization was the erosion of ongoing liaisons between the two communities, including intellectual ones. Nevertheless, as Ravid points out, "the establishment of ghettos did not lead to the breaking off of Jewish contacts with the outside world on any level, much to the consternation of church and state alike."[61] Moreover, as he also indicates, the ghetto provided Jews with a clearly defined place within Christian society. In other words, despite the obvious negative implications of ghetto sequestration, there was a positive side: the Jews were provided a natural residence within the economy of Christian space. The difference between being expelled and being ghettoized is the difference between having no right to live in Christian society and that of becoming an organic part of that society. In this sense, the ghetto, with all its negative implications, could also connote a change for the better, an acknowledgement by Christian society that Jews did belong in some way to their extended community.[62]

The notion of paradox is critical to Robert Bonfil's understanding of

the ghetto experience in his remarkable essay (chapter 15). As he explains, paradox, the mediating element between two opposites, represents a distinct characteristic of transitional periods in history, "a part
of the structural transformation instrumental in inverting the medieval
world and in creating modern views." Most paradoxical of all is Bonfil's
contention that the kabbalah became the most effective mediator between medievalism and modernity in this period. The kabbalah became
"an anchor in the stormy seas aroused by the collapse of medieval
systems of thought" and simultaneously, "an agent of modernity." In
conquering the public sermon, in encouraging revisions in Jewish liturgy,
in proposing alternative times and places for Jewish prayer and study,
and in stimulating the proliferation of confraternities and their extra-
synagogal activities, the kabbalah deeply affected the way Italian Jews
related to both the religious and secular spheres of their lives. In fact, the
growing demarcation of the two spheres, a clear mark of the modern
era, constituted the most profound change engendered by the new spirituality.[63]

Along with religious changes went economic and social ones. The
concentration and economic impoverishment of the ghetto engendered
an enhanced polarization between rich and poor, accompanied by cultural polarization as well. For the poor, their knowledge of Hebrew and
traditional sources conspicuously deteriorated. For the rich, their elitist
cultural activities were paradoxically enhanced. They produced Hebrew
essays, sermons, dramas, and poetry using standard baroque literary
conventions. The seemingly "otherworldly" kabbalist Moses Zacuto
was capable of producing "this worldly" Hebrew drama replete with
Christian metaphors, as Bonfil demonstrates.[64] And despite the insufferable ghetto, some Jews, obviously the most comfortable and the most
privileged, seemed to prefer their present status.[65]

In describing the ghetto era in such a manner, Bonfil strongly urges us
to reconsider the import of the Renaissance for Jewish cultural history.
The beginning of incipient modernism was not the Renaissance, so he
claims, but the ghetto age, as late as the end of the sixteenth and
seventeenth centuries. Moreover, we are entitled to see this later period
not as a continuation of the Renaissance, "a mere blossoming [of Re-
naissance] trends after a long period of germination," but as a distinct
era in itself, that of the baroque, and this latter term, used primarily in a
literary and artistic context, is a relevant category in periodizing a unique
and repercussive era in the Jewish experience.[66]

The full implications of Bonfil's revisionist position for the study of Jewish history have yet to be fully explored by either Bonfil or others. The cultural world of the ghetto still requires closer scrutiny by contemporary researchers. Few historians have employed the category of "baroque" in describing Jewish culture.[67] And several (as this writer) would continue to assign some significance to the Renaissance in the shaping of a novel and even modern Jewish cultural experience. In fact, Bonfil's emphasis on the sharp rupture and discontinuity engendered by the ghetto might be tempered by a greater appreciation of the lines of continuity between the Renaissance and post-Renaissance eras. Nevertheless, Bonfil's new emphasis opens the possibility for a fresh assessment of the ghetto experience with respect to Jewish-Christian relations, Jewish cultural developments, and the ultimate emergence of a modern and secularized temperment, with all its complexities, within the Jewish communities of early modern Europe.

VII

Some of the strands of Jewish life in the ghetto era still to be discussed fall within the purview of Bonfil's synthetic chapter 15. Others lie outside his description and still need to be integrated with his composite portrait. One of these is raised by Mark Cohen in his chapter 16 on Leon Modena, one of the most colorful figures of the Venetian ghetto, and his apologetic work the *Historia de' riti hebraici*.[68] Cohen speaks of a new awareness among Jews and Christians of one another in the seventeenth century, along with "incipient Jewish attempts to reorientate Christian attitudes toward the Jews." Bonfil would surely see this phenomenon as paradoxical: the distancing of the ghetto creates proximity and greater understanding of the other. Be that as it may, Cohen raises the important issue of an emerging sense of political activism, of incipient psychological security allowing Jews to realize that they need not accept their beleagured condition as given, but can take the initiative in defending their community by influencing public opinion.

These first steps of presenting a rehabilitated image of the Jew before the eyes of the non-Jewish world, a kind of "antidefamation" literature written in European languages, constitute a product of an emerging modern, secularized consciousness. One might even suggest that the ghetto, that space confirming the Jews' right to reside within Christian society and to belong to it, facilitates that modicum of self-assurance which encouraged Modena and his colleagues Simone Luzzatto, David de Pomis, and others to take pen in hand in order to demonstrate the benefits Jews offered their Christian neighbors.[69] Surely the pro-Catholic and anti-Protestant perspective of Modena's treatise not only reveals good political sense on his part, as Cohen makes clear, but it might also suggest his enhanced sense of belonging to Catholic society. As a proud resident of the Jewish ghetto and subject to the Catholic state of Venice, he naturally tended to see the world from a Catholic perspective.

Cohen correctly points out that this new political discourse should be seen together with the extensive literature of apologetics written by conversos who had returned to their ancestral faith directed to others who had not yet returned.[70] In either case, whether writing to an educated Christian audience or to educated conversos, the authors strove to go public with their message, to use the power of the press to reach a wider audience of readers, and to encourage them to rethink their opinions on Jews and Judaism. The assumption that "a good press," a mere reeducation through books, could dissipate hostility and the negative image of Judaism in Western civilization would have a long and bitter legacy throughout the modern era.

The connection between presenting a more positive image of Judaism in books and performing choral music in a ghetto synagogue may at first appear tenuous to us, but it was surely not to Leon Modena. For the same author of the *Riti* also conceived of the idea of introducing polyphony in the synagogue. Recruiting his talented friend Salamone de' Rossi to compose music to Hebrew texts, he was eager to fuse Jewish cultural habits with those of the larger Catholic society. As Dan Harrán points out in chapter 17, the music was simply a genus, an aesthetic experience neither Jewish nor Christian in itself. Synagogal music became Jewish only when Jewish texts were employed. Not the style of the music but its purpose was critical in legitimating its usage within the sacred space of the synagogue and within the sacred time of Jewish worship.[71]

The link between Modena's cultural apologetics and liturgical innovation was certainly one of cultural mediation, to use Harrán's expression, of harmonizing differences, and again, paradoxically, of bringing Jewish and Christian cultural sensibilities under one roof in the most Jewish place of all, the synagogue. Furthermore, the new polyphony bespoke the awareness that what Christians think about Jews is important. Reorienting their fallacious assumptions about Judaism through published manuals is one strategy of cultural integration. Another is to transform the synagogue from an unfamiliar and offensive "cacophony of discordant sounds"[72] into a harmony of perfectly blended voices attuned to Christian ears, or even to Jewish ones displaying a budding appreciation of Christian sensibility.

Since the music doesn't matter, but only the words and the intent, why not align the external medium to the accepted tastes of the larger environment? Indeed medium and message could never be confused! And if one is to bring the music of the church into the synagogue, without the message, it should be done in a restrained, conservative, and ambiguous way, as Harrán describes. That studied ambiguity is perhaps more characteristic of the baroque than of "the late Renaissance", as Harrán puts it.[73] The remarkable achievement then of Modena and his friends in remaking the image of the synagogue through the music of the baroque church was not merely an audacious act, not merely a form of accommodation with the outside world, but also an integral part of that restructuring of the Jewish cultural experience that the creators of the ghetto unwittingly had generated.

It should come as no surprise that the same worshippers inspired by the mellifluous sounds of choral production during a wedding ceremony would be subsequently entertained at the wedding feast by Hebrew riddling contests. As the late Dan Pagis describes it in chapter 18, the genre of emblem-riddles emerging from semantic word games challenging the participants in a test of their decoding dexterity, was typically a baroque or mannerist product. Invented by the kabbalist-playwright Moses Zacuto, the riddles rapidly became a popular pastime at weddings and other social occasions, a competition to intrigue and sharpen the wits of the audience.[74] The riddles display that ornate and festive side of the ghetto, at least for the well-to-do; they illustrate the fusion of languages—Hebrew and Italian and Spanish—and cultural tastes; and finally they reveal that baroque sense of obscurity, of searching for a deeper reality below the surface of things. In a sense, the Hebrew riddles were the quintessential product of both the ghetto and the baroque experiences.[75]

Science was another crucial element in the ghetto ambiance. Bonfil himself noticed the heroic image of the physician within the Jewish community, particularly his importance as a cultural mediator between the old and the new.[76] The new landscape was brimming with scientific achievement and discovery; a "revolution" of major significance for the culture of the Western world was taking place. Far removed from the ghetto enclosures, Galileo was peering through his famous telescope, Vesalius was performing his remarkable anatomical experiments, and Bacon and Descartes were reflecting deeply on the new methods of fathoming the natural world from their own distinctive perspectives. Yet the ghetto walls could not filter out the new scientific discourse, just as they could not filter out so much else. When the gates of their locked neighborhood opened at the crack of dawn, young Jewish students were on their way to the great medical schools of Italy; Bologna, Ferrara, and especially Padua. Not all of the great scientific advances took place within the universities; more often than not, the great discoveries were made elsewhere. But medical schools could still be exciting intellectual centers, where original research was fostered and pursued, and where students could be exposed to the latest of the new earth-shattering advances, even within the curricular framework of outdated medical and scientific textbooks.[77] For Jews, as I suggest in chapter 19, the encounter was momentous in opening them to new vistas of knowledge, new languages, new associations, and new values. The communities which sent them to study were energized by their return. Their shared academic experience encouraged them to maintain social and intellectual relationships long after graduation. They were a kind of scientific society among their co-religionists, wedding their naturalistic studies with knowledge of the Torah. More than ever before, Jewish communities were led by men who could creatively fuse their medical and rabbinic expertise.[78]

The new attraction to medical and scientific learning was facilitated by two other factors. In the first place, medicine had been a venerated profession among Jews for centuries. The new exposure to the flood of new scientific books and to the university classroom was simply a natural extension of a traditional Jewish activity. The second factor, however, was unique to the emerging intellectual style of the ghetto. The Maimonidean synthesis of religion and reason, of Arisotelian philosophy and Jewish revelation had been dethroned. The new physics, whatever form it took, was anti-Aristotelian. Physics was divorced from metaphysics, and subsequently Jews could comfortably dabble in the wonders of the natural world without feeling that such involvements threatened their allegiance to Judaism. In the new alliance between religion and science, the latter dealt only with contingent facts while the former was empowered with the absolute authority to determine ultimate values. This did not mean that tensions between science and religion had been fully eliminated, as I point out below. However, it did allow for a revigorated alliance between Judaism and science. With philosophy discredited within the Jewish community, and disassociated from sciences, the pleasures of nature could even be enjoyed by students of the kabbalah. And in a ghetto organically linked to Catholic patterns of thought and behavior, the growing number of rabbis flaunting their medical diplomas before their students and their congregations shared a remarkable kinship with a community of Jesuit clerics, enthusiasts of science in their own right, who proclaimed the majesty of God's creation before their own constituencies in neighborhoods just beyond the ghetto gates.[79]

The striking lines of continuity across the boundaries of the religious cultures of Jews and Christians, in the words of Elliott Horowitz in chapter 20, were not limited to the study of nature, or to musical and poetic creativity. Like their Christian counterparts, Jewish religious and communal leaders were capable of spoiling a good time. As Horowitz demonstrates in his study of the popular celebration on the evening preceding boy's circumcision, "the same shift in post-Tridentine Italy to tone down popular celebrations by means of sacralizing them" is observable among Italian Jews. When the kabbalist rabbi Aaron Berachia of Modena introduced the reading of the Zohar as the centerpiece of the festivity, he quickly transformed the event into a somber occasion. By insisting on the priority of studying texts over the customary celebrations, he succeeded in curtailing feminine participation. Eventually, as Horowitz shows, the rite was performed by confraternity members, those new cells of social organization and communal spirituality sprouting up in the ghetto and beyond it.[80]

In demarcating the boundaries of the sacred and the profane, in separating the sexes, in underscoring the confraternity's central role in the ceremony at the expense of other willing participants, and in transforming a profane event into an occasion of mystical reflection, the community leaders had acted most predictably and reflexively. And ironically, they marched to the beat of a drummer heard far beyond their own neighborhood. The Christian architects of the ghettos had hoped to lead the Jews to the baptismal font through their newly enforced segregated quarters. Instead, they insured the continuity and

resurgence of a proud, resilient minority culture. But in ways unbe-
known to either them or their oppressed Jewish subjects, they had
remade the Jews into a community very much to their own liking, and
very much in their own image.

NOTES

1. J Burckhardt, *The Civilization of the Renaissance in Italy,* trans. S. G. C.
   Middlemore (reprint New York, 1954; first published in 1860 in German).
   See also, W. K. Ferguson, *The Renaissance in Historical Thought* (Cam-
   bridge, Mass., 1948); T. Helton, ed., *The Renaissance: A Reconsideration
   of the Theories and Interpretations of the Age* (Madison, Wis., 1961); A.
   Chastel et al., *The Renaissance: Essays in Interpretation* (London and New
   York, 1982).
2. The literature is too numerous and well known to cite here. I refer, of
   course, to the work of such historians as Natalie Zemon Davis, Peter Burke,
   John Bossy, Keith Thomas, Robert Muchembled, Brian Pullan, Lawrence
   Stone, Carlo Ginzberg, Emmanuel LeRoy Ladurie, and many others.
3. See H. Graetz, *Divrei Yemei Yisrael,* ed. and trans. S. P. Rabinowitz (Warsaw, 1916), vol. 6, chap. 12; S. Dubnov, *Divrei Yemai Am Olam* (Tel Aviv,
   1971–72), vol. 5, pp. 234–54; vol. 6, pp. 37–89; I. Zinberg, *Toledot Sifrut
   Yisrael* (Tel Aviv, 1956), vol. 5, pp. 230–95.
4. See C. Roth, *The Jews in the Renaissance* (New York, 1959); idem, *The
   History of the Jews in Italy* (Philadelphia, 1946); M. A. Shulvass, *The Jews
   in the World of the Renaissance* (Leiden, 1973; first published in Hebrew in
   1955). My formulation here is indebted to that of Robert Bonfil, in his
   revisionist essay, "The Historian's Perception of the Jews in the Italian
   Renaissance: Towards a Reappraisal," *Revue des études juives* 143 (1984):
   59–82.
5. Simonsohn, *History of the Jews in the Duchy of Mantua* (Jerusalem, 1977;
   English translation of the original Hebrew edition published in Tel Aviv,
   1962); I. Barzilay, *Between Reason and Faith: Anti-Rationalism in Italian
   Jewish Thought 1250–1650* (The Hague and Paris, 1967).
6. For a recent historiographical assessment of the work of some of these
   scholars, several of them prominently displayed below, see H. Tirosh-Rothschild, "Jewish Culture in Renaissance Italy: A Methodological Survey,"
   Italia 9 (1990): 63–96. See also my own historiographical essay cited below
   in note 13.
7. On Florence, see U. Cassuto, *Gli Ebrei a Firenze nell'età del Rinascimento*
   (Florence, 1918, 1965; Hebrew translation by M. Hartum, Jerusalem, 1967;
   on Venice, see B. Pullan, *The Jews of Europe and the Inquisition of Venice
   1550–1670* (Oxford, 1983); G. Cozzi, ed., *Gli ebrei e Venezia secoli XIV–*

XVIII (Milan, 1987), with a very extensive bibliography; on Padua, see D. Carpi, ed., *Minute Books of the Council of the Jewish Community of Padua* [*Hebrew*], 2 vols. (Jerusalem, 1973–1979); on Perugia, see A. Toaff, *Gli Ebrei a Perugia* (Perugia, 1975); on Assisi, see A. Toaff, *The Jews in Medieval Assisi 1305–1487* (Florence, 1979); on Verona, see Y. Boksenboim, ed., *Minute Books of the Jewish Community of Verona [Hebrew]*, 3 vols. (Tel Aviv, 1989–90); on Rome, see H. Vogelstein and P. Rieger, *Geschichte der Juden in Rom*, 2 vols. (Berlin, 1896) and A. Milano, *Il Ghetto di Roma* (Rome, 1964); on Milan, see S. Simonsohn, ed., *The Jews in the Duchy of Milan*, 4 vols. (Jerusalem, 1982–86); on Piedmont, see R. Segre, *The Jews in Piedmont*, 3 vols. (Jerusalem, 1986–90); on Mantua, see Simonsohn, *History of the Jews of the Duchy of Mantua*. For further references the reader should consult A. Milano, *Bibliotheca historica Italo-Judaica* (Florence, 1954); idem, *Bibliotheca historica Italo-Judaica: Supplemento 1954–1963* (Florence, 1964) (a supplement for the years 1964–66 was published in *Rassegna mensile di Israel* 32 [1966]); D. Carpi, A. Luzzatto, and M. Moldavi, *Biblioteca Italo-ebraica: Bibliografia per la storia degli Ebrei in Italia 1964–73* (Rome, 1982); and A. Luzzatto, *Biblioteca Italo-ebraica: Bibliografia per la storia degli Ebrei in Italia, 1974–1985* (Rome, 1989).

8. See most recently the collection edited by A. Toaff and S. Schwarzfuchs, *The Mediterranean and the Jews: Banking, Finance, and International Trade in the XVI–XVII Centuries* (Ramat Gan, Israel, 1989), with several essays on Italy. There is also much material in the communal histories listed in the previous note.

9. See especially, K. Stow, *Catholic Thought and Papal Jewry Policy* (New York, 1977); and idem, *Taxation, Community, and State* (Stuttgart, 1982).

10. See especially, V. Colorni, *Legge ebraica e leggi locali* (Milan, 1945).

11. These subjects are treated in great detail in the various communal histories. See R. Bonfil, *Rabbis and Jewish Communities in Renaissance Italy* (Oxford and New York, 1990) on this and on many other areas. See also the recent collection of essays by D. Carpi, *Be-Tarbut ha-Renesans u-ven Homot ha-Getto* (Tel Aviv, 1989). The study of the social and cultural history of Italian Jewry has been thoroughly enriched in recent years by the many edited volumes of Hebrew rabbinical responsa, communal ledgers, and correspondence published by Y. Boksenboim (Tel Aviv University Press).

12. The subject has yet to be fully treated. See generally, the classic essay of G. Scholem, "Zur Geschichte der Anfänge der Christlichen Kabbala," in *Essays Presented to Leo Baeck* (London, 1954), pp. 158–93; F. A. Yates, *The Occult Philosophy in the Elizabethan Age* (London, 1979); idem, *Giordano Bruno and the Hermetic Tradition* (London, 1964); and the recent volume of the late C. Wirszubski, *Pico della Mirandola's Encounter with Jewish Mysticism* (Cambridge, Mass. and London, 1989).

13. In writing this Introduction, I have borrowed freely from two of my pre-

vious essays: "At the Intersection of Cultures: The Historical Legacy of Italian Jewry prior to the Emancipation," in *Art and Jewish Life in Italy*, ed. V. Mann (Los Angeles and Berkeley, 1989), pp. 1–23; and "The Italian Renaissance and Jewish Thought," in *Renaissance Humanism: Foundations, Forms, and Legacy*, ed. A. Rabil, Jr., 3 vols. (Philadelphia, 1987), vol. 1, pp. 382–433.

14. Recent surveys of Jewish life under Roman rule that touch upon ancient Italy include M. Grant, *The Jews in the Roman World* (New York 1973, 1984); and M. Smallwood, *Jewish Life under Roman Rule from Pompey to Diocletian* (Leiden, 1976). On Jewish life in Italy during the Middle Ages, see *Atti della XXVI settimane di studio del Centro Italiano di Studi sull'Alto Medioevo: Gli ebrei nell' Alto Medioevo* (Spoleto, 1980); See also the comprehensive essays by C. Roth, B. Blumenkranz, H. J. Zimmels, and J. Dan, in C. Roth, ed., *The World History of the Jewish People: The Dark Ages*, 2nd ser., vol. 2 (Ramat Gan, 1966).

15. On these new economic opportunities, see S. W. Baron, *A Social and Religious History of the Jews*, vol. 12 (New York, 1967), pp. 159–65; L. Poliakov, *Jewish Bankers and the Holy See*, trans. M. L. Kochan (London, Henley, and Boston, 1977); L. Larner, *Italy in the Age of Dante and Petrarch 1216–1380* (London and New York, 1980), pp. 206–8.

16. For a study of one Jewish intellectual during the Renaissance in close association with Jewish loan bankers, see D. Ruderman, *The World of a Renaissance Jew* (Cincinnati, 1981).

17. All of this is described in the standard histories of Roth and Shulvass. Additional background is found in Bonfil, *Jewish Communities*, and Ruderman, *World of a Renaissance Jew*. See also A. Milano, *Storia degli ebrei in Italia* (Turin, 1963).

18. In addition to the standard histories, see the aforementioned works of Poliakov, Ruderman, *World of a Renaissance Jew*, chap. 7, and A. Milano, "Considerazioni sulla lotta dei Monti di Pieta contro il prestito ebraico," in *Scritti in memoria di Sally Mayer* (Jerusalem, 1956), pp. 199–223; R. Segre, "Bernardino da Feltre, i Monti di Pieta e i banchi ebrei," *Rivista Storica Italiana* 90 (1978): 818–33.

19. Compare, for example, the recent volume, *Jewish Thought in the Sixteenth Century*, ed. B. Cooperman (Cambridge, Mass. and London, 1983), where the Renaissance is a part but not the central focus of the volume.

20. See the references in note 1 above. For a collection of recent assessments of humanism, see A. Rabil, Jr., ed., *Renaissance Humanism: Foundations, Forms and Legacy* 3 vols. (Philadelphia, 1988).

21. C. B. Schmitt, "Towards a Reassessment of Renaissance Aristotelianism," *History of Science* 11 (1973): 159–93; idem, *Aristotle and the Renaissance* (Cambridge, Mass. and London, 1983).

22. See, for example, the many studies of J. Sermoneta, including his critical edition of Hillel ben Shemu'el of Verona, *Sefer Tagmulei ha-Nefesh* (Jerusalem, 1981), and S. Pines, "Scholasticism after Thomas Aquinas in the

Teachings of Hasdai Crescas and His Predecessors," *Israel Academy of Sciences and Humanities Proceedings* 1 (1967): 101ff.

23. On Delmedigo, see M. D. Geffen, "Faith and Reason in Elijah Delmedigo's *Beḥinat ha-Dat* (Examination of the Faith) and the Philosophic Backgrounds of His Work," Ph.D. diss., Columbia University, New York, 1970, and his "Insights into the Life and Thought of Elijah Delmedigo Based on His Published and Unpublished Works," *Proceedings of the American Academy for Jewish Research* 41–42 (1973–74): 68–86. A new edition of the *Beḥinat ha-Dat* was published by J. J. Ross (Tel Aviv, 1984).

24. See below, pp. 174–76. See also B. Kieszkowski, "Les rapports entre Elie Delmedigo et Pic de la Mirandole (d'après le. ms. lat. 6508 de la Bibliothèque Nationale)," *Rinascimento* 2nd ser., 4 (1964): 41–91.

25. See D. Carpi, "R. Judah Messer Leon and His Activity as a Doctor [Hebrew]," *Michael* 1 (1973): 277–301 (reprinted in *Korot* 6 [1974]: 395–415, and in his collection of essays cited in note 11 above, and in abbreviated form in English as "Notes on the Life of Rabbi Judah Messer Leon," in *Studi sull'ebraismo italiano in memoria di Cecil Roth* (Rome, 1974), pp. 37–62; R. Bonfil, introduction to the reproduction of the *Sefer Nofet Ẓufim*, Mantua, c. 1475 (Jerusalem, 1980); and *The Book of the Honeycomb's Flow by Judah Messer Leon,* ed. and trans. I. Rabinowitz (Ithaca, N.Y., 1983).

26. On David, see H. Tirosh Rothschild, *Between Worlds: The Life and Thought of David Ben Judah Messer Leon* (Albany, N.Y., 1990).

27. See below, pp. 69–75, as well as the works of Bonfil and Rabinowitz mentioned in note 25.

28. See below, pp. 45–59. On David ben Judah Messer Leon's humanistic interests, see H. Tirosh-Rothschild, "In Defense of Jewish Humanism," *Jewish History* 3(1988): 31–58.

29. See below, pp. 75–82.

30. See below, p. 59.

31. See below, pp. 85–98. Jewish sermons in Renaissance and baroque Italy have also been discussed in I. Bettan, *Studies in Jewish Preaching* (Cincinnati, 1939); in M. Saperstein, *Jewish Preaching 1200–1800: An Anthology* (New Haven and London, 1989); in J. Dan, *Sifrut ha-Musar ve-ha-Derush (Jerusalem, 1975);* and in D. Ruderman, ed., *Preachers of the Italian Ghetto* (Los Angeles and Berkeley, 1992). See also J. Dan, "Tefillah ve-Dimah of R. Yehudah Moscato [Hebrew]," *Sinai* 76 (1975): 210–32; and idem, "A Consideration of the Hebrew Homiletical Literature during the Italian Renaissance [Hebrew]," *Proceedings of the Sixth World Congress of Jewish Studies* (Jerusalem, 1977), 3: 105–10.

32. In addition to M. Idel's first essay below, chapter 11, see the other references cited in note 12 above.

33. Among the many works on Pico and Ficino and "ancient theology," see P. O. Kristeller, "Giovanni Pico della Mirandola and His Sources," in *L'Opera e il pensiero di Giovanni Pico della Mirandola nella storia della*

umanismo (Florence, 1965), 2 vols.: C. B. Schmitt, "Prisca Theologia e Philosophia Perennis: Due temi del Rinascimento italiano e la loro fortuna," *Il pensiero italiano del Rinascimento e il tempo nostro* (Florence, 1970), pp. 211–36; D. P. Walker, *The Ancient Theology: Studies in Christian Platonism from the Fifteenth to the Eighteenth Century* (Ithaca, N.Y., 1972).
34. See especially, Yates, *Occult Philosophy;* Kristeller, "Pico"; E. Wind, *Pagan Mysteries in the Renaissance* (New York, rev. ed., 1968); D. P. Walker, *Spiritual and Demonic Magic from Ficino to Campanella* (London, 1958).
35. He is treated in Wirszubski's book cited in note 12 above.
36. See the two books of Yates mentioned in note 12. On Egidio, see J. W. O'Malley, S. J., *Giles of Viterbo on Church and Reform: A Study in Renaissance Thought* (Leiden, 1968). On Giorgio, see C. Wirszubski, "Francesco Giorgio's Commentary on Giovanni Pico's Kabbalistic Theses," *Journal of the Warburg and Courtauld Institutes* 37 (1974): 145–56. On Agrippa, see C. G. Nauert, Jr., *Agrippa and the Crisis of Renaissance Thought* (Urbana, Ill., 1965), and the many studies of P. Zambelli. On Reuchlin, see J. Freedman, *The Most Ancient Testimony* (Athens, Ohio, 1983), pp. 71–98. On Postel, see W. J. Bouwsma, "Postel and the Significance of Renaissance Cabalism," in *Renaissance Essays*, ed. P. O. Kristeller and P. P. Weiner (New York, 1968), pp. 252–66 (originally published in the *Journal of the History of Ideas* 15 [1954]: 218–32). Yates stated her controversial thesis on the relationship between hermeticism-kabbalah and science in "The Hermetic Tradition in Renaissance Science," in *Art, Science and History in the Renaissance,* ed. C. S. Singleton (Baltimore, 1967), pp. 255–74.
37. See below, p. 109.
38. Ibid.
39. Bibliography on Leone is quite extensive. Some of the more recent studies include S. Damiens, *Amour et intellect chez Léon l'Hébreu* (Toulouse, 1971); the new Hebrew edition of the *Dialoghi* translated and edited by M. Dorman, entitled *Yehudah Abravanel, Siḥot al ha-Ahavah* (Jerusalem 1983); and the Hebrew collection of essays entitled *The Philosophy of Love of Leone Ebreo,* ed. M. Dorman and Z. Levy (Haifa, 1985); T. A. Perry, *Erotic Spirituality: The Integrative Tradition from Leone Ebreo to John Donne* (University, Ala., 1980); S. Pines, "Medieval Doctrines in Renaissance Garb? Some Jewish and Arabic Sources of Leone Ebreo's Doctrines," in Cooperman, *Jewish Thought,* pp. 365–98.
40. I. Sonne, "On the Question of the Original Language of the *Dialoghi d'amore* of Judah Abravanel [Hebrew]," in *Ziyyunim: Kovez le-Zikhrono shel Y. N. Simḥoni* (Berlin, 1928–29), pp. 142–48, as well as in later studies. Cf. Dorman's introduction to his translation of the *Dialoghi,* pp. 86–95.
41. See below, pp. 182–86.
42. See below, pp. 55–77. Yitzḥak Baer had suggested much earlier the influence of the Italian Renaissance on Solomon Ibn Verga's *Shevet Yehudah.*

See his introduction to *Shevet Yehudah*, ed. A. Shohat (Jerusalem, 1947), pp. 11, 13–15.

43. See below, p. 211.

44. See G. Scholem, *Major Trends in Jewish Mysticism* (New York, 1941), pp. 244–51.

45. See Idel, chapter 11 below.

46. See below, pp. 219–45.

47. Portaleone's discussion on war comprises a large section of his *Sefer Shiltei Gibburim* (Mantua, 1612). A. Melamed, in his Tel Aviv University Ph.D. dissertation, "The Small Sister of the Sciences: Political Thought of Jewish Thinkers in the Italian Renaissance [Hebrew]" (Tel Aviv, 1977), is the only contemporary scholar to study this discussion.

48. Verushalmi, in contrast, treats both works in chapter 6 of this volume.

49. See below, pp. 239–44.

50. Bonfil, "Some Reflections on the Place of Azariah de Rossi's *Me'or Enayim* in the Cultural Milieu of Italian Renaissance Jewry," in Cooperman, *Jewish Thought*, pp. 23–48. He has recently published an anthology of de' Rossi's larger work with an extensive introduction in Hebrew (Jerusalem, 1990). See below, pp. 241–43.

51. See below, pp. 252–69.

52. See G. Scholem, *Major Trends in Jewish Mysticism* (New York, 1941), pp. 244–51; idem, *Sabbatai Zevi, The Mystical Messiah* (Princeton, 1973), pp. 15–22.

53. See below, pp. 283–95.

54. See below, pp. 299–315.

55. Idel summarized his views in his recent book *Kabbalah: New Perspectives* (New Haven, Conn. and London, 1988).

56. See below, pp. 324–37.

57. See below, pp. 345–61.

58. See especially Stow, *Catholic Thought*; idem, "The Burning of the Talmud in 1553 in the Light of Sixteenth Century Catholic Attitudes toward the Talmud," *Bibliothèque d'humanisme et Renaissance* 34 (1972): 435–59; D. Carpi, "The Expulsion of the Jews from the Papal States during the Time of Pope Pius V and the Inquisitional Trials against the Jews of Bologna [Hebrew]" in *Scritti in memoria di Enzo Sereni*, ed. D. Carpi and R. Spiegel (Jerusalem, 1970), pp. 145–65 (reprinted in his collection of essays cited above in note 11); D. Ruderman, "A Jewish Apologetic Treatise from Sixteenth Century Bologna," *Hebrew Union College Annual* 50 (1979): 253–76.

59. See below, p. 373, and also his "The Religious, Economic, and Social Background and Context of the Establishment of the Ghetti in Venice," in Cozzi, *Gli ebrei e Venezia*, pp. 211–59, and his "New Light on the Ghetti of Venice," *Festschrift in Honor of Shlomo Simonsohn*, forthcoming.

60. See below, pp. 386–97.

61. See below, p. 384.

62. This point is also made below by Bonfil, pp. 407–10.
63. See below, pp. 401–5; 410–19. See also his "Cultura e mistica a Venezia nel Cinquecento," in Cozzi, *Gli ebrei e Venezia*, pp. 469–506.
64. See Y. Melkman, "Moshe Zacuto's Play Yesod Olam [Hebrew]," *Sefunot* 10 (1966): 299–333. Additional bibliography on music, theater, and poetry in the ghetto can be found in the notes to Bonfil's chapter 15.
65. See below, pp. 408–9.
66. Ibid., p. 410.
67. See G. Sermonetta, "Aspetti del pensiero moderno nell'Ebraismo tra Rinascimento e eta barocca," *Italia Judaica II: Gli ebrei in Italia tra Rinascimento e eta barocca* (Rome, 1986), pp. 17–35; D. Ruderman, *A Valley of Vision: The Heavenly Journey of Abraham ben Hananiah Yagel* (Philadelphia, 1990), pp. 65–68. On the notion of "baroque," see, for example, F. J. Warnke, *Versions of Baroque: European Literature in the Seventeenth Century* (New Haven, Conn. and London, 1963), and the additional works cited in Ruderman, p. 65, note 192.
68. On Modena, see M. Cohen, trans., *The Autobiography of a Seventeenth Century Venetian Rabbi: Leon Modena's Life of Judah* with intro. by N. Z. Davis, H. Adelman, T. Rabb, and historical notes by B. Ravid and H. Adelman (Princeton, N.J., 1988); H. Adelman, "Success and Failure in the Seventeenth Century Ghetto of Venice: The Life and Thought of Leon Modena," Ph.D. diss., Brandeis University, 1985, and see Cohen's chapter 16 below, pp. 429–73.
69. On the apologetic writing of Luzzatto, see B. C. I. Ravid, *Economics and Toleration in Seventeenth Century Venice* (Jerusalem, 1978); on that of de Pomis, see H. Friedenwald, *The Jews and Medicine* 2 vols., (Baltimore, 1944), 1:31–53.
70. Ibid., p. 429.
71. See below, pp. 482–91.
72. The expression used by the French humanist Francois Tissard when visiting the synagogue of Ferrara at the beginning of the sixteenth century. See Ruderman, *World of a Renaissance Jew*, p. 101.
73. Note the title of Harrán's chapter.
74. See Pagis below, pp. 502–13.
75. For an expanded version of Pagis' study of Hebrew riddles, see his *Al Sod Hatum: Le-Toledot ha-Hiddah ha-ivrit be-Italia u-ve-Holland* (Jerusalem, 1986). An essay that further illustrates the enhanced "baroque" tastes of affluent Jewish families of the ghetto, and which nicely complements the essays of Harrán and Pagis, is that of S. Sabar, "The Use and Meaning of Christian Motifs in Illustrations of Jewish Marriage Contracts in Italy," *Journal of Jewish Art* 10 (1984): 46–63.
76. See below, pp. 405–6.
77. On the mixture of the new and old in Italian medical schools, see especially N. G. Siraisi, *Avicenna in Renaissance Italy* (Princeton, N.J., 1987).
78. See below, pp. 519–43.

79. In addition to my chapter 19 below, see also D. Ruderman, *Kabbalah, Magic, and Science: The Cultural Universe of a Sixteenth-Century Jewish Physician* (Cambridge, Mass. and London, 1988); idem, "The Language of Science as the Language of Faith: An Aspect of Italian Jewish Thought in the Seventeenth- and Eighteenth Centuries," *Festschrift in Honor of Shlomo Simonsohn,* forthcoming.

80. On Jewish confraternities in Italy, see E. Horowitz, "Jewish Confraternities in Seventeenth-Century Verona: A Study in the Social History of Piety," Ph.D. diss., Yale University, 1982, and B. Rivlin, *Arevim Zeh la-Zeh be-Getto Ha-Italki* (Jerusalem 1991).

I

JEWISH CULTURE AND THE RENAISSANCE

A

**New Forms of Hebrew Literary Execution:
Rhetoric, Humanism, and the Jewish Sermon**

1

Jewish Adaptation of Humanist Concepts in Fifteenth- and Sixteenth-Century Italy

Arthur M. Lesley

I

During the fifteenth and sixteenth centuries, there appeared in Hebrew, addressed to a specifically Jewish audience, a number of entirely unprecedented works in genres that the Italian humanists cultivated, such as history, rhetoric, biography, and comedy.[1] At the same time, existing genres of Hebrew writing, such as sermons, letters, poetry, and grammar study, were revised in form, style, and content, so that they conformed more closely to distinctive humanist standards. The humanist features of these Hebrew texts have commonly been treated as "superficial" adornments that their authors "borrowed" from international fashion. One important historian of the Jews in the Renaissance, for example, readily explained such phenomena as illustrations of the Yiddish proverb, *Vi es Kristelt sich, azoi yidlt sich* ("As the Gentile does, so does the Jew").[2] This is an inadequate methodological assumption. To assume that a minority culture that has long survived, such as that of the Jews, automatically imitates whatever it encounters in the surrounding society both ignores the internal dynamics of Jewish life and reduces intercultural relations to simplistic alternatives of borrowing or complete originality. Such schematism betrays its origins in outmoded cultural apologetics.[3] Ample evidence from fifteenth- and sixteenth-century Hebrew literature suggests that this was not reflexive imitation: Hebrew writers carefully selected what they adapted and appropriated from humanist practice and values. The ways in which Jewish scholars selected certain humanist activities and adapted and integrated them into Hebrew discourse are serious topics for the history of Hebrew literature.

Jewish interest in humanist scholarship was anything but automatic. Indeed, Jews could well have been expected to disregard or resist Italian humanism. Aside from the Arabic transmission of Aristotle, Plato, and some scientific writings, Jewish learning simply had no traces of classical antiquity to revive. Furthermore, Rome, which was both the destroyer of the second Temple and the capital of western Christendom, was far from being the object of Jewish nostalgia. Most specifically, relatively few Jews read or wrote Latin, and almost none knew Greek. The most important characteristics of Italian humanism, then, seem at first glance to have been remote from Jewish interest.

Nevertheless, Jews in Italy did not resist or ignore humanism. Instead, they could choose to take advantage of what interested them and disregard the rest, because they felt confident that they possessed a language and literature that was more ancient and perfect than those of the Greeks and Romans. Isaac Abravanel (1437–1508), the leader of the Jewish exiles from Spain in 1492, explained the conception of the transmission of learning that claimed precedence for Hebrew over classical learning in all the arts and sciences:

> Our rabbis of blessed memory long ago investigated the transmission of learning from the school of Shem to the school of Eber, and from there to our father Abraham. From Abraham the art of magic and occult natures came to the sons of Ishmael and of Keturah, as well as astrology and the rest of the investigative sciences. . . . Indeed, it was the sons of Esau who brought the sciences to the Romans and the Greeks, sons of Japheth, when Zepho, son of Eliphas, ruled over them. . . . And this is why the sciences are not found among the other nations descended from Japheth besides these two, the Greeks and the Romans, who at that time were one nation, with a common language. And the wisdom of the children of Israel was as far above them as the heaven is above the earth.[4]

This account of the transmission of learning, formulated by Jewish apologists already in Hellenistic times, defended the priority, perfection, and sufficiency of Hebrew revelation against claims that Greek wisdom, attained through reason, was first and most complete. Christian apologists later adopted the Jewish position, so that Origen could assert, "It seems to me that all the sages of the Greeks borrowed these ideas from Solomon, who had learnt them from the Spirit of God at an age and time long before their own, and that they then put them forward as their own invention."[5] Renaissance Christian thinkers who sought to recover the "ancient theology" also frequently assumed that any similarity between revealed truth and human truth resulted from a garbled pagan account of an original revelation to the Hebrews. In the fifteenth and sixteenth centuries, then, Jews could expect universal assent to their assertion that "On that awesome day at Mount Sinai, [God] crowned us with the whole Torah, which includes all sciences, natural, logical, theological, judicial and political, from which the whole world has drunk."[6] In consequence, Jews believed that they did not automatically need to adopt derivative, though ancient, foreign models for what was already to be found in their own ancient texts.

When, however, Jews first encountered Italian humanist learning, they recognized that, in some areas, their own scholarship was inferior to that of their Christian contemporaries. To overcome this inferiority, they resorted to a strategy for justifying cultural innovation which Jews in earlier periods had used repeatedly: Assuming that all learning was already contained in the Bible, they considered their attempts to remedy current deficiencies to be, not imitation of foreign nations, but rather recovery from the nations of those traces of biblical wisdom—Adamic, Mosaic, or Solomonic—that had been preserved among the nations when the Jews themselves lost it. Faced with their inferiority in certain fields, the Jews looked for evidence that the prophets or the rabbis already knew these fields and then, justified by these precedents, they integrated the new fields into Jewish discourse.

The Jews who first encountered Italian humanism in the fifteenth century were in a social and political situation to benefit from humanist learning, and some of them were already elaborating a grammar-based educational program that made humanism pertinent to their own studies. Between the fourteenth and the seventeenth centuries, Jewish settlements reappeared in Italy north of Rome and disappeared everywhere south of Rome, as well as from Europe west of the Rhine. During the fourteenth and fifteenth centuries, fragile new Jewish communities, created by the terms of *condotte* between communes and loan-bankers, came to be scattered over central and northern Italy. Some lasted only as long as the term of one *condotta,* and, before the sixteenth century, even the largest included no more than two hundred persons.[7] The organization of these new communities was complicated by the continual arrival of refugees from southern Italy, France, Germany, Provence, Spain, and Portugal. The diverse legal, educational, and social practices of the mixed populace were difficult to harmonize, and the authority of leaders was subject to challenge.[8]

The writings of northern Italian Jews from the fifteenth and sixteenth centuries show them to have been responding to their situation by adapting two earlier programs for cultural reform, both of which are based upon study of Hebrew: one program is found in the *Kuzari,* by Yehuda Halevi (1075–1141),[9] and the other in *Sefer Ma'aseh Efod* (1403), by the Aragonese scholar Profiat Duran, known as Efodi.[10] During the fifteenth and sixteenth centuries, Halevi is frequently mentioned and several commentaries on the *Kuzari* were written, clearly signs of a desire to displace the long-dominant Aristotelianism in Jewish philosophy. Efodi's book, an up-to-date grammar even by Latin standards, proposes an educational solution to the political and ethical flaws that crippled Jewish communities in Spain and contributed to their collapse during and following the outbreaks of violence against them in 1391. Efodi diagnoses the flaws of the Jewish communities in Spain to be factionalism, mutual hostility among leaders of the factions, and the personal limitations of leaders, whom he calls "boorish men who were inept in the art of leadership." Efodi continues, "All three of these causes have been responsible for much of our affliction in exile, especially the choice of the private good, each of us being concerned for himself alone, and not knowing or understanding that, in the long run, the security of the parts depends upon the security of the whole."[11] Efodi's critique of Jewish communal leadership in exile focuses on the moral and educational deficiencies of the leaders. To reform leadership, Efodi invokes as models the ancient national rulers, King David and King Solomon, whose wise, just, and effective reigns resulted from their perfect understanding of the Hebrew language, which made all wisdom available to them.

In contrast with these exemplary ancient rulers, contemporary Jewish leaders—Talmudists, philosophers, and kabbalists—neglect the Hebrew of the biblical revelation that is the common source of their rival disciplines. To enable all Jewish factions to understand the Hebrew Bible and derive from it the interpretations useful for communal welfare in their time, Efodi presents a new grammar of biblical Hebrew. Armed with this necessary linguistic education, the factions will no longer be satisfied merely to allegorize the biblical text, like the philosophers; to disregard it, like the Talmudists; or to reduce it to occult meanings, like the kabbalists. They will rather search in the Hebrew Bible for solutions to contemporary problems and, in addition, effectively dispute the biblically based polemics of Christians. A Jewish community united in understanding its ancient texts will withstand all external threats and will repair its faults, to deserve speedy messianic redemption.

Efodi's ambitious claims for the art of Hebrew grammar include the assertion that, by remedying their faulty knowledge of Hebrew, Jews will begin to regain the virtues of pre-exilic Israel and thereby become more worthy of messianic salvation and the return from exile: "I think that my composition, this treatise, is a proof and demonstration that the salvation of the Lord is coming near, His kindness is to be revealed, and though He may delay, he will not be late. . . . 'For there is yet a prophecy for a set term, / A truthful witness for a time that will come. / Even if it tarries, wait for it still; / For it will surely come, without delay' " (Habakkuk 2:3).[12] The closing verse was frequently invoked during the early fifteenth century in Jewish calculations of the imminent coming of the Messiah. The original perfection of Hebrew, as revealed in the Bible, is still available to the Jews, in spite of their own current debasement and their corruption of the language. By dedicated study of Hebrew grammar, as exemplified in the Bible, Jews can revive their studies, their behavior, and their community, to repair the faults that prolong their exile.

Efodi's program, which may be characterized as biblicist hebraism, was readily adaptable to the task of integrating the diverse elements of the new northern Italian Jewish communities. To create a Jewish public discourse where none had existed, the learned leadership in Italy combined an educational program based on grammatical and political study of the Hebrew Bible with some linguistic and political features of Italian humanism. The result was a new and distinct Italian Jewish culture, which innovated several genres of Hebrew composition, notably rhetorical and ethical, and everywhere was recognized as supreme in every kind of Hebrew prose. The program of biblicist hebraism that the Italian Jews established had an affinity with Italian humanist moral and literary studies, but subordinated them to Jewish educational, moral, and political renewal.

Between the middle of the fifteenth century and the middle of the seventeenth century, Jews in Italy adapted each discipline of the *studia humanitatis*—grammar, rhetoric, poetry, history, and political philosophy—to the terms and forms of Hebrew expression. They did this by substituting biblical models for the Greco-Roman models that the humanists imitated.[13] In this way, the Jews made *reductio artium ad sacram scripturam*, the derivation of all arts from the Bible, serve the same functions as Cicero's application of Terence's line: "homo sum; nil humani a me alienum puto."

II

By making the biblical canon, rather than rabbinic medieval usage, normative for Hebrew style and grammar, Efodi took the decisive step for treating the Bible as the Jewish equivalent of classical literature. Although this decision was necessary for making available the disciplinary traditions of Hebrew grammar study and the practice of Hebrew poetry from Spain, it was by no means a natural or inevitable choice. Also, by stating that "The science of language is a science that includes grammar, rhetoric and poetry," Efodi both dignified grammar as a science and made the language arts in Hebrew congruent for the first time with the Latin trivium.[14] Previously, in Jewish scholasticism, following scholasticism in Arabic, grammar was a lowly propaedeutic to the logical arts.[15] Efodi's reclassification of grammar assisted the transference of Jewish scholarship from the Arabic and Islamic cultural background to the Latin and Christian background of Europe.

The achievements of Hebrew grammatical studies in Italy have still been investigated only in part, and their theoretical achievement appears to have been modest. The importance of grammar was its new function, at the beginning and center of Jewish education. Several grammars were composed, and dictionaries of Hebrew and foreign languages were compiled. Serving a new historical perspective, Elijah Levita's examination of the text of the Bible led to the conclusion that the vowels and diacritical marks of the Masoretic text were more recent than the consonants.[16]

Comparative study of Hebrew and the European languages developed to an unprecedented extent during the sixteenth century. Several centuries earlier, in the Arabic cultural setting, comparative study of Hebrew and the cognate languages of Aramaic and Arabic resulted in the first systematic Hebrew grammars. In the sixteenth century, comparison of Hebrew with Latin, Greek, and Italian served mainly to confirm the priority of Hebrew as the language of Adam which only the Jews preserved after the dispersion from the Tower of Babel. Comparison involved the juxtaposition of Italian, Greek, or Latin words with Hebrew words or phrases that had plausibly similar sounds and meanings. For example, the name of the Muse Kalliope could be derived from the Hebrew phrase *Kol Yafeh,* which means "beautiful voice," or "beautiful sound." Latin *uxor* was thought to resemble Hebrew *Ezer,* "helpmate," the term applied to Eve in Genesis. *Hospidale* was connected with *Osef Dalim,* "gathering of poor people," and *accademia* with *Bet Eked,* "house of assembly." The Mantuan scholar, David Provenzal, compiled over two thousand such similarities, to argue that these foreign languages preserved confused traces of the original Hebrew. Such an argument reinforced similar assertions that Jews and some Christian contemporaries made in other fields of learning. It harmonized as well with the kabbalistic ascription of special divine and divinatory power to the Hebrew language.[17]

III

Efodi's formulation of biblicist hebraism from the early fifteenth century became most fruitful for Italian Jews when they combined it with humanist rhetoric. That adaptation became possible once Jews accepted the Latin trivium as the definition of the linguistic arts, so that they could extend the biblical basis of grammar and poetry, the two linguistic arts that Jews studied within Arabic culture, to the third art, rhetoric. Efodi's definitions of the three arts prepared for the Italians' application of biblicist hebraism to the art of rhetoric: "When speech agrees with the elements and laws of the language, without particular sweetness, beauty, dignity or ornament, either in its simple or its complex statements, and is neither deliberately copious nor concise, such an utterance may be called grammatical. . . . When this utterance has sweetness, beauty, dignity and ornament, in both its simple and complex statements, it may be called eloquence *[MeLiTSah],* from the verse, 'How sweet *[NiMLeTSu]* are thy words unto my taste.' (Ps. 119:103) . . . When to these meter is added, the utterance is poetry."[18]

The biblicism that had long characterized Hebrew poetry and grammatical study could now be applied to a hitherto unpracticed linguistic art, rhetoric. Assisted by the power and the variety of applications that rhetoric demonstrated in humanist literature, Hebrew prose compositions could now be written according to humanist norms, but based on biblical models. All that was needed was a methodical analysis of the biblical text according to humanist rhetorical concepts. This was accomplished by Yehuda ben Yehiel, Messer Leon (ca. 1420–ca. 1490), a physician and teacher who was active in Padua, Mantua, and Naples. In *The Book of the Honeycomb's Flow*, printed in Mantua in 1475 but possibly written in Padua in the 1450s, Messer Leon puts the art of rhetoric at the disposal of Hebrew composition by combining a commentary on the *Rhetorica ad Herennium* with a commentary on Averroes' middle commentary on Aristotle's *Rhetoric*, and illustrating their definitions with passages from the Hebrew Bible.[19]

Messer Leon testifies to the process by which he has "recovered" the art of rhetoric for Hebrew: first he learned it from the nations, then he discovered its foundations in the Hebrew Bible: "When I studied the words of the Torah in the way now common amongst most people, I had no idea that the science of Rhetoric was included therein. But once I had studied and investigated Rhetoric . . . out of the treatises written by men of nations other than our own, and afterwards came back to see what is said of her in the Torah and the Holy Scriptures, . . . I saw that it is the Torah which was the giver."[20] Messer Leon goes on to demonstrate in detail the ways that the Hebrew Bible exemplifies all the teachings of rhetoric. Since the Bible contains all of rhetoric and is older than other sources of the art, Messer Leon does not doubt that it is the source of rhetoric. For example, he illustrates all the figures of speech from biblical passages and discovers several uniquely biblical figures: "For most of what we shall say herein, we shall draw upon Book IV of the *Rhetoric [ad Herennium]* written by Tully, and upon the account given by the Philosopher in Book III of his *Rhetoric*. The examples of the figures, however, I have taken from . . . the words of prophecy and the divinely inspired narratives."[21]

Messer Leon also derives the three kinds of rhetoric from biblical practice. Psalm 45, for example, illustrates the norms of epideictic rhetoric and even alludes to the classical prescriptions for this kind. The title of the psalm is, "In the mode of the *SHoSHaHNiM*," a term resembling the number six, *SHeSH*, meaning, Messer Leon says, that the psalmist intended to present "a complete discourse . . . with all its parts—which are six namely, introduction, statement of facts, partition, proof, refutation, and conclusion. . . . You will find many epideictic discourses of censure in Ezekiel, Jeremiah, and in some parts of Isaiah."[22] After careful analysis of psalm 45, Messer Leon concludes: "This psalm, composed through the instrumentality of the Holy Spirit, deals with the Messiah, with his deeds, and with the qualities for which one should praise him—physical attributes, qualities of character, and external circumstances. . . . This discourse, then, belongs in the class of Epideictic and, within this class, in the division of praise."[23]

An example of judicial rhetoric is the speech of the woman of Tekoa to David (2 Samuel 14:1–20). Many passages exemplify deliberative rhetoric. "Much, indeed, of what one finds in the Bible, and nearly all that is said to us in the form of commandments, admonitions, and reproofs . . . are in the category of deliberative oratory." In a similar manner, Messer Leon systematically turns the Hebrew Bible, which was already considered to be the ultimate source of truth and wisdom, into the supreme model of eloquence: "The sum and substance of all that we have said is that the speaker who is a son of our people should adopt his premises from what is found written in these books of Torah; his words will thus be most completely persuasive. . . . In this, as in all matters, our books of Torah rank first."[24] When rhetorical exemplarity is added to the other acknowledged excellences of the Hebrew Bible, it may be analyzed through rhetorical commentary and become the model for various kinds of Hebrew compositions. Hebrew writers in various genres were indebted to this achievement. Although *The Book of the Honeycomb's Flow* was printed only once before the nineteenth century, it had long-lasting influence on Hebrew education in Italy. It enabled other Hebrew writers to apply rhetorical concepts to compositions for which no Hebrew precedents existed, and modified established practice of commentary, composition, and oral address.

IV

Hebrew poetry since the eleventh century, in Spain, Provence, and Italy, had been written according to a set of biblicist hebraic norms, and it was not difficult to find biblical precedent for the writing of Hebrew poetry. Poetry obviously was present in the Bible, although scholars defined it in

different ways: by fixed numbers of metrical feet, by distinctive cantillation marks, by transcription in columns, or by introduction with the
terms *SHiR* or *SHiRah*.[25] There was, however, substantial difficulty in
claiming biblical precedent for writing the kind of Hebrew poetry that
was current in Spain, Provence, and Italy from the eleventh through the
sixteenth centuries.

The sixteenth-century historian, Azariah de Rossi (ca. 1520–78),
proposes solutions to these problems. He refers to a tombstone inscription found in Spain, which was written in the medieval Hebrew poetic
style, but which also mentioned a prince, "Amatziah," whom de Rossi
takes to be the biblical figure.[26] De Rossi concludes that medieval-style
Hebrew poetry was indeed written as early as the biblical period, but
that such poetry was not included in the biblical text because it was used
only for occasional genres, such as funereal inscriptions, rather than for
revealed, prophetic utterance. De Rossi takes the inscription to confirm
that contemporary Hebrew poetry continues Hebrew poetic practice
from biblical times, although it is excused from attempting to emulate
the incompletely understood forms of prophetic poetry that appear in
the Bible. Both kinds of poetry, sharing as they do the same vocabulary,
exemplify the most perfect forms of the Hebrew language, as it was
employed in different genres.

Hebrew writers more easily could claim biblical precedent for a kind
of composition that was not previously practiced in Hebrew, drama.
Yehuda Sommo Portaleone (1527–92), who was active in Mantua, like
Provenzal and de Rossi, wrote a Hebrew "regular" comedy, several
Italian comedies and pastorals, and four dialogues in Italian on the art
of drama. In the dialogues he argues that the biblical book of Job is the
original tragedy: "The sublime genius of the holy legislator Moses, the
famous leader of the Jews, after he had written his five books of divine
law as delivered to him by oracle—nay, from the lips of Almighty God
Himself—in 5550 verses, produced, as is demonstrated in the literature
of the Jews, the magnificent and philosophical tragedy of Job, introducing therein just five human characters."[27] Sommo acknowledges that
Job was not meant to be presented on stage, "but it was cast in the form
of a dialogue or discussion in which various characters took part—that
is to say, in the form assumed by every poem suited for dramatic
presentation." Sommo is not claiming a Hebrew precedent for every
form of drama, or even for those in which he wrote, but only for the

highest kind, for tragedy. He readily concedes the novelty of a Hebrew comedy, in the prologue to his *Comedy of Betrothal:* "What the other languages made a crown for their heads, this holy language made the heel of her shoes."[28] He decided to introduce the genre to Hebrew because: "Those sages thought it a flaw and corruption of the Hebrews that such pleasure and usefulness was absent from our stories. . . . I have therefore decided today to show all the people of the land that the Hebrew language is in no way inferior to any artistry in any foreign language." Given the availability of Job as the original drama, the absence of Hebrew comedy became a challenge to the dignity of Hebrew only when the genre could claim moral utility, through a combination of Horatian and Aristotelian arguments. In response, Sommo says he decided "to compose words which could be told before lords and nobles of the land, words in which pleasure and usefulness would be mingled, and in smooth words . . . condemn individuals who rashly indulge in every vice and, in contrast to such people, . . . praise and draw admiration to those who do good and justice."[29]

The plot of Sommo's comedy is taken from ancient rabbinic *midrash,* so that the matter of the comedy, like its purpose and its efficient cause, the author, are native to Hebrew. Only the comedic form is immediately taken from foreign practice; but since, according to Sommo, Job is the first drama, the form is one more item of ancient Hebrew wisdom now recovered from the nations.

V

Between Flavius Josephus and the sixteenth century, Jewish historiography was a desultory enterprise.[30] Like rhetoric, history had long been neglected in Hebrew, at least in part because the Jewish philosophical tradition disparaged it. According to Jewish philosophers, even the divinely inspired historical narratives of the Bible deserved attention only because they alluded to the eternal truths of physics and metaphysics. The outstanding Jewish philosopher, Maimonides (1135–1204), discouraged the reading of books "as are found among the Arabs describing past events, the governments of kings and Arab genealogy, . . . which neither possess wisdom nor yield profit for the body, but are a sheer waste of time."[31] Like philosophers, Talmudists, and kabbalists, the simple pious recognized no need to study history.

Against this background, the dozen historical works that Jews wrote during the sixteenth century, most of them in Italy, indicate a substantial change in Jewish intellectual life. These historical compositions include a couple of biographies and autobiographies, works which trace the authoritative line of rabbis, a history of the Turkish and Frankish empires, and several accounts of Jewish suffering and salvation, as well as a Portuguese pastoral dialogue on this theme. In addition, earlier Hebrew histories were printed, notably *Sefer Yosippon,* a medieval book that included, with other material, sections translated from a Latin version of Josephus.

The unprecedented, sustained Jewish interest in history resulted when moral and political concerns were combined with the new capabilities of rhetorical composition. Rhetoric guided the formulation of historical material to provide the Hebrew-reading audience with examples of moral and political actions to emulate or avoid. It was, of course, the same motive that led Italian humanist educators to include histories among their studies, as recommended by classical rhetoricians and the historians themselves. Livy had declared: "What chiefly makes the study of history wholesome and profitable is this, that you behold the lessons of every kind of experience set forth as on a conspicuous monument; from these you may choose for yourself and for your own state what to imitate, from these, mark for avoidance what is shameful in the conception and shameful in the result."[32]

Exactly the same didactic motive for studying history is invoked for Hebrew readers in the preface to the second printing of *Yosippon,* in Constantinople, in 1510. The author of the preface, Tam Ibn Yahya, was a Jewish physician to the Turkish sultan, an authoritative figure in Jewish law, and a spokesman for the learned elite of the Iberian exiles. His preface conforms to the established formula of the *accessus ad auctores* and illustrates the way that humanist historiography could be adapted to the values of a Hebrew audience.[33] "Although chronicles regularly exaggerate about things that never were realized, and even invent things that never happened; this book although it belongs to the same genre, is as different from them as truth is from falsehood. . . . The sign of this is that this book is the closest to prophecy of all those that were written after the holy scriptures. It was written before the Mishnah and Talmud, and God's hand was likely on this man while he was writing this book, so that his words were almost prophetic." The assertion that one's own book of history differs from the mass of lying histories can be found throughout sixteenth-century prefaces to histories.

Following the topics of the *accessus,* Ibn Yahya explains the purpose of histories in general, and of this particular book of history:

> Like all histories, this book gives evidence from the past about the future. . . . Contemporaries may learn lessons, each according to his capacity: kings may learn how to win battles and counsellors, to conduct their affairs, "for there is nothing new [under the sun]," and "what is with us now was there in earlier times." Like the histories of other nations, that teach about their origins, the origin of their race, and how they wandered and came to their country, so do we learn from this book about the place from which we were exiled, what it was like, and how we were driven out of our land.[34]

There is no contradiction between the humanist form and values of Ibn Yahya's introduction and his purpose in addressing *Yosippon* to a Jewish audience that was composed, to a large extent, of exiles from Spain. He declares that the reading of this postbiblical, but almost inspired, Jewish history will "strengthen us in our worship of God; and the individual stories, such as those about Daniel, Ahasuerus, and Hannah's sons will sustain our strength to serve God." The Jewish histories that were written in the sixteenth century can all be seen to fulfill the same overall purpose, of providing moral and practical instruction, as well as encouragement for Jewish morale, through presentation of historical examples.

VI

Writings on moral philosophy, which Jewish writers tended to call political philosophy, have always been part of Jewish teaching, so that the most obvious innovation during our period was the use of new literary forms, often narratives, to present the goods and virtues. As in the other fields that correspond to the *studia humanitatis,* Hebrew writers tried to derive their compositions from the most ancient Hebrew texts in the discipline. The biblical book of Proverbs, attributed to King Solomon, fulfilled this function for moral philosophy. Further, Solomon himself was made an exemplary human being and complete sage and ruler, in a voluminous biography. Yohanan Alemanno (1433/34–ca. 1504), a teacher and rabbi who received his medical degree from Messer Leon, wrote this book, *The Song of Solomon's Ascents,* between 1488 and 1492, at the request of Giovanni Pico della Mirandola.[35] Alemanno makes Solomon the Jewish model of the perfect sage and ruler, whose wisdom includes the complete curriculum of studies. Within the biography, Alemanno combines a chronological narrative with a topical arrangement of a wide, eclectic list of goods, arts, sciences, and virtues, taken from philosophy, kabbalah, magic, Jewish law and theology, and humanist sources, to define a *uomo universale,* in Hebrew, a *Hakham Shalem.* The classification of goods, virtues, and sciences most closely conforms to al-Ghazzali's *Criterion of Action,* and the narrative that illustrates it comes from the biblical books of Kings and Chronicles, as well as postbiblical material from varied sources.[36]

Biography had not been cultivated in Hebrew since biblical antiquity, and in Judaism since Philo, as the rabbis avoided turning Moses, Abraham, or David into competitors with the Christian image of Jesus. Alemanno, however, seems to be making Solomon into a Jewish countermodel to Ficino's claim for Jesus: "What else was Christ but a certain living book of moral and divine philosophy, sent from heaven and manifesting the divine idea itself of the virtues to human eyes. . . . Christ is the idea and exemplar of the virtues."[37] Whether Ficino's Christ, Xenophon's Cyrus, or Suetonius's *Divus Augustus* and *Divus Iulius* were his targets, Alemanno announces that he introduced biography to Hebrew in response to the practice of the nations:

> I am very well aware, my son, that you are a wise and understanding man, a Jew who is not used to such long stories telling of a man and his deeds, and who might say that listening to the bleating of this flock of Solomon's virtues wearies the mind. . . . Listen, then, to my two replies to anyone who would seal his ears from hearing more. First, I greatly envied those among all the nations who praise their idols and compose about a single man whole hosts of books, as long as the chronicles of Israel and Judea combined; while we, the community of Jews, do not know how to give two or three particles of praise to one of the holy men of our people. I have therefore opened my mouth to glorify and praise King Solomon, may he rest in peace, with many praises. I undertook to put them into a book in an arrangement that will make it apparent to all the nations that we have as much heart as they. . . . I wrote this book of mine in order . . . to teach the lesson of the wise man who taught in his book [the Song of Songs] that all the virtues and achievements with which he was crowned were vanity compared to the felicity of desire for, and attachment to, the Lord.[38]

Like other Hebrew writers who made innovations in the disciplines that correspond to the *studia humanitatis,* Alemanno establishes a Hebrew original for the genre—in this case, the exemplary life—and then treats that original through distinctive humanist methods. Biblicist hebraism and humanist classicism, although they are distinct, and often opposed, programs of cultural renewal, share enough strategies and values to benefit from each other's methods. Here, Solomon is made an ancient Hebrew exemplar of a system of virtues and sciences that competes with those that Ficino and Pico were proposing.

VII

Already forty years ago, Cecil Roth formulated the essential insight into the way that Hebrew writers appropriated elements of Italian humanism: "The Italian Jews became famous in the Jewish world for their flawless style and composition, in striking contrast to the studied inelegance of their northern European contemporaries. . . . In the same way as the humanistic scholars modelled their prose style on Cicero and Livy, abandoning the barbarous traditions of medieval Church Latin, so their Jewish contemporaries went back to the Bible."[39] It is this essential insight that I have tried to explain and confirm from the texts. Roth did not turn this insight into a guide for further investigation because, as his triumphal prohumanist tone indicates, he wanted only to show that both Jews and Christians were engaged in a clear struggle of Renaissance enlightenment against medieval obscurantism. To show that the Jews belonged to the enlightened camp, Roth adduced an impressive number of Jewish similarities to "Renaissance" traits: individualism, secularism, classicism, and so on. Starting as it did from a polemical caricature of the medieval, and ignoring the inner dynamics of Jewish communities, this argument paradoxically admitted Jews into "the Renaissance" to exactly the degree that they were not behaving as Jews. Our survey here shows, however, that it was not unreflective imitation of a foreign fashion that produced the admired Hebrew of Italian Jews. Instead, the Italian Jews were pursuing a resolutely independent religious and learned program, which they articulated by selectively adapting to their own intellectual heritage the literary, linguistic, and political arts that they could appropriate from humanism. It was in this way that the Jews in fifteenth- and sixteenth-century Italy, a marginal community, succeeded in opening themselves to the world without being assimilated by the world.

NOTES

Research for this paper was supported by the Social Sciences and Humanities Research Council of Canada, to which I express my thanks.

1. There is no adequate survey of Hebrew and other Jewish literature from fifteenth- and sixteenth-century Italy. The most helpful in English is Israel Zinberg, *A History of Jewish Literature*, trans. Bernard Martin (Cincinnati: Hebrew Union College Press and Ktav, 1974), IV.

2. Cecil Roth, *The Jews in the Renaissance* (1959; reprint, New York, Harper and Row, 1965), p. 21.

3. Robert (Reuven) Bonfil. "The Historians' Perception of the Jews in the Italian Renaissance: Towards a Reappraisal," *Revue des Etudes Juives* 143 (Jan.–June 1984), 59–89.

4. Isaac Abravanel, *Commentary on the Pentateuch* [Hebrew] (1862; reprint, Israel: Torah Vada'at, 1956), fol. 33r–v.

5. Origen, Prologue to the Commentary on the Song of Songs. Cited from James L. Kugel, *The Idea of Biblical Poetry* (New Haven, Conn.: Yale University Press, 1981), p. 143, n. 22. On this apologetic strategy, see Harry A. Wolfson, *Philo* (Cambridge, Mass.: Harvard University Press, 1947), 1, 20–22, 141–63.

6. Abraham Farissol, *Magen Avraham*. Cited from David B. Ruderman, *The World of a Renaissance Jew: The Life and Thought of Abraham ben Mordecai Farissol*, Monographs of the Hebrew Union College, 6 (Cincinnati: Hebrew Union College Press, 1981), p. 77, n. 44.

7. Umberto Cassuto, *Gli Ebrei a Firenze nell'età del Rinascimento* (1918; reprint, Firenze: Olschki, 1965), p. 212; Shlomo Simonsohn, *History of the Jews in the Duchy of Mantua*, I [Hebrew] (Jerusalem: Kiryat-Sefer, 1962), 1–10; Moses A. Shulvass, *The Jews in the World of the Renaissance*, trans. Elvin I. Kose (Leiden: Brill, 1973), pp. 1–28.

8. Cecil Roth, "Jewish Society in the Renaissance Environment," in *Jewish Society through the Ages*, ed. Hayim Hillel Ben-Sasson and S. Ettinger (New York: Schocken, 1971), pp. 240–41.

9. Judah Halevi, *The Kuzari: An Argument for the Faith of Israel*, trans. Hartwig Hirschfeld (New York: Schocken, 1964).

10. Profiat Duran, *Sefer Ma'aseh Efod* (1865; reprint, Jerusalem: Makor, 1970). On the historical context, see Yitzhak F. Baer, *A History of the Jews in Christian Spain*, II (Philadelphia: Jewish Publication Society, 1961), 150–60.

11. Baer, pp. 20, 1957; Duran, pp. 191ff.

12. Duran, pp. 177–78; Baer, pp. 159–60.

13. On humanism, see Paul Oskar Kristeller, "Humanist Learning in the Italian Renaissance," in his *Renaissance Thought*, II (New York: Harper, 1965), 3.

14. Duran, p. 42. See Yosef B. Sermoneta, "The Study of the Liberal Arts in Italian Jewish Society in the Fourteenth Century" [Hebrew], in *The City*

and the Community (Jerusalem: Historical Society of Israel, 1968), pp. 249–58.

15. The logical arts were classified as "Categoriae, Perihermenias, Analytica priora, Analytica posteriora, Topica, Sophistica, Rhetorica, Poetica." See Abu-Nasr Al-Farabi, *Catálogo de las Sciencias,* ed. and trans. Ángel González Palencia. 2d ed. (Madrid: n.p., 1953), p. 95.

16. Roth, *Jews in the Renaissance,* pp. 127, 145; Giuseppe (Yosef) B. Sermoneta, Un Glossario filosofico ebraico-italiano del XIII secolo (Rome: Edizioni dell'Ateneo, 1969).

17. Roth, *Jews in the Renaissance,* p. 331; Alexander Altmann, *"Ars Rhetorica* as Reflected in Some Jewish Figures of the Italian Renaissance," in *Jewish Thought in the Sixteenth Century,* ed. Bernard Dov Cooperman (Cambridge, Mass.: Harvard University Press, 1983), p. 20; Gershom G. Scholem, *Kabbalah* (New York: Quadrangle, 1974), pp. 169–74.

18. Duran, pp. 42–43.

19. Judah Messer Leon, *The Book of the Honeycomb's Flow,* ed. and trans. Isaac Rabinowitz (Ithaca, N.Y.: Cornell University Press, 1983). Cf. Robert Bonfil, Introduction to Judah Messer Leon, *Nofet Zufim, on Hebrew Rhetoric* [Hebrew] (Jerusalem: Magnes Press, 1981), pp. 7–69, v–xii.

20. Messer Leon, p. 145.

21. Ibid., pp. 416–17.

22. Ibid., pp. 190–91.

23. Ibid., pp. 172–75.

24. Ibid., pp. 316–17.

25. Kugel, pp. 69–70, 96–134.

26. Kugel, pp. 200–202; Kugel, "The Influence of Moses Ibn Habib's *Darkhei No'am,"* in *Jewish Thought in the Sixteenth Century,* pp. 308–25.

27. Allardyce Nicoll, *The Development of the Theatre,* 5th ed., rev. (New York: Harcourt Brace Jovanovich, 1967), pp. 252–78; Leone de'Sommi, *Quattro dialoghi in materia di rappresentazioni sceniche,* ed. Ferrucio Marotti (Milano: Il Polifilo, 1968), pp. 13–14.

28. Yehuda Sommo mi-Sha'ar Aryeh, *The Comedy of Betrothal* [Hebrew], ed. Hayim Schirmann (Jerusalem: Dvir-Tarshish, 1965), p. 30.

29. Ibid., p. 29.

30. Yosef Hayim Yerushalmi, *Zakhor: Jewish History and Jewish Memory* (Seattle: University of Washington Press, 1982), pp. 31–34; Yerushalmi, "Clio and the Jews," in *American Academy for Jewish Research Jubilee Volume,* 2 (1980), 615.

31. Moses Maimonides, *Commentary on the Mishnah, Sanhedrin* X, 1. Cited from Salo W. Baron, *A Social and Religious History of the Jews,* 2d ed., rev., (Philadelphia: Jewish Publication Society, 1958), VI, 198–99, no. 59.

32. Titus Livius, *Ab urbe condita,* praefatio 10. Cited from A. D. Leeman, *Orationis ratio: The Stylistic Theories and Practice of the Roman Orators, Historians and Philosophers,* 2 vols. (Amsterdam: n.p., 1963), I, 194.

33. Yerushalmi, *Zakhor,* pp. 35–36. See Edwin A. Quain, "The Medieval

accessus ad auctores," *Traditio* 3 (1945), 215–64; Sermoneta, "Study of the Liberal Arts"; *Sefer Yosippon,* ed. A. Hominer (Tel Aviv: Sifriati, 1965), pp. 41–44.

34. *Yosippon,* p. 43.
35. Arthur Lesley, " 'The Song of Solomon's Ascents,' by Yohanan Alemanno: Love and Human Perfection According to a Jewish Associate of Giovanni Pico della Mirandola" (Diss., University of California, Berkeley, 1976), pp. 4–5.
36. Abu Hamid al-Ghazzali, *Sefer Moznei Tsedek,* ed. J. Goldenthal (1839; reprint, Jerusalem: Rare Judaica Publishing House, 1975). See Mohamed Ahmed Sherif, *Ghazali's Theory of Virtue* (Albany: State University of New York, 1975).
37. Marsilio Ficino, *De religione christiana,* XXIII (Basel, 1576), II, 42r–13v. Cited from Charles B. Trinkhaus, *In our Image and Likeness.* 2 vols. (Chicago, University of Chicago Press, 1970), II, 741.
38. Lesley, pp. 55, 472–74.
39. Cecil Roth, *A History of the Jews of Italy* (Philadelphia: Jewish Publication Society, 1916), p. 216.

2

Ars Rhetorica as Reflected in Some Jewish Figures of the Italian Renaissance

Alexander Altmann

Jews living in Renaissance Italy had access to two different philosophical traditions: (1) the Arabic and Judeo-Arabic one, which was inherited from the Middle Ages, and (2) the Latin one, which was being enriched by the discoveries of fresh texts, Latin and Greek, and was being infused with a new spirit, that of humanism. The two traditions did not necessarily converge toward a unified pattern. Their respective attitudes toward the art of rhetoric is a case in point. The Latin sphere of philosophical culture had been able to draw, throughout the medieval period, upon a rich classical legacy that included the writings of Aristotle, Cicero, and Quintilian,[1] while Arabic philosophy had known only Aristotle.[2] The translations of Arabic texts into Latin produced from the twelfth century onward had reinforced the Aristotelian perspective of rhetoric in Latin culture but had hardly changed the overall picture. Rhetoric in the Latin West remained more or less under the dominance of the Ciceronian tradition, no matter how arid and formalistic in its application. The revival of a broader concept of classical rhetoric in the Renaissance was due, to a large extent, to the rediscovery of Quintilian's complete text and of Cicero's *De oratore* in 1416 and 1421 respectively. The Italian Jews of the Renaissance were therefore confronted with two somewhat divergent legacies and, as could have been expected, they were by no means unanimous in the choice of options presented to them. Elijah del

Reprinted by permission of Harvard Center for Jewish Studies from *Jewish Thought in the Sixteenth Century*, edited by Bernard Cooperman, Cambridge, Mass., 1983.

Medigo, for example, seems to have decided to adhere to the medieval orientation,[3] while other prominent figures like Judah ben Yeḥiel Messer Leon, Azariah de Rossi, and Judah Moscato clearly reflect the impact of Renaissance thinking.

What was the role and place of rhetorical art in the Arabic and Judeo-Arabic tradition? Aristotle had defined rhetoric as "the faculty of discovering the possible means of persuasion in reference to any subject whatever" (*Rhetorica*, I.ii.1). Proofs common to all branches of rhetoric were said by him to be of two kinds, example and enthymeme, and to correspond to the use of induction and syllogism in the art of dialectical argumentation, rhetoric being as it were "an offshoot of dialectic" (I.ii.7–8; II.xx.1). As a parallel to the possible "topics" of the dialectical syllogism discussed in *Topica*, Aristotle deals with the specifically rhetorical topics (II.xxiii). The *Rhetorica* does not contrast the art of persuasion and dialectic with the science of demonstration. Aristotle's view concerning the relationship between these three types of argument is spelled out in his logical writings and it may be summed up as follows: The dialectic syllogism and the rhetorical enthymeme proceed from probable premises and arrive at conclusions that are merely probable, whereas strict demonstration or scientific proof is based on incontrovertibly true, i.e., self-evident, premises and reaches equally true conclusions (*Anal. Prior*, II.xxiii, xxvii; *Topica*, I.1). It was this suggestion of a descending scale of logical validity that was seized upon by the Arabic philosophers in determining the place of the *Rhetorica* (and *Poetica*) as the last treatises in the *Organon*, thus highlighting the art of rhetoric as inferior in logical terms to both scientific and dialectical proofs, the difference between dialectic and rhetoric consisting in the kind of probable premises from which they proceed: dialectical probable premises were generally accepted by well-informed people, whereas rhetorical probable premises were accepted by the common people.

This relegation of rhetoric to a logically inferior position, though in accord with Aristotle's stated opinion, tended to ignore the important function that the *Rhetorica* assigns to the art of persuasion in the context of political life and, more precisely, in relation to ethics (*Rhetorica*, I.ii.7). It also failed to attach due prominence to the three kinds of rhetoric (deliberative, forensic, and epideictic), by the careful delineation of which (I.iii.1–6 and passim) Aristotle illuminated the significant role rhetoric exercised in society. By fastening upon the *logical* status of the art, the Arabic philosophers succeeded in downplaying the orator in contrast to the philosopher, and by stressing the close proximity of orator and dialectician, if not their essential identity, they deliberately sought to equate theology and rhetoric. While Aristotle considered oratory the legitimate province of political reality and projected a thoroughly approved use of it in the three kinds of rhetorical activity spelled out in rich detail, the *falāsifa* narrowed down this field of applicability by focusing upon the theologians or preachers of religion as the representatives of a logically faulty rhetoric. To be sure, they did not deny the politically useful role of this particular form of rhetoric, but whereas for Aristotle politics and rhetoric were organically connected, these two elements were now linked in a somewhat artificial manner: For the sake of the common people's happiness—which is the goal of politics—the philosophical truth can be communicated only in the disguise of rhetoric, that is, by proceeding from premises accepted by the common people.

This reading of Aristotle in the light of changed religious and social conditions was initiated by Alfarabi, continued by Avicenna, and perfected by Averroes. Alfarabi's *Kitāb al-Khaṭāba* ("Book of Rhetoric") was part of the lost *Mukhtaṣar al-Manṭiq* ("Abridgment of Logic"), and it has been described by its editor (Jacques Langhade) as a work in which "le point de vue logique prédomine tout au long de l'oeuvre. C'est par des définitions logiques qu'Al-Fārābī commence, et c'est en logicien qu'il continue à envisager et à expliquer la Rhétorique" (p. 26). Alfarabi's lost commentary on the *Rhetorica* seems to have been on a grand scale, but the introduction to it (which is known from Hermann the German's *Didascalia in Rhetoricam Aristotelis ex Glosa Alpharabii,* a simple translation of the introduction and folio 1 of the text) is again heavily weighted on the side of logic. In the words of its editor (Mario Grignaschi), "L'idée maîtresse d'Al-Fārābī" was "que la rhétorique et la poétique font partie de la logique" (p. 139). It is in complete agreement with this idea that Alfarabi's *Iḥṣā' al-'ulūm* ("Enumeration of Sciences") lists rhetoric and poetics as the last topics (nos. 7 and 8) under the rubric of logic *('ilm al-manṭiq).* Avicenna followed this trend. The very first chapter of his rhetoric in *Al-Shifā'* (I.8) is related to Alfarabi's *Kitāb al-Khaṭāba,* as Grignaschi suggested (p. 132). As for Averroes, he wrote a *Middle Commentary (Talkhīṣ)* as well as a *Short Commentary (Jāmi')* on Aristotle's *Rhetorica,* and, according to the incisive analysis of the former by its editor and translator (Charles E. Butterworth), he included rhetoric and poetics in the *Organon* in order to alert the reader to the inferior status of rhetorical and poetical arguments compared with demonstrative and even dialectical proofs. Averroes is said to have indicated the advisability of the use of rhetoric rather than dialectic by the theologians, which tallies with the stance he took in his *Faṣl al-Maqāl* ("The Decisive Treatise"): For every Muslim the Law has offered a specific way to truth according to his nature, through demonstrative, dialectical, or rhetorical methods. In Scripture, dialectical and rhetorical arguments are preferred because it is the purpose of Scripture to teach and guide the majority of men.[4]

Medieval Jewish philosophy adopted this assessment of rhetoric. Moses ibn Ezra's *Poetics (Kitāb al-Muḥāḍara wal-Mudhākara)* opens its chapter on "Rhetoric and Rhetoricians"[5] by defining the art, in the name of Aristotle, as "persuasive speech" but, significantly, adds the qualification "below firm opinion" and further explains that there are five logical arts in all: demonstrative, dialectical, poetical, rhetorical, and sophistical. Maimonides briefly discusses the difference between demonstrative, dialectical, rhetorical, sophistical, and poetical syllogisms in his *Maqāla fī Sana'at al-Mantiq (Milot ha-Higayon)*, ch. VIII. He describes the difference between dialectical and rhetorical proofs as proceeding from generally accepted and traditionally received opinions respectively. Rhetoric is thereby closely associated with religious revealed doctrine. In the *Guide of the Perplexed* there is only a single reference to Aristotle's *Rhetorica* (III, 49), but it must be assumed that his famous interpretation of Rabbi Ishmael's dictum, *dibra tora ki-leshon bney adam*, expresses a distinctly rhetorical advice. "The meaning of this is," says Maimonides (I.26), "that everything that all men are capable of understanding and representing to themselves at first thought *(bi-awwal fikrihi; bi-teḥilat ha-maḥshava)* has been ascribed to Him." The term "at first thought" has a rhetorical connotation. Alfarabi used its equivalent when describing the condition under which the enthymeme (the rhetorical syllogism) becomes persuasive "for the immediate common view" (*fī bādī al-ra'y al-mushtarak;* Langhade and Grignaschi, p. 62; s. note), and Averroes in his *Short Commentary on the Rhetorica* did likewise when defining the enthymeme as a syllogism leading to a conclusion that "corresponds to the immediate view (Butterworth: 'unexamined opinion') previously existing among all or most people" *(bi-ḥasabi bādī al-ra'y . . . ;* Butterworth, pp. 63, 170). The "first" or "immediate" (unexamined) view of the multitude has to be addressed and persuaded by rhetoric, and this is why Maimonides' defense of anthropomorphic language in Scripture amounts to a vindication of rhetoric. Yet the fact remains that for him (and Averroes) scriptural language, however necessary, is *only* rhetoric. Strangely enough, he has little or no use for the artistic element of rhetoric. Aristotle's elaborate discussion of the various elements of style and arrangement evokes no response. He does not refer to this aspect of rhetoric when dealing with the "figurative expressions and rhetorical speeches" of the prophets in *Guide,* II.29, where the hyperbolic language of eschatological passages might have invited some reference to the persuasiveness achieved by certain rhetorical devices. All he mentions in this respect is the fact that "every prophet has a kind of speech peculiar to him," as noted already in the Talmud (*Sanh.* 89a). Rhetoric somehow dwindles down to the comparative evaluation of its place in the hierarchy of logical syllogisms, and its low rank is determined by its function to persuade the multitude, a view that persisted throughout the medieval period and can still be discerned in Elijah del Medigo's *Beḥinat ha-Dat*.[6]

A radically new attitude to the art of rhetoric is manifested in Judah ben Yeḥiel Messer Leon's *Nofet Tzufim,* which was written some time between 1454 and 1474 and appeared in print shortly afterwards (Mantua, 1476–80?) as one of the first Hebrew incunabula. Adolf Jellinek, who republished it (Vienna, 1863), correctly described it on the German title page as a "Rhetorik nach Aristoteles, Cicero und Quintilian, mit besonderer Beziehung auf die Heilige Schrift." In other words, it is a full-fledged treatise on rhetoric, not a manual designed for the benefit of pulpit oratory, as Moritz Steinschneider (*Hebr. Übers.,* 78) suggested. As such, it takes its place alongside some of the major works on the subject that were produced in the fifteenth and sixteenth centuries in response to the Ciceronianism that pervaded the age. Thus, prior to the *Nofet Tzufim* the Greek émigré George of Trebizond known as Trapezuntius (1395–1486), having studied Cicero with Guarino Veronese, wrote his *Rhetoricorum libri quinque* in 1436 or 1437. To the following century belong Philipp Melanchthon's *Institutiones rhetoricae,* Leonard Cox's *Rhetorike* (London, c. 1530) and, perhaps the closest analogue to Messer Leon's work, Thomsas Wilson's *The Arte of Rhetorique* (London, 1585).

Messer Leon's openness to Ciceronian humanism is all the more noteworthy in light of the fact that he also continued the medieval tradition of studying, presenting, and commenting upon Aristotle. In 1453/54 he wrote a compendium of Aristotelian logic *(Mikhlal Yofi)* which, significantly, does not comprise the *Rhetorica* and *Poetica,* a departure from the medieval pattern that may be said to point to the more independent status of these two arts about to emerge. The rhetorical concern is evident already in this early work, for the introduction states the purpose of presenting "old and new subject matters in excellent order *(be-sidur nifla)* and in the utmost degree of elegance and beauty attainable *(be-takhlit ma she-efshar be-erki min ha-hidur ve-ha-yofi)*" so as to duly impress the reader and facilitate his understanding. He wrote, in addition, a commentary on Averroes' *Middle Commentary* to the first five books of the *Organon,* which Jacob Anatoli had translated into Hebrew in 1232. According to his son's report, he also commented on other Aristotelian works.

Messer Leon's *Nofet Tzufim* may be characterized as a judiciously performed synthesis or amalgam of most of the classical texts on rhetoric, selecting from each one what seemed to be the clearest and most felicitous passages dealing with the manifold issues discussed. The following sources are used in the compilation:

1. Aristotle's *Rhetorica (halatza)* as quoted and discussed in Averroes' *Middle Commentary* known to Leon in the Hebrew version by Todros ben Meshullam (1337), to text edited by Jacob Goldenthal (Leipzig, 1842). Leon's use of this version is attested by the terminology he employed; e.g., the term *haspaka* for "persuasion" was obviously taken from Todros' Hebrew version, which renders Arabic *quanā'a* and/or *iqnā'.* Likewise, *siman* (pp. 135, 137) in the sense of "enthymeme" is borrowed from Todros' version, where it translates Arabic *ḍamīr.* Steinschneider already noted that Leon consulted Averroes' *Middle Commentary* rather than the original Aristotle. Yet it is possible that he also knew the Latin version of the *Rhetorica.*

2. The (pseudo-Aristotelian) *Rhetorica ad Alexandrum (ha-halatza asher asa le-Aleksander),* the genuineness of which was first doubted by Erasmus of Rotterdam, is but rarely quoted. It is referred to also as an "abridgment" of the *Rhetorica (Kitzuro she-shalah le-Aleksander;* s. p. 16).

3. Cicero's *De inventione,* known also as the *Rhetorica vetus,* is referred to by Leon as *Tullio ba-halatza ha-yeshana.*

4. (Pseudo-) Cicero's *Rhetorica ad Herrenium,* known also as the

Rhetorica nova, is referred to by Leon as *Tullio ba-halatza ha-ḥadasha.* It was, again, Erasmus who questioned first the genuineness of the work.

5. Fabius Laurentius Victorinus' *Explanationes in Rhetoricam M. Tulli Ciceronis* is referred to by Leon as *Vittorio ha-mefaresh.* The author is a fourth-century rhetorician who is mentioned by St. Augustine (*Confessio* VII.ix), and the work quoted is a commentary on Cicero's *De inventione.*[7]

6. Quintilian's *Institutio oratoria,* the most elaborate and accomplished work in rhetorical literature, is referred to by Leon simply as *Quintiliano ba-perek . . . me-ha-ḥelek ha- . . . (min ha-ma'amar ha- . . .).* It was the impact of the rediscovery of the complete text by Poggio Bracciolini in 1416 that helped to rekindle the enthusiasm for the rhetorical art as a potent element in education. Leon's fulsome quotations from this work in all its parts show the remarkable extent of his familiarity with it.[8]

A major work not quoted by Messer Leon is Cicero's *De oratore,* the complete text of which had been rediscovered by Bishop Gerardo Landriani five years after the find of Quintilian's opus.[9] He probably did not come across this work in either its mutilated form (which had been used by Petrarch) or in its completeness. Otherwise he would have used it, since the image of the orator drawn therein would have suited his purposes.

What motivated Messer Leon to write the *Nofet Tzufim?* It is obvious from the scholarship he invested in this work as well as from the lofty style he employed that he was fascinated by the new look at rhetoric that dominated the era and by the classical texts themselves that he had studied. He could not have failed to notice that the ancient authors (Aristotle, Cicero, Quintilian) were able to illustrate the rhetorical rules by an abundance of quotations from their own literature, and he must therefore have felt the urge to discover the rhetorical dimension also in the Hebrew Bible. It seems that it was the prospect of finding the rhetorical principles embodied in biblical speech that gave wings to his efforts. For this is how he summed up, at the opening of the fourth and last part of his work, what he had so far accomplished (p. 147):

After the foregoing account of the subject-matters of this book and having entered into their domains by searching every section of the writings of the ancient and modern rhetoricians for precious material *[divrey ḥefetz],* it now remains for us to treat the various categories of rhetorical embellishment . . . and most of what we shall have to say thereon will be taken from Cicero's *Rhetorica [ad Herrenium]* and from part III of Aristotle's *Rhetorica.* Yet the illustrations *[ha-meshalim lahem]* I shall adduce from our own glorious sanctuary, from the words of the prophets and from the biblical narratives that "sit first in the kingdom" [Esther 1:14] of rhetorical perfection *[ha-arevut ve-ha-tzaḥut]* and which "cannot be gotten for gold, neither shall the exchange thereof be vessels of fine gold" [Job 28:15, 17].

The assertion that biblical oratory occupied the highest rank in the "kingdom of rhetoric" has to be understood not merely as an expression of piety, but, more particularly, as an attempt to cope with the awareness so characteristic for the Renaissance that there was a common human element, a universal law as it were, that ruled rhetoric, the art of communication, everywhere. The universalism that was all-pervasive in the syncretistic culture of the period made is psychologically imperative for a Jewish traditionalist like Messer Leon to stress the superiority of the Jewish heritage within the commonality of mankind. He was sophisticated enough to realize that the enthusiastic manner in which he applied, to the Hebrew Bible, the rules of rhetoric formulated by the ancient pagans presented some problems. To obviate any misunderstanding he made his position clear at the end of the introduction to *Nofet Tzufim:* Addressing the reader, he emphatically warned him against assuming that it was the conformity of the prophets' speeches to the rhetorical rules of the Gentiles that constituted, in his view, their claim to greatness. One who were to interpret him in this fashion would be utterly wrong. He continued: "Yet if it occurred to you that I turned to those writings because they approximate to the words of the prophets and form a close link with them, you would guess my intent correctly." Classical rhetoric is thus described not as a yardstick for biblical oratory but as an intriguing parallel that caught his fancy. The true facts of the case are not so clear-cut, however. Messer Leon was obviously first drawn to the classical works on the subject, found them highly illuminating, and then sought to discover their rules and devices in the biblical texts. In so doing he brought a hitherto untried method to bear on the comprehension of the Bible. Whereas Maimonides and those following him saw in biblical rhetoric a mere concession to the need of addressing the multitude in terms compatible with their mental capacity, rhetoric now took on the character of a noble art indispensable for effective communication on all levels of public life. It was, above all, the figure of the orator that now commanded a new respect.

The heightened importance attached to oratory and orator is clearly reflected in the *Nofet Tzufim*. Quintilian (II.xv) had passed in review the various definitions of the art of rhetoric previously advanced. They had apparently all taken their cue from the role of the art in sophistry. Hence the tendency to equate rhetoric with persuasiveness, which was adopted also in Aristotle's definition. By contrast, Quintilian professed to have undertaken the task of molding the perfect orator who had to be a good man, and he therefore proposed the definition of rhetoric as "the science of speaking well" *(bene dicendi scientiam)*. This definition was meant to imply that "no man could speak well unless he was good himself." The corollary of this definition was the view that the orator and his art were independent of results (II.xvii). Indeed, the speaker aimed at victory, but if he spoke well, he had lived up to the ideals of his art, even if he was defeated. Like Quintilian, Messer Leon (I.1) reviewed the possible definitions of rhetoric but, unlike Quintilian, he suggested that they all amounted to the same thing and could be squared with Aristotle's. He did not mention the famous definition that Cicero gave in *De optimo genere oratorum* (I.3–4): "The supreme orator, then, is the one whose speech instructs, delights, and moves the minds of his audience," a definition not referred to in Quintilian's discussion either. He quoted instead Cicero's statement in *De inventione* (I.v.6) that the function of eloquence was to persuade by speech. In the end he suggested that one might distinguish between the inner and outer purpose of oratory, the one being the inner quality of the speech ("speaking well"), the other the outer effect ("persuasion"). He saw the inner purpose alluded to in Isa. 50:4, "The Lord hath given me the tongue of them that are taught" *(leshon limudim)*, and the outer purpose indicated by Prov. 10:32, "The lips of the righteous know what is acceptable" *(siftey tzadik yed'un ratzon)*, persuasion being *hafakat ha-ratzon be-ma'amar (persuadere dictione)*. The orator is tacitly identified with the *tzadik* (Quintilian's *vir bonus)*, a view that is not just coincidental but will be pursued later.

Messer Leon is not unmindful of the havoc and misery that may be effected by eloquent speech and, like Cicero *(De inv.* I.i.1) and Quintilian (II.xvi.1–4), he dwells at some length upon the ruin wrought by the wicked whose "tongue walketh through the earth" (Ps. 73:9). This gloomy picture serves, however, only as a counterpoint to the brightness of the portrait he draws of the immense benefit that a nation derives from its great orators. In answer to the question "What is the orator?" *(mahu ha-melitz)*, he now completely identifies himself with Quintilian's idealistic image, which he finds also supported by the commentators: It is impossible for the perfect orator *(ha-melitz ha-shalem)* not to be a "good and righteous man" *(adam tov ve-tzadik)* (I.ii.9). How could he be a leader of men wielding full power of persuasion unless he was utterly sincere *(piv ve-libo shalem)*? Moreover, he had to master the three branches of sciences, viz., the natural, political, and linguistic fields of knowledge, into which Quintilian had divided philosophy. The last-mentioned science (comprising the *artes sermocinales)* included logic, rhetoric and grammar, while natural science embraced the divine science (metaphysics), as Victorinus had pointed out. To be sure, the orator was not supposed to discuss philosophical subjects in all their technical details and in great depth, for persuasion was achieved only if things were presented to the audience in a manner easily comprehensible to all. It is clear, however, that Messer Leon wished to depict the orator as a figure of considerable philosophic erudition, whose words were both eloquent and weighty.

The image of the orator drawn by Messer Leon corresponds to the humanist aspirations which, following Cicero's vision, sought to combine philosophy and rhetoric, a trend that had been initiated by Petrarch and was continued by men like Coluccio Salutati, Leonardo Bruni and, in a way, also by Lorenzo Valla, who would subordinate philosophy to rhetoric.[10] The *Nofet Tzufim* was written prior to the revolution of the "New Logic" that was started by Rudolph Agricola (1444–1485) and was brought to fruition by Peter Ramus (1515–1572). The meaning of that revolt was the creation of a unified field of logic by breaking down the barriers between the *topoi* of dialectic and rhetoric established by Aristotle. It thereby signified the relegation of rhetoric to pure eloquence. It expressed, at its deepest level, a protest against the intrusion of person-to-person communication into the realm of intellectual life, and thus it marked the transition from dialogue to the scientific age of reason.[11] Messer Leon belonged to the "dialogical" humanism of the Renaissance, and to him the nontechnical orator-philosopher represents the ideal figure because of the role he is destined to play in the nation.

This favorable evaluation is articulated in striking fashion by the equation of the orator with the *tzadik,* brief mention of which has already been made. We have here an interpretation of the *tzadik* figure poles apart from the understanding of that term in contemporary Kabbalah. Leon quotes Prov. 10:20, "The tongue of the *tzadik* is as choice silver," and he understands it as a characterization of the orator as a man "perfect in his character and philosophical notions" *(shalem hamidot ve-ha-de'ot)*. There were numerous biblical verses testifying to the same view of the orator, and he concludes the chapter (I.2) by describing the prophets of Israel as the most illustrious representatives of this type. All this, he points out, supported Quintilian's definition of oratory.

The following are a few selected examples of the way in which Messer Leon projected rhetorical rules upon biblical material. In Deut. 32:2, the opening of Moses' farewell song, he (I.4) discovers an affirmation, in poetic language, of the five operations in which, according to Cicero *(De inv. I.vii.9; see also Ad Herr. I.ii.3)* and Quintilian (III.iii.1ff.), the art of rhetoric consists: invention *(inventio, hamtza'a)*; arrangement *(dispositio, seder)*; style *(elocutio, tzahut)*; memory *(memoria, zekhira)*; and delivery *(pronunciatio, remiza)*. Invention and style are said to be alluded to by the term *lekah (likhi)*, which denotes a "taking hold" of the subject-matter as well as the "winning" power achieved by beauty of language. Arrangement and memory are hinted at in the metaphors "dropping as the rain" and "distilling as the dew" respectively. The metaphors "as the small rain upon the tender grass" and "as the showers upon the herb" are interpreted as the persuasive power of the oration, which is attuned to all levels of the audience's understanding. They are also applied to the successful delivery, i.e., the appropriate manner of tone and gesticulation. Moses invoked the testimony of heaven and earth (32:1) for his intention of delivering a speech in which none of the five operations constituting a perfect oration shall be missing. The constrained and artificial manner of Messer Leon's exegesis illustrates his keen desire to find some biblical *locus probandi* for so prominent a rule as the one concerning the five elements of oratory.

Judah's oration before Joseph (Gen. 44:18–34) is seen by Messer Leon as structured according to the sixpartite division of forensic *('itzumi)* speech advocated by Cicero *(De inv. I.xiv.19; Ad Herr. I.iii.7.)*: introduction *(exordium, petiha)*; statement of fact *(narratio, sipur)*; partition *(partitio, hiluk)*; confirmation *(confirmatio, kiyum)*; refutation *(reprehensio or confutatio, hatara)*; and peroration *(conclusio, hatima)*. Leon inaccurately attributed the same division also to Aristotle and

Quintilian, who prescribe, however, only four and five parts respectively (*Rhet,* III.xiii; *Inst. or.* III.ix). In I.7 (p. 24) he does refer, though, to Aristotle's statement (*Rhet.* III.xiii) that in speeches of an epideictic *(mekayem)* or deliberative *('atzati)* kind—as distinct from forensic oratory—only two parts are required: the statement of subject and the proof. He also quotes Cicero's counsel against counterproductive introductions (*De inv.* I.xviii.26) and mentions Quintilian's similar caveat (IV.i.72–73), it being the purpose of the exordium to make the audience attentive *(attentum, makshiv),* well-disposed *(benevolum, mehabev),* and ready to receive instruction *(docilem, mitlamed)* (I.5; *Ad Alex.* XXIX 1436a; *Inst. or.* IV.i.5). The conclusion Messer Leon draws from these various points of view is the realization of the need for a certain flexibility, which he finds confirmed by biblical testimony: "If you consider the Holy Scriptures, you will find that what Aristotle and Quintilian said is undoubtedly true." Only in rare cases, he points out, did biblical speeches contain all six parts. Abigail's oration (1 Sam. 25:24–31), he tries to show, was structured in the following way: statement of fact (24a); exordium (24b). The rest is amplification and rhetorical embellishment. Messer Leon regards this speech as a model of oration hardly matched by any other (p. 26).

Of particular significance is Messer Leon's attention to the style peculiar to biblical oratory. From the *Rhetorica ad Herrenium* (IV.viii.11) he probably took the distinction between three kinds of style called "types" *(figuras, tzurot):* the grand *(gravem, nisa'),* the middle *(mediocrem, beynoni),* and the simple *(extenuatam, shafel).* He (I.14) characterizes the grand style as one employing special or figurative words of utmost elegance or as one of speeches that include amplification *(amplificatio, harhava)*—see II.11; *Ad Herr.* II.xxix.48ff.—and pathetic form *(conquestio, rahmanut;* see *Ad Herr.* III.xiii.24; *De inv.* I..106) or a combination of rhetorical embellishments *(yipuyim halatziyim).* He considers most of the speeches of Isaiah and some of the narrations of Ezekiel the very epitome of grand style.

These specimens of Messer Leon's recourse to biblical rhetoric unmistakably show how profoundly he was impressed by the elaborate structure of the rhetorical art as manifested in the sources at his disposal, and how strongly he felt the need to project those rules upon the biblical material. An almost autobiographical note to this effect occurs in I.13 (pp. 47–48), where he pleads for the study of the secular sciences as help toward an increased awareness of the riches contained in the Holy Scriptures. The "science of rhetoric" *(ḥokhmat ha-halatza)*, he says, is particularly useful in this regard.

For when I had studied the Torah in the habitual way, I had not been able to fathom that it embraced the science [or rhetoric] or part of it. Only after I had learned, searched and mastered it [rhetoric] in all its depth from the writings of the Gentiles, could I visualize, when returning to the Holy Scriptures, what they were like. Now the eyes of my understanding were opened and I saw that there was, in fact, a vast difference *[hevdel muflag]* between the pleasantness and elegance of their speeches *['arevut amareha ve-tzaḥiyuteha]* . . . and all that is found in this [genre] among the rest of the nations, the difference resembling that between "the hyssop out of the wall" and "the cedar that is in Lebanon" [1 Kings 5:13].

Yet for all its emphasis on the uniqueness of the Bible, the aesthetic viewpoint, which Leon pushed to the foreground, contained the seed of secularism, for it saw the Scriptures as great "literature." This approach had been anticipated, under the influence of Aristotle's *Poetica*, in Moses ibn Ezra's *Kitāb al-Muḥāḍara wal-Mudh-ākara* and in Abu'l-Barakāt's *Kitāb al-Muʻtabar* in the twelfth century,[12] but the Middle Ages had not been hospitable to the idea. It was different now in the intellectual climate of Renaissance thought. From Judah Messer Leon's *Nofet Tzufim* the road leads to Azariah de Rossi in the sixteenth century and thence to Robert Lowth and Moses Mendelssohn in the eighteenth.

While Messer Leon applied the classical rules of rhetorical art to the Hebrew Scriptures, Azariah de Rossi took the novel step of referring to them, albeit in limited degree, when dealing with rabbinic Aggadah. In so doing he consciously followed in Messer Leon's footsteps. He quoted him twice in *Imrey Bina* and once in *Matzref la-Kesef*. The first passage[13] draws attention to "the book *Nofet Tzufim* of the great scholar R. Judah known as Messer Leon of Mantua," in particular to the statement at the end of I.13 (cited above), which he sums up in these words: "From the indications of the rhetorical embellishments to which the Gentile scholars alert us we come to recognize how superbly beautiful and pleasant are the Holy Scriptures." He then literally reproduces Messer Leon's concluding remark in which he deprecates the unwillingness of many rabbis to accept the truth from foreign sources. The second passage is more specific. It occurs in a context (I.B. 234–239) discussing the rabbinic use of hyperbole as a rhetorical device and makes corroborative reference to the acknowledgment of the same device by the Gentile rhetoricians as a praiseworthy one, "as you find it stated by their leading writers, Cicero *(Tullio)* in *Topica* IV [should read: X, 44–45] and Quintilian in *Insitutio oratoria (be-ha-latzato)* VII.vi [67–76], from whom the Jewish rhetorician *(ha-melitz ha-yehudi)*, author of the *Nofet Tzufim,* borrowed in IV.43 *(Perek ha-Guzma)*" (p. 236).

Interestingly enough, de Rossi considers it necessary to refer to Gentile support for an oratorical form of expression which, as his Talmudic references show, was fully recognized within the Jewish tradition. He was obviously motivated by the desire to legitimize the use of this kind of interpretation also concerning matters that *prima facie* are asserted as historical facts. For he uses it subsequently in an effort to show that R. Yohanan's statement *(Yoma* 19a) about the number (over 300) of high priests during the Second Temple period was not historical but hyperbolic (ibid.). Quintilian's phrase describing the hyperbole as "an elegant straining of the truth" must have appealed to him. He might have quoted other sources such as Aristotle, *Rhetorica* III.x.15–16 and the *Ad Herenium* IV.xxxiii. The third passage is similar in intent to the second. It is found in *Matzref la-Kesef* II.13 (p. 107, note) and relates to a rabbinic statement *(Ned.* 37b) about the Sinaitic origin of certain masoretic elements. De Rossi considers it a purely rhetorical assertion, "for in all languages do we find essential embellishments *(yipuyim atzmiyim)* and all the more so in this holy and primeval language, as has been shown by the scholarly author of *Nofet Tzufim* who adduced scriptural examples for every form of rhetorical embellishment found therein." It appears from these statements by de Rossi that he valued rhetorical theory as an aid to historical scholarship.

In similar fashion oratorical technique is resorted to as the explanation of the Talmudic-midrashic legend about the strange punishment God decreed upon Titus *(Gittin* 56b; *Pirqey R. Eliezer* 49), which seemed unbelievable to de Rossi as an historical account *(I.B.* 214–219). He quoted "the mellifluous speaker of theirs"—a reference to Cicero—and "our truly wise sages" *(hakhamenu ha-mehukamim be-emet)* who would purposely invent stories of this kind in order to impress people by their fancifulness and thereby drive home certain moral or intellectual verities (p. 217). Oratory as seen from this perspective comes close to poetry, and de Rossi, in a mood of poetic inspiration, felicitously likens the *aggadot* of the rabbis to those groups of angels that are said to arise from the "fiery stream" *(nehar di-nur)*, deliver their song, and, having fulfilled their purpose, return to that element not to be seen again. He takes great pain to collect the numerous rabbinic dicta in which the fluidity of Aggadah is contrasted with the exactness of Halakhah and the rule is laid down that in aggadic matters contentious debate is out of place *(eyn makshin be-aggada)* (*I.B.* 210–212). He has a whole section on poetic theory in which he quotes, among others, Moses ibn Ḥabib's *Darkley No'am* (*I.B.* 477–484). In *Matzref la-Kesef* he refers to Horace's *De arte poetica* (p. 121). He was clearly groping for a rabbinic rhetoric and poetic and he was well equipped to undertake such a task. Yet he remained content to use certain aspects of both in the service of historical research.

Judah Moscato (1530–c. 1593), a contemporary of de Rossi (b. 1513) and his friend and supporter, represented the Hebrew version of the Renaissance in the most accomplished manner. His erudition was steeped in classical, medieval, and Renaissance literature, and his superb Hebrew style exemplified, and did not merely discourse upon, the humanist concern for *ars rhetorica.* Yet there is no lack of direct references to oratorical theory in both his published works, the sermonic collection *Nefutzot Yehuda,*[14] and the commentary on Judah ha-Levi's *Sefer ha-Kuzari* called *Kol Yehuda.*[15] With de Rossi, he shared, among other things, a sense of indebtedness to Messer Leon's pioneering work in Hebrew rhetoric. In Sermon V (fol. 19d) he quoted, *in extenso,* the concluding passage of the introduction to *Nofet Tzufim*[16] in which Messer Leon had sought to define his priorities. Moscato obviously wished to identify himself with the sentiments expressed. He was not, however, an uncritical follower of Messer Leon's outline of rhetoric. He used additional sources such as Cicero's *De partitione oratoria* (19d) and Rudolph Agricola's *De inventione dialectica* (20a), which had been published in 1538 in Paris, and he reached partly different conclusions. He acknowledged five operations of rhetoric instead of six *(Kol Yehuda* on II.72, p. 161f.) and four parts of speech instead of six (*Nefutzot* 19d–20a). He somewhat changed the terminology. The term *haspaka* ("persuasion"), which was an imitation of Arab, *qinā'a,* he replaced by the more idiomatic Hebrew phrase *hafakat ratzon* (20a), which Leon had used only occasionally. Instead of *sipur,* he used *hatza'a* to denote the *narratio* (statement of fact: 19d); and in designating the rhetorical operations by their Italian terms, he referred to *elocutio* (style; *tzaḥut*) as *enunciatione.*

The strong impression that classical rhetoric made upon Moscato's mind is strikingly attested by his attempt to rediscover some of its features in rabbinic sources. Like de Rossi, he applied the urge for projections of this kind to rabbinic literature, seeing that Messer Leon had focused his attention on biblical material. There are two rather bizzare examples of this procedure. The first concerns the aggadic story told in *Sanhedrin* 44b: The angel (Rashi: Gabriel) appointed for the defense of Israel before the heavenly court protests, in exceedingly bold language, against the harsh words uttered by God to Ezekiel (16:3) about the patriarchs. The question is asked whether the angel did not overstep his authority in using such language before God. The answer given is to the effect that he was within his rights, for he bore three names spelling out his legitimate functions: *piskon,* i.e., the one who lays down things before God; *itmon,* i.e., the one who suppresses the sins of Israel; and *sigron,* i.e., he who, having closed the case, does not reopen it. Moscato finds in these three names of the celestial forensic advocate of Israel a reference to three of the four parts of forensic oratory mentioned in Cicero's *De partitione:* statement of fact; proof and refutation; and peroration. What is missing is the exordium, but Moscato is delighted to discover this missing part in the list of four names attributed to the angel *(Metatron)* in *Tikuney ha-Zohar* (no. 57): *piskon, pithon, sigron, itmon. Pithon* stands, of course, for the exordium. The fact that this part is omitted in the Talmudic passage is not disturbing to Moscato, for, as he points out, the introductory part is but a "preparation" to what follows and, besides, may be dispensed with in certain circumstances, as had been stated by Agricola in his *De inventione dialectia* (II.22). To be sure, the Talmudic story could not be taken literally, but it was appropriate to depict, metaphorically, the proceedings in the celestial court in analogy to the rules obtaining in the terrestrial court *(Nefutzot* 19b–20a).

The other example refers to a discussion in *Sanhedrin* 100a where the phrase *ve-'alehu li-terufa* ("and the leaf thereof for healing," Ezek. 47:12) is anagrammatically explained in various ways: 1. The leaf has the power *le-hatir pe shel ma'la,* i.e., to confer eloquence on the dumb; 2. *le-hatir pe shel mata,* i.e., to open the womb of the sterile; 3. *le-to'ar panim shel ba'aley lashon,* i.e., to enliven the facial expression of the speaker. Moscato sees in these three terms an allusion to the five operations of rhetorical art as prescribed by Cicero: the opening of the womb means three of these *(inventione, dispositione,* and *memoria)* for they entail creative activity; the conferment of eloquence denotes the faculty of *enunciatione* (*elocutio,* delivery): and the improvement of facial expression points to *pronunciation,* which includes gesticulation, a subject discussed at length, as Moscato recalls, in the eleventh book of Quintilian's *Institutio oratoria* (*Kol Yehuda* on II.72, pp. 161f.). We may say that it is precisely the far-fetched nature of these cases of eisegesis that illustrates the degree to which Moscato was preoccupied with classical rhetoric.

Indigenous rabbinic oratory comes into its own in Sermon XII, where Moscato elaborates on *Canticles Rabba* (IV:11, 1. The passage chosen by him offers five different views of the verse "Thy lips . . . drop honey —Honey and milk are under thy tongue. . . ," all of which do agree on the application of its praises to the public orator delivering words of Torah, and all of which declare that "If one discourses on the Torah in public and his words are not tasteful *(arevim)* to his hearers. . . , it were better that he had not spoken." Here we have a genuinely rabbinic stress on the elements of persuasive rhetoric, and all Moscato does is to conceptualize the various poetic descriptions of pleasantness presented by the rabbis. They amount, in his view, (1) to the clarity ("sifting") of the material that forms the subject-matter of the oration; (2) to the quality of the disposition ("as honey from the comb"); (3) to the combination of (1) and (2) ("as honey with milk"); (4) to the element of beauty ("as a bride to her husband"). The upshot of his discussion is a summary portrayal of what a public orator discoursing on the Torah should be like: "He must be of pleasant speech, presenting matters in proper order and in conformity to intellectual speculation, being also a man of excellent character." The last condition is best expressed by the rabbinic phrase *"na'e doresh ve-na'e mekayem"* (36c–37b). This image, though authentically rabbinic, conforms, at the same time, to the concept of the ideal orator drawn by Quintilian and eagerly adopted by Messer Leon.

The perfect orator, according to humanist sentiment, is also the perfect man, and this larger perspective was not absent from Moscato's consciousness. In Sermon IX (22d) he permitted himself to quote a lengthy passage from another of his writings—he gave no hint as to its whereabouts—in which he described "the speech of perfect men." There was no "tasteless word" *(mila tefela)* on their lips, he said, and a certain "fragrance and beauty" *(reaḥ tov ve-yofi)* radiated from their faces, for beauty was but the fragrance of goodness *(reaḥ ha-toviut)*, as the Platonists *(ba'aley brit Aflaton)* would say.[17] Moscato linked eloquence of rhetoric also to the dignity of man, another celebrated *topos* of humanist thought, on which Gianozzo Manetti and Pico della Mirandola had written in the fifteenth century.[18] In *Kol Yehuda* (II.68, p. 157), he pointed out that the faculty of speech was the special prerogative of man and that its quality had to be considered the criterion of the rank of a nation. Hence, given the unique character of the Jewish people, its language had to be of the utmost perfection. Moscato shared the belief predominantly held by Jewish scholars (see de Rossi, *Imrey Bina*, 453) that Hebrew was the primeval language, the *lingua Adamica*. In his *Kol Yehuda* (II.67, p. 153ff), Moscato quoted Abraham ibn Ezra's *Safa Brura* in support of his critique of *Genesis Rabba* 18.6, which led him to a new interpretation of this midrashic passage. In his view the burden of the proof that "the Torah was given in the holy tongue" had to be placed upon the fact that the etymologies of proper names offered in the Torah (e.g., Adam: *adama;* Kayin: *kaniti*) could not possibly be regarded as translations from another, earlier tongue because translations invariably left *nomina propria* in their original form. De Rossi, who recalled Isaac Arama's skepticism about the midrashic argument from the consonance of the nouns *ish* ("man") and *isha* ("woman") allegedly peculiar to Hebrew and who adopted Moscato's proof, relates yet another argument which, he says, Moscato had "taught" him: Hebrew is the primeval language, for God, who is perfect, can bestow only perfection. He, who bestowed circularity, the most perfect form (Aristotle, *De coelo* II.iv), upon matter when creating the heaven, could have endowed Adam with but the most perfect language. The argument entails two assumptions: (1) that Hebrew is the most perfect tongue, a view corroborated by de Rossi from a variety of sources; and (2) that the language of the first man was not his own invention but a divine gift. Moscato clearly affirms this view in *Kol Yehuda* when commenting on *Kuzari* II.72 (p. 162): The Hebrew language is not conventional *(muskemet mi-bney adam)* but a *creatio ex nihilo (me'ayin timatze)*, as Ha-Levi's phrase *ha-notzeret ha-beru'a* (Judah ibn Tibbon's rendition of *al-makhlūqa al-mukhtara'a*) means to indicate. The revealed character of Hebrew had been stressed also in *Kuzari* IV.25 and in a passage from Profiat Duran's *Ma'ase Efod* (ch. 3) quoted approvingly by Moscato earlier on (p. 155). From Gen. 2:20, Maimonides (*Guide*, II.30) had inferred that languages, including Hebrew, are conventional, and Naḥmanides (*Commentary on the Torah*, Ex. 30:13) had opposed this doctrine from a mystically inspired position. Moscato explicitly noted (p. 162) that Gen. 2:20 did not disprove the view held by Ha-Levi. As for all other languages, they were conventional.[19] Moscato's position on this issue is clear: The Hebrew language is both *lingua Adamica* and God-given.

What introduces a Renaissance flavor into the medieval texture of this position is Moscato's fondness of syncretistic etymologies. Since Hebrew was the original language of the human race, he found it quite natural that, as he believed, many Hebrew words survived in the other tongues. This belief helped to restore a sense of universal human kinship that the consciousness of Hebrew singularity might have been apt to undermine. Hence the search for words common to many languages, while assuming the primacy of Hebrew, tended, at the same time, to create a bridge between the cultures. It was the counterpart to the intellectual syncretism that permitted Christian Renaissance philosophers to defer, in all innocence, to the pagan deities, and that made it inoffensive in Moscato's eyes to follow the Platonists and Pico in calling the first hypostasis in the process of emanations by the name of the "Son of God" (*Nefutzot* 23c; see Pico, *Discourse on Love* I.iii). It seems that Moscato's excursions into the nebulous region of etymology owed some stimulus to the treatise *Dor ha-Pelaga* written by his friend David Provençal, one of the three Provençal brothers whom de Rossi described as the "upholders of Torah" *(tofsey ha-tora)* in Mantua (*Imrey Bina*, p. 146). In this well-intentioned work, more than two thousand Hebrew words had been collected that were said to be found also in Greek, Latin, Italian and/or other tongues. Examples recorded by de Rossi (*I.B.* 456f.) include the following: *ezer—uxor; pilegesh—paelex, pallakis; osef dalim—hospidale; kol yafe—Kalliope; bet eked—academia.* A list of etymologies found in Moscato's writings has been compiled by Abba Apfelbaum in his valuable monograph on Moscato.[20] Among others, we meet here again *Kalliope*, the first of the nine Muses and protectress of music, as bearing a name derived from Hebrew *kol yafe* (*Nefutzot* 1c). "Music" is said to be a word identical with Hebrew *mezeg* in the sense of a "well-proportioned" arrangement of voices (1b). "Simile" is identical with *mashal* (88c); etc. The most striking etymology concerns the name Moshe (Moses), which is said to be akin *(karov)* to *Musa*, from which name the noun "music" is derived (3c). Moscato adds that, according to some writers, the word music comes from Egyptian *moys,* denoting water, for the art originated near the water (where reeds grow?). This, he says, agrees with Ex. 2:10 ("Moses . . . Because I drew him out of the water"). The same derivation occurs also in the famous encyclo- paedia of the sciences written by the monk and imperial father confessor Gregorius Reisch and known as the *Margarita philosophica,*[21] where also Greek *Musa* is mentioned as a possible derivation. Moscato knew and made use of this work, which he described as "well-known among the Gentiles" (*sefer mefursam etzlam;* 2d), and it is most likely that his etymology is indebted to it. The knowledge of the Egyptian word for water was probably obtained from Philo's *Moses* I.17: "Since he had been taken up from the water, the princess gave him a name derived from this, and called him Moses, for Möu is the Egyptian word for water."

These playful theories as well as the concern for establishing the precise character and origin of the Hebrew language are well part of the larger preoccupation with language as the vehicle of human communica- tion and with the *ars rhetorica* as the ultimate consummation of man's faculty of speech. As we have seen, the three writers whom we have analyzed made a determined effort, each in his own way, to adapt the understanding of the Scriptures and of rabbinic literature to the spirit of Renaissance humanism.

NOTES

1. See Richard McKeon, "Rhetoric in the Middle Ages," *Speculum* 17 (1942), 1–32; James J. Murphy, *Rhetoric in the Middle Ages* (Berkeley, Los Ange- les, London, 1974).

2. See J. Langhade and M. Grignaschi, *Al-Fārābī, Deux ouvrages inédits sur la rhétorique* (Beirut, 1971); Charles E. Butterworth (ed. and tr.), *Averroës' Three Short Commentaries on Aristotle's "Topics," "Rhetoric," and "Poet- ics,"* (Albany, 1977).

3. See below and n. 6.

4. See George F. Hourani, *Averroes on the Harmony of Religion and Philoso- phy* (London, 1961), pp. 45, 49, 63. The logical orientation of the *falāsifa's* approach to the *Rhetoric* (and *Poetics*) was well perceived by Hermann the German. In his Prologue to the "Rhetoric," he wrote: Quod autem hi duo libri logicales sint, nemo dubitat qui libros perspexerit arabum famosorum, Alfarabii videlicet et Avicennae et Avenrosdi et quorundam aliorum. See William F. Boggess, "Hermannus Alemanus's Rhetorical Translations," *Viator*

2 (1971), 249–250. For a discussion of the Averroes Latinus on Poetics, see H. A. Kelly, "Aristotle on Tragedy: The Influence on the 'Poetics' on the Latin Middle Ages," *Viator* 10 (1979), 161–209.

5. See A. S. Halkin, *Moshe ben Yaakov ibn Ezra, Kitāb al-Muḥāḍara wal-Mudhākara—Liber Discussionis et Commemorationis (Poetica Hebraica)* (Jerusalem, 1975), p. 13.

6. See Elijah del Medigo, *Sefer Beḥinat ha-Dat*, ed. by Isaac Reggio (Vienna, 1833), p. 5.

7. For the text, see Charles Halm, *Rhetores latini minores* (Leipzig, 1863), pp. 155–304. Another commentator (on Cicero?) referred to by Leon (pp. 6, 9) as *ha-mefaresh Alano* could not be identified with certainty. Steinschneider (*Die hebräischen Uebersetzungen des Mittelalters und die Juden als Dolmetscher*, 2 vols. (Berlin, 1893), I:79) suggested that Alano was the Italianized form of Aelianus. He obviously had in mind Claudius Aelianus (c. 170–235), the Roman author and teacher of rhetoric, but I have been unable to trace a reference to, let alone a manuscript or printed edition of, a commentary by him on Cicero. No reference to such a commentary occurs in Halm's *Rhetores latini minores*.

8. For the story of the recovery of the text, see James J. Murphy, *Rhetoric*, pp. 357–363.

9. See ibid., 360f.

10. See Hannah Holborn Gray, "Renaissance Humanism: The Pursuit of Eloquence," *Journal of the History of Ideas* (1963) 497–514; Jerrold E. Seigel, *Rhetoric and Philosophy in Renaissance Humanism* (Princeton, N.J., 1968); Eckhard Kessler, *Petrarca und die Geschichte* (Munich, 1978); Jan Lindhardt, *Rhetor. Poeta, Historicus* (Leiden, 1979). Edward E. Hale, Jr., "Ideas on Rhetoric in the Sixteenth Century," *Publications on the Modern Language Association of America*, 17 (1903), 424–444, deals only with sixteenth-century England.

11. See Walter J. Ong, *Ramus, Method and the Decay of Dialogue* (Cambridge, Mass., 1959), pp. 288f.

12. See Shlomo Pines, "Studies in Abu'l-Barakāt al-Baghādī's Poetics and Metaphysics," *The Collected Works of Shlomo Pines, Vol. I: Studies in Abu'l-Barakāt al-Baghdādī Physics and Metaphysics* (Jerusalem-Leiden, 1979), pp. 259–334.

13. Azarya min ha-Adumim, *Sefer Me'or Enayim*, ed. by David Cassel (Vilna, 1866), part III *Imrey Bina [I.B.]*, p. 89.

14. Venice, 1589; quoted here from the Lemberg, 1850 edition.

15. Venice, 1594; quoted here from the Warsaw, 1880 edition.

16. See note 14, p. 104.

17. See Plotinus, *Enneads*, V.i.6; Pico della Mirandola's *Discourse on Love*, II.i: "Love is a species of desire; beauty of good"; Pico's *Discourse* is quoted in *Nefutzot*, 23c.

18. See Paul Oskar Kristeller, *Humanism and Renaissance*, II (Munich, 1976), pp. 110, 120–123.

19. For the theories of language in medieval Islam, see Bernard G. Weiss's article on the subject in *ZDMG*, 124.1 (1974), 33–41.
20. Abba Apfelbaum. *Sefer Toldot Ha-Gaon Rabbi Yehuda Moscato* (Drohobicz, 1900), p. 12.
21. The first edition probably appeared in 1496; the work is quoted here from the 1504 edition, V.i.2.

3

Italian Jewish Preaching: An Overview

Marc Saperstein

On a day between Rosh Hashanah and Yom Kippur, probably in the year 1593, Rabbi Samuel Judah Katzenellenbogen of Padua delivered a eulogy for Judah Moscato. As befits the time of year, he began with a discussion of repentance, proceeding to argue that one of the primary functions of the eulogy was to inspire the listeners to repent. He went on to discuss the qualities of a great scholar: perfection of intellect and behavior, the capacity to communicate wisdom to others, both by capturing the listeners' attention with appealing homiletical material and teaching them the laws they must observe, which are essential for the true felicity of the soul, even though most contemporary congregations do not enjoy listening to the dry halakhic content. At this point the printed text of his sermon reads, "Here I began to recount the praises of the deceased, and to show how these four qualities were present in him to perfection, the conclusion being that we should become inspired by his eulogy and allow the tears to flow for him, look into our deeds, and return to the Lord." [1]

This passage encapsulates for me something of the challenges and frustrations of studying Italian Jewish preaching, and to some extent Jewish preaching in general. Here is a leading Italian rabbi eulogizing perhaps the best known Jewish preacher of his century. We are given some important statements about the function of the eulogy, the proper content and structure of the sermon, the expectations and taste of the average listener. Then we come to the climactic point, where the preacher

Reprinted by permission of the University of California Press from *Preachers of the Italian Ghetto*, edited by David B. Ruderman, Berkeley and Los Angeles, 1992.

turns to Moscato himself. We expect an encomium of the scholarship and piety of Moscato and, what is more important for our purposes, a characterization of his preaching, an indication of his contemporary reputation, an evaluation from a colleague who apparently had a rather different homiletical style. What we get is nothing. This climactic section of the eulogy is deemed unworthy of being recorded, presumably because of its specificity and ephemeral character. What for us (and perhaps for at least some of the listeners) is the most important content has been lost forever.

In *Kabbalah: New Perspectives*, Moshe Idel argues that even after the life work of Gershom Scholem and two generations of his disciples, the literature of Jewish mysticism is by no means fully charted: important schools may never have committed their doctrines to writing, significant works have been lost, certain texts may have arbitrarily been given undue emphasis at the expense of others no less important, and there is as yet no comprehensive bibliographic survey of the literature that does exist.[2] How much more is this true for Jewish sermon literature, which has had no Gershom Scholem to chart the way. The history of Jewish preaching in general, and that of Italy in particular, may best be envisioned as a vast jigsaw puzzle from which 90 percent of the pieces are missing and 75 percent of those that remain lie in a heap on the floor— and for which we have no model picture to tell us what the design should look like. Generalizations about trends or characteristics of the homiletical tradition are like speculations about the design of the puzzle based on individual pieces or small clusters that happen to fit together. And without a clear map of the conventions and continuities of the tradition, all assertions about the novelty or even the significance of a particular preacher or sermon are likely to be precarious and unfounded.

The magnitude of what we lack is astonishing. Leon Modena's *Autobiography* informs us that he preached at three or four places each Sabbath over a period of more than twenty years, and that he had in his possession more than four hundred sermons, but only twenty-one from the early part of his career were published, and the rest have apparently been lost.[3] When we think of the pinnacle of Italian Jewish preaching, Moscato is probably the name that comes first to mind. Yet a contemporary nominated David Provençal, the author of the famous appeal for the founding of a Jewish university, as "the greatest of the Italian preachers in our time." Like most of his other works, all of Provençal's sermons (if written at all) have apparently been lost, leaving us no basis for evaluating the claim.[4] It does, however, give us pause to consider that our standard canon of important Italian Jewish preachers may be highly arbitrary.

The record before the sixteenth century is almost entirely blank: one manuscript by a mid-fifteenth-century preacher, Moses ben Joab of Florence, described and published in part by Umberto Cassuto more than eighty years ago.[5] We have no known extant sermon reacting to the popular anti-Jewish preaching of such Franciscan friars as Bernardino da Siena, John Capistrano, and Bernardino da Feltre; or to the notorious ritual murder charge surrounding Simon of Trent; or to the arrival on Italian soil of refugees from the Iberian peninsula; or to the exploits in Italy of the charismatic David Reubeni, including an audience with Pope Clement VII; or to the burning of the magnificently printed volumes of the Talmud in Rome and Venice; or to the arrest, trial, and execution of former Portuguese New Christians who had returned to Judaism in Ancona and the attempted boycott of that port; or to the papal bull *Cum nimis absurdum* and the establishment of the Ghetto in Rome.

There can be little question that Jewish preachers alluded to, discussed, and interpreted these events in their sermons, nor can it be doubted that the records of these discussions would provide us with precious insight into the strategies of contemporary Jews for accommodating major historical upheavals to their tradition, and conversely, for reinterpreting their tradition in the light of contemporary events. But it apparently did not occur to these preachers that readers removed in space and time from their own congregation would be interested in learning about events in the past, and they therefore had little motivation to write what they said in a permanent form.[6]

Much of the material that exists has yet to be studied. Isaac Hayyim Cantarini of Padua does not appear in any of the lists of great Italian preachers known to me. Yet he may belong in such a list; no one has ever taken a serious look at his homiletical legacy. He left behind what appears to be the largest corpus of Italian Jewish sermons in existence. The *Sefer Zikkaron* of Padua gives the number as "more than a thousand," and a substantial percentage of these are to be found in six large volumes of the Kaufmann Manuscript collection in Budapest (Hebrew MSS 314–319), each one of them devoted to the sermons for a complete year between 1673 and 1682; there may be more such volumes as well.

In many cases there are two sermons for each parashah, one delivered in the morning, the other at the Minhah service. The sermons are written in Italian, in Latin letters, with Hebrew quotations interspersed.[7]

I once thought of looking through the volume containing the sermons for 1676–77 to see if I could find any reaction to the news of the death of Shabbetai Zevi, but I soon realized the enormity of the task: that volume alone runs to 477 pages, and there is no guarantee that the preacher would have referred to the event explicitly as soon as the news reached his community. Needless to say, for someone interested in intellectual or social history during this period, not to mention the history of Jewish preaching or the biography of a many-talented man, these manuscripts may well repay careful study with rich dividends.

The first desideratum is therefore bibliographical: to compile a complete list of all known manuscripts of Italian sermons—let us say through the seventeenth century—to complement the printed works identified by Leopold Zunz and others. Then there is need for a data base that would include a separate entry for each sermon, including the place and approximate date of delivery, the genre (Sabbath or holiday sermon, eulogy, occasional, etc.), the main biblical verses and rabbinic statements discussed, the central subject or thesis, and any historical connection with an individual or an event. This would at least spread out all the known pieces of the puzzle on the table before us and facilitate the process of putting them together.

In addition to actual sermons, related genres need to be considered. Rabbi Henry Sosland has given us a fine edition of Jacob Zahalon's *Or ha-Darshanim,* a manual for preachers from the third quarter of the seventeenth century.[8] But the "Tena'ei ha-Darshan," written by Moses ben Samuel ibn Basa of Blanes is no less worthy of detailed analysis.[9] Nor should the various preaching aids be overlooked, such as works intended to make the preacher's task easier by collecting quotations on various topics, alphabetically arranged, analogous to a host of such works written by Christian contemporaries.[10]

Once the material has been charted, we can define the questions that need to be addressed. Perhaps the most obvious deal with the sermons as a reflection of Italian Jewish culture, as documents in Jewish intellectual history. To what extent can we find evidence in the sermons for the continued vitality of philosophical modes of thought, for the popularization of Kabbalistic doctrines, for the influence of classical motifs or contemporary Christian writings?

What can we say about the native Italian homiletical tradition, and the impact of the Spanish tradition in the wake of the Sephardic immigration? We can outline the broad contours of the Spanish homiletical tradition as it crystallized in the late fifteenth century, and trace its continuity within the Ottoman Empire.[11] The manuscript sermons of Joseph ben Hayyim of Benevento, dating from 1515 until the 1530s, provide an example of preaching on Italian soil very much in the Spanish mold: a verse from the parashah and a passage of aggadah (often from the Zohar) as the basic building blocks, an introduction including a stylized asking of permission *(reshut)* from God, the Torah, and the congregation, followed by a structured investigation of a conceptual problem, sometimes accompanied by an identification of difficulties *(sefeqot)* in the parashah.[12] But the paucity of Italian material from the fifteenth century and the first half of the sixteenth century makes it very difficult to delineate the process by which Spanish Jewish preaching influenced home-grown models.

What is the relationship between Jewish preaching and the Christian preaching of the environment? I am referring not to a rehashing of the debate about the influence of Renaissance rhetorical theory,[13] but to an assessment of the more immediate impact of published Christian sermons and actual Christian preachers. Did the notorious conversionist sermons have an impact on Jewish preaching style, or conversely, did conversionist preachers learn from Jewish practioners the most effective ways to move their audiences?[14] Nor should we forget that Italian Jews did not always need to be coerced to listen to Christian preachers, as we learn from a passing reference to "educated Jews" *(Judei periti)* at a sermon delivered by Egidio da Viterbo in Siena on 11 November 1511.[15]

That Christians attended the sermons of Leon Modena is known to every reader of his *Autobiography;*[16] not as widely known is the passage in which he refers to his own attendance at the sermon of a Christian preacher,[17] and the fact that he owned at least one volume of Savonarola's sermons and an Italian treatise on "The Way to Compose a Sermon."[18] His letter to Samuel Archivolti describes the sermons in *Midbar Yehudah* as a blending of Christian and Jewish homiletics, and he uses the Italian terms *prologhino* and *epiloghino* to characterize the first and last sections of his discourses.[19] All of this bespeaks an openness to what was happening in the pulpits of nearby churches. Extremely important work has been done during the past two decades on various aspects of the history of Italian Christian preaching;[20] the task of integrating this with the Jewish material remains to be accomplished.

Another aspect of this subject relates to the use of Italian literature by Jewish preachers. Extravagant claims have been made; an *Encyclopedia Judaica* article asserts that "like Petrarch, Dante was widely quoted by Italian rabbis of the Renaissance in their sermons."[21] I do not know what evidence could support such a statement. The written texts contain few examples of Jewish preachers using contemporary Italian literature, and there is no reason to assume that such references would be eliminated in the writing, or that those who quoted Italian authors would be predisposed not to write their sermons. Nevertheless, these examples are instructive. Joseph Dan has discussed Moscato's citation of Pico della Mirandola which, though incidental to the preacher's main point, shows that there was apparently nothing extraordinary about using even a Christological interpretation for one's own homiletical purpose.[22]

More impressive are stories used by Leon Modena. The allegory he incorporates into a sermon on repentance, in which Good and Evil exchange garments so that everyone now honors Evil and spurns Good, is presented as one he "heard," probably from a Christian or a Jew conversant with Christian literature. His story, used in the eulogy for a well-known rabbinic scholar, of a young man who tours the world to discover whether he is truly alive or dead, until the answer he receives from a monk is confirmed in a dramatic dialogue with the spirit of a corpse in the cemetery, is attributed explicitly to a "non-Jewish book." While I have still not succeeded in identifying the direct source of the story, it certainly reflects the late medieval and Renaissance preoccupation with death and dying that produced not only the various expressions of the *Danse Macabre* motif but a host of treatises on good living and good dying, including dialogues involving a nonthreatening personification of Death.[23]

What do we know about the training of preachers? For no other country is there such ample evidence for the cultivation of homiletics as an honorable discipline in the paideia as there is for Italian Jewry. The kinds of evidence range from the exemplary sermon of Abraham Farissol dating from the early sixteenth century to the letters of Ellijah ben

Solomon ha-Levi di Vali almost three hundred years later.[24] There seems to have been a special emphasis on students attending services, together with their teacher, to listen to sermons, especially on major preaching occasions. In addition, preaching was actually taught in the schools.[25] Public speaking and the delivery of sermons was to be part of the curriculum in David Provençal's proposed Jewish college in Mantua.[26] The preaching exercises in which Modena participated when he was no older than ten do not seem to have been unusual.[27] The delivery of a sermon by a precocious child may well have had the effect that the playing of a concerto by a young prodigy would have in the age of Mozart. But the actual mechanism for instruction—whether printed collections of sermons were studied and sermons by noted preachers critiqued, and what written guidelines for the preparation of sermons were used in the schools—remains to be fully investigated.

A work like *Medabber Tahapukhot* by Leon Modena's grandson Isaac provides dramatic evidence of the tumultuous politics of the pulpit. Indeed, the ways in which the selection of preachers for various occasions could reveal a hierarchy of prestige, unleashing bitter quarrels, appears as one of the central subjects of the book.[28] Conflicts over the limits of acceptable public discourse—what content could and could not be properly addressed from the pulpit—were part of the same cultural milieu that produced the battles over the printing of the Zohar and the publication of de' Rossi's *Me'or Einayim*.[29] Sometimes these issues were directed to legal authorities who issued formal responsa, but as important as evoking the decisions from above, they reflect problems in the sensibilities and tastes of the listeners in the pews. A full range of such nonsermonic texts is necessary for an adequate reconstruction of the historical dynamic of Italian Jewish preaching.

A final set of questions relates to the writing and printing of sermon collections. Although sermons were undoubtedly delivered in the vernacular throughout the Middle Ages, Italy seems to have produced the first texts of Jewish sermons actually written in a European vernacular language.[30] Why did some Jewish preachers begin to write in Italian in the late sixteenth and seventeenth centuries? What does the transition from Hebrew to Italian in Hebrew characters (Dato), to Italian in Latin characters (Cantarini) reveal about contemporary Jewish culture? Despite the new linguistic variety in the manuscripts, however, printed collections remained in Hebrew. The number of such books published in

Venice between 1585 and 1615, both by Italian and by Ottoman preachers, is an astounding indication of public demand for this kind of literature. Modena decided to prepare a selection of his sermons for print, hoping that the proceeds would help ease his financial pressures, although in this, as in so many other pecuniary matters, he was apparently disappointed.[31]

In addition to the economics of sermon publishing, the format seems worthy of attention. While most collections of Spanish and Ottoman sermons are arranged in accordance with the weekly parashah, most Italian collections are not. We have relatively few ordinary Sabbath sermons, particularly in print; most of them are for special Sabbaths, holidays, occasions in the life cycle or the life of the community. Yet there is abundant evidence that weekly preaching on the parashah was the norm throughout Italy. Could there have been a conscious avoidance of the Sephardic format? We have no answer as yet.

I turn now to a more detailed discussion of certain aspects of Italian preaching. Among other roles, the preacher appears as a guardian of moral and religious standards, and therefore as a critic of the failings of his listeners. Frequently this was just the kind of material the preacher would omit when writing his words for publication, assuming that readers in distant cities would have little interest in the local issues he had addressed.[32] But some of this social criticism has been preserved. If we are careful to distinguish generalized complaints, the commonplaces of the genre of rebuke that recur in almost every generation, from attacks that target a specific, concrete abuse, we may find clues to the stress lines within Jewish society, clues that become more persuasive when the sermon material is integrated with the contemporary responsa literature.[33]

The proper assessment of the sermonic rebuke is not always obvious. I am not quite certain what to make of the accusation, made both by Samuel Katzenellenbogen and by Jacob di Alba, that among those who leave the synagogue after the Tefillah and therefore miss the sermon are congregants who hurry to return to their business affairs.[34] Can they be talking about Jews who engage in work on the Sabbath after attending only part of the Saturday morning service? This would be a violation so serious that one wonders why any rabbi would focus on the much more trivial offense of missing the sermon or insulting the preacher.

Is it then merely a rhetorical device used to discredit those who walk out early by suggesting to the remaining congregation that the exiters *might* be going to work? If so it could not be used to prove that serious Sabbath violation was actually occurring, but only that the possibility of such violation was plausible enough for the listeners not to dismiss the suggestion as absurd. Or could the entire passage be referring not to the Sabbath but to the weekday morning service? If this is the case, it would be evidence of a very different dynamic: the cultivation of the practice of a daily *"devar Torah,"* and the resistance on the part of Jews who were committed enough to attend the service, but resented the homiletical accoutrement as an imposition on their time. As with the Moscato eulogy, Katzenellenbogen leads us to the brink of something rather important but fails to give us quite enough to use it with confidence.

Other passages of rebuke are more straightforward. Cecil Roth wrote that "the employment of adventitious aids to female beauty was a perpetual preoccupation of Renaissance [Christian] preachers and moralists, and it is certain that Jewish women followed (or anticipated) the general fashion."[35] He provided no documentation for this, or for the subsequent assertion that "in Italy generally no sort of ornament was more common than false hair, generally blond, . . . and the wealthy Jewess was able to keep abreast of fashion simply by remodeling her wig."[36] Nevertheless, sixteenth-century Jewish literature does reveal the concern of Jewish moralists with this practice.

In a sermon for the Sabbath of Repentance, Katzenellenbogen turned to the women in the congregation and raised a rather sensitive issue. Women, says the preacher, must heed the moral instruction of the religious authorities even when they do not like it. The example chosen to illustrate the point is one in which the preacher claims the women of his city are particularly susceptible to failure: the prohibition against revealing their hair or adorning themselves with a Gentile wig, which is indistinguishable from their own hair. "In all the Ashkenazi communities, for generations, our ancestors have protested that women must not wear even a silk ribbon that has the color of hair"; the preacher refers to a lengthy legal decision of his in which he argued against authorities who permitted these practices. But this is not, as Roth would suggest, simply a matter of Jewish women being influenced by their surroundings. Katzenellenbogen argues that the fashions of Jewish women are particularly scandalous "in a place where the Gentile women are accustomed to cover their hair, and the nuns strictly prohibit adorning themselves with a wig." The function of the Christian environment is not merely to serve as a source of seduction; the preacher uses his Christian neighbors as a rhetorical goad to bring the listeners back to their own tradition.[37]

Preachers were also exercised by what they considered to be a deterioration of sexual mores. Israel Bettan cited a passage by Azariah Figo condemning the practice (perhaps more widespread in Italy than in other countries?) of recreational gazing at women, both married and single, "an indulgence that must inevitably lead to graver offenses."[38] But this is at most a minor infraction of the traditional code of Jewish norms. A far more serious charge is leveled by Figo elsewhere:

> From then [the destruction of the second Temple] until now, the first two of these sins, namely idolatry and murder, have ceased from the people of Israel. Thank God, there are no reports of a pattern or even a tendency to commit these two sins among our nation—except as a result of compulsion, or in a rare individual case. But the third sin, adultery and incest [gilluy 'arayot], has not been properly guarded against. Jews have violated the rules in these sinful generations in various ways, engaging in all kinds of destructive behavior publicly, out in the open, without any shame or embarrassment.[39]

Unlike the more concrete condemnations by the preachers in Prague 150 years later,[40] this passage remains too vague to be of much value to the social historian, although listeners in the audience may well have thought of specific examples. Nevertheless, the contrast drawn between what the preacher does not consider to be a real problem (the attraction of Christianity, crimes of violence) and what he does (the more serious kind of sexual sins), and the claim that such behavior is tacitly condoned by many Jews, that it can become public knowledge without serious repercussions for the perpetrators, may point to a genuine sense of breakdown in the core of the traditional Jewish ethos.[41]

Financial arrangements also had the potential to create deep conflicts. With considerable power, Azariah Figo addressed the complex problem of impermissible loans. The poor are forced to seek loans from the rich, who "devour their flesh with several forms of clear-cut, open interest." Even worse, in his eyes, is that the sense of sinfulness about such forbidden arrangements has been lost.

> If a group of Jews were to be seen going to a Gentile butcher and were then seen publicly eating pig or other forbidden meat, they would be stoned by all, although this entails only one negative prohibition, for which the punishment is lashes. Yet here we see those who lend money on interest, which involves six transgressions for the lender, as well as others for the borrower, the guarantor, the witnesses and the scribe, and all are silent.[42]

Like the passage about sexual immorality cited above, this reflects a serious gap between the values of the community and the standards of its religious leadership. The prevalent social norms deem the dietary laws to be crucial to Jewish identity even though from a legal standpoint they do not entail the most serious of sins. Taking interest from a fellow Jew has greater legal consequences, but ordinary Jews consider it innocuous. Those who are aware of the prohibition, we are told, show deference to the tradition by hypocritical attempts to avoid the appearance of transgression, through ruses such as an arrangement by which the creditor may live in an apartment without rent. As for the *cambio* [exchange contract], some may be permissible, but many others are totally forbidden, so that even the well-intentioned merchant may unwittingly err. "My quarrel with them, is this," the preacher concludes: "Why don't they consult with experts in these matters, who can provide them with proper guidance?"[43] The passage is extremely rich, revealing the frustrations of religious leaders in the face of economic and social forces they are unable to control.

In addition to areas of major conflict, the sermons may reveal aspects of the norms of social life and *mentalité*. Wedding sermons can hardly avoid reflecting the attitude of the preacher toward women and marriage. The earliest Italian preacher whose sermons are preserved, Moses ben Joab of mid-fifteenth-century Florence, speaking at a betrothal celebration of a certain Abraham of Montalcino, delivered himself of what reads today like a misogynist diatribe, but must have seemed to him like a conventional assessment of woman's limitations and perils. He then proceeds, "What can a man do who wants to find himself a wife? All around him are 'brokers of sin,' who find something good to say about those who have no merit. Today they tell him one thing, tomorrow another, until their combined efforts wear him down. In order to lead him into their trap, they tell him, 'This woman who is coming into your home will bring some dowry! . . . Whoever escapes from the snares of these people like an energetic bird or deer, and finds himself a decent woman has indeed 'found something good.' '" The use of the occasion of a betrothal celebration to incorporate into a religious discourse an attack against the prevailing standards of marriage brokers shows that Italian preachers, though frequently ponderous, were not without humor.[44]

A passage in a sermon by Katzenellenbogen gives us a glimpse of child-rearing practices, that might be related to the burgeoning scholarly literature on attitudes toward children and private life. At issue is an aggadic statement (B. Hag 3a) that small children should be brought to hear sermons, even though they cannot understand them. But this is obvious, the preacher says: if the small children were left home alone, their parents would stand impatiently and resentfully during the sermon, not listening to what was being said but wishing it would end, afraid that their children might be harmed. Thus, "even if parents were not commanded to bring their pre-school children, they would bring them of their own accord out of fear lest they be harmed if they are left at home with no adult around." The preacher does not address here the problem of concentrating on the sermon if the infant or toddler is present in the synagogue, but we have here a rather moving indication of concern for the welfare of small children left without adult supervision.[45]

The fact that Italian preachers such as Katzenellenbogen and Modena made eulogies a significant component of their relatively small selection of published sermons may well have solidified the prestige of that genre as a written text. No consideration of Jewish attitudes toward death and beliefs about the afterlife can claim any semblance of respectability unless it is based on a thorough study of this literature. Though often stylized and filled with conventions and commonplaces, the eulogies also reveal the texture of interpersonal relationships: the feelings of a student for his teacher (or the teacher for a young student), the bonds of genuine friendship, the pain at the loss of a member of the immediate family.[46] No branch of Jewish homiletical literature is more deserving of systematic study.

I will mention one other kind of occasional preaching. Not infrequently, the sermon was used as a vehicle to raise funds for a worthy cause. Each community supported the central institutions of Jewish life through a system of self-imposed taxation, and there were standard funds for free-will offerings. But there were also unusual cases that warranted a special appeal from the pulpit. The causes deemed worthy of such special appeals reflect the shared values of the society, and the arguments used to convince the listeners to give point to a consensus about the expectations of responsibility in Jewish life, in addition to exhibiting one aspect of the rhetorical arsenal at the preacher's disposal.

For example, Moscato devoted a significant part of a sermon for the holiday of Sukkot to an appeal on behalf of the impoverished sick. He notes that this has been "imposed upon me by the [lay] leaders of our people to make known in public their suffering, for their numbers and their need are greater than usual, etc." After dwelling on the importance of charitable giving and the special claim of the impoverished sick, he moves on to other exegetical material, but returns later in the sermon to remind the listeners that he expects their pledges. The entire section is an integral part of the sermon, crafted with no less artistic sophistication than the rest.[47]

Katzenellenbogen delivered a eulogy for R. Zalman Katz of Mantua "in the public square of the ghetto . . . for all the synagogues were closed because of the plague," a circumstance repeated several generations later (in 1657) when Jacob Zahalon preached from the window balcony of a private home to Jews standing in the street below.[48] At this time, when "the line of judgment is stretched out against us," donations to charity are a traditional safeguard from harm. The eulogy ends with a direct appeal: "There is no need to dwell at length on these matters, for I know that your excellencies are not unaware of the great power of this mitzvah of charitable giving, particularly at this perilous time. But I beseech your excellencies to contribute speedily as much as you can, in accordance with the needs of the hour. And I will be the first to perform this mitzvah; see my example and do likewise."[49] In this dramatic gesture, the preacher establishes a model not only for the congregation of listeners, but for subsequent fund-raisers as well.

Even in more normal times, the eulogy was apparently an occasion for appeals on behalf of needy members of the family of the deceased. Leon Modena excelled in this, as in so many other areas. His *Autobiography* reports that as part of his eulogy for a friend in 1616, he exhorted the congregation to take up a collection to provide a dowry for the orphaned daughter. Five hundred ducats were raised, about twice the maximum annual income of Modena's own career, though lower than the dowries he was able to provide for his own daughters, which were by no means high. The achievement was unusual enough to be taken as a model for emulation by Christian preachers who would say on their days of penitence, in order to inspire their audiences to charity, "Did not one Jew in the ghetto raise 500 ducats with one sermon to marry off a young girl?"[50] Unfortunately, he left no known written record of the eloquence of his appeal.

The Days of Awe were often an occasion for pulpit-inspired philanthropy. Azariah Figo devoted part of his sermon on the second day of Rosh Hashanah in 1643 to a collection for the impoverished Jewish community of Jerusalem; forced to pay an enormous tax, they had sent emissaries to all the communities of the Diaspora. Figo's theme-verse is actually only a strategically chosen phrase wrenched from its syntactical context: *Ha-maqom ha-hu³ Adonai yir'eh* (Gen. 22:14). This expresses both the unique providential relationship with the holy city and the hope that "God will see the affliction of that place, and bring it healing and recovery through the extraordinary kindness and generosity of your excellencies, as benefits the sanctity of the place and of this time." The practice of emergency appeals for the land of Israel on the Days of Awe was not an innovation of the past generation.[51]

I hope this sketchy introduction to the riches and challenges of Italian Jewish preaching will serve to whet the appetite for a further investigation of this subject. It is a topic about which much more could be said, but I am already chastened by one of the wisest sentences Leon Modena ever wrote: "In all of the congregations of Italy where I have preached, I never heard anyone complain that the sermon was too short, only that it was too long."[52]

NOTES

1. Samuel Judah Katzenellenbogen, *Sheneim ῾Asar Derashot* (Jerusalem, 1959; reprint of Warsaw, 1876 ed. [for a reason that escapes me, the Warsaw edition identified the author as "MaHaR I Mintz," leading to confusion with the fifteenth-century Talmudic scholar R. Judah Mintz]), p. 21b (page references are to the "Arabic" numerals). Cf. p. 58a, a eulogy for R. Joseph Karo: "After that I went into a recounting of the praise of the deceased *ga³on*," and p. 61a, a eulogy for R. Zalman Katz of Mantua: "After that I began to recount the praise of the deceased *ṣaddiq*." Despite its elliptic character, the eulogy for Karo contains some important historical information. Cf. Robert Bonfil, *Ha-Rabbanut be-³Italyah bi-Tequfat ha-Renesans* (Jerusalem, 1979), p. 194. That the elimination of material about the deceased from the written eulogy was not unique to Katzenellenbogen can be seen from Azariah Figo's eulogy for Abraham Aboab, *Binah le-῾Ittim* (Warsaw, 1866), 75, p. 122c: "I spoke at length on some other such aspects of his personal behavior; I have not written it at length."

2. Moshe Idel, *Kabbalah: New Perspectives* (New Haven, Conn., 1988), pp. 18–21.

3. Mark Cohen, ed., *The Autobiography of a Seventeenth-Century Venetian Rabbi* (Princeton, 1988; henceforth *Autobiography*), pp. 95, 102.

4. Abraham Portaleone, epilogue to *Shilṭei Gibborim* (Jerusalem, 1970), p. 185c. JTS MS Rab 172 was a collection of sermons written "by one of the scholars from the Provençal family in Mantua," and acquired by Leon Modena in Venice in 1595. While some are not without interest, they do not seem to be the work of a master preacher of Moscato's rank, and there were many other members of the family who could have written them.

5. Umberto Cassuto, "Un rabbino fiorentino del secolo XV," *Rivista Israelitica* 3 (1906): 116–28, 224–28; 4 (1907): 33–37, 156–61, 225–29.

6. For a general discussion of the tendency to omit historical references from sermon texts prepared for publication, or to refer to events in a general manner that assumes knowledge by the listener but raises problems for the historian, see my *Jewish Preaching 1200–1800* (New Haven, Conn., 1989), pp. 80–84, and the passage by Azariah Figo cited on p. 86. Cf. also the historical events mentioned by the fifteenth-century preacher Moses ben Joab of Florence: Cassuto, "Un rabbino fiorentino," *RI* 3 (1906): 117–18, and his statement cited in *Jewish Preaching 1200–1800*, p. 18.

7. On Cantarini, see Zalman Shazar, *Ha-Tiqvah li-Shenat HaTaQ* (Jerusalem, 1970), especially pp. 13–15, 18. Another massive manuscript (376 folios) of sermons that, to my knowledge, has not been studied is by Samuel ben Elisha Portaleone: British Library Add. 27,123. Eliezer Nahman Foa, a disciple of Menahem Azariah of Fano, left four manuscript volumes entitled "Goren ʾOrnan" (Mantua MS 59; Jerusalem Institute for Microfilmed Hebrew Manuscripts 842–845), but these are closer to homiletical commentaries than actual sermons. The only extant collection of Jewish sermons larger than Cantarini's from before the nineteenth century are the manuscripts of Saul Levi Morteira of Amsterdam.

8. Henry Sosland, *A Guide for Preachers on Composing and Delivering Sermons: The OR HA-DARSHANIM of Jacob Zahalon* (New York, 1987.

9. Columbia University Ms X893 T15 Q; the text was written in Florence in 1627. Cf. Bonfil, *Ha-Rabbanut*, p. 192; Sosland, *Guide*, pp. 82–83n.

10. Examples from Italy include "Kol Yaʾaqov" by Jacob ben Kalonymos Segal (Columbia University MS X893 J151 Q; cf. Bonfil, *Ha-Rabbanut*, pp. 192–93; Sosland, *Guide*, pp. 83–84n), Leon Modena's "Beit Leḥem Yehudah," an index to *Ein Yaāqov* (see *Autobiography*, p. 226), and Jacob Zahalon's alphabetical index to *Yalqut Shimʿoni* (see Sosland, *Guide*, pp. 73–76). For other such preacher aids by Jews, see Saperstein, *Jewish Preaching 1200–1800*, pp. 16–17, 286.

11. See Saperstein, *Jewish Preaching 1200–1800*, pp. 66–78.

12. Joseph ben Hayyim of Benevento, Parma Hebrew MS 2627 (Deʾ Rossi 1398).

13. Israel Bettan, *Studies in Jewish Preaching: Middle Ages* (Cincinnati, 1939), p. 196; Isaac Barzilay, *Between Reason and Faith* (The Hague and Paris, 1967), pp. 168–69; Isaac Rabinowitz, *The Book of the Honeycomb's Flow*

(Ithaca, 1983), pp. liv–lx; Alexander Altmann, "Ars Rhetorica as Reflected in Some Jewish Figures of the Italian Renaissance," in *Jewish Thought in the Sixteenth Century*, ed. Bernard Cooperman (Cambridge, Mass. 1983); Sosland, *Guide*, pp. 105–7, n. 14, all emphasize the citations of classical rhetoricians by Jewish writers. Joseph Dan, *Sifrut ha-Musar ve-ha-Derush* (Jerusalem, 1975), pp. 190–97, argues that Moscato's sermons should be seen more in the context of the internal Jewish homiletical tradition. I tend to agree with Dan, but for reasons somewhat different than those he adduced.

14. On the forced conversionary sermon in Italy, see S. W. Baron, *A Social and Religious History of the Jews*, 18 vols. (Philadelphia and New York, 1952–1983) 14:50–51 and 323–24, n. 47; Kenneth Stow, *Catholic Thought and Papal Jewry Policy* (New York, 1977), pp. 19–21. I am not aware of any study of the actual rhetorical techniques of these sermons.

15. Ingrid D. Rowland, "Egidio da Viterbo's Defense of Pope Julius II, 1509 and 1511," in *Do Ore Domini: Preacher and Word in the Middle Ages*, ed. Thomas Amos, Eugene Green, and Beverly Kienzle (Kalamazoo, Mich., 1989), pp. 250, 260. Cf. Isaac Arama's description of Spanish Jews impressed by the sermons of Christian preachers and demanding a higher level from their own rabbis: introduction to *'Aqedat Yiṣḥaq*, trans. in Saperstein, *Jewish Preaching 1200–1800*, p. 393.

16. *Autobiography*, pp. 96, 117. Cf. my *Jewish Preaching 1200–1800*, pp. 26, 51, no. 19, and Isaac min ha-Leviyim, *Sefer Medabber Tahapukhot*, ed. Daniel Carpi (Jerusalem, 1985), p. 80. For Montaigne's description of a Jewish sermon he heard in Italy, see my *Jewish Preaching 1200–1800*, p. 9.; for Giordano Bruno's praise of a contemporary Jewish preacher, see Cecil Roth, *The Jews in the Renaissance* (Philadelphia, 1959), pp. 36, 343n.

17. In the Church of San Geremia: *Autobiography*, p. 109; cf. his letter cited by Yosef Yerushalmi, *From Spanish Court to Italian Ghetto* (New York, 1971), pp. 353–54.

18. *Modo di comporre una predica*, by Panigarola (Venice, 1603); see Clemento Ancona, "L'inventario dei beni di Leon da Modena," *Bolletino dell'istituto dis storia della società e dello stato veneziano* 10 (1967): 265–66. I am grateful to Howard Adelman for bringing this article to my attention. Modena himself claims to have written a work called *Matteh Yehudah* "on how to compose a well-ordered sermon" (Sosland, *Guide*, p. 82, n.1).

19. See Saperstein, *Jewish Preaching 1200–1800*, pp. 411–12.

20. Examples of book-length studies include John O'Malley, *Praise and Blame in Renaissance Rome* (Durham, N.C., 1979); Roberto Rusconi, *Predicazione e vita religiosa nella società Italiana: Da Carlo Magna alla controriforma* (Turin, 1981); Carlo Delcorno, *Exemplum e letteratura: Tra Medioevo e Rinascimento* (Bologna, 1989); Daniel Lesnick, *Preaching in Medieval Florence: The Social World of Franciscan and Dominican Spirituality* (Athens, Ga., 1989); B. T. Paton, *Custodians of the Civic Conscience: Preaching Friars and the Communal Ethos in Late Medieval Siena* (Oxford, 1989).

There have also been monumental editions of sermons by the greatest preachers, such as Bernardino da Siena's *Prediche volgari sul Campo di Siena 1427*, vols. 1422 pp. (Milan, 1989).

21. Joseph Sermoneta, "Dante," *EJ* 5:1295. This was apparently based on Cecil Roth's assertion that "any person with the slightest pretext to education was familiar with Dante and with Petrarch. Rabbis quoted them in their sermons" (*The Jews in the Renaissance*, p. 33; note the addition of "widely" in the *EJ* statement). But Roth does not provide a single example of a sermon in which either Dante or Petrarch was quoted. For a more balanced treatment of Jewish knowledge of Italian literature, which does not address its use in sermons, see Moses Shulvass, *The Jews in the World of the Renaissance* (Leiden, 1973), pp. 230–31.

22. Joseph Dan, " 'Inyan be-Sifrut ha-Derush ha-ʾIvrit bi-Tequfat ha-Renesans be-ʾItalyah," *Proceedings of the Sixth World Congress of Jewish Studies* (Jerusalem, 1973), Division C, p. 108.

23. For the stories of Modena, see *Midbar Yehudah* (Venice, 1602), pp. 15a, 76b–77a; Saperstein, "Stories in Jewish Sermons (The 15th–16th Centuries), in *Proceedings of the Ninth World Congress of Jewish Studies* (Jerusalem, 1986), Division C, pp. 105–106; idem, *Jewish Preaching 1200–1800*, pp. 98–99, 342–43. The literature on Christian attitudes toward death in the fifteenth and sixteenth centuries is enormous; see Alberto Tenenti, *Sense de la mort et amour de la vie* (L'Harmattan, 1983 from the Italian ed. of 1957); Jean Delumeau, *Sin and Fear: The Emergence of a Western Guilt Culture* (New York, 1990 from the French ed. of 1983). While the idea that this world was the "land of the dead" was something of a topos (e.g. Delumeau, *Sin and Fear*, 352–53, 459), Modena's story is different from most in that it does not use the macabre (involving the putrefaction of the corpse), or the theme of *memento mori*, but simply the claim that death is true life as its summons to renunciation of this world. Cf. Innocenzo Ringhieri's *Dialoghi della vita e della morte* (Bologna, 1550), set in a cemetery, in which Death serves as a guide to eternal bliss (discussed by Tenenti, *Sense de la mort*, pp. 270–71).

24. David Ruderman, "An Exemplary Sermon from the Classroom of a Jewish Teacher in Renaissance Italy," *Italia* 1 (1978): 7–38. Robert Bonfil, "Shteim ʿEsreh ʾIggerot meʾet R. ʾEliyahu b. R. Shelomoh Raphaʾel ha-Levi (di Vali)," *Sinai* 71 (1972): 167, 184–84.

25. Simhah Assaf, *Meqorot le-Toledot ha-Ḥinukh be-Yisraʾel*, 4 vols. (Tel Aviv, 1930–50) 2:157, 177.

26. See the text in Assaf, *Meqorot le-Toledot*, 2:119, paragraph 12, translated in Jacob Marcus, *The Jew in the Medieval World* (New York, 1965), p. 386.

27. *Autobiography*, pp. 85–86; cf. Saperstein, *Jewish Preaching 1200–1800*, pp. 405–6.

28. For example, Isaac Min ha-Leviyim *Medabber Tahapukhot*, pp. 48–50, 62–63, 74–76, 78–79, 82–83, 104–6.

29. David Kaufmann, "The Dispute about the Sermons of David del Bene of Mantua," *JQR* 8 (1895–96): 513–27. Cf. the responsa of Leon Modena on philosophical and Kabbalistic content in sermons, in Saperstein, *Jewish Preaching 1200–1800*, pp. 406–8.

30. The manuscript sermons of Mordecai Dato; see Robert Bonfil, " 'Aḥat mi-Derashotav shel R. Mordekai Dato," *Italia* 1 (1976): 1–32; Saperstein, *Jewish Preaching 1200–1800*, 41 (and the reservation in n. 41).

31. *Autobiography*, pp. 101–2, 209 n.r, and the letter translated in Saperstein, *Jewish Preaching 1200–1800*, p. 411. In his introduction to *Midbar Yehudah*, Modena speaks of a glut of sermon collections on the market that diminishes their value in the eyes of potential buyers (p. 3a-b, cited in Israel Rosenzweig, *Hogeh Yehudah Mi-Qeṣ ha-Renesans* [Tel Aviv, 1972], p. 45).

32. See the examples cited in Saperstein, *Jewish Preaching 1200–1800*, p. 22.

33. See my discussion of the methodological issues in "Sermons and Jewish Society: The Case of Prague," a volume to be published in the near future by the Harvard Center for Jewish Studies.

34. See Saperstein, *Jewish Preaching 1200–1800*, p. 52, n. 23.

35. Roth, *The Jews in the Renaissance*, p. 48.

36. Cf. Thomas Izbicki, "Pyres of Vanities: Mendicant Preaching on the Vanity of Women and Its Lay Audience," in Amos, *De Ore Domini*, pp. 211–34, esp. pp. 215–16, 219 on hair styles and false hair.

37. Katzenellenbogen, *Sheneim 'Asar Derashot*, p. 9b; cf. Gedaliah Nigal, "Derashotav shel Shemu'el Yehudah Katzenellenbogen," *Sinai* 36 (1971–72): 82. For other examples of Christian behavior used by Jewish preachers as a model worthy of emulation, see my "Christians and Jews—Some Positive Images," in *Christians among Jews and Gentiles*, ed. George Nickelsburg (Philadelphia, 1986) = *HTR* 19:1–3 (1986): 236–46.

38. Figo, *Binah le-'Ittim*, 64, p. 93d; cf. Bettan, *Studies in Jewish Preaching*, p. 237. A different sermon (13, p. 47b) in which Figo complains about the same common phenomenon goes a step further by noting a rationale intended to justify the practice from traditional sources. "Let them not heed deceitful chatter (cf. Ex. 5:9) which claims, 'On the contrary, by this they increase their merit by subduing the erotic impulses [aroused], like those who said, "Let us go on the road leading by the harlots' place and defy our inclination and have our reward" (B. AZ 17a-b).' " Figo concedes that traditional ethical theory recognizes a great merit in overcoming the temptation to sin, which might lead some to conclude that arousing the temptation might play a positive religious role. But "in this generation of ours, with our sins, this is not the way"; the motivation of the young men is not pure, their purpose is only to see what they can see; the practice must therefore be condemned.

39. Figo, *Binah le-'Ittim*, 48, p. 43b.

40. See my "Sermons and Jewish Society" (above, n. 33)

41. Needless to say, such passages from sermons need to be integrated with other types of literature, especially the contemporary responsa, before re-

sponsible conclusions about actual Jewish behavior (as opposed to the consciousness of the religious leadership), can be drawn.

42. Figo, *Binah le'Ittim,* 10, p. 33d; cf. Bettan, *Studies in Jewish Preaching,* p. 239.

43. Figo, *Binah le-'Ittim,* 10, p. 33d. On the complexity of the legal issues relating to the *cambio,* see Stephen Passamaneck, *Insurance in Rabbinic Law* (Edinburgh, 1974). For fifteenth- and sixteenth-century Italian Christian moralists and preachers and their distrust of "letters of exchange" as an attempt to camouflage illicit interest-bearing loans, see Delumeau, *Sin and Fear,* pp. 224–25; for the earlier period, cf. Lesnick, *Preaching in Medieval Florence,* pp. 119–21.

44. Cassuto, "Un rabbino fiorentino," *RI* 4 (1907): 226–27. The last sentence alludes to Prov. 18:22, "One who has found a wife has found something good," frequently used as an ornament on Italian marriage contracts. The elements of humor and wit in Italian Jewish preaching (and in Jewish preaching in general) deserve careful study.

45. Katzenellenbogen, *Sheneim 'Asar Derashot,* p. 10a. The study of Jewish child-rearing practices (as distinct from more formal Jewish education) and their relationship with those of contemporary Christian neighbors (for example, whether the conclusions of Philippe Ariès and his critics have any relevance to the Jewish family) has hardly begun. Pertinent to this passage would be Ariès' claim of a shift in the early modern period from a rather careless indifference toward the child to a regimen involving constant surveillance (*Centuries of Childhood: A Social History of Family Life* [New York, 1962 from the French ed. of 1960], pp. 94–97).

46. For example, Modena's eulogy for his mother delivered at the end of the 30-day mourning period (*Midbar Yehudah,* pp. 51a–55a); cf. Penina Nave, *Yehudah Aryeh mi-Modena, Leqeṭ Ketavim* (Jerusalem, 1968), pp. 143–44. Katzenellenbogen indicates that the prevalent taste considered it inappropriate to discuss in a eulogy the closeness of personal friendship between the preacher and the deceased, but he defends his decision to do so anyway (*Sheneim 'Asar Derashot,* pp. 30a–31a). For recent studies of Italian Christian eulogies, see John McManamon, *Funeral Oratory and the Cultural Ideals of Italian Humanism* (Chapel Hill, N.C., 1989) and the articles by McManaman and Donald Weinstein in *Life and Death in Fifteenth-Century Florence,* ed. Marcel Tetal, Ronald Witt, and Rona Geffen (Durham, N.C., 1989), pp. 68–104.

47. Judah Moscato, *Nefuṣot Yehudah* (Warsaw, 1871), 36, pp. 97c–98a, 99d.

48. See Sosland, *Guide,* p. 26.

49. Katzenellenbogen, *Sheneim 'Asar Derashot,* p. 63b.

50. *Autobiography,* pp. 109, 41–42.

51. Figo, *Binah le-'Ittim,* pp. 13d–14a. Cf. the Florentine preacher Jacob di Alba, *Toledot Ya'aqov* (Venice, 1609), p. 85a:
    We might say, *How lonely does she sit* (Lam. 1:1): the city of God that descended to earth and *became like a widow* sitting on the ground, bereft of all distinction. But

with regard to taxes and exactions, they perform a creation *ex nihilo* upon her; she is *great among the nations, a princess among the states* (Lam. 1:1), for she has existed only so that taxes might be taken from her, making something out of nothing. So it is, in our sins, at present: Jerusalem must pay many kinds of taxes, and if they did not send emissaries from various places, the inhabitants would not be able to endure.

52. Modena, *She'elot u-Teshuvot Ziqnei Yehudah*, ed. Shlomo Simonsohn (Jerusalem, 1957), p. 126. The context is a halakhic question sent to him whether it was permissible for a preacher to turn over an hourglass on the Sabbath to time the sermon so that it would not be a burden on the congregation. For the use of the hourglass by Christian preachers, see Saperstein, *Jewish Preaching 1200–1800*, p. 38, n. 33.

B

The Jewish Encounter with Magic, Ancient
Theology, and Neoplatonism

4

The Magical and Neoplatonic Interpretations of the Kabbalah in the Renaissance

Moshe Idel

I

In Italy of the Renaissance period, Jewish thought developed in a manner unprecedented in earlier stages of Jewish intellectual history. Several of the most creative personalities in Jewish culture were in communication with leading spokesmen of Renaissance thought. This phenomenon is unique: Greek, Arabic and Christian philosophy developed in the absence of any significant oral connection with Jewish culture. Before the Renaissance, Jewish thought exercised no decisive influence upon the major representatives of gentile thought. In those instances where a certain Jewish influence may be detected, that influence originated from a written rather than an oral source.[1] In the Renaissance period, on the other hand, a considerable number of Christian thinkers took instruction from Jews. Among them were the Italians Pico della Mirandola and Egidio da Viterbo, the German Reuchlin, and Tissard, a Frenchman.[2] In addition, Christian scholars had frequent contacts with the numerous Jewish apostates of the time. The new meeting of Christian and Jew was part of the Christian culture's search for ancient wisdom. The Christians themselves initiated these contacts and the following source serves as an illustration of the vigor of this activity:[3]

The author would like to thank Ms. Martelle Gavarin for translating this chapter.

Reprinted by permission of Harvard Center for Jewish Studies from *Jewish Thought in the Sixteenth Century*, edited by Bernard Cooperman, Cambridge, Mass., 1983.

In the last twenty years, knowledge has increased, and people have been seeking everywhere for instruction in Hebrew. Especially after the rise of the sect of Luther,[4] many of the nobles and scholars of the land sought to have thorough knowledge of this glorious science (Kabbalah). They have exhausted themselves in this search, because among our people there are but a small number of men learned in this wisdom, for after the great number of troubles and expulsions, but a few remain. So seven learned men grasp a Jewish man by the hem of his garment and say: 'Be our master in this science!'

Here Rabbi Elijah Menahem Halfan alludes to another aspect of gentile eagerness to learn from the Jews. Not only did the gentiles want instruction in Hebrew; they also wanted to gain access to wider areas of Jewish thought, and particularly to the Kabbalah.[5] In other words Jewish thought became an important subject of discussion among Christian thinkers. This significant change affected the intellectual climate in which Jewish Renaissance culture developed.

Jewish activity in the area of translation is clear evidence of the new Christian attitude to Jewish culture and to the reciprocal Jewish willingness to become involved in Christian culture. Until the end of the fourteenth century, Jews translated many important philosophical works into Hebrew. From the fifteenth century onwards however, Jews and apostates began to translate Jewish books into Latin and Italian or to write part of their own compositions in these languages. In contrast, there are scarcely any translations of philosophical works into Hebrew at this time. The few Hebrew translations were of books authored by Jews: for example, the translation of Judah Abravanel's *Dialoghi d'Amore* and the translation of Rabbi Abraham Herrera's book, *Puerto del Cielo*. Platonic, Neoplatonic and Hermetic writings were translated into Latin and other European languages, but they are not to be found in a Hebrew version. This fact is a clear indication of the change in the direction of translation.

This new development, a lively intellectual meeting of Christian and Jew, had interesting implications for Jewish thought. The outstanding works of medieval Jewish philosophy, *The Book of Beliefs and Opinions, The Kuzari, The Guide for the Perplexed,* and *The Light of God (Or ha-Shem)* were created in response to problems arising from the influence of general intellectual developments upon Jews.[6] Jewish thought in the Renaissance was not reactive in the same way. Here the identification of stimulus and response are not always clear. To determine who was the teacher and who the pupil is not always easy. It is often difficult, therefore, to determine whether a statement of a Jewish author derives ultimately from a Christian source or whether it represents an original development of Jewish thought. The phenomenon was one of mutual openness which began with a Christian desire to learn from Jews and continued with Jewish willingness to absorb ideas developed by the Christian Renaissance. The nature and content of this exchange is well represented in the similarity of views on magic and Kabbalah found in the writings of Pico della Mirandola and Rabbi Yoḥanan Alemanno.

The central topic of this chapter concerns the Neoplatonic and magical interpretations of Kabbalah in the Renaissance period and the way in which such ideas in Jewish sources could have influenced the development of Renaissance culture in general. Before treating the subject in detail, however, it is necessary to consider the general character of Jewish Kabbalah in Italy.

Kabbalah as it developed in Italy differed from that of Spain. In Spain, the primary classical formulation of Kabbalah was cast in terms of myth. This mythical sensibility placed great emphasis upon the theosophical and theurgic meaning of the commandments of Jewish law. Italian kabbalistic theosophy, on the other hand, emphasized the unity and simplicity of the divine emanation and its apprehension by man's intellection, while the theurgic nature of the Kabbalah was correspondingly deemphasized.

Three kabbalists, Rabbi Abraham Abulafia who composed most of his works in Italy, Rabbi Menaḥem Recanati and the author of the book *Ma'arekhet ha-Elohut,* are the central pillars of Italian Kabbalah from its early stage until the beginning of the sixteenth century. Despite the tremendous differences in the thought systems of these figures, I discern in their writing a common conceptual characteristic: the mythical conception of the Divinity which characterized the *Zohar* and the later works of Gikatilla was either unknown to them or incompatible with their way of thought. In the opinion of Abraham Abulafia, belief in the existence of the ten *Sefirot* is worse than the Christian belief in the Trinity.[7] To Recanati, the *Sefirot* are the instruments, not the essence, of God. The author of the *Ma'arekhet* demonstrates a clearly nominalist trend of thought.[8] It follows that a certain similarity exists between the thought of these writers and the philosophical conception of God. After the expulsion, Spanish kabbalists reached Italy and found the Italian school of Kabbalah to be unfamiliar. In the mid-1490s, Rabbi Judah Ḥayyat wrote that in the province of Mantua he had seen "books of the Kabbalah that confuse the unsullied mind," and warned against reading such works.[9] In his two letters to Rabbi Isaac of Pisa, Rabbi Isaac Mar Ḥayyim gave the following advice:[10]

Do not follow the path of those scholars who base themselves upon reason and interpret the words of the Kabbalah so as to agree with philosophy. Rather make Kabbalah the foundation and try to make reason agree with it.

These descriptions underline a similarity between Italian Kabbalah and philosophy which exceeds that found in the writings of Rabbi Menaḥem Recanati and the author of the *Ma'arekhet*.[11] This affinity between Kabbalah and philosophy has an important corollary in the interpretation of the practical commandments of Jewish Law. The Kabbalah emphasizes the theocentric significance of the commandments with kabbalistic awareness enables man to restore the harmony of the Divinity. This concept is fundamental to the Kabbalah of Spain and Safed. Proper evaluation of these kabbalistic schools depends upon recognition of the significance of this principle. It follows that, in this view, a kabbalist is one who above all else lives his life in accordance with the dictates of processes occurring within the system of the *Sefirot*.

Abulafia and the author of the *Ma'arekhet* ignore this notion, and in their teachings Kabbalah loses its theurgic value.[12] The non-theurgic nature of Italian Kabbalah until the sixteenth century facilitated Christian acculturation and acceptance of Kabbalah as a science. The Neoplatonic circles of Florence had an unabrasive encounter with the quasi-philosophical theology of Abulafia, with the kabbalistic theory of the *ma'arekhet* and even with the teaching of Recanati.[13] Furthermore Abulafia's mystical and exegetical system of thought did not depend in essence upon any particular theology. His mystical way was an instrument for all those who sought to narrow the distance between man and the Torah or the Divinity. As H. Wirszubski demonstrated, early in his career Pico had access to Abulafia's thought.[14]

The mutual influence of Jewish and Christian Kabbalah is attested to by a change in the style of Jewish kabbalistic works during the Renaissance. Until the mid-fifteenth century Jewish kabbalistic writings did not contain digressions on other subjects while works of Christian Kabbalah, on the other hand, devoted a considerable, if not a preponderant amount of space to non-kabbalistic material. Pico's *Theses,* his most important kabbalistic composition, contains a very heterogeneous selection of subject matter and a relatively small amount of Kabbalah. Reuchlin set down a weighty amount of Pythagorean and Platonic material alongside his kabbalistic topics. Such is also the case in the writings of Egidio da Viterbo and Francesco Giorgio. From the end of the fifteenth century however, one finds many Jewish authors who utilized the Kabbalah in an eclectic fashion and wrote works incorporating Kabbalah alongside material drawn from other systems of thought. Yoḥanan Alemanno was an outstanding representative of this change as were Isaac and Judah Abravanel, Judah Moscato and Abraham Yagel.

The identification of the lines of influence between the thought of Rabbi Yoḥanan Alemanno and that of his student, Pico della Mirandola, should be attempted within the framework of the general trends described above. It is known that the two scholars met in Florence in the year 1488.[15] If this was their first meeting then several of the ideas which Pico committed to writing between the years 1486 and 1488 were the result of an independent attempt to synthesize various systems of thought. Moreover, similar views appearing in Alemanno's writings were the result of Pico's influence on his teacher. However, if Pico and Alemanno met earlier than 1488, then it is possible that Alemanno's views on the Kabbalah and magic influenced the formulation of Christian Kabbalah as did the writings of Flavius Mithridates.

When treating the question of the direction of influence one should bear in mind also that Alemanno was some twenty years older than Pico and had begun to record his thoughts as early as the year 1470. (It is likely that some of Alemanno's earlier writings have survived in a manuscript collection of his work now at Oxford.[16]) For this reason, I tend to think that Alemanno's thought should be seen as influenced by the general Neoplatonic trend current in Florence. The Florentine interest in magic also left its mark on Alemanno. Alemanno's contribution to his cultural surroundings is represented by his Neoplatonic and magical interpretations of the Kabbalah, interpretations which influenced Pico as well as Jewish writers of the sixteenth century. My discussion is limited to the similarity of their thought and this parallelism permits us to consider Alemanno a Renaissance personality in every respect.[17]

The similarity between the material found in the Christian Kabbalah and that found in Alemanno's writings also deserves attention. In neither case can these works be categorized as kabbalistic in the common sense of the term. For these writers, Kabbalah is but one of several systems of speculation. This accounts for my earlier observation that in every one of Alemanno's compositions one can find much material drawn from non-kabbalistic sources. As a result of this eclecticism, Kabbalah as presented in Alemmano's writings underwent certain metamorphoses, changes which will be discussed in the following pages.

II

One of the most significant contributions of recent Renaissance scholarship has been the recognition of the considerable impact of magic on Renaissance thought.[18] Scholarship has gradually uncovered the influence of doctrines of magic contained in the Hermetic corpus translated by Marsilio Ficino. the literary traces of *Picatrix* are discernible in the writings of several central thinkers such as Giordano Bruno and Tomasso Campanella.[19] Several authors mention another work on magic, the *Sefer Razi'el* attributed to King Solomon.[20] Solomon was also mentioned as the author of other books read by the circle of Lorenzo de' Medici in Florence.[21]

At first, Renaissance magic assumed a philosophical garb woven of Hermetic, Neoplatonic and kabbalistic strands. The demonic elements of magic were rejected by authors such as Ficino and Pico, but these elements came to the fore later and occupied a place of increasing importance in magical literature. The most outstanding representative of this development was Agrippa of Nettesheim.

The study of magic by Jewish scholars also flourished during the same period.[22] Jewish interest was sparked in no small measure by the preoccupation with the subject in Christian intellectual circles. Conceptions of magic known to, and rejected by, Judaism long before the Renaissance now returned to Jewish thought, partially or completely legitimized. Moreover, non-Jewish works on magic which, though they had been translated into Hebrew earlier, had received little attention now enjoyed wider distribution and more frequent mention. New works were also translated from Latin and Italian, and there are references to contacts between Christian and Jewish magicians. All of these provide tangible evidence of the contemporary mutual interest in magic.

The Jewish study of magic was a response to Christianity's new regard for the subject. Nevertheless, Jewish authors had greater freedom of thought than Christian writers who worked under the watchful eye of the Church. As a result, magic could become, for the Jews, a new and comprehensive perspective from which to view all aspects of their tradition.

My general discussion will be preceded by a bibliographical description which charts the increased interest in the study of magic among Jews during the Italian Renaissance.

There are two Hebrew versions of the most important composition on magic, the *Ghayat al-Ḥakim* or *Picatrix*. Both renditions contain abridgments of the larger work.

1) The most important abridgment of the work was made from the Arabic[23] and is entered here under the title, *Takhlit he-Ḥakham*.[24] This version of the work is to be found in two manuscripts, Munich MS 214 f. 46r–101v and Brit. Lib. MS Or. 9861 f. lr–38v. These two manuscripts were copied in Italy at the end of the fifteenth century. During this period, the work was mentioned in Alemanno's curriculum as one of the books on magic which must be perused by anyone who wishes to attain perfection.[25]

2) A fragment of the second abridgment of the *Picatrix* is also relevant to our discussion. This was preserved in two manuscripts which were part of the same codex, New York MS 2470 (ENA 2439) f. lr–10v and New York MS 2465 (ENA 1920) f. lr–5r. These two manuscripts were also copied in Italy. In the first manuscript on page 10r, we read:

This book was translated from Aramaic into Arabic and from Arabic into Hebrew, but this translation is not the first Hebrew translation. From Hebrew it was translated into Latin and from Latin this translation was made, praise to God.

At the end of the second manuscript, we find this (on f. 5r):

The translation of the first chapter of the book *Ghayat al-Ḥakim*, has been completed, thank God, and was translated from a Christian translation, most of which is incorrect, as their translation is in no way clear.

This evidence of the translation of the composition from the Latin *(la'az)* seems to refer to a translation made during the Renaissance period. In any case, the Hebrew translation was made after the first Arabic translation and certainly after the Latin whose approximate date is unknown.[26]

3) A small portion of the Hebrew text of *Picatrix* has been preserved in Oxford MS 1352 (Mic. 228) f. 177r. Neubauer published a section of this text in his catalogue of Oxford manuscripts. This manuscript was also written in Italy.

Three Hebrew translations of *Picatrix* have been preserved in Italian manuscripts written at the end of the fifteenth and the beginning of the sixteenth centuries. At the same time the Latin translation of *Picatrix* was widely disseminated among scholars of the Renaissance. Rabbi Yoḥanan Alemanno, who was involved in the intellectual activities of the type pursued at the Academy of Florence, is one of the few to mention the Hebrew version of the *Picatrix*.

Another work on magic which enjoyed widespread distribution among Christians in the Renaissance is the above mentioned *Sefer Razi'el*. In many respects, this composition differs from the better known *Sefer Razi'el ha-Malakh*. F. Secret has given a detailed description of the content of *Sefer Razi'el*, and I will supplement his remarks by reference to the Hebrew translation which was unknown to him. The composition is found in two manuscripts, the more complete of which is New York JTS MS 8117 f. 59–100. In Oxford MS 1959 f. 98v–131v, a large section of the composition appears in a different and less felicitous version than that of New York MS 8117. Study of the composition indicates that the translation was also made in Italy. Clear evidence of this fact appears on the first page of MS 8117, f. 1r:

In the name of the God of Israel, I shall begin to copy *Sefer Razi'el*. Pay close attention and know that I found this book in two versions, the first in Hebrew and the second in Latin *[latino]*. The names of angels and intelligences *[intien-tzii(!)]* are different in each work but in practical terms there is no difference *(varietati)* in any respect. Since no one who practices may succeed in any of these actions without knowing this book, I have chosen to copy it using each one of the names of the intelligences *[intelientzii]* so that the practitioner will not have to consult other books which have no value whatsoever.

The translator's remarks bear close examination. According to the above quotation, it would seem that the translator had before him two identical compositions whose textual variation concerned only the names of angels. Comparison of this composition (New York JTS MS 8117) with parts of those translations cited by F. Secret indicates that here (MS 8117) we have an actual translation and not merely an integration of different versions. Support for this conclusion may be drawn from the presence in the work itself of Italian words, the product of some individual linguistic imagination, which bear no resemblance to the terminology found in earlier works on Jewish magic. There is proof that this translation was included in Alemanno's curriculum where it is described as a "translation from Latin." Since Alemanno mentions this composition in other places in his writing it is reasonable to assume that the latest date of the translation was the beginning of the 1480s. I have found no other mention of this work by a Jewish source before Alemanno. In the middle of the sixteenth century however, two works named *Sefer Razi'el*, "the long" and "the short," are mentioned in the correspondence of two scholars. It seems that the *Sefer Razi'el* to which I have referred in this chapter was known by the name *Sefer Razi'el ha-Gadol*.[27]

Jews were familiar with the *Liber Clavicula Salomonis (Sefer Mafte'aḥ Shlomo)*, a famous book on magic well known to Christian intellectuals.[28] The *Clavicula* appears to have been mentioned for the first time by Rabbi Asher Lemlin, a German Jewish Kabbalist who lived in northern Italy at the beginning of the sixteenth century.[29] "Solomon, peace be with him, wrote an esoteric book *Sefer ha-Mafteaḥ*, about secret practices. The Christians call that book *Clavicula*."[30] After Lemlin, the book *Sefer Mafte'aḥ Shlomo* is mentioned by Rabbi Gedalya ibn Yaḥya, the author of *Sefer Shalshelet ha-Kabbalah*. Of King Solomon he writes: "He composed books and incantations against the devils and they are named *Mafteaḥ Shlomo*."[31] Close study of the version of *Sefer Mafteaḥ Shlomo* that has reached us[32] reveals that its major part is a translation of material on magic from Christian sources. The translation seems to have been made in Italy between the time of Rabbi Asher Lemlin and the period of writing of *Sefer Shalshelet ha-Kabbalah*. Alemanno, who had great interest in works on magic, especially those ascribed to Solomon,[33] does not mention the book, while Rabbi Asher Lemlin does not refer to it by its usual name, *Mafte'aḥ Shlomo*, but calls it *Ha-Mafte'aḥ ha-Nistar*. It follows that Lemlin was also unfamiliar with the Hebrew version of the work.

In addition to these popular works in the literature of magic, Rabbi Yoḥanan Alemanno also mentions other books which have been preserved thanks to Alemanno's interest in them. For example, in one work, Alemanno copied out an unknown translation of the *Sefer ha-Levana*,[34] an important book on magic. In *Ḥeshek Shlomo*, Alemanno quotes several times from the *Sefer Mlekhet Muskelet*, attributed to Appolonius.³⁵ I found fragments of this book in two Italian manuscripts written in the sixteenth century.³⁶ In Alemanno's writings, the *Sefer ha-Atzamin*³⁷ attributed to Rabbi Abraham ibn Ezra, and the *Sefer ha-Tamar*³⁸ are mentioned. Both compositions were translated from the Arabic a long time before the Renaissance. The *Sefer Pil'ot Olam (The Wonders of the World)* of Albertus Magnus, one of the most important books on magic in Latin in the Middle Ages, was also known to Alemanno.³⁹ It is no less significant that Alemanno himself devoted considerable attention to the topic of magic in one of his works.⁴⁰ He asserts that he has contacts with gentiles who studied similar subjects. In Alemanno's *Collectanaea* we read: "A master of incantations told me that he had tried to find hidden treasure."⁴¹ In the book *Shir ha-Ma'alot* Alemanno makes a second reference to a conversation with a gentile on the subject of magic and reports "what a craftsman told me."⁴² The story concerned the ancient practice of killing a man and turning him into a spirit to guard a treasure. On another occasion, Alemanno relates that he met a gentile in Bologna who discerned Alemanno's character by the art of physiognomy and that his accurate description had greatly impressed Alemanno.⁴³ Dealing with demonic magic, Alemanno stated: "I heard many things of this type from Jews and Christians."⁴⁴

In Judaism as a whole, there were two important conceptions of the possibility of human influence upon the extra-human realms. According to the first, it is man's duty to bring about a unification of the *Sefirot* which constitute, in general kabbalistic theory, the revealed aspect of the Divinity. This view⁴⁵ is singularly theurgic, for man's performance of religious commandments has God as its object. The commandments symbolically represent the dynamic activities and processes of the *Sefirot*. Performance of these actions is accomplished by the prescribed esoteric meditation. In this view, the realm of extra-divine forces is rarely affected by such practices. The resulting divine harmony, however, is beneficial to the world; this is a side effect which depends upon the achievement of the primary goal. One must particularly emphasize the fact that the observance of the commandments is no less a divine than a human necessity. This is expressed in the kabbalistic saying, "Service of God fulfills a divine need" *(avoda tzorekh gavo'ah)*.

In contrast, magic in general acts upon the extra-divine world: the cosmic soul, the world of angels and the forces guiding the constellations and planets. Magic achieves its objectives in various ways. At times, the individual soul cleaves to the cosmic soul; thereby, man may change nature at will, for the cosmic soul directs nature. Other magical texts prescribe actions which cause astral forces to descend into the world and operate in accordance with the magician's will. This type of magic also includes demonic magic. The magician may also utilize talismans, certain materials or things having secret properties which absorb the emanations of higher powers or protect the bearer of the object. These types of magic have one common characteristic: no divine influence is present in the various processes. Generally speaking, magic is neither directed at, nor addressed to, God, nor does God benefit from the magician's activities. In kabbalistic terms these practices are "rituals that serve man" *(avoda tzorekh hedyot)*.

Despite the differences between the kabbalistic and the magical understanding of human activity, the two systems share certain common features. In both conceptions, man has a central role and exercises considerable influence upon processes in many areas. By prayer or incantation, man exerts this influence in an appeal to the *Sefirot* or angels, forces outside himself. Although they are ontologically distinct, the *Sefirot* and the realm of "spirits" contain multiple powers and each of these powers has a unique character and capacity to exert an influence in a particular direction. The kabbalist must first ensure the flow of spiritual emanation from the *Ein Sof* (the Infinite Godhead) to the *Sefirot*. This efflux creates harmony in the divine structure as a whole, and only then may the kabbalist direct his prayers and meditations to any particular *Sefira* in order to achieve a desired effect. This selective employment of sefirotic power is analogous to that of angels who each supervise a certain area. These angels respond to incantations and answer human requests. This similarity between Kabbalah and magic is probably the result of the influence of ancient Jewish magic which was concerned with the incantations of angels. It is reasonable to assume that this doctrine of magic became integrated in the Kabbalah with gnostic and Neoplatonic traditions. Magic was transformed into theurgy once the object of the spiritual efflux became the *Sefira 'Malkhut'* rather than the kabbalist or magician himself.

Renaissance thinkers were aware of the analogy between magic and Kabbalah. In Pico's writings magic and Kabbalah are so often paired that the term "Kabbalah" becomes a synonym for magic. According to Pico, *magia naturalis*,[46] that is natural magic, is an initial and less potent level of Kabbalah which in its entirety is the quintessence of magic.[47] He emphasized that *magia naturalis* shares a common principle with Kabbalah; both are conceived as instruments for the reception of the efflux drawn from higher powers.[48] For Pico, Kabbalah is magic. This interpretation has altered the nature of Kabbalah by transfering its major focus from the realm of the Divinity to that of man. For Pico, the *magia naturalis* described by Marsilio Ficino is simply an initial and less potent level of Kabbalah, although Pico did not leave a detailed explanation of exactly why Kabbalah, the quintessence of magic and the highest achievement attained in the course of human development, is superior.

Pico classified the Kabbalah into "speculative" and "practical" branches, and from various statements in his writings we can identify the content of these branches. "Speculative" Kabbalah included the technique of letter permutation and the doctrine of the interrelation of the three worlds.[49] In another place, Pico offered a division of Kabbalah parallel to that of speculative and practical—namely into the sciences of the *Sefirot* and of the divine names.[50] In yet a third remark, Pico distinguished between letter permutations as one type of Kabbalah and the reception of divine powers as a second type, still superior to *magia naturalis*.[51] From these three statements we see that for Pico, the permutation of letters and the study of the divine names are separate branches of Kabbalah, while the recitation of the divine names and the reception of higher forces are both part of the practical Kabbalah. The exact nature of the latter relationship is not clarified.

There are significant parallels between Pico's classification and that offered by Alemanno and other Jewish kabbalists. For instance, a definition of speculative Kabbalah very similar to Pico's appears in a letter written in Alemanno's intellectual circle:[52]

The speculative part of the Kabbalah concerns knowledge of the interconnection of the three worlds by means of the ten *Sefirot,* and the allusions and secrets of the Torah and the hierarchy of these three worlds and their area of influence.

Scholem[53] has already noted the resemblance between Pico's classification and Abulafia's division of the Kabbalah, in a letter to Rabbi Judah Salomon, into the study of the *Sefirot* and the study of the divine names.[54]

As for Alemanno himself, we can gain some insight into his distinction between magic and Kabbalah by analyzing his proposed curriculum of kabbalistic study. Alemanno advised one to begin the study of the Kabbalah by reading tracts on the doctrine of the *Sefirot*. For example, he recommended the works of Recanati and the book *Ma'arekhet ha-Elohut*.[55] As a further step, Alemanno suggested the writings of Abraham Abulafia and the commentaries on the *Sefer Yetzira*. The study of the corpus of Abraham Abulafia's writings was to be followed by the reading of books on magic, some of which treat the subject of divine names, and most of which discuss techniques for spiritual receptivity.[56]

A two-step technique for the working of miracles found in Alemanno's *Collectanaea* provides us with an excellent approach to that scholar's concept of the relation between Kabbalah and magic.[57] At first the kabbalist recites divine names which he reads to himself from a Torah scroll.

After the external cleansing[58] of the body and an inner change and spiritual purification from all taint, one becomes as clear and pure as the heavens. Once one has divested oneself of all material thoughts, let him read only the Torah and the divine names written there. There shall be revealed awesome secrets and such divine visions as may be emanated upon pure clear souls who are prepared to receive them as the verse said:[59] 'Make ready for three days and wash your clothing.' For there are three preparations: of the exterior (the body), of the interior, and of the imagination.

By reading the Torah as a series of divine names, man receives an initial infusion of power. This reading is preceded by a series of "preparations" which repeat the purifications performed by the Jews before the giving of the Torah at Sinai.

The second stage of the process is described in the continuation of the above quotation. In this, the Torah scroll itself becomes imbued with the spiritual force. At this time, "the writings of God, the spirit of the living God, shall descend upon the written scroll." By the expression, "the writing of God," Alemanno is referring directly to the giving of the Torah at Sinai as described in Exodus. A personal experience of the revelation of the law is a conventional thought in the Kabbalah. What is new and striking in the process described by Alemanno is the similarity of the ceremony to the ritual of dedication found in books of magic.

When a man devotes a great amount of time the intermittent becomes habitual. When he immerses himself in these things, then such a great efflux will come to him that he will be able to cause the spirit of God to descend upon him and hover above him and flutter about him all the day. Not only that, but 'the writing of God, the spirit of the living God' will descend upon the scroll to such a degree that the scroll will give him power to work signs and wonders in the world. And such are the books called 'segretti' and all the incantations are the secret words *[segretti]* which come from evil spirits. Therefore the Torah forbade these practices. The Torah of Moses, however is entirely sealed and closed by the name of the Holy One, blessed be He. Therefore its powers are many and such is the Book of Psalms. This is a great secret, hidden from the eye of the blind and the cunning.

In Alemanno's *Collectanaea,* therefore, we find both elements of Pico's definition of the practical Kabbalah—first the reading of divine names in the Torah, and second, the reception of efflux. The connection between the use of divine names and the reception of emanation is also mentioned in the book, *Sefer Takhlit he-Ḥakham,*[60] a work known to Pico and Alemanno.

Aristotle said . . . in ancient times, divine names had a certain ability to bring spiritual power to earth. At times, these powers descended below. At others, they killed the man who used them.

Neither in Alemanno, nor in the above quotation from *Sefer Takhlit he-Ḥakham* is there any mention of practical Kabbalah. Careful study of Alemanno's statements indicates that the practices he suggests relate to the Torah scroll. The words of the Torah are, in Alemanno's view, a series of names from which meaning may be derived by reference to another source.[61] "The ancient sages said that all the Torah is but one name, and all its words are powerful names and each and every verse is an additional name."

This view originated in the books entitled *Sefer Shimushei Torah* and *Sefer Shimushei Tehilim* and in similar traditions which reached the kabalists Rabbi Ezra and Rabbi Moses ben Naḥman in Gerona. But the doctrines are now given an unequivocally magical interpretation by Alemanno. The Torah read as a series of names is transformed into an instrument of magic.[62]

Anyone who knows the science of the stars and constellations that emanate upon the creatures on earth may interpret the entire Torah according to the signs and rules of astrology. This is true of the masters of both theoretical, as well as practical, astrology. Any man, either good or evil, who knows the work of the pure and impure angels who are superior to the stars may draw their fragrance upon our heads, for he has given a kabbalistic interpretation to the entire Torah. This matter includes the masters of both the speculative and the practical sciences of the *Sefirot.*[63]

The Torah may be read in two ways, astrologically and kabbalistically. Each way has a speculative and a practical part. It seems to me that through the practical interpretation of the Torah (the reading of the divine names), one "may draw their fragrance upon our heads."

If my analysis of Alemanno's view is correct, then his understanding of practical Kabbalah is similar to that of Pico. Both consider the practical Kabbalah to include the use of divine names which are connected to the descent and activation of spiritual forces in the world.

The definitions of practical Kabbalah found in the writings of Pico and Alemanno share another common point. Pico considered as forbidden those kabbalistic practices which employ divine names to charm devils.[64] This distinction between pure and impure forms of practical Kabbalah is suggested by the previous quotation from Alemanno about pure and impure forces above the stars. At the end of the quote cited above from the *Collectanaea*, Alemanno speaks of incantations which are forbidden by the Torah. These are separate from the reading of the Torah in a magical way which is permitted.[65]

Alemanno's remarks appear to contain a thought parallel to material found in *Sefer Takhlit he-Ḥakham*. Immediately after the above quotation we find: "He [i.e. Aristotle] said magical incantations descend upon the globe[?]." Incantations derived from magic are forbidden but not the use of divine names.[66]

For Alemanno then, we have seen that the reading of a Torah scroll became a process for the acquisition of magical powers originating in the emanation of higher forces, and that this process had two stages. The person received an initial pulsation of the divine efflux and only then, after he had become habituated, could he receive the additional efflux, "the spirit of the living God." Alemanno describes this second stage as "bringing down into oneself the spirit of God" (the phrase is from the *Sefer Yetzira*) thus enabling oneself to perform signs and wonders[67]—in my opinion an adaptation of the famous magical formula, *horadat ha-ruḥaniyut*, which appears in many of the texts that Alemanno had before him.[68] The assumption that these are cognate idioms is supported by the fact that the expression occurs within the context of a discussion on magic.

Mention by Alemanno of interpretation of the Torah by the method of practical Kabbalah appears in Paris MS 849. This manuscript was written at the beginning of the sixteenth century. However, it is likely that Alemanno formed his opinion on the matter earlier than that. In the *Beḥinat ha-Dat,* Rabbi Elijah del Medigo opposed those who viewed the Torah and commandments as a means to cause the descent of spiritual forces.

It is impossible to bring spiritual forces into the world in this way as do the magicians who employ forms and talismans. When we examine the words of the Torah, we find that the Torah strenuously opposes this practice for these are idolatrous practices.[69]

One may assume that Del Medigo's remarks are a criticism of Alemanno. Del Medigo was a member of Pico's intellectual circle until about 1490 and probably heard Alemanno's view expressed by intellectual colleagues.

The analogous structure of magic and a kabbalistic reading of the Torah described in Paris MS 849 has an interesting parallel in Alemanno's *Collectanaea.*[70]

The astrologer studies every one of the creatures in relation to one of the seven planets. In the same manner, the kabbalist studies every word of the Torah, as stated before in connection with the commandments of the Torah. That is, he studies the *Sefira* to which it is related. The astrologer studies the movements and governance of the stars. In the same way the kabbalist knows what will happen to people in the future by reference to the influence and efflux of the *Sefirot.* This is in accordance with the activities and movements of those who perform the commandments and divine service. This method is superior to that of the astrologer.[71]

Thus kabbalistic study of the Torah is no longer seen as leading to preoccupation with the hidden processes of divinity. The kabbalist has become a "super-astrologer" who utilizes his knowledge to foresee the future.

A similar conception is again found in Pico's *Theses.*[72] "Sicut vera Astrologia docet nos legere in libro Dei, ita Cabbala docet nos legere in libro legis." (Just as true astrology teaches us to read the books of God, so too does the Kabbalah teach us to read the books of the law.) This statement seems to be analogous to that of Alemanno. The practical side of astrology can be identified with *magia naturalis* for it teaches the way to receive the influx of higher powers. Kabbalah is a higher form of magic because its speculative foundation is, as Pico emphasized here, superior to that of astrology.

In his book, *Shir ha-Ma'alot,* Alemanno declares practical Kabbalah to be superior to astrology, but dismisses astral magic based upon the science of the stars.

The kabbalists say that every limb of a man's body has a spiritual power corresponding to it in the *Sefira Malkhut.* . . . When a man performs one of the commandments by means of one of his corporeal limbs, that limb is readied to become a seat and home for the supernal power which is its likeness. . . . Our patriarch Abraham was the first to discover this wondrous science . . . as proven by his book, *Sefer Yetzira,* which was composed in accordance with this principle. It demonstrates how the likeness of each and every limb is to be found in the celestial spheres and stars and how matters stand in the spiritual world which he terms the world of letters[73] . . . And study how this ancient science resembles the ancient science of astrology which found that every limb and form and corporeal body that exists in the world of change has a likeness in the world of celestial motion[74] in the stars and their forms. The astrologers prepared every thing in a way as to receive the efflux proper to it. However, this is a material craft which is forbidden, flawed and impure. But the wisdom of Abraham is a spiritual craft which is perfect and pure and permitted and his sons,[75] Isaac and Jacob, followed in his path.[76]

Alemanno's words indicate the nature of the new interpretation of the Torah. In his view, the kabbalists learn about future events from the Torah. This method is superior to that of the astrologers who learn from the stars. As demonstrated, practical Kabbalah teaches man how to make contact with magic forces. Thus, Kabbalah was transformed from speculation upon the mysteries of the divinity as an end in itself into a sophisticated means for exerting human influence superior to astrology or magic.

This change in the essence of Kabbalah appeared in both the writings of Alemanno and Pico, his student, but I believe that Alemanno was its source. This opinion is supported not only by the chronological data as given above, but also by the fact that Alemanno's view of Kabbalah as magic belongs to his broader conception, while in Pico's writings the subject received only limited treatment in a few sentences.

As stated before, for Alemanno the Torah had unique properties, and the Kabbalah amounted to instruction in their application. To Alemanno, Moses was a magician who knew how to make use of kabbalistic principles.

The kabbalists believe that Moses, peace be with him, had precise knowledge of the spiritual world which is called the world of *Sefirot* and divine names or the world of letters. Moses knew how to direct his thoughts and prayers so as to improve the divine efflux which the kabbalists call 'channels.'[77] Moses' action caused the channels to emanate upon the lower world in accordance with his will. By means of that efflux, he created anything he wished, just as God created the world by means of various emanations. Whenever he wanted to perform signs and wonders, Moses would pray and utter divine names, words and meditations until he had intensified those emanations. The emanations then descended into the world and created new supra-natural things. With that Moses split the sea, opened up the earth and the like.[78]

Alemanno's view of Moses was not a new one. The idea was an old one found also in many non-Jewish sources.[79] The magic power of the word is described in a kabbalistic context, and here Moses becomes a kabbalistic magician.

Alemanno also used this approach in evaluating prophecy.

A prophet has the power to cause the emanation of divine efflux from *Ein Sof* upon the *hyle* (hylic matter) by the intermediary of the *Sefira Malkhut*. In this way the prophet performs wondrous deeds, impossible in nature.[80]

The Tabernacle and Temple also had a clearly magical function. Alemanno described them as a sort of great talisman which enabled the Jews to receive the divine emanations of the *Sefirot*. In his *Collectanaea*, Alemanno offered four explanations of the nature of the Tabernacle and its vessels of which the third and fourth are relevant.[81]

For the people were educated to believe in the possibility of causing spiritual forces and emanations to descend from above by means of preparations made by man for that purpose, such as talismans, garments, foods and special objects intended to cause the descent of spiritual forces, just as when Moses our master, peace be with him,[82] prepared the golden calf. The intention was only to cause the spiritual forces to descend by means of a physical body. In Ibn Ezra's opinion,[83] they made a figure of Aquarius in mid-sky and Taurus rising, for that had the power necessary to ease their way in the wilderness, a desolate place. In Naḥmanides' opinion,[84] they directed their meditation to the figure of the ox on the left hand side of the *Merkava* in order to be protected from the attribute of strict judgment. Therefore, they had to make an ark and vessels capable of receiving those emanations. The fourth reason was to increase those actions such as the offering of sacrifices, which give protection and cause good emanations to descend and forestall the bad emanations, which descend from the stars and their heavenly courses.[85] The purpose of most of the commandments is to safeguard the prophetic efflux which issues above and descends upon the human intellect. Therefore, it was necessary to have various heavy large vessels and a Tabernacle to contain them.[86]

The Tabernacle is described as a complex talisman which "guards" and "causes the descent" of spiritual forces.

The idea that the Tabernacle "guards" the descent of spiritual forces requires some clarification. From the context it is clear that this is not simply protection against 'evil events.' The term is elucidated by reference to a quotation from one of Alemanno's literary sources, *Sefer Mekor Ḥayyim* [87] of Ibn Zarza.

In the *Book of the Religions of the Prophets*, it is written that Enoch was a great saint and sage who brought nations to the worship of God, blessed be He. At first, he publicized the science of the stars,[88] and he gave each of the inhabitants of the seven climes a religion which conformed to the nature of that climate.[89] He commanded them to observe festivals and offer sacrifices at particular times in accordance with the position of the stars and in keeping with the dominant star in the sky so that the star would guard the efflux of that particular climate. He commanded that some of them should not eat certain foods, but permitted others to eat them.

A similar thought about the purpose of the Torah appears in a responsum of Profiat Duran to Rabbi Meir Crescas.[90]

All agree that the glory of God fills the entire world and that His power extends and emanates upon the creatures in general although they differ in their receptive capacities; thus the vegetative and animal have greater receptivity to divine efflux than the mineral. Man has greater receptivity than all of them. The extent of preparation for, and receptivity to, divine emanation accounts for the hierarchy of beings. Also in the human species, men possess differing degrees of receptivity. The Torah set down the commandments for the purpose of developing this receptivity insofar as possible.

In the case of sacrifices, Duran expresses an opinion similar to that of Alemanno.

The commandment ordained that the sacrifices be seven in number for the first season . . . for the offerant will receive a new spirit of understanding and will be ready to receive prophetic emanation. . . . For by the virtue of the burnt offering future events are revealed insofar as the celebrant intends to receive prophetic emanation.[91]

A similar conception appears in Alemanno's *Collectanaea*. Describing Moses' activity he writes:[92]

I said, I shall ascend to the Lord to receive detailed instruction about the commandments concerning two institutions—one institution safeguards the receptive power and that is the matter of the Tabernacle and its vessels . . .

Alemanno thought that the Temple service was a preparation for the reception of divine emanation. In the expression, "preserving the receptive power,"[93] the term "receptive power" refers to the innate capability of a certain object to receive divine emanation, while, "to preserve the receptive power" is to ensure the continued reception of that power by the object in question. This is but a general definition of the purpose of the Tabernacle. Alemanno's book, *Shir ha-Ma'alot,* contains another description of the Tabernacle which emphasizes the magical character of the Temple institution.[94]

Astrologers, necromancers, chiromancers and masters of pagan crafts have rituals, rules, special places, incense, garments and set times and preparations in order to receive those impure spiritual forces. These descend upon those who manipulate them by means of the relation of those objects to those forces, as the masters of these crafts know. So too, there are activities, foods, garments, preparations and sacrifices, incense and places and times which enable one to receive and cleave to the pure spiritual forces which descend from the world of the *Sefirot.* These actions concern the esoteric knowledge of the Torah and the particulars of the commandments which cause Hebrew souls to cleave to *Malkhut. Malkhut* is the source of oral law which explains all the secrets of the Torah and details of the commandments.

Magic and Kabbalah share a common technique for causing the descent of spiritual forces to earth.[95] They differ, however, in their goal. The magician directs his efforts at the stars from whom he hopes to receive beneficial emanation. The Jews seek to receive, and cleave to, the emanations of the *Sefirot.* In the book, *Sefer Ḥeshek Shlomo,* Alemanno declared the descent of spiritual forces to be the principal goal of the endeavors of King Solomon:[96]

Both Solomon's good, and his unseemly, actions indicate that his lifelong goal was to cause the descent of spiritual forces to earth. He did all this by offering thousands and tens of thousands of sacrifices in order to cause the Holy Spirit to descend upon him[97] . . . and he made a great dwelling for the Lord his God, in order to bring the *Shekhina* to earth.[98]

Alemanno's words fell upon attentive ears and his ideas were echoed by other writers. For instance, Rabbi Isaac ben Yeḥi'el of Pisa,[99] whom Alemanno mentioned in the introduction to his *Shir ha-Ma'alot,*[100] expressed a view of the purpose of the Temple quite similar to Alemanno's in a letter:

To cause a supernal power to descend and perform a certain action, one must minister to that power by means of rituals proper to it. These rituals prepare it [the power] to perform the desired action. . . . The greatest Providence concerns the perfection of the soul and its becoming godly. The noblest service possible is that instructed by the Torah. For after He gave the command concerning the Tabernacle, God said this: 'And I shall dwell in the midst of the Israelites' [Ex. 29:45]. That is to say, it is necessary to safeguard the receptive power so that the supernal powers descend. For the receptive power safeguards the relation [of the upper and lower worlds] by means of particular garments, sacrifices, places and actions, performed at certain times. When one of those particulars is missing, the desired goal will not be achieved. Moreover, harm will replace the hoped-for gain.[101]

This quotation appears with certain changes in two additional versions of the same letter and was included both in the *Commentary on the Ten Sefirot* of Rabbi Yeḥi'el Nissim of Pisa and in the book, *Sha'arei Ḥayyim* of the kabbalist Rabbi Mordekhai Raphael Rossillo. This bibliographical note is tangible evidence of the influence of Alemanno's view of Kabbalah and magic. The repetition of his view by three writers—all Italians—proves that Alemanno's opinions were influential.

As demonstrated above, the phrase "to guard the receptive power" originated in the terminology of magic. In the sources cited above from Alemanno's writings this phrase does not have a kabbalistic connotation. However, in several other discussions, Alemanno explicitly connected "the preservation of the receptive power" to the activity of the *Sefirot*. For example, one finds the following statement:[102]

For our master Moses, peace be with him, demanded only that one safeguard the power of receiving the emanation of the *Sefira Tiferet* which is the purpose of the narratives of the entire Torah and its commandments. For our master Moses, peace be with him, was empowered in this matter, as the verse says, 'That caused his glorious arm [*zroa' tif' arto*—literally, the arm of His Beauty and here the *Sefira Tiferet*] to go at the right hand of Moses' [Isaiah 63:12]. However, he [Moses] did not seek to inquire of the alien women who go around *Tiferet* in what way may the power of receptivity be used to cause the light of the Powers to dwell below. Solomon, on the other hand, was led astray by the alien women because he desired to know how they were able to sustain the adherence of a power to them[103] but he [Solomon] did not safeguard the power of receptivity, for he should not have followed their way.[104]

Solomon repeated this transgression while in the company of the Queen of Sheba, "for he did not safeguard the power of receptivity in thought or deed."[105] This was also the sin of Adam "who did not safeguard the power of receptivity of the *Sefirot* Love, Compassion and Life."[106] Here, the term 'Love' refers to the *Sefira Hesed*.[107] According to the following quotation man's duty is to become a receptacle for the emanation of the *Sefira Malkhut:*

The House of the King: This refers to man's preparation of himself so that each and every one of his limbs will be worthy to receive emanation, so that each [limb] might be a receptacle and contain the efflux proper to itself in a constant manner, just as a man lives in his home permanently and not temporarily. So shall a man prepare all the residences of human habitation—the apartments, upper stories and chambers to receive the efflux which descends constantly upon us. So shall man prepare his intellect, soul and Torah[108] in such a way as to receive wisdom, knowledge and enlightenment from it.[109]

What is the fundamental preparation a man must make in order to receive a constant influx of emanation? Alemanno's answer is based upon the opinion of the "sages of the *Sefira*": the purpose of all commandments is to make a place below for the powers of Love and Compassion, to awaken them and cause them to descend into the lower realms even to "the depth of the grave, and to cause the power of impurity and strict judgment to pass away from the earth."[110]

There are other expressions in Alemanno's writings of this basic idea that the commandments of the Torah enable man to receive the efflux from the *Sefirot*. Alemanno's explanation of prayer will serve as an example of these:[111]

The prayer of those versed in esoteric wisdom is superior to that of the first group for the latter's knowledge of the paths of emanation exceeded that of the former. Therefore they know which prayer suits which particular emanation. Because of the superiority of their knowledge of the character of the emanations and of the manner of preparation for that emanation in a direct manner, they know how to prepare all those things such as human souls which may receive those emanations in accordance with their deeds and their relation to the intelligible.[112]

A more general description appears in the book, *Shir ha-Ma'alot:* "When a man performs one of the commandments by means of one of his corporeal limbs, that limb is prepared to be a seat and home for the supernal spiritual power."[113] This statement bears a close resemblance to that of Rabbi Joseph Gikatilla in his introduction to the book, *Sha'arei Ora*.[114] Alemanno's formulation differs from that of Gikatilla by substitution of the word *bayit* 'home,' for the word *merkava*, a substitution probably intended to stress the fact that man may be filled by the supernal powers. In the continuation of this quotation, Alemanno observes that "all the laws of the Oral Torah" issue from the *Sefira Malkhut,* and are "modeled after its spiritual powers and prepare one to receive wisdom from it." King Solomon learned [115]

to prepare himself and his royal household, and [to order] his wisdom and all his deeds, so as to become an abode for the reception of the glory of *Malkhut* [majesty] by means of it *[Malkhut].* He established courtyard boundaries for it, this being one of the laws of the Oral Torah. . . . By means of his preparations in the construction of the House of the King, he received blessing and perfection in all benefits [both] material [and] spiritual, [as well as in] all the sciences.

According to Alemanno, the Oral Law is also intended to cause the descent of efflux and its reception by the men who are prepared for it. Alemanno's particular esteem of the Oral Torah is also evident in a statement in his book, *Shir ha-Ma'alot:* [116]

Spiritual matters do not descend where there is addition or detraction. The matter resembles the ancient worship of spirits which visited only those who followed the rituals precisely. If the worship of such is bound by restrictions, how much more so must the worship of God be bound by restrictions so that the worshippers neither add nor detract from it. As the verse said: 'You shall not add and you shall not detract' [Deut. 4:2].

This statement amounts to a magical interpretation of the Oral Law which parallels the magical interpretation given to the Written Torah, the phenomenon of prophecy and the institution of the Temple.

This magical interpretation of the fundamental practices of Judaism underlies Alemanno's remarks on the *Sefira Bina* in his untitled composition in Paris MS 849. [117]

The sphere of Saturn is the first sphere beneath the constellations. . . . And they say that Saturn is the true judge and the master of Moses, peace be with him. The angel of Saturn is Michael, the great minister, so called because of his great power in divine matters. He is the ministering angel of Israel [118] as the verse said: 'But only Michael is your minister' [Daniel 10:21]. Because of his exceptional grandeur he was called Michael, as if to say about his great works: 'Mi kha-el' [Who is this one who is as God?] because of his extreme grandeur and spirituality. . . . And the astrologers who described Saturn say that it endows man with profound thought, law and the spiritual sciences, prophecy, sorcery and prognostication and dictates the *shmitot* [the sabbatical years] and *yovlot* [the jubilee years]. The Jewish people and the Hebrew language and the Temple are under its jurisdiction. Saturn's major conjunction is with Libra in Pisces and this occurs to assist the nation and the Torah and its prophets.[119] This planet endows the people with perfection in the sciences and divine matters such as the Torah and its commandments. This is because of its great exaltedness, for it is spiritual and loves what is spiritual, but hates what is corporeal. It is concerned only with thought, understanding and design, esoteric knowledge and divine worship and His Torah. The Sabbath day is in its sway for Saturn causes material existence to cease.

This paragraph is better understood by comparison with a statement of Rabbi Samuel ibn Zarza in his book, *Mekor Ḥayyim.*[120]

Know that the astrologers say that Jupiter who keeps watch over the seventh day has the power to renew the vigor of the corporeal bodies in nature. In truth, the Sabbath day possesses great excellence. To it fall the powers of thought, of understanding and of the maintenance of things. [To it also belong] design, knowledge of the secrets and the service of God, blessed be He. It is the star of Israel, and all the astrologers and Rabbi Joseph ibn Wakar, blessed be his memory, said that Saturn rules over the rational soul, thought and understanding and the existence of things. The Ethiopian, the Sandian [?], the Tabian [?] and the Berber nations and the Jews are under its influence. Of all the parts and the depths of the earth the Temple pertains to Saturn, as does the Hebrew language, the Scriptures and the Torah of Israel.

Alemanno was undoubtedly familiar with the book, *Mekor Ḥayyim,*[121] and he may also have seen a composition of Ibn Wakar dealing with the topic of astrology and spiritual forces. It seems however, that Alemanno did not copy his sources *verbatim.* In Ibn Wakar's account, the influence of Saturn is restricted to the Jews alone, and he omits mention of the other peoples. More important is the addition he makes to the statements of his predecessors, a modification in keeping with his personal views. To Alemanno, Saturn is appointed not only over the Torah of Israel, the Temple in Jerusalem and the Hebrew language, but also over the "spiritual sciences,"[122] magic,[123] sorcery, and prognostication. These additions to the list of Saturn's subjects conform to Alemanno's conception of the magical nature of the Torah, the Oral Law and the Temple.

As demonstrated, Alemanno based his discussions of magic and its relation to Jewish tradition upon writers such as Ibn Wakar, Solomon al-Constantini, Ibn Motot and Samuel Zarza. These authors share certain common assumptions, and this identity of views is the result of mutual influence rather than accident. Ibn Wakar's ideas influenced both Ibn Motot[124] and Zarza,[125] and the latter author knew al-Constantini's work.[126] The intellectual relationship of Ibn Motot and Zarza still needs close examination.[127]

It is useful to briefly characterize the views of this group of writers. First, all these writers attempt to combine philosophical and kabbalistic concepts into a broader system of thought. Second, in all of these attempts at synthesis, the influence of Neoplatonic streams of thought can be discerned in varying degrees. This is particularly true of these authors' renewed interest in, and reliance upon, the thought of Ibn Ezra and Avicenna. Third, these authors refer to several principles present in the Neoplatonic conceptions of Ibn Ezra and Avicenna which deal with the possibility of working miracles. Acceptance of these principles created a receptive ground for the absorption of books on magic by these writers. In this respect, the most important text on magic was *Sefer ha-Atzamim*.[128] Finally, the writings of these authors contain many discussions of the importance of astrology[129] and even of the relationship between magic and astrology.[130]

These writers exercised no major influence upon the development of Jewish thought. The pre-eminence of Ḥasdai Crescas and Joseph Albo in the area of theology and the predominance of the Kabbalah in the second half of the fifteenth century eclipsed the doctrines of most of the authors mentioned. Alemanno's extensive use of these writings, especially those of Ibn Motot and Ibn Wakar, is an exception to the general trend of thought among his Italian Jewish contemporaries. Alemanno's particular interest in these fourteenth-century works was rooted in his search for discussions of magic by Jewish sources. As I have attempted to prove in my article on his curriculum, Alemanno recommended readings on the subject of magic which were connected in one way or another to King Solomon or to the Jews in general. Alemanno utilized these sources on magic in order to construct a comprehensive system of thought which would substantiate the perfection of Judaism in theoretical and practical terms. To Alemanno "praxis" concerns man's ability to receive and command those powers which are emanations of the Divinity.

Alemanno's system of thought is not based upon a simplistic over-evaluation of magic in relation to other areas of thought and action. While the Kabbalah itself was for Alemanno the supreme speculative science, he emphasized elements in the Kabbalah which had only secondary importance in the development of that doctrine as a whole. This interpretation of the Kabbalah gave magic a pre-eminent position. Curiously enough Alemanno selected for this purpose parts of kabbalistic doctrine in which the element of magic had no function. His development of the concept of "guarding the power of receptivity" in kabbalistic contexts is one example of this tendency.

On the other hand, Alemanno adopted without qualm certain conceptions that had been strenuously opposed by the most important Jewish philosophers of the past. Judah ha-Levi stated that:

One who seeks to receive instruction on divine matters [theology] by speculation, reasoning and syllogisms based upon the procedure of causing the descent of spirits and the manufacture of images and talismans is a heretic.[131]

Alemanno's characterization of Solomon's principal activity as "causing the descent of spiritual forces" is an open contradiction of Ha-Levi's view. The denial of the effectiveness of talismanic magic was certainly known to Alemanno from two sources which were familiar to him: Moses Narboni's citation of Averroes' negative attitude to this kind of magic in his *Commentary on the Guide*, I, 63, and Rabbi Nissim of Marseille's attacks on talismanic magic in his *Ma'ase Nissim*. Alemanno had even transcribed this latter passage in his *Collectanaea*.[132] In Florence "causing the descent of spiritual forces" was harshly condemned by Rabbi Moses ben Yo'av who considered this practice to be idolatry in every respect.[133] At the same time, Rabbi Elijah del Medigo dismissed magical interpretation of the Torah of any kind.[134]

Alemanno's revaluation of the element of magic seems to be not only the result of an internal development of Jewish tradition but also the product of outside influence which prompted Alemanno to emphasize the positive attitude to magic in Jewish sources. That influence was, in my opinion, the Neoplatonic school in Florence.[135] The meager biographical information we have about Alemanno does not permit meaningful discussion of the connections Alemanno had with this circle of scholars. It is clear that Alemanno was acquainted with Pico della Mirandola and also possibly with Lorenzo de' Medici; he mentions them in his book, *Shir ha-Ma'alot*, begun in 1488, but it is possible that Alemanno met them or at least had heard about their thought even before that time. In any case, magic occupied no place of particular importance in Alemanno's first composition, the first version of his *Ḥai ha-Olamim*, which was then entitled *Pekaḥ Ko'aḥ*.[136] The introduction and increasing prevalence of Neoplatonic elements in Alemanno's thought can be traced to the inspiration he received from the Neoplatonic school of Florence as we shall see below. I have already mentioned that Alemanno sought out practitioners of magic and quasi-magic and did not restrict himself to the information he received from Hebrew sources. He also appears to have consulted Christian compositions on magic that had not been translated into Hebrew, and it seems that he was familiar with the work *Pil'ot Olam* of Albertus Magnus.

Alemanno had a noteworthy interest in the various manifestations of paganism. This is confirmed by a quotation from his *Collectanaea:* [137]

The books of the ancient *gentili* . . . describe their various idolatrous practices and may the gods confirm everything that our Rabbis of blessed memory say concerning devils of various types of pagan worship. . . . All the idolatrous religions will come together in Rome and they will worship all of them until the coming of the Christian redeemer.

A possible explanation of the identity of the *gentili* and the nature of the "various idolatrous practices" is to be found in a lengthy comment in the *Collectanaea:* [138]

The Chaldeans and Babylonians instituted the science of the heavenly forms [139] and star worship and astrology. Nimrod was chief among them in the "tower which they made." Upon that tower he fashioned a form of Mars to serve as an idol as has been explained. After him, there remained Bel and Nebo of whom Ibn Ezra said that Nebo is the form of a star. Prophecy began with Abraham who disputed with them and cast down their opinions. Isaiah completed this work in his days when he said 'Let now the astrologers, the star-gazers, the monthly prognosticators stand up and save thee from the things that shall come upon thee' [Isaiah 47:13]. The latter reference [i.e., from Isaiah] is to Egypt and its wise men who were entirely preoccupied with the activities of the spirits between heaven and earth, [140] which have a strange effect upon nature. Divine prophecy disagreed with them, and our master Moses, peace be with him, cast them to the ground [141] and proved their lie. Isaiah also said: 'How can ye say unto Pharoah: I am the son of the wise, the son of the ancient Kings?' [Isaiah 19:11] and all that chapter.

This statement of Alemanno contains no clear reference to the books on paganism which he might have read. [142] In my opinion a statement which appears in Paris MS 849, Alemanno's untitled composition, contains a reference to the Hermetic literature, a corpus which greatly influenced the magic of the Renaissance. [143]

The ancient wisdom [144] was so vast that they boasted of it in their books which they attributed to Enoch 'whom the Lord has taken' [Genesis 6:4] and to

Solomon who was wiser than any man and to many perfect men who performed
actions by intermingling various things and comparing qualities in order to
create new forms in gold, silver, vegetable, mineral and animal [matter] which
had never before existed and in order to create divine forms which tell the future,
the laws and the *nomoi*, as well as [to create], spirits of angels, stars and
devils.[145]

I think that this is a description of the Hermetic technique of alchemy
and of images and statues made of precious metals and other vegetable
and animal components which capture the spirits of the gods.[146] Alemanno's statement about divine forms which speak of laws and *nomoi*
also has a parallel in an Arabic source. In his writings, Jabir ibn Ḥayyan
describes the preparation of an artificial man called *"asḥab al-nawamis,"*
that is, the lawgiver.[147]

Alemanno's view of magic did not remain an isolated individual
opinion but can be traced in the compositions of other writers. Alemanno's conception of the Temple and sacrifices was repeated by three other
works.[148] Traces of Alemanno's thought are also to be found in the
writings of Rabbi Issac Abravanel.[149] In his commentary to Exodus 7:8
Abravanel describes the lowest form of spirit life as demons "whose
habitation is beneath the lunar sphere." Use of these demons characterize the activity of the Egyptian magicians. This magic technique is noteworthy: "Those who engage in sorcery prepare the lower bodies to
receive the emanations of demons."[150] Abravanel's commentary on Exodus was written in the year 1506 when Alemanno had completed all
his writings. However, Abravanel had already expressed views similar to
those of Alemanno in his *Commentary on Kings* written in Naples in the
year 1493. There, Abravanel describes the Temple in terms reminiscent
of Alemanno and of the letter of Rabbi Isaac of Pisa. Abravanel states
that Solomon knew the science of talismans hidden from the philosophers and that this was the guarantee of Solomon's success:

The philosophers agree that this lower world of generation and corruption is
conducted by the powers which issue from the celestial spheres. As our rabbis,
blessed be their memory, said: 'There is not a blade of grass below that does not
have a celestial constellation above that strikes it and tells it to grow.' Behold
the men of speculation are unable to apprehend the powers of the stars and the
powers of each one of them in particular, its manner of activity in the lower
world and the way its emanation is drawn into them . . . for the books written
by astrologers on this subject are worthless and a fabrication. When the time of
reckoning comes the writers of those books are lost. Men have exerted them-

selves already to learn how to make talismans which are forms made at particular times in order to cause the descent of efflux from the stars upon particular things. However they did not succeed. It is right that it be so; since they did not apprehend the nature and properties of the celestial bodies, it is impossible that they discern their power or the actions derived from them. Nevertheless since Solomon attained the truth of that science in a wondrous manner and knew its causes, he apprehended what is above and what is below concerning the nature of the celestial beings, their number and disposition as well as the order of their motion. By this he apprehended their true powers which conduct the lowly beings. In matters of practical kingship he made the throne and succeeded as our sages, blessed be their memory, said concerning the works he fashioned in the throne and the forms he made of lions and leopards and other forms which he fashioned to accomplish particular activities.[151]

In another place, Abravanel connected knowledge of the nature of the stars and celestial spheres and their influence to Solomon's knowledge about making talismans and also to the knowledge of "the ways of conduct of each and every one of the spheres and stars, [and] the manner of their service and worship, in order to cause emanation to descend from them upon the earth."[152] In contrast, the prophets knew how to cause "emanation to descend from Him, blessed be He, upon the nation by means of the holy *Sefirot* and the knowledge proper to them in the separate intelligences."[153] King Solomon was also conceived of as one who knew how to cause the emanation of the ministering angels to descend by means of the songs he composed.[154]

By the science of the separate intelligences Solomon composed many poems as the verse said:[155] 'And his songs were 1005.' This has been interpreted as five thousand because it was the custom of the ancients to speak about divine matters in the form of poetry.[156] It seems that he composed a great number of songs for the supernal ministering angels for each one by himself in accordance with the way the angel guided one of the nations in accordance with the ministry and service unique to him. He composed the book of the Song of Songs for God alone who exercises His providence over Israel[157] and for this reason they said:[158] 'All the songs are holy but the Song of Songs is the holy of holies' because all the other songs he made were dedicated to the holy angels but the Song of Songs was uniquely dedicated to Him, blessed be He, for He is the most holy of all. As Solomon's knowledge comprehended spiritual matters and their manner of conduct, he achieved knowledge of the ways and means and preparations necessary to cause emanations to descend for each and every one of the ministering angels over the nations and lands proper to him.

In another context, he states:[159]

All the other songs he composed concern the conduct of the nations by their supernal ministering angels, but they are not included in the Scriptures and are not to be found today. It seems that King Hezekiah and the members of his generation hid them away,[160] so that man should not err and do a like deed, to worship in an alien manner.

The magical capacity of music and its integration in magic ritual is one of the characteristic qualities of the systems if Ficino and Pico,[161] and in a certain measure of Alemanno's as well.[162] His description of Solomon as a composer of songs likely to cause the descent of emanation places Abravanel squarely within the framework of thought which crystallized about the circle of scholars in Florence.

III

In the above, I have attempted to demonstrate how Alemanno employed magical and astrological elements scattered throughout the Judaeo-Arabic tradition in order to give the Kabbalah a new interpretation. This interpretation was the result of intellectual currents in Florence, an atmosphere that lead to a similar interpretation in the writings of Pico. It seems to me that the influence of members of the Italian Renaissance also prompted Alemanno's interest in Neoplatonic literature and his use of it for a new understanding of the Kabbalah.

Although Alemanno cannot be considered a Neoplatonist in the precise sense of the term, there is a striking predominance of the Neoplatonic element in his writings. A clear indication of the predominance of this element is the great number of references to Neoplatonic authors and compositions found in Alemanno's writings. Alemanno was familiar with the greater part of Jewish Neoplatonic literature. This included the works of Isaac Israeli,[163] Ibn Gabirol's *Mekor Hayyim*,[164] *Arugat ha-Bosem* of Moses ibn Ezra,[165] as well as the writings of Abraham ibn Ezra[166] and Rabbi Isaac ibn Latif.[167] Alemanno was greatly interested in the Neoplatonic literature that had been translated from the Arabic into Hebrew; his writings contain many references to the work *Ha-Agulot ha-Ra'ayoniyot* of Al-Batalyusi,[168] a book that exercised a weighty influence on his thought. The book, *Moznei ha-Iyunim*, an elaboration of many of the ideas which appear in *Ha-Agulot ha-Ra'ayoniyot*,[169] is frequently mentioned by Alemanno. From time to time in Alemanno's writings[170] references appear to Al-Ghazali's book, *Mishkat al-Anwar*, a work formulated in a Neoplatonic cast of thought. Alemanno was also acquainted with more specifically Neoplatonic works, such as *Sefer Ha-Atzamim ha-Hamisha* attributed to Empedocles; parts of this work have been preserved because Alemanno copied them into his own writings.[171] Alemanno was especially interested in *Sefer ha-Sibot (Liber de Causis)*. He was familiar with various translations of this work and copied a passage from it into his book, *Hai ha-Olamim*,[172] and into his remarks upon *Hai ben Yoktan*.[173] This same section from *Liber de Causis* appears in Alemanno's book, *Heshek Shlomo*.[174] It is interesting to note that Pico was also familiar with the *Liber de Causis*, and in his writing quoted a portion of the first paragraph of that work without attribution.[175] That same paragraph appears several times in Alemanno's works. This parallelism is a possible indication of Alemanno's influence on Pico, for Pico studied the work *Hai ben Yoktan*[176] with Alemanno. Another selection from *Liber de Causis* (section VI) which is to be found in the book *Imrei Shefer* of Rabbi Abraham Abulafia, is repeated several times in the writings of Alemanno[177] and subsequently various authors copied it from Alemanno. He was intrigued by material from the *Theology of Aristotle*, which he found in the book, *Sefer ha-Ma'alot* of Rabbi Shem Tov ibn Falaquera[178] and in the *Arugat ha-Bosem* of Moses ibn Ezra.[179] Plato's works were known to Alemanno only by name from a list Falaquera had included in the work, *Reshit Hokhma*.[180] However, Alemanno made much use of Plato's *Republic* with the *Commentary* of Averroes.[181]

The most important Platonic and Neoplatonic works were available to Alemanno from the Judaeo-Arabic philosophical tradition. Alemanno exceeded all his Jewish predecessors in the utilization and absorption of Neoplatonic material. Alemanno was unique among his Jewish intellectual contemporaries in his interest in Neoplatonism. His contemporaries, for example Judah Messer Leon, Elijah del Medigo, Obadiah Sforno and David Messer Leon were all Aristotelians. In this respect, Alemanno represents a new trend in the intellectual life of Italian Jewry. The subsequent development of this new interest will be treated below.

Before directing our attention to the Neoplatonic bent of Alemanno's thought, mention should be made of the fact that Alemanno's writings contain references to Neoplatonic compositions which were not translated into Hebrew. It is reasonable to assume that Alemanno knew of these works from his contacts with Renaissance personalities in Florence. In the *Collectanaea*,[182] we read,

Senior Yrhw [!] told me that he found it said in the name of Porphyry that there was a Jewish sect who were holy and ate in such weight and measure that they had no need to relieve themselves.

Further evidence of such Neoplatonic literature is to be found in Alemanno's *Collectanaea*.[183]

The sect of Platonists said that the heavens possess only a rational soul, not an imaginative or vital soul. . . . and the imaginative faculty causes man to love government and dominion, for man imagines himself great when he is honored. In this respect, the human mind is drawn to that work, and is drawn away from the path of reason so that men do not apprehend the rational truths, for then men would not serve them [i.e. the rulers]. The rulers establish pagan practices to kill people or perform acts of sexual immorality or other completely alien practices. This is so that men will not realize the truth, and will thus serve the rulers in perpetuity by means of those alien forms of worship and not serve God. All the world erred in this except the Jews. Porphyry was one of this [idolatrous] sect, and he unashamedly confessed that at one time he wished to kill himself, and said that ever since the nations had stopped worshipping idols all good had ceased. On one occasion, he told his master, named Plotinus,[184] to accompany him to offer a sacrifice. Plotinus answered him that it was more fitting that a god come to offer a sacrifice to him than he to the god because Plotinus belittled this practice, and Porphyry was greatly astonded by this.

Obviously, Alemanno had read Porphyry's *Life of Plotinus*, of which article 10, 34–35 is summarized here. It is even more interesting that the same selection from Porphyry's book appears in an entirely different context in Pico's famous *Oration on the Glory of Man*.[185] Although Alemanno had a negative opinion of Porphyry,[186] his quotation from Porphyry proves that Alemanno had access to Neoplatonic texts which were in circulation among his contemporaries in Florence.

Two of Alemanno's contempories commented on the similarity of Kabbalah and Platonism. Alemanno's teacher Judah Messer Leon said of Kabbalah:[187]

There is to be found among the early exponents of that science in some small measure an approximation in principle of Platonic opinions of an agreeable kind such as would be accessible to an intellectually capable person.

His son, Rabbi David Messer Leon,[188] held the opinion that

Plato is called the divine philosopher, for one who studies his books closely will find there great and tremendous secrets and all their opinions are those of the masters of true Kabbalah.

Although he has a hostile attitude to the Kabbalah, Elijah del Medigo reached the same conclusion as Judah and David Messer Leon. Del Medigo, an Aristotelian, rejected both Platonism and the Kabbalah which followed in its path. The best-known discussion of this issue is to be found in Del Medigo's *Behinat ha-Dat*,[189] where he comments on the statements of the kabbalists:

Most of them agree with statements of the early philosophers, the negligibility of whose opinions are well understood by learned people. Whoever has seen the statements of the Platonists and these [kabbalistic] statements will know that such is the truth. I have already discussed this in another place and therefore I do not wish at this time to discuss the matter.[190]

Del Medigo did, however, elaborate on this matter in his commentary on Averroes' *De Substantia Orbis*.[191]

These beings which are called *Sefirot* in accordance with their degree of reality, act by virtue of the power of the tenth one which they call *Ein Sof*,[192] and by virtue of the emanation reaching the *Sefirot* from It. Therefore all exists by virtue of the power of *Ein Sof*, for the *Sefirot* are emanated from It and depend upon It. Therefore, in their opinion, the world order is derived from them. These opinions were taken from the propositions of the early philosophers, particularly from Plato. In their books, you will find these matters discussed at length. They construct proofs for these ideas in accordance with their own method. They say that one cannot ascribe any name to *Ein Sof*, but *Ein Sof* may be apprehended by the intellect as mentioned by Averroes in the *Incoherence of the Incoherence*.[193] This is known to one who has seen the books of these Platonists and the propositions of the early philosophers. In those books, you will also find statements concerning the *Shmitot* (cosmic sabbaticals), the destruction of the world and its reconstruction as well as the transmigration of souls, so that you can find scarcely any difference between these philosophers and these kabbalists insofar as terms and allusions are concerned. . . . In conclusion, they are nearly identical in principles and topics and in the matter of sacrifices. These statements are very far removed from the words of the peripatetics and their principles.

The above comparison of Kabbalah and Platonism was of a most general kind and did not concern a precise textual comparison of Kabbalah, Platonism and Neoplatonism. Even so, this general characterization is important for an understanding of the way in which the Kabbalah was able to enter into Renaissance intellectual culture. The concurrence of the Kabbalah with certain aspects of ancient philosophy[194] endowed it with the aura of an ancient theology whose vestiges were eagerly sought by Renaissance thinkers. The conceptual proximity of the Kabbalah and Pico's thought in particular enabled the Kabbalah to become part of the efflorescence of Renaissance Platonism. The relationship of Platonism and Kabbalah had no theorectical significance for Jewish philosophers of an Aristotelian bent.[195] Alemanno, who was interested in both Kabbalah and Platonism, tried to find points common to both. Understandably, this search for agreement was not pursued in a critical fashion; in some instances, there was no real connection between the kabbalistic and Platonic conceptions. Furthermore, there was a clear tendency to superimpose Platonic or Neoplatonic formulations upon the Kabbalah. In the process of interpreting the Kabbalah, Alemanno ignored one of its most essential characteristics: the doctrine of *Sefirot* includes a conception of the inner dynamism of the divinity together with the tensions and inner crises that this dynamism entails and man's role in the enhancement and restoration of the system of the *Sefirot*.

Alemanno's attempt to reconcile Kabbalah and Platonism was preceded by the attempts of Rabbi Joseph ibn Wakar and Rabbi Samuel ibn Motot to synthesize Kabbalah and Aristotelian philosophy. In both writers, the system of *Sefirot* was identified with the separate intelligences of Arabic and Jewish Aristotelianism,[196] and their system had influenced Alemanno.

To exemplify Alemanno's attempt to equate Kabbalah and Platonism, I shall review Alemanno's comparison of kabbalistic concepts with the ideas that he found in the writings of one of the most important Neoplatonic philosophers, Proclus. Pico, Alemanno's student and colleague, accorded Proclus an honored place in his *Theses*. Fifty-five of the theses, the *Secundum Proclum,* were based upon the system of Proclus. These fifty-five theses exceeded in number all the theses derived from all the other Neoplatonic philosophers taken together. In addition, Pico also formulated ten theses based upon Abucatem Avenam, whom Pico thought to be the author of *Liber de Causis*.[197] In effect, Proclus appears in another guise in Pico's *Theses*. E. Wind has pointed out the connection between the *Oration on the Glory of Man* and the thought of Proclus.[198] H. Wirszubski, on the other hand, emphasized the influence of Proclus' thought upon a kabbalistic thesis,[199] and so is supported by Alemanno's comparison of certain kabbalistic concepts to ideas which had their origin in Proclus. In his untitled composition in Paris MS 849, Alemanno copied a portion of the second introduction to the book, *Tikunei Zohar,* together with a discussion found in the *Minḥat Yehuda* of Rabbi Judah Hayyat,[200] which concerns our inability to describe the Supreme Cause. I shall quote but a few lines of this text.

The Supreme Court (the *Sefira Keter*) has the attribute of oneness because it is the root of all the *Sefirot* and they are within it *in potentia* and it is within them *in actu*. It is not one of their number by virtue of its superiority to them, so that the effect does not resemble the cause. Therefore, it is not mentioned in Genesis in the chapter of the ten sayings by which the world was created[201] which are the *Sefirot*. However, the word *breshit* [Gen. 1:1] contains an allusion to the Supreme Crown. The beginning—*breshit*—of the numbers is *Ḥokhma*— Wisdom. However, nothing was said of the Master of the Worlds and of His essence; not a single name. This is because He participates in every number, for He is within each number *in actu*. In this aspect is He counted within number and contained within number in a general way. Because of this, it states in the *Book of Creation (Sefer Yetzira):* 'And before one what do you count.'[202] For there is no number at all, even the name One, that applies to what is before the Supreme Crown which is the Master of the Worlds. In Plato's book, *Ha-Atzamim ha-Elyonim,* it says, 'The first cause exceeds number.' However, all language is insufficient to reckon It because of Its unity. However the causes whose light is derived from the light of the First Cause may be numbered.[203]

Alemanno treats the subject of the ineffability of *Ein Sof* on several pages preceding the above quotation. First, he cites the section of *Liber de Causis* whose beginning was mentioned before. After that, he concludes as follows:

Many of the descendents of Shem and Eber saw a vision and many gazed at the *Merkava* and regarded the entire Torah and found neither name, nor word, nor any one letter which signifies the Source of everything in existence, but they found only a reference to the Primary Effect and Simplest Being.[204]

This is an allusion to a remark in the book, *Ma'arekhet ha-Elohut,* which is determined that[205]

there is no allusion of *Ein Sof* in the Torah, the prophets, the hagiographa, or in the words of the sages blessed be their memory, although the 'masters of divine worship' received a brief hint about it.

Here, Alemanno gave a specific example of the correspondence between a negative kabbalistic theology concerning *Ein Sof* and the negative theology of *Liber de Causis,* a similarity which Elijah del Medigo had already sensed.[206]

Another reference to *Liber de Causis* appears in Alemanno's restatement and elaboration of a discussion found in the book, *Minḥat Yehuda.*[207] In this instance, Alemanno speaks of the relationship of *Ein Sof* and *Keter,* the first *Sefira,* the Supreme Crown. For purposes of his discussion, Alemanno draws upon a lengthy discourse of Judah Ḥayyat on this question. In opposition to Rabbi Joseph Gikatilla and Rabbi Elijah di Genazzano,[208] Ḥayyat maintained that *Ein Sof* is not identical with the Supreme Crown, but is to be found above it. Alemanno was interested in Ḥayyat's argumentation but not in the conclusion of the discussion. Alemanno utilized Ḥayyat's proofs in order to prove that the relation of the *Sefira Keter* to the *Sefira Ḥokhma* (Wisdom, the second *Sefira*) is identical to the relation of *Ein Sof* to the Supreme Crown. *Ein Sof,* however, is the source of the efflux which sustains the system of the *Sefirot:*

> The Supreme Crown emanated Wisdom and shines above it [Wisdom] just as *Ein Sof* radiates above the Supreme Crown. In accordance with the principle that everything that exists within the cause exists within the effect, the Supreme Crown relative to *Ḥokhma* has the same value as *Ein Sof* relative to the Supreme Crown: as we have said 'contingent yet not contingent.' *Ein Sof* is the cause of the connection of the *Sefirot* to one another for all of them are joined one to the other by the efflux emanating from *Ein Sof* to all of them, and it joins and unifies and gives existence to all as the philosophers said in the *Liber de Causis* that anything which is the cause of the existence of something else in such a manner that the other thing has no existence other than that coming to it from its cause — if that effect is the cause of something else outside itself in the same way as in the case of the first cause, then the first cause is a truer, more unique and important cause for the existence of the second effect than is the second cause in causing the second effect.[209]

I think that this statement is a clear indication of the significant contribution of *Liber de Causis* and of Kabbalah to Alemanno's thought. As stated before, this passage from *Liber de Causis* was repeated in other parts of Alemanno's writings which were written in the years before the above quotation. The book, *Minḥat Yehuda,* was written between the years 1495 and 1497. Alemanno did not understand Ḥayyat's statement according to its original, literal meaning. Rather, he interpreted Ḥayyat according to the formula of *Liber de Causis,* which he knew well. However, this was not a complete misrepresentation of kabbalistic doctrine but a rechanneling of certain conceptions in a direction unintended by the original author. Alemanno simply restated Ḥayyat's remarks in a philosophical way which removed the mythical element.[210] This is doubly ironic. In his introduction to *Ma'arekhet ha-Elohut*, Hayyat warned against the interpretation of Kabbalah in a philosophical manner such as was done by Rabbi Reuben Tzarfati in his commentary on *Ma'arekhet ha-Elohut*.[211] I have already suggested that this statement in Hayyat's "introduction" was directed against a trend of thought similar to Alemanno's. Alemanno took a particular interest in the very books censured by Hayyat,[212] and Alemanno restated Hayyat's words so as to suit his philosophical conceptions. Alemanno found the quotation from *Sefer Ha-Atzamim ha-Elyonim* in the book, *Imrei Shefer*, of Abraham Abulafia,[213] a kabbalist whom Hayyat condemned in the most explicit terms.[214] Unwittingly Alemanno made certain to reconcile the statement of Hayyat with material found in a composition of Abulafia.

Now let us turn to a consideration of Alemanno's use of that quotation from *Liber de Causis* which he found in Abulafia. In the work *Heshek Shlomo*, Alemanno endeavored to prove the existence of the ten *Sefirot*. After citation of appropriate scriptural verses and mention of Rabbi Nehunya ben ha-Kaneh and Rabbi Simon bar Yohai as adherents of the belief in the existence of the *Sefirot*, Alemanno writes:[215]

But the philosophers among our people did not believe in them and if they mentioned them at all it was to say that they move the heavens[216]. . . . And so too among the gentile sages, there were those who believed in their existence and others who denied them. . . . It follows that the ancients believed in the existence of ten spiritual numbers[217] but the latter day scholars denied it because there is no proof of this. It seems that Plato thought that there are ten spiritual numbers of which one may speak but one may not speak of the first cause due to its great concealment. However they [the numbers] approximate its existence to such an extent that you may call these effects by a name that cannot be ascribed to the movers of corporeal bodies. However, in the opinion of the kabbalists, one may say so of the *Sefirot*, as shall be explained in this our discourse. This is what Plato wrote in the work *Ha-Atzamim Ha-Elyonim* as quoted by Zacharias in the Book *Imrei Shefer*.[218] From this it follows that in Plato's view, the first effects are called *Sefirot* because they may be numbered, unlike the first cause, and therefore he did not call them movers.

Here Plato's theory of ten ideal numbers, as represented in Aristotle, was combined with the opinion of Proclus in the *Liber de Causis* to create the impression that Plato thought that there are ten numbers, separate from matter which may be described, unlike the first cause. These numbers which cannot be described have a relationship to one another of cause and effect. This integration of concepts substantiated Alemanno's claim that the ancients, especially Plato, held a view similar to the kabbalistic conception of the *Sefirot*, as opposed to the opinion of the prophets.[219]

I have proved that Alemanno read the words of Proclus as presented in the various redactions of *Liber de Causis* and understood them to refer to the conception of *Ein Sof* and its relation to the *Sefirot* and their number. This determination was further applied to a discussion of the worlds. An association of this kind is to be found in the book *Shir ha-Ma'alot*. There it is stated that everything that exists in the world of change can be found in some form in all the worlds, the world of motion and in the *Sefirot*.[220]

> Everything which is to be found in the world of change has an analogy in the world of motion and everything that is in the world of motion is in the world of the *Sefirot* . . . for just so the transient beings in the world of change are the image and likeness of the spiritual forms in the world of motion. It is as Alfarabi[221] wrote concerning all the forms which the Indians say are nothing other than spiritual forms known by means of the knowledge of natural phenomena which occur to the men who receive from those forms. The forms found in the world of motion such as the forty-eight forms and the twenty-eight encampments of the moon, point to the spiritual forms existent in the world of the *Sefira*—for example the twenty-eight encampments of the *Shekhina*.

It seems that Alemanno's scheme of the several worlds is based upon a principle formulated by Proclus which was repeated in various ways in the *Liber de Causis*. There it was said that all things are to be found in every world in conformity with the essence of that world.[222]

The kabbalist who, more than any other, followed in the new directions indicated by Alemanno—namely, Abraham Yagel—gave an even more detailed discussion of the topic of the worlds than did Alemanno himself. In his work *Beit Ya'ar ha-Levanon* Yagel took a Neoplatonic conception which he found in the book *De Occulta Philosophia* as the basis for his treatment of the different states of the four primary elements in accordance with the essence of the worlds. Yagel's dependence upon Agrippa becomes obvious if a linear comparison is made of Yagel's remarks with a parallel text in *De Occulta Philosophia*.

Oxford MS 1304 (Reggio 9) *fol. 6r–6v.*	*De Occulta Philosophia I, ch. VIII* *(Hildesheim and N.Y., 1970) p. 18.*
This was the statement of	Est Platonicorum omnium unan-

the philosopher Plato.[223]
Just as in the archetype of
the world
all is in all,
so also in this corporeal
world, all is in all, albeit
in a distinct manner because
of the nature of the separable
things. Therefore the four
elements [224] are not to be
found in isolated form
in this lower world, but
also exist in the celestial
bodies and stars, the angels
and the separate intelligences
and in what is above them in
the archetype of the world,
the Cause of all Causes and
the Principle of all Principles. . . .
However in this world they are
found as dross and matter.

imis sententia
quemadmodum in archetypo
mundo
omnia sunt in omnibus
ita etiam in hoc corporeo
mundo, omnia in omnibus esse
modis tamen diversis pro
natura videlicet suscipientium.
Sic et elementa
nonsolum sunt
in istis
inferioribus sed
in coelis
in stellis in daemonibus in
angelis in ipso
demique;
omnium opifice et archetypo.

Sed in istis inferioribus elementa
sunt crassae quaedam formae im
mensae materiae et materialia
elementa.

In the heavens [they are] as the
powers we have stated [225]
and in the angels [they are]
more perfect and superior
powers than in the heavens.

In coelis autem sunt
elementa per eorum naturas et
vires: modo videlicet coelesti
et multo excellentiori quam
infra lunam.

Above them [angels] there are powers more perfect than, and superior to, the powers in the angels. The world above the angels is called in the language of the kabbalists, the Throne of Glory which is the world of *Beri'a*—creation. The world of *Beri'a* is the shadow of, and the seat for, the supernal *Sefirot* which they [the kabbalists] call the 'World of Emanation.' In the World of *Beri'a* these four powers exist in a more subtle and hidden manner, and it is all the more so in the supernal world of *Atzilut*—emanation, where the powers are most subtle of all. There they [the *Sefirot*] are the root and principle for all of them. From them, all draw sustenance. In that world these four powers are called Grandeur—*Gedula*, which is the element of water; Might—*Gevura*, which is the element of fire; Beauty—*Tiferet*, which is the element of air; and Kingdom—*Malkhut* which is the element of earth. See what the author of *Ma'arekhet ha-Elohut* wrote in the chapter "On the World" *[Sha'ar ha-Olam]*.[226] He said:

I have said in the beginning of the book[227] that there are elements in the lower earth which are three in general and four in particular, because those elements have a great and wondrous root in this. For it is known that everything in existence has a source until the beginning of every thing which is the cause of every effect. The last effect is caused by the one preceding it and that aspect is caused by the aspect which is further beyond it until the aspect of the First Cause, blessed be His name, who is the cause of all.

It is evident that Yagel interpreted the statement which he found in Agrippa to refer to the four worlds of emanation, creation, formation and construction. Of these he mentioned the worlds of emanation and creation. During the course of comparing kabbalistic and Neoplatonic conceptions a change was made in the definition of the essence of the *Sefirot*. They are understood to be the Neoplatonic ideas which descend and become materialized.

For all issues from the Lord of Hosts. He spoke and it was, He commanded and it stood [Ps. 33:9] but the creatures and formations above and below exist by the spirit of His mouth. . . . And the power that is in the lower beings is to be found in the upper worlds in a more subtle, exalted and sublime manner. It is to be found [also] in great purity and clarity in the holy, pure *Sefirot* which are in truth the Ideii for all things. They are the beginning of God's way and all His acts course through the four degrees which are the mystery of the four worlds of emanation, creation, formation and construction.[228]

These *Sefirot*—Ideas—are said to exist in the divine mind:[229]

The meaning of the world *Ideii:* that is to say a simple form, superior to bodies, souls and intelligences.[230] It is absolutely simple, invisible, indivisible and incorporeal; nor is it potentiality within a body. It is eternal and abides in the mind of the Creator and Maker of all, blessed be He. Before a man makes anything, he traces in his mind the form of that thing in quality. So too the form, quality and quantity of the heavens and the earth and their generations were figured within the mind of the Most High before He created them. . . . And in the terminology of the Platonists that first figuration is called *Ideii,* but they do not mean to ascribe multiplicity to a simple substance, God forbid, in any way, nor to imply any change of will at all.

In effect, Yagel set aside the gnostic and dynamic character of the *Sefirot* which constituted one of the principal characteristics of the Kab-balah. He returned to a completely philosophical approach, reminiscent of the formulation of Philo.[231] It is important to emphasize that this shift in theory was not restricted to Yagel alone. It can be found in texts written in Italy in the time period between Alemanno and Yagel. This evidence appears in the *Responsum* of Rabbi Isaac Abravanel to Rabbi Saul ha-Cohen. Abravanel wrote: [232]

For of necessity things exist as a figuration in the mind of the active agent before that thing comes into being. Undoubtedly this image is the world of the *Sefirot* mentioned by the sages of the kabbalists of the true wisdom [who said] that the *Sefirot* are the divine images with which the world was created. Therefore they said that the *Sefirot* are not created but are emanated, and that all of them unite together in Him, blessed be His name, for they are the figuration of His loving-kindness and His willling what He created. In truth, Plato set down the knowledge of the separate general forms.

A similar thought appears in the book *Sha'arei Ḥayyim* which was written in the year 1540. [233]

The upper creatures are a model for the lower creatures. This is because every lower thing has a superior power from which it came into existence. This resembles the relationship of the shadow to the object that casts it. For the one who casts the shadow is the cause of the shadow. Even the ancient philosophers such as Pythagoras and Plato taught and made statements about this. [234] However the matter was not revealed to them in a clear way as it was to the prophets, blessed be their memory, who received it. For the principles stated by Plato resemble this for they are incorporeal forms within the divine mind and that is the cause of the existence of the individuals.

Azaria de' Rossi also [235] pointed out the similarity between the terms 'Sefira' and 'Idea.' It is reasonable to assume that these writers found and utilized a concept mentioned throughout the writings of Marsilio Ficino and Pico della Mirandola; these writers maintained that the Ideas are to be found in God Himself [236] and not only in the general Intellect of Plotinus or in the logos of Philo. From this point of view, Abravanel, the author of *Sha'arei Ḥayyim* and Abraham Yagel continued to develop these topics along lines established during the Renaissance, lines which found expression in the writings of Ficino, Pico and Agrippa.

Detailed examination of the Neoplatonic definition of the *Sefirot* by Italian kabbalists has great significance for an understanding of important developments in the Kabbalah of the sixteenth century. The Kabbalah of Rabbi Isaac Luria (ARI) reached Italy in the version of Israel Sarug. Neoplatonic interpretations of Sarug are to be found in the writings of Abraham Herrera and YaSHaR of Candia. [237] The principal trend of these kabbalists was to divest Lurianic Kabbalah of its mythical garb and to give it a new interpretation. In method and content their efforts resemble the text of Abraham Yagel cited above. The new treatment of Kabbalah was not a synthesis of Kabbalah and philosophy but represented an exegesis of the kabbalistic text which shifted its propositions and descriptions in a direction unanticipated by the original author.

This tendency to force Kabbalah into a Neoplatonic mold consisted in great measure of the superimposition of certain intellectual and conceptual innovations of the Renaissance upon ideas of Jewish origin. This development began in a modest way in the writings of Alemanno. My discussion of certain passages from Alemanno's writings indicates that he placed great emphasis upon the similarity of Kabbalah and Platonic[238] thought. Aided by the various versions of Proclus' teaching Alemanno went beyond emphasis of the intellectual proximity of these systems and introduced a Neoplatonic interpretation of Kabbalah, and Abraham Yagel continued this activity. The essential difference between Alemanno and the later Neoplatonic interpreters of the Kabbalah—Herrera and YaSHaR of Candia—derives from the fact that a greater amount of Neoplatonic literature was available to the latter than to Alemanno. These later writers were much more conversant with Neoplatonic sources and used them in order to explain the new school of Kabbalah of Israel Sarug. Despite these differences, the approach of all the kabbalists mentioned here to their sources was the same, for they shared the same cultural phenomenology. Consciously or not, they ignored the literal meaning of their kabbalistic sources and dressed them in garb which completely changed the original meaning of the kabbalistic texts.

I will conclude my discussion at this point with a very concrete example of this change in interpretation. I have in mind Rabbi Judah Moscato's sermon entitled "The Divine Circle." A detailed analysis of Moscato's understanding of the Jewish sources he quoted in this sermon will have to wait for another time. It will suffice to say that his reading of the sources was dictated by a commonplace Renaissance conception which Moscato mentioned in his sermon:[239]

In the writings of Mercurio Trimesto it is written: The Creator, blessed be He, is a perfect circle whose center is to be found at every point and whose circumference is nowhere.

In his sermon, Moscato interpreted the opinions of Ibn Ezra and the Kabbalists so as to prove the proposition of Hermes Trismegistus that God is a Divine Point or a Divine Circle.[240] These are but a few of Moscato's remarks:

The kabbalists revealed to us a great measure of true wisdom in the matter of the circle. At times they depict it as a crown, surrounding and encompassing all the rest of the *Sefirot* from without. At times they depict it as a point within a circle. I found the following written in the book *Sha'arei Tzedek*.[241] The Crown encompasses all the *Sefirot* and is called *soḥaret* derived from the word *seḥor-seḥor* (around and around).

Here, the homileticist combined two entirely different kabbalistic conceptions in order to construct the same proposition as the pseudo-Hermes. There is something unique about Moscato's method. He did not express himself in a philosophical genre as did Alemanno or Yagel, but expounded his views in a sermon. Here, a conception drawn from outside sources was absorbed into a traditional Jewish literary genre while Moscato voided the Jewish sources of their original meaning in order to accommodate the ideas found by him in Renaissance theology. As proved above, Jewish thinkers had developed their systems under the direct influence of Renaissance ideas. It seems that this particular feature was the reason for their lack of enduring influence. Two main causes contributed to the weakening of the influence of these authors: the printing of the classical kabbalistic literature such as the Zohar and *Ma'arekhet ha-Elohut,* and the increasing impact of the Kabbalah of Safed.[242] In both cases, there is an emphasis on the genuine unmixed Kabbalah. However, it seems to me that Alemanno's influence, directly or indirectly, can be found both in Safed and in Ashkenazi authors, but this must remain a subject for future research.

NOTES

1. This refers particularly to the influence of Maimonides' *Guide of the Perplexed* on Aquinas and the influence of Ibn Gabirol's *Fons Vitae* on Franciscan theology. A peculiar and interesting exception to this lack of cultural exchange through personal communication and instruction is to be found in Byzantine culture. It is reported that a Jew named Elisha was the instructor of Gemistos Plethon.
2. On this personality and his relations with Abraham Farissol see David Ruderman, "Abraham Farissol. An Historical study of His Life and Thought

in the Context of Jewish Communal Life in Renaissance Italy," (Ph.D. diss., Hebrew University, 1974), pp. 170–85.

3. This is the end of an epistle on the history of the Kabbalah written by Rabbi Elijah Menahem Halfan. Jewish Theological Seminary [JTS] MS 1822, f. 154v.

4. For the attitude of Jews to the Lutheran movement see H. H. Ben-Sasson, "The Reformation in Contemporary Jewish Opinion," *Proceedings of the Israel Academy of Sciences and Humanities* 4 (1970), pp. 239–326.

5. Some of the Christian Hebraists in Italy had learned Hebrew as a prerequisite for the study of Kabbalah. See also Ruderman, "Abraham Farissol," p. 173.

6. See E. Schweid, *Feeling and Speculation* [Hebrew] (Ramat Gan, 1970), pp. 17ff.

7. See M. Idel, "Abraham Abulafia's Works and Doctrine," (Ph.D. diss., Hebrew University, 1976), p. 436.

8. For an analysis of these two kabbalists' conception of the *Sefirot* see E. Gottlieb, *Studies in the Literature of the Kabbalah* [Hebrew] (Tel Aviv, 1976), pp. 293–310.

9. *Sefer Ma'arekhet ha-Elohut* (Mantua, 1558), f. 3a–b.

10. Y. Nadav, "An Epistle of the Kabbalist Rabbi Yitzhak Mar Hayyim on the Doctrine of *Tzahtzahot*" [Hebrew], *Tarbitz* 26 (1962–3), p. 458. In his second letter to Rabbi Isaac of Pisa, Rabbi Isaac Mar Hayyim expressed a similar view. This letter was published by A. W. Greenup, "A Kabbalistic Epistle," *JQR*, n.s., 21 (1931), p. 370.

11. Rabbi Reuben Tzarfati's commentary on *Sefer Ma'arekhet ha-Elohut* is particularly representative of this trend. In his commentary, Tzarfati integrates the theology of the *Ma'arekhet* author with the conceptions of Abraham Abulafia. See Gottlieb, *Studies*, pp. 357–69; Idel, "Abraham Abulafia," pp. 12 and 43, n. 48.

12. The term "theurgic" employed here and below refers to the kabbalist's belief in his ability to influence the process and condition of the *Sefirot*.

13. Flavius Mithridates translated several of Abulafia's works as well as Menahem Recanati's commentary on the Torah from Hebrew into Latin. These translations served as one of the most important sources of kabbalistic teaching for Pico. See H. Wirszubski, *Mekubal Notzri Kore ba-Tora [A Christian Kabbalist Reads the Law]* (Jerusalem, 1977), pp. 23 and 30. On an unknown translation of the *Ma'arekhet ha-Elohut* and *Sefer Hayyei ha-Olam ha-Ba* of Abulafia which was made in the circle of Egidio da Viterbo see Idel, "Egidio da Viterbo and Abulafia's Works," *Italia* 3 (1980), pp. 48–50.

14. Wirszubski, *A Christian Kabbalist*, pp. 11 and 17ff.

15. See *Sefer Shir ha-Ma'alot*, Oxford MS 1535, ff. 18r and 20r.

16. This refers to a considerable amount of the material found in Alemanno's *Novellae and Collectanea*, Oxford MS 2234 (Reggio 23). I intend to make a separate study and analysis of the material in this manuscript. Here it

suffices to note that Alemanno collected material during the last third of the fifteenth century, but on the whole made use of it in compositions written between the years 1499 and 1505. For that reason one should not always assume that opinions written in his later works were the result of deliberations made at the time of writing.

17. Rosenthal had a different opinion of Alemanno. In his view, Alemanno was intellectually a medieval figure even though he lived during the Renaissance period. See E. J. F. Rosenthal, "Yohanan Alemanno and Occult Science," *Prismata: Naturwissenschaftgeschichtliche Studien. Fetschrift für Willy Hartner* (Wiesbaden, 1977), p. 356.

18. See in particular D. P. Walker's pioneering study, *Spiritual and Demonic Magic from Ficino to Campanella* (London, 1975).

19. Walker has already made this point. See s.v. "Picatrix" in the index to his *Spiritual and Demonic Magic*. F. Yates added much to Walker's treatment in confirming the literary importance of *Picatrix* during the Renaissance period in her book *Giordano Bruno and the Hermetic Tradition* (London, 1964). See also the important studies of E. Garin, "La diffusione di un manuale di magia," *La Cultura filosofica del rinascimento italiano* (Firenze, 1961), pp. 159–65; "Astrologia e magia: Picatrix," *Lo Zodiaco della vita* (Laterza, 1976), pp. 33–60; and "Postille sull'Ermetismo del rinascimento," *Rinascimento* 16 (1976), pp. 245–6. On the influence of paganism on *Picatrix* see J. Seznec, *The Survival of the Pagan Gods* (Princeton, N.J., 1972). On the Hermetic sources of *Picatrix* see H. and R. Kahane and Angela Pietrangle, "Picatrix and the Talismans," *Romance Philology* 19 (1965–6), pp. 574–93, and D. Pingree, "Some Sources of the Ghāyat al-Ḥakim," *[Journal of the Warburg and Courtauld Inst.]* 43 (1980), 1–15.

20. F. Secret collected a great deal of material on this work in "Sur quelques traductions du Sefer Raziel," *REJ* 128 (1969), pp. 223–45.

21. R. A. Pack, "Almadel Auctor Pseudonimus de Firmitate Sex Scientiarum," *Archives d'Histoire Doctrinale et Littéraire du Moyen Ages [AHDLMA]* 42 (1976), pp. 147ff, esp. 177f.

22. This particular subject has not been discussed in the scholarly literature. Studies of the topic have dealt for the most part with popular superstitions and magical practices but have not considered the place of magic in the intellectual framework of the Renaissance. See M. A. Shulwass, *The Jews in the World of the Renaissance* (Leiden, 1973), pp. 328–32; C. Roth, *The Jews in the Renaissance* (Philadelphia, 1959), pp. 59–63.

23. A detailed description of Munich MS 124 is to be found in M. Steinschneider, *Zur pseudoepigraphischen Literatur* (Berlin, 1862), pp. 28–51. This translation contains certain varia when compared with the original Arabic text and one of these was discussed by M. Plessner, "A Medieval Definition of a Scientific Experiment in the Hebrew Picatrix," *JWCI* 36 (1973), pp. 358–9.

24. In his book *Ma'ase Efod*, Profet Duran refers to this work by this name.

Alemanno knew Duran's book. See Idel, "The Curriculum of Yoḥanan Alemanno" [Hebrew], *Tarbitz* 48 (1980), p. 304, n. 6.

25. See Idel, "Curriculum," p. 311. In his *Collectanaea,* Oxford MS 2234, f. 121r, Alemanno includes a passage from the book *Sefer Megale Amukot* of Rabbi Shlomo ben Ḥanokh al-Constantini who had seen the work in the Arabic original. This reference parallels what is said in *Sefer Megale Amukot,* Vatican MS 59, f. 6r.

26. All the manuscripts of the Latin translation of *Picatrix* date from the fifteenth or sixteenth centuries. See Yates, *Giordano Bruno,* p. 15, n. 3.

27. See I. Sonne, *From Paul the Fourth to Pius the Fifth* [Hebrew] (Jerusalem, 1954), p. 108.

28. L. Thorndike, *History of Magic and Experimental Science* (New York: 1958), II, p. 280.

29. For more information about this kabbalist, see A. Kupfer, "The Visions of Rabbi Asher ben Rav Meir also named Lemlin Reutlingen" [Hebrew], *Kovetz al Yad* 8 (Jerusalem, 1976), pp. 389–423.

30. Budapest, Kaufmann MS 179, p. 134.

31. *Shalshelet ha-Kabbalah* (Jerusalem, 1962), p. 231.

32. See the edition of Gollancz (Jerusalem, 1940). It is noteworthy that an abridgment of *Sefer Mafteaḥ Shlomo* is listed as follows in Coronel's catalogue of manuscripts (London, 1871) p. 12, no. 123: " '*Sefer Mafteaḥ ha-Zahav*': an abridgment of '*Mafteaḥ Shlomo*': an introduction on the writing of amulets with several unusual figures (pictures) and letters." This description does correspond to the content of *Sefer Mafteaḥ Shlomo.* Abraham Colorni translated the Hebrew version of the book into Italian.

33. See Idel, "Curriculum," p. 321ff.

34. See Paris MS 849, f. 64r–v. G. Scholem first noted this in his article, "An Untitled Book of Rabbi Yoḥanan Alemanno" [Hebrew], *Kiryat Sefer* 5 (1929), p. 276. Greenup published another translation: *Sefer ha-Levana* (London, 1912). A fragment of a third translation appears in *Sefer Yesod Olam* of Rabbi Abraham Eskira, Moscow-Ginsburg MS 607, f. 72v. This work is also to be found in Arabic and Latin manuscripts.

35. *Sefer Ḥeshek Shlomo,* Oxford MS 1535, ff. 47v, 48r, 65v, 68r, and 118v. For a bibliography on this work see Rosenthal, "Occult Science" (p. 350–1 and the accompanying notes. I will discuss the subject at another time. References to Apollonius by Alemanno's contemporaries in Italy are contained in Ruderman, "Abraham Farissol," p. 50f and in Walker, *Spiritual and Demonic Magic,* p. 147f.

36. Bar Ilan University MS 286 (formerly Vienna MSx,25), ff. 83r–92v. At the beginning of this section the following appears: "In the book *Shir ha-Ma'alot* of Solomon it is written that about the year 150 of the sixth millenium the scholar Rabbi Shelomo ben Rav Natan translated this composition from Latin into Hebrew. The author was the very ancient Apollonius and the book is called *Mlekhet Muskelet.*" Undoubtedly, this statement relates to what Alemanno said in his book, *Shir ha-Ma'alot* which is an

introductory work to the *Sefer Ḥashek Shlomo*. See Oxford MS 1535, f. 47v and the printed work *Sefer Shaar ha-Ḥeshek* (Halberstadt, s.a.), pp. 8b–9a. There is an important difference between Alemanno's comments in Oxford MS 1535 and *Sefer Shaar ha-Ḥeshek* (which states: "It has been one hundred years") and the remark in Bar Ilan MS 286 ("the year 150"). It follows that the Bar Ilan MS was written fifty years after the composition of *Sefer Shir ha-Ma'alot*, that is to say at the end of the first half of the sixteenth century. About the same time, Rabbi Raphael Shlomo ben Ya'akov Prato copied Budapest Kaufman MS 246. In pp. 3–17 of the Budapest manuscript there are excerpts which are also to be found in the Bar Ilan MS. The Budapest manuscript contains a more complete and linguistically clear version of the excerpts. The translator Raphael Prato worked for Rabbi Yeḥi'el Nissim of Pisa in whose grandfather's house Alemanno was a guest. It is possible that Alemanno himself gathered these excerpts from the book *Mlekhet Muskelet* which was, according to Alemanno's own description, a composition of some two hundred folio pages, much longer than the extant version. A considerable part of the material found in these excerpts also appears in *Sefer Shir ha-Ma'alot*.

37. See Idel, "Curriculum," p. 312, n. 76.
38. Ibid., p. 312, n. 74.
39. Alemanno, *Sefer Shir ha-Ma'alot*, Oxford MS 1535, f. 116r.
40. See Scholem's remarks in the article mentioned above, note 34.
41. Oxford MS 2234, f. 15r.
42. Oxford MS 1535, f. 126r. See also J. Dan "Teraphim: From Popular Belief to a Folktale," *Scripta Hierosolymitana* 27 (1978), pp. 100–2. Compare Alemanno's report with the marginal comment in Oxford MS 2234, f. 68r. and with a story mentioned in M. Bouisson, *La Magie* (Paris, 1958), p. 132.
43. *Collectanaea*, Oxford MS 2234, marginal comments f. 68r.
44. Paris MS 849, f. 47v. At the bottom of folio 20v Alemanno tells of his connections with Paris Ceresarius Mantuano, a former physician who claimed that he knew the secret of immortality. See. G. Scholem in *Kiryat Sefer* 5, p. 274.
45. See Gottlieb, *Studies*, pp. 29–37.
46. On the development of this conception see P. Zambelli, "Le Problème de la magie naturelle à la Renaissance," *Astrologia e religione nel rinascimento* (Wroclaw, 1974), pp. 48–9.
47. Yates elaborated upon the relation of magic and Kabbalah in Pico's writings in *Giordano Bruno*, pp. 86–110.
48. Ibid., pp. 96f.
49. Ibid., p. 95.
50. Giovanni Francesco Pico della Mirandola, *Opera Omna*, (Basel, 1753) p. 107–8; Yates, *Giordano Bruno*, p. 95.
51. Pico, *Opera Omnia*, pp. 180–1; Yates, *Giordano Bruno*, p. 96.
52. Montefiore MS 316, f. 28v. I shall attempt to prove in another article that the letter was written by Rabbi Isaac ben Yeḥi'el of Pisa. A similar definition

appears in the famous address of Rabbi Simone Luzzatto: "E l'altra parte
più teoricale e scientifica che considera la dispendenza di questo mondo
corporale dal spirituale, incorporale et architipo; tengono che vi siano alcuni
principii, e orgini seminarii de tutte le cose sensibili." F. Secret "Un texte
malconnu de Simone Luzzatto sur le Kabbale," *REJ* 118 (1959–60), p. 123.

53. Scholem, "Zur Geschichte der Anfänge der christlichen Kabbalah" in *Essays
Presented to Leo Baeck* (London, 1954), p. 164, n. 1.

54. This was published by A. Jellinek, *Auswahl kabbalisticher Mystik* (Leipzig,
1853), p. 15. Flavius Mithridates translated the letter into Latin and Pico
knew of this text.

55. See Idel, "Curriculum," p. 310, nn. 65, 66.

56. See Idel, "Curriculum," pp. 320ff.

57. Oxford MS 2234, f. 164r.

58. The manuscript in Hebrew reads: *"Ha-Nikayon."*

59. Exodus 19:15.

60. Munich MS 214, f. 51r. See also note 101 below.

61. Paris MS 849, f. 92v. Cf. also f. 6v.

62. See also Scholem's discussion of this matter in his *Pirkei Yesod be-Havanat
ha-Kabala u-Smaleha* [Elements of the Kabbalah and its Symbolism] (Jerusalem: 1976), p. 14ff. In Alemanno's time, several scholars were of the
opinion that the Torah had magical properties which enabled the Jewish
sages to master nature. See the remarks of Rabbi Joseph Yavetz in his
commentary on *Avot* (Warsaw, 1880), p. 68. See also the remarks of S.
Heller-Wilenski, *The Philosophy of Isaac Arama* [Hebrew] (Jerusalem and
Tel-Aviv, 1956), p. 131; *Sefer Minḥat Kena'ot* of Rabbi Yeḥi'el Nissim of
Pisa, and the remarks of YaSHaR of Candia in *Sefer Matzref la-Ḥokhma,*
ch. 4 and 10.

63. Paris MS 849, f. 7v.

64. Pico, *Opera Omnia* p. 181; Yates, *Giordano Bruno,* p. 97.

65. References to a classification of practical Kabbalah according to categories
of pure and impure can be found in the Italian Kabbalah in the first half of
the sixteenth century. Rabbi Elijah Menaḥem Ḥalfan wrote in an epistle:
"First of all the science of the Kabbalah is divided into two parts called the
right side and the left side. Each one of the two parts mentioned is divided
into the speculative and the practical. The right side is all purity and holiness
and divine and angelic names and holy matters. The left side is all [?] and
demons and shells of the impure side." JTS MS 1822, f. 153v. This catego-
rization which considers practical Kabbalah of the left side to be worship of
the "other side" *(sitra aḥra)* is based upon the Zohar which contrasted
magic and Kabbalah. Compare this to the Mazdaic belief which claims that
magic is the ritual worship of Ahriman. See J. Bidez and F. Cumont, *Les
Mages hellenisés* (Paris, 1938), vol. 1, p. 143. See also Profiat Duran's
Klimat ha-foyim, ch. 2, where Jesus is considered a practical Kabbalist who
worked his miracles by the impure side of practical Kabbalah. Compare this
to Pico's statement that Jesus' miracles were not done by magic or by
Kabbalah. See *Opera Omnia,* p. 105 and Yates, Giordano Bruno, p. 106.

66. Munich MS 214, F. 51r.
67. Compare this to a conception appearing in a short composition entitled *Sod Pe'ulat ha-Yetzira*. There a technique of letter combination is described for the reception of the efflux of wisdom. The composition then describes the reception of the holy spirit and the creation of a *golem*. See Idel, "Abraham Abulafia," p. 131.
68. This term appears most frequently throughout the book *Takhlit he-Ḥakham*. See for example Munich MS 214, f. 51r. The expression is also repeated on p. 14 of the work *Sefer ha-Atzamim*, attributed to Ibn Ezra which has been mentioned before. See also *Sefer Megale Amukot* of Shlomo al-Constantini, Vatican MS 59, f. 6rff, and *Sefer Mekor Ḥayyim* of Rabbi Samuel Zarza (Mantua, 1559), f. 6a. Magic based upon "causing a descent" is also known from the literature of the Midrash. See L. Ginzburg, *The Legends of the Jews*, vol. 5, p. 152, n. 56. While the Midrash concerns the descent of the sun and moon, Hermetic magic concerns the descent of the celestial emanations. In *Sefer Takhlit he-Ḥakham* the descent of the spiritual forces is a type of revelation: "For every wise man has power so that some part of the spirit may come to him and awaken him and open up to him what was hidden from him, and this power was described as the perfect nature." On the perfect nature see Scholem, *Elements*, pp. 361–4. About "drawing upon the spiritual forces of the stars" see also Rabbi Baḥya ben Asher's *Commentary on the Torah* to Deut. 18:11. There he quotes material very similar to that found in *Sefer Takhlit he-Ḥakham* from *The Epistle of Galen*. And cf. the statment of Rabbi Moses Cordovero, *Sefer Pardes Rimonim*, Gate 30, ch. 3.
69. *Beḥinat ha-Dat* (Vienna, 1833), pp. 68–9. David Geffen did not identify the person at whom Del Medigo directed his criticism in "Faith and Reason in Elijah del Medigo's Beḥinat ha-Dat and the Philosophical Background of the Work" (Ph.D. diss., Columbia University, 1970), pp. 454–7. See also Idel, "Curriculum," pp. 328–9.
70. Oxford MS 2234, f. 2v. Cf. Naḥmanides' *Commentary on the Torah*, Deut. 32:40. It is important to note that these words of Alemanno in his *Collectanaea* were set down at a very early date, perhaps before the year 1478 or even the year 1470, but the proofs I have for this cannot be included here. This determination is significant in view of the similarity between Alemanno's statement and Pico's theses. The problematic relation of Kabbalah to astrology was discussed in Italy before Alemanno. In the opinion of Rabbi Isaac Dieulosal, the systems of Kabbalah and astrology are compatible. See J. Hacker, "The Connections of Spanish Jewry with Eretz Israel between 1391 and 1492," *Shalem* 1 (1974), p. 145 n. 64 and p. 147.
71. The text should probably read "and the rituals."
72. *Opera Omnia*, p. 113. On the relationship of Kabbalah and astrology in Christian Kabbalah see F. Secret "L'Astrologie et les kabbalistes chrétiens à la Renaissance," *Le Tour Saint-Jacques* 5 (1956), pp. 45–9.
73. The term appears in the writings of the kabbalistic school of Gerona and in texts of the *iyyun* circle. For example see *Sefer Meshiv Dvarim Nekhoḥim*

of Rabbi Ya'akov ben Sheshet, ed. G. Vajda (Jerusalem, 1969), p. 150 and the text published by G. Scholem in his article, "The Development of the Doctrine of the Worlds in Early Kabbalah" [Hebrew], *Tarbitz* 2 (1931), p. 430. It seems that this term is a translation of the Arabic "alam alḥuruf" which appears in the writings of the Ismailliya. See S. Pines, "Note sur l'Ismalijja," *Hermes* 3 (1939), p. 58.

74. The world of change is the lower world because it changes its forms. The world of motion, however, is the middle world because it is in constant motion. Alemanno uses these terms many times in all his books.

75. This appears to be an allusion to BT, *Sanhedrin*, 91a. Compare Alemanno's description of the ancient Jews, found in *Ḥai ha-Olamim*, MS Mantua 21, f. 216v.

76. Oxford MS 1535, f. 104v–105r. The quotation found in the printed version of the work *Shaar ha-Ḥeshek*, f. 33b–34a is quite corrupt.

77. This term is worthy of note. Moses does not repair the divinity but rather the vessels which transmit divine emanation. Compare this to Alemanno's statement in *Sefer Einei ha-Eda*, Jerusalem MS 598, f. 51r–v, concerning the status of man: "Were it not for Him who endows the lower world with perfection as He is perfect, the world would be void and empty, for nothing is called Godly but He. He repairs all the channels and emanations of the supernal and middle worlds, for no one receives that good in its entirety but He. When He receives it, then all the emanations descending to earth are in balance and work to perfection."

78. Oxford MS 2234, f. 8v.

79. See J. Gager, *Moses in Graeco-Roman Paganism* (Nashville, N.Y., 1972), pp. 134–60.

80. *Sefer Ḥeshek Shlomo*, Moscow MS 140, f. 287r.

81. Oxford MS 2234, f. 22v.

82. This attribution of the making of the Golden Calf to Moses is very strange; I have found no parallel to it in Hebrew literature. Cf. L. Smolar and M. Aberbach, "The Golden Calf Episode in Postbiblical Literature," *HUCA* 39 (1968), pp. 91–116. However Giordano Bruno reports in the name of "kabbalists" that Moses made the Calf and the Brass Serpent for magical purposes. *De Imaginum, Signorum et Idearum Compositione Opera Latine Conscripta*, vol. II, *pars* III (Stuttgart, 1962) p. 102: "Cabalistarum doctrina confirmat et exemplum Mosis qui interdum, atque Jovis favorem comparandum vitulum aurem erexit ad Martis item temperadum simul atque Saturni violentem aeneum serpentem adorandum ofiecit." On the conception of the making of the Golden Calf as a technique to cause the descent of spiritual forces, see also *Shaar ha-Ḥeshek*, p. 17b and Rabbi Shlomo Franco's commentary on Ibn Ezra, Munich MS 15, f. 268r–v.

83. See Abraham ibn Ezra's prefatory comment on Exodus 32 in his *Commentary to the Torah*, Ex. 32:1.

84. See Ibn Ezra's *Commentary to the Torah*, Ex. 32:1.

85. This is one of the important rationales for sacrifices found in the writings of Ibn Ezra and his interpreters. For example, the comment of Rabbi Samuel

Zarza in *Mekor Hayyim*, f. 9a and the statement of Rabbi Samuel ben Motot in *Sefer Megilat Starim* (Venice, 1554) ff. 10b, 11a.

86. Compare to the statement of Rabbi Samuel ibn Motot quoted by Alemanno in his *Collectanaea*, Oxford MS 2234, f. 127r: "When Israel observes the Temple service the Holy Spirit rests upon its noble men for the power of the human soul is increased and they prophesy."

87. See f. 9a. On the possible connection between this passage and Hermetic conceptions, see Georges Vajda, *Judah ben Nissim ibn Malka, Philosophe juif marocain* (Paris, 1954), p. 154, n. 1. There is a possible connection between the *Book of the Religions of the Prophets* and the book *Ilot ha-Ruhaniyot* whose content parallels the content of this quotation from Ibn Zarza. See E. Blochet, *Etudes sur le gnosticisme musulman* (Rome, 1913), p. 96. Ibn Zarza's younger contemporary, Profiat Duran, reported in his book *Heshev ha-Efod*, ch. 15, that Hermes is the ancient Enoch who set down the various scriptures. Duran's remark on Enoch was included in the book *Kol Yehuda* of Judah Moscato on *Kuzari* I, i. See also note 89.

88. Compare to *Sefer Heshev ha-Efod*, ch. 15. This is an ancient idea. See A. J. Festugière, *La Révélation d'Hermes Trismegiste* I (Paris, 1959), p. 334; Y. Marquet, "Sabéens et Ihwan al Safa," *Studia Islamica* 24 (1964), p. 58; "Liber Hermetis Mercurii Triplicis de VI Rerum Principium," ed. Th. Silverstein, *AHLDMA* 22 (1955), p. 247: "Hermes . . . astronomiam pruis elucidavit."

89. In Alemanno's opinion "Enoch had sons and daughters and strong and weak descendants and a multitude of laws and religions." *Sefer Einei ha-Eda*, Paris MS 270, f. 125r. In the course of his remarks Alemanno associates astral magic with Enoch's descendants: "Methuselah studied the heavens and their power and constellations. Lemech however, reigned over the upper world so as to cause their spirit to descend to the lower world, to know the future and the spirit of the stars."

It is reasonable to assume that here the roles ascribed to Enoch in the *Book of the Religions of the Prophets*, as a lawgiver, astrologer and magician were reassigned to his descendants. This was in keeping with Alemanno's conception that every generation from Adam to Abraham engaged in the study of a different branch of knowledge. On Enoch as a lawgiver, see also *Sefer Heshek Shlomo*, Berlin MS 832, f. 249r.

90. In the printed edition of *Sefer Ma'ase Efod*, p. 183, included by Alemanno in his *Collectanaea*, MS Oxford 2234, f. 105v with slight variations.

91. *Sefer Ma'ase Efod*, p. 182. Compare to the preface, p. 1.

92. Oxford MS 2234, f. 201b.

93. This expression appeared as early as Ibn Ezra's *Commentary* on Deut. 31:16.

94. *Shaar he-Heshek*, p. 41b. On magic temples and Alemanno see my note, "Magic Temples and Cities in the Middle Ages and the Renaissance," *Jerusalem Studies in Islam and Arabic* 3 (1982). For Alemanno's distinction between holy emanation originating in the world of the *Sefirot* and impure emanation emanating from the world of motion—the world

of the celestial spheres—see his remarks in *Sefer Heshek Shlomo,* MS Moscow 140, f. 100r. There he cites *Sefer ha-Tamar* in support of his position. Alemanno's reference seems to be found on p. 13 of Abuflah's work.

95. Cf. Alemanno's comment in his *Collectanaea,* Oxford MS 2234, f. 95v: "The secret of the world of the letters is that they are forms and seals which receive supernal spiritual emanations as are the seals which receive astral emanations." Undoubtedly, this text refers to talismanic magic: "The seals which receive the emanations of the stars" is a paradigm of kabbalistic seals which function in the same way. The above comment appears at the end of the quotation of Ptolemy from *Centiloquium (Ha-Pri),* book 5, ch. 9 where the subject of talismans is treated. Compare to Paris MS 849, f. 77v. "How does one make a figure for the spirit of the *Sefirot?* He depicted the motion of the letters with the vocalization marks." Here the vocalization marks are an expression of the spirituality of the *Sefirot* that is the efflux of the *Sefirot* while the vocalization points are seals for the *Sefirot.*

96. Oxford MS 1535, f. 15r.

97. On causing the descent of the holy spirit, see the quotation from the *Collectanaea,* f. 164v. which was discussed above.

98. On the extension of the *Shekhina* into the lower world, see Y. Tishbi, *Mishnat ha-Zohar* II, p. 267. This occurrence, however, does not have a magical connotation.

99. Montefiore MS 316, f. 28v. The different versions of this letter include the passage quoted here and were published in my article in *Italia* 4 (1982). I have also analyzed the relation between the writer of this letter and Rabbi Yehiel Nissim of Pisa in my "Three Versions of the Letter of R. Isaac of Pisa(?)," *Kovetz al Yad* (1982).

100. Published in J. Perles, "Les savants juifs à Florence à l'époche de Laurent de Médici," *REJ* 12 (1886), p. 256.

101. The danger involved in the practice of magical rituals without precise attention to their details is mentioned in books on magic. It is reasonable to assume that this quotation is based upon *Sefer ha-Atzamim* which states (f. 13): "If one is not expert and knowledgeable in causing the descent of forces and in the performance of rituals and sacrifices, they will kill him." See also ibid., f. 14–5. This selection also appears in Alemanno. See *Shaar ha-Heshek,* p. 43a and the remarks of *Sefer Takhlit he-Hakham* mentioned above. Munich MS 214, f. 51a.

102. *Shaar ha-Heshek,* p. 16a. Compare to *Sefer Heshek Shlomo,* Oxford MS 1535, f. 146v.

103. *Shaar ha-Heshek,* f. 15r.

104. Ibid., f. 44r.

105. Ibid., loc. cit.

106. Paris MS 849, f. 121v.

107. In the sixteenth century formulations similar to those of Alemanno recur

in texts other than Rabbi Isaac of Pisa's letter and in the book *Shaarei Hayyim*. For example, see the statement of Rabbi Yeḥiel Nissim of Pisa, the nephew of Rabbi Isaac, who writes in *Sefer Minḥat Kena'ot* (Berlin, 1898), pp. 49f: "All these practices are derived from the side of the forces of impurity. Therefore the gentiles made use of them, but the Jews are forbidden to practice them because they are a nation holy unto God. These practices were particularly forbidden in the holy land, for there the power of the holy heaven is revealed more than in other lands, because it is prepared to receive this light and spark." See also *Ma'arekhet ha-Elohut*, f. 6v, and *Avodat ha-Kodesh*, 1, 12.

108. On the Torah as an instrument for the reception of efflux, see the passage from Alemanno's *Collectanaea*, f. 164r.

109. *Shaar ha-Ḥeshek*, f. 33b.

110. Paris MS 849, f. 137v.

111. Oxford MS 2234, f. 3v.

112. Ibid., loc. cit.

113. Edition of Joseph Ben-Shelomo (Jerusalem, 1971) I, p. 49f.

114. *Shaar ha-Ḥeshek*, p. 33b–34a. The term "laws of the Oral law" here parallels the term "the laws" found in the citation from Paris MS 849 together with a discussion of prophecy, language and the Temple. Proof of the identity of the term "the laws" with "the Oral law" is found in the statement of Alemanno which was copied into the book *Ḥai Olamim* from *Sefer Ḥalukat ha-Ḥokhmot* of Alfarabi: "The science of the law is one whereby man may learn a judgment on a matter which a statute of Scripture does not explain or when a statute of Scripture is restricted to certain matters" (Mantua MS 21, f. 195v).

115. Ibid., loc. cit. Compare to Alemanno's remarks on f. 26r–v in the same text. There, he speaks of a Chinese temple built in accordance with the structure of the middle world for the purpose of learning about the emanations of the middle world upon our own. A similar conception also appears in *Picatrix;* see Yates, *Giordano Bruno*, pp. 54–6 and pp. 367–71. On Alemanno's source for the Chinese temple passage see M. Idel, "Magic Temples and Cities in the Middle Ages and the Renaissance. A Passage of Masudi as a Possible Source for Yohanan Alemanno," *Jerusalem Studies in Arabic and Islam* 111 (1981–82: 185–89).

116. *Shaar ha-Ḥeshek*, f. 43b.

117. Paris MS 849, f. 94v. Parallel versions of several parts of this quotation are to be found in material from the commentaries on Ibn Ezra that Alemanno copied into his *Collectanaea*. See Oxford MS 2234, ff. 125v and 128v. This is supplemented by Ibn Zarza's statement which will be quoted in the continuation of this paper. The analogy of *Bina* to the planet Saturn appears in Ibn Wakar and following him in Rabbi Moses Narboni and Ibn Motot.

118. Cf. Georges Vajda, "Recherches sur la synthèse philosophico-kabbalistique de Samuel ibn Motot," *AHDLMA* 27 (1960), p. 59, n. 112.

119. On the origin of religions as linked to the great conjunction of Saturn and Jupiter, see Georges Vajda, *Recherches sur la philosophie et la kabbale dans la pensée juive du moyen âge* (Paris, 1962), p. 264, n. 3.

120. Folio 6, col. 3–4 as compared with Leiden MS Or. 2065. E. Zafran, "Saturn and the Jews," *JWCI* 42 (1979), pp. 16–27 explores the Christian sources.

121. See Oxford MS 1535, ff. 43r, 163v and others. It is possible that Pico had the book in his library. Compare to Kibre, *The Library of Pico della Mirandola* (New York, 1936), p. 160: "Samuel Sarsa, *De Secretis Legis*." Page 149, no. 210 lists a commentary on the Pentateuch. *Sefer Mekor Ḥayyim* is a supercommentary on Ibn Ezra's *Commentary on the Torah.*

122. See Idel, "Curriculum," p. 311, n. 69.

123. In Alemanno's view, magic is to be distinguished from spiritual science because it pertains to pagan worship. In *Shaar ha-Ḥeshek,* f. 44a he says: "Since Saturn is the cause of magic and pagan worship . . . our master Moses, blessed be his memory, had to stand in the breach and guard Israel in the matter of the Torah and commandments which issue from the *Sefira Tiferet* and from all kinds of pagan worship. All kinds of magic issue from Saturn."

124. See Vajda, "Samuel ibn Motot," pp. 31 and 35.

125. See *Sefer Mekor Ḥayyim,* ff. 6b–c.

126. Al-Constantini is mentioned in the book *Mikhlol Yofi* of Ibn Zarza. See C. Sirat, *Ḥanokh b. Salomon al-Constantini* (Jerusalem, 1976), Hebrew part, p. 5.

127. There is a great similarity between several passages of Ibn Zarza's *Mekor Ḥayyim* and Ibn Motot's *Megilat Starim.* For example, compare *Mekor Ḥayyim,* f. 129, col. 3 to *Megilat Starim,* fol. 52. col. 3.

128. See Vajda, *Recherches,* p. 152, n. 2 and *Mekor Ḥayyim,* f. 117, col. 3.

129. See Vajda, *Recherches,* 249–53. Al-Constantini's and Ibn Zarza's astrological conceptions have not yet been the subject of any scholarly study. On the subject of astrology in *Megale Amukot* see Vatican MS 59, ff. 5r–6v, 9r, 10r, and others.

130. See the passage from Rabbi Samuel ibn Motot's book *Meshovev Netivot* translated by Vajda in *Judah ben Nissim,* p. 120f.

131. *Kuzari,* I, 79; III, 23. One must remember that in Alemanno's time, the *Kuzari* of Rabbi Judah ha-Levi enjoyed widespread distribution in Italy. See R. Bonfil, *Ha-Rabanut be-Italya bi-Tkufat ha-Renesans* [The Rabbinate in Renaissance Italy] (Jerusalem, 1979), pp. 186 and 200.

132. See Paris MS 720, f. 32v. Rabbi Nissim was one of the first, perhaps even the first, to mention the book *Ma'ase Nissim.* See Oxford MS 2234, fol. 123r.

133. See his sermons in Montefiore MS 17, ff. 12r, 58r and on. For more details about this author, see Cassuto, *Ha-Yehudim be-Firenze bi-Tkufat ha-Renesans* [The Jews of Renaissance Florence] (Jerusalem, 1966), pp. 194–200.

134. See the above discussion on the subject of the magical interpretation of the Torah.
135. See Yates, *Giordano Bruno*, pp. 80–2, concerning the special esteem of magic in the intellectual circles of Florence.
136. I shall devote a lengthy discussion to this composition and its relation to *Sefer Ḥai Olamim* in another article.
137. Oxford MS 2234, f. 125r.
138. Ibid., fol. 129r.
139. The Hebrew term "tzurot" (forms) has a magical meaning. In this case the word seems to refer to talismans. See M. Steinschneider, *Die hebräischen Übersetzungen des Mittelalters* (Gratz, 1956), p. 846, n. 8.
140. See also the discussion of Rabbi Isaac Abravanel below in the text.
141. Alemanno writes in the book *Einei ha-Eda* that the demons were subdued and subjugated by the Egyptian religion. See Jerusalem MS 8'598, f. 122. Concerning the connection between Egypt and demonic magic in Reuchlin, see H. Zika "Reuchlin's *De Verbo Mirifico* and the Magic Debate of the Late Fifteenth Century," *JWCI* 39 (1976), p. 112, n. 25 and p. 123.
142. This is possibly evidence of the influence of the Brethren of Purity who report the transmission of talismans from the Syrians to the Egyptians and from the Egyptians to the Greeks. See Marquet (above note 88), pp. 36 and 53.
143. Paris MS 849, f. 25r–v. Cf. also Maimonides, *Guide*, III, ch. 29.
144. On the conception of ancient wisdom see note 194.
145. Compare to the thirteenth chapter of Asclepius. See *Corpus Hermeticum*, ed. A. D. Nock and A. J. Festugière (Paris, 1945), pp. 347–9; ed. Scott, I (Oxford, 1926), p. 358. These words of Asclepius were well known during the Renaissance and had a decisive influence upon the thought of Marsilio Ficino. See Walker, *Spiritual and Demonic Magic*, pp. 40–2.
146. See Asclepius, ch. 3, in *Corpus Hermeticum*, ed. Scott, I, p. 338. Concerning the influence of the Hermetic conception of the animation of images on Jabir ibn Ḥayyan, see also the important comments of P. Krauss in his "Jabir ibn Ḥayyan et la science grecque," *Mémoires présentés à l'Institut d'Egypte* 45 (1942), pp. 126–34. On page 133 in note 11, Krauss points out that Proclus in his commentary on the Timeus also considered statues of the gods to have a prophetic character. However, Alemanno's statement has a greater similarity to the conception of Jabar, and Alemanno perhaps preserved a lost Hermetic tradition which influenced the Arab author.
147. Krauss, "Jabir ibn Ḥayyan," pp. 104, 106, 133.
148. See the discussion above concerning the passage from the letter of Rabbi Isaac of Pisa.
149. Concerning the possible influence of some other of Alemanno's conceptions on Abravanel's *Commentary* on Exodus see M. Steinschneider, *Die Handschriftenverzeichnisse des königlichen Bibliothk zu Berlin* (Berlin, 1879), vol. 2, p. 6. See also M. Idel, "Sources of the Circle Images in the 'Dialoghi d'Amore' " [Hebrew], *Iyyun* 28 (1979), p. 160 and note 17.

150. See also B. Netanyahu, *Don Isaac Abravanel* (Philadelphia, 1953), pp. 124–5.
151. Jerusalem ed. (1955), p. 474.
152. Ibid., p. 480.
153. Ibid., loc. cit.
154. Ibid., p. 475. See also ibid., p. 478.
155. Kings I:5, 12.
156. On this subject see D. P. Walker, *The Ancient Theology: Studies in Christian Platonism from the Fifteenth to the Eighteenth Century* (Ithaca, N.Y., 1972) pp. 22–41, and H. Wirszubski, *Shlosha Prakim be-Toldot ha-Kabala ha-Notzrit* [Three Chapters in the History of Christian Kabbalah] (Jerusalem, 1975), pp. 11–27.
157. It is reasonable to assume that in this context the word refers to the *Sefira Malkhut*.
158. BT, *Yadayim*, 86.
159. *Commentary* on Kings, p. 476.
160. BT *Pesaḥim*, f. 56a. Cf. the statement of Rabbi Abraham Yagel in the book *Beit Yaar ha-Levanon* which was published by Isaac Samuel Reggio in *Kerem Ḥemed* 2, pp. 51–2. Yagel was influenced by the statement of Alemanno and by Abravanel's *Commentary* on Kings.
161. See the material in note 156 above and also Walker's comments in *Spiritual and Demonic Magic*, pp. 3–24 and 62–3.
162. See the texts of Alemanno which were published in I. Adler, *Hebrew Writings Concerning Music* (Munich, 1975), pp. 41–5. A detailed discussion of the place of music in Alemanno's thought and particularly of its magic power is the subject of my paper, "The Magic and Theurgic Interpretations of Music in Jewish Sources from the Renaissance to Ḥasidism" (Hebrew), *Yuval* 4 (1982).
163. See *Collectanaea*, Oxford 2234, f. 42v, 58r, 88v.
164. See *Einei ha-Eda*, Paris MS 270, f. 13r: "Two Axioms on the Nature of the Soul Taken from the book *Mekor Ḥayyim* of Shelomo ibn Gabirol." Alemanno proceeds to quote from the *Likutei Mekor Ḥayyim*, III, paragraph 8 (which has a parallel in *Sefer More ha-More*, p. 86) and 10. The work *Mekor Ḥayyim* was known to Rabbi David Messer Leon and Alemanno was a student of his father, Rabbi Judah Messer Leon. See *Sefer Magen David*, Montefiore MS 290, fol. 14a and *Sefer Tehila le-David* (Istanbul, 1576), fol. 42r. Rabbi Isaac Abravanel and his son Judah became acquainted with *Mekor Ḥayyim* while in Italy. Therefore the opinion of D. Kaufmann that "only the living oral tradition of Spanish Jewry" made it possible for Abravanel to know the name of the author of *Mekor Ḥayyim* is not definitive; see D. Kaufmann, *Meḥkarim ba-Sifrut ha-Ivrit shel Yemei ha-Beynayim* [Studies in Hebrew Literature of the Middle Ages] (Jerusalem, 1965), pp. 157–8.
165. See below, note 178 on the *Theology of Aristotle*.
166. In the book *Ḥeshek Shlomo*, Oxford MS 1535, fol. 163v, he says: "And as in the words of the sage Ibn Ezra, who is worthy to be called a sage."

167. See Idel, "Curriculum," pp. 309–10, n. 64.
168. On the influence of Al-Batalyusi on Alemanno, see D. Kaufmann, *Die Spuren Albataljussis in der jüdischen Religionsphilosophie* (Leipzig, 1880), pp. 56–60. See also, M. Idel "Sources," (above, note 149), pp. 160ff. There are more references drawn from the work *Ha-Agulot ha-Ra'ayoniyot* in Alemanno's writings than those noted by Kaufmann.
169. See for example *Sefer Ḥai Olamim*, Mantua MS 21, fol. 14v. and 215r and others. On the different versions of this text, see A. Altmann, "The Ladder of Ascension," *Studies in Mysticism Presented to Gershom Scholem* (Jerusalem, 1967), p. 8, n. 28, and pp. 10–11.
170. For example see *Collectanaea*, Oxford MS 2234, f. 186v–187v.
171. See note 164 above. See D. Kaufmann, *Meḥkarim ba-Sifrut ha-Ivrit shel Yemei ha-Beinayim* (Jerusalem 1962), pp. 78–125. The passage published on pp. 106–112 from Paris MS 301 is taken from the untitled work of Alemanno which is to be found in Paris MS 849 (new listing). Kaufmann did not know of Alemanno's authorship. The material in Kaufmann, *Studies*, pp. 112–181 is from Alemanno's *Collectanaea*. In the copying of the material from the *Collectanaea* several errors, at times very significant ones, were made in the text.
172. Mantua MS 21, f. 22v. See the first entry in this text.
173. Munich MS 59, f. 87v. The passage and its context parallel a discussion in the book *Ḥai Olamim;* see M. Steinschneider, *Alfarabi* (St. Petersburg, 1869) p. 249. Compare to Paris MS 849, fol. 124v and to my discussion below of the statement in the Paris manuscript.
174. Oxford MS 1535, f. 145v–146r.
175. On the similarity of the passage in the *Heptaplus* VI:4 to the first paragraph of *Sefer ha-Sibot*, see O. Bardenhewer, *Die pseudo-Aristotelische Schrift über das reine Gute* (Freiburg, 1882), p. 301. This fact passed unnoticed by the editors of Pico's works. It should be noted that the phrasing of Pico differs from that of the Latin translation of *Liber de Causis*.
176. See the evidence of Giovanni Francesco Pico della Mirandola, *Opera Omnia* (Basel, 1573) p. 1371. The *Heptaplus* was written in 1488 in the same year that Alemanno reports that he had contacts with Pico.
177. See *Collectanaea*, Oxford MS 2234, f. 21v; Paris MS 849, ff. 91r–v and 123r; *Sefer Ḥeshek Shlomo*, Berlin MS 832, f. 83r. In Abulafia and in several of Alemanno's quotations the passage is quoted as *Sefer ha-Atzamim ha-Elyonim*. This passage was published by Steinschneider, *Alfarabi*, pp. 114f.
178. *Collectanaea*, Oxford MS 2234, f. 71v. There Alemanno copied the passages from *Sefer ha-Ma'alot* (Berlin, 1872) which were attributed to Aristotle. One passage found in *Sefer ha-Ma'alot*, pp. 22f parallels the *Theology of Aristotle* I, 1–29 (-*Ennead* IV, 8, 6, 1). Alemanno also made use of this passage in the book *Einei ha'Eda*, Jerusalem MS 598, f. 98r. Another passage is to be found in *Sefer ha-Ma'alot*, p. 26f and parallels the *Theology*, VII, 41–50 (-*Ennead* IV, 8, 8, 1–23). Alemanno also integrates this

material within the text of *Sefer Einei ha-Eda,* Jerusalem MS 598, f. 99v.
On Alemanno's confusion of the *Sefer ha-Ma'alot* with the *Reshit Ḥokhma,*
see M. Steinschneider, *Die hebraischen Übersetzungen,* p. 243 n. 973.
Alemanno was also familiar with the tradition of Aristotle's repentance
which was apparently connected with the attribution of the *Theology* to
Aristotle. This tradition appears in Rabbi Joseph ibn Shem Tov's commentary on *Ethics;* see Oxford MS 1267, f. 171v. It is quoted in Alemanno's
Collectanaea, f. 50r and in a note to *Sefer Ḥeshek Shlomo,* MS Moscow, f.
105r. On this tradition see S. Munk, *Mélanges de philosophie juive et
arabe* (Paris, 1953), p. 249, n. 3.
179. In the *Collectanaea,* MS Oxford 2234, f. 72r a comment appears with the
attribution "from a commentary on *Kuzari.* . . ." This comment concerns
the ascent of the soul in a version similar to that of Moses ibn Ezra in the
book *Arugat ha-Bosem* as published in *Zion* 2 (1842), p. 121. This parallels a passage in *Sefer ha-Ma'alot,* p. 22. Concerning the content and
literary history of this passage, see A. Altmann and S. M. Stern, *Isaac
Israeli* (Oxford, 1958) pp. 191–2.
180. See *Collectanaea,* Oxford MS 2234, f. 140r–v which parallels *Sefer Reshit
Ḥokhma* (Berlin, 1902), p. 77.
181. See Idel, "Curriculum," p. 306, n. 32.
182. Oxford MS 2234, f. 22r.
183. Ibid., f. 125r.
184. In the marginal note at the bottom of f. 210r of *Sefer Ḥeshek Shlomo,*
Moscow MS 140, Plotinus is described as the disciple of "Orieno," that is
of Origen. It seems that this is a corruption of the authentic tradition that
both Plotinus and Origen were disciples of Ammonius Saccas.
185. See Pico, *Opera Omnia* (Basel, 1557), p. 328.
186. Also compare to Alemanno's comment on the page margin of *Sefer Ḥeshek
Shlomo,* Moscow MS 140, f. 105r. There he states that Mani and Porphyry
desired to obliterate the Torah.
187. In his letter to the worthies of Florence published by S. Asaf, *Sefer Minḥa
le-David* [Hebrew] (Jerusalem, 1935), p. 227. For the Renaissance background of this quotation and the one following it see Scholem, "Anfänge
der christlichen Kabbalah," pp. 192f.
188. *Magen David,* Montefiore MS 290, f. 25 published by Schechter, "Notes
sur David Messer Leon," *REJ* 24(1892), p. 122.
189. Ed. I. D. Reggio (Vienna, 1833), p. 48.
190. No serious attempt has been made to discover which work Del Medigo
has in mind here. See Reggio's notes ad loc.; Ruderman, "Abraham Farissol," p. 75, and D. Geffen, "Faith and Reason in Elijah del Medigo's
Beḥinat Ha-Dat and the Philosophic Backgrounds of the Work," (Ph.D.
diss., Columbia University, 1970), pp. 435f. (who did not discuss the
matter although he had seen the discussion of Kabbalah contained in the
commentary on *etzem ha-galgal*).
191. Paris MS 968, f. 41r–v. Comp. Bohdan Kieszkowski, "Les rapports entre

Elie del Medigo et Pic de la Mirandole," *Rinascimento* 4 (1964), pp. 58–61; F. Secret, *Les kabbalistes chrétiens de la Renaissance* (Paris, 1964), pp. 30–1 and 42, n. 24.

192. This passage concerns a kabbalistic conception in which *Ein Sof* is identical with the Supreme Crown (*Keter*, the first *Sefira*). The most important exponent of this idea in the Spanish school was Rabbi Joseph Gikatilla. Two kabbalistic contemporaries of Del Medigo in Italy also held this view: Rabbi Elijah ben Benjamin of Genazzano, the author of *Sefer Igeret Ha-mudot* and the Spanish kabbalist, Rabbi Isaac ben Samuel Mar Ḥayyim who lived in Naples at a period when Del Medigo was writing *Sefer Beḥinat Ha-Dat*. In his composition Del Medigo demonstrates a familiarity with the dispute over the problem of the identity of *Ein Sof* with the Supreme Crown.

193. Chapter 4.

194. On the ancient theology, see D. P. Walker, *Studies in Christian Platonism from the Fifteenth to the Eighteenth Century* (Duckworth, 1972), pp. 1–131 and Ch. B. Schmitt, "Perennial Philosophy: From Agostino Steuco to Leibniz," *Journal of the History of Ideas* 27 (1966), pp. 505–31. Alemanno makes much use of this term and its place in Alemanno's writings deserves a special study.

195. This is also true of David Messer Leon whose knowledge of Kabbalah was quite limited. He tried as far as possible to reconcile Kabbalah with reason. See Schechter's article, note 188 above, pp. 125f. A portion of the kabbalistic material found in *Sefer Magen David* was copied from Rabbi Isaac Mar Ḥayyim as Gottlieb established. See his *Studies,* pp. 404–22.

196. See Vajda, "Samuel ibn Motot" p. 35.

197. Neither Bardenhewer in his edition of *Liber de Causis* nor Dodds in his edition of Proclus' *Elements of Theology* comments upon the literary history of this other version of Proclus which found its way to Pico. I do not know of another source which attributes the *Liber de Causis* to Abucatem Avenam. It is possible that this is a corruption of the name Abu Nasir Alfarabi who was thought to be the author of the work. See Bardenhewer's remarks in his edition of *Liber de Causis,* pp. 309f. It is noteworthy that the third thesis based on *Liber de Causis* parallels what is quoted in the *Heptaplus* in content but not in language, see above.

198. E. Wind, *Pagan Mysteries in the Renaissance* (Penguin Books, 1967) pp. 134, 174.

199. Wirszubski, *A Christian Kabbalist,* pp. 16–8. The passage discussed by Wind is well interpreted by the thesis that Wirzubski analyzed. Both scholars however did not perceive the connection between these two discussions by Pico. I hope to elaborate on the subject in a later article.

200. *Sefer Minḥat Yehuda* in *Sefer Ma'arekhet ha-Elohut* (Mantua, 1558), f. 41b–42a. This passage is quoted without attribution of the author or work. Such is the case in Alemanno's *Collectanaea,* Oxford MS 2234, f.

158r. On Alemanno and Rabbi Judah Ḥayyat see the appendix to my article, "Curriculum," pp. 330–1.

201. BT *Rosh ha-Shana*, f. 32a.

202. *Sefer Yetzira* 1:5.

203. Paris MS 849, f. 123a. On *Sefer ha-Atzamim ha-Elyonim* which is but another title of *Sefer ha-Sibot*, see note 177 above.

204. Paris MS 849, f. 91v.

205. *Sefer ha-Ma'arekhet*, f. 82b. Compare what is said in Paris MS 859, f. 29b with Vatican MS 428, f. 55r ("Not a single allusion to the First Cause is to be found in the Torah") and with the statements in a commentary on the ten *Sefirot*, Vatican MS 224, f. 121r.

206. The commentary on *etzem ha-galgal* was completed as of 1485 and it is possible that Alemanno was familiar with it. See Steinschneider, "Elia del Medigo," *H.B.* 21 (1881–2), p. 68. It is significant that the work *Beit Ya'ar ha-Levanon* of Abraham Yagel contains a broader discussion of negative theology than that found in Alemanno. Yagel compares the kabbalistic concept of *Ein Sof* with the passage from *Sefer ha-Sibot* that Alemanno cited from the work of Abulafia on the one hand, and with the Hermetic conception on the other. Alemanno's comparison of *Ein Sof* and the First Cause of *Sefer ha-Sibot* served as an inspiration for Yagel's discussion. On the subject of negative theology and its relation to the concept of *Ein Sof* see also *Sefer Sha'ar ha-Shamayim* of Abraham Herrera, part IV, ch. 4.

207. *Sefer Ma'arekhet ha-Elohut*, p. 44.

208. As to the identity of the person whom he names "the author of the tract," ff. 41r and 42v, see Gottlieb, *Studies*, p. 430, n. 25 who suggests Rabbi Elijah of Genazzano.

209. Paris MS 849, fol. 124v.

210. Alemanno tends to remove dictations from the Zohar from Ḥayyat's writings and also to replace Ḥayyat's mythical expressions with philosophical formulations. For example Ḥayyat writes: "All the *Sefirot* ascend to it *(Keter)* to receive a reward." Alemanno's version reads "that all of them ascend to the Supreme Crown and the Supreme Crown receives efflux and existence from *Ein Sof*." The replacement of the expression "to receive a reward" by "receives efflux and existence" is evidence of Alemanno's trend of thought.

211. See *Sefer Ma'arekhet ha-Elohut*, f. 114r.

212. See Idel, "Curriculum," Appendix, pp. 330–1.

213. See Munich MS 285, f. 3a–b.

214. *Sefer Ma'arekhet ha-Elohut*, f. 3b.

215. Berlin MS 832, f. 83a–b.

216. For Rabbi Moses Narboni's opinion on the subject, see A. Altmann, "Moses Narboni's Epistle on Shiur Qoma," *Jewish Medieval and Renaissance Studies* (ed. A. Altmann, Cambridge, Mass., 1967), pp. 243–5.

Rabbi Abraham ben Eliezer ha-Levi, Alemanno's contemporary, writes that "In the opinion of several of our contemporary Spanish sages who pursue philosophical studies there are ten spiritual degrees called angels . . . and they say that these degrees are the ten *Sefirot.*" *Sefer Masoret ha-Hokhma,* ed. G. Scholem, *Kiryat Sefer* 2 (1925), p. 126.

217. In the section omitted, Alemanno quotes Aristotle's *Metaphysics* M (13) 1084, which deals with the numbers and ideas. Alemanno refers to the Platonic concept that these are corresponding ideas for only the numbers 1–10, which Aristotle mentioned in order to refute it. On the views of Plato and Aristotle on the ideal numbers, see L. Robin, *La théorie platonicienne des idées et des nombres d'après Aristote* (Hildesheim, 1963), pp. 267 ff. On the comparison between Pythagorean numbers and the *Sefirot,* see also Simone Luzzatto in the reference found in note 52 above.

218. See note 213 above.

219. On the similarity of Plato and the Prophets see *Sefer Hashek Shlomo,* Oxford MS 1535, f. 162v and on, and also Idel, "Curriculum," pp. 325, 331–2, nn. 55–56.

220. See *Shir ha-Ma'alot,* Oxford MS 1535, f. 63r–v. In another part of *Heshek Shlomo,* Moscow MS 140, f. 23r, Alemanno speaks of "the forms which ascend from form to form in order until they come to the First Form which is the Form of all Forms, for It is the Form of the World in entirety, for all of them (the forms) are made for Its purpose, for they have no other purpose but to imitate those abiding forms which are in Him all together in the simplest most excellent and most encompassing and eternal manner possible." On the forms in God, see Simon van den Bergh, *Averroes: Tahafut al Tahafut* (Oxford, 1954), II, pp. 88–9. On the form of the body limbs and their connection to the stars, see F. Cumont, "Astrologia," *Révue archéologique* 3(1916), pp. 7–10; A Sharf, *The Universe of Shabbetai Donnolo* (Warminster, 1976), pp. 52ff.

221. I am not familiar with any such opinion in Alfarabi. However, in *Sefer Takhlit he-Hakham,* Munich MS 214, f. 46r–47v, the twenty-eight encampments of the moon are mentioned and the author notes that this is the opinion of the Indians. On the Indians and records of the twenty-eight encampments and their literary history, see M. Plessner, "Hermes Trismegistus and Arab Science," *Studia Islamica* 2 (1954), pp. 57f; Cornelius Agrippa, *De occulta philosophia,* II, ch. 33.

222. See paragraph 5 of *Sefer ha-Sibot* which is the paragraph quoted by Alemanno from *Imrei Shefer:* "For what is possessed by the effect is also possessed by the cause, but in the cause it is of a more exalted, worthy and superior way;" Paris MS 849, f. 91v. See also paragraphs 7 and 11 of *Sefer ha-Sibot* and Pico's first thesis in the "Secundum Proclum."

223. Yagel changed the wording of Agrippa who claimed that this was the opinion of all the Platonists. Among the Neoplatonist thinkers it seems

that Agrippa's statement most closely resembles the conception of Proclus. The idea that in the world of archetypes "all is in all" has parallels in the *Elements of Theology* of Proclus, sentences 170, 173, 176.

224. Cf. the opinion of Pico on the elements expressed in the *Theses* and *Heptaplus*, Wirszubski's description of this passage in *A Christian Kabbalist*, pp. 35–6, and also F. H. Gombrich, "Icones Symbolicae: The Visual Image in Neoplatonic Thought," *JWCI* II (1948), pp. 167–8. The remarks of both authors mentioned above are supplemented by Pico's comment in his commentary on the *Canzone de Amore* of G. Benivieni, ch. 12. See also M. Idel, "Prometheus in Jewish Garb" [Hebrew], *Eshkolot*, n.s., 5–6 (1980–81), pp. 124–5.

225. In a section found before this discussion.

226. F. 164a.

227. F. 89b.

228. Oxford MS 1304, f. 10v. In the continuation Yagel reaches certain conclusions about the possibility of magic practices which are based upon the correspondences between the different levels of reality.

229. Ibid., f. 10r. Again the source for Yagel's statement is to be found in Agrippa, *De occulta philosophia* I, ch. 11: "Platonici omnia inferiora ferunt esse ideata a superioribus ideis: ideam autem definiunt esse formam supra corpora animas mentes, unam simplicem puram immutabilem incorporem at aeternam; atque eandem idearum omnium esse naturam, ponunt autem ideas primo in ipso quidem bono, hoc est Deo, per cause modum solum." Compare also *De occulta philosophia* III, ch. 10.

230. The elevation of the Platonic ideas to a level higher than that of the separate intelligences also appears in the writings of Yagel's contemporary, Rabbi Judah Moscato in *Nefutzot Yehuda*, sermon 8 (Lwow, 1859), ff. 33b–34a. Moscato follows Pico and calls the place of the ideas by the name "The First Creature." However, in Moscato one does not find the identification of *Sefirot* with Ideas. On this sermon see Y. Dan, "Hebrew Homiletical Literature in Renaissance Italy" [Hebrew], *Proceedings of the Sixth World Congress of Jewish Studies* (Jerusalem, 1977), pp. 107f. The term "first creature" is common in the writings of Rabbi Isaac ibn Latif whose writings were known both to Pico and to Moscato. Yagel knew Moscato; see *Beit Ya'ar ha-Levanon*, Oxford MS 1306, f. 23r.

231. See H. A. Wolfson, "Extradeical and Intradeical Interpretations of Platonic Ideas," *Religious Philosophy* (Cambridge, Mass., 1965), p. 37.

232. (Venice, 1574), f. 12d.

233. Florence, Laurenziana, Plut. II, 38, f. 91v. The passage also appears in a later version of this composition in Munich MS 49, f. 38v.

234. Compare to the statement of Rabbi Yeḥi'el Nissim of Pisa in the book *Minḥat Kena'ot* (Berlin, 1898), p. 49: "Everything possesses a power proper to itself which is the cause of its existence and being. For this reason Plato inclined to this opinion when he propounded his general principles

called forms." See also ibid., pp. 53 and 84. In another article I will discuss the connection between Rabbi Yeḥi'el and Rabbi Mordekhai Rossillo.

235. See *Sefer Me'or Einayim, Imrei Bina,* ch. 4. See also the statements of Simone Luzzatto in his *Ma'amar al Yehudei Venetziya* [Hebrew: *Discourse on the Jews of Venice*] (Jerusalem, 1950), pp. 144–5; for the original Italian see note 52 above.

236. On the opinion of Ficino see, E. F. Rice, *The Renaissance Idea of Wisdom* (Cambridge, Mass., 1958), pp. 61ff. On Pico's view see *Commento sopra Canzone de Amore Composta de Girolamo Benivieni,* ch. 12.

237. See G. Scholem, "Was Israel Sarug a Disciple of the Ari?" [Hebrew] *Zion* 5 (1930), pp. 214–43. See also, Scholem's essay *Avraham Cohen Herrera, Ba'al Sha'ar ha-Shamayim: Ḥayyav, Yetzirato ve-Hashpa'ato* [Abraham Cohen Herrera, Author of *Shaar he-Shamayaim:* his Life, his Works and their Influence] (Jerusalem, 1978), pp. 34–46.

238. This follows Scholem's opinion in his essay *Abraham Cohen Herrera,* pp. 35f.

239. See *Sefer Nefutzot Yehuda,* sermon 31 (Warsaw, 1871), p. 80a. The definition offered by Moscato has as its source a twelfth-century work, *Liber XXIV Philosophorum;* see C. Baumkehr, *Das pseudo-hermetische Buch der XXIV. Meister* (Münster, 1937), p. 208. On the dissemination of this concept see D. Mahnke, *Unendliche Sphäre und Allmittelpunkt* (Halle, 1937). This may be supplemented by Yates, *Giordano Bruno,* p. 247; H. Wirszubski, "Francesco Giorgio's commentary on Giovanni Pico's Kabbalistic Theses," *JWCI* 27 (1974), p. 154; and G. Poulet, *The Metamorphoses of the Circle* (Baltimore, 1966), pp. 1–14.

240. The term "the divine circle" appears already in the book *Beḥinat Olam* of Rabbi Yedaya ha-Penini as David Kaufmann already noted, "Die Spuren al-Batlajusis in der juedischen Religions philosophie," *Jahresbericht der landes-Rabbinerschule in Budapest* 3 (1880): 64. However, Moscato's conception differs absolutely from that of Al-Batalyusi. The conception of the intellectual circle appears in the writings of Renaissance authors as I have shown in my article, "Sources" (note 149 above). See also I. E. Barzilay, *Between Reason and Faith* (The Hague and Paris, 1967), p. 175.

241. In *Sefer Sha'arei Tzedek* of Rabbi Joseph Gikatilla I did not find the same wording as in Moscato, although the idea is to be found in Gikatilla's writings. See Gottlieb, *Studies,* p. 152 and note 158. I do not know of any use of the word "soḥaret" as a term for *Keter.*

242. Highly significant is the fact that anti-philosophical attitudes are held by supporters of the printing of the *Zohar.* Cf. Y. Tishby, "The Polemic on the Book of the *Zohar* in the Sixteenth Century in Italy" [Hebrew], *Perakim, Yearbook of the Schocken Institute* (1966–7), pp. 180–1.

5

The Place of the *Dialoghi d'amore* in Contemporaneous Jewish Thought

Arthur M. Lesley

Study of the *Dialoghi d'amore* has naturally concentrated on its contribution to Renaissance Platonism in philosophy, poetry, and the visual arts, but enough remains unexplained in the peculiar syncretism of the work to justify an attempt to reconstruct its original setting and meaning.[1] The posthumous success of the work with a wide audience, in Italian, Latin, Spanish, and French, tends to obscure the question of why it was written in Hebrew, for a Jewish audience, over thirty years before its publication in Italian. The success of the work in addressing a European audience has led analysis of it to focus on remote, classical sources —Aristotle, Plato, and Plotinus—rather than on the topics of discussion among Jews in Italy during the 1490s. Until the original setting of the *Dialoghi* can be reconstructed, it will be appropriate to say of its author, Yehuda Abravanel (Leone Ebreo), what his character Philo says to Sophia about Aristotle: 'i libri suoi erano editi e non editi: editi solamente a quegli che gli hanno intesi da esso.' ('his books, though published, were not public, but public only to those who heard him interpret them').[2]

The general neglect of the origins of the *Dialoghi d'amore* has been broken only by examination of the sparse evidence for the biography of the author and by speculation on which language was 'lingua sua,' the

Reprinted by permission of Dovehouse Editions Canada from *Ficino and Renaissance Neoplatonism*, edited by Konrad Eisenbichler and Olga Zorzi Pugliese, University of Toronto Italian Studies 1, Toronto, 1986.

one in which he composed the work.[3] By taking as axiomatic the conclusion of Carlo Dionisotti and Isaiah Sonne, that the *Dialoghi* were written in Hebrew, around 1502, the original significance of the work, the reaction of its original audience, and the reasons for its neglect until the 1535 printing all begin to be tractable questions.

As will be seen, both the date and the language of Dionisotti's conclusion conform to the contents of the work and to a reasonable reconstruction of its purpose. Neither a Latin, Italian, Spanish, or French work would have been addressed to a Jewish community at that time and, at a later time, this kind of Hebrew work would not have been attempted. The hostile response to the *Dialoghi* that is found in a Hebrew letter of 1506, as will be seen, indicates the lively, albeit antagonistic, interest that it aroused among Jews at that time. Only a work written in Hebrew would have raised a challenge to Jewish thought sufficient to provoke such opposition: a vernacular work, one addressed to Christians, could have been ignored. And if a vernacular *Dialoghi* had been written at this early date, its thirty years of obscurity would be even more difficult to explain than the oblivion of the Hebrew one.

It is worth recalling the function of Hebrew for Jewish communities. Although Hebrew was not the exclusive spoken language of any Jewish community between the time of the Mishnah (200 C.E.) and twentieth-century Israel, it continued to be the learned language, parallel to Latin, as well as the language of Bible study and prayer, for all European Jewish communities. The extent of the use of Hebrew for scholarship is indicated by the fact that translations of Averroes, Avicenna, and other philosophers were being made for Giovanni Pico della Mirandola, Domenico Grimani, and others, from Hebrew translations.[4]

Original works, of course, continued to be written in Hebrew. Abraham Farissol records having participated in a series of religious debates with a Dominican and a Franciscan at the Este court in Ferrara in 1487. In response to their requests, he supplied them with a copy of his arguments 'in their language,' but only after writing them in Hebrew.[5] In contrast, Jewish works in the vernacular were rare at this time. Later, in 1550, Samuel Usque wrote a major work, *Consolation for the Tribulations of Israel,* in Portuguese, but this, like other Portuguese writings of that time for Jews, was addressed to those who had been Christians, entirely out of touch with Hebrew for two or three generations. Also, by that time the vernacular languages had greatly increased their capacity to deal with subjects that previously had been treated only in Latin.

In addition to these arguments for a Hebrew original of the *Dialoghi d'amore*, there may also be cited the five Italian manuscripts of the third dialogue that have recently been discovered. One, discussed by Dionisotti, and the other four, which so far have not been described, are apparently all different from each other and from the printed text, but differ only stylistically, as would different translations, rather than in content.[6] With greater probability on the side of a Hebrew original than of any other, most of our attention may be concentrated on the circumstances that confirm the date of 1502, found in the text, as accurate for the composition of the work.

Recent study of the several currents of Jewish intellectual life in late fifteenth-century Italy makes it possible to situate the *Dialoghi d'amore* within the particular circumstances of Jewish thought of the time; to recover, in Hebrew terms, the generic identification of the work; and, with the evidence of a Hebrew letter from 1506, to reconstruct some of the reasons for the oblivion into which the work fell until Christians in Rome published it and gave it a place in European literature.

The place of the *Dialoghi* in Hebrew discourse obviously is connected with the social and political circumstances of the Jews in Italy, the major features of which ought to be kept in mind. At the end of the fifteenth century, Jews were scattered along the northern half of the Italian peninsula, in a wide variety of jurisdictions. Except for the old Jewish settlements in Sicily, Naples, and Rome, Jews were, north of Rome, in new, impermanent settlements of dozens of persons, rather than larger numbers. During the fourteenth century, local authorities in those regions had begun to allow Jews to resettle for short periods, which could be renewed or discontinued, for the purpose of carrying on loan-banking. The household of each loan-banker could include a miniature Jewish community of teachers, servants, butcher, and physician, along with the extended family of the banker. During the sixteenth century some of these new settlements established more formal communal institutions, as they became more permanent. A further complication for these Jewish communities was the heterogeneity of their population. Although some were composed mainly of southern Italian Jews, and others, of German Jews, there was an increasing mixture of migrants, notably those who had been expelled from France, Provence, and Spain. The sudden expulsion of 150,000 Jews from Spain in 1492 led to a considerable period of Jewish migration, and thousands passed through Italy and settled there. They were culturally distinct and had to be integrated into the communities in which they settled.

The differences between all these groups included such things as the language of daily speech, customs, educational traditions, and methods of applying Jewish law. All Jewish communities would share study of the Bible and rabbinic literature, as well as preaching and the practice of making legal decisions, but beyond these fundamentals there was great variety. Several 'national' groups of Jews had philosophical traditions, which continued the Arabic transmission of the Aristotelian canon, commentaries, and methods. Maimonides was the central Jewish philosopher, Averroes the most important commentator on Aristotle, and the Christian scholastics were increasingly studied.[7] Other communities ignored or suppressed philosophy. Some had one or several schools of Cabala practiced among them. In addition to these divergences among Jews from different regions outside Italy, there were distinctive Italian practices. One distinctive Italian Jewish development was a humanist movement, based upon the adaptation of Latin rhetoric to the Hebrew Bible. Unlike both philosophers and Cabalists, the Hebrew rhetoricians discussed all topics before any audience, instead of restricting their teaching to the initiated.

The political situation which the demographic, economic, and cultural circumstances created was dominated by four critical necessities. The existence of each Jewish community in Italy, and indeed of all of them together, in the era of total expulsion from Spain, France, Provence, and Portugal, depended on the ability of representatives of the Jews in conducting relations with the Italian authorities. Equally fundamental was the need to estabish legitimate leadership in communities where there could be no traditional leadership. Closely related to this was the necessity of conciliating, if not integrating, diverse populations within particular communities. Finally, these scattered and weak Jewish communities needed to communicate with others and to establish means for coordinating intercommunal relations, both for dealing with Italian authorities and for establishing lines of authority and obligation in such matters as religious law. These political considerations were a factor in intellectual life as well. Appropriate learning was a characteristic of an authoritative figure in what was, in a way, a society of tiny courts in the shadow of the neighbouring Italian courts. Wealth, ancestry, learning, and influence with the authorities gained ascendancy among Jewish communities. Any literary composition by a member of the élite was, then, a political as well as an erudite gesture.

This factor must be considered in understanding the reaction to the *Dialoghi d'amore*. Yehuda Abravanel, as a learned physician with eminent clients, as a member of a wealthy, well-placed family, as an exile from Portugal and Spain, and as the son of the outstanding Biblical commentator and leader of the Spanish Jews, was a candidate for influence among Jews in Italy. Precisely where the intellectual tendency of the *Dialoghi* would place him among the various communities and schools of thought will be apparent after these have been represented by their self-characterizations and by descriptions of them provided by their rivals.

Polemical occasions, on which spokesmen for each group define themselves and their opponents, are generally revealing. It is important to note whom they are criticizing and excluding from conciliation, as well as what they consider to be the core of their own teachings. The dispute which provided the basis for the following survey of Jewish intellectual life occurred in 1490–91, just before Yehuda Abravanel and his father arrived in Naples in 1492. This dispute is particularly interesting because it may well have been provoked by the appearance of the Hebrew work that bears the closest resemblance to the *Dialoghi*.

Elijah del Medigo (c. 1460–93), a rabbi and physician from Candia, Crete, was Giovanni Pico's first Hebrew consultant, beginning in Padua in 1481.[8] In his *Examination of Religion,* written in December 1490, del Medigo identifies himself as a Maimonidean of the Averroist school, whose major interests are metaphysics, natural science, and logic. As he wrote to Pico, 'I have no stronger desire than to leave behind a student who is truly knowledgeable and understands the teachings of the peripatetics; and I believe that this desire will be realizd by you.[9] Del Medigo explains frequently that this professional interest does not lead to conflicts with Jewish study of the Bible and rabbinic writings, because the topics of discussion and the methods of each discipline are distinct:

I do not think that the words of the Torah are explained through the method of philosophy, nor does the former [Torah] need the latter [philosophy]. No one thinks this way, according to my point of view, except for someone who is neither an adherent of Torah nor a philosopher. . . . Moreover, no one would think me in error because in my philosophic works I deal with the philosophers according to their methodology.[10]

Del Medigo's 'modified version of the double-truth theory' asserts that reason and revelation do not contradict each other on basic principles, but that if there is an apparent contradiction, reason must concede the point to revelation. Del Medigo respects the distinct methods of both rabbinic legal reasoning and the demonstrative, syllogistic proofs of physics. The way to avoid apparent conflicts between the two is to employ only the proper method of each field for studying its canonical texts and subject matter.

> Therefore my way differs from that of many self-styled philosophers of our people, who teach the meanings of the Torah and science and mix together the two disciplines, the religious and the speculative methods, the general and the specific, as if to be mediators between the religionists and the philosophers . . . with the result that these men are neither Torah scholars nor scientists. I think that they were brought to this by hatred of the other sects and their explanations. They are, nevertheless, worthy to be given the benefit of the doubt, since they seem only to want to magnify the Torah . . . and since their statements are much closer to rational study, and thus they leave a place for reason, and do not reject it, as do some from the other sects.[11]

Del Medigo's insistence on the appropriateness of the method of study to its particular subject directly opposes, it should be noted, the specific virtue of rhetoric, namely its applicability to all topics.

Del Medigo attacks the Cabalists most forcefully, especially in a letter to Pico, where he is trying to dissuade his student from pursuing his interest in 'isto benedicto Chabala,' a phrase in which more than one scholar has found the word 'benedicto' to be sarcastic.[12] He also criticizes " 'a few people, [who] from their love of Plato's method" use the demonstrations of Aristotle to explain the riddles of Plato, . . . because they think that there is truth in every type of wisdom.'[13] To emphasize the philosophic calm that his beliefs allow him, del Medigo caricatures the other sects as brawlers:

> The people of this sect [Cabalists] call the other sect [mediators] heretics and raise their confused alarms among the masses; and the sect of the self-styled philosophers say that the Cabalists are stupid fools, who extinguish the light of the Torah. And hatred has been great . . . especially among the ignorant of the two sects, so that the Torah has almost been made into many Torahs.[14]

At the end of *The Examination of Religion,* del Medigo recommends that the authorities of the Jewish community condemn to death, apparently as equivalent to false prophets, 'those who reveal the secret of God to those who are unfit to know it,'[15] that is, those who publicize and perhaps print syncretistic or Cabalistic teachings, especially explanations for divine commandments. It is worth noting that del Medigo's offence is also a defence; he appears to have been subjected to criticism for having printed scientific works in Latin.[16]

Spokesmen for del Medigo's opponents, either explicitly or by implication, were also each defending a valuable principle, against his principle of *Lehrfreiheit.* In 1491 the Cabalist Rabbi Isaac Mar Ḥayyim wrote to Isaac da Pisa, a member of the outstanding Jewish banking family in Florence, on a disputed fine point of Cabala, to advocate subjugating rational investigation to the presumed relevation of Cabala:

I do not admonish you, my lord, who are wise as an angel, but remind, that since you are investigating these things, you must not follow those scholars who make reason the root and interpret the words of Cabala in a manner conforming to speculation, rather, you must make Cabala the root, and try to make reason conform to it.[17]

These remarks can be understood as referring to those whom del Medigo called 'mediators,' and a recent investigator has identified the culprit in question as a scholar in da Pisa's household, Yohanan Alemanno, who will be discussed shortly.

In addition to dedicated Averroists and uncompromising Cabalists, there were moralists who traced the troubles of the Jews to philosophy. Yosef Yavets, an exile from Spain who was among those associated with Isaac Abravanel in Naples, developed the argument in his *Or ha-Ḥayyim (The Light of Life).* He particularly attacks the philosophers for their double truth:

They, 'the blind,' interpret David's admonition to Solomon, 'And thou, Solomon my son, know thou the God of thy father' (I Chronicles 28:9) as if addressed only to Solomon, distinct from the whole mass of Israelites. This is supposedly knowledge of God gained by demonstration, which the mass cannot attain. Why did these fools not look at the end of the same verse, 'and serve [la'avod] Him [with a whole heart and a wiling mind]'? Perhaps they misread it as, 'and destroy [le'abed] Him—God forbid![18]

Yavets continues in the next chapter:

We were commanded not to go after the reasonings of opinion. Know, my son, that just as we were commanded not to pursue the appetites of our instincts, but rather to do the commandments of our blessed God, so were we commanded not to go along the paths of syllogisms, as our reason is inclined to do. For just as the evil impulse naturally loves to commit transgressions and despises commandments of prohibitions, . . . just so, human reason misleads man naturally, and loves the concepts that it understands, meanwhile despising the veracious opinions of the Torah, the beliefs in reward and punishment, divine revelation, resurrection of the dead, and a great day of judgment, which are contrary to rational proof. Therefore a person must accustom himself to being mindful of the commandments, which are divine concepts, in order to be rescued from the ambush of the human reason, which lurks in wait for man at all times.[19]

A political angle is revealed in Yavets's contrast between simple, faithful Jews, who will be rewarded with eternal bliss, and the élite, who aspire to conjunction with the active intellect:

If there be by chance, God forbid, some ignorant woman who, barren of wisdom and understanding, is unable to conceive of God but in material terms, but on the other hand scrupulously keeps all the commandments and, never transgressing, longs in her heart for her Creator, being ready to sacrifice her very life for God's Law—and indeed, she did suffer greatly on its account—such a woman is kept in much higher regard by the Lord than all those self-styled, wise intellectuls.[20]

Whether or not this populist model of piety is as accurate a description of events in Spain as some historians credit it to be, its bitterness towards the Spanish élite's intellectuality leaves no room for compromise with rationalists.

These three tendencies—Averroism, Cabalism, and moralism—of which other examples could be given, attempt to avoid a conflict between reason and revelation either by suppressing claimants for the other side, or by isolating reason and revelation from each other. As voices of polarization, they appear difficult to conciliate. It is interesting, however, to note that they agree on blaming the 'mediators,' those described as trying to reconcile reason with revelation, evidently through recourse to rhetorical and Platonic discourse, and through rational examination of the Cabala. These are exactly the qualities that would characterize Yehuda Abravanel's *Dialoghi d'amore,* so whoever was the target for this condemnation in 1491 would be a forerunner of the author of the *Dialoghi.*

In the decade before the composition of the *Dialoghi d'amore,* apparently the most notable violator of the borders between reason and revelation, and the precise target of both del Medigo and Mar Ḥayyim was Yohanan Alemanno. Alemanno (1433/4–c. 1504), a physician, rabbi, biblical commentator, teacher, Cabalist, and philosopher, was Pico's other long-time Jewish collaborator. Apparently descended from the last Rabbi of Paris before the expulsion in 1394, Alemanno was active in Padua, Mantua, Florence, and possibly Bologna. He was acquainted with Agostino Nifo, Alberto Pio, and the Mantuan humanist magician, Paride da Ceresara; and Alemanno's son, Isaac, was Gianfrancesco Pico's Hebrew teacher.[21] Alemanno's own statements candidly identify him as one of the 'mediators' whom del Medigo blamed:

> How well I know that they will say, 'This one explicitly leaves the paradise of scientific philosophy, without arriving at the speech of a mystic. Where, then, is he?' Necessity has forced me, in explaining this Song of Songs, to leave the ways of philosophy, for it belongs to a different world and to a different science. For the hearts of the ancients are like the gate to a hall, and if they are like mystic angels, we are like human scientists. It is therefore inescapably necessary to rise to the wave of mysticism and Cabala, because this Song is of this genre, as Moses of Narbonne, the first among the latter-day scientists said. . . . [On the meaning of the sacrifices in the Bible, we must follow the explanations of the Cabalists.] . . . Necessity has brought me to speak of these ways in a middle manner, between mysticism and science. This I have done by citing proof as far as possible from science, to elucidate mysticism. But on some subjects, this is impossible. I shall therefore do as Averroes did in *The Incoherence of the Incoherence* and Ibn Tufayl, in *The Quality of Attachment*. They say numerous times, 'We refer this matter to prophecy.' For of course the giver of the Torah understood its way, and he and the prophets knew its source. Therefore, our words shall be as if neither scientific nor mystical, but as if on the mean between them.[22]

Alemanno recognizes that this choice of crossing disciplinary boundaries, in the manner of rhetoricians, will make him vulnerable to criticism. He makes it, nevertheless, because he considers the double-truth strategy and the obscurity of technical philosophical discussion to be open to abuse by those who mean to be obscurantists. He equally opposes those philosophers' disregard for kinds of knowledge that are not included in Aristotle's canon:

> For all kinds of wisdom are worthy of study, because they all support each other and are mutually connected . . . for there is no kind of knowledge that has not its hour, and no science that has not its place. . . . who attains felicity will intend

to rise in order, through each science to what is above it ... I shall tell others just what I say to myself: 'Wisdom is one and inclusive.'[23]

He announces his intention of teaching the unified truth to all audiences:

Everything that I see in the clouds will they, the many, also see, unlike their fathers. *They* took the way of the Lord in one manner on earth, but in another manner they went and spoke to the whole people. ... This in one of two ways: either they deliberately hid the light from their neighbors, to rise through obscurity upon their backs, and to subjugate them beneath the soles of their feet; or they imagined to themselves that the great lights would wound the eyes of those here with us today, so that evening shadows and faint images would be better for their health, and to themselves alone they would give the perfect light.[24]

Alemanno's interpretive versatility enables him to recover ancient wisdom. Drawing upon an argument used since Hellenistic times, he asserts that the ancient Israelites possessed all learning from revelation, so that, in his time, it is permissible for Jews to investigate or practise a field that was previously cultivated only by the nations. Alemanno uses the argument, more plausibly than justifiers of philosophy, to justify magic, astrology, alchemy, and the equivalent of what was known among the Christians as the ancient theology. He writes, in a notebook entry that lists his central teachings:

Ancient opinions. They appear new, although they are old and are very useful. ... Clearly a person cannot acquire wisdom unless he rises ... from the wisdom of the moderns to the wisdom of the ancients. ... Not only the doctrines of Aristotle and Plato and their predecessors among the nations; but also the most ancient, such as the teachers of the Talmud and the Mishnah, the prophets and Moses, as well as the patriarchs of the world, such as Abraham, Enoch, Methuselah, Seth and Adam, as far as is possible. The wisdom of the ancients, especially of the ancient Hebrews, is not like the wisdom of modern men. For the ancient wisdom is about matters that are certain, is expressed in a few decisive words about the essence of being, principles and particulars of the sciences, without leaving the slightest doubt in the mind. ... The knowledge of the modern nations is derived from examples, syllogisms and proofs that remain dubious to people, because of the many arguments that support contrary interpretations.[25]

By rendering permissible for Jews any kind of learning, method, or item of information, the invocation of the ancients opposes Jewish scholastic philosophy to teachings, such as Cabala, which can claim great antiquity and the certainty of revelation. The reaction to such a claim by someone like del Medigo is easy to imagine, especially when Alemanno goes on to teach all this to any audience. Instead of excluding any dubious kind of learning from legitimate study, as del Medigo, Yavets, and Mar Ḥayyim do, Alemanno applies a strategy of inclusiveness, which rhetoric makes possible. Just as Moses and the other prophets knew everything through revelation, and taught it through figurative language to all the Israelites and, in theory, to all humanity, Alemanno could do the same through the use of rhetoric.

Aristotle provides the basis for this strategy. In the *Rhetoric* he distinguishes rhetoric from all other arts, each of which

can instruct or persuade about its own particular subject matter. . . . But rhetoric we look upon as the power of observing the means of persuasion on almost any subject presented to us; and that is why we say that, in its technical character, it is not concerned with any special or definite class of subjects. The duty of rhetoric is to deal with such matters as we deliberate upon without arts or systems to guide us, in the hearing of persons who cannot take in at a glance a complicated argument, or follow a long chain of reasoning.[26]

What Alemanno considers the central virtue of rhetoric is what del Medigo considers its greatest danger. It transgresses disciplinary boundaries and then discusses the topics of each discipline for an untrained audience. When the subject is philosophy, the absence of disciplinary terminology, methods, and preparation makes disciplined argument impossible. Del Medigo would respond by saying that what can be understood only in the technical discussion of a distinct discipline must be concealed from general knowledge. The intellectual, political, and 'national' differences between these two distinguished, Padua-educated physicians and rabbis could not be clearer: Alemanno, the philosopher-Cabalist rhetorician, intends to combine wisdom with eloquence to demonstrate the unity of truth to a general audience, whereas del Medigo, the logician, natural scientist, and metaphysician is willing to appeal to the Jewish authorities to suppress those who would contravene the truce of the 'double truth,' and expose his arcane activity to the ignorant scrutiny of the crowd. The Florentine, descended from French and German Jewish 'nobility,' is opposed by the Venetian subject from Crete. This opposition, which would be generally duplicated by the successors of each—Alemanno by Yehuda Abravanel, and del Medigo by Saul Cohen Ashkenazi—obviously makes facile generalizations about 'mediaeval' and 'Renaissance' thinkers inapplicable.

Alemanno employed rhetoric to integrate conclusions from such disparate disciplines as philosophy and Cabala in order, it appears, to unify the diverse Jewish communities of central and northern Italy. Composed of Italian, French, German, and Spanish Jews, whose wide divergences could not be eliminated by suppressing certain tendencies, these communities might be harmoniously unified through an application of the model of Florence under Lorenzo de' Medici. Proud of living in Florence, Alemanno makes an effort to show that he has acquired the virtues of the city, which he actually calls 'the just state,' the goal of mediaeval political thought in the Jewish philosophical tradition: 'From them [the Florentines] I have learned the art of gathering all the opinions scattered in Israel, separated by opposition, and how to unify them in a harmony conducive to the true and the just.[27] Isaac Abravanel similarly preferred republican governments, preeminently Venice, the city in which he spent the last years of his life.[28]

It is Alemanno's commentary on the Song of Songs, *Ḥesheq Shlomo (The Desire of Solomon)*, that provides the best precedent in Hebrew for Yehuda Abravanel's *Dialoghi d'amore*. Alemanno interprets the Song of Songs to be an allegorical dialogue that teaches how to achieve attachment *(Devekut)* to God. The highest means of attaining this attachment is through the *sefira Tiferet*, or Beauty, the seventh of ten divine aspects or emanations, according to one major system of Cabala. Alemanno's commentary on the Song, like the *Dialoghi*, addresses a general Hebrew audience on a wide variety of topics, and in non-technical language proposes solutions from Biblical study and Cabala for complex problems of Averroism. Indeed, it could be said that Alemanno's voluminous commentary on the Song of Songs stands in the same relation to the *Dialoghi* as Marsilio Ficino's commentary on the *Symposium* to his *Platonic Theology*: the commentary on a classical text prepares for systematic study of some of the same questions.

But why should Alemanno's effort have required the development that Abravanel gave it? The answer is that, whereas Alemanno was content to provide, from Jewish sources such as the Song of Songs, an equivalent of the Platonism that Ficino and his colleagues derived from Plato, notably from the *Symposium*, Abravanel had to take up the apologetic task on the basis of the same Platonic texts. The most that Alemanno actually discusses Plato is in invoking his authority from apocryphal statements, such as Plato's concession that he could not understand the Jewish conception of God because it surpassed human capacity.[29] Abravanel, in contrast, must argue with sufficient effectiveness to justify Sofia's remark, 'Mi place vederti fare Platone mosaico e del numero de "cabalisti' " ('I am content that you are able to reconicle Plato's opinion with that of Moses and the Cabbalists').[30] Ficino and Pico made Plato into a support for Christianity; Abravanel had to show that Plato was no less a Jew. And if the Florentines could turn pagan myths into secret avowals of Christian truth, if they christened pagan myths, Abravanel would circumcise them.

It will be necessary to trace the response to Platonism and ancient theology in Alemanno and Abravanel, to show their advancement along the same course. The challenge of Pico's platonizing Cabalism for the sake of Christianity provoked Alemanno to make an analogous combination of Cabala and philosophy, but on the basis of traditional Jewish sources that would yield similar doctrines. Where Pico referred to the *Symposium*, Alemanno referred to the Song of Songs. The correspondence of the biblical to the Platonic book has been explained best in Chaim Wirszubski's studies of Pico's Christian Cabalism:

. . . From this may be derived the conclusion that the divinely inspired Solomon and the divine Plato intended the same meaning. It goes without saying that *mors osculi,* or more precisely, the allegorical interpretation given to death by the kiss, is the connecting link between Plato's *Symposium* and the Song of Songs.[31]

The challenge of Pico's discussion of divine and human love, and Alemanno's response, may be compared with Abravanel's discussion of the topic in the *Dialoghi*.[32] Pico concludes a major part of the argument of the *Heptaplus:*

If what we say is true, that the extremes can be joined together only through the mean: and if that is truly to be called a mean which has already united the extremes in itself; and if that ineffable dispensation by which the Word is made flesh occurs only in Christ: then it is through Christ alone that the flesh can ascend to the Word.[33]

This Christian explanation of the attainment of immortal bliss is, of course, not satisfactory to Alemanno, who, in his various books, finds different solutions to the problems that he shares with Pico. To this justification of the doctrine of Incarnation, Alemanno responds:

We cannot evade the question by asserting that there is no connection of desire [ḥesheq] between God and us, because the prophets have amply asserted that there is one, from each side. Moses wrote, 'Yet it was to your fathers that the Lord was drawn in his passion *[ḥesheq]* for them' (Deuteronomy 10:15). And David wrote, 'Because he hath set his love *[ḥesheq]* upon Me, therefore will I deliver him' (Psalm 91:14). Therefore we cannot deny the existence of this mutual desire, even though we cannot understand its essence, because of the extreme contrast between our nature and the uniqueness of God. This is like what Aristotle says about affection between the beautiful and the ugly; although the ugly one may love the beautiful one only for his beauty, the beautiful one will not love the ugly one, because of his ugliness. Similarly, although we desire God because of His perfection, He will not desire us, because of our imperfection.

If, however, we can show that there is some connection between the separate intellect and the material intellect, we can dispel this perplexity.

Between the extremes of difference between God and us there is a middle term. . . . Let us say, then, that the common or median quality in the desire between God and us, his opposites, is the Good. The good for man is not to become absolutely separated from matter, but only this way to a degree; and the good for God is not—God forbid!—that He become material, but only that His overflow become attached to matter in an attachment that perfects the flaws in everything outside Him.

Alemanno goes on to explain seven means of ascent to the attachment to the good that is common to men and God, and then illustrates them from the life of King Solomon, the presumed author of the Song of Songs, and, by Alemanno's account, the supreme ancient theologian.[34]

Such reformulation for the sake of his own religious community of what Alemanno finds in Pico is adequate as long as each side is content to address only its own community. When, however, the conversionary, polemical address to the other community becomes important, that other community will defend itself. Platonism, especially combined with Christian Cabalism, could be a potent challenge to weak, vulnerable Jewish communities, which were not intellectually unified or fortified for the challenge of the times. Plato could become important for Jewish thinkers to discuss once Christians began using his thought against the Jews. In a letter, Ficino reminds Domenico Benivieni of an occasion on which the two of them and Pico were among the participants in debates between Flavius Mithridates, the apostate from Judaism, and two Jewish physicians, likely to have been Elijah del Medigo and Abraham Farissol.

They insist that the divine words of the prophets do not refer at all to Jesus but were intended in another sense. They turn them all in a different direction, so far as they are able, wresting them from our hands, nor does it seem that they will be easy to refute unless the divine Plato enters the debate, the invincible defender of the holy religion.[35]

Jews could respond to the challenge of Christianity that was reinforced by Plato and Cabala in two ways: by rejecting Plato and Cabala, and consequently Christianity; or by making Plato and Cabala serve Judaism instead. The first response, of course, is characteristic of Elijah del Medigo, and the second, of Yehuda Abravanel, in the *Dialoghi d'amore*.

From a somewhat cryptic, but definitely sarcastic letter of 1506, we have what could be the first reaction of Jewish readers to the Hebrew original of the *Dialoghi*. Saul Cohen Ashkenazi (1496–1523), a peripatetic student of Elijah del Medigo, and also a Candian, who had been the original addressee of the *Examination of Religion,* presented a dozen technical philosophical questions to Isaac Abravanel. Claiming not to be acquainted with those of Isaac's works that a double-truth Averroist would have to condemn, Ashkenazi pointedly asks both Isaac and Yehuda key questions about philosophy that seem to be aimed at undercutting the method and conclusions of their writings. Ashkenazi appears to be trying either to stump the two Abravanels, to point out the philosophical flaws in their 'mediating' writings, to catch them disagreeing, or to force them to disagree explicitly with the authority of Maimonides or Averroes. Any of the results on these questions would discredit what Ashkenazi must have considered their frivolous, rhetorical arguments and conclusions. His Socratic irony is particularly cutting in reference to Yehuda:

Please bring these obscure questions of mine to the attention of your dear son, my brother, the exalted, most elevated and sublime universal sage, Rabbi Yehuda, may God preserve him, if he happens to be there [in Venice]. He will restore my soul and provide for my old age if he answers my inquiries. For I have heard it said that Yehuda rises laudably from study to study along the ascending path to the wisdom of philosophy and its roots, in whatever language and writing, and in exposition of the greatness of the Commentator [Averroes], his statements, his arguments and his demonstrations. And after these things he draws himself along a marvelous path, precious with learning, and utters primeval riddles, to understand fable and eloquence, both divine and of the Torah, that are available to every man.[36]

By the values of Ashkenazi and his late teacher, del Medigo, the Abravanels have violated the disciplinary integrity of Maimonidean philosophy by rhetorically teaching the masses topics that can only be discussed in specialized, philosophic discourse, and have taught things that cannot be demonstrated in such discourse. Yehuda has directly contradicted the proper course of intellectual development outlined by Maimonides in *The Guide of the Perplexed,* by squandering his supposedly philosophical attention on riddles, fables, and eloquence.[37] In peripatetic terms, the *Dialoghi* add up to just this, and no more. The letter does not further specify the character of the work, but the suppressed violence of the reaction, which is indicated by the seriousness of the dozen inquiries, suggests that a substantial, powerful work, which could not he ignored, has drawn the questioner's attention. In addressing such respected communal figures, Ashkenazi cannot openly attack them, so he hopes to embarrass them, to silence such performances in the future. A more precise account of the criticisms that the dozen questions imply will require detailed comparison of the *Dialoghi* with the questions.

The reaction of Saul Cohen Ashkenazi to the *Dialoghi* reflects a polarization of the reactions of Jewish readers that would more or less duplicate the range of reactions to Alemanno's work in 1490. Peripatetics, like Elijah del Medigo and his student, Saul Cohen Ashkenazi, would not consider rhetorical discourse, pagan myths, and Plato to be a fit means of proving anything. Cabalists would not need, and so would not welcome, confirmation of their opinions by syncretists. The inclusive, harmonizing strategy for conciliating diverse communities and scholarly tendencies would seem to have failed again.

Still, why did Jewish syncretists, or 'mediators,' not preserve the Hebrew text that became, thirty years later, popular in translation, so that one Jewish writer translated it into Spanish, and several others translated excerpts back into Hebrew? These are questions that certainly cannot be answered now. All that can be said is that it would be even more astonishing for an Italian original to have remained in oblivion for so long, before being published and meeting with such great success.

Shlomo Pines, the outstanding historian of mediaeval Jewish philosophy, notes in a recent article that the *Dialoghi d'amore* 'though written in Italian is in many passages a typical product of the Judaeo-Arabic philosophical tradition in its final phase': he goes on to give an elegiac account of what specialists in Renaissance literature and Platonism instead would celebrate, namely the popularity of the *Dialoghi* and their influence in that literature:

The *Dialoghi,* a treatise that is perhaps, chronologically speaking, the last important work that was produced by the Jewish mediaeval philosophical tradition,
had become a favorite topic for polite conversation and literary composition. It
is a bizarre fact that the long history of that tradition may, in a meaningful
sense, be regarded as ending upon this note.[38]

Elijah del Medigo and Saul Cohen Ashkenazi would altogether agree.
What renders one kind of discourse memorable consigns the other to
oblivion.

NOTES

Research for this chapter was supported by a stipend from the Social Sciences
and Humanities Research Council of Canada, for which I express my gratitude.

1. T. Anthony Perry, *Erotic Spirituality: The Integrative Tradition from Leone
Ebreo to John Donne* (University, Alabama: Alabama University Press,
1980): Isaiah Sonne, "Traces of the *Dialogues of Love* in Hebrew Literature," [Hebrew] *Tarbiz.* 3, No. 3 (1932), pp. 287–313; John Charles Nel-
son, *Renaissance Theory of Love: The Context of Giordano Bruno's "Er-
otci Furori"* (New York and London: Columbia University Press, 1958).
2. Leone Ebreo (Giuda Abardanel), *Dialoghi d'amore,* ed. Santino Caramella
(Bari: Laterza, 1929). p. 102: Leone Ebreo, *The Philosophy of Love (Dialoghi d'amore),* trans. F. Friedeberg-Seeley and Jean H. Barnes (London: The
Soncino Press, 1937), p. 115.
3. Carlo Dionisotti, "Appunti su Leone Ebreo." *Italia medioevale e umanistica*
2 (1959), pp. 407–28; Isaiah Sonne, "On the Question of the Original
Language of Yehuda Abravanel's *Dialoghi d'amore"* [Hebrew], in, *Tsiyyu-
nim: Kovets le-Zikhrono shel Y. N. Simhoni* (Berlin: Eshkol, 1929), pp.
142–48.
4. David Geffen, "Insight into the Life and Thought of Elijah del Medigo
Based on his Published and Unpublished Works," *Proceedings of the American Academy for Jewish Research* 41–42 (1973–74), pp. 72 n. 13, 85–
86.
5. David B. Ruderman, *The World of a Renaissance Jew: The Life and Thought
of Abraham ben Mordecai Farissol.* Monographs of the Hebrew Union
College, No. 6 (Cincinnati: Hebrew Union College Press, 1981), p. 58 n. 9.
6. I thank Paul Oskar Kristeller for this information, from a conversation in
August 1976.
7. Shlomo Pines, "Scholasticism after Thomas Aquinas and the Teachings of
Hasdai Crescas and his Predecessors," *Proceedings of the Israel Academy of
Sciences and Humanities* 1, No. 10 (1976).
8. M. David Geffen, "Faith and Reason in Elijah del Medigo's *Beḥinat Ha-*

Dat and the Philosophic Backgrounds of the Work," (Doctoral dissertation, Columbia University 1970; Alfred L. Ivry, "Remnants of Jewish Averroism in the Renaissance," in *Jewish Thought in the Sixteen Century,* ed. Bernard Dov Cooperman (Cambridge, Mass.: Harvard University Press, 1983), pp. 243–65.

9. '. . . nullum enim desiderium ita intensum habeo sicut dimmittere post me hominem meum vere scientem et in doctrina peripatetica intelligentem, quod desiderium per te erit completum.' Cited in Jules Dukas. *Recherches sur l'histoire littéraire du quinziene siècle* (Paris: Léon Techener, 1876), p. 65.

10. Geffen, "Insight into Elijah del Medigo," p. 82 n. 46. My translation.

11. Eliyahu del Medigo, *Sefer Behinat ha-Dat,* ed. I. S. Reggio (Vienna: A. E. von Schmid, 1833), pp. 52–53. My translation.

12. Dukas, *Recherches,* p. 62. Cf. Bohdan Kieszkowski, "Les rapports entre Elie del Medigo et Pic de la Mirandole," *Rinascimento* 4 (1964), p. 52 n. 1.

13. Geffen, "Faith and Reason," pp. 19–20.

14. Del Medigo, *Behinat ha-Dat,* p. 51. My translation.

15. Ibid., p. 78..

16. Mortiz Steinschneider, "Miscellen," *Monatsschrift für Geschichte und Wissenschaft des Judenthums* 37 (1893), pp. 185–188.

17. Moshe Idel, "Between the Concept of Essence and the Concepts of 'Instruments' in Kabbalah during the Renaissance." [Hebrew] *Italiah* 3, Nos. 1–2 (1983), p. 90. My translation.

18. Yosef Yavets, *Sefer Or ha-Hayyim* (Lublin: N. Hershenborn, 1910), p. 74. My translation.

19. Ibid., pp. 75–76.

20. Cited from Isaac E. Barzilay, *Between Reason and Faith: Anti-Rationalism in Italian Jewish Thought, 1250–1650,* Publications in Near and Middle East Studies, Columbia University, Series A, vol. 10 (The Hague: Mouton, 1967), p. 139.

21. Arthur Lesley, *"The Song of Solomon's Ascents,* by Yohanan Alemanno: Love and Human Perfection According to a Jewish Associate of Giovanni Pico della Mirandola," (Doctoral dissertation. University of California, Berkeley, 1976), pp. 4–50.

22. Yohanan Alemanno, *Sefer Hesheq Shlomo,* British Museum, MS. Or. 2854, fol. 162r–v; Berlin, Preussisches Staatsbibliothek, MS Steinschneider 8, fols. 119v–120r.

23. Yohanan Alemanno, *Sefer 'Ene ha-'Edah,* New York, Jewish Theological Seminary, MS. 888, fol. 6v.

24. Yohanan Alemanno, *Sefer Hai ha-'Olamim,* Mantua, MS. Ebr. 21, fols. 1r–2r.

25. Oxford, Bodleian MS. Reggio 23, fols. 141v–142v.

26. Aristotle, *Rhetoric* 1, 2 (1355b–1357a. Cited from *The Basic Works of Aristotle,* ed. Richard McKeon (New York: Random House, 1941), pp. 1328–32.

27. Lesley, *"The Songs of Solomon's Ascents,"* pp. 77, 331–32.

28. *Medieval Political Philosophy*, ed. Ralph Lerner and Muhsin Mahdi (Ithaca, N.Y.: Cornell University Press, 1963), pp. 265–67.

29. Alemanno, *Sefer Hesheq Shlomo*, Oxford Bodleian MS. Laud. or. 103, fol. 133r.

30. Leone Ebreo, *Dialoghi*, p. 251; idem, *Philosophy of Love*, p. 296.

31. Chaim Wirszubski, *Three Chapters in the History of Christian Kabbala* [Hebrew] (Jerusalem: Mossad Bialik, 1975), p. 15. My translation.

32. Leone Ebreo, *Dialoghi*, esp. pp. 251ff., 298ff.; idem, *Philosophy of Love*, pp. 298ff., 327ff.

33. Pico della Mirandola, *On the Dignity of Man*, . . . *Heptaplus*, trans. Douglas Carmichael (Indianapolis: Bobbs-Merrill, 1965), pp. 145–46.

34. Lesley, *"The Song of Solomon's Ascents,"* pp. 174–80, 534–540.

35. "Interfuisti et tu disputationibus quae in aedibus Ioannis Pici Mirandulensis ante alios admirandi saepe tractatae sunt atque tractantur, ubi Helia et Abraam hebrei medici atque peripatetici adversus Guilielmum siculum disserunt. Oracula prophetarum ad Iesum minime pertinere, sed alio quodam sensu dicta contendunt, convertentes aliorsumomnia e manibusque nostris pro viribus extorquentes, neque facile convinci posse videntur nisi divinus Platoprodeat in iudicium, invictus religionis sanctae patronus . . ." Marsilio Ficino, *Opera* 1 (Basel, 1576) p. 873; Cited from Ruderman, *Farissol*, pp. 40–41.

36. *She'elot . . . ha-Rav Shaul Kohen* (Venice, 1574), fol. 2v. My translation.

37. Moses Maimonides, *The Guide of the Perplexed*, trans. Shlomo Pines (Chicago and London: University of Chicago Press, 1969), part I, ch. 34, pp. 72–79.

38. Shlomo Pines, "Medieval Doctrines in Renaissance Garb: Some Jewish and Arabic Sources of Leone Ebreo's Doctrines," in *Jewish Thought in the Sixteenth Century*, ed. Cooperman, p. 391.

C

Jewish Historical Writing in the Sixteenth Century

6

Clio and the Jews: Reflections on Jewish Historiography in the Sixteenth Century

Yosef Hayim Yerushalmi

The fiftieth anniversary of the American Academy for Jewish Research seems to me a propitious time, not only for celebration, but for pause and reflection. While, happily, research into all corridors and corners of the Jewish past has burgeoned far beyond what the small group that founded the Academy could have anticipated five decades ago, it is curious that a sophisticated history of Jewish historiography, one that would examine its theoretical underpinnings, its methods and goals, remains a desideratum. With but few exceptions there seems to be almost a reticence on the part of Judaic scholars to examine and articulate the latent assumptions of the enterprise in which they are engaged. The lag is especially striking at a time when, partly as a result of the ongoing crisis of the historicist view of the world, the general history of historiography as well as the theory and practice of the historian continue to be subjects of intense and widespread concern reflected in a vast and growing literature. If, as I am persuaded, modern historicism may be even more problematic when viewed within Jewish frameworks, the task of clarification becomes all the more urgent.

This chapter is a lightly expanded version of a Hebrew lecture given by me in June of 1977 to the combined faculties of the Institute of Jewish Studies at the Hebrew University in Jerusalem. While adding some necessary footnotes, I have deliberately eschewed an extensive and cumbersome apparatus, and have thus made no attempt to give a bibliography of existing monographs on sixteenth-century Jewish historiography or on individual historical works.

Reprinted by permission of the American Academy for Jewish Research from the *Proceedings of the American Academy for Jewish Research*, vols. 46–47, Jerusalem, 1980.

The following chapter, then, is submitted to this volume, not so much in an effort to offer a detailed account of sixteenth-century Jewish historiography per se, as in a spirit of introspection concerning the nature and place of Jewish historiography within the broader context of Jewish experience.

That the sixteenth century witnessed a noteworthy resurgence of Jewish historical writing has been, of course, long recognized, though the phenomenon has yet to be properly analyzed and evaluated. Within the span of a hundred years no less than ten important historical works were produced by Jews: Solomon Ibn Verga's "Scepter of Judah" *(Shebet Yehudah);* Abraham Zacuto's "Book of Genealogies" *(Sefer Yuḥasin);* Elijah Capsali's "Minor Order of Elijah" *(Seder Eliyahu Zuta),* and his Chronicle of Venice *(Dibrey ha-yamim le-malkhut Veneẓiah);* Samuel Usque's Portuguese "Consolation for the Tribulations of Israel" *(Consolaçam as tribulaçoens de Israel);* Joseph ha-Kohen's "Vale of Tears" *('Emek ha-bakha)* and his "History of the Kings of France and of the Ottoman Turkish Sultans" *(Dibrey ha-yamim le-malkhey-Ẓarefat u-malkhey bet Ottoman ha-Togar);* Gedaliah Ibn Yahia's "Chain of Tradition" *(Shalshelet ha-Kabbalah);* Azariah de' Rossi's "Light of the Eyes" *(Me'or 'Einayim);* David Gans' "Sprout of David" *(Ẓemaḥ David).*

These works are of interest, not only for the historical data that can be extracted from them, nor even for the light they cast on the age in which they were written. In their ensemble they offer a valuable key with which to probe certain overarching aspects of the relation of Jews to historical knowledge generally, both before and after.

I

Any attempt to come to grips with sixteenth-century Jewish historiography must entail an assessment of what preceded it. This is no simple matter, for there are fundamental divisions of opinion as to whether one can even speak at all of Jewish historiography between Josephus Flavius and modern times. Some would deny its existence altogether. Others have argued that a ramified historical literature was created. Such debates often come to grief over essentially semantic issues. Very much depends upon how the term "historiography" is defined and conceived. On the whole it seems to me that the negators have proceeded out of a tacit modern bias which assumes that the only historiography worthy of the name must be, if not critical or analytic, at least vaguely secular. Clearly, however, such approaches merely enable one to dismiss almost any medieval historical work, and thus preclude any discussion at the very outset.

At the other pole are those who would broaden the perimeters of historiography to embrace any text that has an historical dimension, or that exhibits any interest whatever in history, with a blithe indifference to its avowed aim or its literary form. Here are two instructive instances of this approach:

To this day Moritz Steinschneider's *Die Geschichtsliteratur der Juden,* published in 1905, serves as the standard bibliographical guide to Jewish historical literature from the close of the Talmudic period to the early nineteenth century. But what is *Geschichtsliteratur?* In his introduction Steinschneider cautioned correctly that history is not to be confused with its raw materials. However, the book itself (several other hands were eventually involved in it) stubbornly defies this principle. It is, in essence, a listing of more than three hundred compositions and texts, most of which cannot properly be subsumed under even the most elastic definition of historiography. A handful of historical works are interspersed among such items as private letters, elegies, penitential prayers, Judah Halevi's *Kuzari,* folk-tales and reports of miracles, communal statutes— it would seem almost as if no literary or documentary genre is absent. Like all the works of the master of Jewish bibliography, this one too is packed with information of importance for a variety of fields. For anyone interested in Jewish historiography, however, Steinschneider's list only serves, by its very nature, to blur the issues.

Some thirty-five years later there appeared in Jerusalem an edition of the "diary" of the famous sixteenth-century messianic adventurer David Reubeni *(Sippur David ha-Reubeni)* prepared by A. Z. Aescoly. This book bears also a preliminary title-page, upon which the following is inscribed: *Historiographical Library of the Palestine Historical and Ethnographical Society, Volume I/II.* For the moment we need not pause to inquire whether Reubeni's so-called diary should be considered a work of historiography or merely an historical source. More germane to our concerns is the general introduction to the projected series, entitled "The Historiographical Library and its Program," written by the historian Ben Zion Dinaburg (Dinur) in the name of the Society.[1] "This historiographical library," he states, "belongs to the literature of ingathering. We want to gather into this library all the historiographical works from biblical times until the beginning of modern Jewish historiography." The formulation is instructive: "From biblical times until . . ." with no cae-sura along the way. There is here an obvious hint at continuity, as though somehow no significant interruption had ever occurred in the historiographical creativity of the Jewish people. I do not think I am mistaken in my impression. Coming to the Middle Ages, Dinur write:

> As for Jewish historiography in the Middle Ages (until the Haskalah period), we are of the opinion that as a matter of priority there is need for a detailed bibliographic-literary survey that will present clear and precise information con-cerning the entire historiographical legacy which has reached us from this period embracing more than a thousand years. This historiographical legacy is by no means poor even in quantity. The number of historiographical works and frag-ments from this period may reach into the hundreds.

The claim for a medieval Jewish historiographical legacy of such dimensions must seem astonishing, until we read further and realize what is meant:

> The historical ideas which were active and influential in the course of the generations found expression and manifestation not only in the historiographical literature. They frequently defined themselves with great clarity and fullness in other literary forms, in every age, from the prophetic literature of ancient times to the literature of mysticism and ethics, enlightenment and scholarship, in more recent times.

In short, the plan for a "historiographical library" traversed far be-yond the bounds of historiography. The notion was to include not only the recorded historical recollections of the Jewish people, but also its meditations on its place among the nations and on its future destiny, as these expressed themselves in any and all literary forms. The details can be read in the Hebrew original and need not be repeated here. It was, in its way, a grandiose project, never executed. Perhaps it had its own intrinsic virtues. But once again we are confronted with a blatant ten-dency to stretch the concept of "historiography" to comprise phenom-ena that, whatever the definition, can hardly be squeezed into such a rubric without bursting it asunder and rendering it meaningless.

Now I am not prepared to offer a fixed definition of historiography, nor do the purposes of this chapter require it. In the end, any such definition will prove, if not arbitrary, then either artificial or restrictive. However, if the term is to be used responsibly and not be allowed to turn into a random receptacle, one characteristic should be isolated without which I believe it altogether impossible to understand the phenomenon that the term is meant to represent.

The minimal condition to be satisfied emanates from the very word "historiography" in its literal and etymological meaning—and that is simply, the "writing of history"—in the sense of recording events out of the human past. Whatever its other aims, qualities and contents, a "historiographical" work must be anchored in a recital of concrete events that possess a temporal specificity. Those events need not be political. They may be biographical, social, literary. But they must be there. This precondition, to be sure, does not tell us what historiography is. But at least it helps us to differentiate what is *not* historiography.

Historiography is not to be equated with "ideas of history," nor with an interest in historical processes, nor with attitudes and reactions to historical events, nor with efforts to unveil the "meaning" of history. Though any of these elements may be present in an historiographical work, none of them is a decisive feature. For historiography represents a very specific activity, not to be confused with others. At its source lies an impulse to record events of the past that, for one reason or another, are seen as worthy of remembrance.

By contrast, the quest for meaning in history can be pursued in various ways and through different literary genres that have an intrinsic connection with historiography. Indeed, this is largely how it has been pursued. Interpretations of history, whether explicit or implicit, can be found abundantly in works of philosophy, theology, exegesis, mythology, belles-lettres, often without a single mention of historical events or personalities, and with no attempt to relate to them. The distinction would seem to be elementary, and yet it is consistently ignored. At an international symposium on medieval historiography held some years ago at Harvard, much of the discussion centered around Joachim da Fiore. Yet no matter how one may view the importance of Joachite ideas in the evolution of certain Western conceptions of history, I doubt that the admission of the Calabrian abbot to the agenda helped clarify the topic at hand which, one assumed, concerned the writing of history during the Middle Ages.

The same distinctions apply in the Jewish sphere as well. The prophets of Israel may have held highly articulate views about history, and some of the biblical historians may have absorbed those views and written their chronicles on prophetic assumptions, but the prophets were surely not historians, nor, then as now, were the historians prophets. If we leap momentarily to the sixteenth century and compare, say, Rabbi Judah Loew (Maharal) of Prague with his compatriot David Gans, we may easily agree that Maharal had by far the more profound views on the course and meaning of Jewish history. Nevertheless it is Gans, and not he, who was the historian. Similarly, we can often find important historical data in works belonging to various genres, yet the aim of these works is not at all historiographical, and it is not this which characterizes them. In the biblical commentaries of Isaac Abravanel, for example, as well as in his messianic treatises, there are scattered clusters of historical information whose significance is manifest, but this material remains incidental to the whole. Abravanel himself apparently understood the difference and, as is well known, he began to write a separate historical work to be called "Days of Yore" *(Yemot 'olam)*.[2]

These observations, tentative and incomplete as they are, will suffice to orient us toward the subject at hand.

II

We possess, in all branches of Jewish literary creativity in the Middle Ages, a wealth of thought on the position of the Jewish people in history, of *ideas* of Jewish history, but comparatively little interest in *recording* the mundane historical experiences of the Jews since they went into exile. In light of what has been said thus far, the paradox is only apparent. As to whether a Jewish historiography existed before the sixteenth century—such a sharp formulation of the question can only obscure the real problem, which is of a more subtle order. For two things seem to me equally clear: Historical works were certainly written by medieval Jews, although, taken together, they do not constitute a historiographical phenomenon of the sort that is to be found among other peoples in whose midst Jews lived. *Iggeret Rab Sherira, Yosippon,* the Hebrew chronicles of the Crusades, and other known works, are certainly historical compositions, not to be removed arbitrarily from the category of "historiography" because of criteria alien to the times in which they were written. Nevertheless, no historiographical tradition ever emerged out of these, no genre with fixed conventions and continuity. The historical words that were written appeared only sporadically.

By and large the distance between them in time and space is significant, the periods of silence long. Only in one well-defined area can one speak at all of a genre, and that is the literature of the so-called "chain of tradition" of the Oral Law *(shalshelet ha-kabbalah)*, which dealt with the transmission of rabbinic law and doctrine, and with the luminaries who were its bearers through the ages. Only this type of historiography achieved legitimacy and found a home within Judaism, and here alone can one discover a certain continuity of effort, from the anonymous "Order of Mishnaic and Talmudic Sages" *(Seder tanna'im va-'amora'im)* in the ninth century, to the "Order of the Generations" *(Seder hadorot)* of Yehiel Heilprin in the eighteenth. Yet for all the variations they exhibit, and despite their significance as historical sources for us today, most of the many compositions of this type did not come into being out of a desire to write the history of the Jewish people. Their chief impulses lay elsewhere, in response to those heretics and antagonists who denied the validity of the Oral Law, in the practical need to determine points of law according to earlier and later authorities, and in a natural curiosity about the evolution of Jewish jurisprudence. Biographical details concerning the rabbis who were the links in the chain of tradition are generally scanty at best, and historical events are scattered about almost haphazardly. At any rate, if we except the literature of the "chain of tradition" there is no historiographical genre in medieval Judaism, only isolated historical works, but these hardly add up to a "legacy."

What I have sketched here is not a retrospective construct. There were Jews in the Middle Ages who understood that such was the situation. Already Moses Ibn Ezra complained about "indolence" and even "sin" on the part of Jews in the neglect of both the Hebrew language and the writing of history:

> ... and they did not succeed to polish their language, to write their chronicles, and to remember their history and traditions. It would have been fitting that they should not have ignored and despised such matters. Behold . . . all the other nations have exerted themselves to write their histories, and to excel in them . . .[3]

This written in the twelfth century, and by a Jew living in the midst of a Muslim culture. At the end of the fifteenth century Solomon Ibn Verga, who grew up in Christian Spain, concludes the third chapter of his *Shebet Yehudah* as follows:

Thus is it found in the chronicles of the kings of Persia which were brought to the king of Spain, according to the custom of the Christians, for they seek to know the things that happened of old in order to take counsel from them, and this because of their distinction and enlightenment.[4]

Significantly, for Ibn Verga it is a *Christian* custom to read historical chronicles, and here there is a note of envy that is at the same time an implicit criticism of his fellow Jews.

Nor is it possible to agree with those would find an organic connection between various Jewish historical compositions merely because they happened to be written within a certain span of time. One hears, for instance, about "epochs of historical creativity" in the tenth and twelfth centuries,[5] but such an artificial periodization does not convince. Other than a rough chronological coincidence, it is hard to discover a unifying factor around which to group the recital of the events of the Second Commonwealth in *Yosippon,* the description of the affairs of the Babylonian exilarchate in *Sippur Nathan ha-Babli,* and the history of Talmudic and Gaonic sages presented in *Iggeret Rab Sherira,* though all three were written in the tenth century. Again, there is no discernible link between Ibn Daud's *Sefer ha-kabbalah,* written against a background of the collapse of Jewish life in Muslim Spain, and the Hebrew Crusade chronicles in Germany, that would justify the suggestion of an "epoch of Jewish historiography" in the twelfth century. At best one may view the Crusade chronicles as a discrete unit, flowing out of a great catastrophe and a common spiritual outlook. Even so, no similar phenomenon is known to us from other times and places in the Middle Ages.

I must emphasize that in what I have outlined thus far, no criticism is intended or implied against the Jews of the past. I do not happen to be among those who would fault medieval Jewry for not writing more history. Quite to the contrary, I can conceive that there may yet arise a future generation that will demand of us why we were so preoccupied, not to say obsessed, with history. The writing of history is far from a natural and ubiquitous human activity to be found in every age and in every culture. If Jews in the Middle Ages wrote relatively little history, that does not point to a flaw or lacuna in their civilization, nor, as has sometimes been alleged, that they lived "outside history." It merely shows that they did not regard historiography as vital to themselves. There were three highways of religious and intellectual creativity among medieval Jews—Halakhah, philosophy and Kabbalah, each of which offered an all-embracing world-view, and none of which required history in order to be cultivated or validated. These alone led to ultimate truths, to spiritual felicity, and to self-knowledge. In comparison, historical works were at best a form of diversion or, at worst, a waste of time.

It is not that Jews felt the past to be irrelevant to the present. But the relevant past was, for them, the distant, ancient past, the periods of the First and Second Temples. What had happened then had determined what had occurred since, and even provided the explanation for what was now transpiring.

With this in mind we can perhaps better understand why it was that *Yosippon* loomed as the single most important chronicle in the eyes of medieval Jews. Apart from the Bible itself, this was the only available work that offered a detailed account of ancient events in the fateful period whose repercussions were felt to extend to all subsequent generations. When, in the thirteenth century, Judah Mosconi enumerates the many virtues of the book, he writes: "For we can read in it the deeds of our ancestors because of whose sins our city was destroyed . . . and they ate the sour grapes, but our teeth are set on edge."[6] And when, in the generation of the Spanish and Portuguese exiles, Tam Ibn Yahia sponsored a new edition of *Yosippon* published in Constantinople in 1510, he stated in his introduction:

And I, in the midst of the exile, wallowing in the blood of the upheavals that are overtaking my people and nation, was roused by my soul and spirit to be among those who have helped to print this book, for this is the one that has laid bare the source of the misfortunes of the House of Judah.[7]

Moreover, the book had the good fortune to be accepted as an original work written by Josephus Flavius in the aftermath of the destruction of the Second Temple. Thereby *Yosippon* acquired a halo of authority in the eyes of Jews that was vouchsafed to no other medieval historical work, and that would have been denied it altogether if it had been regarded as the work of a Jew living in southern Italy in the tenth century. Much of the attitude toward *Yosippon* in particular and, by contrast, to historiography in general, is revealed in the following statement by Tam Ibn Yahia:

Although it is characteristic of historical works to exaggerate things that never existed, to add to them, to invent things that never were, nevertheless this book *[Yosippon]*, although it is part of the same genre, is completely distinct from them, and it is the difference between truth and falsehood. For all the words of this book are righteousness and truth, and there is no wrong within it. And the mark of this is that of all the books written after the Holy Scriptures this is [chronologically] closest to prophecy, having been written before the Mishnah and the Talmud.[8]

In the same manner we begin to understand why, besides the literature of the "chain of tradition," whose very aim necessitated a survey of all the generations of halakhic endeavor in order to argue their unbroken continuity, there is not a single medieval Jewish chronicle that attempts to give a continuous history of what had occurred since the destruction of the Second Temple. The chronological span is generally short, with most compositions confined to contemporary events or those close to the time of the author, usually relating what happened during a persecution. There is little or no attempt to bridge events from one generation to another. More significantly, in most cases there is little search for specific explanations of what had occurred, and in fact the events described are not regarded essentially as novelties. Only in two instances can one detect a full consciousness that something genuinely new has happened and that there is a special importance to the events themselves. In Ibn Daud's *Sefer ha-kabbalah* there is a keen awareness of certain processes as a result of which, in his view, spiritual and cultural hegemony among the Jews passed first from Babylonia to the Iberian Peninsula, and in his own time from Muslim to Christian Spain. In the Crusade chronicles there is a palpable sense of the terrifying shift in the relations between Jewry and Christendom, and an expression of astonished awe at this first instance of Jewish mass martyrdom on European soil. But Ibn Daud and the authors of the Crusade chronicles are, in this sense, exceptional rather than exemplary. On the whole, medieval Jewish chronicles tend to assimilate events to old and established conceptual frameworks. Persecution and suffering are, after all, the result of the conditions of exile, and exile itself is the bitter fruit of ancient sins. It is important to realize that there is also no real desire to find novelty in passing events. On the contrary, we find a pronounced tendency to subsume major new events to familiar archetypes, perhaps because even terrible events are less terrifying when viewed in patterns rather than in their bewildering specificity. Thus the new oppressor is Haman and the court-Jew is Mordecai. Christendom is Edom or Esau, and Islam is

Ishmael. Samuel ha-Nagid is David, and the Andalusian landscape is biblical. The essential contours of the relationship between Israel and the Gentiles have been delineated long ago in the Aggadah, and there is little or no interest in the history of contemporary nations. In periods of acute messianic tension there may be a spurt of interest in global events and so, for example, we have texts stemming from the first century after the rise of Islam as a world power out of which we can reconstruct minute details of the progress of the Arab conquests.[9] But there is no historiography here, only a desperate apocalyptic equation. The Arab conquests are seen, in essence, as the wars of Gog and Magog which are to bring an end to history.

Not that there was a waning in the vitality of Jewish collective memory in the Middle Ages, but that it did not express itself or function through historiography. Jewish historical memory had other channels: synagogal poetry *(selihot* and *piyyutim); Memorbücher,* whose lists of martyrs were kept by the community; special fast-days; "Second Purims." That which was placed into such vessels, that which was transfigured liturgically and ritually, was endowed with a chance for survival and permanence. Ordinary chronicles and historical texts were neglected and forgotten, unless (and here again I refer to the literature of the "chain of tradition") they were of halakhic significance, or were embedded in halakhic or theological works. Most medieval Jewish historical writings went down to oblivion, and they are in our hands today only because they were rediscovered and published by scholars in modern times. Should one desire to know what was the medieval historiographical "legacy" available to Jewish readers after the year 1500, it is only necessary to glance at the development of Hebrew printing. In addition to the ever popular *Yosippon,* only four historical works out of the past were printed in the course of the sixteenth century: *Iggeret Rab Sherira, Seder 'Olam Rabba* and *Seder 'Olam Zuta,* and the *Sefer ha-kabbalah* of Ibn Daud[10] (which usually included his brief sketches of the history of the Second Commonwealth and of the Roman emperors). This was, in effect, the entire "Historiographical library" that remained in general circulation from all the preceding generations.

Even if we take into consideration everything that had been written, in the final analysis the Jewish historiographical literature of the Middle Ages was sparse enough, and modern attempts to inflate its dimensions only prove how important historiography is to us. Here I must stress once again that if medieval Jews generally did not write history it was not out of lack of talent, nor even for lack of knowledge, but primarily because they felt no need to do so. It just was not sufficiently important to them, for reasons I have suggested. None of the other explanations usually advanced will suffice. It has been said that sufferings and persecutions numbered the historical creativity of the Jews, that they wrote no history because, lacking a state and political power, they had no history to write about, or that it was because they had neither royal chroniclers nor monks who could devote themselves to historical writing. Such explanations are, however, no more than a form of second-guessing, and they are ultimately self-liquidating. All the aforementioned factors were equally true of the Jewish people in the sixteenth century. Yet in that time a corpus of Jewish historiography was created which surpassed, in scope and quality, all that had come before.

III

Only in the sixteenth century do we encounter, for the first time, a cultural phenomenon within Jewry that can be recognized with little hesitation as genuinely historiographical, though each book that was produced was quite different from the other. As we noted at the outset, ten major works were written. Of their eight authors, five were either exiles from Spain and Portugal or descendants of exiles (Ibn Verga, Zacuto, Usque, Joseph ha-Kohen, Gedaliah Ibn Yahia). One, Elijah, Capsali of Crete, was profoundly influenced by Spanish refugees. Only two, Azariah de' Rossi and David Gans, emerge out of a non-Sephardic ambiance (Mantua and Prague, respectively), and their books present special problems. Patently, the primary stimulus to the rise of Jewish historiography in the sixteenth century was the tremendous catastrophe that had overtaken the Jews in the Iberian Peninsula. That is to say, for the first time we encounter a ramified historiographical response to a great historic event. So far as we know, no event in the Middle Ages, not even the Crusades, engendered a comparable literature. In addition to the historical works proper, almost all branches of sixteenth-century Jewish literature are replete with accounts of the Spanish Expulsion of 1492, of the forced conversion that followed in Portugal only five years later, and of the sufferings of the exiles on land and sea. Yet this had hardly been the first expulsion of a European Jewry. The expulsion from

France in 1306, while not of the same dimensions, had been no paltry affair. Gersonides had written of the number of French exiles as "twice those who emerged from Egypt."[11] But except for the passage in his commentary on the Pentateuch there are almost no references in fourteenth-century Jewish texts to that great upheaval. The contrast is glaring.

Certainly there must have been more than one reason for this. But above all, there is a highly articulate feeling among the generations following the expulsion from Spain that something unprecedented had taken place. Not only that an abrupt end had come to a great and venerable Jewry, but also something beyond that. Precisely because this expulsion was not the first but, in a sense, the *last,* it was felt to have altered the face of Jewry and of history itself. When Abravanel enumerates the various European expulsions that began from England in 1290, he perceives the expulsion from Spain as the climax and culmination of a process that has shifted the Jewish people, globally, from the West to the East.[12] The larger significance of the Spanish Expulsion is that because of it Western Europe has been emptied of Jews. When Abraham Zacuto compares the expulsions from Spain and Portugal with the earlier French expulsion, he understands the radical difference. Relating that a forebear of his had been among the Jewish refugees from France who had found an immediate haven across the border in Spain, he exclaims: "And from France they came to Spain. But we faced the enemies on one side, and the sea on the other!"[13]

That historical crisis should stimulate historical writing comes as no surprise. To take but one pertinent instance, Hans Baron has shown the nexus between the rise of Italian humanist historiography and the breakdown of the republican system in the Italian city-states.[14] The resemblance ends there, however. Except for Azariah de' Rossi, we do not find that the spirit of Italian humanist historiography was absorbed into sixteenth-century Jewish historiography, though some Jewish historians drew information from it. The elements of humanist culture that crop up in the works of Joseph ha-Kohen or Gedaliah Ibn Yahia should not mislead us in this respect, for in the end they remain external trappings. Nor, as is commonly supposed, does the *Shebet Yehudah* of Ibn Verga betray influences of the Italian Renaissance.[15] Recent research has shown that Ibn Verga never came to Italy, but died in Flanders shortly after fleeing from Portugal.[16] If there are external influences in his book they should be sought, as I have long supposed, in the Iberian cultural milieu that was closest to him. But in general, the dynamics of Jewish historiography after the Spanish Expulsion are imminent to itself and related to what had happened within Jewry. Jews who were "wallowing in the blood of the upheavals" wanted to understand the meaning of those upheavals and, as Ibn Verga put it, "Why this enormous wrath?"

IV

Jewish historiography in the generations following the expulsion from Spain does not only constitute a novum, but was felt as such. The awareness of novelty is expressed most vividly by Joseph ha-Kohen, in an exultant passage that deliberately echoes the biblical Song of Deborah:

> All my people is aware that no author has arisen in Israel comparable to Yosippon the priest, who wrote of the war of the land of Judea and of Jerusalem. The chroniclers ceased in Israel, they ceased, until I, Joseph, did arise, until I did arise, a chronicler in Israel! And I set my heart to write as a remembrance in a book the bulk of the troubles that have been visited upon us in Gentile lands, from the day that Judah was exiled from its land until the present day.[17]

For all the hyperbole in this passage, it deserves special attention. Joseph ha-Kohen was acquainted with the Jewish historical works of others and drew from them ("I gleaned among the sheaves after the harvesters, whatever my hand could find"). Nonetheless, he considers himself a new creature. Since Yosippon (and let us remember that for him Yosippon was Josephus Flavius of the first century), "the chroniclers ceased in Israel." He states this as something of common knowledge ("all my people knows"), and in terms of the psychology revealed, this testimony is impressive. There is here a consciousness that to write history is something new for Jews, a new beginning after a very long hiatus. Yet if, as he has tacitly admitted, there were historical works in former ages, whence does this feeling arise? What is there about his manner of writing history that enables him to style himself the first Jewish historian since Josephus? Indeed, since we are concerned here not with Joseph ha-Kohen alone, we may well broaden the question. What, in essence, are the novelties within sixteenth-century Jewish historiography as a whole?

To begin with, these works cover a temporal and geographical span far beyond anything that can be found previously. They do not focus merely upon this or that persecution or set of events, but attempt, within the limits of the data available to their authors, a coherent and consecutive survey of many centuries, in an expansive and detailed narration.

A new element is the prominence assigned to postbiblical Jewish history. For the first time we sense a keen interest in the entire course of Jewish history from the destruction of the Second Temple down to the authors' own time. The *Shebet Yehudah* is concerned almost exclusively with events that have occurred since the loss of Jewish independence and especially during the Middle Ages. Joseph ha-Kohen begins his *'Emek ha-bakha:* "And it came to pass *after* all the glory had departed from Jerusalem." If he opens his *Dibrey ha-yamim* with "Adam begat Seth," it is only in order to establish the genealogies of the nations, and after half a page he plunges the reader into the seventh century of the Common Era and the rise of Islam. In Usque's Portuguese work there is a clear triple periodization based, not upon the literary history of scholars and sages, but upon the larger rhythms of Jewish history: the periods of the First and the Second Temples, and a third period that comprises "all the tribulations Israel has suffered since the loss of the Second Temple, destroyed by the Romans, until this day." To this third period he devotes as much space as to the other two combined.

This points also to a new attitude toward the history of Jewry in exile. While, by and large, the Jewish historians of the sixteenth century believe, no less than prior generations, that "for our sins were we exiled," and that "the fathers ate sour grapes and the teeth of the sons are set on edge," they do not regard this as a warrant to gloss over the history of those very sons. On the contrary, they lavish their attention upon it. Thus they bestow a new value upon the events that have transpired over the entire course of the Middle Ages. They seem to recognize implicitly that these events too have a meaning for the present and the future which cannot be grasped merely by focusing attention on ancient times, and that they are therefore worth recalling. All this marks a significant change in outlook.

A final novelty is the renewed interest in the history of the nations, especially of the contemporary nations, in which a desire to know various aspects of non-Jewish history combines with an incipient recognition that Jewish destinies are affected by the interplay of relations between certain of the great powers. To these categories belong such books as Capsali's Chronicle of Venice, and large portions of his *Seder Eliyahu Zuta*[18] which are devoted to the history of the Ottoman Empire. In fact, for all its archaic theological presuppositions, the latter work may properly be regarded as a first attempt to write Jewish history within the framework of general history. From Joseph ha-Kohen we possess not only the chronicle of the kings of France and Turkey, but his Hebrew translations (with insertions of his own) of Francisco López de Gómara's *Historia general de las Indias (Ha-India ha-ḥadashah)* and *La conquista de Mexico (Sefer Fernando Cortes)*.[19] On another level mention should also be made of the various sections dealing with general history in Zacuto's *Sefer Yuḥasin* and Ibn Yahia's *Shalshelet ha-Kabbalah*.[20] And of course the entire second part of David Gans' *Zemaḥ David*, although, as already indicated, this book arises out of a different cultural setting.

Taken together, the features enumerated thus far are impressive enough, and for that very reason there is no need to inflate their proportions. Jewish historiography in the wake of the Spanish expulsion marks a leap forward when viewed over and against what had preceded it. Within other perspectives its stature tends to diminish. It never reached the level of critical insight to be found in the best of general historical scholarship contemporary with it. Moreover, although ten full-fledged historical works following so closely upon one another mark, for Jews, a period of relatively intense historiographical activity, they do represent but a tiny fraction of the sum of sixteenth-century Jewish literature.

Yet these reservations do not absolve us of our primary duty, which is to evaluate this corpus of historiography within its own context, as one among a gamut of Jewish responses to the trauma of the expulsion from Spain. From this vantage-point the work of the sixteenth-century Jewish historians may properly be seen as a significant attempt, however tentative, to pave the way among Jews toward a concern with the historical dimension of their existence. In itself this phenomenon was laden with potential for future development and, had it continued, who knows where it might not have led. Seen in retrospect, however, we must conclude that it was an attempt that failed.

It was not, essentially, a failure of the historians, though their limitations are obvious in themselves and deserve to be spelled out.

For all their innovations, they could not free themselves from conceptions and modes of thought that had been deeply rooted among Jews for many ages. We have said that events since the destruction of the Second Temple received a new appreciation, and so they did. But in general these events are perceived as important, not because of any casual connection between them, but because the historians seek to find within them hints, configurations, and meanings that lie beyond them. The historical episodes that Usque narrates derive their significance, not from any intrinsic links they might have to one another, but from his conviction that these events are fulfillments of biblical prophecies that predicted what would happen to the Jewish people in exile. By his own time, Usque believed, even the most dire of biblical prophecies had come to pass, and hence redemption was imminent. All that was lacking was that the Portuguese Marranos return openly to Judaism.

Messianic impulses are discernible in both the *'Emek ha-bakha* and *Dibrey ha-yamim* of Joseph ha-Kohen, even though his messianism is generally restrained and often veiled. He himself hints at the messianic framework in a passage repeated in both books, declaring: "The expulsions from France as well as this exceedingly bitter exile [i.e., from Spain] have roused me to compose this book, so that the Children of Israel may know what [the Gentiles] have done to us in their lands, their courts and their castles, *for behold the days approach.*"[21] Behind the "Chronicle of the Kings of France and of the Ottoman Turkish Sultans" there hovers a venerable apocalyptic tradition. Although, characteristically, Joseph ha-Kohen does not allow apocalyptic elements to erupt into the foreground, his book is not a mere exercise in French and Turkish history, but an attempt to trace the age-old struggle between Christendom and Islam, whose leading contemporary standard-bearers were perceived by him as France and the Ottoman Empire. The explicit history remains that of Gog and Magog.

The messianic theme of the *Seder Eliyahu Zuta* is so dominant as to leave no doubt of Elijah Capsali's intentions. The entire book is messianic history at its most exuberant. It is saturated with biblical messianic language and typologies, and the Turkish sultans are cast in the redemptive image of Cyrus the Great.

In Ibn Verga's *Shebet Yehudah* there is, by contrast, not a trace of messianism, and in several respects its boldness and originality are impressive. Ibn Verga alone transfers the concept of "natural cause" *(ha-sibbah ha-tib'it)* from the sphere of philosophy and science to history and, as Yitzhak Baer has shown, it is he who went farthest in exploring the mundane causes of Jewish historical suffering generally, and of the Spanish Expulsion in particular. Still, it remains a fundamental error to consider Ibn Verga, as some have, to be merely a rationalist with a precociously secular conception of Jewish history. The truth is that his use of "natural cause" by no means precludes or contradicts the notion of divine providence. A close reading of the book will also reveal to what extent Ibn Verga was still bound by attitudes that had crystalized ages ago among the Hispano-Jewish aristocracy and no longer corresponded to the historical realities of his time.[22]

All of these features, however regressive they might seem to modern eyes, do not detract from the essential achievements of the historians. A mixture of old and new is to be expected in the initial phases of almost any cultural development. The fate of sixteenth-century Jewish historiography was ultimately determined by an inheritance of a different order—the attitude among Jews toward historical works generally.

We have noted that historiography had never become a legitimate and recognized genre in medieval Judaism. This meant that except for Zacuto and Ibn Yahia, who continued to write within the familiar and accepted mold of the "chain of tradition," the Jewish historians of the sixteenth century found no available slot into which to fit their work. Each, in fact, had to create his own individual forms. But though it made their task more difficult, it is not even this that ultimately defeated them. Something else had passed over from centuries gone by, namely, the relative low esteem in which historical works of any kind were held by most Jews. Despite their own occasional disclaimers (we shall examine these shortly), it can hardly be doubted that the sixteenth-century historians felt themselves engaged in something that was of high seriousness and purpose. Whether they were taken by the Jewish public as seriously as they deserved, or even correctly understood, is questionable.

Though the reading public of the past is silent almost by definition, there are indirect ways of gauging the attitudes with which our authors had to contend. Most of the historical works under consideration are preceded by introductions filled with apology for the very fact that the writer is dealing with history at all, and offering a host of reasons to justify such a concern. Why was all this necessary? Because the historian knew very well the nature of the audience that awaited him. If even Zacuto, writing within a literary tradition in which distinguished rabbinic scholars of the past had already participated, still feels called upon to declare with a self-deprecatory shrug—"I cannot presume to say that it is a deep science, for because of my sins, as a result of the many persecutions and the want of a livelihood, I have neither strength nor wisdom"[23]—then how much more is there need for special pleading when David Gans presents his detailed chronology of the Gentile nations. These and other apologia go far beyond conventional literary protestations of modesty. Here it is not really the authors' capacities that are at issue, but the value of the enterprise itself. All the introductions sound a common note. It is as though the historian were saying in the same breath: "Dear reader, although both of us know what I am writing is unimportant, nevertheless it is important. . .."

A somewhat whimsical but revealing example of another kind can be found in the first edition of the *Dibrey ha-yamim* (Sabbionetta, 1554). We recall the exultant cry of Joseph ha-Kohen in his preface to the work: "The chroniclers ceased, they ceased . . . until I arose." But in old printed books it is worthwhile to read all the preliminary matter. In this instance, along with the author's introduction, the following verses are inscribed:

> When the author's nephew, Zeraḥiah Halevi,
> Saw the glory of this book, and the nectar of its honeycombed words,
> The Lord lifted his spirit and he began to speak.
> So he opened his mouth with song and hymn, and declared:
> *Let anyone who delights in a time that was before ours*
> *Take this chronicle and read it when his sleep wanders,* [italics mine]
> For in it he will see the history of the nations,
> And should he merit to witness the end of our exile,
> He will understand the difference between the destiny of the Gentile kings
> and of our Messiah.

Leaving aside the somewhat curious ending, we may focus upon the lines I have placed in italics. Faint praise this, one might say, in a poem purporting to extol the book. After all, even Bach's "Goldberg Variations," though composed expressly for a case of insomnia, were not intended exclusively for nocturnal performances. Certainly we understand that there is a biblicism lurking behind Zeraḥiah Halevi's lines (Esther 6:1, "On that night the king's sleep wandered, and he commanded to bring the book of records and chronicles . . ."). But it is also more than a neat turn of a biblical phrase, and deserves to be taken seriously. Historical chronicles are to be read "when sleep wanders" *(bi-*

nedod shenah), for otherwise such reading is *bittul Torah,* a waste of time that could otherwise be devoted to the serious study of sacred texts. In fact, Zerahiah's attitude is by no means unusual. Despite Tam Ibn Yahia's veneration for *Yosippon,* he is at pains to add in his introduction to the work that especially "the merchants who are immersed in temporal successes, and who have not turned to the Torah in their leisure time, will delight in reading it."[24]

Of all the historical works, Ibn Verga's *Shebet Yehudah* was to enjoy the widest popularity. I have examined no less than seventeen different editions printed from the mid-sixteenth century to the end of the eighteenth, and there may be others. What was at the heart of this extraordinary success? How was the book read, and what did its readers see in it? I think one may safely assume that only isolated readers grasped Ibn Verga's intentions in exploring the Spanish expulsion and the situation of Jews in Christian society. There are sufficient indications that what seems central to us in the book was not what attracted most readers, but rather other matters. It is interesting, for example, to follow the metamorphoses in the texts of the title-pages of the *Shebet Yehudah,* for these were aimed at focusing the reader's attention on what were considered the highlights within. Already in the title-page of the first edition (Adrianople, 1553), published more than four decades after Solomon Ibn Verga's death, the following description of the book is given (the words are not of the author, but of the editor, Joseph Ibn Verga, or the printer):

> This is a book of the generations of Israel, and of the many misfortunes that have come upon the Jews in the lands of the nations. . . . And so it tells of the blood-libel, how many times its falsehood was revealed and made public, and Israel emerged delivered. Similarly, it speaks of religious disputations that were held in the presence of kings, as well as the ceremony of installing the princes [i.e., the exilarchs] in various periods. . . . Finally, it depicts the structure of the Temple and its inner precincts, the service of the High Priest when he came to his chamber before the Day of Atonement, and the order of the Passover sacrifice, which we shall yet see with our own eyes, as we were promised by our Creator, the lord of compassion.

What is so frustrating about this harbinger of the modern publisher's blurb is the fact that technically each detail is correct, yet the total impression is so far removed from the inner spirit of the book. By the time we come to the third edition, a Yiddish translation printed in Krakow in 1591 "for ordinary householders, men and women" *(far gemayne baale-batim, man un vayber)* we can see from the title-page that the *Shebet Yehudah* has been transmuted perceptually into a standard piece of edifying folk-literature:

One will find in it marvelous stories of what happened to our fathers in exile, and how many times they underwent martyrdom, the book also specifying in which times and in which countries it all happened, so that a person's heart will be roused to the fear of God. May the Blessed Lord in His infinite mercy and grace continue to keep His people from all evil calamities, and send us the redeemer, Messiah son of David, speedily and in our own days.

More examples could be adduced, but the point remains. The attitude toward historiography among sixteenth-century readers was no different, by and large, from what it had been in prior ages. An historical work was regarded as something pleasant and diverting in moments of leisure, and at best a source of moral uplift. Works concerned with the history of Gentile nations were still described generically as "books of wars" *(sifrey milḥamot)*, and in halakhic literature opinions continued divided about whether one is permitted to read them, and when, and in what language.[25]

V

Still, one Jewish historical work of the sixteenth century, though not a chronicle, was received with sufficient seriousness to produce some very interesting repercussions. I have in mind Azariah de' Rossi's collection of historical and antiquarian essays, entitled *Me'or 'Einayim* and first published in Mantua in 1573–75. Unlike the other books with which we have been dealing, the *Me'or 'Einayim* has no links to the Spanish expulsion and the spiritual crisis it provoked. It is rather the fruit of a creative encounter, in the mind of an Italian rabbi, between Jewish tradition and Italian Renaissance culture. Unlike so many other books written by Italian Jews which display a veneer of humanistic learning, here the humanist spirit has penetrated the very vitals of the work, and only here do we find the real beginnings of historical criticism. The *Me'or 'Einayim* remains the most audacious Jewish historical work of the sixteenth century. Its essential daring lies in Azariah's reluctance to set up predetermined boundaries between his general and Jewish knowledge, in his readiness to allow a genuine confrontation between the two spheres, and in his acceptance of the conclusions that seemed to flow out of it.

For our present purpose the most instructive aspect of the book lies in what it reveals about the audience and the spiritual climate of the time. Throughout his writing Azariah shows himself particularly sensitive to public opinion. He writes with utmost care, and is even prepared to make certain compromises so long as they do not involve basic principles. Time and again he interrupts his discussions in order to comment on the objections he anticipates from his potential readers. Thus, in speaking of various Talmudic references to the massacre of Alexandrian Jewry:

> Let us now turn back to the city of Alexandria. Our eyes behold three different passages concerning it, for the Jerusalem Talmud has stated that the evil murderer was Trajan . . . and the Babylonian Talmud in tractate Sukkah said it was Alexander of Macedon, while in tractate Gittin it changed its opinion to write that it was Hadrian. And if we have now begun to investigate the [historical] truth of these matters, that is not because of the thing in itself, for what was—*[mai de-havah havah]*, but only because we are concerned that the words of our sages in relating well-known events should not appear to contradict one another.[26]

Later on, in the same chapter:

> At any rate, even were we to admit that some stories reached the ears of the sages with some distortion, and that this is how they related them to us, that in no way diminishes their stature. . . . And even though this chapter consists mostly of inconsequential investigations *[ḥakirot shel mah be-khakh]*, for it will be said "what was—was, and there is in it no relevance to law or observance," still, the refined soul yearns to know the truth of everything.[27]

And again, in his strictures on the computation of the traditional Jewish era of Creation:

> Before we leave this subject it will become clear that the manner in which they, of blessed memory, computed the years was considered a noble science whose worth was known and proclaimed by every enlightened person. However, I can foresee that you will say to yourself, dear reader: "But surely such an investigation is completely farfetched *[hilkheta de-meshiḥa, lit: "law for the time of the Messiah"]* and even worse, for what have we to do with all this, considering that what was—was, several thousand years ago or more?"[28]

There are many such passages in the *Me'or 'Einayim,* and they demonstrate vividly the reactions that Azariah expected from his readers. He was wary of them on two counts. His overall concern was that they had a low opinion of any historical investigation. "What was—was." This phrase seems to sum up for him the prevalent Jewish mood, and it surfaces so frequently in the book as to be almost a leitmotif. More specifically, however, he suspected that some of the contents of the book would be construed as a denigration of the Talmudic sages.

As it turned out, his worries were not in vain. The book was printed and immediately attacked. In various Italian Jewish communities it was placed under rabbinic ban.[29] Rumblings were heard from Prague and from Safed in Palestine.[30] Some rose in defense of the book. But the question remains—what, in essence, stirred up the tempest? Azariah was no heretic, but a respected physician-scholar whose personal piety was not in question. Mantua was a center of Jewish intellectuals well attuned to the cultural currents of the time. Indeed, most of the Italian rabbis who signed the ban were not obscurantists, but men of fairly broad secular culture.

Could it really have been Azariah's debunking of the rabbinic legend about the gnat that entered Titus' head through the nose and finally killed him?[31] Azariah himself relates that there were Jews who sharply criticized this passage in his book and regarded what he had done as an insult to the sages. But could the critique of such an *aggadah* really have seemed like a novelty in the sixteenth century? Did there not already exist long and recognized traditions within Judaism, whether philosophical or kabbalistic, which could not accept rabbinic *aggadot* literally, and which strove to reinterpret them rationally or mystically, at times to the most radical extremes? In what manner, then, had Azariah de' Rossi transgressed?

I would suggest that the answer lies, not in the fact of Azariah's criticism, but in its source, method and conclusion. Philosophic and kabbalistic critiques and reinterpretations of *aggadah* possessed an age-old legitimacy even though, to be sure, there still remained Jews in Azariah's time who would not accept even these.[32] The essential innovation in Azariah's approach lay in his attempt to evaluate *aggadot*, not within the framework of philosophy or Kabbalah, each a source of truth for its partisans, but by the use of profane history which few, if any, would accept as a truth by which the words of the sages might be judged. Worse than that, Azariah ventured to employ non-Jewish historical sources for this purpose, drawn from Greek, Roman and Christian writers. Above all, he did not flinch from the conclusions that emerged out of the comparison, even when these affected so sensitive an area as calendar computation. As for Titus' gnat, Azariah would not reinterpret the legend metaphorically or allegorically, nor did he spiritualize it in any way in order to salvage it. Citing Roman and other historians as to the actual date and cause of Titus' death, he dismissed the story as historically untrue. Such historical critiques could not yet be tolerated, let alone assimilated, by Azariah's Jewish contemporaries. On the contrary, it is perhaps a token of the flexibility of Italian Jewry that the ban upon the book (it was not pronounced against the author, and only required that special permission be obtained by those who wanted to read it) was not always enforced stringently, and there were some who continued to read it in subsequent generations. Azariah's experiment, however, remained his alone. There were no heirs to his method.

In a vital sense that is true of sixteenth-century Jewish historiography as a whole. In retrospect we see it as a sudden flowering, and an equally abrupt withering. It produces no real continuity and has no parallel for the next two hundred years. At the end of the sixteenth century those who still sought the meaning of Jewish historical suffering and of the length of exile found it in the Kabbalah of Isaac Luria and his disciples, and it is surely more than coincidence that a people that did not yet dream of defining itself in historical categories should find the key to its history in an awesome metahistorical myth.

I do not mean by this to imply in any way that sixteenth-century historiography and Lurianic Kabbalah stood in a consciously competitive relationship in which the latter was "victorious." Though both were ultimately related to the Spanish expulsion, each represented a separate response with its own inner dynamics. If I juxtapose the two, it is not in order to suggest an organic lateral relationship, but because of what the juxtaposition reveals about the mentality of Jews. That the historiographical effort proved abortive, while the Lurianic myth permeated ever-widening circles in Jewry, seems to me a datum of no small consequence for an understanding of important facets of that mentality. Whatever Lurianic Kabbalah may have meant to Jews (and Gershom Scholem has unveiled for us both its conceptual audacity and overwhelming pathos), its rapid reception by the Jewish world is significant in itself. Clearly, the bulk of Jewry was unprepared to tolerate history in imminent terms. It is as though, with the culminating tragedy of the expulsion from Spain, Jewish history had become opaque, and could not yield a satisfactory meaning even when, as among most of the historians, it was viewed religiously. Patently, however, Jews were spiritually and psychologically prepared for that which Lurianic Kabbalah offered them: a mythic interpretation of history that lay beyond history, and endowed the individual with the power to participate actively in hastening its messianic liquidation.

For us, both the Jewish historiography and the Kabbalah of the sixteenth century have become "history." Not only are we equidistant from both; we also study both—historically. But if we style ourselves historians and do not aspire to be kabbalists, that should not indulge us in the illusion that we have salvaged the one over the other.

There is no continuum between sixteenth-century Jewish historiography and Jewish historical scholarship as we know it and practice it in modern times. The rupture has been complete and decisive. To the degree that we have become historians (and there is no Jewish scholarly discipline today that is not historical), our roots lie in other soil. The fact that, in 1794, the *Me'or 'Einayim* was republished by the Maskilim in Berlin should not mislead us in this respect. At that time the *Historisches Journal* had already appeared in Göttingen for more than two decades, Barthold Niebuhr was eighteen years old, and Ranke would be born a year later. We are not the heirs of Azariah de' Rossi, but of these men and others, and the mode whereby we came into this inheritance has implications of its own. If the historical consciousness of the modern West is the result of gradual and coherent developments within European culture, Jews absorbed it abruptly when they plunged into that culture in the nineteenth century. The quest for Jewish history inaugurated by *Wissenschaft des Judentums* emanated from the convergence of a religious collapse from within and assimilation from without.[33] These observations involve neither judgment nor regret, both irrelevant in face of what seems, in retrospect, to have been inevitable.[34] In the measure that we have become modern Western men and women, the historical outlook is now part of our innermost selves.

As a result, Jewish scholars since the nineteenth century have been building, at an ever-accelerating rate, a vast edifice of historical research. Whether, despite what has been achieved, one can say even now that historiography has found a home within Jewry at large is another matter. Whether contemporary Jewry, having lived through its own unparalleled cataclysm, looks to history for meaning, or awaits a new myth, will also bear discussion. These and other queries arise, unsummoned, "when sleep wanders," even though one knows that the work will continue in the morning.

NOTES

1. *Sippur David Ha-Reubeni*, ed. A. Z. Aescoly (Jerusalem, 1940), pp. v–xii.
2. See Abravanel, *Ma'ayeney ha-yeshu'ah* (Ferrara, 1551), Ma'ayan II, Tomer 3, fol. 21v.
3. Moses Ibn Ezra, *Kitab al-Muḥādara wal-Mudhākara*, ed. with Hebrew tr. by A. S. Halkin (Jerusalem, 1975), pp. 50f.
4. *Shebet Yehudah*, ed. A. Shohat, int. by Y. Baer (Jerusalem, 1947), p. 21.
5. See H. H. Ben-Sasson, "Li-megamot ha-kronografiah ha-Yehudit shel yemey ha-benayim," in *Historionim v'askolot historiot* (Jerusalem, 1963), p. 30.
6. First printed in *Ozar Tob* (supplement to *Magazin für die Wissenschaft des Judenthums*) (Berlin, 1877–78), pp. 17ff. Reprinted in *Sefer Yosippon*, ed. H. Hominer (Jerusalem, 1965), p. 37.
7. Reprinted by Hominer, *op. cit.*, p. 41.
8. *Ibid.*, p. 43.
9. Most of the important apocalyptic texts of this period are assembled in Y. Eben-Shmuel, *Midreshey ge'ulah*, 2nd ed. (Jerusalem, 1954). Cf. also B. Lewis, "An Apocalyptic Vision of Islamic History" [analysis and translation of *Tefilat R. Shimon bar Yohai*], *Bulletin of the School of Oriental and African Studies*, XIII (1949–51), 308–338.
10. Sherira's epistle was first printed with Zacuto's *Yuḥusin* (Constantinople, 1566). The other three works were generally printed together in one volume (Mantua, 1513–14; Venice, 1545; Basel, 1580).
11. Gersonides, *Perush 'al ha-Torah*, on Lev. 26:38.
12. Abravanel, *Perush nebi'im aḥaronim*, on Is. 43:6.
13. Zacuto, *Sefer Yuḥasin*, ed. H. Filipowski, int. by A. H. Freimann (Frankfurt a.M., 1924), p. 223.
14. See Hans Baron, *The Crisis of the Early Italian Renaissance*, 2 vols. (Princeton, 1955), especially chs. 1–3.
15. This view derives from Yitzhak Baer. See his introduction to Shohat's edition of *Shebet Yehudah*, pp. 11, 13f., as well as his "He'arot ḥadashot le-Sefer Shebet Yehudah," *Tarbiz*, VI (1934–35), 152–179, and *Galut* (Eng. tr.) (New York, 1947), pp. 77ff.
16. See M. Benayahu, "Makor 'al megorashey Sefarad be-Portugal ve-ẓetam 'aḥarey gezerat RaSaV le-Saloniki," *Sefunot*, XI (1971–78), 233–265.
17. Joseph b. Joshua ha-Kohen, *Sefer dibrey ha-yamim le-malkhey Ẓarefat u-malkhey Bet Ottoman ha-Togar* (ed. Amsterdam, 1733), preface.

18. See now the recent edition of both the *Seder Eliyahu Zuta* and the Venetian chronicle by A. Shmuelevitz, S. Simonsohn and M. Benayahu, 2 vols. (Jerusalem, 1976–77).

19. Both works are extant in four manuscripts: Paris (Alliance, H81A); Berlin (160); New York (Columbia University, K82); Moscow (Günzberg, 212). All of these also contain his Hebrew version of Joannes Boemius' historical-geographical work *Omnium gentium mores, leges et ritus.*

20. To these we may also properly add the account of the reign of Suleiman the Magnificent in the Judeo-Spanish *Extremos y grandezas de Constantinople*, written by the sixteenth-century Salonikan rabbi Moses Almosnino.

21. *'Emek ha-bakha*, ed. M. Letteris (Krakow, 1895), pp. 102f.; *Sefer dibrey ha-yamim*, ed. cit, Pt. I, fol. 36v. Cf. also the account of the martyred messianic enthusiast Solomon Molkho in the latter work (Pt. II, fol. 19v), introduced by the significant phrase: "And a shoot came forth from Portugal *(wa-yeze hoter mi-Portugal)*, Solomon Molkho was his name."

22. See Y. H. Yerushalmi, *The Lisbon Massacre of 1506 and the Royal Image in the "Shebet Yehudah"* (Cincinnati, 1976), Supplement No. 1, *Hebrew Union College Annual.*

23. Yuhasin, ed. cit., Author's introduction, p. 1.

24. *Yosippon*, ed. Hominer, p. 43. Compare, in the seventeenth century, Joseph Delmedigo's list of recommended readings to the Karaite Zerah ben Menahem. The historical works, largely those with which we have been dealing, are endorsed "for cheering the soul when one is sad" *(le-ta'anug ha-nefesh bi-she'at ha-'izabon)*. For the text, see S. Assaf, *Mekorot le-toledot ha-hinnukh be-Yisrael* (Tel-Aviv, 1936), I, 101.

25. See, for example, Joseph Karo, *Shulhan 'Arukh*, Orah hayyim, no. 307:16, and the gloss of Moses Isserles *ad loc.*

26. *Sefer Me'or 'Einayim*, ed. D. Cassel (Vilna, 1866; reprinted, Jerusalem, 1970), I, 182. The phrase *mai de-havah* derives from the Talmud (Yoma, fol. 5v), where the question of the manner in which Aaron and his sons were dressed in their priestly garments is temporarily rejected as being of purely antiquarian interest ("what was—was"). On Azariah's methodology as a whole, see Salo Baron, "La méthode historique d'Azaria de' Rossi," *REJ*, LXXXVI (1928), 151–175; LXXXVII (1929), 43–78.

27. *Me'or 'Einayim*, I, 189.

28. *Ibid.*, II, 275.

29. See David Kaufmann, "Contributions à l'histoire des luttes d'Azaria de Rossi," *REJ*, XXXIII (1896), 77–87; *idem*, "La défense de lire le Meor Enayim d'Azaria de Rossi," *REJ*, XXXVIII (1899), 280–281. Cf. S. Z. H. Halberstamm, "Sheloshah ketabim 'al debar Sefer Me'or 'Einayim," in *Tehilah le-Mosheh* (Leipzig, 1896), Steinschneider Festschrift; Hebrew Section, pp. 1–8.

30. See the attack of Judah Loew b. Bezalel (Maharal), *Be'er ha-golah* (New York, 1969), pp. 126–141, and the report of a ban issued by Joseph Karo

on his deathbed, published by Kaufmann in his aforementioned article in *REJ*, XXXIII.

31. *Me'or 'Einayim*, I, 214–219.

32. A striking instance in the sixteenth century, though perhaps an isolated one, of the most extreme antagonism to non-literal interpretation of *aggadah*, is provided by the Safed Mishnaic scholar Joseph Ashkenazi. See G. Scholem, "Yediot ḥadashot 'al R. Yosef Ashkenazi, ha-Tanna mi-Ẓefat," *Tarbiz*, XXVIII (1959), 59–89, 201–233.

33. The change can be seen within the span of a generation. Compare, for example, the discussion of the uses of history in *Me'assef*, I (1784), 7–28, where the function of history is still perceived as ancillary to traditional religious concerns, and Immanuel Wolf's famous manifesto of 1822 "On the Concept of a Science of Judaism" (Eng. tr. by L. Kochan in *Leo Baeck Institute Yearbook*, II [1957], 194–204), in which historical studies are assigned the central role of clarifying "the fundamental idea of Judaism," and "the scientific [i.e. historico-critical] attitude" is hailed as "the characteristic of our time."

34. I refer here only to the absorption by Jews of the historical spirit and method. The specific deficiencies or biases of nineteenth-century *Wissenschaft* are a separate matter, and need not detain us here.

7

How Golden Was the Age of the Renaissance in Jewish Historiography?

Robert Bonfil

I

It is more or less a commonplace that "le XVIe siècle est un point culminant de l'historiographie juive." In formulating this statement in one of his earlier essays,[1] Salo W. Baron was probably influenced by the views on historical writing which were current in the first decades of this century (those of Fueter, Barnes, and so on). Indeed, the statement seems to stem from the belief that the Middle Ages did not produce any real historiography, and that Jewish writings during this period were quite naturally to be considered as reflecting this general condition. Baron himself stated this view clearly in the next sentence: "Après les grandes productions de l'antiquité, le moyen-âge juif—*pas plus d'ailleurs que le moyen-âge chrétien* [my italics]—n'avait connu aucune oeuvre historique dans le véritable sens du terme." Oddly enough, however, in the revised English translation of the same essay, as it appeared thirty-five years later,[2] the words italicized above had disappeared. Why did Baron remove the *terminus comparationis?* Was this simply an unintentional omission, or should we rather infer that in Baron's later historical outlook, the comparison with the Christian Middle Ages appeared irrelevant to the exposition of the Jewish case? If so, why did he not remove the entire introductory section, which sets out to show that medieval Jewry indeed "failed to bring forth any major historical work in the true

Reprinted by permission of the author and Wesleyan University from *History and Theory* 27 (1988).

sense of that term"? Should we infer that in Baron's revised view, medieval Christianity did produce some major historical works, while medieval Jewry did not?

The pertinence of these questions to the subject of the present enquiry is not immediately obvious. At first glance, it may seem that a study of Jewish historiography in the Renaissance and Baroque periods[3] need not concern itself with the medieval antecedents of the genre. Indeed, no fewer than ten substantial Jewish works of history were composed during the sixteenth and seventeenth centuries. Is not this evidence sufficient to plunge us into our subject *in medias res,* leaving aside the issue of the medieval concern with the past, which, as is well known, has recently become an object of dispute?[4] Yet the two issues are closely related: to deal with the "Golden Age" of Jewish historiography as an exception, and to interpret it as such, is obviously quite different from treating it as a normal expression of reality, to be interpreted within the context to which it belongs.

If we accept the traditional view whereby neither Christians nor Jews had produced any historiography as such during the Middle Ages, we should obviously interpret the later Jewish efflorescence of historiographical production as an integral part of the general "Renaissance" of historiography in the West, whatever the significance of this "rebirth" and its chronological parameters. For instance, if we adhere to R. G. Collingwood's opinion that "in the sense in which Gibbon and Mommsen were historians, there was no such thing as an historian before the 18th century,"[5] we might quite naturally extend his general statement to include the Jews, and apply to them the general framework of the emergence of modern historiography. Within this framework, such questions may be asked as: did the Jewish historians adopt the same genres as were current in Christian literature? did they ask the same kind of questions? did they adopt similar methods and explanations? did they intend to accomplish social, cultural, or political aims of a similar kind? and so on. If we prefer to date the emergence of modern historiography to the fifteenth or sixteenth century, the analytical process in the cases of both Jewish and non-Jewish historiography would be no different from the methodological point of view. In any case, the two parallel "Renaissance" productions would be studied comparatively in the same terms. On the other hand, one might argue that while a premodern Christian historiography existed, it did not have its counterpart among the Jews.

In this case, while the Christian "Renaissance" production should be interpreted in terms of *change,* the Jewish production should be thought of in terms of *emergence.* The "ontological" issue would thus take precedence over the "phenomenological" one.

Few scholars have shown awareness of the need to adopt such a comparative approach. Is this an expression of the general failure to study Jewish history as organically linked to general history, and the convention of treating it as somehow pertaining to the realm of the "other"? Is it a corollary of the essentially Judeo-Christian cultural tradition of the West which has bequeathed to us the idea that Jewish otherness is to be conceived as total, implying the near-essential difference of everything that belongs to Jewish existence in history? Indeed, in such an overall antithetical framework, an antithesis in the realm of historiography would, at least *prima facie,* follow quite naturally as a part of the whole structure in which knowledge is organized. On the other hand, the attempt to adopt a comparative approach within this framework might reveal itself as very problematic. Although it is not always easy to follow the argument in all its ramifications, one may assume that for non-Jews such an approach might imply some unnecessary confrontation with unpleasant components of anti-Jewishness in their own culture, while for Jews, the implication might be perceived in terms of some equally disagreeable alienation.[6] The tendency to avoid the whole question may thus be quite understandable. However, it is not the less regrettable.

Baron's decision to delete in 1964, after World War II, the words he wrote in 1928 may well be an expression of unwillingness to deal with the general question. Nevertheless, in Baron's case the point might well pass unobserved. In the essay in question, he deals with specific aspects related to the single figure which is the subject of his study, and this might be done without paying too much attention to the linkage with the non-Jewish, general framework. Thus, after the sentence referring to Christian medieval production was deleted, the opening statement that "the sixteenth century represents one of the high points in Jewish historiography" became ambiguous enough to leave the whole question pending. Whether or not Baron subsequently took up a position in his *Social and Religious History of the Jews* remains open to more than one interpretation.[7]

Be that as it may, the problem has recently been put forward by Yosef

Haim Yerushalmi in a highly provocative little book.[8] Without any
reference to the question of the emergence of modern historical science,
and in fact without any working definition of history and/or historiography, Yerushalmi presents Jewish historiography as totally isolated,
and suggests an approach to its dynamics in terms of the possible factors
that determined essential changes in Jewish thought. For him, Jewish
historiography is a product of the Jewish inception into modernity. The
Jewish historian is "a new creature in Jewish history"; his "lineage does
not extend beyond the second decade of the nineteenth century."[9] According to Yerushalmi, it was the ideology of the *Wissenschaft des
Judentums* that gave birth to Jewish historiography, in answer to the
crisis-laden emergence of the Jews from the ghetto.[10] While the premodern period was characterized by "the absence of interaction" between
Jews and non-Jews in the sphere of historiography, the modern period,
on the contrary, was characterized by "a deep and ubiquitous interaction
with modern historicism."[11] This in itself was only one aspect of what
we might, in Foucault's mode, call the "inversion of the structure" which
took place at the passage from premodern to modern times. In the realm
of philosophy things went exactly the opposite way. However, unlike
Foucault, Yerushalmi does not seek to explain these inversions by means
of an analysis of the changes that occurred in the conception of science
and of scientific method. Having established a nexus between "assimilation" and "historiography," he rather concludes that "the modern effort
to reconstruct the Jewish past begins at a time that witnesses a sharp
break in the continuity of Jewish living and hence also an ever-growing
decay of Jewish group memory."[12] Thus "history becomes what it had
never been before—the faith of fallen Jews."[13] We need not follow
Yerushalmi further in the development of this thesis. It will be enough
to note that, given the scheme, it is only natural to conclude that before
the second decade of the nineteenth century, there was no such thing as
Jewish historiography. Instead, there was a very strong perception of
"memory," expressed in a variety of literary genres, such as liturgical
poetry and hagiography.

Yet, puzzlingly enough, Yerushalmi concedes that there were some
notable exceptions to confirm the rule of the general absence of Jewish
historiography in premodern times. The production of the sixteenth and
seventeenth centuries was one such exception. In fact, Yerushalmi clearly
states that "only in the sixteenth century do we encounter within Jewry

a cultural phenomenon that can be recognized with little hesitation as genuinely historiographical."[14] But, even after conceding that much, he does not venture to dwell on comparative phenomenological questions. It is the "ontological" issue which absorbs the whole of Yerushalmi's attention. Others might ask themselves whether the Jewish historiography of the sixteenth and seventeenth centuries still belonged to the tradition of the Middle Ages or whether it was a Renaissance phenomenon;[15] they might ask how this historiography expressed the dialectical interplay between external events and immanent trends.[16] Yerushalmi, in focusing on the "ontological" issue, totally absolves himself from such questions. By stating that the Jewish historiographical production of the sixteenth and seventeenth centuries was virtually a unique exception, he leaves aside all phenomenological questions and limits himself to treating the emergence of the exceptional phenomenon. Thus, in searching for an exceptional circumstance that would account for the emergence of the exceptional phenomenon, Yerushalmi unhesitatingly points to the expulsion of the Jews from Spain;[17] for, as he has argued, albeit in connection with another school of historical scholarship, historiography emerges from the consciousness of a "sharp break in the continuity of Jewish living."

Was such a major crisis a sufficient condition for the emergence of historiography? Could a novel historical consciousness develop without secularization and assimilation? To put it in Yerushalmi's terms, could such a consciousness develop without the need of a "faith for fallen believers"? These questions are never addressed, as if exceptions did not deserve comparative phenomenological consideration. Yet the answers to some carefully selected phenomenological questions might well confirm or possibly weaken his main thesis. Moreover, the failure to address these questions may obscure other, more fundamental questions. For instance, we have already mentioned the question of definition, which seems to be crucial to the "ontological" aspect of our subject. If Jost or Graetz were indeed the first Jewish historians, in the sense in which Gibbon and Mommsen were historians, how "historiographical" were the works of sixteenth- and seventeenth-century Jewish "historians" and chroniclers who, by general consensus, were never as effective as the most successful Renaissance historians, such as Guicciardini or Machiavelli (themselves unworthy of inclusion in Collingwood's historians' club)? Does Yerushalmi disagree with Collingwood's sharp distinction between modern and premodern historiography? If so, would not an explicit and well-reasoned statement to that effect do away with the extraordinariness of sixteenth- and seventeenth-century Jewish historiography? Or does Yerushalmi agree with Collingwood? If so, would not the exceptional Jewish production of that period cease to be "historiographical," together with its contemporary non-Jewish "historical" production? One might add many other questions of this kind. In fact, one of the main characteristics of Yerushalmi's book seems to be rhetorical ambiguity, an intriguing mixture of certainty and doubt.[18] However, a critique of this book is not my purpose here. If I have lingered on Yerushalmi's argument, I have done so mainly because in substituting the "ontological" for the phenomenological issue, he has so much altered the terms of reference which now define the field, that a preliminary re-establishment of some kind of *status quo ante* seemed to me desirable.

Indeed, in what follows I would suggest adopting a different approach. I shall propose that the schema contrasting Jewish with non-Jewish does not provide an adequate overall context for historical interpretation; it is therefore insufficient as a framework for understanding Jewish historiographical production where this is not specifically related to the essence of Jewish otherness. For examples of such issues, besides the "ontological" question itself, one may cite the attitude towards historical explanation; the relevance of history, and particularly ancient history, for the cultural definition of the self; or the supposed opposition between "medieval" as essentially "God-oriented" and "Renaissance" as "man-oriented;" and so on. In fact, I would assume that there was no essential difference between Jews and Christians concerning such issues, either in the premodern period or in the modern world. Keeping that in mind, I would maintain that to focus on the "ontological" question not only leaves basic questions unanswered but also increases the risk of distorting the overall picture. I would, therefore, attempt first to eliminate this risk, and then bring the discussion back to the comparative phenomenological approach. It is within this framework that the difference between being a Jew and being a Christian should be considered as concurring in shaping the varieties of response to the peculiar challenges of the times.

II

The first important point which calls for modification is the common-place that the Jewish historiographic production of the sixteenth and seventeenth centuries was exceptionally rich. To justify this claim almost all the literary works, however loosely related to history, that were produced by Jews over a period of some two hundred years (from roughly the mid-fifteenth to the mid-seventeenth century) have been grouped under the heading of "Jewish historiography." This seems to me to be patently wrong.[19] Moreover, I would suggest, next to questioning the richness of this production, its status as an exceptional phenomenon must also be questioned.

To begin with, I would argue that the assumption of monolithic richness cannot withstand comparison with the non-Jewish historical output of the same period, even without taking into account the well-established dissimilarities between Renaissance and Baroque writings.[20] In fact, only a handful of Jewish works may legitimately be classified as belonging to Renaissance or Baroque historiography. Most of the Jewish works usually thus reckoned should be excluded from this category on the grounds that both in subject matter and in literary genre, they do not accord with such notions of historical writings as were current at the time.

In the fifteenth and sixteenth centuries, history was universally understood as *narratio rerum gestarum*. It told the story of "memorable" events in which exemplary men were involved and which might be cited to teach moral or political lessons. Thus historical writing was exclusively narrative and its subject matter was confined to political and military affairs and to *dramatis personae* who were usually kings and princes, leaders and men of arms. Of course, such a narrow definition should not be used rigidly to exclude everything else. Historians made room also for anecdotes and accounts of notable deeds which were considered worth recording as paradigmatic or because they were bizarre or intriguing and could provide an entertaining diversion from the main theme. Such stories would be included even if the *dramatis personae* were women or commoners who were not directly involved in political and military affairs. But if political and military affairs had become secondary to other themes, authors might not really think of themselves as writing history. Nor would they consider themselves historians if they were to choose a literary genre other than the narrative, as did a number of medieval authors.[21] Contemporaries would hardly accept this kind of ambiguity. Thus, whatever the style of writing, one could certainly not claim to be writing history when the work was what Italians would define as *utili e dilettevoli ragionamenti*,[22] even if it was based on what we would recognize as sound, critical, historical research. This is why it would seem inappropriate to include in the category of Renaissance or Baroque historiography even Azaria de Rossi's *Meor Enayim*, a huge work which consists of a collection of truly historical essays in the erudite mode that the *Wissenschaft des Judentums* school would later on greatly appreciate.[23] It seems even less appropriate to consider as genuine historical writing Samuel Usque's *Consolacam as tribulacoens de Israel*, which is in fact a pastoral, allegorical dialogue, using historical themes in a rhetorical framework of argumentation. Neither should we unreservedly add to our list Abraham Zacuto's *Sefer Yuhasin* (Book of Genealogies), which is an erudite epigone of the medieval "Chains of Tradition," however important it may be for the factual accuracy and historical information which it provides about specific events of Jewish history. For the same reason we may have to reject as genuine historiography Gedaliah Ibn Yahia's *Shalshelet ha-Kabbalah* (Chain of Tradition), although it contains much historical narrative.

Renaissance and Baroque historians also agreed, much more so than did their medieval predecessors, that an historian should not lie. Commitment to truth certainly allows for the selection or embellishment of facts, tendentiousness, or whatever else historians might consider as conforming with the Ciceronian idea of history as *exhornatio rerum*. But they should not lie. They should not administer to their readers edifying and imaginative tales camouflaged as history. This is not to say that charlatans did not exist or that historians did not occasionally include in their works stories taken from some pamphlet or other which had been manufactured by a charlatan, not realizing that their source was unreliable. Such accidents may occur even to modern historians, notwithstanding the infinitely more refined techniques of verification at their disposal. *A fortiori* our Renaissance or Baroque colleagues might have fallen into unintentional error owing to their insufficient means of checking information. Yet it was clear that one's readers should not be offered known fairy tales in the guise of history. The fanciful presentation of the persecutions of the Jews, as set out in Solomon Ibn Verga's *Shebet Yehudah* (The Scepter of Judah), cannot be considered as truly historical, however important this work may be for analyzing the perception of Jewish suffering in the wake of the Spanish Expulsion.

Thus all in all the only works that belong properly to the category of Renaissance and Baroque historiography are Eliyahu Capsali's *Seder Olam Zuta* (The Minor Order of Elijah), which is a history of the Ottoman Turks, including a chronicle of Venice and chapters of contemporary Jewish history; Joseph ha-Cohen's *Divrey ha-Yamim le malkhey Tsarefat u-beth Ottoman ha-Togar* (History of the French and Ottoman Kings), including all the persecutions of the Jews that had come to the author's knowledge and were subsequently assembled separately in *Emek ha-Bakha* (The Vale of Tears);[24] David Ganz's *Zemach David* (The Sprout of David), which is a hybrid work: the first part is an account of Jewish history, echoing strongly the old "Chains of Tradition," while in the second part there appears an epitome of world history, viewed from the standpoint of German and Polish chroniclers. To these one might also add Josef Sambari's *Divrey Yosef* (The Sayings of Josef), which is a universal chronicle, beginning with the creation of the world and ending in 1672. A considerable effort of imagination would be required to suppose that fewer than half a dozen works constitute an exceptionally rich harvest over a period of almost two hundred years, during which printing was available and history was held in high esteem.

It could be contended that I have been pushing the argument too far. Perhaps we should not altogether exclude from consideration works which a centuries-old tradition has seen as historical writings, and which, from a modern point of view, could in fact and with some justification be thus seen. Yet even were we prepared to admit such writings to the historiographical canon, that canon would not be enriched as a result. Rather, its ultimate poverty would be highlighted by the contrast with non-Jewish historiography. In fact, while the scanty and imprecise (in terms of literary genre) medieval Jewish production did not really differ from its non-Jewish counterpart which was equally sparse and loosely defined, this was no longer true in the Renaissance and Baroque periods. The quantitatively poor Jewish production of the latter periods should now be compared with the extraordinary richness of non-Jewish historiography. Thus, if with regard to the Middle Ages the comparison was between half a dozen Jewish books and two or three dozen non-Jewish ones—a reasonable proportion, given the demographic and existential conditions of Jewish life in the Christian Middle Ages—with regards to the sixteenth and seventeenth centuries little more than half a dozen Jewish books are to be compared with hundreds of non-Jewish works which belong clearly and substantially to the historical genre,[25] and to these should be added a few hundred more in which the historical element would equal that of the Jewish works under consideration. In fact, if we value consistency we cannot maintain a loose definition of literary genre for the Jewish production, while insisting on a narrow definition of the non-Jewish. The contrast between them would thus be sharpened rather than blurred.

Not only was Jewish historiographical writing much less than exceptionally rich during our period, it did not even encounter the favor of the Jewish public. It hardly provided a valid response to the special challenge that those troubled times presented to the Jewish readership. In fact, it is difficult to say how many of these books were ever read, unlike most of the books of history composed by non-Jews. To begin with, none of the works that we might describe as genuine Jewish historical writing was printed more than once, and some were not printed at all (Capsali's and Sambari's).[26] Even those that did reach print do not seem to have circulated widely. There may be indirect proof of this in the fact that they have not become rare, as did popular editions which enjoyed large distribution. Statistical evidence based on the detailed analysis of the libraries of Mantuan Jews at the turn of the sixteenth century fully confirms this point. People did not usually keep this kind of historical writing in their private libraries.[27]

On the other hand, even a quick scanning of catalogues of printed Jewish books would immediately show that the best-sellers of Jewish historical writing continued to be, as in the Middle Ages, the *Yosippon* and the various "Chains of Tradition," among which should be included Zacuto's *Sefer Yuhasin* and the old chronologies of Jewish knowledge: the *Seder Olam Rabba*, the *Seder Olam Zuta*, and Ibn David's *Sefer ha-Kabbalah*. Further, it would not be farfetched to add to the *Yosippon* some other little books and pamphlets, belonging ultimately to the same literary genre: for instance, *The Gests of Alexander*, which was indeed included in contemporary editions of the *Yosippon; Eldad ha-Dani*, the haggadic part of which is concerned with the lost tribes of Israel; or some medieval midrashic elaborations of biblical themes like *Divrey ha-*

Yamim shel Moshe rabbenu (The Chronicle of Moses, our Master).[28]
According to modern scholars, the popularity of such *midrashim* might
even have yielded to some new production, such as the *Sefer ha-Yashar,*
first printed in Venice in 1625.[29]

It would thus seem that in the very period in which the definition of
the historical genre became more rigorous than in the Middle Ages, and
history enjoyed much higher esteem, the Jewish response to the impact
of reality at the historiographical level was to take refuge in a conservative attachment to old models, of which a fairly important component
was the flight into the realm of the imaginary. When they did not apply
themselves to rabbinical chronologies, the Jews gave precedence to a
literary production which was more pertinent to myth than to history.
Does this constitute a proof that they were unresponsive to the historiographical challenge of the times? It does not seem so. As far as literary
genre is concerned, the mythical production that interested the Jews was
very close to the classical conception of history which was current at the
time: it narrated truly Jewish *axiologa,* and it was properly focused on
political and military themes, in much the same way as was current in
non-Jewish historiography. The Renaissance discovery of antiquity might
even have invested it with some nobility, since it could be presented as
the "Ancient History" of the Jews. Thus the exceptionally poor harvest
of historiographical writings among the Jews during this period cannot
be said to have resulted from a lack of interest in history as such. Rather,
their interest in historical writing continued to be satisfied by a production of a kind which was no longer sufficient for the non-Jewish public.
How should we interpret this fact?

III

Answers should probably be sought in more than one direction. On the
cultural level, this situation may be seen as a particular aspect of Jewish
perplexity at the almost ubiquitous process of refinement of definitions,
a process which had been set in motion by medieval and Renaissance
thought. This process came increasingly to challenge the Jewish condition and to question the Jews' relation to society as a whole. One may
see in it a particular expression of the ever more powerful tendency to
exclude the Jews from the social framework, by this time increasingly
influenced by the rise of intolerance and anti-Jewish sentiment to unprec-

edented heights. More concrete expressions of this trend were the numerous expulsions (of which the Spanish is perhaps the most striking),
the spread of ghettoes, and so on. In other words, before this trend was
arrested and eventually reversed, the Renaissance attitude to the relationship between Jews and non-Jews was increasingly to strengthen the
medieval view of the relationship as sheer opposition. The more refined
the definitions, the more acute the opposition between the two camps,
as sensed by both Jews and non-Jews. This attitude applied to all areas
of life and assumed Jewish destiny to be radically opposed to that of the
non-Jews, in much the same way as God was opposed to the Devil and
Salvation to Damnation.[30] Inevitably, this in turn affected the Jewish
perception of history and the historian's task. As was suggested above,
the difficulties sensed by modern historians, whether Jewish or not, in
defining and handling Jewish history may well, at least in part, arise
from the same cultural tradition, a tradition of opposition which is still
very much alive.

Indeed, the very conception of history as a narrative of political and
military events may itself be a part of that refinement of definitions
which the orientation toward Antiquity of humanism and the Renaissance had bequeathed to the Baroque period. History could no longer
accommodate liturgical poetry or hagiography, as it had done during the
Middle Ages. In a sense, the situation became similar to that faced by
fourth-century ecclesiastical historiography, as outlined by Arnaldo
Momigliano in one of his finest essays.[31] By making "Pagan historiography" the main concern of the historian, Renaissance historiography
confronted the Jews with a problem similar to the one which was
encountered centuries earlier by Eusebius and the early Christian historiographers. In Momigliano's view, Eusebius' success lay in that his
history did not attempt to reinterpret in Christian terms the existing
pagan military, political, and diplomatic history. Following in the footsteps of Jewish-Hellenistic historiography, he introduced a "new type of
historical exposition," characterized, *inter alia,* by the central position
of doctrinal controversies and by the marginality of military and political
events, which at most might provide the setting for a providential apologetic history of the Christians. This kind of historiography was handed
down through the Middle Ages, prolonging the divorce from political
history. I would surmise that during the Middle Ages, such a divorce
suited the Jewish perception of the *axiologa* worth recording for poster-

ity. During the period, this Jewish writers of "Chains of Tradition"-type history could feel confident that their work was history as much as was "ecclesiastical history," a genre whose legitimacy had been strongly affirmed by the followers of Eusebius and reinforced by the loose conception of history which prevailed at the time. This type of history filled the vacuum created by the total absence of contemporary Jewish political and military history, while for the aesthetic and emotional satisfaction provided by tales of wars and kings the Jews were compelled to turn to the ancient history of Israel at the time of its independence in the Holy Land. From time to time they would turn to the histories of other peoples—a pursuit of doubtful merit from the orthodox point of view but nonetheless not uncommon, to judge by the various Hebrew versions of the *Romance of Alexander* and the Arthurian legend,[32] which circulated in the Middle Ages and were written and read in the medieval romance mode.[33]

In any event, until the humanists' revolutionary approach to the writing of history, Jews and Christians shared the same literary conventions and historical sensibilities. For both Jews and Christians "no real historiography founded upon the political experience of Herodotus, Thucydides, Livy, and Tacitus was transmitted to the Middle Ages," and "when in the fifteenth and sixteenth centuries the humanists rediscovered their Herodotus, Thucydides, Livy, and Tacitus they rediscovered something for which there was no plain alternative."[34] But, while the break between pagan and Christian history introduced by the ecclesiastical historiography of the fourth century paradoxically helped historians such as Machiavelli and Guicciardini to turn to "real" historiography, there were no Jewish counterparts to Machiavelli or Guicciardini. This was not simply because the Jews did not happen to produce such intellectual giants of their own. The difference between the Jewish and Christian responses to the humanist challenge was rooted in the profound difference of the historical contexts in which the two respective communities were operating. The Jews had long ceased to have kings and conduct wars. As far as Jewish history was concerned, the humanistic historiographical model was irrelevant. Jews could not but feel unable to respond to the challenge of current categories of historical practice. They were finally forced to give up. It was, I suggest, as a result of the rebirth of political and military historiography that Jewish historiography was finally pushed out of the main stream. Following this interpretation, the Jewish production of the Renaissance and Baroque periods should in fact be considered as the swan song of medieval Jewish historiography.

The various facts adduced in the previous section can be explained within this schematic framework. To be sure, the first instinctive response was to cling to the old model and keep it alive. It is thus not surprising that we witness not only the success of the traditional Jewish "ecclesiastical histories" such as Ibn Daud's *Sefer ha-Kabbalah,* populated by rabbis with their literary works, but also the production of new ones, such as Zacuto's *Yuhasin.* After all, the Jews continued to be a nation in the way in which Eusebius conceived the Christians to be a nation when he borrowed from them the Jewish version of history, including the Jewish scheme of redemption and of sacred time governing chronology. Hence, like Eusebius, yet apparently without any clear consciousness of it, Jews would not persist alone in the Flavian tradition of opposing a Jewish conception of history to Greco-Roman history. That by this time such attempts had become extremely out of date hardly calls for demonstration.

Some Jews courageously explored new roads. The most eloquent of these, who came close to a genuinely historical mode of writing by contemporary standards, were Eliyahu Capsali, Joseph ha-Cohen, and David Ganz. Gedaliah Ibn Yahia may be added to their ranks, although not without some reservations. By adopting the methods of ecclesiastical history, they tried to do what Eusebius and his followers had done, yet in a different way. They assigned a place to Jewish history within the framework imposed by the literary genre of history as a narrative of political and military deeds. Their methods and areas of concern are quite distinct from one another, as a result of the diversity of the historical contexts of their lives and cultures. A thorough examination of their works in the light of all these factors is yet to be undertaken. However, some general remarks may be offered at this point.

All these authors were involved in a truly novel type of Jewish literary production. Although most historians may have a strong feeling of solitude when at work on their particular "patch," some more than others are imbued with the consciousness of the originality and novelty of their enterprise. Joseph ha-Cohen experienced this intensely and he did not hesitate to express his feelings at the opening of his book. Yerushalmi vividly characterizes ha-Cohen's words as ''an exultant passage that deliberately echoes the biblical Song of Deborah'':

All my people is aware that no author has arisen in Israel comparable to Yosippon the priest, who wrote of the war of the land of Judea and of Jerusalem. The chronicles ceased in Israel, they ceased, until I, Joseph, did arise, until I did arise, a chronicler in Israel![35]

I would certainly agree with most of Yerushalmi's remarks on this point: like Joseph ha-Cohen, all these writers indeed extended their range far beyond previously accepted boundaries; all assigned prominence to post-biblical Jewish history; all certainly showed much interest in non-Jewish history, especially the history of contemporary peoples.[36] I would add that all of them openly broke with the tradition of paying lip service to the idea of history as an unworthy intellectual occupation for a good Jew. On the contrary, they did not refrain from presenting the wars of kings and princes as a subject matter worthy of being put into biblical language, thus offering them to the Jewish public as strongly deserving attention. As even a glance at the preface of *Seder Eliyahu Zuta* immediately shows, Capsali, who wrote his book in the 1520s, was perhaps much more aware of, and faithful to, the rhetorical ideal of historical writing than was Joseph ha-Cohen some decades later. Indeed, his preface certainly deserves to be considered as a masterpiece of medieval *accessus ad auctores* in which the dignity of history is so deeply felt that the author senses his own inability to meet the challenge adequately. In his highly rhetorical Hebrew prose which is almost impossible to translate, dotted with biblical phrases, most of them pointing automatically to some traditional midrashic interpretation, Capsali would even extend the medieval conception of the prophet as a perfect *rhetor* in order to include his Ciceronian equivalent, that is, the historian.[37]

However, the historical method employed by all these writers clearly reveals the persistence of an intimate, somehow structural, similarity with "ecclesiastical history." In fact, just as the fourth-century Christian writers considered the pagan *breviaria* as sufficient sources of knowledge, mostly because they were devoid of religious content, the Jewish historians confined themselves to epitomes of general history.[38] By their choice of material they convey the idea that, notwithstanding their natural interest in anecdotes and curiosities, in which the histories they could read abounded, and notwithstanding the amount of space they were compelled to dedicate to general history, they still conceived it as ancillary to Jewish history—the subject that really interested them. In other words, the general history which they reported so extensively was no more than a convenient setting for Jewish history. Their main focus ultimately remained the "Jewish question." A thorough examination of the ways in which these authors had used their sources, and of their principles of selection and transplantation of themes and details, would certainly reveal a great deal about the particular mode of their reading the lessons of history with their own aims always in view. This kind of study is at present only in its initial stages. However, at least one general remark may be ventured safely even now.

Such a reaction to reality was certainly most natural. Historiography always appears to be a mode of adapting the perception of the self in response to major changes in reality. From their very beginnings, the historiographical traditions to which Western thought is indebted were the products of a similar reaction. Indeed, as Arnaldo Momigliano has taught us,[39] both the Jewish and the Greek historiography that flourished in the fifth century B.C. may be considered as parallel reactions to the same reality—that of the Persian Empire. The "flourishing" of Jewish historiography in our period may also be considered as an expression of the authors' attempt to find their place in the overall framework of the changes which they were witnessing. That these were times of major upheaval hardly needs to be stressed. Therefore, in a very broad sense, one might say that this historiographical output was but a part of the general Jewish endeavor to redefine, by means of this particular literary genre, Jewish identity at the dawn of the modern era.

While it may well be that the expulsion of Spanish Jewry had played some role in shaping a new Jewish consciousness, there is no reason whatsoever to think of it as a factor of exclusive or even primary importance. *Post hoc* is certainly not equivalent to *propter hoc* as a category of historical explanation. In fact, only Joseph ha-Cohen explicitly accorded any importance to the expulsion of the Jews from Spain in the formation of his historical outlook, when he declared that "[t]he expulsions from France as well as this exceedingly bitter exile [that is, from Spain] have aroused me to compose this book, so that the Children of Israel may know what they [the Gentiles] have done to us in their lands, their courts and their castles."[40] Even so, he mentions the expulsion from Spain together with other expulsions which he knew, and he does not accord it more space than other disasters. One might even say that he passes over the event in near-silence. In any case, as far as the other authors are concerned, the allegedly extraordinary importance of the Spanish tragedy for the "emergence" of Jewish historiography in our period is not supported by any substantial evidence. We have already shown that one cannot speak of an emergence. It is even less permissible to assume *a priori* the existence of a link between those writers' primary motivations and the Spanish tragedy.[41] Until some truly convincing evidence is produced, one should not succumb to the inclination of modern historians who, perhaps under the impact of World War II, have taken such a link for granted. On the contrary, a good dose of healthy epistemological skepticism, urging one to reconsider the expediency of inserting the Spanish issue into a much larger framework, would be preferable.

Be that it may, the problem of defining the essence of Jewish history in relation to general history—itself quite narrowly defined as specified above—was a real one. It presented itself then in much the same way as it presents itself, *mutatis mutandis,* to every modern historian. The works I am discussing here represent different solutions to this problem. All were ultimately highly unsatisfactory. I would even venture to say that they were total failures.

Working as he was within the medieval categories of thought, Joseph ha-Cohen inevitably achieved only an exacerbation of the opposition between Jewish and non-Jewish history. In fact, as he himself said, his intention was to tell "what *they* have done to *us* in *their* lands, *their* courts and *their* castles" (my italics). In his case the result was thus inevitably to sharpen the medieval dichotomy between Jewish and non-Jewish. This dichotomy now came to underline a whole set of oppositions which were not necessarily pertinent to historiography alone: active versus passive, joyful versus lachrymose. For Joseph ha-Cohen, lachrymose was simply homologous, almost synonymous, with Jewish, in just the same way as were passivity, absence of political power, of military force, and of *axiologa* in the Thucydidean sense of the word. Following such premises, his history inevitably became a history of the Other interspersed with a history of the Self, while mediation between them was accomplished by the theme of the suffering imposed on the Jews by the Other. The common arena on which the action was played out thus came to be a Vale of Tears, *Emek ha-Bakha,* as Joseph actually called the compendium of Jewish history excerpted from his general *Divrey ha-Yamim.* According to him, the story was not only a sad one; it amounted in effect to the history of the Other in which was implied the affirmation that a real history of the Jews could not be written. It is not surprising that the work did not meet with contemporary favor. Quite possibly Joseph ha-Cohen himself became aware of this difficulty. Indeed, although he continued to update his book until his last days, he excerpted *Emek ha-Bakha* from *Divrey ha-Yamim* only some five years after its publication. In the light of the poor reception of the complete work, he might have thought that *Emek ha-Bakha,* however "medieval," would better satisfy his co-religionists. Further research, in which I am at present engaged, will, I hope, shed more light on the matter.

David Ganz attempted a somewhat different solution to the problem of defining Jewish history in relation to general history. He wrote two parallel stories: one was the history of the Gentiles, a history of kings and wars which was as entertaining and exciting as such a history was expected to be according to the literary taste of the time; the other was the history of the Jews, a history of rabbis and literary works, tedious and sleep-inducing, like other "Chains of Tradition." Yet he carefully avoided the narrative of persecutions and expulsions, asserting that he had a good reason for doing so,[42] but without revealing it to his readers. May we assume that he deliberately chose to separate the two histories, and eliminated the only mediating link he could perceive, because he sensed that it did not really provide a satisfactory answer to the problem? Rather than mixing two stories of different natures, better to tell them separately. Thus the dichotomy between the profane, violent, and material history of the Other, and the sacred, peaceful, and spiritual history of the Self was squarely denied a mediation. Ganz's solution to the problem of the proper way of writing Jewish history was perhaps a far better answer than that of Joseph ha-Cohen. Yet it was still hardly satisfactory.

To my mind, the most successful work to have been written within the conventional historical literary genre of the epoch was that of Capsali. It is a pity that its true originality has not yet attracted sufficient scholarly scrutiny. The recent and only available edition of Capsali's work has not been joined by a comparative study of his sources nor by any attempt to focus on the cultural milieu to which the work properly belongs. In any case, even a superficial reading would immediately show that it was the most outstanding attempt of its time to write history in Hebrew. Capsali had a proper rhetorical conception of history. More than any other Jewish historian, he considered himself an *exhornator rerum* in the Ciceronian mode. He accorded a far more important place to style and aesthetic effect than to the facts he picked out of his sources. Thus his rhetorical conflation of narrative was ultimately more successful than other contemporary writings in concealing the dichotomy between the Other and the Self behind the artistic accomplishment. Yet if Capsali's history was indeed a notable example of how general history might have been written in Hebrew, it obviously failed to answer the question of how such a history should be viewed as relevant to the special demands of Jewish self-consciousness. It may be a beautiful history, stylistically perfect, aesthetically satisfactory, and excitingly entertaining. However, it is not a *Jewish* history. It remains the history of the Other. As such, it could hardly have been taken as an answer to Jewish cultural necessities. In any event, Capsali's history was not published until very recently, and the author never had the opportunity to test the public's reaction to his labor.

To conclude, history—that is, history according to the classic pagan definition—became irrelevant to the history of the Jewish people, mainly because it posed a problem that remained practically insoluble until very recently, when that definition of history was relinquished in favor of, for example, cultural history, intellectual history, social and religious history, or *histoire des mentalités*. Nowhere did the Jews possess political and military *axiologa* of their own. Therefore they appeared not to have a history at all, and this was one of the many expressions of the difference between the Jewish and non-Jewish conditions. In our context, the distinction was, quite simply, between people who had history and people who did not. This would obviously discourage any Jew from venturing into historiography, even if he were not himself inclined to reject history as an intellectual occupation. Without any further refinement of definition, historiography would mean for him the writing down of such deeds as were relevant to the self-perception of the Other, and this would be too high a price to pay for the indisputable pleasure of dedicating his time to this kind of occupation—the price of basic alienation, which is generally unacceptable even to incorrigibly erudite men. Viewed from this standpoint, I would argue that the Jewish historiographical production of the Renaissance and Baroque periods was in fact the expression of the unsuccessful attempt by a handful of individuals to come to grips with this problem. Their failure was the inevitable result of the essential incompatibility of the subject matter of history, as conceived in those days, and the destiny of their people the world over.

In this sense, the Jewish historiographical production of the Renaissance and Baroque periods may be considered as one of the saddest expressions of the medieval Jewish attempt to retain historiography within the range of normal intellectual activities befitting the Jewish condition.

For ordinary people, flight into the realm of the imaginary might, on the level of historiography, be the equivalent of the general trend of excluding the Jews from the non-Jewish world at the turn of the sixteenth century. It may even be said that the tendency to embark on this kind of flight was reinforced by the confluence of two contradictory forces, one essentially centripetal and the other centrifugal. The first paralleled the already established fact that among the urban *menu peuple* of the sixteenth century, medieval popular literature, which for centuries had effectively mediated between oral and written culture, continued to enjoy great favor. In other words, in Jewish society, the *Chronicle of Moses* or *The Gests of Alexander* played the same role as that played by the *Roman de la Rose* or the *Calendrier historial* in that part of Christian society that might be considered equivalent to the majority of European Jews, that is, people of quite low social standing.[43] Most of these productions possessed a genuinely Jewish exotic flavor, important in providing some relief from the suffocating atmosphere of overcrowded and stench-ridden ghettoes. The uncritical plunge into the mythical tales of the past, whose veracity remained almost always unchallenged, may have offered a means of escape far more realistic than the messianic chimera.

The centrifugal force was represented by the effects of restructuring, as perceived by the Jews. In fact, one of the first clear results of their integration into the non-Jewish world, an integration to which their resistance was gradually diminishing, was the adoption of non-Jewish languages as creative languages—a phenomenon which had been widespread in the earlier Middle Ages, but which progressively waned as the Middle Ages were drawing to an end. The dawn of the early modern era witnessed a gradual reversal of this situation. The less the Jews felt culturally opposed to non-Jews, the less they found it necessary to import from outside, by means of translation and adaptation, works that might easily be read in the original language. The diffusion of the vernacular obviously made the process easier. Consequently, while Hebrew became more and more confined to creativity specifically committed to Jewishness, for all other fields the vernaculars were amply sufficient. Should we venture to draw quantitative conclusions from the scanty historiographical production of the period under consideration, we may conclude that it was not by mere coincidence that the disappearance of Hebrew historiography, which throughout our period was synonymous with Jewish historiography, was very much favored by the increasing adoption by Jews of the vernacular as a language of cultural creativity—first in Italy and later in Eastern Europe and the Ottoman Empire.

IV

There was one notable exception to the picture drawn above: Azariah de Rossi and his book *Meor Einayim*.[44] As we have already noted, this was not *narratio rerum gestarum,* whether Jewish or Gentile, and so certainly not history in the then current meaning of the word. Yet, at least in one sense, it was genuine history. In his highly erudite essays, de Rossi presented the results of thorough and meticulous research on specific themes, most of which may rightly be called themes of ancient history: the significance of the apocryphal book known as the *Letter of Aristeas;* the place of Philo in the cultural and religious tradition of the Jewish people; the history of human creativity, such as linguistics, poetry, and so on; the significance of rabbinic legends; the High Priest's garments and the splendors of the Temple of Jerusalem; the synchronizing of biblical and extra-biblical chronology; the calculation of the age of the universe; Daniel's prophecy of seventy weeks; and even messianic and eschatological speculation. Only one theme was of some immediate topical interest: the essay on the earthquake of 1571 in Ferrara, where de Rossi lived. However, even this essay was more a motley and erudite digression on the nature of earthquakes, based mostly on classical literature, than an historical *compte rendu*. Thus, notwithstanding its tedious erudition, one might say that the essential character of de Rossi's work brings it much closer than Capsali's or Joseph ha-Cohen's to our modern views of what historical research should be. In that sense it is certainly not without reason that de Rossi has been called "the first to teach Israel the science of scholarship which is the basis of learning— for by means of it, truth is distinguished from falsehood."[45]

In fact, even if de Rossi somewhat nonchalantly departed from the current practice of history by openly justifying his adoption of the literary genre proper to *utili et dilettevoli ragionamenti*,[46] he certainly maintained that ultimately, he was writing history. He was led to this seemingly not quite historical literary genre, so he claimed, by purely aesthetic considerations. Indeed, his intellectual occupation seemed to him comparable to a stroll through a botanical garden: his attention would shift from one flower to another, as a means of procuring intellectual pleasure, following each passing inclination. De Rossi most likely had borrowed the image of the garden from the title of Pedro Mexia's *Silva de varia lecion,* which he read in Italian translation. It is nonetheless difficult not to sense the exoticism of such an image in this context. Yet if this image might serve as a justification for the dilettantism of his essays, their utility also had to be defended. It is highly significant, I would suggest, that his line of defense was to place his work squarely within the category of history.

De Rossi's way of argumentation could at this point be highly misleading. In fact, one may *prima facie* form the impression of being faced with the old problem of the legitimacy of history as an occupation worthy of orthodox Jews. Having referred to Livy's view of history as teaching by example to search for the useful and to avoid the harmful, he goes on to say:

Yet, this might be true for the Gentiles, who did not have the privilege of seeing the Light of the perfect Law and the other Holy Scriptures; therefore they proceed through the darkness of human knowledge. . . . However, we the people of Abraham's God who are devoted to His service, need not engage in this kind of research. His Law and precepts should suffice to enlighten the darkness. . . . His perfect law and the books of the Prophets contain many reports of experiences and observations on matters which either preceded or followed the promulgation of the Law. In this fashion we are able to penetrate the truth of everything useful to us. . . . We therefore have no need of expending our physical and literary energies on matters which, among the other nations, constantly lead to conflicting interpretations.[47]

What, then, are the relevance and purpose of history for Jews? According to Azariah that purpose is threefold:

First, it is to establish truth . . . and Truth is in effect God's own seal, the virtue of all beautiful souls and the good worthy of being sought after by all. Second, and more important, is that in the process of this inquiry we shall have occasion to understand better some biblical passages. . . . And a third reason, not to be dismissed, is that through this discussion such issues will be truly clarified as are relevant to the time of the Messiah, whose coming, according to many reliable sources, is imminent.[48]

This text is clearly ambivalent. For one thing, it appears to defend the orthodoxy of historical research within the narrow traditional utilitarian perspective of religious study. If that was all, one should obviously agree with Baron's conclusion that "it is sad to think that a people who had once played a most magnificent creative role in the domain of history should have come to such an impasse!"[49] However, I would maintain that there was much more to it than that. To present history as principally a search for truth for its own sake, because this is one aspect of the essential link between the human soul and God, makes the second and third motives which are listed in our text as justifications of history clearly subordinate to the first, notwithstanding the rhetorical characterization of the better understanding of obscure scriptural passages as more important. In fact, everything appears in this context as a consequence of the primary aim of establishing truth. This is a very modern trait of historical thought. Yet I would further suggest that its real importance lies in that, having detached himself from the current practice of history, but nevertheless claiming that what he was writing was history, de Rossi was placing this particular kind of intellectual pursuit within the realm of the most relevant activities which aim at satisfying the natural thirst of "beautiful" Jewish souls. In this, de Rossi presents one of the most revolutionary views of what Jewish history should be: delving into the past in order to establish truth, as a means of procuring the intellectual pleasure of knowledge, knowledge to which a "beautiful" Jewish soul should naturally aspire. In other words, de Rossi in his own way was affirming the relevance of history to the definition of the cultural identity of the self. Instead of pursuing the impossible goal of integrating Jewish within non-Jewish history, as Capsali or Joseph ha-Cohen had tried to do, de Rossi took quite a different way. Should he have chosen to write history by following the current practice, he would hardly have been able to make his point as firmly as he did, however nonchalantly. We shall not speculate here on what degree of consciousness was implied in this hesitant inception of a "New History" of the Jewish people. Yet there is no doubt that this is what we are facing. A history which is relevant to Jews might include only what was really important to them.

Such a conception immediately poses the question of selection, notwithstanding de Rossi's apparently insouciant attempt to minimize it by the allegory of the botanical garden. Indeed, what was the relevance of de Rossi's historical interests to the "beautiful" Jewish souls of his time? As Baron has already pointed out,[50] de Rossi's detached studies are intrinsically connected in their clearly apologetic aim. In fact, as I believe I have demonstrated elsewhere,[51] the contemporaneity of the apparently "antique" topics discussed by de Rossi consisted in that almost all of them were relevant to the defense of Judaism in the particular religious and cultural context of Jewish life in sixteenth-century Italy. This defense required a response to the challenge of interpreting Scripture in a manner consonant with both reason and experience; it meant refuting the attacks on rabbinic literature of both Christians and Jewish apostates; it sought to discredit messianic calculations of the "historical" sort; it also meant fostering the conscience of Jewish nationalism. To achieve this goal, de Rossi firmly believed, it was both necessary and sufficient to discover God's seal in the book of history, in other words, to unveil the truth. If one argues, for example, that traditional chronology is a mere convention, and therefore the 420 years of the alleged duration of the Second Temple are not to be taken at face value, the Christian claim of the historicity of the linkage between the Crucifixion of Jesus and the Jewish tragedy becomes equally open to question.

Obviously, one must not confuse apology, as understood by de Rossi, with plain propaganda. The kind of apology to which de Rossi had recourse was in fact a restructuring of the perception of Jewish cultural identity in the face of the accusation that Judaism was irrational, incoherent with its own tradition, and ultimately immoral. Such a restructuring would indeed imply self-criticism and even the bankruptcy of long established beliefs. In his mighty effort of erudition, instinctively following the procedure which is usually adopted in similar situations,[52] de Rossi attempted to show that his apology fell decidedly within the range of Jewish orthodoxy. As a matter of fact, his conviction was barely recognizable as proper Jewish propaganda, and he was attacked by some of his co-religionists on the grounds that he was actually spreading heretical ideas, while some Christians interpreted these same ideas as a prelude to his conversion to Christianity. All were obviously wrong, confusing epistemological, scientific doubt with weakness of faith.[53] Yet this misunderstanding may be used as further proof of the objective earnestness of de Rossi's effort.

In light of what has been said, it would appear that de Rossi's work must be seen as yet another variety of the Jewish response to the challenge of reality on the level of historiography, roughly following the path traced by ecclesiastical historiography as well as by contemporary trends. In fact, as Momigliano put it, it was precisely the survival of ecclesiastical historiography which, merging with the antiquarian type of sixteenth- and seventeenth-century erudition, made it possible to broaden the political and military Renaissance perspective of history and to bring about the slow inception of modern history. The shifting of focus in historiography from literature to science, to which modern historicism is largely indebted, is in fact well rooted in the now quite unreadable, mostly ecclesiastical historiography of those centuries.[54] De Rossi's *Meor Einayim* was a "New History" of the Jews.[55] In fact it was an ecclesiastical historiography of the new early modern variety: it followed the erudite method of Baroque ecclesiastical and antiquarian historiography, it adopted philological criticism as its main tool, it focused on doctrinal rather than political or military topics, it sacrificed style and rhetoric to analytical reasoning and logical demonstration, and it was practically unreadable for pleasure. In this sense, I would argue, one should understand de Rossi's affinity to polymaths such as Sigonio and Panvinio as based not only on their status as the epigones of Flavio Biondo's school.[56] In the same sense one should stress de Rossi's affinity with all other European representatives of erudite scholarship of his age.[57] His work may thus be considered as a further, particular witness of the widespread "conviction that the old histories would not do and that a breakthrough was needed."[58] Like his non-Jewish contemporaries, he had confidence in erudite historical research as a means of fostering, as objectively as possible, his nationalistic perception of Jewish identity. French historians such as Pasquier and La Popelinière behaved in much the same way.[59]

One might ask why there was no sequel to de Rossi's attempt. This was certainly not a consequence of the controversy it had raised on publication. As Zunz has stressed,[60] despite the controversy, the book was held in high esteem all over the Jewish world. Those who were prepared to struggle through it could fine much satisfaction and would cite it on appropriate occasions. David Ganz, living in Prague, the Maharal's city, would delve into it and use it extensively; so occasionally did Manasseh ben Israel in Amsterdam. Nor was the dearth of de Rossi followers a consequence of the allegedly exceptional and brief emergence of the sense of the past during the Renaissance and Baroque periods, not to surface again until the nineteenth century. In other words, it was not only by natural extinction as an abnormal and premature birth of the sense of the past among Jews that the book appeared to die with the death of its author. It was rather, I would suggest, because sheer erudition can never take the place of history and the time had not yet come for a "New History" among both Jews and non-Jews.

Renaissance and Baroque Jewish historical writing appears as the sad epilogue of medieval Jewish historiography. This is so mainly because it had failed to make sense of Jewish history as a living history in diaspora conditions. Ultimately, this was an impossible enterprise, given the current terms of reference whereby history continued to be written mainly as political and military narrative. The time had not yet come for a cultural history of some sort, which might have provided a possible answer to the crisis of Renaissance historiography.[61] The monumental works of antiquarian scholarship would in the end content themselves with the ancillary role of "faire la toilette des texts à publier"[62] in order to provide the documentary evidence scientifically supporting memory history. So long as Jews could not become the actors of a really "New History," they could hardly conceive of a real historiography of their own. For Jewish historiography, radical change could indeed be achieved only in one of two ways: by transforming the Jews into actors of political and military history, or by radically changing the very conception of history. But while the first alternative was obviously ruled out under the diaspora conditions in which the Jewish people lived, the time had not yet come for the second, and most certainly not for the rejection of the "lachrymose conception of Jewish History," as Baron would have it. Yet, this failure was not rooted in lachrymosity—itself a possible incentive rather than an obstacle to memory, which is always a prerequisite of history. Failure was due to the fact that, until recently, lachrymosity was equivalent to marginality, to passivity, and finally to negativity. One does not register under the heading of *res gestae,* worthy of being recorded, what is almost exclusively done by the Other. Might not the sense of unease about their craft which modern Jewish historians have displayed be an unhappy residue of the medieval failure to accord full legitimacy to a "New History" for diaspora Jews? Might not this sense represent an unconscious rejection of memory, rather than a conscious aspiration to fill the vacuum of faith on the part of fallen believers?

NOTES

1. Salo W. Baron, "La méthode historique d'Azaria de Rossi," *Revue des Etudes Juives* 86 (1928), 151.
2. Salo W. Baron, "Azariah de' Rossi's Historical Method," in Baron, *History and Jewish Historians* (Philadelphia, 1964), 205. The English version of the above quotation reads as follows: "The sixteenth century represents one of the high points in Jewish historiography. In contrast to its ancestors' imposing productions during the biblical and Hellenistic antiquity, medieval Jewry failed to bring forth any major historical work in the true sense of that term." In fact, the English version of the essay shows very little real revision. As far as I can see, the sentence quoted here is one of the very few where revision is evident.
3. The terms Renaissance and Baroque are used here in a purely chronological sense.
4. For Christian historical writing, it will suffice to mention here Peter Burke, *The Renaissance Sense of the Past* (New York, 1969), and Bernard Guenée, *Histoire et culture historique dans l'occident médiéval* (Paris, 1980). For the Jewish production see below.
5. R. G. Collingwood, *Speculum Mentis* (Oxford, 1924), 204; and *The Idea of History* (Oxford, 1946), 209.
6. As I shall try to show, the question was already clearly posed in the sixteenth century and it has come down to us in similar terms.
7. Salo W. Baron, *A Social and Religious History of the Jews* (New York, 1958), V, chap. 28: "Homilies and Histories." It is perhaps all the more striking that to date (after the publication of the eighteenth volume of that *History*) Baron has not devoted a special chapter to Jewish historiography of the sixteenth and seventeenth centuries.
8. Yosef Haim Yerushalmi, *Zakhor: Jewish History and Jewish Memory* (Seattle and London, 1982). Yerushalmi had already put forward most of his ideas on the issue in his "Clio and the Jews," *American Academy for Jewish Research Jubilee Volume* [Proceedings of the American Academy for Jewish Research 46–47 (1978–1979)] (Jerusalem, 1980)), II, 607–638. See chapter 6 of this volume.
9. Yerushalmi, *Zakhor*, 81.
10. "Modern Jewish historiography began precipitously out of that assimilation from without and collapse from within which characterized the sudden emergence of Jews out of the ghetto. It originated, not as scholarly curiosity, but as ideology, one of a gamut of responses to the crisis of Jewish emancipation and the struggle to attain it." *Zakhor*, 84.

11. *Ibid.*, 85.
12. *Ibid.*, 86.
13. *Idem.*
14. *Ibid.*, 58.
15. Here too, expectations will depend upon one's basic historical outlook, as will the presentation of the findings. One scholar, for instance, may find no Renaissance impact upon Jewish historical writing of the sixteenth century, while another would find this impact remarkably present, or would otherwise attempt to produce some harmonious presentation of contradictory findings. For a recent schematic contribution on this particular point, see *Avraham Melamed*, "The Perception of Jewish History in Italian Jewish Thought of the Sixteenth and Seventeenth Century, a Reexamination," in *Italia Judaica—"Gli ebrei in Italia tra Rinascimento ed Eta barocca," Atti del II Convegno Internazional, Genova 10–15 giugno 1984* (Rome, 1986), 139–170.
16. H. H. Ben-Sasson, "Li-megamoth ha-Chronographia ha-Yehudith shel Yemei ha-Beinayim u-Beayoteha [Trends and Problems in Medieval Jewish Chronography]," in *Historians and Historical Schools: Lectures Delivered at the Seventh Convention of the Historical Society of Israel, December 1961* (Jerusalem, 1962), 29–46.
17. Yerushalmi does not, on the whole, seem to depart from the traditional scheme of historical interpretation in terms of external-non-Jewish-challenge/internal-Jewish-response, this in itself being no more than a particular variation of the general scheme that almost totally opposes Jewish to non-Jewish. In fact, it is precisely within this scheme that, as far as the premodern historiographical production is concerned, Yerushalmi pushes the argument *ad limitem* and proposes to deal almost exclusively with the "ontological" issue. Since, in that scheme, the main questions are how much internal influence is detectable inside Jewish life and how the external pressure of events influences the course of internal evolution, it follows that major external events must always have priority over all others. For most Jewish historians, the expulsion from the Iberian Peninsula was just such a major event, and thus it naturally seemed necessary to attribute to it a definitive role in the emergence of a Jewish historiographical consciousness. What Gershom Scholem did in his presentation of the mystical trends of that epoch is exactly what Yerushalmi does in studying Jewish historiography.
18. The very structure of the book, a collection of four public lectures, is in itself ambiguous. It is accompanied by rich bibliographical references, yet these very rarely seem intended to support the author's statements. Hence these statements, notwithstanding their clear, often overtly polemical formulation, leave much room to guess at various underlying levels of uncertainty. As in the examples mentioned above, major open questions are dealt with as if they had long been closed. All this conveys the impression of extreme assurance, while in fact the entire book ultimately leads to the confession of fundamental uncertainty, arising from the historian's episte-

mological, even professional doubt. A book subtitled *Jewish History and Jewish Memory*, in which the difference between these two crucial terms is nowhere clearly defined but is left to the understanding (or, perhaps, the imagination) of the reader, finally serves as a justification of the author's confessed aspiration to blur the boundaries and reintegrate memory within history. It is as if the assertion of the difference was but an incidental by-product of the author's own imperfect self-consciousness. It is perhaps this pervasive rhetorical ambiguity that has determined much of the good fortune which this book has recently enjoyed. Further to my critique of particular points in Yerushalmi's *Zakhor* see: Roberto Bonfil, "Esiste una storiografia ebraica medioevale?" in *Aspetti della Storiografia Ebracia: Atti del IV Congresso internazionale dell'AISG (= Associazione Italiana per lo Studio del Guidaismo), S. Miniato, 7–10 novembre 1983* (Rome, 1987), 227–247; Bonfil, "Riflessioni sulla storiografia ebracia in Italia nel Cinquecento," in *Italia Judacia*, 55–66. In any event, Yerushalmi's main theses should be compared with those of Bernard Lewis, *History Remembered, Recovered, Invented* (Princeton, 1975), especially the first chapter. As the reader will easily perceive, I myself feel much closer to Lewis than to Yerushalmi.

19. The practice is, at least in origin, a by-product of the still common tendency to extend the chronological boundaries of the "Jewish Renaissance" beyond any reasonable limits, in order to include in it every possible expression of Jewish culture that might indicate openness toward the non-Jewish world or acculturation perceived essentially as assimilation (cf. Robert Bonfil, "The Historian's Perception of the Jews in the Italian Renaissance: Towards a Reappraisal," *Revue des Etudes Juives* 143 [1984], 59–82). In focusing on the catastrophe of the expulsion of the Jews from Spain, Yerushalmi obviously departs from this general framework, while still maintaining the validity of the factual "evidence." Yet should we adhere to Yerushalmi's overall thesis and consider Jewish historiography as arising from some ideology of secularization and assimilation, we may ask why the emergence of that historiography should not be dated to the sixteenth century, thus obviating the need to consider it as an exceptional response to the exceptional event of the exodus from the Iberian Peninsula. In any case, as will be stated below, we have no reason to maintain that the main stimulus for historiographical production was the catastrophe suffered by Spanish Jewry.

20. Eric Cochrane, "The Transition from Renaissance to Baroque: The Case of Italian Historiography," *History and Theory* 19 (1980), 21–38.

21. D. Ray, "Medieval Historiography through the Twelfth Century: Problems and Progress of Research," *Viator* 5 (1974), 33–59.

22. I borrow the expression for Galeazzo Capella's *L'antropologia* (Venice, 1533), fol. 3b. Capella certainly knew very well what writing history meant, for he himself wrote history.

23. For bibliographical information on most of the works cited in the present chapters, the reader is referred to Yerushalmi's *Zakhor*; for works not mentioned by Yerushalmi, see the relevant items in the *Encyclopaedia Ju-*

daica (Jerusalem, 1971). Some supplementary information will be supplied here, where necessary.

24. It was on this title that Salo W. Baron apparently drew in coining his striking expression "lachrymose Jewish history."

25. For the sake of comparison, the following selected references will suffice: F. Smith Fussner, *The Historical Revolution: English Historical Writing and Thought, 1580–1640* (London, 1962); Claude-Gilbert Dubois, *La conception de l'histoire en France au XVIe siècle (1560–1610)* (Paris, 1977); Eric Cochrane, *Historians and Historiography in the Italian Renaissance* (Chicago and London, 1981).

26. I deliberately exclude Joseph ha-Cohen's *Emek ha-Bakha*, which is in fact a part of his *Divrey ha-Yamim*. One should however keep in mind that *Emek ha-Bakhah* was not printed until the nineteenth century.

27. The results of this analysis have recently become available in Zipora Baruchson's as yet unpublished Ph.D. dissertation, "The Private Libraries of North Italian Jews at the Close of the Renaissance" (Bar-Ilan University, 1985).

28. The *Yosippon* was printed at least five times up to the end of the sixteenth century: Mantua *ca.* 1475, Constantinople 1510, Basle 1541 (with Latin translation), Venice 1544, Cracow 1589. *Sefer Yuhasin, Sefer ha-Kabbalah,* and *Seder Olam* were printed at least twice each, sometimes in joint editions; *Sefer Yuhasin:* Constantinople 1566 (together with *Sefer ha-Kabbalah*) and Cracow 1580–1581 (together with *Seder Olam*); *Seder Olam Rabba* and *Seder Olam Zuta:* Mantua 1513, Venice 1545, Basle 1580 (twice), and Cracow 1580–1581 (the first three together with *Sefer ha-Kabbalah* and the last together with *Sefer Yuhasin*); *Sefer ha-Kabbalah;* Mantua 1513, Venice 1545, Constantinople 1566, Basle 1580 (sometimes with *Seder Olam* and sometimes with *Sefer Yuhasin,* as previously listed). *Divrey ha-yamim shel Moshe rabbenu* was printed twice, together with various other compositions of the same kind: Constantinople 1517 and Venice 1544. *Eldad ha-Dani* was printed only once, in Mantua, *ca.* 1478. On *Divrey ha-yamim shel Moshe rabbenu,* see Avigdor Shinan, "The Chronicle of Moses—the Genre, Time, Sources and Literary Nature of a Medieval Hebrew Story," *Ha-Sifrut/Literature* 6 (1975–1976), 100–116. On *The Gests of Alexander* see *The Book of the Gests of Alexander of Macedon, Sefer Toledot Alexandros ha-Makdoni: A Medieval Hebrew Version of the Alexander Romance, by Immanuel ben Jacob Bonfils,* ed. and transl. with introduction and notes by Israel J. Kazis (Cambridge, Mass, 1962); *Aliloth Alexander Mokdon* [= The Gests of Alexander of Macedon], ed. with an introduction by Joseph Dan (Jerusalem, 1969). On *Eldad ha-Dani* see the introduction to *The Ritual of Eldad ha-Dani,* reconstructed and edited by Max Schlossinger (Leipzig and New York, 1908).

29. See *Sefer ha-Yashar,* ed. with introduction by Joseph Dan (Jerusalem, 1986) and the bibliographical references appended to the introduction.

30. Cf. John Boswell, *Christianity, Social Tolerance and Homosexuality* (Chicago, 1980).

31. Arnaldo Momigliano, "Pagan Christian Historiography in the Fourth Century," in *The Conflict between Paganism and Christianity in the Fourth Century*, ed. Arnaldo Momigliano (Oxford, 1963), 79–99.

32. On *The Gests of Alexander*, see above, note 28. On the Arthurian legend, see *King Artus: A Hebrew Arturian Romance of 1279*, ed. and transl. with cultural and historical commentary by Curt Leviant (New York, 1969).

33. In this connection it must be said that the terminology adopted by Jews who were increasingly oriented towards halakhic formulations was highly misleading in unconditionally labelling history as irrelevant to Jewish self-perception, and consequently in condemming, apparently without reservations, the reading or writing of history as a waste of time. The Jews continued to define history quite strictly as a narrative of wars and kings. Since they no longer had any warrior kings of their own, this kind of history had become irrelevant to them. But narratives of kings and wars did not make up the whole of history, as Eusebius had taught, nor can they be considered the most important part of it.

34. Momigliano, "Pagan and Christian Historiography in the Fourth Century," 89.

35. Joseph ha-Cohen, Preface to *Divrey ha-Yamim le-malkhey Tsarefath u-veth Ottoman ha-Togar*, Sabbioneta 1553; cf. Yerushalmi, *Zakhor*, 61. I follow Yerushalmi's translation.

36. Yerushalmi, *Zakhor*, 60–63.

37. *Seder Eliyahu Zuta*, ed. Aryeh Shmuelevitz [a.o.] (Jerusalem, 1975), 1, 7–21. For the persistence of the medieval conception of the prophet as a perfect *rhetor* in sixteenth-century Jewish Italian thought, the cultural area to which Capsali belongs, see Robert Bonfil, *Rabbis and Jewish Communities in Renaissance Italy* (Oxford, 1990). For the Ciceronian reference, cf. the famous passage in *De oratore* II, 36: "Historia vero testis temporum, lux veritatis, vita memoriae, magistra vitae, nuntia vetustatis, qua voce alia, nisi oratoris ímmortalitate commendature?"

38. Bonfil, "Riflessioni sulla storiografia ebraica in Italia nel Cinquecento," 57–61.

39. Arnaldo Momigliano, *Essays of Ancient and Modern Historiography* (Oxford, 1977), 25–35. More bibliographical information on this essay is given in *Problêmes d'historiographie ancienne et moderne* (Paris, 1983), 91–103.

40. Joseph ha-Cohen, *Divrey ha-Yamim*, Sabbioneta 1553, f. 113v. This passage is cited by Yerushalmi (*Zakhor*, 64), whose translation I follow. I have deliberately suppressed the concluding phrase ("for behold the days approach"), in which Yerushalmi sees proof "that there were powerful messianic stimuli to the whole of sixteenth-century Jewish historiography"; cf. also his "Messianic Impulses in Joseph ha-Kohen," in *Jewish Thought in the Sixteenth Century*, ed. Bernard Dov Cooperman (Cambridge, Mass, 1983), 460–487. I would prefer to situate this phrase within the general framework of similar biblical phrases tacked onto Joseph ha-Cohen's own

dull Hebrew to give it some biblical flavor. For this expression itself see Amos iv, 2; iv, 4; and so on.

41. Yerushalmi's endeavor to substantiate such a link is mostly rhetorical and hardly convincing. Although some of the authors of Jewish historical works in the sixteenth century were admittedly exiles from the Iberian Peninsula or descendants of such exiles, this fact should not be considered sufficient to establish a relationship between the catastrophe of Spanish Jewry and historical writing. Even less persuasive is the likelihood that those who had no connection whatever with Spain might have been influenced by Spanish refugees who had come to live among them, or by their books. See Yerushalmi, *Zakhor*, 58; and cf. Ivan Marcus, "Beyond the Sephardic Mystique," *ORIM—A Jewish Journal at Yale* 1 (1985), 35–53.

42. David Ganz, *Zemah David: A Chronicle of World History* (Prague, 1592), ed. with an introduction and notes by Mordechai Breuer (Jerusalem, 1983), 118, and cf. Breuer's introduction, xx.

43. Cf. Natalie Z. Davis, *Society and Culture in Early Modern France* (Stanford, 1975), chap. 7: "Printing and the People," 189–226.

44. This author and his book have attracted much greater scholarly interest than any other Jewish author of an historical work. Apart from the essay by Baron listed above (note 2), reference should be made to the following: Salo W. Baron, "Azariah de' Rossi: A Biographical Sketch" (revised translation from the Hebrew text, published in *Eshkol, Hebrew Encyclopedia* [Berlin, 1929], I, cols. 689–693), reprinted in his *History and Jewish Historians*, 167–173, 405; Baron, "Azariah de' Rossi's Attitude to Life," in *Jewish Studies in Memory of Israel Abrahams* (New York, 1927), 12–52, reprinted in *History and Jewish Historians*, 174–204, 406–422; Robert Bonfil, "Some Reflections on the Place of Azariah de Rossi's *Meor Enayim* in the Cultural Milieu of Italian Renaissance Jewry," in *Jewish Thought in the Sixteenth Century*, 23–48; Joanna Weinberg, "Azariah dei Rossi: Towards a Reappraisal of the Last Years of His Life," *Annali della Scuola Normale Superiore di Pisa*, ser. 3, 8, 2 (1978), 493–511; J. Weinberg, "Azaria de' Rossi and Septuagint Traditions," *Italia: Studi e Ricerche sulla Storia, la Cultura e la Letteratura degli Ebrei d'Italia* 5 (1985), 7–35; J. Weinberg, "Azariah de' Rossi and the Forgeries of Annius of Viterbo," in *Aspetti della Storiografia Ebracia: Atti del IV Congresso internazionale dell'AISG (= Associazione Italian per lo Studio del Guidaismo), S. Miniato, 7–10 novembre 1983* (Rome, 1987), 23–47. (See chap. 8 of this volume).

45. Leopold Zunz, "Toledoth R. Azariah min ha-Adummim," *Kerem Hemed* 5 (1841), 139.

46. *Meor Einayim*, chap. i (in David Cassel's edition, Vilna 1864–1866: pp. 78–81).

47. *Meor Einayim*, chap. 27 (in Cassel's ed.: p. 264); cf. Baron, "Azariah de' Rossi's Historical Method," 423, whose translation I have followed with slight modifications.

48. *Meor Einayim*, chap. 28 (in Cassel's ed.: pp. 275–276); cf. Baron, "Azariah

de' Rossi's Attitude to Life," 195–196 and *Meor Einayim*, chap. 15 (in Cassel's ed.: pp. 206–207).

49. Baron, "Azariah de' Rossi's Attitude to Life," 207.

50. *Ibid.*, 212.

51. Bonfil, "Some Reflections."

52. Cf. John H. Elliott, *The Old and the New, 1492–1650* (Cambridge, 1970).

53. We cannot here follow the details of the controversy that ensued on the publication of de Rossi's book. It is sufficient to recall that a close reading of all the extant evidence has clearly established that it was neither historical criticism as such nor de Rossi's independent attitudes that were at stake. Most of the criticism coming from Italian Jews was based on a misunderstanding of some marginal statements, which might be interpreted as skeptical of the Kabbalistic tradition. How mistaken this reaction was is demonstrated by de Rossi's willingness to delete the incriminating passages and proceed to a revision of the entire chapter. As long as his main thesis was not affected, de Rossi was ready to accept censorship and give up independence. For more details, see Bonfil, "Some Reflections."

54. Momigliano, "Pagan and Christian Historiography"; Momigliano, "Ancient History and the Antiquarian," *Journal of the Warburg and Courtauld Institutes* 13 (1950), 285–315 (reprinted in *Contributo alla storia degli studi classici* [Rome, 1955]); George Huppert, *The Idea of Perfect History: Historical Erudition and Historical Philosophy in Renaissance France* (Urbana, Chicago and London, 1970).

55. As Huppert observes (*The Idea of Perfect History*, 9, note 8), the phrase "New History" was already used by la Popelinière in the title of his *Dessein de l'historie nouvelle des francois* (Paris, 1599). "The idea that a new kind of history was in the making and that they were its artisans—not only as opposed to the medieval chronicles but also new when compared to the histories of the Ancients; in short altogether new" is, in Huppert's view, clearly stated by all the authors he studies, the French historians and theoreticians of history, from Jean Bodin to Henri La Popelinière.

56. Cf. Baron, "Azariah de' Rossi's Historical Method," 209.

57. In this context the remark by J. Weinberg ("Azariah de' Rossi and . . . Annius of Viterbo," 25, note 8) that northern European antiquarian scholarship was certainly as important as the Italian, seems very pertinent.

58. The wording is that used by Huppert (*The Idea of Perfect History*, 25) with reference to the French authors he studies.

59. Cf. Huppert, *The Idea of Perfect History, passim* and particularly chapter iv: "The Origins of the Nation."

60. Zunz, "Toledoth R. Azariah min ha-Adummim."

61. Cochrane, "The Transition from Renaissance to Baroque."

62. The phrase was borrowed from Henri-Irenée Marrou, *De la connsaissance historique* (Paris 1954), 30.

8

Azariah de' Rossi and the Forgeries of Annius of Viterbo

Joanna Weinberg

"He was the first to teach Israel the science of scholarship which is the basis of learning—for by means of it, truth is distinguished from falsehood"[1]. These words, which were written in 1841 by Leopold Zunz about the subject of his biographical article, Azariah de' Rossi, reflected a widely-held opinion among nineteenth-century Jewish scholars. Azariah de' Rossi, on whom Zunz lavished such great praise, was the sixteenth-century Italian Jewish historiographer whose *magnum opus*, the *Me'or 'Enayim (Light of the Eyes)* was first printed in 1573 in the author's birthplace Mantua.[2] The nineteenth-century evaluation, although certainly not unjustified, needs to be qualified. De' Rossi possessed a vast erudition. There is not one subject discussed by him in which he does not present an impressive array of diverse sources ranging from the Old Testament and Maimonides to Augustine and Pico della Mirandola. The pre-requisite for any fair assessment of de' Rossi's scholarship must therefore be to give due consideration to the numerous primary and secondary sources which he used and which form an integral part of his argumentation and his historical method in general.[3] In

This is an expanded form of a paper given at the *IV Convegno di studi giudaici* in an Italian version translated by Mirko Tavono, I am indebted to Arnaldo Momigliano, Jill Kraye, Anthony Grafton, Giulio Lepschy and Peter Majer who read various drafts of the paper and submitted many valuable insights and criticism which were taken into account in the writing of this final version.

Reprinted by permission from *Aspetti della Storiografia Ebraica,* Atti del IV Convegno internazionale dell AISG, San Miniato, 1983 (Rome 1987).

particular, such an evaluation must take account of the sixteenth-century writings which appear to have dictated not only his method of research, but also to a certain extent, his choice of subject-matter.

The *Me'or 'Enayim* was an innovation in Hebrew literature. While previous Jewish historians had restricted their work to chronicles or to accounts of the "chain of Rabbinic tradition", de' Rossi, on his own admission, chose to adopt as his model of writing the form of "miscellanea" compilation used by antiquarians, philologists and encyclopaedists of the time.[4] He decided to write essays, as Salo Baron has described de' Rossi's work[5], on various problems of Jewish history, particularly of the Hellenistic period which had either been totally neglected by his predecessors or else inadequately treated. The juxtaposition of a number of loosely-related subjects was not a characteristic of miscellanies alone. Jean Bodin's *Methodus ad facilem historiarium cognitionem* (Paris 1566), for example, was not a pure and simple discussion of how to study history, but embraced subjects ranging from universal history which included Jewish history, to geography, the age of the universe and the origin of peoples. Pierfrancesco Giambullari's dialogue on the origin of the Tuscan language[6] which de' Rossi had read, included subject-matter tangential to the main discourse, such as the Hebrew calendar and details of Biblical chronology. Similarly, de' Rossi's *Me'or 'Enayim* covered a wide variety of subjects, encompassing the origins of the Septuagint, Philo, Jewish chronology, geography and the antiquity of the Hebrew language, script and vowels.[7]

Until quite recently, most appraisals of de' Rossi's contribution to Jewish historiography were influenced by the nineteenth-century perspective. Two scholars succeeded in putting an end to the repetitive and encomious references to the "father of Jewish historiography". In an article first published in 1928, Salo Baron compared the *Me'or 'Enayim* to the antiquarian writings of de' Rossi's time.[8] He regarded de' Rossi's particular originality in source criticism to consist not so much in its form and method, but rather in the broad foundation on which de' Rossi built his argument, in his synthesis of evidence from different periods and peoples. Baron also detected de' Rossi's apologetic stance, which affected "his sincere although rather timid love for the truth".

The apologetic and polemical nature of the *Me'or 'Enayim* was further stressed by Roberto Bonfil, firstly in a general article on Italian Jews of the Renaissance (1975)[9] and then in a paper on the cultural milieu of the *Me'or 'Enayim* (1980)[10]. Bonfil regarded the apologetic strain prevalent in the whole work as the key to its understanding. In his view, the *Me'or 'Enayim* was de' Rossi's response to the anti-Jewish atmosphere of Counter Reformation Italy.

While certainly not denying that de' Rossi's discussions were sometimes polemically motivated[11], I would propose that the principal task of the interpreter of de' Rossi's work must be to acknowledge the Christian scholarly world in which de' Rossi was so obviously immersed. (In fact, a high level of scholarship may be seen to be one of the byproducts of the Counter Reformation.) Only when such an analysis has been accomplished will it be possible to determine the underlying motivations which led de' Rossi to write the book. The polemical and apologetic elements in the book cannot be the master-key to a work which in so many ways presents itself as a Jewish counterpart to contemporary Christian scholarship. The majority of subjects treated by de' Rossi were already under discussion by Christian scholars of all descriptions: Protestants, Catholics, Italians and northern Europeans. A most notable feature of de' Rossi's discourse on the origins of the Septuagint, for example, is his expertise in the relevant Christian literature on the subject. He could even show himself familiar with the debate which arose among such scholars as Augustinus Steuchus and Sebastian Münster regarding the authorship of the extant version of the Vulgate[12]. Whatever the subject, de' Rossi consulted the current textbooks. In each case, de' Rossi culled the relevant facts or evidence from these texts. Having divested the requisite data of any religious or political bias, he then applied it to his own discussion of Jewish history. Such a method was consistent with his own pronouncement in chapter two of the *Me'or 'Enayim* that he would use non-Jewish sources for the clarification of any intellectual problem provided that "there is no hint of heresy and they do not make light of our Torah"[13].

One of the main sections of the book in which the non-Jewish or rather non-Rabbinic evidence is particularly crucial to de' Rossi's argument is the *Yeme 'Olam* ("Days of Old"), a critique of Rabbinic chronology in which he challenged the traditional computations for the age of the universe[14]. With the exception of chronological tables, all aspects of contemporary chronological writings are represented in de' Rossi's discourse: astronomical and calendrical data; Scriptural interpretation with particular reference to Daniel's prophecy of the seventy weeks;

calculation of the age of the universe; the synchronizing of Biblical and extra-Biblical chronology; Messianic and eschatological speculation[15]. All these topics were treated by de' Rossi in relation to three specific periods in Jewish history: the Egyptian exile, the middle part of the first Temple period and the beginning of the second Commonwealth. In the course of the discussion, de' Rossi continually repeats (hoping to preempt the criticism which was in fact to follow the publication of the book) that the conclusions drawn from his investigation could not have any practical, legal repercussions. A hundred years or so added to the Rabbinic *aera mundi* computation need not be regarded as of anything but academic consequence. In his opinion, the Rabbinic calculation had never been intended to indicate the precise date. Rather, it was a mere convention "which was established sensibly and intelligently by the formulator of our calendar. Thus you can clearly see that addition or subtraction or years can in no way disrupt or defer any of the fixed times in our calendar"[16].

De' Rossi was not the first Jew to question Rabbinic tradition regarding chronology. Writers such as the twelfth-century author of the *Sefer Ha-Qabbalah (Book of Tradition)*, Abraham ibn Daud, and the fifteenth-century Bible exegete, Isaac Abarbanel, had either implicitly or explicitly confronted the same questions. Ibn Daud's motive in tampering with Scriptural and Rabbinic computations of key periods in Jewish history was to establish a schematic structure with implied apocalyptic overtones[17]. De' Rossi's critique of Rabbinic chronology was, however, novel in that he did not supplant his rejection of the Rabbinic view with yet another artificial scheme of world or Jewish history. Nor did he indulge in Messianic chronology. In fact, he devoted an entire chapter to rigorously combatting the fashionable Messianic speculation for the year 1575, a date which in Hebrew lent itself to eschatalogical significance, given its correspondence to the word Shilo in the verse, "The sceptre shall not depart from Judah ... until Shilo come" (*Gen.*, 49.10)[18]. Furthermore, unlike Abarbanel, he did not openly attack Christological analysis of Old Testament history[19]. He simply selected the necessary evidence from the relevant texts, thereby attempting to solve the problems within the Jewish tradition while silently and simultaneously dismissing the Christian views.

On two occasions in his commentary on *Genesis*, the sixteenth-century Bible exegete and philosopher, Obadiah Sforno, refers to a certain

Berosus whose views regarding Noah concurred with those of the Rabbis. Sforno's allusions to Noah's pious conduct motivated by altruism
and to Ham's use of magic in castrating his father are too brief to tell us
much about Sforno's exegetical method[20]. But, in a more general way,
they do shed light on the scholarly pursuits of some of Sforno's contemporaries: their search for texts from antiquity which could both corroborate and complement Scripture, and their quest for evidence from the
past which might describe the origins of mankind and the genealogies of
Noah and his sons to whom they traced their descent.

The source of Sforno's information was not the authentic Berosus,
only fragments of which remain, but rather was derived from a forgery
which was first published in Rome in 1498 and immediately became one
of the best-sellers of the day[21]. The ps. Berosus was printed in a collection of writings most of which purported to be the lost works of ancient
authors. They included the writings of Xenophon, Fabius Pictor, Myrsi-
lus Lesbius, Cato the Elder, Archilochus, Metasthenes the Persian and
Philo the Jew. These works were both edited and annotated by their
author, the Dominican monk Annius of Viterbo[22]. The *Opera* also
contained the *Quaestiones Annianae* which discussed the antiquity of
Annius' home-town Viterbo, and two "unpublished" fragments of the
Itineraria Antonii Pii and a history of the Kings of Spain. All these works
were accompanied by commentaries also written by Annius. The texts
framed by the commentaries had all the appearances of medieval annotated editions of Scripture. Text and commentary complemented each
other and a carefully constructed unity was imposed on the different
works. Annius claimed to have acquired the text of Berosus from two
Armenians and to have discovered the other texts in Mantua[23]. With
surprising uniformity, all these texts discovered by Annius were preserved in Latin. A semblance of authenticity was achieved because all
the Annian authors had at least been mentioned in ancient sources. The
central texts of Berosus, Metasthenes and Philo supplied a complete
history of the Middle East from the time of Adam. These writers, according to Annius, were reliable historians unlike those rivals of the Italians,
the Greeks, who spoke only "per opiniones". The Babylonian archivist,
Berosus the Chaldean, listed genealogies of Kings and described events
which had occurred in ante-diluvian times. According to Annius, his
testimony disproved the Greek myths and the works of such writers as
Herodotus, Hellanicus and Ephorus among whom there was no consensus of opinion[24]. Ps. Metasthenes continued the history from the point

at which the account of ps. Berosus ended[25]. The ps. Philonic *Breviarium de temporibus* gave a complete chronology of all four monarchies of Persia, Babylon, Greece and Rome[26].

In the preface to the 1512 Parisian edition of the Annian texts, Iodocus Badius stated that although Annius' main aim was patriotic (i.e. to demonstrate the antiquity of Etruria in general, and his native-town of Viterbo in particular which, according to Annian sources, was founded by Noah-Janus when he came to Italy after the flood), he also provided valuable information on the pedigree of European royalty and on the genealogy of Jesus[27]. In other words, as Albano Biondi pointed out, Badius elicted three objectives in Annius' work: patriotic, historical and religious[28]. And yet, the true motivation of the fakes (for which Annius was appointed to one of the highest offices of the Catholic Church, *magister sacri palatii,* by the Borgian Pope Alexander VI) still eludes scholars. It is obvious that Annius wished to "convince the world that his own native place Viterbo had been a cradle of civilization with a history and traditions compared to which even those of Rome paled into insignificance"[29]. But various other factors must be taken into account. "Aware of the rising star of Spanish influence in Italian politics" Annius dedicated his work to the Spanish monarchs Ferdinand and Isabella[30]. Spanish patriotic sentiments would have been well-satisfied by the Annian discourse on the antiquity of Spain, which was given a notable pre-history including an appearance in the country by Hercules, son of Osiris[31]. But as Tigerstedt has pointed out, Annius also endowed France and Germany with similarly glorious pre-histories[32]. Tigerstedt cast a different perspective on the inspiration of the forgeries when he interpreted the pervasive anti-Greek bias of the works as an attack on humanists' preoccupation with the "glories that were Greece"[33]. Biondi, however, refined Tigerstedt's thesis by pointing out that Annius' preference for *Chaldaerorum veritas* as opposed to *Graecorum vanitas* was an expression of his disapproval that the ancient theology and philosophy with which Noah had illuminated the West had been supplanted by Greek fables and culture[34]. In this respect, Annius' syncretistic forgeries, which extolled the ancient wisdom underlying Christian traditions, could be seen as a parallel tradition to the syncretism expressed in other forgeries popular at the time such as the Hermetic writings or the Chaldaic oracles[35]. To a certain extent, the Annian forgeries (like the Hermetic writings) attained the status of "appendices to Holy Writ"[36].

"Nobody invents a fake unless there is a demand for it", stated Fritz

Saxl[37]. That Annius correctly gauged the interest of his prospective readers is fully attested by the wide dissemination which his fakes had among scholars of the calibre of Erasmus, Jean Bodin and Sebastian Münster, to name but a few. As Eugenio Garin has stated, Annius' forgeries belonged as much to the culture of the Renaissance as the works of Machiavelli, Pomponazzi, Erasmus and Agrippa, Rabelais and Montaigne, Folengo and Giordano Bruno[38]. From the end of the fifteenth century, every scholar interested in ancient chronology or in the origins of peoples (particularly his own) referred to the Annian "discoveries". It is true that the texts were submitted to rigorous and scathing denunciation by such critical thinkers as Juan Luis Vives, Melchor Cano and Antonio Agustìn. But their outcry did not dissuade the majority of scholars from exploiting the attractive Annian products to their full. De' Rossi was no exception, nor was he the first or the last Jew to make use of the texts. As we have seen, Sforno made fleeting allusion to Annius' Berosus. At the beginning of section two of the *Tsemaḥ David,* which dealt with universal chronology, the German chronicler David Ganz referred to the use of Berosus by de' Rossi and by Cyriacus Spangenberg. Ganz stated his own intention of citing Berosus, despite the fact that he had failed to divulge the name of his sources, "because he is the first Gentile historian known to us by name"[39].

Of the sixteenth-century writers who used the Annian material and whose works de' Rossi knew and cited extensively, most were either unquestioning followers of Annius, or at least argued in favor of the genuineness of his fragments. The exception was Mercator, whose *Chronologia* de' Rossi read only after he had completed the first version of the *Me'or 'Enayim*[40]. Two writers who raised the issue of authenticity were Sebastian Münster and Pierfrancesco Giambullari. While de' Rossi quoted Giambullari only once, but on a significant occasion, as we shall see, Münster works were cited extensively throughout the *Me'or 'Enayim.* In fact, a large proportion of the subjects which Münster treated in separate works constitutes the themes of individual chapters in De' Rossi's book[41]. For example, as I have shown elsewhere, de' Rossi's thesis on the Aramaic origins of the Septuagint is based, to a certain extent, on the distinction which Münster had already made in his *Chaldaica Grammatica* between *lingua Hebraeorum* and *lingua Hebraica*[42]. Of particular relevance to the present study is Münster's evaluation of the medieval Hebrew compilation, the *Josippon,* which had been erroneously attributed to Josephus[43]. Münster published a Latin edition of the work (Basel 1541) with a preface entitled, *Praefatio in Iosephum Hebraicum in qua disputatur num haec editio Flavii sit Iosephi an alterius cuiusdam Iudaei.* The preface was intended to disprove the opinions of those who had rejected the Flavian authorship of the work on the grounds that Josephus had not known Hebrew. In addition, Münster argued that the anachronistic references to Bulgarians, Lombards, Franks and Goths were simply glosses to the text which were interpolated by Jews at a later date[44]. In his examination of the textual tradition of the *Josippon,* de' Rossi explicitly upheld Münster's view on the later interpolations, but as regards the authenticity issue he was silent[45]. Of course, de' Rossi may not have wanted to cast aspersions on a work which had been quoted by such respectable Jews as David Kimhi, Saadiah and Abarbanel; alternatively, I think more probably, de' Rossi was showing allegiance to Münster by silently upholding his view. As regards the Annian forgeries, Münster, thorough scholar that he was, and always abreast of the latest scholarly debates, took the precaution of discussing the authenticity of the Annian Berosus, which he was using in his *Cosmographia* for his discussion of the peoples of antiquity. Münster argued against Annius' detractors that the text of Berosus contained correct *(sic)* references to Hebrew words[46]. Since Annius was writing at a time when monks were ignorant of Hebrew the work could not have been forged. Münster did, however, concede that the work contained occasional lapses from the truth.

Münster's rather weak argument, which disregarded Annius' own declaration that he had received help for his Hebrew and Aramaic etymologies from a certain "Samuel Talmudista", must have satisfied de' Rossi when he read the *Cosmographia*[47]. As with the *Josippon,* de' Rossi seems to have been prepared to accept Münster's conclusions without further argument. In any case, it must be remembered that de' Rossi was not really in a position to evaluate the authenticity of Greek and Latin works. He knew little Greek and had read Greek texts including Josephus and Philo only in Latin translation. Melchor Cano, in his scathing critique of Annius, pointed out that the Annian Philo bore no resemblance to the eloquent Philo praised by antiquity for his intellect, erudition and grandiloquence; the style of the Annian Philo was that of the "uncultured and vulgar who know nothing of finesse and elegance"[48]. De' Rossi did not have the competence to perceive such stylistic differences. It should be noted, however, that he had displayed such acute faculties in assessing texts written in Rabbinic Hebrew that he could correctly discern that the commentary on Chronicles attributed to Rashi was not genuine[49].

It was the opinion of Antonio Possevino that even the scholars who had discerned the fictitiousness of the Annian texts continued to utilize them because they shed light on Scriptural history[50]. Indeed, the clarification of Scripture was one of the reasons offered by de' Rossi to account for his study of chronology[51]. Similarly, Johannes Lucidus Samotheus, whose *Opusculum de emendationibus temporum* frequently cited by de' Rossi, was to a large extent a shortened form of Annian ancient history, stressed the importance of chronological evidence for a complete understanding of the literal sense of Scripture[52]. In his view, Scripture was of paramount importance. Authoritative, too, were all the writers whose works had been accepted into the Canon of the Church. As regards all other histories, he merely followed Annius, claiming to be formulating an accurate chronological study because the ancient and reliable authors cited by him concurred with Scripture[53].

As Anthony Grafton pointed out, even before Scaliger, some scholars used astronomical and calendrical data in conjunction with historical sources and combined Near Eastern and Classical studies for their work on chronology[54]. De' Rossi's chronological writing is therefore clearly to be seen in the framework of pre-Scaligerian scholarship. He combined calendrical and historical data when dealing with the complicated and controversial problems of Jewish chronology. He also elucidated Scripture and Talmudic statements by means of the sources of classical antiquity. Like Lucidus and other chronologers of the time, de' Rossi used the Annian forgeries as an essential part of his discourse. In fact, he translated ps. Metasthenes and ps. Philo into Hebrew in chapters thirty-one and thirty-two. These texts were to be used as sources for the history of the first and second Temple periods because, in his view, their authors provided impartial evidence[55]: "If, regarding a story of an event of the past relevant to this subject, we come across evidence of various writers from among the scholars of different nationalities and tongues who, in order to attain fame, studied, elaborated and recorded those events with no ulterior motive but to inform mankind of their occurrence, one will realize that a scholar may allow this evidence to be heard amidst the array of the reports and to base our position on the basis of their (statements)". This was a criterion which de' Rossi derived from the Talmudic method of evaluating evidence where greater credence was given to those witnesses who had no vested interests in the issue at stake. Accordingly, de' Rossi selected passages from Xenophon[56], Josephus[57] and Eusebius' *Chronicon*[58] as well as the entire texts of ps. Metasthenes and ps. Philo and set them out as the primary source materials in the first chapters of the section in preparation for the detailed and complicated discussions of the following chapters. His translations are, on the whole, faithful to Annius' Latin texts (he used the Lyons 1554 edition). However, it should be noted, he translated the title of ps. Metasthenes' work *De iudicio temporum (On the Appraisal of the Times)* as *Mi-Seder Ha-Zemanim (On the Order of the Times)*. While being an accurate description of its contents since it contains a list of Kings of Babylon and Persia until Seleucus Nikanor, this title does not convey the meaning of *De iudicio temporum*[59].

The ps. Philonic text traces the line of Solomon's successors and presents a list of the high-priests who ministered from the Alexandrian period until Philo's own time. From his remarks in the preface and in his commentary to the *Breviarium,* Annius disclosed that his main objective in presenting the text was to resolve the problem of the contradictory evidence in the Gospels of Matthew and Luke regarding Jesus' genealogy[60]. Needless to say, de' Rossi completely disregards Annius' arguments on this subject. His purpose in using the text was simply to find evidence by which he could corroborate the view of the medieval Jewish commentators who rejected the Rabbinic computation of 410 years for the period, a figure which was calculated on the basis of the reigns of the Kings of Israel rather than on the longer span of the Kings of Judah. While rejecting Josephus' computations for this period, de' Rossi followed his Christian contemporaries who "took on trust" Philo's computations, especially because his view concurred with those of Ibn Daud, Kimhi and Abarbanel in calculating 430 years for the period[61]. The ps. Philonic text was not however faultless; de' Rossi disagreed with ps. Philo for his reckoning of Amon's rule which was based on the Septuagint reading of Scripture, a detail which was also mentioned by Johannes Lucidus[62]. Nevertheless, de' Rossi was satisfied that ps. Philo's evidence adequately demonstrated that the Rabbinic calculation, and consequently also the traditional computation for the age of the universe, had to be emended.

Problematic, too, was the length of the second Temple period. Scriptural evidence was fragmentary here and subject to widely divergent interpretation. The problem relating to the duration of the second Temple period, which was 420 years according to Jewish tradition, arose from the computations given in the historical Midrash, the *Seder 'Olam Rabbah*[63] and in tractate *'Avodah Zarah* (9a) of the Babylonian Talmud: "The Persian rule lasted 34 years of the Temple period; the Greek Empire 180 years; the Hasmonean dynasty 103 years; the Herodian dynasty 103 years". Since work on the building of the second Temple was begun in 517 B.C. and Alexander defeated Darius in 334, the Persian rule must have lasted about 193 years and not 34 years of the second Temple period. The intricacies of the question to which de' Rossi devotes a detailed examination in chapters thirty-six to thirty-nine need not concern us here. What is relevant, however, is that for the purpose of resolving the problem and invalidating the Rabbinic computation, de' Rossi cites among other works, the basic source-book on Persian history, ps. Metasthenes' *De iudicio temporum*. Since ps. Metasthenes opens his work with a discussion of the criteria according to which the reliability of historians may be judged, the reader might well believe that the subsequent information imparted by Metasthenes satisfied de' Rossi' own criteria[64]. Metasthenes writes (de' Rossi's translation)[65]: "Whosoever wishes to write on matters of chronology ought not to follow popular hearsay or the opinion of one of the ancients. When this is their objective, they do in fact mislead both themselves and others. Indeed, we would not go wrong if we follow the chronicles belonging to the monarchies which govern the world and ban all other chroniclers on the grounds that their statements are spurious . . . Furthermore, these writers are not all to be accepted; we only trust the priests of that kingdom to whom were entrusted private and public information on all events. Such a man was Berosus the Chaldean. He wrote the history of the Assyrians according to the order which he found in the ancient digests . . ." Confident in the reliability of his source, de' Rossi could thus proceed to calculate the length of the second Commonwealth. In the final analysis, however, although de' Rossi certainly showed preference for ps. Metasthenes' figures rather than the Rabbinic ones, he admitted that he could not supply exact computations, thereby preventing Messianic speculators, whether Jewish or Christian, from finding corroboration for their computations in the works of even the most trustworthy authorities.

De' Rossi's criticisms of the Talmudic sages were always expressed in an apologetic vein and he generally juxtaposed a defence of the Rabbis' position with his criticism. One of de' Rossi's most hostile critics, the "Maharal of Prague", detected this method whereby de' Rossi paid lip service to Rabbinic authority and accused him of employing such feeble arguments that he undermined their case to an even greater extent[66]. The eclectic use of sources which characterizes de' Rossi's style of argumentation led him to confirm Rabbinic opinion even from the works of non-Jewish writers. The same Annian authors on whose authority he had disproved Rabbinic chronology could also be used by him to support Talmudic opinion on another area of Jewish history. A case in point concerns the Samaritan Temple, which according to one Rabbinic tradition was erected on Mt. Gerizim before the time of Alexander of Macedon and destroyed by his command as a result of the intercession of the high-priest Simeon the Just[67]. Another Rabbinic account recorded that a statue of a dove had been found on the peak of Mt. Gerizim in the time of Rabbi Meir (A.D. 130–160), in other words, subsequent to its purported date of destruction[68]. Further contradictory evidence was supplied by Josephus who stated that the Samaritan Temple had been built with the permission of Alexander of Macedon and destroyed two hundred years later by John Hyrcanus[69]. The Annian data were introduced by de' Rossi in an attempt to arbitrate between all these conflicting pieces of information. In fact, he did not even have to consult Annius himself; a collation of all the relevant material collected from the Annian sources was provided by Johannes Lucidus' chronicle[70]. According to ps. Berosus and ps. Metasthenes, the fourth ruler of ancient Babylon was Semiramis. Various legends had built up about Semiramis who had been nurtured by doves[71]. Annius related that after her death, Semiramis was worshipped as a goddess and the dove became used as the emblem of Babylon[72]. Allusions to the dove as symbol of the Babylonians were also found in Scripture, as in the verse. "He has left the covert like a lion; for their land is desolate because of the fierce anger of the dove ... (*Jer.*, 25–38).

In respect to this evidence, de' Rossi cited the Scriptural record of the first settlement of Samaritans by the King of Assyria and Babylon in Shechem, Samaria, in which area Mt. Gerizim was located. On the basis of the Scriptural and Annian evidence, de' Rossi then put forward his own original idea. He surmised that the Samaritans would have erected a statue of a dove on the peak of Mt. Gerizim as a sign of their allegiance to the Babylonians whose emblem the dove was[73]. The collation of Annian and Scriptural data provided a neat solution to the problem; and as a consequence, de' Rossi did not have to reject the Talmudic evidence which reported traces of idol-worship on the top of Mt. Gerizim before and after the time of Alexander of Macedon. The Annian fabrications thus served as a link between Scripture and Talmud.

The subject of the language spoken in antiquity engaged many Renaissance scholars. Just as humanists like Valla and Poggio discussed the question whether the literary Latin known to them was also the spoken language of the ancient Romans[74], so, too, there was a prevalent interest in tracing the origins of all languages and peoples and also in identifying the *Ursprache* and determining its relation to other languages.

The story of Babel was the starting-point from which ever philogical study proceeded. Two Scriptural verses provided the basic evidence. "And the whole earth was of one language and one speech" (*Gen.*, 11.1), and "Therefore was it called Babel because the Lord did there confound the language of all the earth and from there did the Lord scatter them abroad upon the face of all the earth" (*Gen.*, 11.9) The problem which confronted the philologists of the sixteenth century was how to provide a unifying link between the one pre-existing language and the multiplicity of seemingly diverse languages[75]. The idea that the language of the Old Testament was the first language of humanity did not originate in the sixteenth century, but the method by which the links were made was different from earlier discussions of the same sources[76].

Of course Annius, who was well-acquainted with the interests of his prospective readers, had a proposal to make regarding the language of antiquity; the predominance of Etruria as a centre of ancient culture had to be asserted in respect to its language as well. Noah, the founder of Western civilization, must have bequeathed the ante-diluvian language to Etruscans as well as to Chaldeans. It thus followed that the Etruscan language was derived from Hebrew or Aramaic.

The subject of the *Ursprache* also attracted de' Rossi's attention and in chapter fifty-seven of his work he attempted to prove that the Holy Tongue was the first language of mankind. And at least in this subject he was not at odds with his Jewish contemporaries. In his *Dor Ha-Pelagah*, David Provenzali, de' Rossi's teacher, had attempted to trace by affinities the presence of Hebrew in other languages[77]. De Rossi's

friend and mentor Judah Moscato appears to have discussed the subject
with de' Rossi, and he also dealt with it in his commentary to Judah
Halevi's *Cuzari*[78].

In the course of his argument, de' Rossi made use of the Annian
Berosus; but according to his own eclectic system, he ignored some of
the more outlandish elements, while selecting the material more reminiscent of the Scriptural stories[79]. For example, he appeared to accept
Annius' euhemeristic identification of Noah with Janus:

> Now the above-mentioned Berosus could not attribute the confusion of lan-
> guages to God because he was not acquainted with the name of God. At the
> beginning of book four, he wrote that when Noah saw that the human species
> was beginning to multiply, he divided Asia, Africa and Europe among his
> progeny and despatched each man and his family to his own designated country,
> And he said that a hundred and thirty one years after the flood, Nimrod founded
> the city of Babel and its wondrous tower, but was unable to complete their
> construction. Towards the end of book three, he wrote that Noah was called
> Iano, a name derived from the word for wine *[yayin]*; and the name of his wife
> was Tithea, but she was also called Aretia which name is a derivative of the
> word *erets* which means earth. This was because she was the mother of all the
> inhabitants of the world. After her death, she was called Esta, a name connected
> with the word meaning fire *[esh]* because she ascended to the highest of all
> elements, to heaven. Other examples are given which demonstrate the prevalent
> use of the Holy Tongue in those generations[80].

De' Rossi then referred to Annius' *Fragmenta Catonis* in which Ar-
ezzo is listed as one of the twelve cities of antiquity founded by Noah-
Janus, who named the city after his wife Vesta[81]. (Annius' obvious
purpose in proposing this toponym—to prove that the names of the
Etruscan cities of Italy were not Latin in origin[82]—appears to have
escaped de' Rossi's notice.)

De' Rossi continued his argument by citing Pierfrancesco Giambullari's dialogue on the origins of the Tuscan language. However, de' Rossi
was still indirectly using Annius' work; for Giambullari gave Annius'
theory its fullest exposition. Acknowledging his debt to his friend Giambattista Gelli[83], who had also treated the origins of the Florentine language, by making him one of the main interlocutors of his dialogue,
Giambullari attempted to assert the linguistic autonomy of the Tuscan
language by claiming that Etruscan, and not Latin was its forbear[84]. The
political significance of this theory has been elucidated by Cipriani who
has demonstrated Giambullari's attempt to legitimize the new regime of

the Grand Duke Cosimo de' Medici by endowing it with a noble Etruscan past. Since Etruscan civilization preceded that of Greece, Cosimo's dominion was inextricably linked with the history of all humanity[85].

Like Annius, Giambullari stated that an expert knowledge of Aramaic or Hebrew was required for the study of Etruscan[86]. (He constantly confuses Hebrew with Aramaic[87].) Obviously entertaining certain scruples about utilizing the Annian texts, Giambullari felt obliged to present an apologia for his citation from authors other than Moses for the story of the flood[88]. His attempts to absolve himself of any charge of impiety towards the sacred text could well have been made by de' Rossi. He denied any mistrust of the Scriptural account, which after all was above suspicion, and lightly dismissed his own investigations as satisfying the cravings of an enquiring mind such as his own[89]. After producing some typical Annian etymologies, Curzio, one of the interlocutors, considered the reasons which had prompted scholars to dismiss the work as an Annian fabrication[90]. But Gello tried to maintain a neutral position since it was impossible to compare it to the original Greek text. In response to Curzio's scepticism about the truth of the account of Noah's visit to Italy after the flood, Gello used Johannes Lucidus' evidence in support of Annius, presumably unaware of the Annian inspiration of all Lucidus' comments on this subject.

De' Rossi appears not to have taken this part of the work into account nor does he indicate any awareness of the political nature of the linguistic problem treated by Giambullari. He only cites the passage in which Giambullari gives a list of the words which, according to Giambullari, derived from Hebrew: "ambasceria" from *baser;* "misura" from *mesura;* "carbone" from *harbone qayits* etc.[91]. Influenced by such etymological gymnastics, de' Rossi then describes a meeting of the Jewish accademia in Ferrara. When one of the participants had objected to the use of a Greek word to describe a Jewish gathering, de' Rossi had appeased his fellow scholar by proposing that the word "accademia" actually derived from the Biblical expression *'beth 'eqed ro'im'* (2 K., 10.12)[92]. While ignoring the fact that both Annius and Giambullari display poor knowledge of the language that both claim to be the *Ursprache,* de' Rossi utilized their proofs which accorded with his own and that of the Jewish tradition. Thus he could conclude: "These words supply us with convincing evidence that the Holy Tongue is the antecedent and father of all languages since its imprint is specially recognizable and has left its vestiges in every one of those languages"[93].

A chapter on the antiquity of the Hebrew script follows de' Rossi's discourse on language. According to de' Rossi, language and script were both Adamic and divine in origin. Adam had been created with the faculty of language to enable him to be the recipient of the divine message; the art of writing was similarly divinely bestowed on him for the purpose of transmitting a written legacy to his descendants[94]. As with the subject of language, de' Rossi was supplied with a wealth of material including Kabbalist writings from the Jewish tradition which asserted the antiquity of the Hebrew or Ashuri script[95]. A precise dating of the origin of the script was given in *Mishnah Avoth* which enumerates the script among the ten things which were created on the sixth day of creation at twilight[96]. In characteristic fashion, however, de' Rossi supplied the main Jewish sources and then turned to the secular texts for corroboration of the thesis he was propounding. The complete disregard for the context of the statements which he cited is also typical of his method of discussion.

Walter Stevens has clearly demonstrated how Annius was intent on proving that historical records pre-existed the flood and that they were preserved in Babylon until the time of Berosus. In this way Annius was able to consolidate his myth of the Babylonian archivist who had access to ante-diluvian records[97]. Annius' argument was built on the *topos* of the ante-diluvian books, found in medieval historiography and mainly based on a passage in Josephus' Antiquities. In addition, a statement of Pliny (also quoted by de' Rossi)[98] about the existence of the Assyrian script from time immemorial was used by Annius as a means of refuting a current notion that hieroglyphics were the oldest form of writing[99].

A general statement based on the Annian material gave the first indication that de' Rossi intended to investigate ancient history the Annian way. "At the beginning of book one, the ancient writer Berosus the Chaldean wrote that prior to the flood there existed wise men who predicted the future and inscribed their prophesies on marble"[100]. This was then followed by the oft-quoted passage from Josephus which was intended to demonstrate how the arts survived the flood. According to Josephus, the sons of Seth did not want their inventions to be lost in the two universal catastrophes predicted by Adam[101]. The Sethites therefore constructed two pillars, one of brick, the other of stone, and inscribed their inventions on both pillars. The pillar of brick disappeared in the deluge, but the pillar of stone was reported by Josephus to "exist to this day in the land of Seiris"[102]. De' Rossi then quoted a Christian Apostle who, in his letter of rules *(sedarim)*, referred to these columns as having been built by Enoch. Enoch is said to have engraved his prediction of a universal deluge and a universal conflagration on these columns.

What is striking here is the omission of the name of the Apostle. Only in Jude, 14 is there a vague allusion to Enoch's prophecy of God's future judgement on mankind[103].

The puzzle is solved by a consultation of Annius' commentary to book one of Berosus. Annius writes: "As is shown in Genesis, the holy prophet Enoch was born 1034 years before the deluge. Jude the Apostle, called Tadeus, testifies in his Canon that Enoch predicted both the flood of water as well as the final conflagration. According to Josephus, he recorded his prophecies on two columns, one of bronze, the other of brick"[104]. Here we are presented with de' Rossi's source complete with the citation from Josephus. Evidently unable to trace the quotation to any Apostle, de' Rossi was forced to be slightly vague in his reference. Annius' conflation of various traditions regarding the predictions of the early generations of mankind and the origin of written documentation was taken on trust by de' Rossi and used by him as a means of presenting a series of links in a chain of tradition which corroborated the Rabbinic view of the antiquity of the Hebrew script.

Robert Tate has written that what differentiated sixteenth-century scholars from their medieval predecessors was the choice of written authority to be accepted. "New circumstances can create new expedients all the more acceptable if they derive their validity from classical authority"[105]. Seeking to resolve problems of Jewish history by means of the most accessible and best-documented evidence, de' Rossi showed himself to be a typical sixteenth-century scholar. His use of the Annian fabrications demonstrated his familiarity with the *locus classicus* for ancient chronology. In accepting the authenticity of the Annian texts de' Rossi kept company with the Protestant polymath, Sebastian Münster, whose scholarly interests were so strikingly similar to his own. The forgeries had attained the status of "appendices to Holy Writ" and it required the critical acumen of a Melchor Cano or Joseph Scaliger to point out that the fakes neither clarified nor confirmed Scripture. The syncretistic nature of the forgeries had a great correspondence to elements in the Jewish tradition, so too, the Annian forgeries appealed to him because they could be used to emend or confirm Rabbinic tradition.

Had Zunz and his contemporaries examined the sixteenth-century context of de' Rossi's researches, they might have been led to qualify their eulogistic assessment of his scholarly contribution, for when de' Rossi presented his *ḥiddushim*, that is, his "original findings", he usually meant the term "original" to be understood solely in respect to his Jewish readers. And what was novel to Jews was not necessarily novel to the scholarly-reading public at large. But de' Rossi was writing for Jews in his *Me'or 'Enayim;* and his use of the popular Annian texts to solve the historical problems posed by Rabbinic tradition was a new venture in Jewish historiography.

NOTES

1. *Toledoth le-R Azariah min Ha-Adummim* "Kerem Hemed" 5 (1841), 131–158: 139. The article included S. Rappoport's additional notes and was continued in *"Kerem Hemed"* 7 *(1843), 119–124.* The article was reprinted at the end of Benjacob's edition of the *Me'or Enayim,* Vilna 1863–5.
2. The printing of the ed. pr. was in two stages: 1) The original text November 1573, the last printing of which was published in September 1574. To this text, de' Rossi added two more pages (195–6) in which he described his negotiations with some Venetian Rabbis who had objected to some of the contents of the book. On this printing, see I. Mehlmann in *Genuzoth Sefarim,* Jerusalem 1976, 21–39. 2) A revised text emended according to the stipulations of the Venetian Rabbis, the final revised text of which was published April 1575. Subsequent editions of the book were published in Berlin 1794 (ed. I. Satanow); Vienna 1829–1830; Vilna 1863–5 (ed. I. Benjacob and includes the latter works of de' Rossi, *Matsref La-Kesef* and *Tsedeq 'Olamim);* Vilna 1864–6 (ed. D. Cassel and includes the *Matsref La-Kesef, Tsedeq 'Olamim* and various poems of de' Rossi. This edition was reprinted in Jerusalem 1970); Warsaw 1899 (ed. Z. H. Jaffe. Cassel's edition is used.) All references in this article will be to the Cassel edition.
3. S. Baron already indicated the need for such research in 1928. See n. 1, p. 422, in his *Azariah de' Rossi's historical method,* in *History and Jewish Historians,* Philadelphia 1964.
4. Ch. 1, 78–79. He states that this style of 'variegated and eclectic study' was an innovation in Hebrew literature. By the time he was writing, there were many examples of published "miscellanea". His essays are not comparable to the type of "miscellanea" written by Poliziano and Beroaldo which are basically devoted to textual criticism. His work bears more similarity to Pedro Mexia's *Silva de varia leçion* and Antonio de Guevara's Letters which he had read and which had been reprinted many times in the sixteenth century and translated into Italian.

5. S. Baron, *Azariah de' Rossi's historical method*, 210.
6. *Il Gello: Ragionamenti de la prima et antica origine della toscana e particolarmente della lingua fiorentina*, Firenze 1546. On Giambullari, see below.
7. The best general survey of the work still remains S. Baron's three essays in *History and Jewish Historians*, 167–239.
8. This was subsequently published as *Azariah de' Rossi's historic method* (quoted in *supra*, note 3). Baron compared de' Rossi's method to that of Carlo Sigonio, Onofrio Panvinio and Robortello. On the basis of examination of his source material, I would also stress the importance of northern-European antiquarian scholarship as a point of comparison, particularly with regard to his Septuagint studies.
9. *Expressions of the unity of the people of Israel in Italy during the Renaissance* [Hebrew], "Sinai" 76 (1975), 40.
10. *Some reflections on the place of Azariah de Rossi's MEOR ENAYIM in the cultural milieu of Italian Renaissance Jewry*, in *Jewish thought in the sixteenth century*, ed. B. D. Cooperman, Cambridge, Mass., 1983, 23–48.
11. One example of polemical discourse may be detected in de' Rossi's attack on Elijah Levita's *Masoreth Ha-Masoreth* (Venice 1938) in which Levita argued with good reason that the Hebrew vowel-system had been invented by the Tiberian Masoretes after the redaction of the Talmud. In arguing in favour of the antiquity of the vowel-points in ch. 59, de' Rossi was assuming a somewhat conservative stance which was not consistent with the more critical position he took with regard to such controversial issues as the age of the universe. It seems quite likely that de' Rossi was upholding such a position in this case as a response to the medieval Christian view which continued to be re-stated that the Jews had invented the vowel-points in order to conceal the true meaning of Scripture and suppress the Christian truth. Such a view had been propounded by Jacob Perez de Valencia in the Prologue to his commentary to the Psalms (tract. VI), a work which de' Rossi had read.
12. De' Rossi alludes to this in ch. 9, 148. Steuchus, in *Vulgata editio an sit divi Hieronymi*, Ludguni 1538, 222–235, argued that the elegance of the existing version of the Vulgate indicated that Jerome must have written it. Münster, like Erasmus and Xantes Pagninus, argued that it was not Jerome's on the basis of the discrepancies between the Vulgate and Jerome's *Liber Heb. Quaest. in Genesim*. (See Münster's introduction to his Latin translation of the O.T.)
13. Ch. 2, 81. This chapter is devoted to arguments based on Rabbinic sources to prove that the study of non-Jewish literature was never forbidden *per se*, but only vetoed as a precautionary measure to prevent Jews' absorption in non-Jewish culture.
14. Chs. 29–44, 275–382. The controversy over the publication of the book was particularly directed against this section of the work. On the controversy, see D. Kaufmann, *Contributions à la histoire des luttes d'Azaria de Rossi*, REJ 33 (1896), 77–87; I. Mehlmann, *Genuzoth Sefarim* (*supra*, note

2). See also R. Bonfil, *Some reflections*, 25–31, who shows that the negative response to the book was over-emphasized by scholars and that the controversy "was little more than a tempest in a teapot". De' Rossi was forced to include Moses Provenzali's critique of the *Yeme 'Olam'* in the text, but he reaffirmed his position by writing a reply, and both documents were published as a kind of appendix to the book. De' Rossi made a second attempt to prove his theories by writing the *Matsref La-Kesef (The Refinement of Silver)* and the *Tsedeq 'Olamim (Everlasting Righteousness)* which were never published in his lifetime (the ed. pr. was Edinburgh 1854). Publishers may have been disinclined to cause further controversy by publishing these works. Attention should also be drawn to de' Rossi's references subsequent to the publication of the *Me'or 'Enayim* to his impoverished state and to his persecution by his co-religionists, another indication of his controversial position occasioned by the publication of his chronological theories. On this, see my article in *Annali della scuola normale superiore di Pisa*, ser. III, (1978), 493–511.

15. The contemporary interest in the subject may be demonstrated by de' Rossi's selection of ch. 35 from this section of the book for translation into Italian for Giacomo Boncompagni, "general governatore dello stato ecclesiastico". The translation is in Ms. Bodleian, Mich 308, 133*v*–135*v*.

16. Ch. 35, 305–306.

17. This has been proven by G. Cohen in his excellent edition and English translation of Ibn Daud. See his ch. *The symmetry of history*, 189–222, in *The book of tradition*, (1967), London 1969.

18. On the messianic issue, see D. Tamar, *The messianic expectation in Italy for the year 1575'* [Hebrew] "Sefunot" 2 (1958), 61–88, reprinted in his *Studies in the History of the Jewish People in Erets Israel*, Jerusalem 1970, 11–38. Tamar links the Messianic fervour of the time to the Papal persecution of Jews during this period. Bonfil *The place of Azariah de' Rossi*, 41, views de' Rossi's discussion of the Messianic issue in the context of Judaeo-Christian debates on the subject and therefore regards de' Rossi's treatment as an attempt to defend the Jewish position.

19. See, for example, Abarbanel's *Mayane Ha-Yeshuah (Fountains of Salvation)*, Ferrara 1551, a commentary on *Daniel*, 10.8, in which he attacks Christian calculations of Daniel's prophecy of the seventy weeks including those of Nicholas of Lyra, Bede and the Bishop of Burgos, and then gives an alternative calculation for the dates indicated in the prophecy.

20. A. I. Baumgarten, *Sforno and Berossus*, JJS 25 (1974), 313–316, was the first to indicate Sforno's use of Annius. The references are found on *Gen.*, 6.9 and 9.22.

21. *Opera diversorum auctorum de antiquitatibus loquentium*. It was printed by Eucharius Silber. A list of more than sixteen editions of the works (including translations) published between 1498 and 1583 is given in W. Stevens, unpublished diss. Cornell 1974, *Berosus Chaldaeus: Counterfeit and fictive editors of the early sixteenth century*.

22. There is an enormous bibliography on the subject of the fakes, most of which is to be found in disparate articles. W. Stevens's diss. (quoted above) gives an excellent summary of the contents of the texts. E. Fumagalli, *Aneddoti della vita di Annio da Viterbo*, "Archivum fratrum Praedicatorum" 50 (1980), 167–169, gives the latest report on biographical details of Annius' life. An unpublished ms. was published in *Annio da Viterbo: Documenti e ricerche*, a cura di G. B. Caporali, Roma 1981. For further details on the subject, see R. Weiss, *Traccia per una biografia di Annio da Viterbo'*, "Italia medievale e umanistica" 5 (1962), 425–441 and *An unknown epigraphic tract by Annius of Viterbo*, in *Italian Studies to E. R. Vincent*, ed. C. P. Brand et al., Cambridge 1962, pp. 101–120; E. N. Tigerstedt, *Joannes Annius and Graecia mendax*, in *Classical, Medieval and Renaissance Studies in Honour of B. L. Ullman*, II, Rome 1964, pp. 293–310; A. D. Momigliano, review of H. J. Erasmus, *The origins of Rome*, Assen 1962 "Rivista storica italiana" 75, (1963), 390–394, reprinted in *Terzo Contributo*, Rome 1966, [II], 769–774; R. Tate, *Mythology in Spanish historiography*, "Hispanic Review" 22 (1954), 1–18, and *Nebrija the historian*, "Bulletin of Hispanic Studies" 34 (1957), 124–146, reprinted in his *Esayos Sobre la Historiografia paninsular del Siglo XV* (Madrid, 1970), 183–211; O. A. Danielsson, *Annius von Viterbo über die Gründungsgeschichte Roms*, in *Corolla archeologica. . . . Gustavo Adolpho dedicata*, Lund 1932, 1–16; R. E. Asher, *Myth, legend and history in Renaissance France*, "Studi francesi" 39 (1969), 409–419; O. Gruppe *Geschichte der klassischen Mythologie and Religionsgeschichte*, Leipzig 1912, 19–21; A. Biondi, *Annio da Viterbo e un aspetto dell'orientalismo di Guillaume Postel*, "Bollettino della società di studi valdesi" 113, n. 132 (1972), 49–67.
23. On the identity of the Armenians, see Weiss, *Traccia*, 431.
24. See Annius' comment to Metasthenes, *De iudicio temporum*, Lyon 1554, I, 361–362. All references henceforth shall be to the Lyons edition.
25. He gives a list of the Kings of Media from Sardanapalus until "Seleucus Nikanor in our own time."
26. The *Breviarium* presents a brief chronological list from Adam to Solomon and then gives a more detailed description of Solomon's successors, the Kings and high-priests of Israel with reference to the Kings of the four monarchies and ends with a reference to Agrippinus, Agrippa the third of his own time.
27. "Ioannes Annius Viterbensis . . . antiquitatum . . . indagator et illustrator solertissimus. Qui tametsi ad patriae suae exaltationem praecipue respexisse visus est multa tamen quae ad regum regnorumque Christianorum immo ad Christi ipsius generationes et primordia cognoscenda faciant adducit". This preface is quoted by Biondi, Annio da Viterbo, 51.
28. *Ibid.*
29. Weiss, *An unknown*, 101.
30. Tate, *Mythology*, 12.
31. The work was entitled, *De primis temporibus et quatuor ac viginti regibus primis Hispaniae*. Tate has shown, (*Mythology* 12), that Annius was using

the thirteenth-century chronicle of Ximénez de Rada, Archbishop of Toledo, for this work. The account of Hercules' arrival in Spain thus linked the antiquity of Spain with the classical world and also signalled its priority over Greece and Rome.

32. Tigerstedt, *Joannes Annius*, 306.

33. *Ibid.*, 307ff.

34. Biondi, *Annio da Viterbo*, 55–56.

35. *Ibid.*, 49. Reference to the Hermetic texts in conjunction with Annius is also made by P. Mattiangelli, *Annio da Viterbo, ispiratore di cicli pittorici* in *Annio da Viterbo*, a cura di *Caporali (supra*, nota 22), 257–339: 275, who points out that Annius also refers to the "Egyptian Hermes".

36. Biondi, *Annio da Viterbo*, 60–61. Biondi makes this point with specific reference to Guillaume Postel, who regarded the Noachide traditions as the basis for his project of religious restoration. In his *De Etruriae . . . origine, religione, institutis et moribus,* Florentiae 1551, Postel makes Noah's coming to Italy as representative of his own prophetic mission helped by the rebirth of the "true" historians. De' Rossi never referred to Postel, although he did know the work of his friend Moses Basola. It is interesting to note that de' Rossi also read the Hermetic writings in Ficino's translation and that he stated the intention of translating the *Asclepius* and *Pimander* into Hebrew. De' Rossi, like most of his contemporaries, did not question the authenticity of the Hermetic writings and accepted that Hermes had lived in the time of Moses and had been influenced by the teachings of the Torah. See ch. 4, 100–101.

37. F. Saxl, *Lectures* I, London 1957, 186. Saxl discusses the Annian inspiration of Pinturicchio's frescoes in the Borgian apartments in the Vatican. On the Egyptian element in the frescoes, see E. Iversen, *The myth of Egypt and its hieroglyphs in European tradition*, Copenhagen 1961, 63ff. and P. Mattiangeli, *Annio da Viterbo (supra*, note 35).

38. E. Garin, *La cultura del Rinascimento*, Firenze 1976 (1967[1]), 58.

39. David Ganz (1541–1613) was a pupil of the "Maharal of Prague". His *Tsemaḥ David* (ed. pr. Prague 1592) was dependent on the work of de' Rossi and Gedalya ibn Yahya. The reference to Berosus occurs in the introduction to part II (N.Y 1966, 67), in which he defends the use of non-Jewish literature in a manner reminiscent of de' Rossi. Ganz also states that Abraham Zacuto (1452–   C. 1515 had used (ps.) Berosus on his list of Egyptian Kings given in the final section of his chronicle *Sefer Yuḥasin*. (This section presents world history, synchronizing dates and events with relevant periods of Jewish history.)

40. De' Rossi refers to Mercator's *Chronologia* (Cologne 1569) in ch. 41, 361 regarding the identification of Ptolemy's Nabonassar with the Biblical Shalmanassar. (On the history of this question, see the article by A. Grafton, *From* De die natali *to* De emendatione temporum: *The origins and setting of Scaliger's chronology,* "Journal of the Warburg and Courtauld Institutes" 48 (1985), 100–143. At the beginning of the *Chronologia*, Mercator elaborates on the fictitiousness of the Annian texts and indicates that such fabri-

cations cannot be used for any discourse on chronology. Whether de' Rossi took Mercator's introduction into account or not, he still continued to use the Annian texts for his later work, the *Matsref La-Kesef,* although very infrequently. Moreover, Mercator, himself, sometimes used the fakes.

41. Münster's work on Aramaic and introduction on the antiquity of Hebrew and Aramaic in the *Chaldaica Grammatica,* Basileae 1527 correspond to ch. 57; the *Kalendarium Hebraicum* with chs. of *Yeme Olam;* the *Cosmographia* with ch. II in which de' Rossi appraised Rabbinic notions of geography in the light of the discoveries of the New World.

42. See my article, *Azariah de' Rossi and LXX tradition, Italia,* V, 1–2 (1985), 7–35.

43. On the *Josippon,* see D. Flusser, *The Josippon [Hebrew],* II (Jerusalem 1980).

44. Münster's text of the *Josippon* is entitled: *Josephus hebraicus diu desideratus et nunc ex Constantinopolitano exemplari iuxta Hebraismum . . . illustratus,* Basileae 1541. A5*v* ". . . et citantur quaedam gentes quae longe post Iosephi tempora in mundo surrexerunt ut sunt Franci, Gothi, Lombardi, Bulgari et haec plane arguunt Iosepho quaedam accessisse per posteros Iudaeos expositionis et praefationis gratia . . .".

45. Ch. 19, 233–234. It should be noted that de' Rossi did not have a high regard for the book. He called it "an unfundamental work" (pag. 234). The textual tradition of the *Josippon* is treated in ch. 19 which is devoted to the subject of textual corruption. De' Rossi, like many of his contemporaries, attributes main cause of textual corruption to copyists' errors, the insertion of marginal glosses into the body of the text and the intentional alteration of the text by readers. Scribal error is the convenient excuse usually used by de' Rossi in order to account for discrepancies or anomalies in texts.

46. *Cosmographiae universalis lib. VI,* Basileae 1554, 272:
. . . Berosum quidam reiiciunt, idque ob id, quod ille aut liber sub eius nomine evulgatus non concordet cum reliquis scriptoribus. Quicquid sit, hoc unum scio, quantum attinet ad hebraica vocabula, quorum multa sunt in eius fragmentis, nullam in eis inveniri imposturam, quin haec cogunt me fidem adhibere autori et libro eius, potissimum quod eo tempore quando Berosus per monachum quendam est publicatus, nemo fuerit inter Christianos qui Hebraicam calluerit linguam. Alioquin quis indoctis monachis dixisset quid Estha, Maia, Arecia et Ruha significaverint, qui linguarum penitus rudes fuerunt. Non tamen inficias eo, quin bono authori aliquid falsi sit admixtum?

47. F. Secret, *Edigio da Viterbo et quelques-uns de ses contemporains,* "Augustiniana" 16 (1966), 371–385, attempts to identify "Samuel Talmudista" with Samuel Zarfati, doctor to Pope Alexander VI. The evidence is most inconclusive. Samuel the Talmudist may well have been yet another of Annius' fakes.

48. *Melchor Cano, De locis theologicis,* Louvain 1564, bk II, 626–669: 636, "Non ergo Philo Iudaeus cuius ingenium, eruditionem, facundiam, celebravit antiquitas, auctor illius libelli fuit . . . sed ubique non modo indocte et indiserte, verum inculte etiam atque inornate loquitur . . .".

49. Ch. 20, 238–239. With regard to the comm. to *I Chr., 5.36*, he writes, "But surely anyone who is familiar with his language will easily judge that the passage is not written in his customary style".

50. Antonio Possevino (1534–1612), *Apparatus ad omnium gentium historiam,* Venetus 1597, part 4, ch. 1, 139, ". . . Ne quem autem fallat Berosi nomen, qui non ita multos ante annos erutus in lucem praestantibus etiam viris imposuit, eo magis hoc loco dicendum est quod cum legitimos Berosi partus una cum aliis interiisse certum sit ac ita (cum retento errore necesse fuit) plures tandem crediderunt non desunt tamen qui istius suppositii uti et reliquam Annii Viterbensis lectionem divinae hostoriae percipendae licet a seipsis commentitiam habitam extiment utilem". Then follows a list of authors who had accepted or rejected the Annian texts.

51. Ch. 29, 276.

52. It seems quite probable that Johannes Lucidus Samotheus is to be identified with the Dominican Giovanni Tolosani (d. 1549). This has been shown by D. Marzi, *La questione della riforma del calendario,* Firenze 1896, 148–149. Lucidus, *Opusculum de emendationibus temporum,* (Venetiis 1537), Venetiis 1545, 2*v*, ". . . Erit igitur opusculum hoc perutile non modo illis qui seculares et humanas literas discunt sed ipsis praecipue qui literalem sensum in scripturis divinis quaerunt . . .".

53. *Ibid.,* 2*r*, ". . . Et quoniam, uti dictum est, apud Hebraeos Philo, apud Chaldaeoos Berosus, apud Persas Metasthenes, apud Graecos Eusebius excerpta monarchia Medorum et Persarum et apud Latinos Hieronymus presbyter scripturis divinis una conveniunt ideo maximam authoritatem inter antiquos chronographos obtinent . . .".

54. A. Grafton, *Joseph Scaliger and historical chronology: The rise and fall of a discipline,* "History and Theory" 160, 164.

55. Ch. 29, 276.

56. In ch. 30, he translated into Hebrew a Latin version of *Cyropaedia* 8:6, 7, 8 and of the beginning of the *Anabasis* for the purpose of identifying the Kings of Persia reigning before and during the second Temple period.

57. Josephus, *Antiquitates* X end; XI *passim;* XII, are translated in ch. 33 from Gelenius' Latin translation for succession of Median and Persian Kings until the time of Alexander of Macedon and for names of high-priests ministering over the same period.

58. Eusebius, *Chronicorum lib.* The table of 14 Kings from Cyrus to Darius is translated in ch. 34 from Sichard's ed. of Chronicles, Basileae 1529 (PG, 19, 343–344). De' Rossi also refers to statements of Quintus Curtius and Jerome on the subject.

59. I can find no reason for de' Rossi's translation. Perhaps he was unable to find an equivalent Hebrew word to express the sense of *iudicium.* Annius, in his comm. to Metasthenes (pag. 359), asserts that *de censura temporum* would be a more appropriate title for the work since it is above all an emendation of incorrect (i.e. private opinion) chronology.

60. Annius prefaces his commentary to ps. Philo with a *Quaestionale prooe-*

mium concerning Jesus' genealogy. On the basis of his fictitious text of Philo he attempts to show against Nicholas of Lyra that there is no discrepancy between the data for Jesus' genealogy given in Matthew and Luke. He states that Matthew gives the genealogy of Joseph, Luke that of Mary. He feigns surprise that the *Breviarium* had been ignored by theologians since it provided such clear proofs against the Jews.

61. Ch. 35, 295.
62. *Ibid.*, ". . . In his reckoning, he followed the LXX reading, for where Scripture reads, Amon was 22 years when he began to reign and he reigned 2 years in Jerusalem' (II. K. 21.19), the LXX reads, 'he reigned 12 years' ". This is mentioned by Samotheus the Christian [i.e. Lucidus] in bk. 2, ch. 9. But once these ten years are discounted from Philo's reckoning, his figure accords exactly with those who reckon 430 years".
63. *Seder Olam Rabbah*, ch. 30, ed. B. Ratner, Vilna 1897, 141–143.
64. On the rules of assessing evidence given by Annius, see A. Biondi, ed. M. Cano. *L'autorità della storia profana*, Torino 1973, XXXVff., and W. Goez, *Die Anfänge der historischen Methoden-Reflexion in der italienischen Renaissance und ihre Aufnahme in der Geschichtsschreibung des deutschen Humanismus*, "Arch. für Kulturgesch." 56 (1974), 25–48.
65. Ch. 31, 270. De' Rossi's translation is not completely literal.
     Ps. Metasthenes, 360–361: Qui de temporibus parant necesse est illos non solo auditu et opinione chronographiam scribere ne quum per opiniones scribunt, uti Graeci, cum ipsis pariter et se et alios decipiant et per omnem vitam aberrent. Verum absque ullo errore fiet si solos annales duarum monarchiarum assecuti, caeteros omnes ut fabulatores reiecerimus . . . Neque tamen omnes recipiendi sunt qui de his regibus scribunt sed solum sacerdotes illius regni penes quos est publica et probata fides annalium suorum, qualis est Berosus. Nam is Chaldaeus omne tempus Assyriorum digesit ex antiquorum annalibus . . . .
66. Judah Loew b. Bezalel (Maharal of Prague), *Be'er Ha-Golah*, Prague 1589 [Jerusalem 1971], 'Be'er' 6, 130.
67. *Yoma'* 69a; *Megillath Ta'anith* 9 (De' Rossi used ed. Mantua 1513), ed. H. Lichtenstein, HUCA 8–9 (1931–1932), 339–340. De' Rossi treats this subject in ch. 21, 241–242.
68. *Hullin*, 6a.
69. *Ant.* XI, 306–312; XII, 254–258.
70. Lucidus, *Opusculus* (*supra*, note 52), 4, ch. I, 35–36.
71. See Diodorus Siculus, 2, ch. 4. Annius on Berosus 5, 185–186, writes, "Diodorus scribit . . . Semiramidem natam ex dea Ascalonita eamque dictam Semiramidem quod Semiramis lingua Syra dicantur aves a quibus nutrita sit . . .". As regards the origin of the name, de' Rossi suggests that it derives from the root "to sing".
72. Annius to ps-Berosus, states that Semiramis turned into a dove when she died. De' Rossi omits to include this detail in his account, presumably because he found it too incredible. J. J. Scaliger refers to the legends about the two Semirames in his *Animadversiones in Chronologica Eusebii*, Lugduni Batavorum 1606, 35–36 and includes a reference to de' Rossi's treat-

ment of the subject. I am grateful to A. Grafton who pointed this out to me.

73. Pag. 242 end.

74. On this subject, see M. Tavoni, *Latino, grammatica, volgare: Studi di una dialettica dell'umanesimo*, Padova 1984.

75. On this subject, see M. Dubois, *Mythe et langage au seizième siècle*, Bordeaux 1970.

76. For a comprehensive study of this theme, see A. Borst, *Der Turmbau von Babel*, 3, I, Stuttgart 1960.

77. The work does not appear to be extant. De' Rossi refers to it in ch. 57, 456.

78. See ch. 57, 454. Moscato treats the subject in his commentary *Qol Yehudah* to *Cuzari* 2, 68, Vilna 1594.

79. De' Rossi makes no references to Annius' "Rabbi Samuel" or "Samuel Talmudista, noster linguarum interpretes", Annius' informant for Hebrew and Aramaic etymology.

80. Ch. 57, 456. On Annius' euhemerism, see H. J. Erasmus, *The origins of Rome in historiography from Petrarch to Perizonius*, Assen 1962, 41.

81. Pag. 456.

82. Annius to ps. Berosus bk. 3, I, 128, and to ps. Cato, 116, "Sane sciendum est . . . haec . . . nomina ante Latinam fuisse . . .".

83. Gelli wrote the *Origine di Firenze* which was published between 1542 and 1545 and dedicated it to Cosimo de' Medici. The work which had a limited diffusion followed Annian notions. On Gelli, see A. de Gaetano, *G. Gelli and the Florentine Academy. The rebellion against Latin*, Florence 1976. Giambullari writes of Gelli, 6, ". . . nel principio ho introdotto a parlare il nostro Giovambattista Gelli . . . che dal cognome suo voglio chiamare . . .".

84. Giambullari (1495–1555) had held various positions: he was Canon of San Lorenzo in Florence; capellano of Volterra; Custodian of the Laurenziana Library of Florence. Apart from his *Il Gello*, he also wrote a *Storia dell-'Europa*, Firenze 1566 which has been discussed by C. Dionisotti, in '*Medio evo barbaro e cinquecento italiano*', "*Lettere italiane*" 24 (1972), 421–430. There were two early editions of *Il Gello*, Firenze 1546 and 1549. All references here will be to the edition of 1546.

85. G. Cipriani, *Il mito etrusco nel Rinascimento italiano*, Firenze 1980.

86. *Il. Gello*, 6, "Perché la maggior parte de nostri nomi non dependono dal latino ma dall'etrusco il quale si puo male intendere ne tempi nostri senza una ottima cognitione di queste altre lingue, della Hebrea dico et della caldea lequali uscirono donde la Etrusca, come nel presente ragionamento . . . agevolmente potrà vedersi . . .".

87. See, e.g. 68 where he attempts to prove that the name Firenze derived from the Aramaic word for flower and then gives *Numbers* 8.4 and *Isaiah*, 5.24 as his references.

88. Pag. 11.

89. *Ibid.*, ". . . Non gia perche io non creda allui, come certo credere si debbe: Ma per satisfattione maggiore de' troppo curiosi, come forse son'io . . .".

90. Pag. 13. It is suggested that the reason for the suspicion about the Annian
text was only caused by the fact of its preservation over such a long period
of time, "... perché a dotti appare impossibile che egli si sia mantenuto
cotanto. Perilche si crede per molti che Beroso che hoggi è tra mano, sia
piu tosto fintione dello Annio che opera del vero Beroso ...".

91. Pag. 55, "... Diciamo noi adunque, ambasciata, imbasciadore, ed ambasceria, da bascer che a loro significa nuntiare ... carbone da carbon che la
estrema ed ultima siccità arsiccia ...". The "mesura misura" etymology is
not given in either of the editions of the Gello, but it does occur in
Augustinus Steuchus' Recognitio veteris testamenti, Venetiis 1529
(9r) which de' Rossi quotes frequently. "Mensura enim nomen est hebraicum ...".

92. The phrase means "meeting-place of shepherds" according to the interpretation of the Targum ascribed to Jonathan b. Uzziel to which de' Rossi
refers. He states (pag. 457), "In other words, an assembly of men is
meant".

93. Pag. 457.

94. Ch. 58, 465.

95. The actual form of the original script was a matter of controversy among
the Talmudic sages, some claiming that it had been the Ashuri script
currently used, others, the Ivri script. See Sanhedrin 21a and de' Rossi's
discussion of all the relevant sources, 466–470.

96. Avoth 5.6. Annius has Berosus state that letters and disciplinae were
infused into Adam by God. He also records another opinion according to
which the Chaldeans are said to have possessed the complete history of
mankind which had been written down and transmitted by Adam and
other patriarchs.

97. W. Stevens, Berosus Chaldaeus (supra, note 21), ch. 2, 59–76. Stevens
points out the use of the topos in John Cassian's Collationes (5th c.),
Godfrey of Viterbo's Historia Adamae (12th c.) and by Petrus Comestor.

98. Pliny, Nat. Hist., VII, 56, 192–193, "Litteras semper arbitror Assyriis
fuisse" and note that Pliny later refers to Berosus when discussing
the length of time over which astronomical observations had been written down. He then concludes, "... ex quo apparet aeternus litterarum
usus".

99. Annius, I, 59. Annius objects to the use of the word "aeternus" by Pliny
and argues with the help of Diodorus Siculus that the Chaldeans had
attributed the origin of writing to Adam.

100. Pag. 466. This quotation follows his citation of Pliny and brief references
to Augustine, De civ. Dei 18:39 and Quaestiones in Exodum 69, who also
argued that writing had originated in antiquity, but asserted that there was
no precise date for its invention, "... Hic sane significatur quod ante
legem datam, habuerint Hebraei litteras quae quando coeperint esse, nescio
utrum valeat indagari ...". The citation from bk. 1 of Berosus (I, 62) is
not literal and de' Rossi also includes a passage from pag. 74. "Tum multi

praedicabant et vaticinabantur et lapidibus excidebant . . .", but translates "marble" instead of "stone".

101. *Ant.* 1, 70–72. For a discussion of this passage, see C. E. Lutz, *"Remigius' Ideas on the seven liberal Arts,* "Medievalia et Humanistica" 10 (1956), 41–42, who discusses how Seth takes precedent over Enoch as a prophet. See also T. W. Franxman, *Genesis and the Jewish Antiquities of Flavius Josephus,* Rome 1979, 79–80, who gives all the sources of tradition underlying Josephus' statement and then says, "Who derived what from whom and how, are questions that are still open to speculation".

102. Seiris has not been identified. De' Rossi incorrectly translates "Syria" for "Seiris". Similarly, he wrongly translates the passage and writes: "And he [i.e. Josephus] saw the column of marble . . .".

103. "And Enoch also, the seventh from Adam, prophesied of these saying, Behold the Lord cometh with ten thousands of his saints" and v. 15, 'To execute judgement upon all. . .".

104. Annius comm. to bk. I of Berosus, 69, "Nam, ut patet Genesis v cap. Sanctus propheta Enoch natus est ante inundationem terrarum anno 34 supra mille, qui teste Iuda Apostolo cognomine Thadeo in sua canonica prophetavit de iudicio futuro tam aquarum diluvii quam ultimae conflagrationis et ea teste Josephi in primo de antiquitate Iudaica inscribit duabus columnis, altera aerea, altera lateritia.".

105. Tate. *Nebrija* (*supra,* note 22), 131.

D

Sixteenth-Century Messianism and Kabbalah and Their Transformations in Italy

9

Messianic Expectations and Spiritualization of Religious Life in the Sixteenth Century

Rachel Elior

The expulsion from Spain in 1492 left a deep impression on its generation and on the generations to follow throughout the course of the
sixteenth century[1]. The banishment was not perceived as mere historical
circumstance nor as an arbitrary political consideration that could be
compensated for within a realistic historical framework, but rather, as
part of a wide-ranging, comprehensive process, of which the expulsion
was only one manifestation among many.

The leaders of the Jewish community, the Rabbis, the sages, and the
spiritual leadership pondered the reason underlying exile and sought
explanation and meaning for the catastrophe which uprooted the major
part of the Jewish People.

The research of Baer, Aescoli, Ben Sasson, and Scholem[2] has revealed
that the majority of the spiritual leaders interpreted the expulsion in
religious terms, some of these leaders, in particular Yitzhak Karo and
Joseph Hayon[3] interpreting it as divine punishment and as the abandonment by providence of the people of Israel. Others, in despair and unable
to find reasonable answers to the meaning of the torments of the expulsion, yearned for spiritual redemption and expressed various degrees of
detachment from mundane life while striving to attain cultural segregation and a comprehensive spiritualization of all Jewish life[4].

This article is the revised and annotated version of a lecture presented at the meeting of
the Second Congress of the European Association for Jewish Studies, held in Oxford,
England, 22–26 July 1984.

Reprinted by permission of *Revue des Études juives* 145 (1986).

Other attempts to confront the new realities of this post-expulsion period can be found in messianic propaganda such as the apocalyptic writings of Abraham ben Eliezer[5] and his circle; in the homiletics of Shlomo Turiel about the coming Redemption[6]; in letters purporting to reveal the ten lost tribes[7]; in the detailed messianic calculations by the anonymous author of *Galia Raza*[8]; in the pseudo-Zoharic writings of Joseph ibn Shraga[9]; and in the chronicles of Eliahu Kapsali[10], to name but a few. Their common contention defined the expulsion as the foundation and backdrop for the coming redemption, and the associated catastrophies as pre-messianic tribulations[11]. This apocalyptic trend was further elaborated by Isaac Abravanel in *Yeshu'ot Meshiḥo*, and later by Solomon Molkho who offered a political-messianic interpretation of the expulsion in his letters and revelations[12]. This interpretation was based in part on the views of the apocalyptical writers aforementioned, but proceeded to integrate realistic means and political dimensions into the messianic apocalypse[13].

We shall focus our attention on one dimension of the many solutions offered, i.e., the mystical ideology behind the radical spiritualization within religious life which occurred at the turn of the century and continued during the course of most of the sixteenth century wherever exiles from Spain settled.

The primary contention is that this spiritualization was motivated by intensive messianic expectation and was founded on the vital connection as formulated in *Tikkuney Zohar*, between the revelation of the kabbalistic secrets through the propagation of the *Zohar* and the attempts to hasten the coming of the Messiah.

This connection not only was discussed in every kabbalistic book of the sixteenth century but was also pondered on its actual implication for the coming redemption[14]. It was first stated in *Minḥat Yehudah* in 1498: "Hence it is explained that the *Zohar* was destined to be hidden until the last generation when it shall be revealed unto man; by virtue of its students the Messiah will come, for the earth shall be full of the knowledge of the Lord and that will be the reason for his coming".

The process of spiritualization of religion was propagated by the Kabbalah and the kabbalistic teachers who intended to generate a fundamental change in Jewish religious life in accordance with the spiritual introspection inherent in mystical thought. This process was expressed realistically in terms of a struggle to establish a new position for the Kabbalah in relation to the *peshaṭ* and the Halakha[15].

After the expulsion from Spain, kabbalism underwent a complete transformation. It acquired a new orientation when it formed a conjunction with the contemporary messianic tendencies[16]. The kabbalists suggested a new interpretation of religious life and a new historical perspective on the destiny of the people of Israel, while boldly challenging, and firmly criticizing, the common, predominant perception of religion. Kabbalism strived to establish its claim to spiritual priority within all aspects of Judaism. This becomes immediately apparent in the transformation of the Kabbalah from the elitist-esoteric concern of an elect few, into a popular doctrine readily available to wide circles. The former esoteric, theosophical interest in the earlier Kabbalah, living harmoniously side by side with the conventions of the Halakha, disappeared, and in its place we find a doctrine promoting radical changes in Jewish life for the purpose of advancing the messianic era[17].

The kabbalistic literature that was written from the turn of the sixteenth century onwards, and the diversified testimonies of strong contempt and opposition[18] that the new orientation of the Kabbalah raised in different quarters, testify to the various stages in the formation of alternative religious norms. The culmination of these efforts is to be found in the introduction to Ḥayyim Vital's magnum opus *Etz Ḥayyim*[19]. This introduction is a bold religious document, expressing a transformation of religious awareness. Unlike the rest of this work, the introduction is not a part of the Lurianic Kabbalah but rather a summary of the struggle for the new position which the Kabbalah sought to attain in the sixteenth century. Each of the contentions presented in his introduction was stated previously in the kabbalistic literature of the generation of the expulsion. In other words, the introduction to *Etz Ḥayyim* does not announce the new spiritual point of view of the sixteenth century but sums it up.

Vital wrote his introduction to *Etz Ḥayyim* as a program to transform the religious world in which he was living. He wished to change the accepted order-of-priorities which viewed halakhic interpretation as the focal point of Judaism, and which placed the Kabbalah alongside the Halakha but only in a marginal, esoteric role. He strove to amend the misconception of perceiving the Ṭorah only as law, and to restore it to its true pre-eminent spiritual position. He identified the spiritual perception of the Torah with the Kabbalah, in which he included the talmudic *ma'ase merkavah*, the *Zohar*, and also kabbalistic books based upon holy visions, and current divine revelations[20].

The kabbalists attempted to clarify the relationship between the spiritual archetype of the Torah, and the law, i.e., between the eternal holy Torah through which the world was created and between the Pentateuch which we possess. They contended that undoubtedly, it was not the literal Torah—peshaṭ—which possesses holy substance and creative cosmic powers, but rather there must exist some inner meaning which expresses this dimension to *ma'ase merkavah* (Ezekiel's vision of the throne) and *ma'aseh bereshit* (the creation) as well as to the holy names of God:

"The literal Torah, its stories, its laws and its commandments, when they remain literal, express no awareness and knowledge of the Lord, blessed by he; on the contrary, there are laws and commandments which the rational mind cannot fathom, almost all the Biblical commandments and especially their legal details are unbearable for the mind—and, if this is so, where is the splendor of the Torah, its beauty, and its greatness"[21]?

This inner meaning, "its splendor, beauty, and greatness", in their opinion, is to be found in the Kabbalah of the *Zohar*. The kabbalistic argument is based upon the assumption that the scriptures and the law possess a concealed stratum. Discovering and deciphering this layer is the paramount vocation of the kabbalistic literature[22] as well as the expression of its messianic perspective. Thus the scholarly tendencies concerned entirely with the law and with the peshaṭ, or with arbitrary reasonable interpretation, are a direct contradiction to the basis of the mystical perception and its messianic perspective and should be rejected, opposed, and contested.

Ḥayyim Vital was writing under the inspiration of the renowned fourteenth century kabbalist books *Raya Mehemna* and *Tikkuney Zohar* which he and his contemporaries believed to have been written in the second century by Simon Bar Yoḥay. Their anonymous author formed a polarization between two aspects of the Torah which he named Etz ha-Ḥayyim and Etz ha-Da'at, the Torah of the tree of life and the Torah of the tree of knowledge[23].

The former represents the superior spiritual, eternal holy Torah which will be prevalent in the messianic future, while the latter relates to the inferior Torah which we already possess and which emphasizes its literal dimensions and its legal aspects. The theories of *Raya Mehemna* and *Tikkuney Zohar* were discussed comprehensively by Baer, Scholem, Tishby, and others in relation to fourteenth century Spain, and kabbalistic theology. The current research of G. Sed-Rajna and J. Katz[24] has concerned itself with some implications of the two dimensions of the Torah as elaborated by Vital. However, it seems that the role of the two Torot or the polarization between law and spirit within the new status which the Kabbalah attempted to attain in the sixteenth century, has not been sufficiently appreciated.

R. Ḥayyim Vital argued that the Kabbalah is the Torat-Etz-Ḥayyim while the Halakha, or in his words the Mishna and the peshaṭ, are Torat-Etz-ha-da'at. Vital re-affirms the inherent hierarchy existing between the two Torot and he promulgates the superior Torat-Etz-Ḥayyim as expressed by the Kabbalah. Furthermore, he contended that the literal perception of the Torah and Halakha as prevailing in all aspects of daily life, to be an expression of the era of the exile, while the Kabbalah is the expression of the new messianic era, thought to be immanent. He concluded that the coming of the redemption depends primarily on the study of Kabbalah and of the acknowledgement of its authority, validity, and priority.

In addition to the identification between Kabbalah and Torat-Etz-Ḥayyim on one side, and between Kabbalah and the Torah of redemption on the other, Vital and his contemporaries viewed the Kabbalah as the current expression in the successive heritage of the oral law as well as the ancient mystical tradition of *heikhalot* literature and *ma'ase merkavah*.

Vital, the chief formulator of the Lurianic Kabbalah, presents in his introduction a summary of the opinions of kabbalists from the time of the expulsion until his own time. The introduction contains not a hint of the novel Lurianic perception but rather, a summary of the opinions of R. Yehuda Ḥayaṭ, who wrote *Minḥat Yehudah* at the turn of the century; the contentions of the anonymous author of *Ohel Mo'ed* (circa 1500), as well as the ideas of Asher of Lamlien (circa 1500), of Solomon Molkho (circa 1530); the contentions of the Libyan kabbalist Simon ibn Lavi who wrote *Ketem Paz* (circa 1550); the Byzantine author of *Galia Raza* (written between 1543 and 1553); and the arguments of Matitiahu Delaqroṭ (circa 1560), and Solomon of Turiel on redemption (circa 1560).

The common denominators uniting all these kabbalists, living through and after the expulsion and spread throughout the diaspora, were: (1) the negation of the concept that the Torah taken literally has sufficient religious and spiritual meaning and provides true knowledge of God; (2) the denial of the relevance of rational criteria of the human mind in interpretation of the Torah in its inner meaning, divine perspective, and messianic vocation.

The kabbalists developed and elaborated this new hierarchy between the Halakha and the Kabbalah. They argued that the former signifies Torat-Etz-ha-Da'at and therefore originates from a lesser divine source in a like manner as Meṭaṭron and the world of creation. Therefore, the Mishna and the peshaṭ reflect material interests and are confined to anthropocentric concerns, to the period of the exile and to this world alone. The Kabbalah signifies Torat-Etz-Ḥayyim and originates from the highest divine source, "the world of emanation". It is considered to be the eternal divine Torah and encompasses theocentric concerns and relates to the coming messianic era.

Vital states: "regarding the Torah in its literality, which is the Torah of the Mundane world, it is worthless when compared to the Messianic Torah and the Torah of the world to come . . .". He did not hesitate to state bluntly: "Regarding the Mishna, there can be no doubt that the Mishna's literal aspects are but veils, shells, and outer wrappings when compared to the hidden mysteries which are inherent and insinuated in its inner aspects [i.e. the Kabbalah] since all literalness is only of this world and belongs to the lesser material affairs"[25].

Thus, they contended that the literal perception of the scriptures was a severe misconception and distortion of their true nature. Further, they argued that not only the scriptures but also the entire Talmud is also based upon the secrets of the Torah—and thus those who disregard this important foundation when studying, are "blind and thoughtless and evil doers". Vital concludes:

"As it was said according to the *Zohar*, in the portion of Pinhas, the Tannaim and the Amoraim compiled all of the Talmud upon the basis of the secrets of the Torah. There can be no doubt that those who study only the Babylonian Talmud are groping like a blind man against a wall, they are studying only the outer wrappings of the Torah and they have no eyes to discern the inner secrets of the Torah which are hidden within. Not at random did they rule what is impure and what is holy, what is prohibited and what is permitted [. . .] rather, from the esoteric dimension of the Torah they judged as the kabbalist knows [. . .] those who are engaged in the Mishna without contemplating its secrets and arbitrarily pass judgement without relating to its esoteric aspects and hidden secrets are blind . . ."[26].

The kabbalists attempted to endow the Torah with meaning above its literality and beyond its legal dimensions, as well as to transcend its perspective, beyond post-historical and rational considerations. However, it should be strongly affirmed that these thinkers were not antinomian—rather—they wished to argue that, lacking another dimension beyond the law, behind the peshaṭ, by reading the Bible only as law, all true religious significance is lost and all messianic expectations are denied.

The Kabbalah thus suggests a new criterion for the true meaning of the Halakha and contends that the legal literature which for all appearances seems to have been founded upon reason and tradition, is actually founded upon the secrets of the Kabbalah and as such it should be studied, and acted upon. The anonymous author of *Galia Raza* claims: "The peshaṭ is insufficient to explain the Talmud properly; it can only be elucidated by its secrets and esoteric meanings"[27].

The argument as to the mystical meaning of the Talmud was first raised in the fourteenth century in the books of the *Kana* and *Pliah*[28]. Later, it was further elaborated in *Galia Raza* and *Ketem Paz*[29]. *Galia Raza* was written to exemplify the correct interpretation of the peshaṭ according to its true mystical meaning. The author argues:

"Hence, we have evidence that the measures of the ritual bath were constituted esoterically according to the secrets; thus we ought to believe faithfully that all the quantities and all the measures that our sages constituted in all our commandments are allusions to heavenly, spiritual matters and that the earthly rates are paralleled in heavenly measures"[30].

The kabbalists strove to shatter and undermine the legitimacy of rational consideration and the literal perception utilized to understand the Halakha, to explain the reasons for the commandments and to interpret the law. They emphasized the esoteric stratum behind the Biblical stories, the mystical reasoning behind the commandments, and the kabbalistic interpretation of halakhic consideration.

However it should be stated that the struggle is not between kabbalah and the Halakha but between two different principles of interpretation of the Halakha: the mystical-spiritual interpretation with its eschatological perspective on the one hand and the rational-literal interpretation with its realistic perspective on the other.

The severe criticism of the *peshaṭ,* which included sharp attacks on its exponents, is obviously a criticism of the dominant traditional establishment and accepted authority which was organized around *peshaṭ* and *din,* literality and law [31]. There can be but a small doubt that it was the eschatological orientation, which dominated this generation, that inspired this daring criticism of the rabbinical establishment, as well as the literal-legal system, and motivated a new perception of spiritual priorities and the religious hierarchy. This radical tendency, challenging the study of *peshaṭ,* is best exemplified in Vital's description:

"When the lesser scholars of the Torah observe the major scholars preoccupying themselves with the pursuit of the literal meaning of the text *(peshaṭim)* rather than with the study of the Kabbalah [they must conclude] that the major scholars have degenerated into the heresy of denying the validity of the truth while insisting that the only meaning of Torah is the *peshaṭ* [. . .]. The situation is desperate since it is only by means of the Kabbalah that redemption can be brought about while to refrain from it would delay the restoration of our temple and our glory" [32].

This description reflects a criticism that was shared by many kabbalists on rabbinical authority. As a result an alternative power was proposed; the kabbalists were formulating a new religious authority—an authority drawn not from knowledge, tradition or rabbinical power, but rather from pneumatic inspiration: "The secrets of the Torah and its esoteric being cannot be acquired by man in material study, only from the divine abundance as emanated from his supreme holiness by celestial messengers and angels or by Eliyah the prophet . . ." [33].

The kabbalists emphasized that their own spiritual authority was based upon the ancient tradition of the *Zohar* in conjunction with divine revelations and holy visions. These were considered to be various types of contemporary prophecy. This is borne out fully by the statements with which they introduce their works.

Asher of Lamlien wrote in his letter to Moses Hefetz in 1500—"I am the lowest of people, writing these letters, not through my wisdom but only according to the secrets that I have been shown from Heaven" [34].

Solomon Molkho wrote: "After I was sealed with the seal of my creator, I was shown great secrets and I was told the holy secrets of the Kabbalah and my heart was illuminated" [35]. Later on he wrote: "As regards the vision that I reported from Monastir . . .".

Yehudah Albotini stated in the introduction to his book *Sullam ḥa-'Aliyyah* (Ladder of Ascension): "I write this to record that which I was shown from Heaven" [36].

The anonymous author of *Galia Raza* repeated a number of times that "everything I wrote was prompted by a revelation from Heaven which I experienced in my sleep by means of nightly visions"[37].

Joseph Karo, while reporting the words of his maggid (celestial mentor), a personification of the Mishnah, wrote: "therefore listen to what I command you for I am the Mishnah speaking through you—I come to reveal to you sublime and esoteric matters"[38].

Regarding Solomon Alkabetz, the celestial mentor assures Joseph Karo that, "whatever he wrote to you in the name of his redeeming angel is true"[39].

Thus, inspired by direct revelation and freed from the confines of tradition, the new Kabbalah was able to suggest new ideas and methods, attributed to a divine source: "Blessed is the Lord of Israel who revealed unto me those sublime secrets that had never been revealed to any man since Simon Bar Yoḥay"[40].

The kabbalists bitterly contested human reason as the legitimate and sole source of authority. Their authority was based upon contemporary divine revelations linked to the tradition of revelations from the earlier kabbalistic literature and the mystical-visionary conceptions of the *Zohar.*

This new visionary Kabbalah was reflected in a number of books, such as the *Answering Angel,* the Visions of R. Asher of Lamlien, Solomon Molkho's *Ḥayat Hakane, Galia Raza,* Joseph Karo's *Maggid Meisharim,* and Ḥayyim Vital's *Book of Visions*[41].

This literature reflects one of the most prominent characteristics of the period—the preference for spiritual reality of vision and revelation, over the disappointing and arbitrary historical reality. This tendency culminated in transcending historical circumstance, rational consideration, and reality into revelation, redemption, and meta-history.

Pneumatic inspiration and revelation were not awaited passively, but actively initiated and encouraged by mystical and magical means, by the use of sacred names and by practical Kabbalah[42].

It appears that the kabbalistic texts, written under visionary inspiration, were primarily interested in eschatological prospects and their relation to the dualistic perception. The active motivation behind many of the induced visions and the spontaneous revelations (on reading the Torah as Torat-Etz-Ḥayyim), was the desire to achieve an accurate understanding of the eschatological process alluded to in the verses of the Torah as well as the hidden meaning behind historical events. One of the basic principles in the perception of redemption of all generations is the conception of the redemption as the final result of a catastrophe, of a tremendous struggle, as a conflict between the forces of good against the forces of evil, both on Earth and in Heaven[43].

This struggle is often pictured in apocalyptic terms, and likewise in psychological terms as a spiritual redemption in which man frees man himself from inner evil. At other times, it is perceived as a struggle between the universal principles of good and of evil.

The traditional Jewish perception of redemption (except that of Maimonides and his followers) has often described the image of the opponent as Satan, the Hated One; thus the concept of redemption has always included the conquering and humiliation of this figure[44]. The theological assumption pressed and emphasized in the sixteenth century is that both the holy and the profane are immanent in Heaven and Earth. The kabbalists read the scriptures as expressing the dialectics of this duality and interpreted the commandments as reflecting the dual ontological perception of reality, and thus, giving assistance to holiness in its struggle with evil. It was Joseph Karo who stated: "[. . .] all of the Torah is composed of the positive law and the prohibitory law; positive law refers to the holy spheres and prohibitory law is relegated to the evil spheres of the Satan [. . .]"[45]. Simon ibn Lavi preceded him in suggesting that: "[. . .] the laws of purity and impurity are the principle and foundation of all the Scriptures since the knowledge of purities and impurities is the secret of the holiness and of defilements"[46]. The author of *Galia Raza* argues that—"on this matter [of duality] all the Torah is founded"[47].

The new kabbalistic interpretation of the hidden status of the *peshaṭ* relates mainly to two points:

1) the dualistic perception which views the world in its entirety as divided between the domains of holiness and evil, *qeddushah* and *kelipah;*
2) the search for this dualistic perception as found in the scriptures and its significance in the struggle between the two forces, while viewing it as various stages of the messianic process which will inevitably culminate in the coming of the Messiah.

The dualistic ontology, as inspired by the *Zohar* and elaborated in the various visions and revelations, was the central idea around which all the eschatological historiosophy was anchored. Moses Kordovero set out in *Or Yaqqar* that: "[. . .] by perfection of the [kabbalistic] worship, the humiliation of the gentile will occur and their rule will be overthrown, and is understood according to what is known that this world includes two supermundane systems, one holy and one profane [. . .]"[48].

The kabbalistic writers of the post-expulsion period tried to force apocalyptic meaning into every word of the scriptures. This can be exemplified best by Abraham Ben Eliezer ha-Levi's contention: "Behold Scripture in its entirety is filled with allusions to the future redemption"[49]. But gradually, the two concepts of exile and redemption lost their concrete, political, historical meanings and were identified with the cosmic principles of holiness and Satan while arguing that exile is the result of the victory of the evil-forces over the holy ones. All religious life was oriented to assist the holy forces (incarnated in the *shekhinah* as the representative of holiness and redemption), and to combat the *kelipah* and *sitra aḥra,* that dominate the exile. In other words, the messianic expectations were not passive but active and were not directed towards historical planes and realistic aims but rather towards Heaven[50]. The prayers, the performance of the commandments and principally the study of the Kabbalah—all composed from divine words and endowed with absolute powers—were all infused with messianic meaning or with the perception of struggle between the two cosmic forces. The secret function of kabbalistic worship was to serve as a magical weapon to be wielded in the continuing, everlasting struggle. The prayers, the commandments, study of the scripture and above all the study of the Kabbalah, were weapons which were endowed with unlimited powers of purification and destruction, so that they might annihilate all the forces of defilement and strengthen all the powers of holiness. Thus the basic concept of traditional Jewish theology concerning exile and redemption lost its historical significance and realistic perspective and acquired a purely spiritual character, concerning itself with a mythical, spiritual state.

The post-expulsion and visionary Kabbalah offered a comprehensive historiosophical perception of the history of the people of Israel, based upon a mythical dualistic conception of the forces of good and evil. This Kabbalah applied the new spiritual authority derived from holy visions to interpret the scriptures according to an eschatological orientation. As such, it explained the commandments and laws according to their contribution to the forthcoming messianic conflict between holiness and the forces of evil. This perception suggests that the entire history of the people of Israel is occurring between the opposite poles of exile and redemption. Exile and redemption are not considered realistic, historic events but rather the reflection of the mythical struggle between the forces of evil and of holiness. The historical passage from exile to redemption was presented as stages in the struggle between the two cosmic forces. The historiosophical perception transcends realistic historical events. It expresses a deep conviction that there is a hidden history which strives towards an apocalyptic era. The messianic expectations became the historiosophical framework for all the history of Israel which were then interpreted according to eschatological destiny[51]. The study and teaching of the Kabbalah became the means of hastening the advance of the messianic era by revealing the true hidden meaning of the scripture and the law.

In summary, the five principal characteristics of this new form of mystical interpretation were:

1) the acute messianic expectation that motivated the majority of the changes in religious life in the sixteenth century;
2) the struggle to attain a new authoritative position for the Kabbalah as the hidden meaning of the scriptures and the law and as their dominant legitimate interpretation, while challenging the prevailing legal system with its literal interpretation;
3) the comprehensive process of spiritualization which was accompanied by the revival and expansion of the dualistic ontology as the leading interpretative perception of the hidden meaning of the Torah, of the law and of history;
4) the development of the visionary Kabbalah and the pneumatic authority of the vision and of esoteric experience as an alternative to the existing legal authority and rational criteria. Those visions were acknowledged as the prime source of inspiration and authority to the new perceptions of the law according to Torat-Etz-Hayyim;
5) the formation of a new historiosophical perception arguing the inner meaning of external events and emphasizing the messianic perspective of history.

These factors created a fundamental change in religious norms which was characterized by a detachment from realistic confinements and historical considerations—a change without which neither Lurianic Kabbalah nor the Sabbatian movement could have come about. Lurianic Kabbalah was not a pioneering messianic strain within Kabbalah, as is commonly believed, but rather the culmination of a gradual detachment from historical and rational frameworks and constant messianic preoccupation which characterized the post expulsion period.

NOTES

1. Cf. H. H. Ben Sasson, "Exile and Redemption Through the Eyes of the Spanish Exiles", *Yitzhak F. Baer Jubilee Volume*, Jerusalem, 1960, pp. 216–277; J. Hacker, "New Chronicles on the Expulsion of the Jews from Spain", *I. F. Baer Memorial Volume, Zion* XLIV 1–4, Jerusalem 1979, pp. 201–228.
2. I. Baer, *Galut*, Berlin, 1936, pp. 49–69; A. Z. Aescoli, *Jewish Messianic Movements*, Jerusalem, 1956, pp. 236–280; H. Ben Sasson, *ibid.*; G. Scholem, *Shabbetai Zvi*, Tel Aviv, 1967, pp. 9–18; *idem, Major Trends in Jewish Mysticism*, New York, 1967, pp. 244–251; *idem*, "The Idea of Redemption in the Kabbalah", *Devarim Bego*, Tel Aviv 1975, pp. 201–206.
3. Yitzhak Karo, *Toldot Yitzhak*, Mantua 1558, *Parashat Bereshit* (cf. *Encyclopaedia Judaica*, V, col. 193f.); Joseph Hayon, *Perush Tehilim*, Saloniki, 1522, p. 166; Isaac Abravanel, *Perush Ezekiel*, Pisaro, 1520, ch. 20; *idem, Ma'ayanai ha-Yeshua', Ma'ayan* 12, ch. 2. Cf. H. Ben Sasson *ibid.*, pp. 216–219.
4. Some representatives of these tendencies: Yehudah Hayyat, the author of *Minhat Yehudah, Ma'arekhet Elohut*, Mantua, 1558, introduction (cf. *Encyclopaedia Judaica* VII, 1005); Immanuel of Benvenuto, the editor of various kabbalistic books; Simon ibn Lavi, *Ketem Paz*, Jerba, 1940.
5. Abraham ha-Levi, *Mišra Kitrin* (Constantinople 1510); cf. *Kiryat Sefer* II, 1925, pp. 101–104, 269–273 and *Kiryat Sefer* VII, 1930, pp. 149–165, 440–456.
6. See G. Scholem, "A Homily on Redemption by Shlomo of the House of Toriel", *Sefunot* I, 1951, pp. 62–79.
7. A. Neubauer, "The Ten Lost Tribes", *Kovetz Al-Yad* 4, 1888, p. 35. A. Yaari, *Igrot Eretz Ysrael*, Tel Aviv, 1950, pp. 175–177 and 184–185, cf. D. Tamar, "A Letter Concerning the Ten Lost Tribes", *Sefunot* VI, 1962, pp. 305–310. Aescoli, *op. cit.*, pp. 316–328.
8. Cf. R. Elior, *Galia Raza*, critical edition, Research projects of the Institute of Jewish Studies. The Hebrew University, publication series I, Jerusalem, 1981; *idem*, "The Dispute on the Position of the Kabbalah in the 16th Century", *Jerusalem Studies in Jewish Thought*, I, 1981, pp. 177–190.
9. British Museum Manuscript Add. 27034 p. 3–4a; cf. G. Scholem, "R. Joseph ibn Shraga", *Kiryat Sefer* 7, 1930, pp. 151f. and *Kiryat Sefer* 8,

1931–1932, pp. 262–265; idem, *Encyclopaedia Judaica* X, col. 243–244; A. Marx. *R.E.J.* 61, 1911, pp. 137f.

10. Cf. British Museum Manuscript Add. Or. 19.971. C. Berlin, "A Sixteenth Century Hebrew Chronicle", *Studies in Jewish Bibliography . . . in Honor of J. E. Kiev*, New York, 1971, pp. 21–44.

11. Cf. C. Scholem, *Kabbala*, Jerusalem, 1974, pp. 67–79. Rabbi Joseph ben Shaltiel ha-Cohen wrote in 1495: "I suppose that the troubles that happened to the Jews in the Christian world from 1490–1495 . . . are the premessianic tribulations". Vatican manuscript 187, end of *Sefer ha-Pliah*. This explanation is to be compared with the exegesis of I. Abravanel on Isaiah 43:6 (Pisaro 1520) and with *Ketem Paz* p. 12a.

12. Cf. Solomon Molkho, *Ḥayat Kane* (Amsterdam 1660?); *idem, Sefer ha-Mefo'ar*, Saloniki, 1529; cf. Aescoli, *op. cit.*, 266–280.

13. Messianic movements were organized around kabbalists such as Solomon Molkho and Asher of Lamlien. Cf. Graetz, *History of the Jews* (Hebrew) vol. 7, p. 401. E. Kopfer, "The Visions of R. Asher ben Meir, known as Lamlien", *Kovetz Al-Yad*, N.S. 18, 1976, pp. 387–423.

14. Cf. Yehuda Ḥayyat, *Minḥat Yehudah*, introduction; *Galia Raza*, p. 64. Moses Kordovero *Or Yaqqar*, vol. II, Jerusalem, 1962, p. 104. G. Scholem, "Homily" (n. 6 above), p. 63.

15. Different aspects of this struggle can be found relating to the controversy around reincarnation: cf. E. Gottlieb, *Studies in the Kabbalah Literature*, ed. J. Hacker, Tel Aviv, 1976, pp. 370–396; in the contemporary rabbinical responsa relating the status of the Kabbalah (cf. J. Katz, "Post Zoharic Relations Between Halakhah and Kabbalah", *Da'at* 4, 1980, pp. 54–74 and R. Elior, "The Dispute . . .", *art. cit.*), as well as the polemic concerning the publication of the *Zohar* (cf. I. Tishby, *Studies in Kabbalah and its Branches*, Jerusalem, 1982, pp. 79–130): J. Katz, *Halakhah and Kabbalah*, Jerusalem, 1984.

16. Cf. G. Scholem, *Major Trends. . .* , pp. 244–251.

17. *Mishra Kitrin*, Constantinople, 1510, p. 176; cf. *Ketem Paz*, pp. 12a–13b, 20b, 68a, 135a, 171a; *Galia Raza*, ms. Oxford, Opp. 104 p. 174a; *Ma'arek-het Elohut*, introduction.

18. Cf. Eliahu Mizrachi, *Responsa*, Constantinople, 1560, article 1, p. 2b; *Minḥat Yehudah*, introduction; *Ohel Mo'ed*, ms. Cambridge, Add. 673 (8) 1/2 pp. 13a-b, 18b, 54b, 55a; Solomon Molkho, *Sefer he-Mefo'ar*, p. 51, author's apology, *Galia Raza*, ms. Oxford Opp. 526, f. 50b and ms. Oxford Opp. 104, ff. 111b-112a; *Ketem Paz*, pp. 23b, 144a, 171a, 208b; Jacob Yaabetz, *Or Ḥayyim*, Warsaw, 1871, p. 6a; Jacob Cohen of Gazolo, *Sefer Tikhune Zohar*, Mantua, 1558, printer's note.

19. Ḥayyim Vital, *Etz Ḥayyim*, Warsaw, 1890, introduction to the Gate of Introductions, pp. 1–10; cf. G. Sed-Rajna, "Le Rôle de la Kabbale dans la tradition juive selon Ḥayyim Vital", *Revue de l'Histoire des Religions*, 168, 1965, pp. 177–196; J. Katz, "Halakha and Kabbala as Competing Subjects of Study", *Da'at* 7, 1981, pp. 61–63.

20. Cf. *Etz Ḥayyim*, p. 2. Vital writes in his introduction: "The inner soul of the Torah is called the secrets of the Torah which are called *ma'ase merkavah*, which is the Kabbalah".

21. *Ibid.*, p. 5; cf. Matitiahu Delaqrot, *Book of Memorials*, ms. Oxford, Opp. 439, introduction: "Why did the Torah tell in length the stories about the sinners . . . if it does not allude to hidden secrets?"; cf. Eliahu Ginzano, *Iggeret Ḥamudot*, "All the commandments are hints to heavenly secrets from the depth of reality, which were not given in vain, even the stories which seem literal have significant value", cf. *Galia Raza*, p. 65.

22. G. Scholem, "The Meaning of the Torah in Jewish Mysticism", *On the Kabbala and its Symbolism*, New York, 1965, p. 32–86; cf. pp. 66–70 for the radical meaning of the new spiritual conception; cf. *idem, The Messianic Idea in Judaism*, New York, 1971.

23. *Etz Ḥayyim*, introduction, p. 5. "Halakha and Kabbala . . .", *art. cit.*

24. G. Sed-Rajna, *art. cit.*; J. Katz, pp. 37–68.

25. *Etz Ḥayyim*, introduction, p. 2; cf. introduction, pp. 4–6.

26. *Ibid.* p. 5; cf. *Galia Raza*, p. 8, introduction.

27. Ms. Oxford Opp. 104, f. 75b.

28. Cf. G. Scholem, *Major Trends. . .*, *op. cit.*, pp. 211 and 244.

29. *Ketem Paz*, p. 12a–b.

30. *Galia Raza*, p. 30.

31. It is interesting to note that Vital, who transferred the strong social and religious criticism from *Tikkuney Zohar* and *Raya Mehemna* to his own generation, viewed the scholarly renaissance of the literal-rational studies of his period with deep criticism. He refused to relate to the external developments (which were concerned with the system of *peshaṭ*), occurring in Safed, Damascus, Turkey, and Italy, as possessing any spiritual significance. On the contrary, he saw them as a distortion of religion and as a misunderstanding of the new pre-messianic reality.

32. Cf. *Etz Ḥayyim*, introduction, p. 4.

33. *Ibid.* p. 6; cf. Moses Kordovero, *Raya Mehemna*, with the commentary *Or Yaqqar; ms.* Modena 1–16 Li, f. 31b: "[. . .] It has been said that the Torah is the supreme spiritually emanated substance which expanded into the lesser worlds. It is divine perception and it cannot be attained except by prophecy since it is not within the realm of human, corporeal knowledge. Its precepts do not spring from material reason as natural matters perceived by empirical perception, but it is divine and its principles are from prophecy [. . .]".

34. Cf. E. Kopfer, *art. cit.*, p. 412.

35. Solomon Molkho, *Ḥayat ha-Kane*, Paris, 1938, p. 5.

36. Judah Albotini, *Sullam ha-'Aliyyah*, in *Kiryat Sefer* 2, 1924–1925, p. 138. *Idem, Kiryat Sefer* 22, 1945, pp. 161f. G. Scholem, *Catalogue of Kabbalistic Manuscripts*, Jerusalem, 1930, pp. 225–230; cf. M. Benayahu, "R. Yehudah Albotini", *Sinai* 36, 1955, pp. 239f.

37. *Galia Raza*, ms. Oxford Opp. 104b, 146b; cf. R. Elior, *Galia Raza, op. cit.,* introduction p. 15, text pp. 9, 11, 157.
38. Joseph Karo, *Maggid Meisharim*, Jerusalem, 1960, pp. 37, 51. Cf. R. J. Werblowsky, *Joseph Karo, Lawyer and Mystic*, Oxford, 1962, pp. 9–23, 257–286.
39. *Maggid Meisharim*, p. 157f.
40. *Galia Raza*, pp. 9 and 39.
41. Cf. R. J. Werblowsky, *op. cit,* pp. 38–83, "the answering angel"; G. Scholem, "The Maggid of Joseph Taytazak", *Sefunot* 11, 1967–1978, pp. 47–112; M. Idel, "Inquiries into the Doctrine of Sefer ha-Meshiv", *Sefunot* 17, 1983, pp. 185–266.
42. We possess vast literature of mystical and magical instructions for the purpose of attaining the different stages of revelation or prophecy. Books such as Vital's *Gates of Holiness* and Albotini's *Ladder of Ascension*, belong to this category.
43. Cf. G. Scholem, *The Messianic Idea in Judaism*, New York, 1971, pp. 1–36, *idem, Devarim Bego, op. cit.,* pp. 196–198.
44. J. Dan, "The Beginning of the Messianic Myth in 13th Century Kabbalah", in *Messianism and Eschatology*, Jerusalem, 1984, p. 251f; for a description of the later stages of this perception in the Lurianic Kabbalah cf. I. Tishby, *Torat ha-ra' we-ha-kelipah be-qaballat ha-Ari*, Jerusalem, 1965, pp. 62–143.
45. Joseph Karo, *Maggid Meisharim, op. cit.,* p. 126.
46. *Ketem Paz*, f. 12b.
47. *Galia Raza*, p. 49f.
48. *Or Yaqqar*, IV, p. 155.
49. Abraham ben Eliezer ha-Levi, *Mishra Kitrin*, f. 16a.
50. Cf. G. Scholem, *Major Trends. . . , op. cit.,* p. 248.
51. Cf. R. Elior, "The Doctrine of Metempsychosis in *Galia Raza*", *Studies in Jewish Mysticism presented in Isaiah Tishby*, Jerusalem Studies in Jewish Thought, III (1–2), 1984, pp. 207–240.

10

Hope against Hope: Jewish and Christian Messianic Expectations in the Late Middle Ages

David B. Ruderman

In the year 1473, Francesco da Meleto, a young Florentine with delusions of prophetic grandeur, journeyed to the city of Constantinople with a companion of his native city, Benedetto Manetti. There he sought from a number of Jewish legal scholars opinions regarding the time of the coming of the Messiah and the ultimate conversion of the Jews to Christianity.[1] He was especially pleased to gain the acquaintance of one notable Rabbi who secretly confessed to him, so he claimed, that all the Jews would convert to the Christian faith if "the Messiah for whom they had waited will not come during the entire year of our salvation, 1484."[2] The Jew based his prediction on the Book of Daniel, refusing to elaborate but claiming nevertheless that this view was not merely his own but also that "of all the other masters of their law."[3] Delighted that the Jews of his generation were ready to confirm his wildest fantasy regarding their imminent conversion, Meleto returned to Italy where he preached

An earlier version of this chapter was presented at a conference 6eld at Columbia University on April 13–14, 1981, entitled "Perspectives on Jewish Messianism." I have revised and updated this work as a modest tribute to my teacher, Professor Haim Beinart, whose recent articles on *converso* messianism have greatly stimulated some of my own reflections here.

Reprinted by permission of the Ben-Zvi Institute for the Study of Jewish Communities in the East from *Exile and Diaspora: Studies in the History of the Jewish People* presented to *Haim Beinart*, edited by Avraham Grossman, Aharon Mirsky, Yosef Kaplan, Jerusalem, 1991.

and composed treatises predicting the end of days and the ultimate conversion of the Jews and Moslems. In his *Convivio de'segreti della scriptura santa*, written some time after 1513, he records the Rabbi's remarks, adding his own clarifications with respect to the Daniel prophecies. Daniel must have indicated, so he claimed, that "in this time their great persecution begins, brought about by the kings of Spain and Portugal," representing no less than the universal flagellation of Christ's enemies which precedes the renovation of the Catholic Church.[4] Meleto had certified beyond doubt by Jewish counsel and by the evidence of Jewish suffering that the end of their "blasphemy" was at hand, leading undeniably to the universal redemption of all mankind.

Some years earlier, some time between 1456 and 1467, an Italian Jew named Isaac Dieulosal composed a Hebrew work on the appearance of Halley's comet in Italy in 1456 in which he wrote:

So I saw, according to what was told to me, that many Christian scholars spoke and wrote about the message of this star. All their opinion and intention was for the purpose of making their people upright to restore them to good from their evil and despicable actions. And priests and preachers rose up each day, spreading out all over in order to inform and warn them (their Christian constituency). I zealously have sought the Lord, the God of Israel and his people and (thus) I say: "How is this act appropriate to God, blessed be He, that they (the Christians) will assume a task and a skill not bestowed on them while the children of our people whose strength lies (in the utterances) of the mouth and in prayer and repentance, will neglect their skill given to them from their fathers? . . . I declared that our holy Torah would not be inferior to their useless conversation. . . . These people whose task is not such will repent while Israel whose faith it is, will not repent and will stand in tribulations? . . . For this act (the appearance of the comet) is a marvelously divine act to cause us to repent for it is a sign of the Messiah and the approach of the time of perfection and redemption. . . .[5]

For Isaac the Jew, the comet of 1456 had to be a sign of the approaching redemption of Israel, for how else might one explain the frenzied reactions of his Christian neighbors who were convinced beyond doubt of the authenticity of this portent of approaching doom? If Christian priests had admonished their faithful to repent, how could Jews fail to respond any differently?[6] Although embarrassed by the fact that Christians could teach a lesson to Jews about the time of redemption, Isaac nevertheless had no misgivings about the appropriateness of Jews imitating this example, As Meleto, the Christian, had verified his own millennial expectations by appeal to Jewish authorities, so Isaac the Jew sought similar confirmation of his own messianic expectations by appeal to Christian authorities.

The reactions of Meleto and Dieulosal offer striking evidence of the interrelation of two apparently distinct cultural phenomena—Jewish and Christian messianic speculation and activity at the end of the Middle Ages.[7] Given the close social and cultural liaisons on so many other levels between Jewish and Christian societies in the fifteenth and sixteenth centuries, such shared messianic attitudes should hardly come as a surprise. Yet students of messianic activity in the Jewish communities of this period have usually viewed Jewish messianism as primarily an internal Jewish phenomenon. It is already a commonplace in Jewish historiography that the upsurge of messianic activity among Jews, beginning at the end of the fifteenth century and lasting well into the eighteenth century, was a direct response to the expulsion of the Jews from Spain in 1492. More than any other event, the dramatic ejection of Spanish Jewry constituted the major catalyst in precipitating messianic stirrings among Jews and Marranos alike. Spanish exiles who settled in Italy, Turkey and Palestine became the primary agents of messianic passion; in Safed they also were responsible for the creative fusion of Kabbalah and messianism, which marked the most lasting innovation of sixteenth century Jewish thought.[8]

This understanding of Jewish messianism, so persuasively argued by Yiẓḥak Baer and Gershom Scholem, among others, is certainly not incorrect but perhaps requires refinement and modification. One need not deny the significance of 1492 while, at the same time, enlarging the context for understanding Jewish messianism in this period. The questions that I would like to pose are these: To what extent is Jewish messianism in the late Middle Ages a manifestation of forces acutely present in the larger society shared by Jews and Christians alike? Can one discern in this period Christian influence on Jewish messianic activity as well as Jewish influence on Christian millennial stirrings? In what ways might Jewish messianism in the fifteenth and sixteenth centuries be considered an expression of conformity and assimilation to Christian culture, and in what ways might it also constitute a primary assertion of Jewish uniqueness and estrangement from Christian society?

Few historians, to my knowledge, have examined Jewish messianic expectations primarily in the context of similar expectations in the

Christian world during the medieval or early modern period.[9] I would like here to begin such an examination, with the hope of answering at least partially the questions I have posed, restricting myself primarily to the period of the fifteenth and sixteenth centuries. Yet any impressions I may draw for this decisive period would likely be suggestive for earlier and later periods as well.

Christian Influences on Jewish Messianism

Let me begin by delineating the potential influence of ideas, events and personalities in the Christian world of this era on the shaping of Jewish messianic consciousness. Excluding, for the moment, the undeniable impact of the Spanish expulsion, what other "contact situations"[10] between Jews and Christians might have aroused expectation of the imminent coming of the Messiah within the Jewish community?

Isaac's reaction to the comment of 1456 as a clear portent of the Messiah's arrival is hardly an isolated occurrence; rather it fits into an entire pattern of intercultural receptivity to astrological events commonly shared by Christians and Jews throughout this period. The significance of astrological beliefs as a critical factor in Renaissance culture in general and for Christian millennial expectations in particular has been noted sufficiently by historians of late medieval-Renaissance culture. One need only examine the outpouring of astrological prognostications regarding comets and planetary conjunctions and their impact on European society at the end of the fifteenth and beginning of the sixteenth century to appreciate the potency of such speculations in heightening visions of the Apocalypse, the Apostolic Pope and the imminent golden age. At the end of the fifteenth century such prognosticators as Paul of Middleberg, Antonio Torquato and George Lichtenberg among many others, profoundly aroused contradictory anticipations of approaching doom and regeneration throughout Europe.[11] And their predictions were no less fascinating for astrological enthusiasts within the Jewish community. Every major astrological event in the second half of the fifteenth century and the first half of the sixteenth century attracted simultaneously and with remarkable regularity the attention of both Jews and Christians. A good example of such astrological ecumenicity is that of Meleto's testimony of the Turkish Rabbi's prediction for 1484. It seems more than a coincidence that this Jew pointed especially to the completion of "an astrological great year," a year heralded by a large group of

Christian astrologers as one of spectacular changes for Christians. 1484 was also the year of Savonarola's prophetic awakening, the year of religious renovation according to Giovanni Nanni of Viterbo as well as the year of the public appearance of the strange hermetic prophet Giovanni Mercurio da Correggio in Italy.[12] Nor was the Constantinople Rabbi the only member of his community to appraise the eschatological significance of that year. As far away as Ferrara, Abraham b. Mordecai Farissol recorded his impressions of the Christian prophet Correggio while revealing an intimate awareness of the relation of astrological great years such as 1484 to the birth of prophecy.[13]

But 1484 is only one instance of similarly shared perceptions among Jews and Christians regarding years of astrological significance beginning in our period in 1456 and including such dates as 1467–8, 1484, 1500, 1503–4, 1517, and 1530–1, to mention only the most prominent. Any student of Jewish messianism is aware that each of these dates played important roles in the cosmic plans of such distinguished Jewish prognosticators as Abraham Zakut, Bonet de Lattes, Abraham Eliezer Ha-Levi, Isaac Abravanel and many others. But less emphasis has been placed on the fact that each of these dates coincides precisely with the calculations of Christian speculators. One more example should suffice. Moshe Idel has recently pointed out how Yohanan Alemanno copied a prognostication of an anonymous Italian astrologer who predicted that after considerable Jewish suffering, a prophet would appear during the great conjunction of October, 1503.[14] For Alemanno, the rise of such a prophet suggested unmistakably the coming of the Jewish Messiah. The fact that a Jewish savant copied verbatim a Christian expert to confirm his own eschatology is remarkable in itself. What is even more revealing, however, is the incredible concurrence regarding the prominence of this date (or one approximating it) among Jews and Christians alike. A list of such names would comprise a virtual "who's who" of messianic prognosticators in the early sixteenth century: Jews, Isaac Abravanel, Abraham Zakut, Joseph Ibn Shraga, Bonet de Lattes, Abraham Farissol, Asher Lemlein, the author of *Sefer ha-Meshiv*, and Christians, Antonio Torquato, Girolamo Torella, Albert of Trent, Sandro Botticelli, Antonio da Rieti, Sebastian Brant and more.[15] Such an overwhelming accord regarding the eschatological import of one year suggests beyond doubt the insufficiency of explaining Jewish messianic expectations for 1503–4 solely on the basis of their temporal proximity to 1492.

Besides astrological portents, major historical events that significantly transformed the face of European civilization in this period directly affected the messianic sensibilities of Jews and Christians alike. Living under the same skies as their Christian contemporaries, Jews evidently could not ignore the eschatological messages, so apparent to Christians, of the conquest of Constantinople in 1453, the French Charles VIII's invasion of Italy in 1494, the dramatic appearance of Luther in 1517, the sack of Rome by the German Charles V in 1527, and the sensational discoveries of the New World. With no exception, each of these events figures prominently in the messianic thinking of contemporary Jews who appear to be impressed by them, either because of the momentous transformations such happenings were generating within Christian society as a whole or because of the hysterical millennial excitement they were evoking among Christians. Jews totally concurred with the assessment of many Christians that the fall of Constantinople and the sack of Rome were blatant signs of the imminent destruction of the Christian Empire.[16] The messianic significance of the discoveries of the New World profoundly shaped the thinking of Christians like Columbus and the Franciscan Gerónimo de Medieta, and of Jews like Abraham Farissol, Abraham Yagel, Samuel Usque, and Yohanan Alemanno.[17]

Even the messianic significance of Luther's challenge to the hegemony of the Catholic Church did not go unnoticed by at least one contemporary Jewish observer. For Abraham Eliezer Ha-Levi, writing from Jerusalem, Luther appeared as a kind of secret Jew, rebelling not only against Papal authority but against the essence of Christianity itself. Luther clearly signified the beginning of a process whereby Christians would begin to draw closely to Judaism in the advent of the messianic Age.[18] More than that of any other Jewish thinker, Ha-Levi's view of contemporary historical events as messianic theophanies in an elaborate cosmic plan reveals the extent to which cataclysmic changes in European civilization as a whole—beyond the single event of 1492—deeply stirred the apocalyptic tendencies of some contemporary Jews.

A further illustration of how historical events in Christian society affected Jewish messianic thinking is the case of Charles VIII's dramatic invasion of Italy in 1494. The Christian messianic prophecies associated with his campaign, emanating out of France and Italy, especially that of Savonarola, have long been known.[19] That certain Jews also attributed eschatological importance to the French king's campaign is less known and certainly less understandable. Yet it appears that Charles' appearance in Italy did arouse messianic interest among contemporary Jews who saw him as an element in the unfolding messianic drama if not the true Messiah himself. A Jewish scribe added to a manuscript of *Sefer Peliah* a comment that the invasion of Charles VIII was indeed a clear manifestation of apocalyptic agitation, the messianic birth pangs preceding the Messiah, who would definitely appear in 1503.[20] In his *Opus Davidicum*, written in Italy in 1497, the Franciscan priest Johannes Angelus Terzois de Legonissa also points to Jewish messianic reactions related to Charles' expedition. Writing to demonstrate the Davidic origin of the French king, Johannes also refers to the Jewish persecutions in his age, a penitential fervor among Jews and even the beginning of their immigration to Israel.[21] That Joseph Ha-Cohen, in his history of kings of France and Turkey, also assigned to Charles VIII an eschatological role in his own construction of world history has been recently argued by Yosef Hayyim Yerushalmi.[22] All three pieces of evidence suggest that Jewish messianic anticipation could be induced not only by events directly affecting Jews but also by circumstances that had little or no obvious relation to Jews. Since Jews nevertheless were attentive to the messianic overtones of Charles' actions, they seem clearly to be influenced in this case by the apocalyptic designs of their Christian contemporaries.

Another example of the impact of Christian activity on Jewish eschatological thinking also needs to be recalled. By the early sixteenth century, Jews, especially those in Italy, could not help noticing that a sizable number of Christians were studying Hebrew and especially the Kabbalah. "And since," wrote Abraham Azulai, "the messianic king will appear through the merits [of this study] and through none other, it behooves us not to be remiss."[23] Moreover, others of Azulai's generation surely saw the unraveling of the secrets of Jewish mysticism to non-Jews as a precondition for hastening the advent of redemption. Both Abraham Ha-Levi and Isaac de Lattes articulated identical views, and the same idea was held by a number of Christian Kabbalists as well.[24] I shall return to the important function of the Kabbalah as a vehicle for the illumination of divine mysteries among Christians and thus an incontrovertible sign of the Messiah's coming.

To recapitulate, it would appear that Jewish messianic stirrings in the fifteenth and sixteenth centuries were directly influenced by a concatenation of astrological and historical events in the Christian world (other than 1492) which precipitated similar messianic reactions among Christians. These events, together with a Christian awakening of interest in Judaism and arcane Hebrew texts, served to confirm and reinforce expectations among Jews that the Messiah was indeed approaching.

Jewish Influences on Christian Messianism

Let me now turn to the reverse side of the interaction: the potential influence of Jews, Judaism and specifically Jewish messianic behavior on Christian millennial stirrings of this period.[25] The cosmic role of the Jews in the eschatological blueprint of ancient and medieval Christendom was still an essential feature of fifteenth and sixteenth century Christian millennialism. The primary function that Jews were to play in the Last Judgment was that they would convert. Thus St. Augustine wrote:

And in connection with that judgment the following events will come to pass, as we have learned. Elijah the Tishbite shall come; the Jew shall believe; Anti-Christ shall persecute; Christ shall judge; the dead shall rise; the good and the wicked shall be separated; the world shall be burned and renewed.[26]

Kenneth Stow, in his book on sixteenth century Papal Jewry policy, has sufficiently demonstrated the critical link between Christian eschatological hopes and preoccupations with Jewish conversion throughout the sixteenth century.[27] I need only mention here that this link is highly prominent in almost every Christian apocalyptic scenario of the period. The theme of imminent conversion of the Jews is obsessively displayed on almost every page of Francesco da Meleto's *Convivio*, already referred to above.[28] But Meleto is only one example of many Florentine visionaries, Franciscan missionaries, political Joachimites or Christian Kabbalists who not only reproduce the stock scenarios of the Anti-Christ, last emperor, angelic pastor, and conversion of the Jews, and the Final World Sabbath, but also place unmistakable emphasis on the Jewish component of this spectacle.[29] This tendency is especially accentuated in Spanish formulations of the Conquest of the New World as the fulfilment of prophecies of the Apocalypse. Thus Gerónimo de Mendieta could announce that in the holy task of the Spanish nation of leading all non-believers to the promised land of the Church, the Jews would be the first and easiest group to approach the baptismal font.[30]

Reinforcing Christian expectations of the imminence of Jewish conversion was the awareness of the punishment and persecution meted out to contemporary Jews, especially those of the Spanish kingdom. The nexus between Jewish (and Marrano) suffering and the ultimate conversion to Christianity is obvious to Mendieta: "I am firmly convinced," he writes, "that as those Catholic monarchs (Ferdinand and Isabella) were granted the mission of beginning to extirpate those three diabolical squadrons, 'Perfidious' Judaism, 'false' Mohammedanism, and 'blind' idolatry along with the fourth squadron of the heretics whose remedy and medicine is the Holy Inquisition, in like manner . . . completing the task has been reserved for their royal successors: final conversion of all the peoples of the earth to the bosom of the Church."[31] Catholics and Protestants alike took notice of the expulsion of the Jews from Spain and placed it squarely in their own assorted visions of the Apocalypse and the destruction of the Anti-Christ.[32]

But some fifteenth and sixteenth century Christians were also cognizant, to a surprising degree, of every major manifestation of Jewish messianic activity in their era. The extent to which contemporary Jewish messianic ferment infected them is difficult to gauge. But there is no doubt that they took notice and that what they saw in the Jewish community served to reinforce their own messianic proclivities. Clearly a best-seller among Jewish and Christian prognosticators of this period was Abraham bar Ḥiyyah's *Megillat ha-Megaleh*. The Latin translation of his astrological calculations on the Messiah, particularly the section on great conjunctions, was readily available to Christians who seemed genuinely impressed by his predictions. Abraham bar Ḥiyyah, alias Sasadorda, is mentioned by Alonso de Espina, Pierre d'Ailley, Pico della Mirandola, Paolo Orlandini, Savonarola, and he probably influenced Francesco da Meleto, among many others.[33] The frequency with which contemporary Jews utilize these same computations is equally impressive.[34]

But Christians were informed of Jewish messianic speculation by means other than Jewish books. Meleto's journey to Constantinople to familiarize himself with the "oral" teachings of the Jews on the Messiah is a clear indication of the importance of such teachings to at least some Christians in confirming their own eschatological schemes. In his lionization of Charles VIII's messianic role, Johannes Angelus not only glorified the French king's Davidic ancestry but also seemed genuinely impressed that some contemporary Jews themselves took Charles to be a clear sign of the approaching messianic age. Despite Johannes' obvious distaste for Jews of his era, he nevertheless felt that their own advocacy of the French king lent credence to his propaganda campaign on behalf of Charles.[35]

Numerous other examples of Christian awareness of Jewish messianism are easily forthcoming. The Florentine chronicler of Savonarola's mission, Piero Parenti, is not oblivious to Jewish and Moslem messianic prophecies of imminent realization in his own day.[36] Cardinal Bathazar del Rio, in his inaugural speech before the Fifth Lateran Council, mentions the diffusion of prophets in his own day among "gli infedeli, ebrei e musulmani."[37] The widespread interest in the messianic calculations of Jewish astrologers such as Abraham Zakut and Bonet de Lattes is well known.[38] A marvelous indication of both the diffusion and longevity of Jewish messianic prophecies within the Christian world is the evidence supplied by Gershom Scholem concerning a *menorah* held by the Rabbis of Constantinople. According to information available to a Canon in Pressberg, writing in 1750, the Rabbis of Constantinople had received a *menorah* (with the date 1532 inscribed on it) in the fifteenth century from R. Levi ben Ḥabib of Jerusalem, considered to be a clear manifestation of the approaching redemption.[39]

That sixteenth century Christians took note and were even fascinated by Jewish messianic figures, years before Shabbatai Zevi's dramatic appearance, is well known and need only be mentioned briefly here. David Ganz reports that many Christians were impressed by Asher Lemlein.[40] The German humanist Sebastian Münster even describes Lemlein in a brief passage.[41] David Reuveni's appearance in Italy intrigued many Christians not the least of whom included the Pope himself and Cardinal Giles of Viterbo.[42] No less notable a scholar than Giambatista Ramusio was charged with interviewing Reuveni in Venice.[43] Shlomo Molcho writes about his Christian following who came faithfully to listen to his sermons.[44] He was protected by the Pope despite his suspect heretical leanings.[45] J. A. Widmanstat, another distinguished German scholar, notices the Jewish flag carried by Molcho.[46] And a week before he drafted the Augsburg Confession, in 1530, the most authoritative statement of Lutheran faith, Philip Melanchthon appears to have reacted directly to Molcho in explicitly condemning Jewish chiliasm.[47]

It is impossible to assess the significance of all such references to Jewish messianism among Christians. What is clear is that a Christian community nurturing its own apocalyptic fantasies found more than casual interest in both contemporary Jewish messianic speculation and the more dramatic spectacle of Jewish messianic pretenders in their day.[48] Christian messianic expectations in the fifteenth and sixteenth centuries undoubtedly would have flourished with or without corresponding ideas and patterns of behavior within the Jewish community, just as Jewish messianism in the same period would have captivated the minds and hearts of contemporary Jews whether or not Jews were aware of analogous Christian stirrings. Nevertheless there is sufficient evidence to suggest that some cross-fertilization of messianic ideas did transpire and that Jewish and Christian messianic fears and hopes did intersect on numerous levels, at least serving to reinforce and reconfirm already implanted and fully matured visions of the approaching end.

Christian Kabbalists and the Marranos

Any discussion of such mutual influences remains incomplete without reference to two critical elements in the history of late medieval messianism among Jews and Christians: the Christian Kabbalah as a potential receptacle of Jewish messianic ideas into the Christian community, on the one hand, and the Marranos as a potential channel for Christian messianic ideas into the Jewish community, on the other.

Not every Christian attracted to the study of Jewish mystical sources in the fifteenth and sixteenth centuries was also an apocalyptic visionary; Pico is the most obvious illustration.[49] Nevertheless, it is more than a coincidence that a prominent number of Christian kabbalists fervently believed in the imminent coming of the Apocalypse and were preoccupied with various eschatological schema of the approaching end. In fact, there is sufficient evidence to suggest that for some of them the study of Hebrew and kabbalistic sources contributed most heavily to their sensation of tense expectation in the immediate consummation of the world. In particular, Pietro Galatino,[50] Giles of Viterbo[51] and Guillaume Postel[52] exhibit most conspicuously the confluence of kabbalistic ideas and messianic agitation among Christians. All three were conscious of living in the last age because of the newly discovered Hebrew mysteries that were now placed at their disposal. Each of them gave particular emphasis to the study of Hebrew as a unifying principle of the approaching golden age; each of them weighed heavily the conversion of the Jews as a significant dimension of their eschatological schemes; and each, like many contemporary Jews, saw their study of kabbalah as a primary instrument of spiritual illumination galvanizing the divine energies of the universe, propelling all mankind towards the approaching religious climax. Through their study of the kabbalah, all the mysteries of divine creation would be deciphered, signaling the approaching redemption. All three probably knew each other and nurtured close relationships with contemporary Jewish savants.[53] More than any other Christian group, they demonstrate dramatically the profound impression Jewish eschatology left on contemporary Christian culture.

Only the general outlines of the specific Jewish content of their messianic visions have yet been delineated, but already it is apparent that one critical source shaping their views were the writings of the thirteenth century kabbalist Abraham Abulafia. What must have been appealing to them was his view of messianism as a spiritual process whereby the Messiah as a perfect mystic would illuminate the true interpretation of the law, thus bringing about a new religious teaching of ecumenical harmony.[54] Abulafia's writings were widely known among sixteenth century Jews—men like Asher Lemlein, Shlomo Molcho and a number of kabbalists in the circle of Isaac Luria[55]—and profoundly affected their own messianic stirrings. Undoubtedly, one of the key components engendering a common universe of messianic discourse among certain sixteenth century Jews and Christians was the noticeable impact Abulafian ideas left on each community.

Marranos returning to Judaism, on the other hand, seem to offer the most likely conduit for the passage of Christian millenary ideas into the Jewish community.[56] Gershom Scholem has sensibly cautioned us, however, not to exaggerate the potential Christian influences of such individuals on Jewish messianism. Certain developments are imminent in the nature of all religious phenomena; a common religious motif need not be labeled Christian or Jewish when one compares analogous developments in two contiguous systems of religious speculation.[57] Nevertheless, Scholem readily admits that certain Marranos in the seventeenth century unquestionably infected Sabbatian ideology with Christian notions of the Messiah, particularly those found among heretical rather than orthodox traditions of Christianity.[58] Although not a Marrano himself, Nathan of Gaza may reflect some of this influence in the blatantly Christian character of his religious terminology.[59] The sermons of the former Marrano Moses Abudiente (d. 1688) betray Christian typological exegesis on the Messiah.[60] And most astonishing in this regard is the conscious acknowledgment on the part of Abraham Cardozo that his view of the Jewish Messiah is shaped unmistakably by his Christian upbringing. Thus he informs his brother on the accuracy of his messianic belief by arguing:

And if the Christians say the same, what harm can come to us from the truth? They took it from the sages of Israel. To what extent is it entangled in Augustine's Book on the City of God, being a contemporary of the sages of the Gemara, with whom he conversed and from whom he learned? Shall we abandon the truth for fear of the lie? No benefit at all shall emerge for our opponents by conceding that which is certain . . .[61]

Cardozo has no hesitation in identifying Isaiah's suffering servant with the Messiah and accuses earlier Jewish exegetes of "fleeing from Idumean arguments" by denying this interpretation. As Yosef Yerushalmi argues, one need not impugn Abraham's conscious Jewish loyalties when identifying in his messianic theology the Christian elements which he could not dislodge.[62]

If Christian influence on Marrano eschatologies is discernible in the seventeenth century, what about in earlier periods? As in the case of the Marranos attracted to Sabbatianism, messianic stirrings among their fifteenth and sixteenth century ancestors need not be attributable to Christian inspiration. Yet it seems plausible enough to assume that a Marrano raised for a long period of time in a totally Christian environment could not, in returning to Judaism, totally divorce himself from Christian modes of thinking and behavior. Even when violently uprooting himself from his Christian past, the Marrano might unconsciously assimilate traces of the conceptual background he so willingly repudiates. Such a pattern of behavior is suggested by the heightened anticipation of the Messiah's coming among fifteenth and sixteenth century Marranos. For some time now, students of Jewish messianism in the period preceding and immediately following the Spanish expulsion have known of the considerable evidence available from Inquisitional testimony on messianic stirrings among Marranos both in and outside of Spain.[63] Such evidence for Yiẓḥak Baer was not necessarily the product of a Christian environment since "*Conversos* and Jews were one people united by bonds of religion, destiny and messianic hope."[64] Yet as the case of Abraham Cardozo suggests, fervent loyalty to the Jewish community is in no way incompatible with Christian influence. How else might one explain the messianic imagery of the Marrano visions described by Baer: visions of the Turk as Anti-Christ or the prophetess of Herrara who sees purgatory and the souls of the dead before penance? It seems to me that a systematic investigation of expressions of messianic anticipation among Marranos, taking into account especially their psychological makeup and the free and imaginative associations of their visions, would yield more hints of the subliminal as well as self-conscious penetration of Christian ideas into their messianic behavior.

Such hints are dramatically suggested, for example, in the sermons of the most illustrious sixteenth century messianic prophet of Marrano ancestry, Shlomo Molcho. In his collection entitled *Sefer ha-Mefo'ar*, he introduces the same Christian messianic typology of Isaiah 53 in speaking about the Messiah of Israel.[65] This he fuses with an elaborate identification of the characters of the Job allegory cast unmistakably in a contemporary eschatological setting. Thus Job represents Israel, Elihu-Elijah, Eliphaz-Edom or Rome, Bildad-Ishmael or Turkey, the latter two characters to be destroyed along with all of Israel's enemies by the Messiah the son of Joseph.[66] Molcho had undoubtedly familiarized himself with the themes of Jewish apocalyptic literature like the *Book of Zerubbabel* printed in Constantinople in 1519, and need not have availed himself of parallel Christian messianic typologies current in his generation. Yet alternatively, his graphic depiction of the person of the Messiah, his constant emphasis on the redemption of the poor and downtrodden,[67] and especially his almost histrionic apocalyptic scenes of the utter devastation of Edom reminiscent of visions of the coming of the Anti-Christ,[68] might all betray his Christian upbringing. These allusions, taken together with his complex personality traits, his aspiration to die as a martyr, and the unusual receptivity his prophecies were accorded in the Christian world, recommend him as a prime candidate for the transference of Christian eschatological ideas into Judaism.[69] The potential Christian source of Molcho's messianic disposition is all the more interesting given the profound impact he had on such sixteenth century Rabbinic luminaries as Joseph Taitaẓak and Joseph Karo.[70]

LURIANIC MESSIANISM AND ITS SIXTEENTH CENTURY
CHRISTIAN COUNTERPARTS

In light of the evidence we have considered so far, it seems safe to acknowledge a certain degree of mutual interaction between Jewish and Christian messianic beliefs and activity in the fifteenth and sixteenth centuries. Such an acknowledgment need not exaggerate the importance of such mutuality nor blur the obvious dissimilarities between the two faiths, but it does suggest the extent to which late medieval messianic expectations constitute a clearly visible reflection of shared mental attitudes and behavior among Jews and Christians.

Yet such a guarded conclusion still appears somewhat imbalanced and certainly incomplete without calling attention, albeit briefly, to at least one major area of Jewish messianism which clearly does not intersect with Christian millennial forms, revealing independence and originality rather than confluence or commonality. What I am proposing is that an overall comparison of Jewish and Christian messianism in this period might also adumbrate, from a perspective previously unnoticed, the marked features of Jewish messianism which define the uniqueness and novelty of its conception in the sixteenth century.

I am referring especially to the ideology of Lurianic kabbalah, generally viewed as the most dramatic and influential expression of Jewish messianic anticipation of this period.[71] When reflecting initially on the messianic myth of creation and redemption of Isaac Luria, I was especially intrigued by the possibility of structural similarity, if not influence, between Luria's conception of *Tikkun* and the Catholic ideal of reform as articulated by certain sixteenth century exponents of Church renewal.[72] Such outrageously dissimilar notions would appear to have little in common with each other. Yet a favorable comparison of the meaning of both ideals and their social setting need not be dismissed out of hand. Besides the obvious linguistic similarity between *Tikkun* and *Reformatio* or *Renovatio,* other similarities come to mind. *Tikkun,* or the process of restoring or mending an ideal order through the spiritual and mystical activity of man, is nothing less than a bold and dramatic vision of mission and reform—the mystic is charged with the task of reuniting the scattered fragments of creation and healing the sickness of the cosmos by first purifying his own soul through acts of piety and spiritual meditation.[73]

How different is this ideal from that of the Pauline doctrine of reform expounded by sixteenth century Catholic reformers? For Ignatius Loyola and his disciples in the Society for Jesus, personal salvation depended upon a spiritual regeneration brought out by human effort, beginning with the purging and cleansing of each individual Christian soul. The typical Catholic reformer, as dramatically portrayed in Ignatius' *Spiritual Exercises,* was a mystic guide engaged in spiritual battle with evil attempting to transform himself and his spiritual devotées before transforming the world.[74] What was critical for the Catholic reformers, like the Safed mystics yet unlike the quietistic fatalism of either Luther or Calvin, was the importance of human free will and human effort in effecting reform.[75] To Loyola is attributed the saying: "We must work as if success depended on ourselves and not God."[76] The mystical reformer directs all of his spiritual energies to eradicating sin, to ascetic denial, to mental concentration on biblical and religious subjects, intense prayer and meditation, in order to raise each individual soul to the bliss of eternal life.

If one could remove for a moment the specific content feeding the spiritual lives of both kinds of mystics, how different would Lurianic and Loyolan piety actually be? A zealous drive for spiritual rejuvenation, eradication of evil, repentance and love of God grounded in the communal life of devout brotherhoods and elevated by a sense of divine mission and spiritual élitism marked the religious vision of both.[77]

Yet the comparison is misleading in one major respect.[78] The ideal of human reform and spiritual perfection articulated by Loyola and his disciples is never embedded in an eschatological context. Christian reform may lead to spiritual salvation, but it is forcefully detached from any apocalyptic vision of the end of days. On the contrary, the Loyolan ideal of human perfectibility would have little in common with the visions of sixteenth century Christian apocalyptics. More often than not, the latter had little desire to refashion human personality or society. Their vision of dramatic upheaval rested on social withdrawal rather than engagement; change would be effected by divine intervention rather than human effort. The only human roles were to gather together, to await signs of the coming doom, to listen to the prophets, to purify oneself and to pray. And more often than not, prognosticators of the Last Judgment and the Golden Age would find the social activity of the army of mystical reformers unworthy of serious attention.[79] Even within a figure like Giles of Viterbo, where the two tendencies of human reform and millennial expectation seem to coalesce, the chasm between passive apocalypticism and active reform is remarkably preserved. Giles' reform measures have nothing to do with his eschatology. History for Giles was to be consummated by divine energies, not human ones.[80]

How alien this dichotomy seems to the Lurianic formulation. The spiritual reform of the pious mystic constitutes the primary instrument of rescuing the divine *Shekhina* from imprisonment in the realm of the *kelipah*. Man alone and not God holds the keys to earthly salvation. Man alone is empowered to bring about the Messiah. The redemption of Israel is not the result of a sudden and dramatic divine intervention outside the realm of history; it is rather a logical and necessary fruition of human endeavor achieved within the historical realm.[81]

The only sixteenth century Christians who would allow the coadunation of human activity and messianic anticipation were not reformers but dissenters. For the radical reformers, reform was too gradual and lengthy a process; radical rupture with the immedite past, repudiation of existing authority, whether ecclesiastic or secular, and the implementation of a new social order informed their eschatological visions. They lived with the gripping conviction that the restoration for which they yearned could only be gained by the eradication of social and spiritual ills, not by their progressive amelioration. Coloring their messianic activism were the charges and countercharges of heresy versus orthodoxy, legitimate dissent versus the discipline of Church authority.[82]

And uniquely between these two extremes of Church reform purged of messianic anticipation, on the one hand, and Church revolt fused with intense expectancy of disaster and rebirth on the other, lies the original conception of Lurianic messianism—neither mystic dissent nor withdrawal but a gradualistic human reform firmly grounded in a cosmic myth of renewal and restoration. When viewed against the background of Catholic reform and Protestant rebellion, the uniqueness of the Lurianic conception is thus brought sharply into focus. It forcefully reminds us that the recognition of apparent similarities and even mutually shared perceptions ought not obscure the unmistakable dissimilarities underlying Christian and Jewish visions of the messianic future at the end of the Middle Ages.

NOTES

1. On Francesco da Meleto, see C. Vasoli, "La profezia di Francesco da Meleto," *Archivio di filosofia, Umanesimo e Ermeneutica* 3 (1963): 27–80; S. Bongi, "Francesco da Meleto un profeta fiorentino atiempi del Machiavello," *Archivio storico italiano*, series v, 3 (1889): 62–70; D. Weinstein, *Savonarola and Florence, Prophecy and Patriotism in the Renaissance*, Princeton, 1970, pp. 353–57; and E. Garin, "Paolo Orlandini e il profeta Francesco da Meleto," in *La cultura filosofica del Rinascimento italiano*, Florence, 1961, pp. 213–23.

   Another Christian prophet named Johannes Baptista Italus visited Constantinople at about the same time and, like Meleto, predicted that the Jews would convert in 1517. See G. H. Williams, *The Radical Reformation* (Philadelphia, 1961), pp. 18–19, 255; R. Schwoebel, *The Shadow of the Crescent: The Renaissance Image of the Turk (1453–1517)*, New York, 1969, p. 220. Williams suggests that Italus and Meleto may be the same person.

2. Vasoli, *op. cit.*, pp. 56–57.

3. *Ibid.*, p. 57. Only a few years earlier, letters written by *Conversos* in Constantinople regarding the birth of the Messiah and his imminent public appearance were received in Valencia, Spain. See Y. Baer, "The Messianic Movement in Spain in the Period of the Expulsion" (Hebrew), *Me'asef Zion* 5 (1933): 63–64; idem, *A History of the Jewish Christian Spain* 2 vols. (Philadelphia, 1961–66) II, pp. 292–95; idem, *Die Juden im Christlichen Spanien* 2 vols. (Berlin, 1929–36) II, no. 392.

4. Vasoli, *op. cit.*, p. 57.

5. J. Hacker, "The Immigration of Spanish Jews to the Land of Israel and their Bond to It Between 1391 and 1492" (Hebrew), *Shalem* 1 (1973–74); 143–44.

6. In addition to the references Hacker brings on the comet of 1456 (*ibid.*, p. 119, nn. 48 and 49), see L. Thorndike, *A History of Magic and Experimental Science*, vol. 4, New York, 1934, pp. 413–14. Reports that Pope Calixtus III was so alarmed by two comets that appeared in Rome that year that he ordered the reading of special prayers and the ringing of bells seem to confirm Isaac's testimony. See also G. Celoria, "Sull'apparizione della cometa di Halley avvenuta nell'anno 1456," *Rendiconti del R. Istituto Lombardo*, 2nd series, 18 (1885): 112–25. For a later discussion of cometary theory in the writings of an Italian Jew, see D. Ruderman, "The Receptivity of Jewish Thought to the New Astronomy of the Seventeenth Century: The Case of Abraham ben Hananiyah Yagel," *Jews in Italy: Studies Dedicated to the Memory of U. Cassuto on the 100th Anniversary of His Birth*, Jerusalem, 1988.

7. Most studies of Christian messianism generally make distinctions between

messianism, millenarianism and apocalypticism. See for example, Y. Talmon, "Millenarianism," *International Encyclopedia of the Social Sciences* 10 (1968): 349; N. Cohn, "Medieval Millenarism: Its Bearing on the Comparative Study of Millenarian Movements," in S. L. Thrupp, ed., *Millennial Dreams in Action, Comparative Studies in Society and History*, supplement 2 (The Hague, 1962), p. 31; B. McGinn, *Visions of the End, Apocalyptic Traditions in the Middle Ages*, New York, 1979, pp. 26–36, who prefers the term "apocalypticism." Studies of Jewish messianism usually employ the term "messianism." For the purposes of this paper, I have utilized the "loose" definition of messianism by R. J. Z.. Werblowsky ("Messiah and Messianic Movements" in *Encyclopaedia Britannica, Macropaedia*, vol. II [Chicago, 1979], p. 1017): ". . . beliefs or theories regarding an eschatological (concerning the last times) improvement of the state of man or the world, and a final consummation of history," while using the other two terms more or less interchangeably. I have also avoided the term "messianic movement" in referring to the phenomena described below. On the distinction between messianic "ideology" and "movement," see Werblowsky, p. 1017, and see S. Sharot, "Jewish Millenarianism: A Comparison of Medieval Communities," *Comparative Studies in Society and History* 22 (1980): 395, n. 5. Sharot's essay subsequently has appeared in somewhat expanded form as Chapter 5 of his *Messianism, Mysticism, and Magic: A Sociological Analysis of Jewish Religious Movements*, Chapel Hill, 1982.

8. See especially, Baer, "The Messianic Movement," G. Scholem, *Major Trends in Jewish Mysticism*, New York, 1941, pp. 241–47; *idem, Sabbatai Zevi, The Mystical Messiah*, Princeton, 1973, pp. 18ff.; H. H. Ben Sasson, "Exile and Redemption Through the Eyes of the Spanish Exiles," (Hebrew), in *Yiṣḥak F. Baer Jubilee Volume*, ed. S. W. Baron, B. Dinur et al., Jerusalem, 1960, pp. 216–27; A. Z. Aescoly, *Ha-Tenu'ot Ha-Meshiḥiot be-Yisrael*, Jerusalem, 1956, pp. 231ff.; A. H. Silver, *A History of Messianic Speculation in Israel*, Boston, 1959, pp. 110ff. See most recently, I. Tishby, "Genizah Fragments of a Messianic-Mystical Text on the Expulsion from Spain and Portugal" (Hebrew), *Zion* 47 (1983): 55–102; 347–85; and his book, *Meshiḥiut Be-Dor Gerushe Sefarad Ve-Portugal*, Jerusalem, 1985; R. Shatz, "An Outline of the Image of the Political-Messianic Arousal after the Spanish Expulsion" (Hebrew), *Da'at* II (1982–83): 53–66; R. Elior, "Messianic Expectations and Spiritualization of Religious Life in the Sixteenth Century," *REJ* 145 (1986): 35–49.

9. See Sharot's article (n. 7 above) which offers some comparison of a general nature. Sharot's conclusions seem to confirm my own on the inadequacy of general sociological models for explaining such complex phenomena as Jewish messianism. Cf. McGinn, *Visions of the End*, pp. 29ff. For other partial attempts to compare Jewish and Christian messianism, see Scholem, *Sabbatai Zevi*, pp. 93ff. and Y. H. Yerushalmi, *From Spanish Court to Italian Ghetto*, New York, 1971, pp. 307ff.

10. On the use of the term, see D. J. Geanakoplos, *Interaction of the "Sibling" Byzantine and Western Culture in the Middle Ages*, New Haven and London, 1976, pp. 3–4.

11. See for example, C. Vasoli, "Temi mistici e profetici alla fine del Quattrocento," in *Studi sulla cultura del Rinascimento*, Manduria, 1968, pp. 180–240; D. Cantimori, *Eretici italiani del Cinquecento, ricerche storiche*, Florence, 1939; reprinted, 1967, pp. 12ff.; E. Garin, *Lo zodiaco della vita, la polemica sull'astrologia dal Trecento al Cinquecento*, Rome and Bari, 1976, especially chapter 1; idem, "L'attesa dell'età nuova e la 'Renovatio' " in *L'età nuova, ricerche di storia della cultura dal XII al XVI secolo*, Naples, 1969, pp. 81–111; Weinstein, *Savonarola*, especially, pp. 88ff.; A. Chastel, "L'Antéchrist à la Renaissance," *Cristianesimo e ragion di Stato, L'umanesimo e il demoniaco nell'arte*, Atti del II Congresso Internazionale di Studi Umanistici, ed. by E. Castelli, Rome, 1953, pp. 177–86; M. Reeves, *The Influence of Prophecy in the Later Middle Ages, A Study in Joachimism*, Oxford, 1969; Thorndike, *History*, 4, pp. 467–84; G. Tognetti, "Note sul profetismo nel Rinascimento et la letteratura relativa," *Bullettino dell-'Istituto storico italiano per il Medio Evo* 82 (1970): 129–57.

12. On 1484, see Weinstein, *Savonarola*, pp. 88ff.; on Nanni, see Garin, *La cultura filosofica*, pp. 188ff. and R. Weiss, "Traccia per una biografia di Annio da Viterbo," *Italia medioevale e umanistica* 5 (1962): 425–41; on Correggio, see D. Ruderman, "Giovanni Mercurio da Correggio's Appearance in Italy as Seen Through the Eyes of an Italian Jew," *Renaissance Quarterly* 28 (1975): 309–22. For an alternative explanation of the importance of 1484 in messianic prognostications, see Tishby, "Genizah Fragments," pp. 381ff.

13. Ruderman, "Giovanni Mercurio da Correggio's Appearance," and idem, *The World of a Renaissance Jew, The Life and Though of Abraham ben Mordecai Farissol*, Cincinnati, 1981, chapter 10.

14. M. Beit-Arié and M. Idel, "A Treatise on (the Calculation of) the End and Astrology by R. Abraham Zakut" (Hebrew), *Kiryat Sefer* 54 (1979): 180–82 and M. Idel, "On R. Yoḥanan Alemanno and 'Ma'amar Ḥozeh' " (Hebrew), *Kiryat Sefer* 54 (1979): 875–76.

15. Idel has already noted the significance of this date for some of these individuals (see "A Treatise on the End," p. 282, nn. 44, 45; and "On R. Yoḥanan Alemanno," p. 826, n. 19 for further bibliography; and compare also Tishby, p. 365). for Abravanel, see B. Netanyahu, *Don Isaac Abravanel, Statesman and Philosopher*, Philadelphia, 1953, p. 218; for Lemlein, see Aescoly, *Ha-Tenu'ot*, pp. 307ff.; for Torquato, see Thorndike, *op. cit.* 4, pp. 468–70; 5, p. 179 and Garin, "L'attesa dell'età nuova," pp. 105ff.; for Albert of Trent, see D. Weinstein, "The Apocalypse in Sixteenth Century Florence, The Vision of Albert of Trent," in *Renaissance Studies in Honor of Hans Baron*, ed. A. Molho and J. A. Tedeschi, Dekalb, Illinois, 1971, pp. 311–31; for Botticelli, see Weinstein, *Savonarola*, pp. 335; for Rieti, see Weinstein, "Albert of Trent," pp. 314ff.; for Brant, see G. Strauss, ed. and

trans., *Manifestations of Discontent in Germany on the Eve of the Reformation*, Bloomington and London, 1971, p. 224. Undoubtedly, a more comprehensive search would reveal more such references.

16. See for example, for 1453, Baer, "The Messianic Movement," p. 61; G. Scholem, "The Maggid of R. Yosef Taitaẓak and the Visions Ascribed to Him," (Hebrew) *Sefunot* II (1971–8): 79; H. Beinart, *Anusim be-Din Ha-Inquisiẓia*, Tel Aviv, 1965, pp. 19, 54–55; Hacker, "Immigration," pp. 116ff. Tishby, *op. cit.*, pp. 354ff. and pp. 364ff. where the author also emphasizes the messianic importance of the Turkish victory at Lepanto. For 1527, see for example, M. Beit-Arié, "An Epistle on the Matter of the Ten Tribes by R. Abraham b. Eliezer Ha-Levi" (Hebrew), *Koveẓ al Yad* 6 (16) (1962): 372–73; H. H. Ben Sasson, "The Reformation in Contemporary Jewish Eyes" (Hebrew), *Proceedings of the Israel Academy of Sciences and Humanities* 4 (1970): pp. 75–76, 86.

17. On Christian interest, see for example, J. L. Phelan, *The Millennial Kingdom of the Franciscans in the New World, A Study of the Writings of Gerónimo de Mendieta (1525–1604)*, Berkeley and Los Angeles, 1956; M. Bataillon, "Évangélisme et millénarisme au Nouveau Monde," in *Courants religieux et humanisme à la fin du xve au début du xvie siècle;* on Usque's interest, see M. Cohen, ed. *Samuel Usque's Consolations for the Tribulations of Israel*, Philadelphia, 1965, pp. 220ff.; on Yagel's interest, see the selection from *Sefer Be'er Sheva* mistitled *Beit Ya'ar ha-Levanon*) published in *Koveẓ Al Yad* IV (1888): 37ff. On Farissol's interest and additional references on the entire subject, see Ruderman, *The World of A Renaissance Jew*, chapter 11.

18. G. Scholem, "New Researches on R. Abraham b. Eliezer Ha-Levi" (Hebrew), *Kiryat Sefer* 7 (1930): 161ff., 444ff.; Ben-Sasson, "Reformation," pp. 76ff.

19. See Weinstein, *Savonarola*, pp. 166ff.; Reeves, *The Influence of Prophecy*, pp. 320ff.

20. S. Krauss, "Le Roi de France Charles VIII et les espérances messianiques," *REJ* 51 (1906): 87–96.

21. A. Linder, "L'Expédition Italienne de Charleś VIII et les espérances messianiques des Juifs, Temoignage du manuscrit B. N. Lat. 5971A," *REJ* 137 (1978): 179–86.

22. Y. Yerushalmi, "Messianic Impulses in Joseph Ha-Kohen," in *Jewish Thought in the Sixteenth Century*, ed. B. D. Cooperman, Cambridge, Mass., 1983, pp. 460–87.

23. Quoted by Scholem, *Sabbatai Ẓevi*, p. 22.

24. See Scholem," Abraham Eliezer Ha-Levi" (Hebrew), *Kiryat Sefer* 7 (1930): 445; Introduction to Isaac Lattes' edition to the *Sefer ha-Zohar* quoted in K. Stow, *Catholic Thought and Papal Jewry Policy 1555–1593*, New York, 1977, p. 251. On this idea among Christian kabbalists, see below.

25. For Sabbatian influences on seventeenth century Christian millennialism, see Scholem, *Sabbatai Ẓevi*, pp. 101ff.

26. St. Augustine, *The City of God*, trans. M. Dodds, bk. 20, c. 30, p. 762.

27. Stow, *Catholic Thought and Papal Jewry Policy*, chapter 11.
28. See note 1 above.
29. For a comprehensive survey, see Reeves, *The Influence of Prophecy*.
30. See Phelan, *The Millennial Kingdom*, p. 16.
31. Quoted by Phelan, p. 13.
32. Some examples include Francesco da Meleto (in Vasoli, "La profezia," p. 57); Girolamo Torrella (Thorndike 4, p. 584); Johannes Angelus (Linder, p. 183); and Guillaume Postel (W. J. Bousma, *Concordia Mundi, The Career and Thought of Guillaume Postel* [1510–1581], Cambridge, Mass., 1957, p. 206). Other Christian references to the Spanish expulsion are mentioned in J. Hacker, "Some Letters on the Expulsion of the Jews from Spain and Sicily" (Hebrew), *Studies in the History of Jewish Society . . . Presented to Professor Jacob Katz*, Jerusalem, 1980, p. 64, note 2, especially the references to the works of Shmueli and Baron. One should also add to the above list Jean Bodin's *Heptaplomeres* and Johann Reuchlin's *De Arte Cabalistica*.
33. See Garin, "L'attesa," pp. 92ff. and J. Guttmann, Introduction to *Sefer Megillat Ha-Megale*, ed. A. Poznansky, Berlin, 1924; reprinted Jerusalem, 1968, pp. xxviiiff.
34. See Guttmann, pp. xxi ff. and Beit-Arié and Idel, "A Treatise on the End," p. 181, n. 37.
35. See note 21 above.
36. Vasoli, "Temi mistici," p. 224.
37. *Ibid.*
38. See especially, C. Roth, "The Last Years of Abraham Zakut," *Sefarad* 9 (1947): 445–54; D. Goldschmidt, "Bonetto Latis e i suoi scritti latini e italiani," in *Scritti in memoria di Enzo Sereni*, Jerusalem, 1970, pp. 88–94.
39. Scholem, "R. Abraham Eliezer Ha-Levi" (Hebrew), *Kiryat Sefer* 7 (1930): 163ff., 441.
40. Aescoly, *Ha-Tenu'ot*, p. 308.
41. *Ibid.*, pp. 309–10.
42. A. Z. Aescoly, ed. *Sippur David Ha-Reuveni*, Jerusalem, 1940, pp. 44–57, 171–78; idem, *Ha Tenu'ot*, pp. 354–59.
43. Aescoly, *Sippur*, pp. 183–89; idem, *Ha-Tenu'ot*, p. 381–84.
44. Aescoly, *Ha-Tenu'ot*, p. 386.
45. *Ibid.*, pp. 379–80.
46. *Ibid.*, p. 411.
47. Scholem, *Sabbatai Ẓevi*, p. 100; J. H. Leith, *Creeds of the Churches*, Garden City, N.Y., 1963, p. 73.
48. One might note here the preponderance of "heretical" Catholics or at least those outside "mainstream" Christianity who were especially attracted to manifestations of Jewish messianism. This interesting phenomenon merits further investigation.
49. Yet a number of intellectuals in Pico's circle were attracted to apocalypticism. See C. Vasoli, "Giovanni Nesi tra Donato Acciaivoli e Girolamo Savonarola. Testi editi e inediti, "in *Umanesimo e teologia tra '400 e '500,*

ed. A. F. Verde *et al.*, Pistoia, 1973, pp. 103–79; Weinstein, *Savonarola*, chap. 6; Garin, *La cultura filosofica*, pp. 180ff.

50. P.A. Kleinhaus, "De Vita et Operibus Petri Galatino O. F. M. scientiarum biblicarum cultoris (c. 1460–1540)," *Antonianium* I (1926), pp. 147–79, 327–56; Reeves, *The Influence of Prophecy*, pp. 234–38, 358, 366–67, 442–47.

51. J. W. O'Malley, *Giles of Viterbo: On Church and Reform, A Study in Renaissance Thought*, Leiden, 1968, Reeves. *The Influence of Prophecy*, pp. 235, 267–68, 270–71, 364–66, 441–42.

52. W. J. Bousma, *Concordia Mundi: The Career and Thought of Guillaume Postel (1510–1581)*, Cambridge, Mass., 1957; F. Secret, "Guillaume Postel et les courants prophétiques de la Renaissance," *Studi Francesci* I (1957): 375–95; Reeves, *The Influence of Prophecy*, pp. 287–89, 381–84, 479–81: M. Kuntz, *Guillaume Postel, Prophet of the Restitution of All Things: His Life and Thought*, The Hague, 1981.

53. Secret, "Guillaume Postel," pp. 371–81.

54. M. Idel, "The Writings of R. Abraham Abulafia and His Teaching" (Hebrew), PhD. dissertation, Hebrew University, Jerusalem, 1976, pp. 395–433; A. Berger, "The Messianic Self-Consciousness of Abraham Abulafia," J. L. Blau *et al.*, *Essays on Jewish Life and Thought*, New York, 1959, pp. 55–61.

55. On Abulafia's influence on Lemlein, see E. Kupfer, "The Visions of R. Asher b. Meir Lemlein of Reutlingen" (Hebrew), *Kovez al Yad* 8 (18) (1976): 397; on Molcho, see Idel, "Abulafia," p. 417; on the mystics of Safed, see R. J. Z. Werblowsky, *Joseph Karo, Lawyer and Mystic*, Philadelphia, 1977, pp. 38–39; Scholem, "Ha-Mekkubal R. Abraham Eliezer Ha-Levi" (Hebrew), *Kiryat Sefer* 2 (1925): 107, n. 4.

56. The "Jewish" influence of the Marranos on Christian millenary movements also merits further scrutiny, particularly the case of Brother Melchior and the Alumbrados of sixteenth century Spain. See G. H. Williams, *The Radical Reformation*, pp. 7–8; M. Bataillon, *Erasme et L'Espagne*, Paris, 1937, pp. 65ff.

57. Scholem, *Sabbatai Zevi*, p. 796.

58. *Ibid.*

59. *Ibid.*, pp. 282–85.

60. *Ibid.*, pp. 583–86.

61. Quoted from Yerushalmi, p. 336.

62. *Ibid.*, pp. 337–38; cf. Yerushalmi's discussion of Sabbatianism and Sebastianism, pp. 307ff.

63. See references in note 3 above; Yerushalmi, pp. 303–6, Sharot, *Messianism*, pp. 76–114 and now H. Beinart, "A Prophesying Movement in Cordova in 1499–1502" (Hebrew), in *Yizhak F. Baer Memorial Volume, Zion* 44 (1979): 190–200; *idem*, "The Prophetess Inés and her Movement in Peubla de Alcocer and Talarrubias" (Hebrew), *Tarbiz* 51 (1981): 631–58; *idem*, "The Prophetess Inés and Her Movement in her Hometown Herrera" (He-

brew), *Studies in Jewish Mysticism etc. presented to I. Tishby:* Jerusalem, 1986, pp. 459–506, *idem,* "Conversos of Chillón and Siruela and the Prophecies of Maria Goméz and Inés, the Daughter of Juan Esteban" (Hebrew), *Zion* 48 (1983): 241–72; and the other references to Beinart's work in Tishby, "Genizah Fragments," p. 355, note 206.

64. Baer, *A History of the Jews,* II, p. 424.
65. S. Molcho, *Sefer Ha-Mefo'ar,* Amsterdam, 1709, pp. 15a–15b. This has already been noticed by Scholem, *Sabbatai Zevi,* pp. 54, 309, no. 292.
66. Molcho, *Sefer Ha-Mefo'ar,* pp. 16b–17a.
67. See for example, pp. 15b, 20b, 21a.
68. See for example his sermon on "The Great Sabbath," pp. 22aff.
69. One of the primary sources for Molcho's biography is his book of visions entitled *Hayyat Kanel,* Amsterdam, 1658?. Another fascinating example of the transference of Christian eschatology to Judaism is found in the *Sefer ha-Meshiv.* See the illuminating article of M. Idel, "The Attitude to Christianity in the Sefer ha-Meshiv" (Hebrew), *Zion* 46 (1981): 77–91, especially 88–91. Idel even suggests the possibility of the author's converso ancestry (see p. 78 there).
70. Cf. Werblowsky, *Joseph Karo,* pp. 97ff.; Scholem, "The Maggid," p. 70.
71. For a useful summary, see Scholem, *Major Trends,* pp. 244–86 or Scholem, *Sabbatai Zevi,* chapter 1, as well as I. Tishby, *Torat ha-Ra ve-ha-kelipah bekabbalat ha-Ari,* Jerusalem, 1966.
72. On Lurianic *Tikkun,* see Scholem, *Major Trends,* pp. 268ff.; Scholem, *Sabbatai Zevi,* pp. 40ff. On the general concept of reform in early Christianity, see G. B. Ladner, *The Idea of Reform: Its Impact on Christian Thought and Action in the Age of the Fathers,* Cambridge, Mass., 1959.; N.Y. 1967. For the sixteenth century, see O'Malley, *Giles of Viterbo,* pp. 1ff; H. O. Evennett, *The Spirit of the Counter-Reformation,* Cambridge, 1968; H. Daniel-Rops, *The Catholic Reformation,* London, 1962; R. E. McNalley, "The Council of Trent, *The Spiritual Exercises* and the Catholic Reform," *Church History* 34 (1965): 36–49; J. C. Olin, *The Catholic Reformation: Savonarola to Ignatius Loyola,* New York, 1969; idem, "Erasmus and Reform," in *Desiderius Erasmus, Christian Humanism and the Reformation,* New York, 1965, pp. 1–21; Marocchi, *La riforma cattolica, documenti e testimonianze,* Brescia, 1967, 2 vols.; P. Janell, *The Catholic Reformation,* Milwaukee, 1963, pp. 183ff. On the general background of Church renewal, see the more recent works of J. Delumeau, *Catholicism between Luther and Voltaire,* London-Philadelphia, 1977; A. D. Wright, *The Counter-Reformation: Catholic Europe and the Non-Christian World,* London, 1982, with extensive bibliography.
73. Besides the two works of Scholem, see Werblowsky, *Joseph Karo,* chapter 4; Tishby, pp. 113ff.
74. *The Spiritual Exercises of St. Ignatius,* translated by A. Mottola, introduction by R. W. Gleason, Garden City, N.Y., 1964.
75. On the importance of human effort in Catholic reform, see especially Janell,

p. 153; Evennett, pp. 36ff.; Daniel-Rops, p. 35. For the Lurianic kabbalists, see the works of Scholem, Tishby, and Werblowsky as well as B. Sack, "The Mystical Theology of Solomon Alkabez" (Hebrew). Ph.D. dissertation, Brandeis University, 1978, pp. 171ff.

76. Quoted by Daniel-Rops, p. 35.

77. The parallel between the Catholic and Lurianic spiritual brotherhoods is especially interesting. On the latter, see Werblowsky, *Joseph Karo*, pp. 58ff and D. Tamar, "On the Associations of Safed" (Hebrew), in *Meḥkarim be-toledot Ha-Yehudim be-Ereẓ Yisra'el u-ve-Italya*, Jerusalem, 1970, pp. 95–100.

78. It is also misleading because some of the Lurian mystics, such as Ḥayyim Vital, engaged in techniques of spiritual preparation not only to make themselves worthy of God, as Loyola, but for magical purposes as well. On this, see Werblowsky, *Joseph Karo*, p. 48.

79. On the diverging paths of Christian reform and apocalyptical withdrawal, see the suggestive comments of G. Tellenbach, *Church, State and Christian Society at the Time of the Investiture Contest*, trans. by R. F. Bennett, Oxford, 1966, pp. 25ff.; McGinn, *Visions of the End*, p. 32; E. J. Hobsbawm, *Primitive Rebels: Studies in Archaic Forms of Social Movement in the 19th and 20th Centuries*, Manchester, 1959, pp. 58–59; cf. also, Werblowsky's distinctions between eschatological and reformative, active and passive messianism in *Encyclopaedia Britannica* 11, 1021; E. L. Tuveson, *Millennium and Utopia, A Study in the Background of the Idea of Progress*, Berkeley and Los Angeles, 1949, pp. 17–30. However, note the evidence Reeves brings for Jesuit reformers who were influenced by Joachimite ideas (Reeves, *The Influence of Prophecy*, pp. 274–76, 278–80, 287–88, 382). Postel himself viewed the Jesuits as the principal agency of reform and part of an eschatological divine pattern, but the Jesuits later expelled him.

80. O'Malley, *Giles of Viterbo*, p. 148.

81. This is fully described in the works of Scholem and Tishby cited in note 71 above.

82. See especially, Williams, *The Radical Reformation*, pp. 857–65. Cf. Strauss, *Manifestations of Discontent* and L. H. Zuck, *Christianity and Revolution, Radical Christian Testimonies 1520–1650*. Philadelphia, 1975; N. Cohn, *The Pursuit of the Millennium: Revolutionary Millenarians and Mystical Anarchists of the Middle Ages*, expanded and revised London, 1970; S. Ozment, *Mysticism and Dissent, Religious Ideology and Social Protest in the 16th Century*, New Haven and London, 1973.

11

Particularism and Universalism in Kabbalah, 1480–1650

Moshe Idel

I

With the conclusion of the Jewish exodus from the Iberian Peninsula, Kabbalah had lost its oldest and most vital stronghold. Though it was originally an alien lore to the Andalusian and Castilian culture of the Jews, Kabbalah succeeded in infiltrating into the major centers of Jewish creativity in Northern Spain, Barcelona, and Toledo with their smaller satellite towns and to establish itself as the inner interpretation of Judaism. From the beginning of the thirteenth century until the Expulsion, Kabbalah was gradually absorbed, adapted, and cultivated among a considerable part of the Spanish Jewish elite, whence it radiated in all directions: the Franco-Ashkenazi provinces, Italy, North Africa, Byzantine, and the Mameluk Empire. However, almost all of these centers remained under the dominant influence of Spanish Kabbalah.

I would like to survey the history of Spanish Kabbalah as a sequence of four stages:

A. The philosophical interpretation of the earlier esoteric traditions, which reached Catalonia from Provence and the Franco-Ashkenazi Jewish centers. This mainly Catalonian stage is manifested in three differing approaches:

(1) The Geronese center,[1] whose main figures were R. Ezra, R. Azriel, and R. Jacob ben Sheshet, mingled the theosophical and theurgical traditions which they received directly from the Provençal

center with Neoplatonic concepts. Crucial for the understanding of this Kabbalistic school, in contrast to the ecstatic Kabbalah, is the importance of theurgic activity (i.e., operations intended to influence the theosophical structure). This Kabbalistic school was active between approximately 1200 and 1260.

(2) The Ecstatic Kabbalah, which seems to have emerged in Barcelona, where Abraham Abulafia had studied Ashkenazic traditions concerning combinatory techniques,[2] which he merged with Aristotelian—mainly Maimonidean—speculations. If there was a circle which elaborated upon this type of Kabbalah, it cannot be traced any later than the early seventies of the thirteenth century.[3]

(3) A thinker who flourished in the mid-thirteenth century, R. Isaac ibn Latif, apparently independent of any crystallized Kabbalistic group, cultivated a peculiar type of Neoplatonic theosophy.[4]

B. Mythical Kabbalah, which flourished in Castile in the second half of the thirteenth century and early fourteenth century.[5] This branch of Kabbalah encompasses several smaller circles: the school of the brothers R. Jacob and Isaac ha-Cohen and their followers, the circle of R. Moses de Leon and R. Joseph Gikatilla, the *Zohar* and the huge literature connected to it. Roughly speaking, all these groups were interested in complex theosophies, generally nonphilosophical and at times even antiphilosophical in their essential approaches.

C. Still in Castile, we find between 1330 and 1400 significant attempts to interpret Kabbalah philosophically. The main exponents of this trend are R. Joseph ibn Waqqar and R. Samuel ibn Zarza, who envisioned Kabbalah as the highest human lore without, however, rejecting the importance of astronomy, astrology, occult sciences, and philosophy.[6] Heavily influenced by stage A, these authors only rarely refer to the basic concepts of stage B, notwithstanding their proximity in both space and time.

D. Following the sad events of 1391, acid antiphilosophical treatises on Kabbalah were composed, again in Castile. The most important contributions to Kabbalah in general and to antiphilosophical polemics in Judaism in particular until the Expulsion were R. Shem Tov ben Shem Tov's *Sefer ha-Emunot* and the anonymous *Sefer ha-Meshiv*.[7] These works draw mainly upon Kabbalistic treatises composed in stage B, almost totally ignoring those written in stage A.

The first book does not contain a demonization of philosophy—

or Christianity—notwithstanding its acid attacks against Jewish philosophy. R. Shem Tov's critique is conducted in a rather analytical
way, pointing out the extreme dangers for religion inherent in the
philosophical approach. The latter is characterized, as we shall see
later on, by a demonization of philosophy in general, without both-
ering to detail the weak points of this "satanic" lore. We may
therefore assume that during the few decades that separate the writing of these two works, a considerable shift in the negative evaluation of philosophy is notable in Kabbalistic literature.

The Expulsion found Spanish Kabbalah in its extreme antiphilosophical phase. However, this approach, which had ripened in the Iberian
Peninsula during the previous hundred years, was in fact unknown
beyond the boundary of Castile. Italian Kabbalah was then decisively
influenced by the first three stages of Spanish Kabbalah, and its preponderant inclination was prophilosophical.[8] Less philosophically biased
were Byzantium and Northern and Central Europe, in which no clear
direction had as yet emerged in the wake of the arrival of the various
waves of Kabbalistic thought from Spain. Northern Africa was only
slightly concerned with Kabbalah, and the scanty references to this lore
betray mainly speculative—and only secondarily mythical—interests.
Our knowledge of Kabbalah in fifteenth-century Palestine is close to nil.

II

At the time of the Expulsion, there were only two active, consolidated
interpretations of Kabbalah: (a) the Spanish one, rooted in classical
Kabbalistic texts such as the *Zohar,* was mythical and antiphilosophical,
and already had behind it a short history, with strong particularistic
tendencies, namely, as a lore unique to the Jews; and (b) the emerging
philosophical Kabbalah in Italy, backed by thirteenth- and fourteenth-
century ecstatic and speculative Spanish Kabbalah, on the one hand, and
consonant with the Renaissance thought flourishing then in the circle of
Marsilio Ficino and Pico della Mirandola, on the other. The Italian
Kabbalah, both Jewish and Christian, drew upon relatively non-"classical" Kabbalah: i.e., that of R. Abraham Abulafia, R. Isaac ibn Latif and
the fourteenth-century authors listed in stage C.

The eradication of Spanish Jewry created the possibility of a meeting

and confrontation between these two phases of Kabbalah as living entities; this meeting indeed took place in Italy, and there were more than
mere frictions. I should like to focus upon the main lines of evolution of
these two types of Kabbalah either independently or in confrontation
with one another. *Mutatis mutandis,* Italian Kabbalah may be viewed as
a continuation of stages A and C of Spanish Kabbalah, while most
North-African, Ashkenazic, and Safedian Kabbalah constituted the heirs
of stages B and D.

The first pair of conflicting attitudes to be considered here is that of
the esoteric versus the exoteric view of Kabbalah. Though Kabbalah is
commonly regarded as an esoteric lore, the emphasis upon its esotericism
is most obvious in the mythical phases, B and D, the other stages A and
C being less valued in this feature of Kabbalah. The Geronese Kabbalists
seem to have been the first propagators of Kabbalah in public. Abraham
Abulafia even tried to convince Christians of the truth of his version of
Kabbalah, after he failed to convince Jews in Spain, Greece, and Italy of
his Kabbalistic and messianic claims. R. Judah ben Nissim ibn Malkah
devoted two treatises in Arabic to issues related to Kabbalah; later on,
R. Joseph ibn Waqqar wrote a concordance between Kabbalah and
philosophy in Arabic, indeed a rather bizarre way to confine Kabbalah
to Jewish circles alone. This open approach to Kabbalah is inherent in
its speculative interpretation; the philosophization of Kabbalah is intrin-
sicly also its translation into, and sometimes even reduction to, the
commonly shared philosophical jargon. In Spain, this terminology was
derived from a few Neoplatonic sources in Gerona, or from the Avicen-
nian-Averroistic school in the fourteenth century. In Italy, such scholars
as Johanan Alemanno, David Messer Leon, Abraham de Balmes, and
Judah Abravanel (Leone Ebreo) introduced further Neoplatonic and
Aristotelian conceptions in their casting of Kabbalah into a philosophical mold. This avenue was later further broadened by Abraham Herrera,
Abraham Yagel, Joseph Delmedigo of Candia, and Menasseh ben Israel.[9] Exposing Kabbalah philosophically is tantamount to an efface-
ment of its idiosyncracy, and opens the way for anyone expert in philosophy—Jew as well as Gentile—to understand it.

This approach was facilitated by the assumption shared by most of
the above-mentioned authors, namely, that non-Jewish philosophy, mainly
Greek and particularly that of Plato, was originally taken from ancient
Jewish masters. Given this ultimate Jewish extraction of Greek lore, it

may legitimately be used to expose the other remnants of ancient Jewish lore: Kabbalah. This Judaizing of philosophy also has another goal: it combated the theory, elaborated since Ficino and Pico, of the pagan origin of ancient theology, independent of, albeit similar to, the true religion as it was embodied in the Old and New Testaments.[10]

Another testimony to this exoteric turn in Kabbalah is the appearance of a new branch of Christian theology: Christian Kabbalah. The major contributions to its emergence were indeed made by apostates: Flavius Mithridates, Paulus Riccius, Felix Pratensis, etc., who translated the most important Kabbalistic treatises into Latin and Italian, thereby making their contents available to a Christian audience. Their activity cannot be seen as part of a change in the understanding of Kabbalah among the Jews; nevertheless, the contribution of Jewish persons to the spread of Kabbalistic lore among the Christians must also be taken into account. It is obvious that R. Elijah Delmedigo was instrumental in procuring Kabbalistic manuscripts for Pico;[11] we may assume that the relationship between Johanan Alemanno and Pico, or Eliahu (Bahur) Levita and Egidio da Viterbo, left their impression on the Christian theologians' knowledge of Kabbalah. No wonder that in sixteenth-century Italy we witness an interest in the halakhic interdiction against disclosing Jewish esotericism to Gentiles.[12] One Kabbalist, after describing the eagerness of the Christians to study Kabbalah under Jewish tutorship, recommends that the Jews answer the request of the Christian nobles in these words:[13]

> In my house there is neither bread nor clothes, and the books [i.e. the Kabbalistic works] are very rare, and those which are in our hands are written in an awkward and highly symbolic language, which it is impossible to understand without an instructor who will transmit their theses mouth to mouth, since the ancient ones [Kabbalists] concealed their intention in that [difficult] language.

Indeed, not very elegant pretexts, and I doubt if they were effective, given the large amounts of money Christians were able and willing to invest in order to study the ancient Jewish lore.

In a letter to R. Abraham of Perugia, R. Elijah Halfan's elder contemporary, a certain R. Israel, refrains from sending his messianic calculations to Italy:[14]

> In my opinion, it is dangerous to send them[15] to you, since, as we were told, many of our brothers,[16] the sons of Esau learn the Hebrew language . . . and who will write something hither, when it is prone to fall in their hands.

Again, he indicates that his messianic speculations are esoteric issues and therefore: [17]

I refrained [from] sending you these folios of the *Iggeret Sod ha-Ge'ulah*,[18] and you who are my masters are concealing the knowledge, and the secret of God is [intended] to those who fear Him, all the sons of the covenant may see it, but it shall not be done so to every nation.

Therefore, sensitive matters concerning the eschaton, which were fraught with deep anti-Christian feelings, must be kept out of the reach of Italian Jews, lest they be transmitted to Christians. Indeed, according to the author, this is a very reasonable imperative, the punishment for whose transgression is banishment.[19]

An interesting refraction of the Christian readiness to study Kabbalah appears in R. Hayyim Vital's diary of dreams. In one of his dreams, he was forcibly taken to the "Caesar of Rome" who, in a private interview, appeals to the Kabbalist, saying: [20]

"I know that there is no one wiser and more erudite in the Kabbalah than you are. I wish you to let me know the secrets of the Torah[21] and some of the divine names[22] of your God, since I have already recognized the truth; therefore, do not be afraid that I have sent to bring you, since I indeed love you." Then I let him know something of this lore; and I woke up.

This dream, which took place in 1607, represents, together with R. Israel's view adduced above, both the awareness of the Kabbalists that Christians are interested in acquiring knowledge of the foremost Jewish esoteric lore, as well as the Jewish opposition—in the case of the above-cited epistle—or hesitation[23]—in the case of Vital—to transferring this knowledge to their religious enemies. Among the Christian figures interested in Kabbalah, we must mention not only such lay intellectuals as Pico, Ficino, Reuchlin, or Cornelius Agrippa, but also a cardinal—Egidio da Viterbo—and even a Pope, Clemens VII.[24] This Judeo-Christian cooperation is not evidenced by overt statements or descriptions, since the Jews were legally prohibited from disclosing the secrets of the Torah to Gentiles; this activity was done in the shadow of the studies of Christian nobles and dignitaries, but, I suppose, would have been vigorously denied in public by the Jewish masters.

Limited as it may have been, this cultural cooperation of Jewish and Christian scholars had an amazing impact on the dissemination of Kabbalah. A short comparative survey of the printing and propagation of

Kabbalistic treatises until the end of the first half of the sixteenth century will clarify this point. The first printed Kabbalistic works were those written by Christians or apostates; Pico della Mirandola's *Theses,* Reuchlin's two books on Kabbalah, Paulus Riccius translations and theses and, above all, Francesco Giorgio's *De Harmonia Mundi* deeply influenced European occultism in Italy, Germany, France, Bohemia, and England.[25] At the same time that the Kabbalah was cultivated in small Jewish elites, which used manuscripts exclusively, the Christian intelligentsia were studying the principles of Kabbalah in a number of printed handbooks. Moreover, the Christians were not only pioneers in printing Kabbalistic books in Latin, which they themselves authored; in at least one instance, it is obvious that a Christian editor printed Kabbalistic material in Hebrew, a part of it being extant solely in this edition, while others are rare samples of Kabbalistic texts.[26] The willingness of Christians to propagate Kabbalistic lore thus contributed, in at least one clearcut case, to the preservation of Hebrew material. Earlier Jewish Kabbalistic traditions have likewise been preserved solely in the Latin version of Paulus Riccius.[27] All these activities, as well as a multitude of translations in Latin,[28] were accomplished before the first massive printing of Hebrew Kabbalistic works at the end of the 1550s. Significantly enough, G. Postel, who was, *inter alia,* also deeply influenced by Kabbalah, encouraged the printing of the *Zohar*—a subject of bitter controversy in Jewish circles.[29] Ironically enough, the first disseminators of esoteric Jewish lore were Christians and apostates.

III

A distinctive feature of particularistic Kabbalah was the continuous transmission of Kabbalistic lore from masters to students; thus, Spanish Kabbalah did not disappear with the destruction of its stronghold, but was preserved, transmitted, and elaborated by the offsprings of the exiles and their disciples. The Spanish Kabbalists established groups of students, either in Turkey or in Jerusalem and in Safed, where the traditions learned in Spain were directly passed down, the written form of transmission being only one way of teaching Kabbalah. Isaac Luria, for example, learned the Spanish mystical tradition orally from David ibn Zimra. An interesting example of continuous transmission is Abraham ha-Levi: he drew upon the partially pre-Expulsion Kabbalistic school of

Sefer ha-Meshiv, but also mentions his master of Kabbalah, R. Isaac Gakon,[30] who was the student of R. Isaac de Leon. The latter is quoted as the author of a passage remarkably close to *Sefer ha-Meshiv*;[31] thus, Abraham ha-Levi's affinity to the ideas of *Sefer ha-Meshiv* also seems to stem from oral study. On the other hand, Abraham ha-Levi's eschatological views, as explicated in *Perush le-Nevu'at ha-Yeled* (Commentary on the Visions of the Child), were studied in Jerusalem by "those who are perfect" in his own lifetime.[32]

Most of the active Kabbalists in Italy at the end of the fifteenth century were autodidacts; David Messer Leon studied Kabbalah, seemingly alone, in a hostile environment.[33] Alemanno, who studied under Judah Messer Leon, an anti-Kabbalistic thinker,[34] never mentions any other teacher, and all he knew about Kabbalah seems to have been extracted almost exclusively from written books. As far as Abraham de Balmes is concerned, we have no knowledge of his studying Kabbalah with any teacher.

This basic difference between the Kabbalah of the Spaniards and that of the Italians may explain the latter's readiness to explain it according to alien concepts; as there were no authoritative masters to limit their hermeneutical freedom by imposing the basic meaning of the Kabbalistic texts as "genuine" Kabbalah, persons like David Messer Leon, Alemanno, and de Balmes could freely use and superimpose philosophical nomenclature on Kabbalah. No wonder that Spanish Kabbalists who arrived in Italy protested against the "speculative Kabbalah," which was opposed by them to the authentic "prophetic" or "revealed Kabbalah,"[35] which seems to stand for the Zoharic Kabbalah.[36] The fact that Italian Kabbalists were autodidacts may have contributed to their willingness to disclose the contents of Kabbalah to Christian scholars; one who was not part of a long series of Kabbalists who orally transmitted this lore, presumably in a dense atmosphere of esotericism, had little reason not to impart whatever he learned by himself or his own syntheses to those interested in ancient Jewish theology.

I would now like to dwell briefly upon a related issue which is of paramount importance for the later development of Kabbalah. The particularistic Kabbalah, since its emergence in Spain, proposed revelation as the main means of attaining Kabbalistic secrets.[37] Since the end of the fifteenth century, in Spain, North Africa, Byzantium, Eastern Europe, but especially in the Land of Israel, revelatory experiences gradually came to the forefront of Jewish awareness. This was, in my opinion, part of a deep restructuring of the Jewish mind,[38] complemented by a gradual retreat of philosophy within the economy of Jewish culture and the ascent of asceticism in the practices of the Jewish elite.[39] I surmise that this was an organic development only marginally touched by external factors. At exactly the same period, namely the end of the fifteenth century and the beginning of the sixteenth the appearance of revelations became more manifest in an Ashkenazic figure like R. Asher Lemlein; among the exiles of Spain in Turkey, in the anonymous author of *Sefer Kaf ha-Ketoret* and in *Sefer Gallei Razaya;* or in R. Judah Albotini's work *Sullam ha-ʿAliyah* in Jerusalem. This evolution became more evident in the Kabbalah of Safed, flourished thereafter among Sabbatian figures, and reached its peak in early Hasidism.[40] The universalistic Kabbalah was only partially interested in revelations or mystical techniques, as the writings of David Messer Leon, Alemanno, Moscato, Yagel, Delmedigo, and Herrera convincingly demonstrate. We witness here the dichotomy of revelation-reason as inherent in the diversification of Kabbalistic trends in our period.

IV

The universalistic perception of Kabbalah, embraced by some Jewish Kabbalists living in Italy and by Christian intellectuals in Europe, was a secondary by-product of the initial contacts of Spanish Kabbalah with Renaissance culture during the period 1480–1650; the mainstream of Kabbalistic creativity had only little to do with this cultural symbiosis. The major centers of Kabbalistic thought after the Expulsion—Northern Africa, the Ottoman Empire, and Palestine—continued the impetus of stage D of Spanish Kabbalah, only rarely combined with some influences of Renaissance culture, and occasionally integrating the ecstatic Kabbalah of Abulafia and his followers. In our context, it is pertinent to compare the principal features of this mainstream with those of the universalistic Kabbalah. Its outstanding characteristic is a sharp antiphilosophical attitude. While an examination of the variety of post-Expulsion expressions against philosophy is beyond the scope of this discussion, I should like to elaborate upon a few of them which are particularly relevant for a comparative survey of the two main types of Kabbalah. The first quotation stems from the anonymous commentary on the

Psalms named *Kaf ha-Ketoret*, which was probably composed in former Byzantine territory,[41] apparently in the first decade[42] of the sixteenth century:[43]

"A perverse heart shall depart from me, [I will know no] evil matter."[44] These are the wise men of philosophy, who pervert their heart by the [study of] physics according to the views of the philosophers, who are confused in the land, shut in by the wilderness.[45] . . . But some of the wise men of our nation did not cry to God to show them a tree, but they cried to Aristotle[46] the wicked, and he showed them his venom, a tree,[47] according to his wisdom from the side of Sammael the wicked, who is his god. And they provided power to Sammael the wicked, who reached a higher degree than he [previously] was. . . . [When he died] the soul of a great wise man was brought before God in the supernal academy, and they asked him: "What did you study?" And he spoke about the philosophical divine sciences.[48] [Then] God cries to him, in His role of head of the academy: "A perverse heart shall depart from me," and He Himself causes him to descend in the great abyss.[49]

As against the Judaization of philosophy among the Italian Jews, here our anonymous Kabbalist, continuing a certain Spanish trend,[50] manifestly demonizes it; demonic venom has infiltrated into Judaism and its success enhances the power of Sammael. The gap between Kabbalah and philosophy is therefore irreducible; according to this Kabbalist, salvation will be possible only when philosophy is forgotten and the works of R. Simeon bar Yohai, namely the *Zohar*, are widespread.[51]

However, the demonization of philosophy is complemented by a demonization of Christianity; against the Christian portrait of Judaism as "synagoga diaboli," those Kabbalists who demonized philosophy perceived Christianity as an "ecclesia diaboli."[52] This antiphilosophical, anti-Christian, and demonological Kabbalah influenced certain Kabbalistic works written in the Ottoman Empire in the sixteenth century: R. Abraham ha-Levi's works,[53] *Sefer Gallei Razaya*,[54] R. Isaac Ezovi's *Agudat Ezov*,[55] R. Moshe Cordovero,[56] R. Ovadia Hamon,[57] R. Hayyim Vital in Safed[58] and, directly[59] and indirectly,[60] seventeenth-century Ashkenazic Kabbalah[61] and Sabbatianism.[62] In the East, the particularistic trend of Kabbalah became prevalent; philosophy was denigrated as was Christianity. Kabbalah again became the singular Jewish lore which cannot and should not be translated into alien terminology or a foreign language, nor taught directly to Gentiles. In Luria, the emphasis upon the esoteric nature of Kabbalah reached its peak; only a few elite Kabbalists were permitted to attend his lectures,[63] as was also Vital's practice.[64]

The reaction against philosophy in the second half of the sixteenth century is deserving of closer scrutiny; Isaac Luria and his Polish friend R. Joseph Ashkenazi not only opposed philosophy, but also those Kabbalistic treatises which were influenced by philosophical thought.[65] The scope of "authentic" Kabbalah was drastically limited and, for Luria, only Kabbalistic works which were composed as the result of revelations were considered authoritative.[66]

We may describe stage D of the Spanish Kabbalah, and that Kabbalah which continued it, including the Lurianic one, as a withdrawal from alien influences and concentration upon some basic concepts, found already in stage B, which had hitherto not come to the forefront. The expansion of the range of Kabbalah in Italy so far beyond its normal boundaries as to include Platonic thought ended in a process of disintegration of the basic ground of Kabbalah: a dynamic theosophy and theurgy. It is exactly these two domains that were manifestly reinforced by Lurianic Kabbalah; through the "purification" of Kabbalah of "alien" influences, its idiosyncratic religious thought was put in relief beyond the former stages of conservative Kabbalah. This last point is highly significant for an understanding of Kabbalistic creativity: the withdrawal of Kabbalah from large-scale influences from outside allowed for more intense creative effort and far-reaching intellectual results; this is true of the Zohar, Lurianic Kabbalah, and Hasidism. On the other hand, the openness to extraneous concepts has only rarely produced systems which represented milestones in the history of Kabbalistic thought. As far as Kabbalah is concerned, it would seem that the intense interaction with alien thought effaced its particular structures, whereas the endeavor to avoid them catalyzed the emergence of more important works.

V

The continuity of stages B and D of Spanish Kabbalah into the Lurianic one may be demonstrated in a short survey of the problem of the origin of evil. The view that evil stems from the highest divine realm is already explicit in the Zohar and works written in its intellectual environment, such as those of Joseph of Hamdam and David ben Judah he-Hasid.[67] These Kabbalists affirmed that the ultimate source of evil is the Divine

thought, or that the appearance of the evil forces preceded that of the
holy ones. These views were reiterated in stage D by R. Shem Tov ben
Shem Tov[68] and by the anonymous author of Kabbalistic responsa
previously attributed to R. Joseph Gikatilla.[69] Following the Expulsion,
a long and continuous series of Kabbalists reiterated this theme in their
works: R. Joseph Alcastiel,[70] R. Judah Ḥayyat,[71] R. Meir ibn Gabbai,[72]
R. Judah Ḥallena,[73] and R. Mattitiahu Delacrut,[74] to mention only a
few names.[75] Luria was therefore the heir to a certain traditional conception of the source of evil, a point which renders doubtful the construc-
tions of affinities between his Kabbalah and certain historical events.[76]
Moreover, it seems to me that Luria was less an innovator of daring new
ideas than the constructor of a more comprehensive system out of earlier
Kabbalistic traditions.

This conservative perception of Luria's thought seems to me relevant
for our understanding of the formation of his system in general. As we
know, Scholem proposed a well-known theory on the ultimate origin of
some of Luria's basic views on the dramatic events of Expulsion and
Exile; according to this view, Luria gave expression, in Kabbalistic
terminology, to the dreadful fate of the Iberian Peninsula, and his Kabbalistic thought is presented by Scholem as an attempt to cope with the
plight of the people of Israel after the Expulsion.[77] This type of explanation takes into account historical elements whose actual influence on
doctrinal issues is rather difficult to demonstrate, while the inner development of Kabbalah as a mystical-mythical system is thereby neglected.
The elucidation of the origins of such crucial conceptions in Lurianic
Kabbalah as *Zimzum* (Withdrawal), *Shevirat ha-kelim* (Breaking), and
Adam Qadmon or *Tiqqun* (Restoration) must be conducted against the
background of existing traditions before we turn to other solutions. As I
have already pointed out, at least on the issue of the supernal origin of
evil, Luria is but a later link in the chain of Kabbalistic thought; this is,
in my opinion, also the case as far as the other key notions are concerned.[78] But whatever extent Kabbalistic texts may be partial or fuller
sources for Luria's system, it seems to me reasonable that the nexus
between history and doctrine, Expulsion and Exile, on the one hand,
and Kabbalah, on the other, is highly hypothetical, for several reasons:

1. The Spanish Kabbalists, who underwent the hardest ordeals, never
mixed personal events with doctrinal discussions, as we learn from their
works. Even close perusal of R. Judah Hayyat's *Minḥat Yehudah* reveals

no allusions to the Expulsion, except for the famous autobiographical preface. This also seems to be the situation with regard to other Kabbalists. Indeed, the lengthy Kabbalistic works of R. Meir ibn Gabbai, R. Abraham Adrutiel, and R. Joseph Alashkar never combine the Expulsion with Kabbalah or interpret this historical event according to Kabbalistic notions.[79] This is also true of David ibn Zimra, one of Luria's masters. However, discussions of the religious causes of the Expulsion, including attempts at theodicy, occur in the works of thinkers who cannot be regarded as Kabbalists in the technical meaning of the word, such as Isaac Abravanel, Joseph Jabez, and R. Isaac Arama.[80] Moreover, some Jewish historiographers even saw the arrival of masses of Jews in close proximity to the Land of Israel as part of the eschatological scheme, which came about partly as a result of the initiative of the Spanish ruler, inspired by God, to expel the Jews from his land.[81]

2. As an intellectual reaction to a "catastrophic" Expulsion cannot be viewed as a concern of the Spanish Kabbalists themselves, we must, according to Scholem, postpone the Kabbalistic reaction to this event, and to Exile in general, to that generation which did not experience the drama of Expulsion. Moreover, we must also suppose that the Kabbalistic response to Expulsion was produced not only in the land of Israel —itself a rather interesting paradox—but also by an individual who was of Ashkenazic extraction. Why should the young Luria, who undertook upon himself various ascetic practices, have regarded the dislocation of Spanish Jewry as a catastrophe, if its ultimate result was the arrival of Kabbalists in the Land of Israel and the emergence of an intense religious life in Safed? It seems to me that we must understand what appears to be Luria's indifference toward the Expulsion against the wider background of Jewish response to it. An examination of the treatment of the Expulsion will easily reveal that the only Jews who were impressed by and interested in this event were, almost exclusively, Spanish Jews.[82] Italian and Ashkenazic Jewry were probably ready to help their brethren, but not to interiorize their expulsion. I shall offer one example: Johanan Alemanno, who wrote most of his voluminous works immediately after the Expulsion in an environment where Spanish Jews were influential, never mentions this historical event.[83] Though Alemanno was more historically oriented, his contemporary and compatriot R. Asher Lemlein, a messianic visionary who composed his works and propagated his ascetic and messianic message during the decade

following the Expulsion, offers no eschatological perception, or even mention, of the Expulsion in his extant writings. We know that he had contact with Spanish Kabbalists, but his attitude toward Spanish Kabbalah was negative.[84]

Any attempt to overemphasize the centrality of the "catastrophic" nature of the Expulsion must not underrate this indifference. As far as Luria's own interest in the Expulsion is concerned, it seems to be no greater than that of Alemanno and Lemlein: nil. Insofar as I could survey his authentic writings, the Expulsion is never mentioned. This also seems to hold true regarding the attitude of Hayyim Vital: an Italian by origin, he seems to ignore the historical dimension of the Expulsion, to say nothing of its metaphysical impact on his Kabbalah. The total absence of this issue weighs, in my opinon, far more heavily than any intellectual construction.

Therefore, I propose to exchange the conceptual explanation of the emergence of Lurianic Kabbalah on historical grounds for a reevaluation of the extant, though neglected, Kabbalistic material in print and manuscript.[85] As interesting as the broader speculations may be, they never engage either in detailed analysis of Lurianic texts or in detailed description of the way history was metamorphosed into mythical Kabbalah; as we well know, the absence of evidence corroborating a certain hypothesis cannot be successfully substituted by bright insights or eloquent formulations.

Thus, the alternation of speculative and mythical elements in Spanish Kabbalah and thereafter is tantamount with the ascent, respectively, of universalistic and particularistic features. I am not quite sure that this is only part of an inner rhythm of Kabbalah, as has been assumed by Isaiah Tishby.[86] I would suggest that stages A and C in Spanish Kabbalah were induced by speculative interest in the intellectual environments of their times, as the emergence of the Renaissance thought had contributed in one way or another to the cultivation of an open and intellectualistic approach to Kabbalah.[87] The understanding of the processes which conditioned the peculiar ways in which Kabbalah developed must naturally take into account more than one line of explanation: both the inner, endogenous or organic processes[88] and external influences molded Kabbalah, just as they molded other types of thought. However, I am highly doubtful whether historical events played such a dominant role as they are supposed to have, according to modern scholarship.

NOTES

1. See Gershom Scholem, *Origins of the Kabbalah*, trans. A. Arkush, ed. R. Z. Zwi Werblowsky (Princeton, 1987), 365–460; idem, *Kabbalah* (Jerusalem, 1974), 48–52. I would like to point out that I exclude Nahmanides' Kabbalah from this trend of thought, *inter alia*, because of his negative attitude to philosophy.
2. See Moshe Idel, *R. Abraham Abulafia's Works and Doctrines* (Heb.), Ph.D. dissertation, Hebrew University (Jerusalem: 1976), 255–56. On Abulafia in general, see Gershom Scholem, *Major Trends in Jewish Mysticism* (New York, 1967), 119–55.
3. I assume that this circle was active in Barcelona. By the middle of the 1270s, Abulafia had left Spain forever, and the interest in the ecstatic-linguistic Kabbalah drastically declined there, although it continued its evolution elsewhere. See also Scholem, *Kabbalah* (n. 1 above), 53–55.
4. On this figure, see Sara O. Heller-Wilensky, "Isaac Ibn Latif: Philosopher or Kabbalist?" in *Jewish Medieval and Renaissance Studies*, ed. Alexander Altmann (Cambridge, Mass., 1967), 185–223; Scholem, *Kabbalah* (n. 1 above), 52–54.
5. See Scholem, *Kabbalah* (n. above), 55–61.
6. See Moshe Idel, "The Magical and Neoplatonic Interpretations of the Kabbalah in the Renaissance," in *Jewish Thought in the Sixteenth Century*, ed. Bernard D. Cooperman (Cambridge, Mass., 1983), 209–11.
7. See Moshe Idel, "Inquiries into the Thought of *Sefer ha-Meshiv*" (Heb.), *Sefunot* 2, no. 17 (1980): 185–266, especially 232–43.
8. See Idel, "The Magical and Neoplatonic Interpretations" (n. 6 above), 188–89.
9. Alexander Altmann, "Lurianic Kabbala in a Platonic Key: Abraham Cohen Herrera's *Puerta del Cielo*," *Hebrew Union College Annual* 53 (1982): 317–55; Moshe Idel, "Kabbalah, Platonism and *Prisca Theologia*—The Case of R. Menasseh ben Israel," in *Menasseh ben Israel and his World*, ed. Y. Kaplan, Henry Mechoulan, and Richard H. Popkin (Leiden, 1989), 207–19; idem, "Major Currents in Italian Kabbalah between 1560–1660," in *Italia Judaica* 2 (Rome, 1986), 2: 243–62 (see chapter 12 of the present volume); David Ruderman, *Kabbalah, Magic and Science, The Cultural Universe of a Sixteenth-Century Jewish Physician* (Cambridge, Mass., 1988).
10. On the entire problem, see Moshe Idel, "Kabbalah and the Ancient Philosophy in R. Isaac and Jehudah Abravanel" (Heb.), in *Filosofiyah ha-ahavah shel Yehudah Abarvanel*, ed. M. Dorman and Z. Levi (Tel Aviv, 1985), 73–112. On the proud attitude of Jews in Italy toward their cultural heritage, see Reuven Bonfil, "Expressions of Uniqueness of the Jewish People in Italy in the Renaissance Period" (Heb.), *Sinai* 76 (1975): 36–46.
11. See Bohdan Kieszkowski, "Les rapports entre Elie del Medigo et Pic de la Mirandole," *Rinascimento* 4 (1964): 41–90.

12. See David Kaufmann, "Elia Menahem Chalfan on Jews Teaching Hebrew to Non-Jews," *JQR* 9 (O.S.) (1896): 500–508; Meir Benayahu, "Kabbalah and Halakhah—A Confrontation" (Heb.), *Da'at* 5 (1980): 90, 94, etc. The entire issue is deserving of closer study.

13. This is part of the end of R. Eliahu Menahem Halfan's epistle on the history of Kabbalah, MS. New York JTS 1822, fol. 154b. On the relationship between a Jewish teacher and his Christian student, see David B. Ruderman, *The World of a Renaissance Jew: The Life and Thought of Abraham ben Mordecai Farissol* (Cincinnati, 1981), 98–106.

14. Cf. the version printed in Abraham David, "A Jerusalemite Epistle from the beginning of the Ottoman Empire in the Land of Israel" (Heb.), in *Peraqim be-toledot Yerushalayim be-reshit ha-Empiryah ha-'Ottomanit* (Jerusalem, 1979), 59. David proposes there the authorship of R. Abraham ha-Levi (ibid. 46–47). Kaufmann, "Elia Menahem Chalfan (n. 12 above) has already referred to this text in his discussion on the interdiction against disclosing Kabbalistic secrets to Gentiles (p. 500, n. 5).

15. He refers to *Perush le-nevu'at ha-yeled* by R. Abraham ben Eliezer ha-Levi.

16. This designation of the Christians is rather curious if the epistle was indeed authored by R. Abraham ha-Levi (see n. 14 above). Even in the most positive descriptions of the Christians, they were never called by R. Abraham ha-Levi "brothers"; see, e.g., the text printed by Ira Robinson, "Two Letters of Abraham ben Eliezer Ha-Levi," in *Studies in Medieval Jewish History and Literature,* ed. Isadore Twersky, (Cambridge, Mass., 1984), 2: 409.

17. David, "A Jerusalemite Epistle" (n. 14 above), p. 59.

18. This is another treatise by R. Abraham ha-Levi.

19. David, "A Jerusalemite Epistle" (n. 14 above), p. 59. On the sharp Jewish reaction to the emerging Christian Kabbalah, see Ruderman, *The World* (n. 13 above), 51–56; M. Idel, "Differing Perceptions of Kabbalah in the Early 17th Century," in *Jewish Thought in the Seventeenth Century,* ed. Isadore Twersky and Bernard Septimus (Cambridge, Mass., 1987), 166–71.

20. *Sefer ha-Ḥezyonot,* ed. A. Z. Aescoli (Jerusalem, 1954), 68. On some other aspects of this passage, see Idel, "Shelomo Molkho qua Magician" (Heb.), *Sefunot* 3, no. 18 (1985): 216–17.

21. I.e., speculative Kabbalah.

22. I.e., practical Kabbalah.

23. It seems to me that this coercive and imaginary meeting with a high Christian dignitary—be it the pope or an emperor—reflects, more than Vital's willingness to reveal Kabbalistic lore, his quest for recognition as the authoritative Kabbalist of his day.

24. See Idel, "Shelomo Molkho" (n. 20 above), 218.

25. See the studies of F. A. Yates, who reiterated the importance of Kabbalah for the understanding of a long series of intellectual issues in European culture. Even if her evaluation is sometimes exaggerated, the studies opened an important avenue for appreciation of the contribution of various mystical

elements, including Kabbalah, to the intellectual structures of the fifteenth–eighteenth centuries.

26. I refer to the Genoan Polyglot of Psalms printed in 1516, in which I was able to identify Hebrew fragments of one of R. Abraham Abulafia's lost works. I hope to elaborate upon this topic elsewhere.

27. See M. Idel, "The Concept of the Torah in the Hekhalot Literature and its Metamorphoses in Kabbalah" (Heb.), *Meḥqerey Yerushalayim be-Maḥshevet Yisra'el* 1 (1981): 76–77.

28. See François Secret's bio-bibliographical survey in *Les Kabbalistes chrétiens de la Renaissance* (Paris, 1964).

29. See Isaiah Tishby, *Hikrei Qabbalah u-sheluḥoteha* (Jerusalem, 1982), 1: 97–99.

30. See *Masoret ha-Ḥokhmah*, published by Gershom Scholem in *Kiryat Sefer*, 2 (1925): 126. Interestingly enough, there he describes his master as someone who received Kabbalah orally from other masters.

31. See Idel, "Inquiries" (no. 7 above), 262–63.

32. See the Epistle from Jerusalem (n. 14 above), 59.

33. See his account printed in Salomon Schechter, "Notes sur Messer David Leon," *REJ* 24 (1892): 121.

34. See n. 33 above.

35. See Moshe Idel, "Between the Concept of Sefirot as Essence and Instruments in the Kabbalah of the Period of Renaissance" (Heb.), *Italia* 3 (1982): 89–90; idem, "The Study Program of R. Yohanan Alemanno" (Heb.), *Tarbiz* 47 (1979): 330–31.

36. See Moshe Idel, "R. Judah Hallewa and his *Zofenat Pa'aneah*" (Heb.), in *Shalem*, ed. J. Hacker (Jerusalem, 1984), 4: 129, n. 64.

37. See Idel, "Inquiries" (n. 7 above), 239–43.

38. Another prominent phenomenon partially related to our subject is the emergence of the "negative" revelations of the *dybbuk*, a possessive phenomenon which was less than marginal in the medieval period, and which became widespread at exactly the same time as positive revelations came to the forefront. I hope to dedicate a separate inquiry to the interrelation and overlapping of "negative" and "positive" revelation,

39. See R. Z. J. Werblowsky, *Joseph Karo, Lawyer and Mystic* (Philadelphia, 1977), 38–83, 133–38, 149–51; Ira Robinson, "Messianic Prayer Vigil in Jerusalem in the Early Sixteenth Century," *JQR* 72 (N.S.) (1981), 32–42; and Moshe Idel, "On *Mishmarot* and Messianism in Jerusalem in the 16th–17th Centuries" *(Heb.)*, *Shalem* 5 (1987): 83–90.

40. I hope to deal with this broadening of revelatory phenomena in a special study. For the time being, see the supposition by Rahel Elior, "The Kabbalists of Dra'a" (Heb.), *Pe'amim* 24 (1985): 36–73, that some pneumatic phenomena among Morroccan Jewish Kabbalists are the results of Muslim Berberian mysticism (see pp. 66–67). Since no conclusive evidence is adduced to substantiate this hypothesis, I tend to see these phenomena, too, as part of an inner development of Kabbalah.

41. See Idel, "Inquiries" (n. 7 above), 196, n. 60.
42. This fact will be elaborated elsewhere.
43. The Hebrew text was printed in Idel, "Inquiries" (n. 7 above), 234–36, where some aspects of the text were analyzed.
44. Ps. 101:4.
45. Ex. 14:3.
46. In Hebrew, the spelling is intended to facilitate the pun: Aristotle = venom.
47. Seemingly the tree of knowledge or philosophy, as against the former tree of life, namely Kabbalah.
48. I.e., metaphysics.
49. A Kabbalistic designation for hell.
50. See Idel, "Inquiries" (n. 7 above), 232–34.
51. See the text printed by Idel, "Inquiries" (n. 7 above), 237.
52. See Moshe Idel, "The Attitude to Christianity in Sefer ha-Meshiv," Immanuel 12 (1981): 77–95.
53. See, for the first time being, Idel "Inquiries" (n. 7 above), 201–4, 244–50.
54. See Idel, "The Attitude" (n. 52 above), 84–85, 88.
55. See Idel, "Inquiries" (n. 7 above), 200.
56. Ibid., 193–94.
57. Ibid., 194–95.
58. Ibid., 201.
59. Fragments of Sefer ha-Meshiv were copied in Prague.
60. Through the intermediary of Gallei Razaya. See, e.g., the quotation of a passage from this book which reflects the views of Kaf ha-Ketoret in R. Nathan Shapira of Cracow's Megalle 'Amuqot, no. 193; see Gershom Scholem, "On the Account of R. Joseph della Reina" (Heb.), in Studies in Jewish Religious and Intellectual History Presented to Alexander Altmann, ed. S. Stein and R. Loewe (University, Ala., 1979), 107–17, and Twersky and Septimus, Jewish Thought in the Seventeenth Century (n. 19 above), 221–55.
61. See Yehudah Liebes, "Mysticism and Reality: Towards a Portrait of the Martyr and Kabbalist, R. Samson of Ostropoler" (Heb.), Tarbiz 52 (1983): 93–108 (English translation in Jewish Thought in the Seventeenth Century, 221–56).
62. See Gershom Scholem, Sabbatai Ṣevi, The Mystical Messiah: 1626–1676 (Bollingen Series 93 [Princeton, 1975]), 122, n. 45, pp. 203, 210, 805–6.
63. See Scholem, Major Trends (n. 2 above), 256.
64. Ibid.
65. See Gershom Scholem, "New Information on R. Joseph Ashkenazi, the Tanna of Safed" (Heb.), Tarbiz 28 (1959): 59–89; in his attack on Maimonides, he uses the criticism of R. Shem Tov ben Shem Tov, Tarbiz, idem, 201–2; see also Isadore Twersky, "R. Joseph Ashkenazi and the Sefer Mishneh Torah of Maimonides" (Heb.), Salo Baron Festschrift 3 (Jerusalem, 1975), 183–94.
66. Idel, "Inquiries" (n. 7 above), 239–43.

67. See M. Idel, "The Evil Thought of the Deity" (Heb.), *Tarbiz* 49 (1980): 356–64.
68. See *Sefer ha-Emunot*, fol. 32a, 48ab, 78b, 95b, etc.
69. See Gershom Scholem in *Jacob Freimann Festschrift* (Berlin, 1937), 170.
70. Gershom Scholem, "On the Knowledge of Kabbalah in Spain in the Eve of Expulsion" (Heb.), *Tarbiz* 24 (1955): 182.
71. *Minhat Yehudah* in *Ma'arekhet ha-Elohut* (Mantua, 1558), fol. 19b, 115b.
72. *'Avodat ha-Qodesh* (Jerusalem, 1973), fol. 1b–c, 95b, 97b. Ibn Gabbai's statements are clear enough and I see no reason for Joseph Dan's assertion that he "obscured" the problem of the origin of evil. See his "No Evil Descends from Heaven," in *Jewish Thought in the Sixteenth Century*, ed. Bernard D. Cooperman (Cambridge, Mass., 1983), 101. No reference was supplied to substantiate the assertion of "obscuration." See also his "The Concept of Evil and Demonology in R. Menasseh ben Israel's book *Nishmat Hayyim*" (Heb.), in *Mehqerey Aggadah u-folklor Yehudi*, ed. I. Ben-Ami and J. Dan (Jerusalem, 1983), 263–64; Dan enumerates there (p. 264) that R. Abraham ben Eliezer ha-Levi and the anonymous author of *Gallei Razaya* are proposing views on evil influenced by the crisis of the Expulsion. As no exact reference was supplied, and I could find no reason to support this hypothesis, I assume that these Kabbalists were just continuing the views of the circle of Kabbalists who produced *Sefer ha-Meshiv* (see nn. 30, 53, 79).
73. See M. Idel, "The Evil Thought of the Diety," 363–64.
74. Idem, 363 and additional sources to be discussed elsewhere.
75. The material referred to in the previous notes was ignored by scholars who dealt with Luria's view of evil; hence the "revolutionary" or "drastic" descriptions of the Lurianic view on this issue characteristic of Isaiah Tishby, *Torat ha-ra' veha-qelipah be-Qabbalat ha-ar'i* (Jerusalem, 1984), 11. and of Dan's paper, "No Evil" (n. 72 above), 90, 103. Without an examination of pre-Lurianic Kabbalistic literature, any discussion of his "innovations" is highly haphazard; cf. n. 85 below.
76. Dan, "No Evil" (n. 72 above), 103; Scholem, *Sabbatai Sevi* (n. 62 above), 44–45. I doubt whether there is any connection between the scanty remarks on the nature of evil as part of the divine structure, and what is considered by Dan, following Scholem, to be the rapid propagation of Lurianic Kabbalah. Since no evidence was adduced to substantiate this theory, there is indeed no way to analyze the reasons for this proposal. I would only like to point out that the acceptance of Lurianic Kabbalah in its Sarugian form was clearly achieved by a suppression of its discussions on the nature of evil; see the works of R. Abraham Herrera and R. Joseph Delmedigo. This neutralization of the aspect of evil prepared the way for philosophization of this type of Kabbalah. On the other hand, the demonology of some early seventeenth-century Ashkenazi Kabbalists is not Lurianic, but mostly pre-Lurianic in nature.
77. Scholem, *Major Trends* (n. 2 above), 248–50; see also the eloquent sum-

mary of this view of Scholem by Joseph Dan, "The Historical Perceptions of the Late Professor Gershom Scholem" (Heb.) *Zion* 47 (1982): 169.

78. Berakha Zak, "The Concept of Zimzum in R. Moshe Cordovero" (Heb, *Tarbiz* 58 (1984): 207–37. I am preparing a study of the treatments of the concept of Zimzum in pre-Expulsion Kabbalah. See meanwhile, Scholem, *Major Trends*, 264; idem, "For the Knowledge" (n. 70 above), 72–74; On the early source of the Lurianic concept of Adam Qadmon, see Idel, "The Image of Man Above the Sefirot" (Heb.), *Da'at* 4 (1980): 49–51.

79. I would like to emphasize that even R. Abraham ben Eliezer ha-Levi, who was highly interested in messianic views and calculations, never mentioned the Expulsion as a crucial event in the eschatological scheme. Moreover, in his Kabbalistic works, as distinct from his messianic one, Expulsion or messianism are never mentioned. In general, his messianism is either a continuation of motifs found in *Sefer ha-Ketoret,* or messianic interpretations of historical events after the Expulsion; see also n. 72 above.

The issue of messianism in the generations immediately preceding and following the Expulsion is a rather complex topic. Schematizing and obviously simplifying, I would conceive the highest peak of this phenomenon as being connected to the *Book of the Meshiv,* written before the Expulsion and the Kabbalistic works written under its direct or indirect influence, such as *Kaf ha-Ketoret* and *Sefer Gallei Razaya.* Probably, the same influence may be detected also in the case of R. Shelomo Molkho's writings. This activistic messianism, based mainly on an anomian activity—i.e., not a halakhic type of activity—was rejected in Lurianic Kabbalah, whose messianic component—though present—is less obvious and crucial than it is described in modern scholarship. The whole subject is worthy of a detailed analysis; see, meanwhile, Idel, "Shelomo Molkho" (n. 20 above) and idem, "Types of Redemptive Activity in the Middle Ages" (Heb.), in *Messianism and Eschatology,* ed. Zvi Baras (Jerusalem, 1983), 278–79.

The proper discussion of messianism cannot be conducted without a balanced survey of the entire corpus of expressions of messianic hopes and activities. Only after a comparison of the various degrees of intensity of messianic "enthusiasm" or frenzy implicit in the pertinent texts, will we be able to correctly assess the "messianic" nature of Lurianic Kabbalah, which is hitherto one of the still unproved cornerstones of modern historiosophy.

80. See Hayyim Hillel Ben-Sasson, "Exile and Redemption through the Eyes of the Spanish Exiles" (Heb.), in *Sefer Yovel le-Yitzhak Baer,* ed. S. W. Baron, B. Dinur, S. Ettinger, I. Halperin (Jerusalem, 1960), 216–27.

81. Ibid., 226–27.

82. My first impression was confirmed by the very similar evaluation of my friend Prof. Robert Bonfil, who was kind enough to discuss this issue with me.

83. Alemmano was otherwise interested in various historical events, though he never had pretensions to be an historian.

An issue which seems to be pertinent to our discussion, but which cannot be elaborated here, is the cause of the flowering of historical writing among Jews in Italy, in comparison to the indifference to this genre among the Jews in the Orient, in the Ottoman Empire, and in the Land of Israel. However, we ought not to limit this indifference to the impact of the Lurianic mythical approach alone, but should also include the spread of the particularistic kind of Kabbalah in general. Compare Yosef Hayyim Yerushalmi, *Zakhor: Jewish History and Jewish Memory* (Seattle and London, 1982), 73–74. Spanish Jews while in the Iberian Peninsula, and afterwards while in non-Italian countries, did not produce much historical writing; thus, it would be implausible to attribute the renascence of historical writing among Italian Jews and Sefardi Jews living in Italy to the Expulsion. On the affinity between Jewish historiography and the Italian interest in history, see Robert Bonfil, "How Golden Was the Age of the Renaissance in Jewish Historiography?" *History and Theory* 27 (1988): 78–102 (see chapter 7 of the present volume).

84. See Ephraim Kupfer, "The Visions of R. Asher ben Meir Lemlein Reutlingen" (Heb.), *Kovez ʿal Yad* 8, no 18 (1976): 387–423, as well as MS. Budapest Kaufmann 179, fol. 121–72.

85. Scholem's advice in *Major Trends* (n. 2 above), 259—"These connections between Luria and a few half-forgotten Spanish Kabbalists still await an adequate historical analysis"—is as relevant today as it was in 1939. See above the articles referred to in nn. 6, 67, 78.

86. See Isaiah Tishby, *Netivey Emunah u-Minut* (Ramat Gan, 1966), 23–24. I am not quite sure that this alternation is only part of an inner rhythm of Kabbalah, as has apparently been assumed by Tishby.

87. According to Tishby (ibid., p. 24), the immanent processes of the development of Kabbalistic thought are without any direct affinity to external factors.

88. See the approach proposed by Robert Bonfil, *Ha-Rabbanut be-Italyah be-tequfat ha-Renesans* (Jerusalem, 1979), 173–206, who offers a more balanced view of Jewish cultural development in Renaissance Italy, taking into account the inner processes, far more so than earlier historians, who tended to explain Jewish culture of that period as the result of external influences. See also his article "The Historian's Perception of the Jews in the Italian Renaissance, Towards a Reappraisal" *Revue des Etudes Juives* 143 (1984): 59–82, esp. 80–82.

12

Major Currents in Italian Kabbalah between 1560 and 1660

Moshe Idel

1

The aim of this survey of Jewish Kabbalah in Italy is neither bibliographical nor merely historical. I am interested in highlighting one major thesis, which may explain some important developments of Italian Kabbalah. This thesis is: the peculiar nature of the Kabbalah as it emerged in the works of some Kabbalists at the end of the 15th century and early 16th century: R. David Messer Leon, Abraham de Balmes and mainly R. Johanan Alemanno constitute the blue-print for the further developments in Italian Kabbalah until the 17th century, either by direct influence, or by indirect one, exercised through a long chain of intermediary sources. I should like to describe some major features of this brand of Kabbalah:

a) Kabbalah is viewed as an ancient Jewish lore, esoterical in its historical expressions, which can in principle be understood and explained in a philosophical way. This assumption underlines the writings of at least four thinkers, who were contemporaries and lived in Northern Italy: R. Yohanan Alemanno[1], R. David Messer Leon[2], R. Abraham de Balmes[3], and R. Isaac of Pisa[4]. The first three were the students of R. Yehudah Messer Leon who was an opponent of Kabbalah, as well

Reprinted by permission of Istituto Poligrafico e Zeccia dello Stato from *Italia Judaica 2: gli Ebrei in Italia Tra Rinascimento Ed Eta Barocca*, Alti del II Convegno internazionale, Genova 1984 (Rome 1986).

as an Aristotelian-oriented philosopher[5]. His students, however, became deeply interested in Kabbalah and tended to use also the Neoplatonic philosophy[6] in order to elucidate the content of the Kabbalistic body of literature in addition to Aristotelian works.

b) Some Italian Kabbalists like Alemanno and Isaac da Pisa[7], as well as
others under their influence[8], conceived of Kabbalah as a magical
lore, namely a technique to draw downwards the supernal efflux,
from the world of *Sefirot* and collect it for the sake of using it. This
perception represents an important change in the nature of Kabbalah
as it appears in the Zoharic literature which is mainly a theurgical
lore, namely a technique intended to cause changes in the inner
structure of the *Sefirot,* viewing the attainment of an inner harmony
or union[9].

c) Kabbalah, though an ancient Jewish lore, may be disclosed to the
larger public, and in some cases it seems that this permission includes
even the Christians. Therefore, Kabbalah is now viewed mainly as an
exoterical wisdom, since its content can be interpreted in a speculative manner.[10].

The first two features constitute a continuation of certain conceptions
found already in Spanish Kabbalah in the second half of the 14th century, in the writings of R. Joseph ben Wakkar, R. Samuel ibn Motot and
R. Samuel Sarsa, etc. The philosophical-magical trend of Kabbalah was
rejected by the 15th century Spanish Kabbalists, who focused on the
theosophical tendency of the *Book of the Zohar*[11]. However, this rejected Spanish tradition concerning Kabbalah was accepted by the late
15th century Italian Kabbalists, like R. Yohanan Alemanno.

When the Spanish Kabbalists reached Northern Italy at the end of the
15th century, clashes between their theosophical-theurgical Kabbalah,
and the Italian magical-philosophical Kabbalah became inevitable. Certain passages in the writings of R. Isaac Mar Hayyim[12], R. Joseph ibn
Shragu[13], and R. Yehudah Hayyat[14], are clear evidence of the intellectual controversies between Spaniards and Italian Kabbalists[15].

At the beginning of the 16th century, the gap between the two approaches seems to be bridged to a certain extent. In Alemanno's later
writings, Zoharic passages, translated into Hebrew, are inserted[16]. The
various versions of the commentaries on the ten *Sefirot* of R. Yehiel
Nissim of Pisa and R. Mordekhai Raphael Rossello are striking evidence

of the increasing importance the Spanish Kabbalah received even among Italian Kabbalists who followed Alemanno and R. Isaac of Pisa[17]. On the other hand, as we shall see later, Spanish Kabbalists, who arrived in Northern Italy and the Ottoman Empire, also suffered the impact of Italian Kabbalah.

Before surveying the fate of the 15th century Kabbalah in later periods of Italian Kabbalah, I should like to remark that at the middle of the 16th century, the philosophical-magical Kabbalah flourishing in Italy found its way also beyond the Italian borders. Here I should like to point out the fact that Ashkenazi authors, like R. Matitiahu Delacrut[18], studied Kabbalah in Italy, and served as vehicles for the transmission of the peculiar brand of Kabbalah in Poland and Central Europe. The most important Ashkenazi figure who was influenced by Italian philosophical-magical Kabbalah is the famous R. Moshe Isserles (Rema)[19].

II

The peculiar brand of Kabbalah represented by R. Yohanan Alemanno and his followers remained in manuscripts; none of their writings expressing the philosophical-magical interpretations of Kabbalah found its way to the larger public, neither had they been disseminated in a large number of manuscripts. However, its influence on some important figures of Jewish Italian thought is considerable enough and it constitutes an uninterrupted continuation of this special perception of Kabbalah from the end of the 15th century until the beginnings of the 17th century. The following survey of this line of Italian Kabbalah is important not only for the very fact of establishing a historical filiation for certain limited tendencies in the 16th century Kabbalah; it may enable us to understand better a broader phenomenon: why was R. Moses Cordovero's Kabbalah accepted so easily and, later on, the philosophical interpretation of the Sarugian Kabbalah. Let us therefore discuss the impact of Alemanno's writing in the period which concerns us.

a) Almost all of Alemanno's works reached us in their autographical form. But, the greatest part of the manuscripts other than the autographs was copied by two important scribes, who influenced by their activity the direction of Kabbalah in Italy and elsewhere: R. Isaac Joshua de Lattes and his son-in-law, R. Abraham ben Meshullam of San Angelo. They were in possession of most of Alemanno's autographs, a fact which

seems to be the result of a certain familiar relation, and some of Alemanno's works were copies by them, sometimes with random notes including
interesting reactions to the content they copied[20]. Alemanno is mentioned in one of R. Abraham's *Responsa*[21]. R. Isaac de Lattes indicates
in a colophon of his copy of Alemanno's *Heshek Shelomo*[22]:

> This book named Heshek Shelomo was accomplished by me, Isaac Yehoshua,
> the son of R. Emmanuel of Lattes, from the copy copied by my dear and
> righteous son in law R. Abraham, the son of Meshullam Angelo, who compared
> it to the book [i.e. to the autograph] itself, and I have accomplished it today 17
> Elul, 328 of the fifth millennium.

Therefore at least the autograph of *Heshek Shelomo* was in the hands
of R. Abraham, and he copied it before 1568.

It is evident that R. Isaac de Lattes had thoroughly studied Alemanno's commentary on the *Song of Songs;* in his copy of Alemanno's *Eine
ha-Edah,* a fragment of a commentary on Genesis, de Lattes frequently
refers in marginal notes to the parallel discussions found in *Heshek
Shelomo*[23]. Besides these two important works of Alemanno, at least
one more work was copied by R. Abraham of San Angelo: it is his *Hei
ha-Olamim*[24].

No wonder, therefore, that these two Kabbalists were interested in
Alemanno and quoted him.

Almost all the works of Alemanno were in the possession of R.
Abraham Yagel, a Kabbalist who will be the subject of some of our
further comments. Since his literary output is much greater than that of
the above-mentioned Kabbalists, we can easily perceive in it the profound influence of the 15th century Kabbalist; Alemanno is quoted by
him at least fifteen times and the identifiable passages stem from all the
known works of Alemanno[25]. Moreover, various remarks written by
Yagel's hand are extant in Alemanno's autograph of *Collectanaea* from
various medieval sources[26].

We may conclude our short survey with the assumption that more
than a century after his death, Alemanno was still influencial among
some important Jewish figures, his works being preserved, copied and
quoted. The hypothesis that the philosophical-magical view of Kabbalah
was shared by Northern Italian Jews of the second part of the 16th
century can be strengthened by the fact that two of the sources of
Alemanno's perception of Kabbalah were printed at that period. R.
Samuel Sarsa's voluminous *Makor Hayyim* was published in Mantua in

1559 whereas R. Samuel Motot's *Megilat Setarim* had already been printed in Venice in 1554. These works, which combine R. Abraham ibn Ezra's thought with Kabbalah and astral magic, moulded Alemanno's views, while otherwise they were neglected by all the important trends of Jewish thought. Their appearance in press contributed to the dissemination of ideas akin to those of Alemanno, of R. Isaac of Pisa, of Yehiel Nissim of Pisa and R. Mordekhai Rossello[27].

A philosophical perception of Kabbalah, which may be considered independent of Alemanno's works, is found in the work of R. Berakhiel ben Meshullam Kafman (born in Mantua in 1485); in his *Lev Adam*[28], Kabbalah is considered to be the "inner philosophy" and on this line he built up his thought[29]. His work was not published in the period we analyse here. However, it seems that his influence can be detected in at least three well-known authors: R. Yehudah Moscato, the famous Mantuan preacher quoted the *Chapters of R. Berakhiel* several times in his commentary on R. Yehudah ha-Levi's *Kuzari*[30]. These are lengthy citations which reflect the high respect Moscato had for R. Berakhiel. It is therefore probable that the tendency to interpret Kabbalah philosophically, which is evident in Moscato's homilies, *Nefuzot Yehudah*[31], results, at least partially, from the influence of R. Berakhiel's work. R. Isaac of Lattes, too, refers to R. Berakhiel in an important document, his decision on the problem whether it is permitted to publish the *Zohar*[32], and so did also his friend, R. Emmanuel of Benivenito in a similar context[33]. Likewise, R. Berakhiel is quoted by R. Abraham Yagel, another important representative of philosophical Kabbalah in Italy, who was influenced also by Moscato[34]. Therefore we have hard evidence for the continuation of Italian Kabbalistic thought, widespread in the hundred years before 1560, in the writings of some leading Jewish thinkers in the next hundred years.

III

This atmosphere which encouraged a speculative understanding of Kabbalah was the background of the warm reception in Italy of the writings of two important Safedian Kabbalists: R. Moses Cordovero, and R. Shelomo ha-Levi Alkabetz. Mainly the Kabbalah of Cordovero was enthusiastically accepted by Italian Jewish Kabbalists and it turned, in the third quarter of the 16th century, into the most authoritative brand of Kabbalah. Before discussing this process of integration of Cordovero's writings, let us turn for a moment to the starting point of his Kabbalah.

After the Expulsion, the spanish Kabbalah spread mainly in two important directions: the Northern itinerary, including Italy and the former Byzantine provinces; and, the second, the Southern itinerary which includes the Maghreb and Egypt[35]. The Northern itinerary contributed something novel to the further development of Kabbalah. The Jewish Kabbalists encountered in Northern Italy, and to a certain extent also in the Ottoman empire, the emerging ideas of Christian and Jewish Renaissance, which consist, as far as we are interested, in the magical and philosophical interpretation of Kabbalah, as well as the attempt to develop a comprehensive perception of knowledge and universe. This encounter was sometimes difficult, given the divergences between the mythical orientation of Spanish Kabbalah and the more speculative tendency of the Italian one. However, even the frictions between these two brands are clear evidence of such an encounter. One of the Kabbalists who left Spain and experienced this type of encounter was R. Shelomo ha-Levi Alkabetz. For some years, which were apparently his formative period, Alkabetz lived in the company of R. Yoseph Taitazak, a distinguished Spanish scholar, who was heavily influenced by Christian scholastics, as J. B. Sermoneta has convincingly demonstrated[36]. Likewise, he was aware of the philosophical perception of Kabbalah as exposed by R. David Messer Leon, who was also a resident of the Ottoman Empire. Alkabetz was the probable intermediary who transmitted Messer Leon's views to Palestine, when they were known to and discussed by Cordovero[37]. This encounter of Kabbalah and philosophy, which took place in the Ottoman Empire, had important repercussions on Alkabetz's thought; he integrated philosophical images and ideas, though often he disapproved of the superiority of philosophy[38]. Some of them served him, and those influenced by him, to create a more complex view of Kabbalah. He left the former Byzantium area and reached Safed, and thereby he contributed to the emergence of a relatively novel approach to Kabbalah there, whose main exponent was his relative and friend R. Moses Cordovero. In the latter's *magnum opus, Pardes Rimmonium,* obvious traces of magical perceptions of Kabbalah, views of love as a cosmic force and awareness of the philosophical Kabbalah, can be detected[39]. All of them, combined with the "authentic" Spanish Kabbalah, which focused on the Zoharic literature, were exposed in a systematic way, which turned *Pardes Rimmonium* into a *Summa Kabbalistica* influential throughout the whole Jewish world. However, the impact of Cordovero's works in Italy is exceptional[40]. Kabbalists like R. Mordekhai Dato[41] and R. Menahem Azariah of Fano[42], to name only the famous names, were fervent disciples of Cordovero, whom they venerated at least as Cordovero's followers in Safed did. It is worth emphasizing that Cordovero's and Alkabetz's works play an important role in the Italian Kabbalah because of the intrinsic values they reflect as well as because of the celebrity of their authors. This statement notwithstanding, I should like to highlight also the deep consonance between prior tendencies in Italian Kabbalah, and the Cordoverian system which included some of them in a larger and more complex intellectual construction. This affinity, stemming from common sources, allowed an undisturbed and immediate acceptance of the works of Cordovero and Alkabetz in Italy.

Formal evidence of the profound influence of Cordovero in Italy is the very composition of commentaries on his *Pardes Rimmonim:* R. Samuel Gallico's *Assis Rimmonim,* to which Mordekhai Dato added some additions, and R. Menahem Azariah's *Pelah Rimmon* and his disciple's abridgement, together with additions to *Pardes Rimmonim.* Also R. Eliah de Vidas' *Reshit Hokhmah,* which is basically a popularization of Cordovero's Kabbalah, was widespread in Italy in various abridgements[43]. It is instructive to point out that the Italian Kabbalists, though deeply influenced by Cordovero's thought, did not produce abridgements of *Or Yakkar,* his commentary on the *Zohar*[44]. Moreover, in obvious contrast to their Safedian contemporaries, who composed a whole literature intended to comment on the *Zohar,* the Italian Kabbalists did not comment upon this Kabbalistic book; this fact is reflective of the different frame of mind of Kabbalists in Italy, who preferred Cordovero's speculative digest of mythical Kabbalah of the *Zohar,* in *lieu* of a direct approach to this central opus of Kabbalistic literature.

IV

The early nineties of the 16th century are decisive years for the history of Kabbalah in general and in the Kabbalah in Italy in particular. The theosophical-theurgical Kabbalah of R. Isaac Luria, which was limited for twenty years to a small circle of Kabbalists in Safed and Jerusalem, reached Northern Italy and was propagated by the intensive oral and literary activity of R. Israel Sarug[45] and his disciples and followers[46]. Though the Kabbalah of Sarug departs from the authentic teachings of Luria in more than one point, it still remained a highly mythical wisdom, which differed substantially from the philosophical Kabbalistic trends of Italian Kabbalists. Given the speculative Kabbalistic tradition dominant in Italy, and the deep influence of Cordovero, a clash between Sarug's Kabbalah and Italian Kabbalah would seem reasonable. However, the aggressive dissemination of Lurianic Kabbalah by Sarug passed without any resistance from the side of the Italians. His Kabbalah was almost immediately accepted by important Kabbalists, led by R. Menahem Azariah of Fano, the paragon of Italian kabbalah[47]. Was this drastic change a failure of nerves of the philosophical orientation of Italian Kabbalah? Was it overcome instantly by the activity of one single Kabbalist, even if he posed as a disciple of the legendary Luria? *Prima facie,* this seems to be the situation; Sarugian Kabbalah became almost unanimously accepted. However, a more profound study of the sources may reveal a more complex picture, in which philosophical Kabbalah will assume an important role.

As Isaiah Tishby has already convincingly proved, strong allegiance to Cordoverian Kabbalah[48] is evident from the perusal of the works of Sarugian Kabbalists like R. Menahem Azariah of Fano and his student Aharon Berakhiah of Modena, years after they met Sarug. The acceptance of Sarug's authority as a Kabbalist and his Kabbalah as superior to Cordovero's does not imply a total desertion of the latter's works and doctrines. This important finding of Tishby can be corroborated by further evidence.

In the early twenties of the 17th century, R. Jacob ben Kalonimus of the Levites, the son-in-law of R. Yehudah Arieh of Modena and a pupil of the Kabbalist R. Ezra of Fano, composed a booklet *Nahalat Yaacov,* defending Kabbalah against the arguments of Modena[49]. A perusal of its manuscripts, which is very instructive for the understanding of the composition of *Ari Nohem*[50], shows that he is defending solely the Zoharic and Cordoverian Kabbalah, without even one reference to Luria or Sarug. We may conclude that either the Lurianic Kabbalah was not attacked, and therefore there was no need to defend it, or if it was criticized, R. Jacob was not a disciple of Luria's Kabbalah and accordingly he did not respond to these attacks. Out of the two possibilities, the first one seems to be more plausible; if this assumption is correct, then we can conclude that thirty years after the arrival of Sarug in Venice and the dissemination of his Kabbalah, there were still Kabbalists who could neglect any discussion of this brand of Kabbalah, and remain totally faithful to Cordovero's doctrine. Again we may supplement the previous remark with a short note on *Ari Nohem:* this comprehensive criticism of Kabbalah in general was mainly directed at the doctrines of Cordovero from one side, but against the legends surrounding Luria's life or Sarug's personality. Hence, it seems that Cordovero's Kabbalistic system remained the symbol of Kabbalah whereas the Lurianic ideas, though influential among the Kabbalistic elite, were rather marginal in the consciousness of certain circles.

Other striking evidence in this direction is found in the works of R. Abraham Yagel. In his voluminous books he did not allow a significant place for Lurianic Kabbalah; as far as I could peruse the almost one thousand manuscript folios of his autographs that have reached us, Sarug is never mentioned, though the bulk of the literary activity of Yagel took place in the early 17th century. Though Luria and Vital are respectfully mentioned and considered supreme Kabbalistic authorities, their books, or doctrines are never mentioned, let alone influential. Interestingly enough, Vital is referred to by these words[51]:

> the wondrous teacher Rabbi Hayyim Vitalo
> his student [i.e. Luria's] about whom I heard
> said that he is the father [i.e. head] of all
> the Kabbalists of that province.

The manner in which Vital is mentioned, "I heard said", shows that he had no first-hand knowledge of Vital's books; moreover, his description as head of the Kabbalists of that province may imply that Vital was not considered, despite the recognition of his greatness as a Kabbalist, the authority in matters of Kabbalah for the Italian Kabbalists. On the other hand, Cordovero is considered by Yagel to be the very metamorphosis of R. Shimeon bar Yohai, the author of the *Zohar*[52]. By the way of metempsychosis, the soul of bar Yohai came to elucidate the obscurities of the *Zohar,* for the benefit of Cordovero's generation. It seems obvious that such a perception of Cordovero's genesis and activity reveals an appreciation of his Kabbalah, which is apparently superior even to that of Luria and Vital.

These remarks demonstrate that the reversal from Cordoverian Kabbalah to the Lurianic or Sarugian one was neither complete nor immediate; a generation after the beginning of Sarug's activity in Italy, there were still Kabbalists who could produce learned works, even very lengthy ones like Yagel's, without even mentioning Lurianic concepts.

Moreover, the situation seems to be complicated even in the circles of the Kabbalists who adhered to the teachings in a philosophical manner[53]. One of the outstanding students of Sarug, R. Abraham Herrera, received the main Lurianic teachings directly from his master but his own works present a philosophical interpretation of the mythical Kabbalah[54]. The main vein of his interpretation is the Renaissance Neoplatonism, which is extensively employed in order to transform the Kabbalah into a speculative system. The same tendency is easily noticed also in the work of R. Yoseph Shelomo del Medigo; he studied at the University of Padua and he became acquainted with Sarugian texts without receiving oral instruction from Sarug. Though he seems to be unaware of the tendency to philosophize the Sarugian Kabbalah, displayed by Herrera, del Medigo follows the same direction[55]. The single meaningful difference between them is that to the Neoplatonic sources employed by both of them, del Medigo added also an atomistic interpretation, using extensively the names and teachings of the ancient atomists and eventually also atomistic views of Giordano Bruno[56]. These two Kabbalists, who are among the first to use Lurianic texts and concepts, actually neutralized the mystical and anthropomorphic features of this Kabbalah perceiving it in accordance with the philosophical conceptions *en vogue* among their Christian contemporaries. Herrera and del Medigo introduced, apparently independently, an array of Neoplatonic authors and titles, more than any other Jewish Kabbalist, or even philosopher, had done beforehand. The same phenomenon is evident also in the writings of R. Abraham Yagel, whose Kabbalah is independent from Sarug's teachings. Therefore, exactly at the same period when the most mythical brand of Kabbalah became influential in Italy, we witness also another significant event: three Kabbalists, contemporaries of Sarug, whose intellectual education was deeply influenced by the Renaissance culture, vigorously expressed their philosophical knowledge in the way they perceive the Kabbalah. The more mythical the Kabbalah was, the more philosophical was the manner in which it was interpreted[57]. The question may be asked which type of thought was prevalent: the Kabbalah, even in its Lurianic form, or the Neoplatonic philosophy which was massively being infused in the Kabbalistic discussion. In my opinion, the latter possibility seems to be more likely. We may conclude our concise survey with the remark that even when Lurianic Kabbalah reached Italy, the philosophical interpretation of the esoteric lore was not diminished, but on the contrary, it reached its peak. It constitutes the Jewish counterpart to the Renaissance and Baroque rationalization of myth. At least in the case of R. Abraham Yagel, we can indicate that he firmly belongs to the Jewish philosophical Kabbalah, as it was formulated in the works of Yohanan Alemanno one hundred years beforehand, given the direct references to all the latter's works.

Furthermore, Yagel extensively quotes from a wide array of Neoplatonic texts, the most important being Chaleidius' commentary on Plato's *Timaeus*[58] or Renaissance Neoplatonic texts, sometimes indirectly through Cornelius Agrippa's *De Occulta Philosophia*[59], and a long series of Patristic and medieval Christian theologians[60]. Likewise, he subscribed to the Renaissance view of *prisca theologia*[61] and he brings together Kabbalistic views with Hermetic and "Zoroastrian" ones[62]. However, in the case of the other two Kabbalists, Herrara and del Medigo, no direct impact of Alemanno on their books can presently be demonstrated. Though an indirect influence cannot be ruled out, its importance seems to be negligible. Nevertheless, at least from the phenomenological point of view, their speculative interpretation of Kabbalah represents only a later metamorphosis of the perception of the Kabbalah which was crystallized in Northern Italy at the end of the 15th century.

The impact of Renaissance thought on the works of the above-mentioned Kabbalists cannot be exaggerated. It represents an almost unrestrained openness to Italian thought which was strong enough to change some basic features of Lurianic or other types of Kabbalah which were accepted as autoritative Jewish theology. However, this massive influence of alien sources on the writings of Herrara, del Medigo, or Yagel contributed to the rejection of their works from the mainstream of Jewish Kabbalah. Yagel's Kabbalistic work, *Bet Ya'ar ha-Levanon*, was never printed, Herrera's writings in Spanish influenced Christian Kabbalah, via the Latin translation in *De Cabala Denudata*, much more than Jewish Kabbalists; del Medigo's works, though printed, were generally quoted by Kabbalists in order to argue against them. The single important author who seems to follow those authors' line is R. Menashe ben Israel, the Rabbi of Amsterdam whose Kabbalistic views are beyond the scope of our discussion. From our point of view, the intellectual profile of R. Barukh ben Barukh may also be interesting[63]. Though he received his education in Salonika, he was active at the end of the 16th century and early 17th century in several important cities in Northern Italy; he was both interested in medieval philosophy including Thomas Aquinas, and in the Sarugian Kabbalah upon which he has written short footnotes[64]. R. Barukh was also influential in the Venetian Kabbalistic mystical group named *Shomerim la-Boker*.

V

In Italy, no major Kabbalist continued the tradition of combining Renaissance culture with Kabbalistic concepts. Since the beginning of the 17th century the arena was gradually occupied by the literary activity of the most important disciple of Sarug, R. Menahem Azariah of Fano[65]. Incontestably, he was the head of the Kabbalists in Italy from the eighties of the 16th century, and after contacts with Lurianic material which arrived from Jerusalem[66] and after his encounter with Sarug, he became a fervent Lurianic Kabbalist. His literary activity had a deep influence on Italian Kabbalah, as well as on the study of Kabbalah until the Hasidic masters in Russia and Poland at the end of the 18th century. R. Menahem Azariah, contrary to the above-mentioned Kabbalists, refrained himself from citing alien sources and his writings are composed in a manner akin to Vital's or Sarug's books. He faithfully continued their tradition, and taught it to his students. However, at least in one important case, he differs from his predecessors. The most intriguing concept of Lurianic Kabbalah, the doctrine of contraction or withdrawal in the bosom of Divinity—*Zimzum*—in order to make space for the creation, is interpreted by R. Menahem Azariah in a novel fashion. According to him[67], the contraction did not take place in the *Ein Sof*, namely the innermost Divinity, named by him as *Ba'al ha-Razon*, the owner of will[68], but in the Will, which is only an aspect of Godhead. This interpretation comes to neutralize the Lurianic assertion that there is any change in Godhead Himself, and it seems that the influence of philosophical thought is evident. Hence, it is plausible to conclude that the acceptance of Lurianic Kabbalah among those whom we may rightly call orthodox Kabbalists in Italy has an obvious flavour of speculative thought. Interestingly enough, the peculiar speculative interpretation of contraction in R. Menahem Azariah's work became influential in the further development of Kabbalah, through the writings of other Italian Kabbalists: R. Moses Hayyim Luzzato[69] and R. Joseph Ergas[70].

However, the possible philosophical implication of Menahem Azariah of Fano's view of contraction is a major exception in the general orthodox way he accepted Lurianism. Through his works and those of his students, orthodox Lurianism, mostly in its Sarugian version, became prevalent and the tendency to interpret it philosophically gradually vanished. The success of the mythical Kabbalah was overt and the later writings of R. Joseph Hamiz, R. Moses Zacuto or R. Natan Sharpira of Jerusalem, who was active in his last years in Reggio, are conclusive evidence. The foundation of mystical societies in Northern Italy, like *Shomerim la-Boker,* represents the beginning of a tendency to isolate from the Christian environment, and to cultivate a more exclusively Jewish way of living.

VI

As described above, the Italian Kabbalists from the end of the 15th century onwards conceived of the magical influence as an important activity; we face here not an ascent of popular witchcraft but the perception of magic as part of the "scientific" explanation of the universe, which supplies the new "intellectuals" with "technological" instructions, which are in some cases the very halakhic way of life[71], together with certain additions, like musical incantations[72]. This trend of Kabbalah remains influential not only in the first part of the 16th century, as in the work of R. Berakhiel and R. Moses Cordovero[73]; it reached its apex in the writings of R. Abraham Yagel, at the end of the 16th century and the beginning of the 17th[74]. Mostly in his encyclopedical *Beit Ya'ar ha-Levanon* Yagel presents a very detailed picture of magic, viewed as a part of Kabbalah. His major sources are Alemanno's anthology on magic and demonology and several major Christian works on magic like Roger Bacon's[75] and Albertus Magnus' books on natural magic[76], Cornelius Agrippa of Netesheim's *De Occulta Philosophia*[77], Giulio Camillo's *Teatro*[78], and even the *Life of Appolonius*[79]. In his medical work, *Moshia Hosim,* or in his *Gei Hizzaiyon,* magical elements are easily visible, testifying thereby that the magical perception of Kabbalah is part of Yagel's more comprehensive *Weltanschauung*. More than any of his intellectual predecessors, Yagel was ready to quote approvingly from the most notorious magical writings of Christian tradition. This intensive usage of Christian magic is unique in the literature of Jewish Kabbalah.

VII

The philosophical interpretation of Kabbalah by Jewish authors had a striking parallel in the same phenomenon in Christian Kabbalah. Pico della Mirandola, Johannes Reuchlin, Francesco Giorgio, apparently under the partial influence of Jewish Kabbalists, cast Kabbalah in a philosophical key. The affinities between these two brands of Kabbalah served as a bridge between the two religions.

The contours of Judaism and Christianity became more and more vague, the barriers were crossed by Kabbalists to the other side and the fascination of Christian Kabbalah grew as time passed. Since the end of the 15th century, Kabbalah played a similar role in Italy to the one played by Jewish philosophy in Spain since the 14th century. The two brands of theology, which in their primary phases strengthened Jewish religion, turned more and more pernicious, partly because they absorbed speculative elements which were accepted also by the surrounding alien cultures. To put it in other words: the gap between Judaism and Christianity can be easily reduced when Kabbalah, conceived as the quintessence of Judaism, is interpreted in philosophical terms, similar to or eventually identical with those employed by the Christian Renaissance theologian in order to interpret the tenets of Christianity.

The attitudes towards this blurring of religious boundaries differ between Jewish thinkers. A Kabbalist like R. Eliah Menahem Halfan, who in one of his *Responsa* explicitly opposed the dissemination of Jewish esoteric lore among Gentiles[80], cannot refrain from indicating that the Gentiles, who once were not aware of Jewish secrets and despised the Jews, now—namely in the middle of the 16th century—worship God by means of this lore, because of the Will of God, which inspired them to study Kabbalah[81]. Therefore, in his eyes, the dissemination of Kabbalah is part of the Divine design and its propagation among the Christians has eschatological overtones. This spread of Kabbalah—and Halfan stresses that he intends the speculative one—may contribute to the messianic event when, I quote, "the time will come and we shall become one nation and worship God and He will be one and His name One"[82].

The significance of the phrase "we shall become one nation" when it comes immediately after the discussion of Christians' fervent study of Kabbalah is obvious, it is a part of the conversion of Christians to Judaism via Kabbalah.

Since the end of the 15th century onwards, conversions of Jewish Kabbalists to Christianity turned into a phenomenon and the mention of the most famous names is sufficient to prove the existence of such a change: Flavious Mithridates, Paulus Ricius, Felix Prato or S. Rittangelus. Even Abraham Yagel, whom I mentioned several times here, was suspected of having converted in his last years. Strangely enough, the Kabbalah which was one of the most peculiar Jewish domains of literary creation, turned in its exoterical and speculative form into a problem for Jewish theology.

Kabbalah became suspect at the beginning of the 17th century[83]; authors like R. Yehudah del Bene or R. Azariah Figo were reticent towards the esoteric lore. Their contemporary, R. Yehudah Arieh of Modena, was much more explicit; he launched the fiercest attack on Kabbalah ever composed by a Jewish Rabbi; one of the most important arguments against the cultivation of Kabbalah among the Jews was the assertion that it served as a powerful instrument in the hands of Christians, in their attempts to convert Jews[84]; time and again Modena points out that Christians interpret Kabbalistic concepts for Christological purposes. However, the historical aspect of Christian missionary usage of Kabbalah is only one of the dangers of Kabbalah. Modena was aware of the fascination of the literature of Christian Kabbalah in his own entourage. His most talented student, R. Yoseph Hamiz, delved not only into the study of Jewish Kabbalah, a turn Modena was not able to stop; he became interested also in Pico della Mirandola's works. The spectre of apostasy out of mystical reason became one major drive which urges Modena's criticism of Kabbalah. Interestingly enough, Hamiz was, at least in the first steps of his study of Kabbalah, interested in Abulafian mysticism[85], which combines Maimonidean philosophy with mystical linguistics, and in Jewish philosophical treatises. He asserted, as he reported to his master, that every Kabbalistic concept can be explained philosophically. It seems probable, therefore, that there is some affinity between Hamez's interest in Christian Kabbalah and his indication that he can expose Kabbalah philosophically.

This alleged affinity can be the result of the perception that Kabbalah is a kind of *philosophia perennis* which was transmitted by the Jewish authorities like Jeremiah or R. Simeon the Just, to Greek philosophers[86]. But, Modena continued, this assumption is absurd since there is a clear-cut interdiction to revealing Jewish secrets to Gentiles and it is inconceivable that the famous figures mentioned in this context would flagrantly transgress this interdiction[87]. The truth is the very opposite to the assertion of the philosophical Kabbalist. Greek lore is not the result of the influence of Jewish mysticism but vice versa: Kabbalah emerged, according to Modena, as a result of the impact of medieval Neoplatonic philosophy on Jews[88]. Therefore the similarity between Kabbalah and alien culture is not the effect of the dissemination of Jewish lore among the Gentile nations, but the import of alien thought into Judaism, an import which, in Modena's opinion, has pernicious consequences. Therefore, the working hypothesis of the philosophical Kabbalah, that it may use alien sources in order to faithfully interpret Kabbalah, is employed by Modena in order to combat the authenticity of Kabbalah as a Jewish lore.

VIII

The findings of the previous discussion may enable us to draw certain conclusions about the nature of Kabbalah in Italy in the period analyzed, as well as about the character of Jewish culture in general.

a) There was an overt predilection among Italian Jewry towards a speculative perception of Kabbalah. This tendency is prominent in comparison with the contemporary Jewish thought in Germany, Poland and Palestine[89], therein the speculative elements stem from the Italian soil.

b) This predilection is the result of the combination of earlier elements, which were formulated at the end of the 15th century in Northern Italy, with a predisposition of Italian Jews to accept achievements of Renaissance culture.[90]. It is worth stressing that whereas at the end of the 15th century Jews contributed substantially to the formation of certain concepts important for the general Renaissance—Alemanno's view of Kabbalistic magic or Leone Ebreo's concept of love—after the middle of the 16th century Jewish thought became more passive and considerably moulded by the more powerful Christian culture: the works of Azariah de' Rossi, Yehudah Moscato or Abraham Portaleone testify to this process. As Kabbalists, del Medigo, Yagel or Herrera are examples of a comprehensive process of a large-scale aculturation of Renaissance culture. This process, which was limited to elitistic circles, "shines with its maximum brilliance, at the moment when it attempts to die"[91].

c). This view of Italian Kabbalists runs against the description of Jewish Italian thought as basically anti-rationalistic, as Isaac Barzilay attempted to show[92].

NOTES

1. See M. IDEL, *The Magical and Neoplatonic Interpretations of the Kabbalah in the Renaissance*, in *Jewish Thought in the Sixteenth Century*, ed. B. D. COOPERMAN, Cambridge (Mass.)—London 1983, pp. 215–229 [hereafter, IDEL, *The Magical and Neoplatonic Interpretation[s]*, and the studies referred to in n. 4 below.

2. See S. SCHECHTER, *Notes sur Messer David Leon*, in "Revue des Études Juives", and H. TIROSH-ROTHSCHILD, *Sefirot as the Essence of God in the Writings of David Messer Leon*, in "The American Journal of Sociology", 7–8 (1982–1983), pp. 409–425 [hereafter, TIROSH-ROTHSCHILD, *Sefirot as the Essence*].

3. See his *Commentary on Ten Sefirot*, extant in manuscript form, which will be published and analyzed by the present author elsewhere.

4. See M. IDEL, *The Epistle of R. Isaac of Pisa (?) in its Three Versions*, in "Kovetz Al-Yad", n.s., 10 (1982), pp. 163–214 [Hebrew] [hereafter, IDEL, *The Epistle of R. Isaac of Pisa (?)*]; ID., *Vasi e Sefirot: sostanzialità e infinità ipersostanziale nelle teorie cabbalistiche del Rinascimento*, in "Italia", III (1982), n. 1–2, pp. 102–111 [Hebrew] [hereafter, IDEL, *Vasi e Sefirot*].

5. On this author and his writings, see the preface by Robert Bonfil to Jehudah's *Nofet Zufim* (Jerusalem 1981) where the bibliographical references are brought up-to-date. On his negative attitude towards Kabbalah, see the letter printed in S. ASSAF, *Sefer Minha le-David*, Jerusalem 1935, p. 227 [Hebrew]. On the similar and negative attitude to Kabbalah, see also Messer Leon's famous contemporary, R. Eliah del Medigo's view discussed by IDEL, *The Magical and Neoplatonic Interpretations*, pp. 218–229; D. RUDERMAN, *The World of a Renaissance Jew: The Life and Thought of Abraham ben Mordecai Farissol*, Cincinnati 1981, pp. 52–56, [hereafter, RUDERMAN, *The World*]. See also the testimony of R. David Messer Leon, printed by Schechter (n. 2 above), p. 121.

6. On Alemanno's Neoplatonism, see Idel, *The Magical and Neoplatonic Interpretations,* pp. 215 ff.; on David Messer Leon's Neoplatonism, see Tirosh-Rothschild, *Sefirot as the Essence,* p. 420. On Isaac de Pisa's usage of Neoplatonic views, see Idel, *The Epistle of R. Isaac of Pisa (?),* pp. 173, 178, 186, 204.

7. Idel, *The Epistle of R. Isaac of Pisa (?),* pp. 166–168; see Idel, *The Magical and Neoplatonic Interpretations,* pp. 191 ff.

8. See below, our discussion on R. Abraham Yagel.

9. See Idel, *Vasi e Sefirot,* p. 93, n. 37–39; Idel, *The Magical and Neoplatonic Interpretations,* pp. 210–211. The magical interpretation of Kabbalah influential among Christian theologians since Pico, seemingly under the direct influence of Italian Jewish Kabbalists. See also Ruderman, *The World,* pp. 35–40.

10. A combination of philosophical perception of Kabbalah with an exoterical view, which permits open discussion of Kabbalistic issues, is found in R. Berakhiel Kafman; on his philosophical Kabbalah, see below; on his exoterism, see: I. Tishby, *Studies in Kabbalah and its Branches,* Jerusalem 1982, p. 103 [hereafter, Tishby, *Studies*].

11. The influence of the *Zohar* on 15th century and early 16th century Italian Kabbalah is scanty; see R. Bonfil, *The Rabbinate in Renaissance Italy,* Jerusalem 1979, p. 179 [Hebrew] [hereafter, Bonfil, *The Rabbinate*]; Moshe Idel's review of Bonfil's book in "Pa'amim", 4 (1980), n. 2, p. 101 [Hebrew]; and Id., *The Study Program of R. Yohanan Alemanno,* in "Tarbiz", 48 (1977), pp. 329–330 [Hebrew] [hereafter, Idel, *The Study Program*].

12. See Idel, *Vasi e Sefirot,* pp. 89–90.

13. See his critical remarks addressed to R. Asher Lemlein, a Northern Italian Kabbalist who was influenced by Abulafia's philosophical Kabbalah; cf. A. Marx, *Le Faux Messie Ascher Laemmlein,* in "Revue des Études Juives", 61 (1911), pp. 135–138; E. Kupfer, *The Visions of R. Asher ben Meir, named Lemlein Reutlingen,* in "Kovez al-Yad", n.s., 8 (18) (1976), pp. 387–423 [Hebrew]. The tension between R. Asher and the Spanish Kabbalah is overt. I hope to deal with this issue elsewhere at length.

14. Idel, *The Study Program,* pp. 330–331.

15. Compare the view expressed by Tirosh-Rothschild, *Sefirot as the Essence,* p. 412, according to which the 13th and 14th century Spanish synthesis of Kabbalah with philosophy was brought by Spanish Kabbalists of the Expulsion period to Italy; however, the study of Alemanno's earliest texts, written around 1470, demonstrates that he was acquainted with the Spanish philosophical-magical Kabbalah years before the Expulsion.

16. See his quotations in his last work, *Eine ha-Edah;* the very usage of the Zoharic texts in Hebrew translation is evidence that the public for which Alemanno wrote his book could not understand the original Aramaic of the *Zohar;* compare also to R. Isaac Mar Hayyim's explicit assertion that he translated a passage of the *Zohar* into Hebrew, since "you are not accustomed in this country [i.e., Italy] to the [language of] Jerusalemite transla-

tion [i.e. Aramaic]". Printed in A. W. GREENUP, *A Kabbalistic Epistle by Isaac B. Hayyim Sephardi*, in "Jewish Quarterly Review", n.s., XXI (1931), p. 370.

17. See IDEL, *The Epistle of R. Isaac of Pisa (?)*, pp. 170–171; IDEL, *Vasi e Sefirot*, pp. 108–111.

18. He was influenced by the third version of R. Isaac of Pisa's epistle and by Abraham Abulafia's Kabbalah; this issue will be the subject of a separate study.

19. See IDEL, *Vasi e Sefirot*, p. 110.

20. *Ibid.*, pp. 101–102, and R. Abraham of San Angelo's note in ms. Oxford 1663, f. 23 a.

21. Printed in I. SONNE, *From Paulo IV to Pius VI*, Jerusalem 1954, p. 135 [Hebrew].

22. Ms. Berlin Qu. 832, f. 275; see the description of M. STEINSCHNEIDER, *Die Handschiften-Verzeichnisse der Königlichen Bibliothek zu Berlin*, II, Berlin 1897, pp. 5–6. This manuscript was seen by HiDa (R. Hayyim Joseph David Azulai) and described in his *Shem Gedolim*, Ma'arekhet Sefarim, H: no. 118.

23. See ms. New York, JTS 889 Hi-99 No. 1958 f. 18 *v*, (where he refers to his copy of *Heshek Shelomo*), ff. 51 *r*, 58 *v* (where he refers to R. Abraham's copy), and 36 *r*, 63 *v*, 71 *r*, 84 *v*, 92 *v*, 120 *r*.

24. Ms. New York, JTS Rab. 1586, f. 2073.

25. To these quotations, a special discussion will be dedicated by the present author.

26. See IDEL, *The Study Program*, p. 330, n. 154.

27. See IDEL, *The Epistle of R. Isaac of Pisa (?)*, pp. 165–169. The possible impact of a certain passage by Motot on Isaac and Jehudah Abravanel is discussed in: M. Idel, "On Kabbalah and Ancient Theology in Isaac and Judah Abravanel." [in Hebrew] in M. Dorman and Z. Levy, eds, *The Philosophy of Leone Ebreo, Four Lectures* (Tel Aviv, 1988), pp. 90–93 [Hebrew].

28. Extant in two manuscripts: ms. Budapest, 128, and ms. Moscow; only a fragment of it was printed in *Ha-Meassef*. See n. 29 below. See also R. BONFIL, *The Rabbinate*, which is discussed in M. IDEL, *On Kabbalah* . . . cited (n. 27 above).

29. See *Ha-Meassef*, ed. RABINOVITZ, I, St. Petersburg 1902, p. 11.

30. See Moscato's *Kol Yehudah* on *Kuzari*, IV, 2; IV, 3; IV, 25.

31. See IDEL, *The Magical and Neoplatonic Interpretations*, pp. 228–229.

32. See TISHBY, *Studies*, pp. 102–103.

33. *Ibid.*, p. 105, n. 88. A question of utmost importance for our discussion, which cannot be elaborated upon in this framework, is the relation between the type of Kabbalah which was influential among the Kabbalists who printed the *Zohar*, versus the type of Kabbalah prevalent among the opponents to the printing of the *Zohar*. The view accepted by some scholars, under Tishby's influence (See *Studies*, pp. 180–182) that the publication of

the *Zohar* was considered to be a way of combatting the dissemination of philosophy, requires qualification and the whole problem deserves a detailed re-examination.

34. See *Beer Sheva*, ms. Oxford 1306, ff. 21 *r*, 24 *v*.
35. See M. IDEL, *R. Yehudah Hallewa and his "Zafenat Pa'aneah"*, in *Shalem*, 4 (ed. J. HACKER), Jerusalem 1984, pp. 119–121 [Hebrew].
36. J. B. SERMONETA, *Scholastic Philosophical Literature in Rabbi Joseph Taitasak's Porat Yosef*, in "Sefunot", 11 (1971–1977), pp. 135–185 [Hebrew].
37. See G. SCHOLEM, *Kabbalah*, Jerusalem 1974, p. 69; E. GOTTLIEB, *Studies in the Kabbala Literature* (ed. HACKER), Tel Aviv 1976, pp. 402–422 [Hebrew]; B. SACK, *The Mystical Theology of Solomon Alkabez* (Ph. D. Thesis, Brandeis University, 1977), pp. 21–24, 36–38 [Hebrew]. As Tirosh-Rothschild has proved (see here *Sefirot as the Essence*, p. 416) David Messer Leon, like Taitasak, was influenced by Thomistic views.
    On Cordovero's discussion of Messer Leon's speculative view of *Sefirot*, see J. BEN SHELOMO, *The Mystical Theology of Moses Cordovero*, Jerusalem 1965, pp. 102 ff. [Hebrew] [hereafter, BEN-SHELOMO, *The Mystical Theology*].
38. See B. SACK, *R. Solomon Alkabetz's Attitude Towards Philosophical Studies*, in *Eshel Beer-Sheva—Studies in Jewish Thought* (eds. G. BLIDSTEIN, R. BONFIL, Y. SALMON), I, Beer Sheva 1976, pp. 288–306 [Hebrew]; ID., *The Parable of Three Lights in the 'Book Ayelet Ahavim' by R. Shelomo ha-Levi Alkabetz*, in *Studies in Jewish Religious and Intellectual History Presented to Alexander Altmann* (eds. S. STEIN, R. LOEWE), Alabama 1979, pp. 53–61 [Hebrew].
39. See BEN-SHELOMO, *THe Mystical Theology*, pp. 23 ff.; M. IDEL, *R. Yehudah Hallewa . . .* cited (n. 35 above), p. 120, n. 11.
40. See TISHBY, *Studies*, pp. 131–146; Y. JACOBSON, *The Doctrine of Redemption of Rabbi Mordecai Dato* (Ph. D. Thesis, Hebrew University, 1982), pp. 120–121 [Hebrew] [hereafter, JACOBSON, *The Doctrine of Redemption*].
41. JACOBSON, *The Doctrine of Redemption*, pp. 36–40.
42. TISHBY, *Studies*, p. 185.
43. See M. PACHTER, *Sefer Reshit Hokhmah by R. Eliahu de Vidas and its Abridgements*, in "Kiriat Sefer", 47 (1972), pp. 696–698, 704–705, 709–710 [Hebrew].
44. However, Cordovero's commentary on the *Zohar* was known in manuscripts—one of them copied by R. Abraham ben Meshullam of San Angelo (see TISHBY, *Studies*, p. 143, n. 68)—circulating in Italy (*Ibid*, pp. 142, 153–154).
45. See G. SCHOLEM, *Israel Sarug—Disciple of Luria*, in "Zion", V (1949), pp. 204–213 [Hebrew].
46. TISHBY, *Studies*, p. 131 and A. ALTMANN, *Notes on the Development of Rabbi Menahem Azariah Fano's Kabbalistic Doctrine*, in *Studies in Jewish Mysticism Presented to Isaiah Tishby*, Jerusalem 1984, pp. 241–267 [Hebrew] [hereafter, ALTMANN, *Notes*].

47. TISHBY, *Studies,* pp. 177–254.
48. As happened to some Palestinian Kabbalists, according to TISHBY, *Studies,* p. 251.
49. Ms. Oxford, 1955, ff. 1 *r*-91 *r;* the texts between 1 *r*-75 *r* are an introduction to Kabbalah using classical Kabbalistic sources such as the books of R. Joseph Gikatilla and R. Menahem Recanati, and recurrently referring to *Pardes Rimmonim,* without any mention of either Luria or Sarug; folios 76 *r*-91 *r* are dedicated to the defence of the *Zohar.*
50. See e.g. Modena's criticism of Cordovero's Kabbalistic concept of prayer, analyzed in M. IDEL, *Differing Conceptions of Kabbalah in the Early 17th Century,* in *Jewish Thought in the 17th Century,* Cambridge, Ma. 1987 [hereafter, IDEL, *Differing Conceptions*], par. H.
51. Ms. Oxford, 1304, f. 50.
52. Ms. Oxford 1304, f. 50. On Yagel's relation with R. Menaham Azariah, see also D. RUDERMAN, *Three Contemporary Perceptions of a Polish Wunderkind of the Seventeenth Century,* in *Association for Jewish Studies Review* 4 *(1979), pp. 153, 157. The view of Cordovero as connected by metempsychosis with Zakharia ben Jehodaiah is found in a Lurianic source; see R. HAYYIM VITAL's Sefer ha-Gilgulim,* Vilna 1886, p. 142; however, Vital does not mention R. Shimeon bar Yohai in this context.
53. On the whole problem, see IDEL, *Differing Conceptions* (n. 50 above), par. I.
54. See A. ALTMANN, *Lurianic Kabbala in a Platonic Key: Abraham Cohen Herrera's Puerta del Cielo,* in "Hebrew Union College Annual", 53 (1982), pp. 317–355, K. KRABBENHOFT, *Abraham Cohen Herrera and Platonic Theology,* (Ph. D. Thesis, New York University, 1982).
55. This subject requires a detailed study, although the evidence is clear as far as it concerns the philosophization of Kabbalah. See, meanwhile, ALTMANN, *Notes* (n. 46 above), p. 254, n. 50, 255, n. 55.
56. See IDEL, *Differing Conceptions,* par. I.
57. It would be interesting to compare the Renaissance openness toward ancient mythology, and the latter's philosophical understanding to the Kabbalists' eagerness to accept Lurianic mythologumena, tempered by speculative interpretations. See D. C. ALLEN, *Mysteriously Meant,* Baltimore-London 1970, pp. 279–311. The perception of the Renaissance usage of mythology, as described by Jean Seznec, possesses a certain affinity to the philosophization of Kabbalah in the same period. "Mythology still plays a considerable role (even more so than in the past) but it is fatally submerged in allegory", J. SEZNEC, *The Survival of the Pagan Gods—The Mythological Tradition and its Place in Renaissance Humanism and Art,* Princeton 1972, p. 287.
58. Ms. Oxford, 1303, f. 50 *a.*
59. See IDEL, *Magical and Neoplatonic Interpretations,* pp. 224–226.
60. Ms. Oxford, 1303, ff. 38 *b*-39 *b;* Yagel mentions Origenes, Gregorius, Augustinus.

61. See M. IDEL, *Prometheus in a Hebrew Garb,* in "Eshkolot" n.s., 5–6 (1980–1981), pp. 120–127 [Hebrew].
62. Ms. Oxford, 1304, ff. 47 *b*-48 *a.* On "Zoroaster" in Renaissance, see K. H. DANNENFELD, *The Pseudo-Zoroastrian Oracles in the Renaissance,* in "Studies in the Renaissance", 4 (1957), pp. 7–28; on Kabbalistic interpretations of pseudo-Zoroastrian statements in Pico's theses, see C. WIRSZUBSKI, *Three Studies in Christian Kabbala,* Jerusalem 1975, pp. 28–38 [Hebrew]; Zoroaster was already quoted in R. Eliah of Genazano. See IDEL, *Differing Conceptions,* par. D.
63. On this author, and his literary activity, see M. BENAYAHU, *Relations between Greek and Italian Jewry,* Tel Aviv 1980, pp. 169–193 [Hebrew].
64. R. Barukh represents a good example of interest in both Kabbalah and Aristotelian thought. It is noteworthy that Aristotelian philosophy, mainly in its Averroistic version, remained a living tradition among Jewish Italian thinkers: Jehudah Messer Leon, his son, R. David, Alemanno, R. Obadiah Sforno and R. Jacob Mantino. Sforno's Averroism was analyzed by R. BONFIL, *The Doctrine of the Human Soul and its Holiness in the Thought of R. Obadiah Sforno,* in *Eshel Beer-Sheva—Studies in Jewish Thought . . .* cited (n. 38 above), pp. 200–257. Sforno did not accept Kabbalah at all; however, his contemporary, the famous translator of Averroes into Latin, Jacob Mantino, was, in contrast with the impression someone may have received from the existing bibliography, interested in Kabbalah.
65. On his activity, see R. BONFIL, *New Information on R. Menahem Azariah of Fano's Life and His Period,* in *Jewish Thought in the 17h Century.* (N. 50 above).
66. Cf. ALTMANN, *Notes,* (n. 46 above), p. 258.
67. See *Pelah ha-Rimmon,* IV, ch. 2–4.
68. The phrase "ba'al ha-razon" stems from Maimonides' *Guide to the Perplexed,* I:2.
69. See M. PAKHTER, *The Secret of Contraction in RaMHal's Doctrine and its Influence on the Doctrine of the Mitnagdism;* paper submitted to a symposium on 18th century Jewish thought (Harvard University 1984).
70. *Shomer 'Emunim,* II, par. 23–30, Lemberg 1859, pp. 67–69.
71. See IDEL, *The Magical and Neoplatonic Interpretations,* pp. 208–209.
72. See M. IDEL, *The Magical and Theurgic Interpretation of Music in Jewish Sources from the Renaissance to Hassidism,* in *Yuval—Studies of the Jewish Music Research Centre* (eds. I. ADLER, B. BAYER), Jerusalem 1982, vol. 4, pp. 33–62 [Hebrew].
73. Both are interested, like Alemanno, in linguistic magic; see the quotation from R. Berakhiel's *Chapters* in Moscato's *Kol Yehudah:* IV, 25.
74. Ms. Oxford, 1303, ff. 41 *r,* 118 *v*-119 *r,* referring to the anonymous treatise of Alemanno, extant in ms. Paris (BN) 849.
75. Ms. Oxford, 1303, f. 46.
76. Ms. Oxford, 1306, f. 17. See also f. 53 *v,* and in *Beit Ya'ar ha-Levanon,* ms. Oxford, 1304, ff. 10 *v,* 13 *r.*

77. On Agrippa's influence on Yagel see IDEL, *The Magical and Neoplatonic Interpretations*, pp. 224–226.
78. Ms. Oxford, 1303, f. 46.
79. *Beit Ya'ar ha-Levanon*, ms. Oxford, 1305, f. 109 r.
80. See D. KAUFMAN, *Elia Menachem Chalfan on Jews Teaching Hebrew to Non-Jews*, in "Jewish Quarterly Review", (OS), 9 (1896–1897), pp. 500–508.
81. See his unprinted epistle on the history of Kabbalah extant in the autographic manuscript, New York, JTS, 1822, f. 154. See also IDEL, *Magical and Neoplatonic Interpretations*, pp. 186–187, and H. HILLEL BEN SASSON, *The Reformation in Contemporary Jewish Eyes*, in *Proceedings of the Israel Academy of Science and Humanities*, 4 (1970), pp. 71–72 ([Hebrew].
82. Ms New York, JTS, 1822, f. 154.
83. On the desire to use Kabbalah to promote conversion, see the bibliography referred to in K. R. STOW, *The Burning of the Talmud in 1553 in the Light of 16th Century Catholic Attitudes toward the Talmud*, in "Bibliothèque d'Humanisme et Renaissance", 34 (1977), p. 457, n. 42; IDEL, *Differing Conceptions*, nn. 127, 141.
184. *Ari Nohem*, p. 96. See IDEL, *Differing Conceptions*, n. 152.
85. See M. IDEL, *Abraham Abulafia's Works and Doctrines* (Ph.D. Thesis, Hebrew University, Jerusalem, 1976), pp. 31–32 [Hebrew].
86. The relation between the perception of Kabbalah as an ancient Jewish lore and the concepts of *philosophia perennis* or *prisca theologia* is an important problem which deserves a separate study; see C. SCHMITT, *Prisca Theologia e Philosophia Perennis: due temi del Rinascimento italiano e la loro fortuna*, in *Il pensiero italiano del Rinascimento e il tempo nostro*, Firenze 1970, pp. 211–236, esp. p. 227, n. 49.
87. On the whole question, see IDEL, *Differing Conceptions*, par. C.
88. This statement holds also in connection with earlier stages of Italian Kabbalah; see IDEL, *The Magical and Neoplatonic Interpretations*, pp. 188–189.
89. Compare the anti-rationalistic outburst of R. J. ASHKENAZI, *The Tanna of Safed*; cfr. G. SCHOLEM, *New Information on R. Joseph Ashkenazi, the "Tanna" of Safed*, in "Tarbiz", 28 (1959), pp. 59–89, 201–235, esp. pp. 85–88 [Hebrew]; M. IDEL, *Inquiries into the Doctrine of Sefer ha-Meshiv*, in "Sefunòt", n.s., 2, XVII (1983), pp. 232–243 [Hebrew].
90. See M. SHULVASS, *The Knowledge of Antiquity among the Italian Jews of the Renaissance*, in "Proceedings of the American Academy for Jewish Research", (1948), pp. 291–299; his conclusion (p. 299) fairly presents the situation in the baroque period, ". . . the Jews, did not get totally absorbed in the pursuits of the Renaissance, as did certain parts of the Christian population . . . they only adopted the culture of the Renaissance in a 'moderate' form". See also, A. ALTMANN, *Essays in Jewish Intellectual History*, Hanover-London 1981, pp. 97–118.
91. Cfr. R. BARTHES, *Writing Degree Zero*, Boston 1967, p. 38.

92. The dichotomy between Kabbalists, who are described as "representatives of a 'spiritual asceticism'" and Renaissance Jews, labelled as "immoral licentiousness" espoused by I. BARZILAY, *Yoseph Shlomo Delmedigo,* p. 231, is an oversimplification of the more complex situation at the end of the 16th century in Italy. Kabbalah and Kabbalists were instrumental in introducing alien elements, mostly renaissancian, into Jewish theology, whereas non-Kabbalists, such as Figo, tried to limit the infiltration of alien concepts into Jewish thought. The tension between a more conservative Judaism and a more open one can be located even among various types of Kabbalists.

II

**JEWISH CULTURE IN THE SETTING
OF THE GHETTO**

A

The Significance of the Ghetto
in Shaping Jewish Society and Culture

13

From Geographical Realia to Historiographical Symbol: The Odyssey of the Word *Ghetto*

Benjamin C. I. Ravid

The phenomenon of the Jewish quarter in preemancipation Europe, one of the most basic features of the life of the Jews, still awaits a comprehensive and definitive treatment. Such an undertaking ideally requires a systematic investigation of the specific conditions under which the Jews resided until the eighteenth century, and indeed in some areas well into the nineteenth. First, the origins of the Jewish settlement, an event often completely shrouded in darkness or illuminated only by the dim light of dubious legend, must be carefully examined. Then a precise distinction must always be maintained between three forms of Jewish quarters: (1) voluntary Jewish quarters; (2) quarters assigned to the Jews, either for their convenience or for their protection, as an inducement for them to settle in an area, without however establishing a legally exclusive Jewish quarter; (3) the compulsory segregated Jewish quarter in which all Jews were required to live and in which no Christians were permitted to live. Upon encountering a legally compulsory and exclusive segregated Jewish quarter, the researcher must investigate several problems, including the pressure, often emanating from clerical circles, leading to its establishment; the attitude of the authorities, who may have instituted a compulsory and exclusive quarter as a compromise between freedom of residence and expulsion; the nature of the new, proposed Jewish quarter; the reaction of the Jews to the new situation; the actual implementation of the segregatory legislation, which was often delayed, and its subsequent enforcement. Finally, despite the special function of the Jewish quarter in the specific context of Jewish-Christian relations and the Christian attitude toward Judaism, it must also be placed in the general context of the residential patterns of other groups, both native and foreign, in the location under investigation.

Accordingly, any serious attempt to engage in comprehensive research on the ghettos of Venice raises at least four significant, yet inadequately researched, sets of questions:

1. The main issue: the origin of the word *ghetto* in Venice (including an examination of the foundries supposedly once existing on the site of the ghetto), the establishment of the three ghettos of that city, and the subsequent history of those areas (i.e., specific matters of topography, demography, and administration, as distinct from a general religious-cultural history of the Jews of the city).
2. As background: the history of the development of Jewish quarters both in Christian Europe and under the rule of Islam, and where applicable, the later enactment of compulsory and segregated Jewish quarters.
3. As parallel context: the wider issue of the phenomenon of special residential quarters, both voluntary and compulsory, for certain elements of the native population—usually for social and moral reasons —and also for foreigners, usually for economic or religious reasons.
4. As postscript: the history of the changing nuance of the word *ghetto* from the time it was first used in connection with the Jews until the present.

The investigation of these problems is of special relevance and interest in view of the general importance of Venice in European history, its significance as a center of Jewish life and culture, and the fact that the Venetian experience gave rise to the widely used and later on equally misused and misunderstood term *ghetto*. The following represents a summary of current research which I plan to present more extensively in the future.

I

From their earliest diaspora days onward, Jews chose freely, for a variety of religious and social reasons, to live close together, as did many other groups residing in foreign lands. This tendency was strengthened in the eleventh and twelfth centuries, as the secular authorities, primarily in the Germanic lands and reconquista Spain, offered Jews special quarters as an inducement to settle in their realms. These quarters, often referred to as the Jewish quarter or street in the vernacular of the country, were neither compulsory nor segregated. Jews continued to have contacts on all levels—economic, intellectual, and social—with their Christian neighbors. However, the Catholic church always looked askance at these relationships, and in 1179 the third Lateran Council stipulated that henceforth Christians should not dwell together with Jews. To become effective, this vague policy statement had to be translated into legislation by the numerous European secular authorities, and on the whole, only infrequently were laws confining the Jews to segregated quarters enacted in the Middle Ages and not always were those laws actually implemented. The few segregated Jewish quarters which indeed were then established were never called ghettos, since the term originated in Venice and came to be associated with the Jews only in the sixteenth century.

While the Venetian government permitted individual Jews to reside in the city of Venice, it never officially authorized Jews to settle in it as a group in the Middle Ages, with the exception of the brief period from 1382 to 1397. However, the government did allow Jewish moneylenders to live on the mainland, across the lagoon in Mestre and in Padua and elsewhere, and the terms of the charter of those moneylenders of Mestre allowed them to seek refuge in Venice in case of war. Understandably, in 1509, during the war of the League of Cambrai, as the enemies of Venice overran the Venetian mainland, Jewish moneylenders residing there were among the many refugees who fled to Venice. Soon afterward, when the Venetian government recovered those mainland territories, it ordered the refugees to return home. However, it realized that allowing the Jews to stay in the city was doubly beneficial: first, they could be required to provide the hard-pressed treasury with substantial annual payments, and second, allowing them to engage in moneylending in the city itself would be convenient for the needy poor, whose numbers had been swelled by war. Accordingly, in 1513 the government issued a five-year charter which authorized the Jews to stay in the city and to lend money in it.

Jewish moneylending was clearly very important. In addition to giving the government an additional source of revenue and assisting in promoting urban tranquillity, it also had great significance in the religious sphere. Since Christians as well as Jews adhered to the biblical commandment which forbade members of the same faith to lend money to each other at interest, the presence of Jewish pawnbrokers lending money on interest on loan-pledges to the Christian poor rendered it unnecessary for Christians to engage in that activity in violation of the religious tradition. Thus, the Jewish moneylenders not only helped to solve the socioeconomic problems of an increasingly urbanized economy, but also made it less necessary for Christians to violate church law by lending money at interest to fellow Christians. Consequently, the Venetian government periodically renewed charters allowing Jews to engage in moneylending down to the end of the Republic in 1797.

While the Venetian government tolerated the presence of the Jews in the city, many Venetians were upset by the new phenomenon of the presence of Jews all over the city, and the clergy preached against them, especially at Eastertime when anti-Jewish sentiment tended to intensify, demanding their expulsion. As a compromise, on 29 March 1516, the Venetian Senate took action. The preamble to legislation of that day asserted that although the Jews had been permitted to live in Venice primarily for the safety of the loan-pledges of Christian Venetians which were in their hands, nevertheless no God-fearing inhabitant of the city desired that they should dwell spread out all over it, living in the same houses as Christians and going wherever they pleased day and night, allegedly committing many detestable things to the grave offense of God and against the laws of the Republic. The legislation of the Senate required all Jews then living in the city and those who were to come in the future to go and reside on the island known as the *ghetto nuovo* (the new ghetto). Gates were to be erected in two places, and locked at sunset (not midnight as sometimes erroneously asserted) and only opened again at sunrise, with a substantial fine levied against any Jew caught outside after hours. The Christian inhabitants of the ghetto were required to vacate their premises, and as an incentive for landlords to comply, the Jews were required to pay them a rent one-third higher than that previously paid, with that increase exempt from taxation.

Thus the ghetto of Venice came into being. Clearly, the word *ghetto* is of Venetian rather than of Jewish origin, as has sometimes been conjectured. It is encountered in Venetian sources from the fourteenth and fifteenth centuries, and today it is generally presumed that the word derives from the Italian verb *gettare* (to pour or to cast), because of the previous presence of foundries in the area.

Despite the attempts of the Jews to ward off segregation in this new compulsory area, the Venetian government was adamant; while willing to make minor concessions on a few administrative details, it was unwilling to yield on the general principle that all the Jews in the city had to live in the ghetto. The presence of the Jews was necessary for economic reasons, and the ghetto was the institution that relegated them to their appropriate permanent position in Christian society.

Some twenty-five years later, in 1541, a group of visiting Levantine Jewish merchants complained to the Venetian government that there was not sufficient room for themselves and their merchandise in the ghetto and requested additional space. The government investigated and found their complaint to be valid. Noting, in the context of a larger plan designed to make Venice more attractive to foreign merchants, that the greater part of the imports from the Ottoman Balkans was handled by these Jewish merchants, it granted their request. It ordered that twenty dwellings in the not yet fully built-up area known as the *ghetto vecchio* (the old ghetto), located across the canal from the ghetto nuovo, be walled up, joined by a footbridge to the ghetto nuovo, and assigned to the Jewish merchants, who were only allowed to stay there temporarily without their families. However, these restrictions were soon disregarded as the merchants settled in the ghetto vecchio with their families for lengthy periods.

The word *ghetto* was not for long to remain confined only to the city of Venice. In 1555, as a part of the new hostile Counter-Reformation attitude toward the Jews, Pope Paul IV, shortly after his inauguration, issued the bull *Cum Nimis Absurdum* which sought severely to restrict the Jews. Its first paragraph provided that henceforth in all places in the papal states the Jews were to live on a single street, and should it not suffice, then on as many adjacent ones as should be necessary, separated from Christians, with only one entrance and exit. Accordingly, that same year the Jews of Rome were required to move into a new compulsory enclosed quarter in that city, which, as far as is known today, apparently was first called a ghetto in the bull *Dudum a Felicis* of Pius IV in 1562.

Influenced by the papal example, many local Italian authorities instituted special compulsory quarters for the Jews. Following the Venetian and now also Roman nomenclature, these new residential areas were given the name of ghetto. Indeed, that word was used in the legislation which required the Jews to move into the newly designated areas. Thus, for example, an edict issued in Tuscany in 1571 required all the Jews living in the region of Florence either to leave or to go permanently to live in the ghetto set aside for them in the city of Florence. Similar legislation, issued in 1572, confining the Jews of the region of Siena to a segregated area in the city of Siena, also specifically referred to that area as the ghetto. The word *ghetto* was used in Hebrew documents by the Jews of Padua in 1582, in connection with the compulsory Jewish quarter contemplated for their residence, and when in 1601 the city council of Padua, which had been under Venetian rule since 1405, finally decided after years of discussion and negotiation to implement the segregation of the Jews into a special enclosed area, it referred to that area as a ghetto. The word *ghetto* also was used by the Jews of Mantua in 1610, after the government had indicated its intention to establish one, but before the actual implementation.

Significantly, this new usage of the word *ghetto* for a compulsory Jewish quarter came into usage also in Venice. In 1630, the Jewish merchants in the city requested that the ghetto be enlarged for the sake of some additional wealthy families of Jewish merchants who, they claimed, would come to the city if they had suitable living quarters. Very sharp objections were raised both by the Christian landlords who owned the buildings in the ghetto as well as by those Jews who had built additional stories, on the grounds that expanding the ghetto might lead to their own dwellings going unrented. Thereupon, to demonstrate that they did not seek the enlargement of the ghetto for their own sake but only for that of the newcomers, the Jewish merchants offered a guarantee of three thousand ducats that twenty additional Jewish families would come, with that sum to be prorated if necessary according to the number of families that did not actually arrive. The Senate, always concerned with attracting merchants to the city in order to enhance trade and no doubt especially so after the plague of 1630–31, accepted this offer and in March 1633 provided that an area containing twenty dwellings located across from the ghetto nuovo in a direction almost opposite from the ghetto vecchio be enclosed and joined to the ghetto nuovo by a footbridge over the canal. This area was not designated by any name in the Senate legislation of 1633, but almost immediately it was being referred to by the Venetian authorities as the *ghetto nuovissimo*, i.e., the newest ghetto.

In light of developments elsewhere, it is understandable that when a third compulsory Jewish quarter was established in Venice, it was referred to as a ghetto. And since in Venice there already existed areas called the old ghetto (ghetto vecchio) and the new ghetto (ghetto nouvo), this third ghetto became known as the newest ghetto (ghetto nuovissimo). However, the ghetto nuovissimo differed from the ghetto nuovo and the ghetto vecchio in one important respect. While the latter two designations had been in use prior to the residence of the Jews in those locations and apparently owed their origin to the former presence of foundries in the area, the ghetto nuovissimo had never been the site of a foundry. Rather, it was called the ghetto nuovissimo because it was the site of the newest compulsory, segregated, walled-up Jewish quarter. The term *ghetto* had come full circle in its city of origin: from an original specific usage as a foundry in Venice, to a generic usage in other cities designating a compulsory, segregated, walled-in Jewish quarter with no relation to a foundry, and then to that generic usage also in Venice.

II

The initial sunset closing time of the ghetto gates established by the Venetian government in 1516 was extended slightly a few weeks later at the request of the Jews, until the first hour of the night in summer and the second hour of the night in winter (presumably a necessary concession since it got darker considerably earlier in winter). Only Jewish doctors treating Christian patients and Jewish merchants who had to attend to their business seem to have been routinely allowed to be outside after hours, but on occasion other Jews, including representatives of the Jewish community who had to negotiate charter renewals with the government, singers and dancers who performed especially at carnival time, and individuals who had special skills and needs, were granted the privilege on a one-time basis, often only until a specified hour of the night. Only extremely rarely indeed was permission granted to reside outside the ghetto.

While apparently the hour of closing of the ghetto gates was very slightly modified by administrative rulings over the decades, in 1738 the Senate for the first time incorporated the hours of the opening and closing of the ghetto gates in the charter of the Jews, restoring the original provisions of sunrise and sunset. The charter of 1760 extended the closing hour to the second hour of the night in the summer and the fourth hour of the night in winter, while the charter of 1788 more liberally fixed it as midnight without any seasonal qualifications. That charter was only slightly over a year away from its expiration when in May 1797, as the conquering army of Napoleon Bonaparte stood poised across the lagoon at Mestre, the Venetian government dissolved itself in favor of a municipal council. Shortly afterward, the special restrictive charter system of the Jews of Venice, with all that it entailed, came to an end, and the ghetto gates were torn down.

III

Although the complex attitude of Christianity toward Judaism and the Jews must always be kept in mind when discussing legislation of Christian authorities on the matter of Jewish quarters, nevertheless it is instructive to consider briefly Venetian provisions requiring other groups in the city to live in compulsory quarters.

Merchants from the Germanic lands were required, from at least the early fourteenth century on, to go with their merchandise directly to reside in a special building known as the Fondaco dei Tedeschi. Initially, this provision had been instituted to make evasion of customs, duty payments and the violation of certain Venetian commercial laws more difficult, but it assumed religious significance after the Reformation when it also had the effect of hampering somewhat the spread of new Protestant ideas and practices in the city by restricting the freedom of residence of merchants from the North.

For a while in the fourteenth and fifteenth centuries, the Venetian government followed the practice adopted also in some other European cities at that time of attempting to confine prostitutes to certain houses. Presumably even less successful was legislation requiring prostitutes and pimps to be recognizable through the wearing of yellow items of clothing, a step reminiscent of the Jewish badge which had been introduced in 1397 and replaced by a hat in 1497.

The segregation of the Jews served as a precedent for the segregation of the Moslem Ottoman Turkish merchants in Venice. Apparently, the initial impetus for providing them with their own quarters came from the Turks themselves. After their internment as enemy subjects in Venice during the Venetian-Ottoman war of 1570–73, according to the papal nuncio in Venice, the Turks requested from the Venetian government, for the convenience of their trade, a place of their own similar to the Jews who had their ghetto. The Venetian government was for the most part favorably inclined toward this idea for various reasons, and discussed several proposals for almost fifty years. Finally, in 1621, it required the Turkish merchants to live in a certain building which was first to be carefully isolated from its surroundings in a manner reminiscent of those provisions which had been made for the isolation of the ghetto nuovo and vecchio, and subsequently this building became known as the Fondaco dei Turchi. Yet, interestingly, not all Venetians favored this segregation of the Turks. An anonymous memorandum of 1602 urged the government not to grant the Turks a fondaco, claiming among other things that the concentration of many Turks in one place would be very dangerous and lead to the erection of mosques and to the worship of Mohammed, causing greater scandal than that provoked by the Jews and the Protestant Germans; additionally it asserted that the pernicious innovation of a fondaco would further the political aims of the Turks, who, headed by one sultan and possessing great naval power, were in a position to harm Venice much more than were the Jews, who were without any head or prince and everywhere depressed.

These arguments, taken together with the comment of the Catholic patriarch of Venice, Girolamo Querini, in 1528 that the Greek Orthodox Christians in Venice, whose freedom of worship was severely restricted, were worse than the Jews, serve as a reminder of the complexity of the attitudes held toward the Jews in Renaissance Venice, as indeed in most other times and places.

IV

While the word *ghetto* had never been applied to a Jewish quarter prior to 1516, compulsory, segregated and enclosed Jewish quarters had existed prior to 1516 in a few places; for example, the Jewish quarter of Frankfurt, established in 1462, may perhaps be the best-known and longest-lasting institution of its kind. Thus, the oft-encountered statement that the first ghetto was established in Venice in 1516 is correct in a technical, linguistic sense but in a wider context, misleading. Although the institution of the compulsory, exclusive and enclosed Jewish quarter was called a ghetto for the first time in Venice in 1516, it was not unknown prior to then. In short, to apply the term *ghetto* to an area prior to 1516 is anachronistic, while to state that the first ghetto was established in 1516 is somewhat of a misrepresentation.

The Jewish ghetto of Venice was apparently first mentioned in the Hebrew language in the *Diary* of David Ha-Reuveni, who came to Venice in the winter of 1523–24. Realizing that many of his readers would not know what he meant, he explained the word in a gloss as he related that "I went with R. Moses to the ghetto, the place of the Jews." The word *ghetto* first seems to have appeared in print in the English language in Thomas Coryat's travelogue *Coryat's Crudities* (London, 1611) in connection with his visit to Venice. Coryat also felt the need to explain the word: "It was at a place where the whole fraternity of the Jews dwelleth together, which is called the ghetto." It should be noted that the ghetto is not encountered in Shakespeare's *Merchant of Venice* (London, 1596); Shylock also fared better than his real-life coreligionists in that he was not subjected to wearing a special yellow hat; additionally, both he and Antonio would have been severely punished by the Venetian authorities for their transaction, for Jewish moneylending was restricted to small-scale pawnbroking, with loans limited to three ducats per pledge.

In later years, the Venetian origin of the word *ghetto* came to be forgotten, as it was used exclusively in its secondary meaning as referring to compulsory Jewish quarters, and much ink was spilled by eighteenth-nineteenth-, and twentieth-century authors in attempts to ascertain its etymology. Subsequently, in a process that has not yet been traced, the word *ghetto* came to be used in a looser sense to refer to any area densely populated by Jews, even in places where they had freedom of residence and could and did live in the same districts and houses as Christians. Eventually it came to be the general designation for areas densely inhabited by members of any minority group, almost always for voluntary socioeconomic reasons rather than for compulsory legal ones as had been the case with the initial Jewish ghetto. Indeed, the ghetto has even been extended to the animal world; an article in the *Wall Street Journal,* discussing the mating habits of South African flamingos, related that "they want mud to build their nests—180-pound mounts they slap together in ghettos of up to 60,000." Thus while the institution which had given birth to the word *ghetto* had long come to an end, the word assumed a life of its own and entered the general everyday vocabulary, similar to other words emerging from the Jewish experience, such as *diaspora* and *holocaust.*

It must be noted that the varied usages of the word *ghetto* in different senses has created a certain blurring of the historical reality, especially when the word is used loosely in phrases such as "the age of the ghetto," "out of the ghetto," and "ghetto mentality," which are so often applied to the Jewish experience especially in Central and Eastern Europe in the seventeenth, eighteenth, and even nineteenth centuries. Actually, the word can be used in the original Counter-Reformation Italian sense of a compulsory and segregated Jewish quarter only in connection with the Jewish experience in a few places in the Germanic lands, and certainly not at all with that in Poland-Russia. Although up to the Russian Revolution of 1917 many Jews lived in small towns and rural villages that were predominantly Jewish, they were never confined to specific, segregated, walled-up quarters apart from their Christian neighbors. Despite the general Russian restriction that officially no Jew could live outside the Pale of Settlement (i.e., basically the Polish territory annexed by Russia in the late eighteenth-century partitions of Poland), the Pale never possessed the one essential characteristic of the ghetto, because within it the Jews were not segregated in walled-up quarters apart from their Christian neighbors. Additionally, the requirement that all Jews were to live within the Pale was not always enforced; indeed, at certain times, specific groups of Jews such as agriculturalists, holders of university degrees, merchants of the first guild, artisans, and army veterans were granted official permission to live outside the Pale. If the word *ghetto* is to be used in its original literal sense in connection with Eastern Europe, then it must be asserted that the age of the ghetto arrived there only after the German invasions during the Second World War. However, there was a basic difference: unlike those ghettos of earlier days which were designed to provide the Jews with a clearly defined, permanent place in Christian society, these twentieth-century ghettos constituted merely a temporary stage on the planned road to total liquidation.

Of course the use of the word *ghetto* is even more misleading when applied to the experience of Jewish immigrants in North America, with its completely different legal traditions, religious heritage, and social environment. In this context, the word *ghetto* used in expressions such as "ghetto life" and "ghetto mentality" is intended by those who use it to refer primarily to the Eastern European pattern of Jewish life and certain of its manifold manifestations, often in a critical sense, and has nothing to do with the institution of the ghetto as it originated on the Italian peninsula.

To a great extent because of the negative connotations of the word *ghetto*, the nature of Jewish life in the ghetto is often misunderstood. The establishment of ghettos did not lead, as perhaps most readily revealed in the autobiography of Leon Modena, to the breaking off of Jewish contacts with the outside world on any level, from the highest to the lowest, much to the consternation of church and state alike. Additionally, apart from the question of whether the ghetto succeeded in fulfilling the expectations of those in the outside world who desired its establishment, from the internal Jewish perspective many evaluations of the alleged impact of the ghetto upon the cultural and intellectual life of the Jews and their mentality require substantial revision. For example, an investigation of the cultural life inside the ghetto of Venice and the extent to which external trends penetrated it—as attested by the writings of Leon Modena, Simone Luzzatto, and Sara Copia Sullam—leads to a reevaluation of the alleged negative impact of the ghetto in the intellectual and cultural spheres. In general, the determining element in Jewish self-expression and creativity was not so much the circumstance of whether or not Jews were required to live in a ghetto, but rather the nature of the outside environment and whether it offered an attractive supplement to traditional Jewish genres of intellectual activity. In all places, Jewish culture should be examined in the context of the environment, and developments—especially those subjectively evaluated as undesirable—not merely attributed to the alleged impact of the ghetto.

In conclusion, an extended investigation of why the word *ghetto* is used so loosely and imprecisely in Jewish history and contemporary sociology would reveal many complex motivations. The most common reason is no doubt merely a simple casual use of the word without any thought or awareness of its origin and nature. Others, however, are somewhat less innocent and may involve a desire, proceeding from either religious, nationalistic, or psychological considerations—often almost instinctive or barely conscious—to portray the life of the Jews in the preemancipation European diaspora unfavorably. Thus the word *ghetto* has become a value concept with negative connotations, rather than a descriptive word indicating a particular legal, residential system under which Jews lived. The result has been to blur the historical reality of one of the basic aspects of Jewish survival, the Jewish quarter, and thus gives additional urgency to the need for its systematic examination.

REFERENCES

This article is based primarily on B. Ravid, "The Religious, Economic and Social Background and Context of the Establishment of the Ghetti of Venice," in *Gli Ebrei e Venezia*, ed. G. Cozzi (Venice, 1987), 211–59; idem, "The Establishment of the Ghetto Nuovissimo of Venice," in *Jews in Italy: Studies Dedicated to the Memory of Umberto Cassuto on the 100th Anniversary of His Birth*, H. Beinart, ed. (Jerusalem, 1988), 35–54; idem, "The Venetian Ghetto in Historical Perspective," in *The Autobiography of a Seventeenth-Century Venetian Rabbi: Leon Modena's Life of Judah*, trans. and ed. M. R. Cohen (Princeton, 1988), 279–85; and idem, "New Light on the Ghetti of Venice," to appear in the Festschrift in Honor of Shlomo Simonsohn. See also S. Baron, *A Social and Religious History of the Jews*, 18 vols. (Philadelphia, 1952–83), 9:32–36, 11:87–96, 14:114–20; and S. Rawidowicz, "On the Concept of Galut," in his *Israel: The Ever-Dying People and Other Essays* (Rutherford, N.J., 1986), 96–117.

14

The Consciousness of Closure: Roman Jewry and Its *Ghet*

Kenneth R. Stow

In 1555, Paul IV enclosed the Jews of Rome within the walls of what would eventually be known as the Roman Ghetto. A ghetto already existed, of course, that of Venice, established by the Serenissima in 1516. Yet, although the Venetian area of forced Jewish residence was called from the start "the ghetto"—clearly after the previous name of the place (meaning foundry) where this residential area was established—in Rome, the name *ghetto* was not at first used. Originally, in fact, Jews did not abstractly conceive of their residential area as a place and a space requiring a name. The first documented Jewish reference known to me to the new residential situation—which occurred in September 1555— noted simply (in Hebrew) that "the Pope has ordered the Jews to live [lit., to be] together."[1]

Jews and other contemporaries normally called the new residential zone the *serraglio,* or, more specifically, the *serraglio degli hebrei*— incidentally, the same name used to refer to the area near the Roman Porta Ripetta, previously known as the Ortaccio, where Pius V and Sixtus V intended to enclose Roman prostitutes. The name *serraglio* was widely accepted. Isaac Piatelli, the Jews' own notary, who drew his acts in Hebrew and whose career spanned 60 years, used *serraglio* until the end of his days in 1605. However, in May 1589, Rabbi Pompeo del Borgo, also a Jewish notary, who had been drawing acts (in Italian) since 1578—that is, already for more than a decade—dropped the customary *serraglio,* and, in its stead, he referred to *nostro (our) Ghet.* Pompeo repeated this usage on other occasions, sometimes spelling the word *gette*.[2] Following his example, a third Jewish notary, Simone de Castelnuovo, spoke of the *gete, gette, ghet,* even the *ghetto.* To be sure, these notaries, in particular, Pompeo never completely deserted *serraglio,* but some form of *ghet* or *gette* became the established norm. For Roman Jewry, the *serraglio* had become the *ghetto,* or, more simply—and frequently—the *ghet.*

Admittedly, the name *ghetto* had previously been used to specify Jewish quarters beside those in the original Ghetto of Venice. As early as 1536, Rabbi David ha Cohen of Corfu applied the name to the quay (jetty, *getto)* in Genova where Jews fleeing Spain in 1492 were retained in quarantine. This usage has led to the speculation that the name may actually come from *gettare,* or the Latin *jactare,* (to throw).[3] More probably, R. David was making the specific Venetian name into a generic one referring to any area of enforced Jewish residence. The same process—applying the specific to the general—might also explain Pompeo del Borgo's usage. But should we draw this facile conclusion, we would be ignoring why it took Roman Jews thirty-four years (from 1555 to 1589) to switch from *serraglio* to some form of *ghetto,* and why Pompeo himself did not make the switch until he had been at work as a notary for over ten years. Perhaps, therefore, some event occurred in the year 1589, which may more properly account for Pompeo's switch? Moreover, why did Pompeo adopt specifically *ghet, gette,* etc.—forms that in terms of both their spelling and their then current Italian pronunciation were homologous with the Hebrew word, *get* (with a hard g), meaning a bill of divorce? Could it be that in the Jews' initially casual reference in 1555 to their residential district—saying that the pope simply willed that the Jews live together—they were optimistically hiding from the truth; by switching to the pointed *ghet*—a switch that was of course made by others than Pompeo alone—the Jews were signifying a new awareness? Namely, that they had finally understood that there was to be no going back: The ghetto was to be a permanent institution and fact of life; and the Jews themselves had been given a bill of divorce, at once physical and emotional, relegating them to the margins of Roman Christian society.

At first glance, such a suggestion seems to be preposterous. Pompeo del Borgo, as already mentioned, began to use *ghet* in May 1589. This *was* immediately after an important event; however, that event was one which should have buoyed up Jewish spirits, not made Jews think in terms of a "divorce." For in February 1589, the then reigning pope, Sixtus V, had enlarged the Roman ghetto, adding to it the sector that eventually was called via Fiumara. And the pope had acted ostensibly to relieve the ghetto's unbearable overcrowding. In addition, to suggest that the Jews were irrevocably "divorced" from Christian society during the reign of Sixtus V seems contrary to fact. Historians have invariably described as moderate the main lines of Sixtus V's policies toward the Jews.[4] They were a respite from the draconian precedents set by Paul IV and Pius V, not to mention from the actions of Sixtus' immediate predecessor, Gregory XIII. In particular, Sixtus cancelled Pius V's 1569 decree expelling the Jews from all places of the Papal State except Rome and Ancona. And a number of Jews, who received banking licenses, did reestablish residences in various papal State localities. Sixtus also eased many commercial restrictions imposed by Gregory and Pius V, and he further seems to have encouraged some notable Jewish business ventures. A somewhat shadowy figure known as Magino was even given an exclusive patent on a glass-making process, and he, together with other Jews, was also called upon to increase the production of silk worms and cloth.[5]

Furthermore, we do not have to view these programs as acts of papal magnanimity; no papal Jewry policy, for that matter, should ever be viewed in such moralizing, rather than historically proper, analytical terms. Rather, Sixtus' actions, as just described, correspond to his overall policies, and they fit in well with his image as politician and head of state. It was his desire, as is so well known, to expand wherever possible the financial base and independence of the Papal State. Sixtus was also a practical man, seeking to keep the poor out of debt. And that included the Jews, whose ability to meet tax payments was rapidly deteriorating thanks to previous papal financial sanctions. To avoid the embarrassment of supporting the Jewish community with ecclesiastical charity, it was necessary to allow Jews to grow economically, even if that entailed raising the permitted interest rate to as high as 24 percent. Even Paul IV, after all, had only regulated interest rates, not cancelled them entirely. Why should Sixtus V not follow suit? Besides, the regrowth of Jewish banking and the new revenues it generated did more than aid the Jews to liquidate their debts—which the papacy, and Sixtus in particular (once again in accord with his overall programs) had otherwise begun to fund by having Jews invest in various governmental securities known as *Monti*.[6] The revenues of Jewish banking also allowed Sixtus to impose new business taxes, which he indeed did collect from Jews who opened loan banks outside of Rome. More importantly, the banks scattered throughout the Papal State provided agricultural credit to poor farmers, a group Sixtus was especially concerned to assist, just as he also emphasized that Roman Jewish bankers were to supply credit to poor urban wool workers.[7]

Even the expansion of the ghetto may be said to have accorded with Sixtus' broader political needs. One of his aims had been to revive the sluggish Roman wool industry. Toward this end, he had appointed Cardinal Santa Croce as chief administrator.[8] As it turned out, however, the cardinal was also the prime owner of real estate—27 percent of it, in fact—on the land that in 1589 was to be enclosed within ghetto walls.[9] This enclosure was a godsend to owners. Eventually ghetto rents were regulated. But in these early ghetto years, rents steadily increased. Furthermore, there was immediate profit in leasing houses to Jews, who scrambled to purchase a long-term lease, the *cazaga*—actually the name of an old Jewish leasing device—but still had to pay the owner (either directly or through a subtenant) an annual rent. Most of all, as soon as a house was placed within ghetto walls, its own walls rose higher—by as many as three or four stories—to accommodate the numerous applicants for previously unavailable housing. Jewish notarial texts describe this building activity in detail. Against this backdrop, one may easily venture that one reason behind the expansion of the ghetto, and particularly on the via Fiumara site, was Cardinal Santa Croce's direct urging and Sixtus V's reciprocal sense of obligation to a devoted civil servant. The expansion of the ghetto also profited another papal faithful, namely, the architect Domenico Fontana, who planned and executed so many of Sixtus' grandiose projects. Fontana built the ghetto's new walls and gates, and in return was given an annual stipend that his heirs continued to collect through the end of the ghetto period in 1870.[10] Finally, although only indirectly related to the ghetto's expansion, we should not be surprised to find as an owner of property there one Camilla Peretti—Sixtus' sister!—who was the titular owner of property originally purchased by the pope himself. If this was so, then Sixtus' attitude toward the Jews and the ghetto was also integral to his policy of Peretti familial aggrandizement. Camilla certainly was supposed to benefit from Magino's silk enterprises. The letter granting Magino his franchise also awarded Camilla one-half of all Magino's profits.[11]

Yet should we not be warned by what Paolo Prodi has so recently affirmed? The Papal State was a *Tempelstadt,* and its head was a religious leader. Aims of statecraft and faith often intertwined; they became indistinguishable and naturally reinforcing. I have indirectly supported this argument in a book that appeared more or less simultaneously with Prodi's, in 1982, arguing that modes of papal taxation of the Jews were dependent on papal conversionary goals, as well as on fiscal ones.[12] The policies of Sixtus V, whether they were those related to the Jews, the Church, or the Papal State, were no exception to this schema. Indeed, our discussion here would be faulty were it to insist that purely pragmatic political or economic motives alone governed Sixtus' policies toward the Jews.

The concept of an enclosed ghetto was highly compatible with the sixteenth-century papacy's overall program of reform. The otherwise massively threatened Catholic world had to be defended, not only from the Lutherans, but also from the so-called "Jewish contamination" that ecclesiastical radicals had always feared. The surest way to this end was through segregation and enclosure. The ghetto thus responded to St. Paul's warning in Galatians that a little leaven sours the dough, that too much contact with Jews imperils Christian salvation, and that given too much Jewish provocation, it was best to dismiss Esau, the son of the servant woman Hagar, in order to protect Isaac, the son of Sara the freewoman (Gal. 4:21–5:13), that is, to dismiss the Jew, whom the Church had persistently identified with Esau; the Church, of course, being Jacob, Israel—indeed, the *Verus Israel.* And when the Ghetto proved insufficient to enclose all the Papal State's Jewries, the excess Jewish population was to be expelled, as in fact it was, by Pius V, in 1569.

At the same time, the ghetto was pictured as the locus of a massive conversionary program. It made the Jews a captive audience for the obligatory sermons initiated by Gregory XIII, the first pope ever to make attendance at such sermons truly compulsory.[13] Gathered into the ghetto, Jews might also be more easily controlled, ensuring that they would have no access to their supposedly blasphemous Talmud (which was said to dissuade them from seeing Christian truth). Such control further ensured

that any unfortunate who even breathed a word about a Catholic preference could be whisked straightaway to the *Domus cathecumenorum*
(the House of Converts). Most of all, the ghetto was the scene where
canon law could be unmitigatedly enforced, to convince the Jews through
the application of "pious lashes"—a term first used by Alexander of
Hales in the thirteenth century, revived by the convert Abner of Burgos
in the fourteenth century, and adopted by the Camaldulese monks Quir-
ini and Giustiniani in the sixteenth—that Christianity was the more
worthy faith.[14] To apply such "lashes" was also the undoubted vision of
Paul IV, the ghetto's founder. I personally am convinced that Paul IV
took this drastic action in the belief that he was living in an apocalyptic
moment, certainly in one of total social ruin. The time for the Jews'
conversion had at last arrived. If not actually that, the ghetto allowed
for a by now necessary fiction. The centuries-old ecclesiastical policy of
living with the Jews could theoretically be maintained, even though,
with the exception of the ghetto, the Jews had been shut out from the
Christian fold. Alternately, the ghetto was a way to pretend openly that
all had changed, even though it could be argued that what had changed
in fact was only the Jews' physical circumstances and the degree to
which they must bow before canonical limitation.[15]

The probability that sixteenth-century popes following Paul IV would
have identified with any, or all, of these goals is extremely high. As Paolo
Simoncelli is now arguing, subsequent to Paul IV's election in 1555, and
perhaps more precisely from 1549, with the election of Julius III, the
papacy was ever more dominated by inquisitors and friars; and Counter
Reformation, or Catholic Restoration (to avoid arguments over terms)
programs were becoming identifiable with those of the Roman Inquisition itself. Notably, the one rent in this fabric was Pius IV. Pius had
sharp differences with the Inquisition, and it was precisely Pius IV who
mitigated the harshest restrictions imposed by Paul IV's bull establishing
the ghetto, *Cum nimis absurdum*.[16]

As for Sixtus V, was he not a Franciscan, the general of the order,
appointed by the one-time chief inquisitor, Ghislieri (Pius V); and was
he not previously a devoted follower of that other chief inquisitor,
Carafa (Paul IV)? One must logically expect that Sixtus would follow
the lead of these two in heavily restricting the Jews, just as he otherwise
pursued their initiative to restrain the exuberance of Roman society as a
whole. And, indeed, this is precisely what happened. Moreover, Sixtus

quite likely viewed his restriction of both Romans and Jews as being two sides of the same coin. Hence, if he insisted that even visitors to Rome be bound by the city's sumptuary laws, he also required Jews to wear the yellow Jewish *biretta* (as Paul IV had first ordered), except while on journeys. Similarly, his austere new ghetto walls mirror the grandiosity and cold formality with which he invested all his architectural projects —both executed, as we have already noted, by the same architect.[17] Sixtus further ordered that within Roman prisons, Jews be relegated to special cells, apart from Christian prisoners. For like other contemporary popes, Sixtus perceived prisons as places of penance and reform; he may well have seen the Jews' special cells as an extension of the "penitential" ghetto itself.[18]

One may further point to the parallel between Sixtus' attitude toward unorthodox Catholic books—ratified at the Council of Trent and concretized in the well-known "Index of Prohibited Books"—and his approach to the Jewish Talmud. Here, as in the first condemnation of the Talmud in the thirteenth century—as well as of suspect Christian literature—the ultimate object was to turn readers away from heresy and channel them toward approved doctrines and right belief. Thus, reversing the decree of 1553 that led to the Talmud's burning in various Italian cities, Sixtus authorized the publication of a censored version of its text. This censored version, however, never materialized. Following the admonitions of Cardinals Bellarmine and Sirleto, the utopian Tommaso Campanella, the humanist Andrea Masio, and the devoted converts and teachers of Jewish converts, Fabiano Fioghi and Fino Fini, the aim was to produce a text purified of so-called false rabbinic accretions whose remaining purportedly Christological teachings, it was hoped, would induce Jews to convert. Such a sophisticated level of textual manipulation was never achieved.[19]

Where Sixtus' attitudes toward Jews and non-Jews most directly intersected was in the matter of prostitutes. Just as Sixtus enlarged the ghetto, so he revived Pius V's intention of enclosing prostitutes within the *ortaccio* of the Campus Martius. Prostitutes were also to be forced to attend morally uplifting sermons, much as Sixtus remedied the imprecision of Gregory XIII's original edict concerning sermons delivered to the Jews. The latter had only indicated that these sermons were to be delivered weekly in a central location. Attendance was left unregulated. Sixtus decreed that all male Jews must attend these sermons at least six times a year. Like Jews, too, prostitutes were not to appear in public during Holy Week, and they were to wear a special garb, the *spurniglia*. Nor were they to mix in church with honest Christian women, bathe publicly in the Tiber, or ply their trade in taverns and restaurants. All of these restrictions had parallels in the canons governing Jewish behavior.[20] The issue was one of contamination, and it is noteworthy that although Sixtus widened Jewish business opportunities, he prohibited Jews from resuming the purveying of foodstuffs to Christians—a once-important source of Jewish livelihood that Paul IV, in 1555, had cut off.[21] To sell food to Christians bordered on violating the canons condemning the mixed dining of Christians and Jews. Even more threateningly, Sixtus' prohibition recalls late thirteenth-century Southern French laws forbidding Jews from touching food in the marketplace, lest what they touched and left unpurchased might later contaminate a Christian consumer.[22]

Sixtus V's policies toward the Jews were thus only superficially permissive ones. Instead they were as austere—and as full of Catholic Restoration fervor—as were his policies toward the entire Roman population. Even Sixtus' apparent attempt to aid the Jews financially by admitting them to participate in various *Monti* ultimately achieved the precisely opposite end; the Jewish community was saddled with an ever-larger debt, which its ever-dwindling resources could not service. Once again, Sixtus was following the lead of Paul IV and Pius V, both of whom had weighed down the Jews with numerous fines and monetary penalties. And this Sixtus surely knew, just as he must have known that these penalties had first been imposed in the hope of bringing despairing Jews to convert.[23]

By 1589, therefore, the Jews had good reason to be suspicious of Sixtus' intentions. Even any initially positive reaction to Sixtus' reversal of Pius V's (1569) decree of expulsion and to the possibility of resettlement in the Papal State must by then have been tempered. Sixtus did allow Jews to reestablish small centers of residence outside of Rome. But the conditions of resettlement were notably vague. Sixtus spoke of "entering" or "dwelling," and also about reopening synagogues closed in 1569. Yet, he did not presuppose actually founding new "communities." Instead, residential or entry patents issued by the papal chancellery, requiring holders to pay an entry fee of 2 scudi and an annual poll tax of 1.2

scudi, imply instability. Most importantly, these patents, as revealed by Ermano Loevinson's study sixty years ago (which concerns other Jews beside the bankers, who were Loevinson's particular interest), clearly distinguish between "entrance" and "dwelling." In fact, more than one-third of the three-hundred patents issued between 1587 and 1590 specify: "entrance with *no* permission to reside."[24] Moreover, the number of specifically mentioned Roman Jews who received these patents, especially to open a bank (which admittedly covered the banker, his family, and his assistants) was a small one. Banks, in any case, and irrespective of any residence permit—were always chartered for a precisely limited duration. Thus, it would appear that the Jews in the revived settlements were either actual, or potential, residents of the Papal State's ghettos. And the continued existence of these ghettos in Rome and in the port-city of Ancona was never doubted.[25] Sixtus' eventual solution to over-crowding in the ghetto—to expand its area rather than to grant exemptions from ghetto residence, let alone to consider the Roman Ghetto's abolition—thus hammered the proverbial nail into the coffin. No matter how overpopulated the ghetto was, Sixtus had obviously decided that Roman Jews were going to live exclusively within its walls.

It was at this point that Jews first referred to *our Ghet*. They could no longer doubt that they had permanently been separated—or, as they themselves put it, "divorced"—from Christian society, and they were at last ready to verbalize an awareness that had previously been suppressed. And suppress their awareness is indeed what they had done. Certain events of everday ghetto life reveal this fact most clearly.

To be sure, daily events in the ghetto usually do not bespeak tension or a sense of urgency. After all, whatever were its real goals, papal policy toward the Jews failed. The Jews lost relatively few of their numbers to conversion, and paradoxically, under pressure, their society immensely solidified. Ghetto neighborhoods, for one, operated effectively. A Jew trying to prove in court his father's identity called twenty-one *neighbors* as witnesses—in preference to a living uncle and aunt.[26] Similarly, ethnic divisions were giving way before a more homogeneous communal body. Jews of varying ethnic backgrounds, for example, were increasingly choosing at random their place of prayer among the ghetto's synagogues, which, in theory, represented Jews who distinctively followed the Italian, Ashkenazi, or Sephardic rite.[27] Jews even maintained a limbo relationship with neophytes, did business with them, and occasionally displayed parental concern—despite latent antipathies.[28] On the level of the individual, too, there was continuity and normality. Acts drawn by Jewish notaries in the years 1585–90 include contracts with musicians to teach grooms dancing and singing in preparation for their nuptials, as well as agreements to form catering firms that provided refreshments at festivities. Jews were apprenticed to other Jews to work as artisans and shopkeepers, rabbis and teachers of the young were hired, and games of chance were highly—some said overly—popular. Jews were ready, it seems, to wager on anything, even, for instance, as they not infrequently did, that the first of three friends to marry would buy the others a hat or a shirt.[29] This is a matter to which we shall shortly return.

On the other hand, the problem of overcrowding left definite traces. The simple act of renting an apartment or a store became a complex ritual. From the time of Sixtus V's pontificate, in particular, departing tenants were obliged to make a formal *rinunzio,* stating that they were leaving of their own free will and that their apartment or store was hence available for rental according to the edict issued by the eleventh-century rabbinic sage, Gershom of Mainz, which stipulated that no Jew may rent a dwelling owned by a non-Jew, if a previous Jewish tenant had been evicted for refusing to pay a higher rent.[30] The tight housing supply was clearly making rent gouging a reality. The number of housing disputes that went to arbitration was also extremely large, especially over questions of who owned the leasing rights (the *cazaga*) to a particular space.[31] When the houses on via Fiumara became available, disputes immediately broke out. And even the relatively strong community, which had been given a hand in the distribution of these dwellings, was unable to resolve them.[32] The new housing was successfully apportioned only when the papal vicar stepped in.[33] If panic is too strong a word to use, we may certainly speak of an acutely perceived housing shortage. The Jews of the Roman Ghetto had sensed that both physically and temperamentally they were being squeezed ever more tightly together.

But let us return to the issue of the marriage wagers. Much more than playful diversions, these were symbolic indicators that Jewish men were putting marriage off—as indeed they were, which was quite a novelty. Where past records are available, it is clear that marriage was a nearly universal Jewish institution; among Jews, there had never existed incentives not to marry—or even not to remarry—such as those which Christian society and its leadership had fostered. Jewish males in sixteenth-century Rome were also marrying relatively early, on average at about age 24, which is somewhat below the age of marrying Rennais-ance male Christians. Any change in the Jewish marriage pattern could thus be expected to be the product of outside stimuli.[34] And this seems to have been precisely the case. In the years preceding Sixtus' pontificate, Jewish marriages in Rome occurred on an average of twenty-two per year. During Sixtus' reign, this ratio fell by a full 13 percent to less than nineteen. Moreover, this lower ratio remained steady in each of Sixtus' five regnal years. At the same time, during these five years—when the Jewish population of Rome and its environs certainly did not shrink—the ratio of Jewish males per family remained virtually constant. This constancy may be seen from the oaths brothers of grooms regularly swore to free the latters' (potentially) childless widows from the obliga-tion of Levirite marriage (see Devt. 25:5–10). For the oath was sworn (directly, or indirectly by their fathers or elder brothers, should they have been minors) by all brothers of the groom. Taken together, these figures mean that the total number of Roman Jewish males of potentially marriageble age remained the same. Yet the number of these males who actually married had decreased.[35] Something other than demographic factors must have been responsible for this downturn.

Ascertaining what actually was responsible is no easy task. Changes in marriage rates like this one normally are produced by complex forces. In our particular case, we must also ask whether the phenomenon being described is the postponement of marriage or a result of Jewish move-ment to localities outside Rome after 1585. More than likely, it was the former. As we just said, the Roman Jewish population did not shrink durign Sixtus' reign; indeed, there was always movement of Jews in and out of the ghetto, guaranteeing a steady demographic level. If anything, the Roman Jewish population may have increased, meaning that the drop in the marriage rate was even greater than that which we reported. Moreover, Jews living, since 1585, in the various localities of the Papal State continued to record their prenuptial agreements before a Roman Jewish notary. Hence, their marriages were included in the above calcu-lations. There is, finally, no evidence of—nor some natural reason like the severe outbreak of illness and death among adult childbearers to account for—a temporary drop in birth rates about 1560–65, which might have meant a constant number of male children per family, but a decrease in the number of those who reached the normal marrying age of 24 by 1565–90. What then caused the nuptial postponements? Quite clearly, we must avoid drawing facile conclusions. But perhaps we will not err in proposing that any hopes aroused among the Jews by the election of the astute, commercially minded Cardinal Montalto (Peretti) to the papal throne as Sixtus V were quickly shattered. It became immediately evident that the new pope planned no relaxation of existing controls. With the exception of those relatively few Jews who could attach themselves to the strictly limited number of banking firms that established extra Roman branches (and settlements), the vast majority of Jews were forced to remain in the extraordinately overcrowded Roman Ghetto. Those who had planned to marry, or at least some 13 percent of them, thus were forced to relinquish their marital plans. They simply had no available physical space in which to initiate their domestic life.

Whatever else Sixtus V did, therefore, it is certain that among prospective Jewish spouses, and probably their parents as well, he succeeded in generating frustration and despair. Jews no longer had the capacity to create marriages at will. And the express cause of this incapacity was their unremitting segregation in the ghetto. Here, nobody needed to tell them, they were certainly different from Christians. Innately, therefore, even in 1585, the Jews must have sensed their particularity and the distance separating them from Christian society. In 1589, the ghetto's enlargement raised that sense from a suppressed, or even unconscious level, to one that was unambiguously verbalized. No wonder that Pompeo del Borgo chose precisely this moment to speak of *nostro*—our— *Ghet*. Eventually, as we learn from the diary of a young girl involuntarily held in the *Domus cathecumenorum,* the equation of *ghetto* and *get* was to become a matter of common, everyday usage.[36]

NOTES

1. Rome, *Archivio Storico Capitolini* (ASC), Sezione III, Notai Ebrei, Fasc. 12, lib. 1, f. 16v-174. On the about-face in papal policy after 1555, see Kenneth Stow, *Catholic Thought and Papal Jewry Policy* (New York, 1977). Aside from erecting the ghetto, the popes forced the Jews to hear missionary sermons, burned their Talmud, insisted on the rigid application of discriminatory canons, especially the one requiring Jews to wear a yellow hat, lowered the rate of permissible interest on loans, outlawed all titles of

honor, and generally limited contacts between Christians and Jews. On the Roman Ghetto itself, see the classic, Attilio Milano, *Il ghetto di Roma* (Rome, 1964), and more recently, K. R. Stow, "Sanctity and the Construction of Space, the Roman Ghetto as Sacred Space," in *Proceedings of the Second Annual Klutznick Chair Conference,* ed. M. Mor, (Omaha, 1991). The first non-Jewish reference to the Roman Ghetto by that name appears in a bull issued in 1562 by Pius IV. This usage was not, however, repeated over the coming decades. It is possible that the available version of the bull, in the *Bullarium Romanum Taurensis Editio* (Turin, 1857–72), 7:168, is a corrupt one; see the similar problem of corrupt readings in this edition noted in n. 21, below.

2. See, e.g., ASC, Sezione III, Notai Ebrei, Fasc. 14 lib. 1, f. 117v ("il nostro Ghet") & 129r; F.6, 1.2, f.167v ("in Ghet, "il gette," and even "il *get*" [in Hebrew letters], all in this one text of 1591); F.5, 1.2, f.112r ("in gette"); and F.11, 1.5, no. 29. On the identical pronunciation of all three forms, as well as for many other examples, see Sandra D. Stow, "The Etymology of 'Ghetto': The Evidence of 16th and 17th Century Roman Jewish Documentation," in *Frank Talmage Memorial Volume,* ed. B. Walfish, (Haifa, 1991).

3. Josef Sermoneta, "Sull'origine della parola 'ghetto,' " in *Studi sull'Ebraismo Italiano in memoria di Cecil Roth,* ed. E. Toaff, (Rome, 1974), 185–202. Cf. Benjamin Ravid, "The Religious, Economic and Social Background and Context of the Establishment of the Ghetti of Venice," in *Gli ebrei e Venezia,* ed. G. Cozzi (Milan, 1986), 244–47, and also Riccardo Calimani, *The Ghetto of Venice,* trans. K. S. Wolfthal (New York, 1987), 129–32.

4. E.g., Milano, *Il ghetto,* 79–82, but especially H. Vogelstein and P. Rieger, *Geschichte der Juden im Rom* (Berlin, 1896), 2:176–83.

5. On Magino, see Milano, *Il ghetto,* 81, and G. Tomassetti, *L'arte della seta in Roma* (Rome, 1881), 2:133. See also the works cited in n. 17, below.

6. See K. R. Stow, *Taxation Community and State* (Stuttgart, 1982), 35, and E. Loevinson, "La concessin de banques de prêts aux Juifs par les Papes," *Revue des Ètudes Juives,* 92–95 (1932–33).

7. On farm credits, see Franca D'Amico, "La qualità della vita nella concezione di Sisto V," Proceedings of the Congress *Sisto V e lo Stato Pontificio,* ed. M. Fagiolo, (Rome, 1991), and on the wool issue, see Flavio Cherubini, *Compendium Bullarii ab Leone Primo usque ad Paulum V* (Rome, 1623), 2:386a–387b, no. 14.

8. On the role of Cardinal S. Croce in Sixtus' administration, see Cherubini, *Compendium.*

9. Archivio di Stato, Roma (ASR), Camerale I, Diversa Cameralia, b.406, f. 17r–v.

10. Milano, *Il ghetto,* 190, and Jean Delumeau, *Vie èconomique et sociale de Rome* (Paris, 1957–59), 837–39. On ghetto rents, see Milano, *Il ghetto,* 198–200.

11. Tomassetti, *L'arte,* 2:146–49.

12. See Paolo Prodi, *Il sovrano pontefice* (Roma, 1982), and K. R. Stow, *Taxation*.

13. See Stow, *Catholic Thought*, 20, n. 59.

14. Ibid., 217–20, and 218, n. 113; Alexander of Hales, *Summa Theologica*, (Quaracchi, 1924–48), 3:729–32; and K. R. Stow, "Expulsion Italian Style: The Case of Lucio Ferraris," *Jewish History* no. 3,1 (1988): 53–55.

15. See Anna Foa, "Il gioco del proselitismo: politica delle conversioni e controllo della violenza nella Roma del Cinquecento," *Ebrei e cristiani nell-'Italia medievale e moderna: conversioni, scambi, contrasti*, ed. M. Luzzati, M. Olivari, A. Veronese (Rome, 1988), 155–70.

16. Paolo Simoncelli, "Inquisizione romana e riforma in Italia," *Rivista Storica Italiana*, 100 (1988): 5–125.

17. On Sixtus' building policies, as well as his other programs, see L. von Ranke, *Storia dei Papi* (FLorence, 1965), 328ff.; Delumeau, *Vie économique* 101–2, 105, 116, 143, 217, 290, 312, 314, 339, 357, 424, 426, 427; and Prodi, *Il Sovrano*, esp. 10, 98, 123.

18. *Quae ordini ecclesiastico, Bullarium Romanum Taurensis Editio* 9:120; and see K. R. Stow, "Delitto e castigo nello stato della chiesa: Gli ebrei nelle carceri Romane da 1572 al 1659," *Italia Judaica, II* (Rome, 1986), 173–92. On prisons and penance, see Vincenzo Paglia, *La pietà dei carcerati* (Rome, 1980).

19. See K. R. Stow, "The Burning of the Talmud in 1553," *Bibliothèque d'Humanisme et Renaissance*, 34 (1972): 435–59.

20. On prostitutes, see Pio Pecchiai, *Roma nel cinquecento* (Bologna, 1948), 374–48, and Delumeau, *Vie économique*, 424–27; for parallel Jewish restrictions, see Stow, *Catholic Thought*, part 1.

21. *Christiana pietas, Bull. Rom.* 8:786 (in Italian), which indicates erroneously that Jews might deal in foodstuffs; now see the more precise French version found in René Moulinas, *Les Juifs du pape en France* (Paris, 1981), 241.

22. Maurice Kriegel, "Un trait de psychologie sociale dans les pays méditerranéens du Bas Moyen Age; le juif comme intouchable," *Annales ESC* 31 (1976): 326–30.

23. Stow, *Taxation*, chap. 3.

24. Loevinson, "La concession," esp. 94:161–68.

25. Bologna should not be considerd an exception to this pattern. If many of the Jews expelled from this city in 1569 returned after 1585 (only to be again expelled definitely in 1593), they still returned to a ghetto.

26. ASC, F.5, lib.2, fols 115r–120v.

27. On the synagogues' social functions and the mixing of the *edoth*, see K. R. Stow, "Sacred Space."

28. E.g., ASC, F.2, 1.3, f.91r; F.2, 1.4, F.40r–v; F.7, 1.2, f.116v; and see K. R. Stow, "A Tale of Uncertainties: Converts in the Roman Ghetto," *Festschrift Shelomo Simonsohn*, ed. D. Carpi (Tel Aviv, 1991).

29. On various aspects of daily life, see, e.g., ASC, F.2, 1.6, f.166r; F.6, 1.2, d.41r; F.10, 1.3, f.42r; F.4, 1.2, f.1005r; F.5, 1.3, ff.84v–85r; F.8, 1.3,

f.107v; F.9, 1.6, f.241v; F.6, 1.1, f.55r; F.12, 1.1, f.55r; F.12, 1.1, ff.34r, 76r, 80r; F.10, 1.2, ff.15v–17r; F.12, 1.1, ff.56v–57r; F.3, 1.2, ff.39v–40r; see, too, K. R. Stow, "Gli ebrei di Roma nell'eta' del Ghetto: problemi storiografici," *La storia degli ebrei nell'Italia medievale: tra filologia e metodologia,* ed. M. G. Muzzarelli and G. Todeschini (Bologna, 1990), 43–57.

30. E.g., ASC, F.9, 1.2, ff.46r, 46v, 75v.
31. E.g., ASC, F.9, 1.2, f.55r.
32. E.g., ASC, F.9, 1.2, ff.73r–v, 75v, 76v, and esp. 78v.
33. As specified in ASR Camerale I, Diversa Cameralia, b. 406, f. 17r–v.
34. See K. R. Stow, "The Jewish Family in the Rhineland in the High Middle Ages, Form and Function," *American Historical Review* 92 (1987): 1085–1110; Shaul Stampfer, "Remarriage among Jews and Christians in Nineteenth-Century Eastern Europe," *Jewish History* 3 /2 (1988): 85–114, but esp. K. R. Stow and S. Debenedetti Stow, "Donne ebree a Roma nell'età del ghetto: affetto, dipendenza, autonomia," *Rassegna Mensile di Israel* 52 (1986): 71–72, on age at marriage in the ghetto.
35. In the period 1580–82 (36 months), there were 65 marriages; in the 64 months of Sixtus' pontificate (1585–1590), there were 101. These figures yield respective ratios of 1.81 marriages/months and 1.56/month, for a drop of 12.6 percent. In the former case, the oaths of *halizah* were taken by 73 males, in the latter, by 92. Adding the grooms, the total number of males becomes 138 and 192, respectively, for an average of 2.12 males/family and 2.05, a negligible difference, considering the vagaries of birth and mortality rates, of 3.3 percent. On the Jewish population in Rome, see *Biblioteca Apostolica Vaticana,* Codice Ottoboniano Latino 2434, cc. 856–57, now cited in Claudio Schiavoni, "Introduzione allo studio delle fonti archivistiche per la storia demografica di Roma, *Genus,* 27 (1971): 384.
36. See the remarks of G. Sermoneta, and the text offered in evidence, in "Tredici giorni nella Casa dei Conversi—dal diario di una giovane ebrea del 18 secolo," *Michael* 1 (1972): 313.

15

Change in the Cultural Patterns of a Jewish Society in Crisis: Italian Jewry at the Close of the Sixteenth Century

Robert Bonfil

In the hundred years prior to the end of the sixteenth century, despite constant pressures to the contrary, the Jews of Italy—who were made up of relatively small and ethnically different groups that traced their origins to lands are far apart as Spain and Turkey—managed with no small success to preserve their diverse ancestral religious traditions. Suddenly, from sometime about 1570, the winds shifted,[1] and Italian Jews became receptive to innovations that led to major changes in their religious practices and attitudes.[2] I say "suddenly," because revolutionary change did not require a revolution. The major changes that occurred apparently were not preceded by an extended period of cultural and social ferment. The opposition to change seems to have been sporadic, limited in scope, of brief duration, and far weaker than might have been expected, certainly with respect to other Jewish societies, where less significant changes in daily life and religious opinion occasionally generated considerable controversy.[3] Problems of intellectual nonconformity, at least at first glance, seem to have affected only slight sensitivities to issues involving authority and institutional and social stability.

This chapter is a revised version of a paper delivered at the Conference on Jewish Societies in Transformation in the Sixteenth and Seventeenth Centuries, held at the Van Leer Institute, Jerusalem, 1986.

Reprinted by permission of *Jewish History* 3 (1988).

Innovations in Jewish attitudes were produced in particular by that unique system of thought and literature known as the kabbalah. These innovations especially affected prayer and daily religious practices. Yet, the two editions of the *Zohar*, published at Mantua in 1558, and at Cremona in 1560, stirred authorities less[4] than did the publication a century earlier of the writings of Levi ben Gershon, which was greeted by the rabbinic ban of Judah Messer Leon.[5] No ban was placed on the *Zohar*. Indeed, judging by the number of bans issued, rabbis of the 1560s seem to have been much more preoccupied with the Tamari-Venturozzo controversy, concerning the problematic divorce of an unlucky Venetian girl,[6] than they were with the publication of the *Zohar*. From a historian's vantage point, rather than as a student of the kabbalah in the specific sense, I believe that the example of the kabbalah is, paradoxically, both unique and paradigmatic in the religious life of Italian Jewry.

Kabbalah penetrated Italian Jewish life in stages.[7] After a long period of restricted kabbalistic intellectual activity in the fifteenth century, interest in the kabbalah steadily grew during the first half of the sixteenth. For many, the kabbalah became an anchor in the stormy seas aroused by the collapse of medieval systems of thought. Toward mid-century, kabbalah crossed the border between esotericism and exotericism, and transformed itself from being essentially a closed system into an open one. Widespread diffusion of the *Zohar* was perhaps the first of the more visible symptoms of this transformation. The next visible sign that the kabbalah had shed its esoteric garb was the initiation of its public teaching, most likely by Rabbi Menahem Azariah da Fano (1548–1620) at Venice in 1575. Soon afterward, kabbalah conquered the public sermon. By the end of the century even ardent opponents occasionally referred to it in their sermons in order to win the interest of kabbalistically oriented audiences. The next step was the revision of prayer and ritual. In 1587–88, a revised prayer book was published; in the early 1580s a short-lived controversy arose over the use of phylacteries on intermediate festival days;[8] and in the same decade, the orientation of kabbalah, which until then had been mainly Zoharic and Cordoverian, became increasingly Lurianic. Perhaps the most obvious symptom of that change was the proliferation of vigils, eventually institutionalized within a large number of confraternal frameworks. The aim of most of these vigils was to exert a mystical influence on the cosmic order that would supposedly hasten the final redemption. The final step was the emergence of Sabbateanism.

In a previous study of Rabbi Menahem Azariah da Fano's attempt to deal with the apparent conflict between Halachah and kabbalah, I argued that Rabbi Menahem introduced innovations into the daily synagogue service in Reggio, apparently without pangs of conscience.[9] In a statement published in the 1600 Venice edition of his Responsa,[10] he informed his correspondent:

I prevented the precentor in my place of residence from beginning the prayer with the Mishnah at the end of *Tamid,* instructing him rather to begin with the opening of the Psalm of the day.

Obviously, Rabbi Menahem felt confident of his authority and was not worried by the possibility of fierce opposition. Such independence in halachic decision making and its open, almost nonchalant expression seem to me to be directly related to a kabbalistic outlook. Of course, such independence may also be discerned in the halachic thinking of many great non-kabbalists as well. Nevertheless, it seems to me that personal confidence in the absolute authority of the *kabbalistica veritas* fostered interpretative independence, directed mainly toward halachic texts. This interpretative independence became a general characteristic of Jewish creativity, even when kabbalah was not openly and directly involved. Thanks to the sociocultural background of Italian Jewry, interpretative independence, self-confidence, and a selective approach to sources—which in modern parlance might be labeled liberalism—had little prospect of provoking a major reaction. On the contrary, in a time of crisis and challenge, mysticism provided Italian Jews with an ample defense, which also gave life a revolutionary meaning. Indeed, Italian Jewry, from the mid-sixteenth century to the mid-seventeenth century, underwent a profound socioeconomic crisis. Its main visible characteristic was the polarization of rich and poor. The poor were very poor and the rich only relatively wealthy. Socioeconomic polarities were paralleled by cultural ones. A small group of highly learned men, most of them wealthy or allied by marriage to wealthy families, confronted a great, uneducated majority incapable of participating in scholarly debates or even understanding them. Learned disagreements on ritual issues could hardly degenerate into institutional crises. Sectarianism flourished "within the establishment" as a kind of tolerated pluralism "within the family." To the common people, who were generally incapable of understanding their essence, most of the debates were adiaphorous. They were reduced to accepting *tout et le contraire de tout,* provided that it did not produce a sense of chaos.

It is also safe to assert that cultural polarization was in part causally related to socioeconomic polarization. Seemingly paradoxical aspects of Jewish communal life were not that at all, because they were relevant only to limited elements in the community. The poor were not in a position to learn much more than the rudimentary Hebrew needed to read the prayers in the *Siddur.* This state of affairs accounts for the sudden deterioration of Hebrew knowledge at a time when learned Jews, most of whom had assimilated certain kabbalistic components into their *Weltanschauung,* were gradually resorting to ever more cryptic and intricate modes of literary expression.

Nevertheless, for all that these things are true, I would like to go one step further and argue that rather than eliminating paradox by means of distinctions like the one just used, we would do well to accept paradox as a distinctive characteristic of transitional periods. We must view paradox not as a puzzle that requires a rational explanation but as a key to interpreting reality. A proper understanding of the phenomenon of historical paradox may be gained by recognizing that throughout the period under consideration various other phenomena present similarly paradoxical characteristics, especially the structural transformation that was instrumental in inverting the medieval world outlook and creating modern views.[11] One particular expression of this transformation is the progressive distancing of what were formerly proximate, yet distinct, entities. The process is clearly visible in all fields of historical reality. One may point to the evolving consciousness of the need to assess distinction in epistemology, specialization in knowledge (which becomes professional knowledge), particularism and nationalism in political outlooks, disjunction in mental attitudes, and the actual praxis of contraries, such as obscene/sublime, sacred/profane, normal/abnormal, clean/dirty, ridiculous/serious, weeping/laughing, illness/health, useful/detrimental, death/life. This process itself logically presents natural shifts of conceptual and axiological attitudes that are necessarily inherent in ongoing examination and individualization. In these shifts the dynamic source of structural change may logically be identified.[12] For example, we may consider as absolutely necessary to proper social function activities that the medievals considered detrimental to the social body; to wit, dissent, critical expression, and opposition to authority. Such shifts always seem to imply paradox. Paradox is essentially a mediating element between opposites, and for mediation to take place obfuscation of the process itself is necessary.[13] A proper understanding of the nature of mediation may serve to avoid the distortion arising from the perception of paradox as simply the presence of opposites. The cultural process outlined above, with kabbalah at its center, may be considered one example of the role of paradox in mediating between opposites. Within Jewish society, kabbalah was one of the most effective mediators between the medieval and the modern worlds, and, as such, functioned as an agent of modernity.

Let us diverge for a moment from the discussion of kabbalah and recall some aspects of a similar role played by medicine in promoting modern concepts of man's knowledge of himself as a living entity within nature.[14] Vesalius, for example, innovatively limited the field of medical discourse to specific knowledge of the human body,[15] which implied renouncing a quest for total knowledge in favor of increasing professional skill. The emphasis on experiment as the way toward specific medical knowledge challenged the earlier conception of scientific knowledge as something achieved via the exegesis of authoritative texts; science became rooted in individual praxis. The modernity of Vesalius's redefinitions may be sensed in the strong component of neutrality he conferred on scientific knowledge. That knowledge was now oriented toward a maximum specialization within a minimal field and was distanced from most other spheres of human intellectual activity, including moral philosophy. Vesalius no longer explained disease in allegorical or otherwise spiritual terms. The correspondence between microcosm and macrocosm implied in Galen's physiological theory of anatomy disappeared, as did the former correspondence between priest and physician.

But incipient modernity may also be perceived in the works of physicians like Leonardo Fioravanti, who considered himself an orthodox exponent of the old outlook.[16] Fioravanti emphasized the singularity of disease, which the physician grasps by means of a detailed description furnished by the patient that is then correlated to the store of received medical knowledge. Yet, Fioravanti also accepted the validity of popular medical experience and old wives tales, as well as the possibility that magical, alchemistic, and astrological forces can affect the human body.

Obscurantist as this methodology is, it contains the kind of experimental observation associated with modern medicine. The old relationship between microcosm and macrocosm—whether in the medieval sense, implying the influence of the stars on man, or in the more recent humanistic sense, implying a conception of the cosmos as serving man—now implied, among other things, mediation between popular and learned knowledge. Physicians were also assuming new political and sociocultural roles within the context of public welfare. In a sense, physicians were replacing the chancellors, the rhetors, and the philosophers of earlier times to become the intellectual par excellence. The proliferation of small tracts giving advice on how to preserve one's health during a plague[17] may be seen as one expression of the new medical discourse that aimed at regulating all human activity—eating, drinking, coitus, etc.

On a sociocultural and political level, it was this redefinition of the field of medicine and the growing faith in the capacity of observation and in the therapeutic powers of drugs or other "natural" substances that resulted in the trend to segregate patients, as has been described by Michel Foucault.[18] Medicine, in passing from its medieval to its modern stage, underwent a transformation with regard to both the nature of medical knowledge and the definition of the objects of medical practice. Modern medicine rests on profound expertise in diagnosis; here, too, distance was placed between proximate opposites in the form of more precise epistemological distinctions between the truly ill and the truly healthy. Such progress implies a more sophisticated use of hospitalization and methods of isolation. Today, improved scientific knowledge has radically transformed the social function of medical segregation. Persons who in the sixteenth and seventeenth centuries would have been doomed to isolation would not be today. This is precisely the kind of paradox we are attempting to illustrate. In order to attain distance, opposites had first to be brought into intense proximity with each other: "unhealthy" people were isolated together, and popular knowledge was brought close to scientific knowledge. The progressive distance placed between intensely proximate opposites resulted in a revision of the categories of opposites and a shifting of elements from one field to another. The result was a new outlook in which apparent opposites ceased to be such, and other concepts, previously thought to belong to the same category, came to be perceived as opposites. The process in itself was one of continuous reconsideration that led to new definitions and newly restructured limits.

A further example of processes of this kind comes from the history of the Jews. How did both Jews and Christians in Italy react to the continued presence of Jews in Christian society? Was the period 1550–1650 a "good" or a "bad" one for Italian Jews? At first glance, it may be claimed that from about 1580 the situation of the Jews in Italy steadily "improved." [19] Jews were permitted to engage in moneylending in most of the places from which they had previously been expelled, including those places where there was no ghetto. [20] In the same years, no persecutions are recorded. This might be defined as an inversion of the previous tendency of Christians to distance themselves from Jews, as well as the beginning of a more "liberal" attitude, to which the Jews might have reacted by taking steps toward integration. For example, as one enlightened scholar has put it, they might have refrained from using their money deceptively or for otherwise forbidden purposes. [21] Yet there is evidence to the contrary. Apart from the ghettos of Venice and Rome, established, respectively, in 1516 and 1555, all the other Italian ghettos were established shortly before 1580, or not long after, particularly in the "relatively quiet" first half of the seventeenth century: [22] Florence, 1571; Siena, 1571; Mirandola, 1602; Verona, 1600; Padua, 1603; Mantua, 1612; Rovigo, 1613; Ferrara, 1624; Modena, 1638; Lugo, Cento, 1639; Urbino, Pesaro, Senigallia, 1634; Reggio Emilia, 1670; Este, 1666; Turin, 1679; Conegliano Veneto, 1675; Casale Monferrato, 1724; Vercelli, 1725; Finale, 1736; Acqui, 1731; Moncalvo, 1732; Correggio, 1779. In some places where a ghetto was established only in the second half of the seventeenth century, the delay was caused solely by practical difficulties, such as the need to solve problems of space, or the reluctance of Christians to give up their property. This was the case in Reggio Emilia, where discussions about a ghetto began in 1611, but where a ghetto was established only in 1670. If establishing ghettos is seen as tantamount to endorsing nonliberal Church policy demanding that Jews be distanced from Christians, it is not clear why most ghettos were established at a time when the Church had apparently inverted its priorities.

There was also the same kind of quizzically growing ambivalence among Jews. Jews describe the atmosphere in the ghettos as oppressive, airless, and insufferable. Comparison with previous periods suggests a deterioration in relations. The Jews believed that they were being regarded with greater contempt than before and felt that it was damaging the Jewish psyche, weakening Jewish cultural vitality, and lowering the level of religious observance. Yet, adapting to the new situation did not seem to displease them. To cite but one example, Rabbi Eliezer Nahman Foa, one of the disciples of Rabbi Menahem Azariah da Fano, drew a clear parallel in his commentary to the Passover Haggadah between the situation of the Jews in Egypt and that of the Jews in his own day. He imaginatively maintained this comparison throughout the entire commentary. The oppression of the Jews in Egypt was reflected in the exorbitant rents demanded by the Egyptians, no doubt alluding to the excessive rents paid in the Italian ghettos. Allegorically interpreting the Passover text, Rabbi Foa wrote that

present exile is bitter in itself and bitter on account of its length and on account of the abuse we suffer from so greatly that it clings to the soul and is very bitter. In previous exiles, we were not abused, but elevated and sought after.[23]

This idealization is uncritical and exaggerated, but it leaves no doubt about Foa's wounded pride and his desire for liberation. Nevertheless, he warned that his fellow Jews

should not make for ourselves a "permanent lodging" in this exile, purchasing homes and fields and vineyards; we should remain strangers in the land, as if each day we were about to return to our land.[24]

Indeed, in his own day, just when it seemed that the Roman Church was actually condoning moneylending, Jews were increasingly being pushed out of true banking activities and forced to invest their available liquid resources in real estate, agriculture, and the breeding of livestock (including pigs). Perhaps this may be seen as a "Jewish" facet of the contemporary Italian "return to the land." Yet, Jews were eventually required to disguise these investments, especially the ownership of real property, since they were often illegal. In any case, Foa's words reveal his awareness of the Jews' economic success, which, given the circumstances, might be considered paradoxical, as Foa himself pointed out. He ascribed it to a miraculous divine decree that bested what he called the gentiles' particular intelligence and their expediency in oppressing the Jews. Commenting upon the passage "And they oppressed us" in the Passover Haggadah, Foa noted that:

Pharaoh and the Egyptians acted with great wisdom; when they rented their houses to the Jews, they raised the rent tenfold,[25] and the same was true in other commercial dealings. But they did not know that they would not succeed in their enterprise. On the contrary, "As they [the Jews] were oppressed, so did they thrive," that is, became wealthier.[26]

Yet, if Jewish wealth conveyed a sense of well-being, its extensiveness also troubled Rabbi Foa, who cautioned against its unrestrained growth. The ambivalence does not end here. Foa was equally troubled by premature attempts to bring about the messianic liberation:

Picking a fruit before it is ripe causes it to spoil; we were warned against precipitating "the end." We must not relive the experience of the previous exile, from which God was forced to liberate us prematurely, causing us to return anew into exile.[27]

Just as in the Egyptian exile Jews were persecuted, so they are being persecuted again, and for the same reason: they have a universal redemptive mission to accomplish, to purify the sparks and repair the damage "caused by original sin."[28] However intense his sense of oppression and his desire for liberation, Foa apparently preferred the status quo to any other more chimerical alternative.

Rabbi Foa belonged to a wealthy family. One may wonder how many other Jews shared his sense of increasing Jewish wealth. The large number of people maintained by charity[29] and the proliferation of charitable confraternities leave no doubt that in Foa's time economic and social gaps widened considerably. However, on closer examination, the growing gaps within the Jewish communities should not be seen as contradicting Foa's paradoxical sense of Jewish wealth. On the contrary, especially on Passover night, when rich and poor alike crowded about a large table in the center of a small ghetto room, all Jews might agree on the ultimate truth of Rabbi Foa's perceptions, each one considering those perceptions from his own social vantage point. As often occurs in situations such as this, the contraction of living space, which brought rich and poor ever closer together, acutely sharpened the Jews' consciousness of even the most subtle social distinctions. Yet, however stifling the ghetto atmosphere was, Jews like Rabbi Foa seem to have preferred the status quo—as if the ghetto provided an optimal framework for carrying on Jewish life. Some Jews even ritually celebrated their incarceration within the ghetto walls.[30] Does this not suggest that the existence of the ghetto led the Jews to reconsider and restructure their perceptions of the proper condition of their existence within Christian society? What is more, segregation in ghettos coexisting with the reintegration of the

Jews into Christian society forced a change in gentile attitudes. The reception of Jews into Christian society was transformed by means of the ghetto from being exceptional and unnatural into being unexceptional and natural.

Could anything be more paradoxical than "closing in order to permit opening," segregation to mediate integration? There were precedents for this in the Middle Ages, but they were justified by stipulating that "the Jews were tolerated for the sake of the poor." From the late sixteenth century, the Jews were just "tolerated."

Cultural and religious issues fit well into this pattern. A superficial glance at the cultural activity within the ghetto reveals paradox. Historians have noted that there was a flowering of Jewish culture in such fields as theater, music, and literature. One would have expected the opposite. It is the Renaissance, not the post-Renaissance world, that is usually credited with an openness toward the non-Jewish environment and with the secularist thisworldliness that is presumably a prerequisite for such a flowering. To be sure, almost all the significant "Jewish contributions" to such fields as music and the theater took place during the post-Renaissance age.[31] Yet this time-gap has normally been explained in terms of a delayed outburst of Renaissance vitality, a blossoming after a long period of germination.

Nevertheless, there is something wrong about associating a "positive Jewish response" to "outer-directed" cultural activities with an openness engendered by liberal attitudes coming from the outside.[32] Such a model posits a clear structural correspondence between openness/closedness, liberal/nonliberal, integration/segregation, progress/regression, evolution/involution, general culture/specifically religious culture, and even good/bad. This is a model that is rooted in *our* view of the world; it may not be valid for interpreting past epochs. I therefore suggest that Jewish "openness" toward outside culture in the fields of theater and music must be viewed within the context of ambivalence and closure. As such, this "openness" must be understood to reflect the process of restructuring that led to an axiological inversion of attitudes.[33]

Literary production is more puzzling. There is evidence that knowledge and use of the Hebrew language waned.[34] This might be interpreted as symptomatic of the cultural impoverishment of a society in decline; such an interpretation would be appropriate with regard to the lower strata of Jewish society, which were dependent upon charity and unable to obtain an adequate Jewish education. But the distancing of the Jews from Hebrew seems to have been much more than a symptom. Simple ignorance, duly lamented by rabbis and teachers, was matched by claims that Italian was enormously rich, in contrast to the poverty of Hebrew.[35] This is a complete reversal of the Jewish Renaissance attitude expressed by Rabbi Judah Messer Leon in his *Nofet Zufim* treatise on Hebrew rhetoric, in which Hebrew is extolled at the expense of other languages, including Ciceronian Latin.[36] The Jews' aversion to Hebrew and their preference for the vernacular at a time of increasing isolation from the outside world was the diametric opposite of the attitude they had adopted at a time of relative openness.

Moreover, from the later sixteenth century, bilingual literary competence ceased to be a mere curiosity and became a common vehicle for literary expression.[37] Much of the poetry written in the seventeenth and eighteenth centuries, mostly for social occasions, contains variously interrelated Hebrew and Italian components. The Hebrew enigma, one of the principal literary expressions of the epoch, frequently contains an Italian key-word organically interwoven in the Hebrew text.[38] I do not intend to discuss the phenomenon of literary paradox, which scholars of both Hebrew and baroque literature in general have recently scrutinized anew,[39] but note that Jewish authors who normally would be characterized as conservative, "antirationalist," and, hence, presumably isolationist in their orientation were au courant with regard to baroque literary trends. A good example is Rabbi Judah del Bene's collection of baroque essays.[40] By contrast, at least one scholar has detected a medieval orientation in the booklet devoted to the art of memory written by that much-praised champion of modernity *ante litteram*, Leon Modena. These observations have led to the revisionist thesis that incipient Jewish modernity should be dated from the mid-seventeenth century rather than from the time of the Renaissance.[41] I suggest a somewhat different interpretation. Leon Modena's introduction of, among other things, non-Jewish medieval texts into Jewish discourse was no less modern than Judah del Bene's display of baroque sensibilities. Of course, Leon Modena's translation of popular foreign works into Hebrew was part and parcel of the medieval Jewish tradition. Jews had long been familiar with translations and literary transplants, as the whole Jewish philosophical, theological, rhetorical, and historical tradition testifies. For centuries, whatever was considered intellectually valid, that is to say, objectively true, was adopted by Jewish writers who also weighed its congruity with "genuine" Jewish thought. In our period, the definition of "objectively true knowledge" seems to have changed. The dynamics of this change do not appear to have been different from those of the other changes we have observed, so that here, too, one senses a paradoxical narrowing of the distance between fields traditionally regarded as remote opposites and a consequential restructuring of these opposites and their assumption of a new identity. This formula also applies to Leon Modena's *Lev Aryeh*.[42] Modena suggested, at times incredulously, that devices normally associated with magic and alchemy be used as means for cultivating the classical art of memory. He did not recommend magic and alchemy per se, but he did effectively advocate the two with authoritative classical knowledge. Just as magic and alchemy "mediated" between old-fashioned medieval popular knowledge and modern experimental science, so they had a mediating function in a Jewish context.

The point is further illustrated by another work of Modena's, the *Zemach Zaddiq*,[43] a typically medieval collection of moral *fioretti, fior di virtù*, containing a great deal of Christian lore presented in Jewish guise.[44] Some years later Abraham Yagel put out a similar booklet, the *Lekach Tov*,[45] a Jewish catechism that drew heavily upon the Jesuit catechism of Peter Canisius. The adoption by Jews of this Christian genre played a mediating role in narrowing the distance between Judaism and Christianity. Yagel succeeded in presenting Augustinian maxims on human salvation and Jesuit definitions of religious faith as authentically Jewish, and he even supported them with relevant talmudic passages. Thus, he effectively bridged the chasm separating Judaism from Christianity. Unwittingly, he made Jewish and Christian believers into virtual allies opposing deism, naturalism, and other forms of contemporary belief. Judah del Bene did the same in the collection of essays mentioned above. From a Maimonidean stance, del Bene regarded the success of Christianity as an integral part of the providential design to defeat paganism and hasten the redemption. In his view, Christianity was an agent of civilization and progress, as indicated by the Christian acceptance of the Hebrew Bible. Writing well into the ghetto period, del Bene viewed Christian toleration of Jews and Jewish tradition as a prelude to the messianic redemption of mankind.[46]

A striking example of Judaism and Christianity being brought together under the same conceptual roof is Rabbi Moses Zacuto's use of

Christian metaphors to describe Jewish concepts. As has been noted,[47] in his drama *Yesod Olam*, Zacuto used imagery adopted from the Christian Passion Play to describe Abraham's trial and condemnation to the burning furnace for having challenged idolatry in his father's home:

> . . . and Thistles a crown upon his head/the streets, to be mocked, he was led/[48]

This brings us back to our original theme. Moses Zacuto was the outstanding kabbalist of baroque Italy. Long before Moses Haim Luzzato, the persona of Zacuto presents us with what has long been considered the enigma of a Janus-like intellectual. On the one hand, he was aware of literary developments and actively took part in contemporary literary life, to the point of creatively participating in literary social events. He was very much of "this world." I would argue that for Zacuto, as for most leading figures of Italian Jewry, kabbalah offered a rich and potent framework for bringing thisworldliness and otherworldliness under the same roof, which, in turn, was a prelude to the subsequent restructuring of the relationship between the two, a restructuring that ultimately led to the birth of the modern religious outlook.

Modern religious perception appears to be characterized less by its concern with public ritual and other tangible devotional expressions than by its preoccupation with inner spirituality and the individual's approach to the sacred. It sharply distinguishes between otherworldliness and thisworldliness and between the sacred and the profane: it emphasizes the contradiction between the realms of the spiritual and the material. In contrast, the medieval mind often considered the proximity of distinct opposites to be natural. The spiritual and the material, individuality of religious expression and public ritual, were not considered contradictory. In the harmonious holistic and organic medieval view of the world, one opposite was interpreted to be the necessary complement to the other. The afterlife, the world to come, was felt to be as near as the ephemeral, material world; the two, in a sense, were interwoven. Metaphysics was at once beyond, but also an extension of, physics. Economics was a branch of philosophical theology. Otherworldliness and thisworldliness, the sacred and the profane, were believed to coexist in a proximity that may seem scandalous to us. I suggest that the historical process that transformed the medieval religious outlook into a

modern one was similar to that which is outlined above, that the separation of realms now considered opposing was preceded by a temporary
and paradoxical intensification of an earlier proximity. Such a transformation occurred in Italian Judaism principally through the agency of the
kabbalah. In its history and nature, kabbalah was particularly suited to
this role. Moreover, kabbalah may also have been an agent of secularism
that enabled Jewish religious space and time to undergo a process of
restructuring parallel to concurrent processes in non-Jewish society. It
has already been noted how Rabbi Menahem Azariah da Fano's kabbalism may have brought him to a Renaissance perception of religious
individualism that strengthened his proclivity to regard personal experience as the only valid kind. I believe that it is possible to go beyond
individual experience to include under this rubric group experience as
well.

In order to be completed, the restructuring of group religious experience required that inner spiritual individualism be brought into ever
closer proximity to the religious practice of the group. Proximity would
then mediate between the two. Our case clearly reveals the stages of the
process. Individualism begins at the level of personal allegiance to a
ritual other than the normative one of the group. Justification for this
deviance is offered in terms of a personal judgment that nonchalantly
dismisses centuries-old tradition, apparently on the grounds that the
right to follow one's inner convictions is a given. Precedents are not
invoked in favor of revolutionary decisions; the binding force of normative custom *(minhag)* is considered irrelevant, in fact, is completely
ignored. Personal opinion is the sole criterion for making decisions.
Rabbi Jacob Israel Finzi of Recanati, who should have followed family
tradition and prayed according to the Italian rite, simply decided:

I have seen that Sephardic prayer texts are better than those of other traditions. . . . I have followed them, for to me they seemed the most authentic. And
since the prayers are fundamentally rooted in kabbalah . . . I have explained
them according to the kabbalah, the true teaching.[49]

Similarly, Rabbi Moses Basola (1480–1560), of French origin, wrote to
one of his students urging him to depart from his usual formula of
prayer and to adopt the French rite,

since in the prayers of the Italians there are many worthless things from which
one should distance himself as much as possible.[50]

These examples are not intended to convey the impression that the process of change proceeded with linear uniformity and without nuance. Nor is it being suggested that the principle of individual freedom to choose a personal way of serving God was ever universally accepted. Difficulties were created by psychological and social inertia and by varying degrees of group cohesion. The watchword was compromise. Moses Basola's student introduced

radical changes in the prayer formula when he prayed privately, but in public prayer, he changed not one iota, lest controversy ensue.[51]

Compromises of this sort must have been typical in these times. Indeed, past practices were stubbornly resistant. Moses Basola's condemnation of the Italian prayer book as being full of nonsense was questioned by Rabbi Yohanan Treves. Treves agreed that the Italian text was problematic, but he also insisted that the force of tradition obligated him to accept it.[52] Doubt provided insufficient reason to abrogate customs rooted in antiquity. One must wonder about the degree of inner religious conviction such a stance reflects.[53] Nevertheless, the double standard of private and public behavior at least kept "public peace." It no doubt also perpetuated the traditional view that the kabbalah was an esoteric body of knowledge that should be cultivated only by a limited few, not disseminated among the public at large.

The complexity of these revolutionary processes, as well as the opposition they encountered, is well illustrated by the publication in 1587–88 of a startlingly new version of the Italian prayer book (Mahzor), replete with marginal notations that proposed numerous emendations. Most of these proposals originated in the circle of Menahem Azariah da Fano.[54] Hundreds of copies of this Mahzor were printed. Since it was not intended for export it may be assumed that the publishers expected many communities to adopt it locally. Yet they did not. Most of the copies remained unsold, even years later.[55] And, by and large, proposed emendations remained dead letters.[56] Only a thorough study of the Italian rite as practiced in the various Italian communities will reveal which emendations were actually adopted. The rejection of the others may well be linked to the transitionary phase of the kabbalah, in which most of the emendations were rooted. It hardly needs to be said that as a system of thought and practice kabbalah was not static. In the same years in which the Mahzor was published, a Lurianic kabbalistic Weltan-

schauung was taking the place of the Cordoverian one. The proposed liturgical emendations in the *Mahzor* were founded on the latter, so that, ipso facto, the earlier, Cordoverian-based revolutionary tendencies were neutralized, including, of course, the innovations proposed in the *Mahzor* itself. Indeed, when the Lurianic kabbalah gained full sway, proposals for change no longer required the justification they once did. However, by that time, the dimensions of the problem had also diminished. Kabbalistic ritual was slowly disappearing from the synagogue service and becoming more visible in the practices of confraternities. Yet it is not the rejection of most emendations that must be underlined here as really significant; it is, rather, the publication of the *Mahzor* itself and the introduction in the whole of those emendations that were actually introduced in it.

The number of Jewish confraternities increased in Italy during the sixteenth century and expanded sharply in the seventeenth and eighteenth centuries.[57] As noted by Elliott Horowitz, "whereas the first generation of confraternities was eclectic in its religious orientation yet stressed benevolent deeds connected with sickness and death, the second generation tended to be more specialized in its religious aims and to stress ritual rather than benevolent piety."[58] That ritual was eventually suffused with kabbalistic elements, even if originally this was not so. The recitation of kabbalistic *tikkunim,* which were available in dozens of editions, became exceedingly popular at seventeenth- and eighteenth-century confraternal gatherings. The *tikkun* was a parasynagogal religious activity, in strict terms a prayer that was usually recited at confraternal gatherings. As such, the *tikkun* was essentially ambivalent: public, yet exclusive; it was a religious ritual, yet, as a rule, it was not performed in the synagogue space that was, by definition, considered sacred. Nevertheless, the marked social aspect of the *tikkun* did not obscure its religious essence as an intervention by means of *kavannah* in cosmic processes. The increased socialization of extra-synagogal religious activities, as well as the appearance of individualism in normative religious decision making, were surely a paradoxical result of the heightened religious sentiment that the kabbalah engendered.

One of the most visible consequences of this process was the restructuring of the space that housed the Jew's spiritual activity: the part inside the synagogue remained essentially unaltered, while that outside the synagogue underwent rapid change. In fact, sacred religious activity, performed in the sacred space of the synagogue, was increasingly being divorced from private religious sentiment, with the latter expressed in a portable space that is best labeled profane. This division made room for these sentiments to be expressed alongside such profane social activities as the coffee break, inevitably accompanied by gossip or even entertainment.[59] In other words, kabbalah made it possible for the sacred to coexist with the profane. Yet this was so only outside the synagogue. Synagogal activities became increasingly sacred.

Events in Venice, which have been carefully investigated, eloquently illustrate this process.[60] In about 1555, Menahem Azariah da Fano instituted public study of the kabbalah at the time of the traditional study hour following the morning prayers. Subsequently, confraternities combined both traditional and kabbalistic study with prayer, so that study was transformed into devotion. Finally, study was divorced from prayer, eventually acquiring its own specific role in the restructuring of modern religious life. There is visual evidence of this transformation of study into devotion. In the Italian ghetto, synagogues were assigned fixed locations, whereas previously they were often situated in private dwellings. The Venetian synagogues, which may still be visited, furnish a striking example of this new attitude. The synagogue fabric became more sacred as society became more profane. This was the beginning of the process that culminated in the nineteenth century, as synagogues were transformed into churchlike edifices.[61]

To sum up, kabbalah may be singled out as a most effective agent of modernity in the sphere of religious activity.[62] Its ambivalent nature, expressed through the socialization of ritual, distanced the sacred from the profane by balancing inner spirituality, uninhibited individualism, and essential otherworldliness against a thisworldliness that was firmly entrenched. Within the limits of this essay, it would be impossible to consider each one of the ambivalent aspects of kabbalah that enabled it to perform its functions. Yet, before closing, we must discuss one more aspect, namely, the relationship between kabbalah and magic—a subject about which we know a good deal, thanks to the studies of Moshe Idel.[63] As noted above, magic fostered ambivalence in medicine and facilitated its mediating role. But kabbalah and magic were so intimately related during the Renaissance that in most Western languages they have become synonymous—not without some justification. After all, magic is a kind of thisworldly operation performed on otherworldly forces. It embodies man's mastery of cosmic forces by means of secret cosmic knowledge, that is, man's mastery of the universe. Magic is thus homologous with kabbalah, for both allow man supremely to affirm his powers over nature.[64] Consequently, kabbalah facilitated the *concordantia oppositorum* that underlies structural inversion.

Proceeding one step further, a relationship between the restructuring of religious space and the restructuring of the whole of Jewish living space that resulted from the establishment of the ghetto may be posited. With respect to the outside world, ghetto space represents enclosure. Perceived from within, it was homologous with interiorization and self-reliance. Professor Jacob Katz has convincingly argued that a kind of detached contact, distancing fields of intellectual interest, characterized the Jewish disposition toward the outside world, in much the same way that the ghetto walls created a physical distinction between the Jews on the inside and the non-Jews on the outside.[65] Yet, enclosure with respect to the Christian world was paralleled by an opening toward the "outside" Jewish world. That is, public lecturing on the kabbalah and public preaching on kabbalistic themes, using kabbalistic terminology, came, essentially, from outside Italy. Rabbi Menahem Azariah da Fano commenced his public lectures at Venice in 1575 while he was under the influence of the kabbalists of Safed. Rabbi Mordecai Dato, the first preacher to deliver unabashedly kabbalistic sermons, initiated his preaching shortly after his return to Italy from Safed.[66] It was in response to the demands of the markets of northeastern Europe that the Cremona edition of the *Zohar* was produced. The Mantuan edition was destined for the Levant. Most other kabbalistically oriented works published in Italy after the mid-sixteenth century were also directed abroad, where, in fact, they had also been composed.[67] The restructuring of intellectual space thus parallels the restructuring of the religious, as well as the physical, space of the Jewish community.

This aspect of restructuring possessed a crucial mediating significance, for it facilitated the eventual blending of antiquated medieval tropes of reasoning and expression—now cloaked in Levantine and Eastern European dress—with innovative ways of thinking that had arisen in the West and were leading to modernization. Technically and geographically, Italian printing presses played a mediating role in this process. It is significant that nearly all the Hebrew books in Italy during the period here studied emanated from Venice. The official reception of Levantine

Jews into the Venetian Jewish community in 1571 initiated a paradigmatic and symbolic restructuring of the physical space of the ghetto that was accompanied by cultural reformation. Books written by authors living in the Ottoman Empire were printed in Italy and distributed in places as far away as Holland and Poland. Books written by Spanish conversos educated and living in the West were printed in Italy and distributed in the East. Inventories of the contents of an average Italian Jewish library show that these books were also circulated in Italy, where they were freely cited by Italian Jewish thinkers, mainly rabbis.

Religious time was also restructured. Kabbalistically oriented nocturnal vigils, like the *Tikkun Hazot,* shattered the traditional threefold division of prayer time. The upheaval was even more marked with respect to the *tikkunim* for festivals, since they inverted the focus of procedures and rituals for the entire festival day.[68] To complete and perhaps to emphasize these changes, the vigils were accompanied by the study of kabbalistic texts, including the *Zohar.* Since the totality of Jewish public spiritual activity was linked to prayer time, the restructuring of this time was homologous with similar changes, as has been identified by Natalie Z. Davis in her comparison of Protestant and Catholic religious behavior and its effects in sixteenth-century Lyons.[69]

In conclusion, it seems clear that the diffusion of the kabbalah contributed to the inception of modernity among Jews because of its paradoxically simultaneous stress on both the distance and proximity between opposites. The restructuring of religious space and time should be seen as symbolic of the restructuring of religious attitudes as a whole. Moreover, this model developed in such a way as to make it homologous with many other historical phenomena, whose interrelations are not always self-evident and which will be clarified only through further investigation.

NOTES

1. Scholarship related to Italian Jewry in the Renaissance and early modern period has flourished in recent decades, but we still lack a recent comprehensive synthesis. Moses A. Shulvass's *The Jews in the World of the Renais-*

sance (Leiden, 1973) is an unrevised translation of the Hebrew edition, which appeared in 1955. One must still refer to Cecil Roth's classic essay, *The Jews in the Renaissance* (Philadelphia, 1959), as well as to his *The History of the Jews of Italy* (Philadelphia, 1946). Attilio Milano's *Storia degli Ebrei in Italia* (Turin, 1963) is also very useful for the *histoire événe-mentielle* of the period. Recent useful monographs, with up-to-date bibliography, are: Shlomo Simonsohn, *History of the Jews in the Duchy of Mantua* (Jerusalem, 1977), Hebrew edition, 1962–1964, and David B. Ruderman, *The World of a Renaissance Jew: The Life and Thought of Abraham Farissol* (Cincinnati, 1981). Especially pertinent here is Robert Bonfil, *Ha-Rabbanut be-Italia bi-Tequfat ha-Renaissance [The Rabbinate in Renaissance Italy]* (Jerusalem, 1979). See the English version of this book, *Rabbis and Jewish Communities in Renaissance Italy*, trans. Jonathan Chipman (Oxford University Press, 1990).

2. The reference is to the period of major demographic and sociocultural change among Italian Jews, especially in the fifteenth century, which witnessed the emigration of French exiles, the southern movement of German Jews, the continuous migration of Italian Jews from the center of the peninsula northward, and, finally, the arrival of refugees from Spain.

3. For instance, the introduction of vernacular preaching and music in the synagogue service with the inception of Reform in Germany.

4. This reaction was carefully analyzed by Isaiah Tishby, "The Controversy about the *Zohar* in the Sixteenth Century in Italy" [in Hebrew], in *P'raqim* —*Yearbook of the Schocken Institute for Jewish Research of the Jewish Theological Seminary of America* 1 (1967–68):131–92.

5. On Messer Leon's ban see the reconstruction of the events and the relevant bibliography in my introduction to the reprinted *editio princeps* of *Sefer Nofet Zufim* (Jerusalem, 1981), 15–17.

6. See Shlomo Simonsohn, "The Scandal of the Tamari-Venturozzo Divorce" [in Hebrew], *Tarbiz* 28 (1959):375–92; Ephraim Kupfer, "Further Clarifications Concerning the Scandal of the Tamari-Venturozzo Divorce" [in Hebrew], *Tarbiz* 38 (1969):54–60; Robert Bonfil, "Aspects of Social and Spiritual Life of the Jews in the Venetian Territories at the Beginning of the Sixteenth Century" [in Hebrew], *Zion* 41 (1976):79–80, n. 64; Pier Cesare Ioly Zorattini, *Processi del S. Uffizio di Venezia contro Ebrei e qiudaizzanti (1561–1570* (Florence, 1982), 24–26.

7. For further detail see Bonfil, *Ha-Rabbanut be-Italia bi-Tequfat ha-Renaissance*, 179–90; idem, "New Information on Rabbi Menahem Azariah da Fano and His Age," in *Studies in the History of Jewish Society in the Middle Ages and in the Modern Period, Presented to Professor Jacob Katz*, ed. Emanuel Etkes and Yosef Salmon (Jerusalem, 1980), 83–135; idem, "Halakhah, Kabbalah and Society; Some Insights Into Rabbi Menahem Azariah da Fano's Inner World," in *Jewish Thought in the Seventeenth Century*, ed. Isadore Twersky and Bernard Septimus (Cambridge, Mass., 1987), 39–61; idem, "Cultura e mistica a Venezia nel Cinquecento," in *Gli Ebrei e Vene-*

zia, secoli XIV–XVII; Atti del Convegno Internazionale Organizzato dall'Istituto di Storia della Società e dello Stato Veneziano della Fondazione Giorgio Cini, Venezia . . . 5–10 quiqno 1983, ed. Gaetano Cozzi (Milano, 1987), 469–506; and, of course, Gershom Scholem's *Major Trends in Jewish Mysticism* (New York, 1941).

8. Recent treatments are: Meir Benayahu, "Kabbalah and Halakhah—A Confrontation," *Daat—Journal of Jewish Philosophy and Kabbalah* 5 (1980):61– 115; Jacob Katz, "Tefillin shel Hol ha-Mo'ed," in *Proceedings of the Seventh World Congress of Jewish Studies* (Jerusalem, 1981), 191–213, reprinted in his collected writings, *Halakhah ve-Kabbalah* (Jerusalem, 1984), 102–24.

9. Bonfil, "Halakhah, Kabbalah and Society."

10. Menahem Azariah da Fano, *Responsa* (Venice, 1600), no. 25.

11. For instance, the works of Michel Foucault, Philippe Aries, Michel Vovelle, Alberto Tenenti, Natalie Zemon Davis.

12. One might even push the argument *ad limitem* and say that were these shifts to affect the totality of the structure a *total inversion* would occur.

13. In fact, I would surmise that rather than eliminating paradox by means of distinctions, we should accept it as a distinctive characteristic of transitional situations. We should shift the emphasis from the meaning of the term as a substantive, i.e., something extraordinary, exceptional (to paradoxon), to the primary meaning of the term in its adjectival form (paradoxos, i.e., para doxan): that which transcends current opinion, rising to the status of ultimate truth. Perhaps it is not by chance that the Stoics emphasized paradox in relation to morality; for morals possess a certain mediating character— between intellect and sentiment, reason and passion, thought and sense. Morals may never rest on straightforward statements like "the heart has reasons that the intellect does not recognize." Rather, they ought to attempt to integrate heart and reason, mediating between them, even if ultimately damaging both. A stimulating treatment of paradox is Rosalie L. Colie, *Paradoxica Epidemica; The Renaissance Tradition of Paradox* (Princeton, 1966). I owe this reference to the kindness of Natalie Z. Davis. Paradox has been discussed in relation to other transitional periods as well in, for instance, Peter Brown, *The Making of Late Antiquity* (Cambridge, Mass., 1978).

14. On these issues see especially Guido Panseni, "Medicina e scienze naturali nei secoli XVI e XVII," in *Storia d'Italia (Einaudi), Annali 3* (Turin, 1980), 345–80. See, too, H. Zimmels, *Magicians, Theologians and Doctors* (London, 1952); V. Nutten, ed., *Galenism—Rise and Decline of a Medical Philosophy* (Ithaca, 1973); C. Webster, *From Paracelsus to Newton; Magic and the Making of Modern Science* (Cambridge, 1982); B. Vickers, ed., *Occult and Scientific Mentalities in the Renaissance* (Cambridge, 1984); David B. Ruderman, *Kabbalah, Magic, and Science: The Cultural Universe of a Sixteenth-Century Jewish Physician* (Cambridge, Mass., 1988).

15. Andreas Vesalius (1514–1564) was born in Brussels and studied in Louvain,

Paris, and Padua. The father of modern anatomy and a pioneer in the field of anatomical dissection, he wrote *Tabulae Anatomicae* (Venice, 1538) and *De humani corporis fabrica libri septem* (Venice, 1548).

16. Leonardo Fioravanti (Bologna, 1518–1588) wrote about medicine, surgery, physics, and alchemy.

17. Significantly enough, Abraham Yagel also composed such a tract. See Ruderman, *Kabbalah, Magic, and Science*, 18, 137.

18. Michel Foucault, *Histoire de la folie à l' Age Classique* (Paris, 1972).

19. This perspective has been adopted by, among others, Jonathan I. Israel, *European Jewry in the Age of Mercantilism* (Oxford, 1985). Israel even speaks of a "re-expansion of Jewish life in Italy at the end of the sixteenth century" (p. 49).

20. Ermanno Loevinson, "La concession des banques des prêts aux Juifs par les Papes du XVIe et XVIIe siècles," *Revue des Études Juives* 92–95 (1932–1933).

21. Loevinson, "La concession des banques," *Revue des Études Juives* 92:27–30.

22. See Milano, *Storia degli Ebrei in Italia*, 525 ff.

23. Eliezer Nahman Foa, *Commentary on the Passover Haggadah* (Jerusalem, 1975), fol. 7v.

24. Ibid., fol. 7v.

25. The allusion is to excessive rent increases in the Italian ghettos.

26. Ibid., fols. 11v–12r. On the sources of Jewish wealth for activities such as the purchase and sale of livestock, see Bonfil, "Halakhah, Kabbalah and Society."

27. Foa, *Commentary on the Passover Haggadah*, fol. 8r.

28. Ibid., fol. 5r. The terminology is that of the Lurianic kabbalah, yet "original sin" is a Christian concept. This is but one more paradox for us to confront.

29. See Bonfil, "Halakhah, Kabbalah and Society."

30. For example, the ceremony carried out by the Jews of Verona on the occasion of the establishment of the ghetto. See Cecil Roth, "La fête de l'institution du ghetto; une célébration particulière à Vérone," *Revue des Études Juives* 79 (1924):163–69 (*Rassegna Mensile di Israel* 3 [1928]:33–39).

31. See Bonfil, *Ha-Rabbanut be-Italia bi-Tequfat ha-Renaissance*, 180, n. 52. On music in Italy see Israel Adler, *La pratique musicale savante dans quelques communautés juives en Europe aux XVIIe et XVIIIe siècles* (Paris, 1966); idem, "The Rise of Art Music in the Italian Ghetto," in *Jewish Medieval and Renaissance Studies*, ed. Alexander Altmann (Cambridge, Mass., 1967), 321–64; further up-to-date bibliographical references may be found in I. Adler, "Three Musical Texts for Hoshana Rabba in Casale Monferrato" [in Hebrew], *Yuval* 5 (1968):51–137 *(The Abraham Zvi Idelsohn Memorial Volume)*. On theater, see Jefim Schirmann, "Theater and Music in Italian Jewish Quarters, XVI–XVIII Centuries" [in Hebrew], *Zion* 29 (1964):61–111 (reprinted in *Studies in the History of Hebrew Poetry*

and Drama, 2 vols. [Jerusalem, 1977], 1:44–94); idem, "The Hebrew Drama in the XVIIth Century" [in Hebrew], *Moznayim* 4 (1938):624–35 (reprinted in *Studies in the History of Hebrew Poetry and Drama,* 1:25–38).

32. See Robert Bonfil, "The Historian's Perception of the Jews in the Italian Renaissance; Towards a Reappraisal," *Revue des Etudes Juives* 143 (1983):59–82.

33. As far as theater is concerned, inversion appears to have been arrested, or at least not to have reached completion. In music, however, even the most conservative and "closed" Jewish groups no longer maintain attitudes similar to those that prevailed in the Middle Ages. The outlook toward music has undergone a revolution within traditional Jewish society, mostly because of Hasidic attitudes, which, of course, are closely linked with kabbalah. See below, nn. 62 and 68.

34. See Bonfil, "Halakhah, Kabbalah and Society."

35. See Judah del Bene, *Sefer Kiss'ot le-veth David* (Verona, 1646), II, 9 (fol. 28v). On del Bene see Isaac E. Barzilay, *Between Reason and Faith: Anti-Rationalism in Italian Jewish Thought, 1250–1640* (The Hague-Paris, 1967), 210–17. Giuseppe Sermoneta argued cogently for the modernity of this writer; see his "Le opere di Leon da Modena e di Jehudah del Bene nel contesto culturale del Seicento Italiano," *Italia Judaica* II (Rome, 1986):17–35.

36. See my introduction to the reprint of the *editio princeps* of *Nofet Zufim* (Jerusalem, 1981).

37. See, for example, Sandra De Benedetti-Stow, "Due poesie biligui inedite contro le donne di Samuel da Castiglione (1553), *Italia—Studi e ricerche sulla cultura e sulla letteratura degli ebrei d'Italia* 2 (1980):7–64.

38. See Dan Pagis, ʿAl Sod Hatum; Le-Toledot ha-Hiddah ha-ʿIvrit be-Italia u-ve-Holland [A Secret Sealed; Hebrew Baroque Emblem-Riddles from Italy and Holland] (Jerusalem, 1986).

39. See Ariel Rathaus, "In Love with the Portrait; Two Hebrew Sonnets from the Seicento" [in Hebrew], *Italia—Studi e ricerche sulla cultura e sulla letteratura degli ebrei d'Italia* 2 (1980):xxx–xlvii; idem, "The Philosophical Poetry of Jehoshua Josef Levi" [in Hebrew], *Italia—Studi e ricerche sulla cultura e sulla letteratura degli ebrei d'Italia* 4 (1985):vii–xxvi.

40. Cf. Barzilay, *Between Reason and Faith,* 210–17.

41. Sermoneta, "Le opere di leon da Modena e di Jehudah del Bene."

42. Venice, 1612.

43. Venice, 1660.

44. The fact was explicitly stated by Modena himself in his autobiography.

45. See S. Maybaum, "Abraham Jaghel's Kathechismus Lekach-Tob," *Lehranstalt für die Wissenschaft des Judenthums in Berlin,* 1892; Ruderman, *Kabbalah, Magic, and Science.*

46. Sermoneta, "Le opere di Leon da Modena e di Jehudah del Bene."

47. See Yosef Melkman, "Moshe Zacuto's Play *Yesod Olam*" [in Hebrew], *Sefunot* 10 (1966): 299–333.

48. *Yesod 'Olam,* ed. A. Berliner (Berlin, 1874), 14. Quoted by Melkman, "Moshe Zacuto's Play," 321.
49. Yacob Israel Finzi, *Commentary to the Prayer Book,* Cambridge MS, Add. 512, fol. 3r.
50. Ruth Lamdan, "Two Writings by R. Moses Basola" [in Hebrew], *Michael* 9 (1985):177.
51. See *She'elot U-Teshuvot Mattanot Ba-Adam,* ed. Yacov Boksenboim (Tel Aviv, 1983), 67, n. 9.
52. Yohanan Treves, *Commentary to the Bologna Edition of the Prayer-Book* (Bologna, 1540–1541), fol. iv. Bv.
53. For a more detailed discussion on this point see Bonfil, "Halakhah, Kabbalah and Society."
54. See Bonfil, "Cultura e mistica a Venezia nel Cinquecento."
55. Shlomo Simonsohn, "Books and Libraries of Mantuan Jews, 1595" [in Hebrew], *Kiryat Sepher* 37 (1961–1962):114.
56. The above statement is based on an examination of some three dozen proposed changes. I am much indebted to Rabbi Menahem Emanuele Artom for his assistance.
57. Elliott S. Horowitz, "Jewish Confraternities in Seventeenth-Century Verona: A Study in the Social History of Piety" (Ph.D. diss., Yale University, 1982).
58. Horowitz, "Jewish Confraternities in Seventeenth-Century Verona."
59. Elliott S. Horowitz, "Coffee, Coffeehouses, and the Nocturnal Rituals of Early Modern Jewry," *Association for Jewish Studies Review* 14 (1989):17–46.
60. See Bonfil, "Cultura e mistica a Venezia nel Cinquecento."
61. Cf. Roberto Bonfil, "La Sinagoga in Italia come luogo di riunionè e preghiera," *Il Centenario del Tempio Israelitico di Firenze; Atti del Convegno 7 Heshvan 5743, 24 ottobre 1982* (Florence, 1985), 36–44.
62. It may be useful to call attention to the similar role of restructuring religious space played by Hasidism from the moment of its inception to the present, as well as to the influence of Italian kabbalists, especially Mose Hayim Luzzatto, on spiritual trends in the places where Hasidism flourished. Cf. n. 33, above, and 68, below.
63. See Moshe Idel, "The Magical and Neoplatonic Interpretations of the Kabbalah in the Renaissance," in *Jewish Thought in the Sixteenth Century,* ed. Bernard D. Cooperman (Cambridge, Mass., 1983), 186–242.
64. If I am correct, this homology might be extended to several other aspects of the complex relationship between thisworldliness and otherworldliness, for instance, that between life and death. In fact, it seems to me that here lies the solution of another paradox, that of the apparently obsessive concern with death in an epoch in which life might have been viewed more optimistically than before. In the baroque perception of the world, death and life indeed appear paradoxically interwoven, as reflected in various literary expressions.

65. See Jacob Katz, *Exclusiveness and Tolerance* (London, 1961), 131 ff.
66. See Roberto Bonfil, "A Sermon by Rabbi Mordekhai Dato" [in Hebrew], *Italia—Studi e ricerche sulla cultura e sulla letteratura degli ebrei d'Italia* 1 (1976):i–xxxii.
67. See Bonfil, "Cultura e mistica a Venezia nel Cinquecento," n. 105.
68. It should be noted that the process of shattering the boundaries of religious time reached its apex in Hasidism, which revolutionized the entire normative system underlying the traditional attitude; by sharpening the importance of *kavvanah*, the traditional division of time into sacred and profane was practically eliminated. *Any time* became fit for religious practice, although, paradoxically, it was stressed that any time *is not* fit for religious practice. Cf. nn. 33 and 62, above.
69. Natalie Z. Davis, *Society and Culture in Early Modern France* (Stanford, Calif., 1975).

B

Cultural Trends in the Age of the Ghetto

16

Leone da Modena's *Riti*: A Seventeenth-Century Plea for Social Toleration of Jews

Mark R. Cohen

Like Simone Luzzatto's *Discorso circa il stato de gl'Hebrei* (1638)[1] and Menasseh ben Israel's *Humble Addresses* (1655) and *Vindiciae Judaeorum* (1656),[2] Leone da Modena's *Historia de' riti hebraici*[3] was one of the first Jewish books composed in European languages for non-Jewish consumption. These works reflected a new awareness among Jews and Christians of one another at the beginning of the seventeenth century and represented incipient Jewish attempts to re-orient Christian attitudes towards the Jews.[4] Especially in Holland and in Italy, where Jews of a certain level of secular cultural attainment mingled more freely with Christians than elsewhere, traditionally derisive attitudes towards the Jews and Judaism offended Jewish sensibilities and called for intellectual response. While the *Discorso* and the two tracts of Menasseh ben Israel were avowedly apologetic essays, designed to convince Christian rulers to tolerate Jewish settlements in their midst, the *Riti* was ostensibly only a straightforward description of Jewish religious practice without any

I would like to thank Professor Ismar Schorsch of the Institute for Advanced Studies in the Humanities in New York City for first suggesting that I study the *Riti* and for his helpful comments about my research. My friend and colleague, Ivan George Marcus, read the final manuscript and offered many helpful criticisms. I would like to express my special gratitude to Professor Gerson D. Cohen, Chancellor of the Jewish Theological Seminary of America, for the constantly enriching advice which helped me sharpen my thoughts and my writing. Professor Cohen also directed my attention to many of the secondary works which are cited in the notes.

Reprinted from *Jewish Social Studies* 34 (1972).

political axe to grind. Closer examination will reveal that the *Riti* was as tendentious as the other three contemporary polemical treatises, but in a more subtle way and for a different purpose. Its primary goal was to advance the social integration of Jews into Christian society.

It was on the apologetic nature of the *Riti* that scholarly opinion on the book was divided during the last half of the nineteenth and even into the first decades of the twentieth century. Salamon Rubin, the Hebrew translator of the *Riti* (1867), correctly detected Modena's apologetic motive in omitting certain rituals traditionally repugnant to Christian writers. Unfortunately, Rubin failed to support his suggestion, because in evidence he invoked a Christian work written a century *after* Modena had completed the *Riti:* the manual of Jewish ceremonies compiled by the apostate Paul Christian Kirchner and amplified by Sebastian Jungendres.[5]

Graetz, on the other hand, completely overlooked the apologetic purpose of the *Riti* and condemned its author for publishing such a detailed exposé of Judaism, which Graetz thought could only bring ridicule upon the religion and its adherents.[6]

Curiously, subsequent commentators on the *Riti* tended to focus their attention more on Graetz's harsh indictment than on the work itself. In his Hebrew biography of Leone da Modena, Nehemiah Libowitz lashed out at Graetz and charged him with projecting upon Modena his own embarrassment with Jewish observance. Modena had composed the *Riti* to defend the Jews, Libowitz insisted, and to prove his point he compared a number of passages in the book with the *Shevet Yehuda* and showed that Modena was responding to many of the same anti-Jewish calumnies that Ibn Verga had.[7] Ludwig Blau, in his edition of Modena's Hebrew correspondence, criticized Graetz in a similar vein for having branded Modena a "traitor to Judaism." Referring to a Hebrew letter of 1640 in which Modena stated explicitly that he had written the *Riti* to put an end to Christian derision of the Jews, Blau argued that Graetz had completely misunderstood the book.[8] Similarly, Ottolenghi and Cassuto, commenting briefly on the significance of the *Riti,* took Graetz to task and stressed the positive contribution which Modena had made with his apologetic treatise.[9] (In a more recent bibliographical article on the vicissitudes of the *Riti* Nino Samaja touched on the apologetical content of the work too, without reference, however, to Graetz.[10])

Graetz was clearly unfair in his evaluation of the *Riti,* and Libowitz,

Blau, Ottolenghi, and Cassuto were justified in taking exception to his severe strictures. Remarkably, none of these scholars actually examined the *Riti* in any depth. This is unfortunate since an investigation of the contents of the book in its historical setting would have disclosed its particular kind of social polemic.

ORIGINS OF THE *RITI*[11]

The origins and publishing vicissitudes of the *Riti*, treated in some detail by Roth, Ottolenghi, and Samaja,[12] constitute a rather fascinating vignette of seventeenth-century Italian Jewish life. By combining substantial bits of information culled from a well-known passage in Modena's own autobiographical journal, *Hayye Yehuda*,[13] from documents in the archives of the Holy Office in Venice, as well as from Modena's correspondence, it is possible to reconstruct the general outlines of the book's history. Modena composed the treatise in about 1616 for an "English nobleman" who, in turn, wished to present it to his sovereign, James I (r. 1603–25).[14] Hand-written copies of the work circulated in English Christian circles for years before the first printed edition appeared on the Continent.[15] In fact, consideration of Italian ecclesiastical censorship inhibited Modena from publishing the book for almost twenty years.

In September, 1634, however, he wrote to an English correspondent that at the behest of "certain friends and patrons" he had begun considering publication of the manuscript, but only "in Paris in order to avoid censorship here."[16] Indeed, in the spring of 1635 he entrusted a manuscript of the *Riti* to Jacques Gaffarel,[17] the French Christian mystic and Hebraist, upon the latter's promise to publish it in France. When, however, on April 9, 1637, Modena received word from Gaffarel that he had fulfilled his pledge, renewed fears of censorial objection to certain passages in the book led the Italian rabbi to the rather drastic step of voluntarily submitting a manuscript to the Holy Office for scrutiny.[18] The archives of the Venetian Holy Office confirm that this was done on April 28. After reading the work the Inquisitorial examiner ruled it unfit for publication as it stood and singled out two parts as unacceptable: the final chapter, listing the thirteen articles of Maimonides; and a section devoted to the doctrine of transmigration of souls. Modena was further admonished not to print or even circulate the manuscript without permission and was advised to inform the Holy Office of any other such works that came to his attention. The ruling of the Holy Office was handed down on May 14.[19]

This fear of censorship which drove Modena to the point of self-incrimination was a real one. During that period of counter reformation, when the Catholic Church was ever on guard against deviations, Jews in Italy were as cautious as others about what they published.[20] That is why Modena allowed the *Riti* to remain in manuscript for so many years and consented to publish it, as he admitted in the "Proemio" to the book, only upon the insistence of Christian acquaintances.[21] Indeed, he probably had the specter of the ecclesiastical censor before him when he wrote in that same introduction:

> In my writing I have, in truth, forgotten that I am a Jew, and have considered myself as a plain and neutral relator only. I do not deny, however, that I have endeavored to avoid (giving the reader cause for) derision (of the Jews) on account of their many ceremonies. But at the same time I have not had in mind either to defend them or to find excuses for them, since I have intended only to inform, not to persuade.[22]

This candid passage, which Graetz, incidentally, interpreted as a betrayal of the Jews, was rather a protest of objectivity designed to divert the scrutinizing eye of the Inquisition away from the *Riti*.[23]

It is ironic, therefore, that the Holy Office's first awareness of the *Riti* should have come as a result of Modena's own disclosure. Doubly ironic is the fact that about the same time as the Inquisitor was rendering his verdict on the manuscript, Modena received his first copy of the newly-printed Paris edition and found, much to his surprise, that Gaffarel had already edited out the passages Modena had fretted over.[24] "Nevertheless," he informs us in *Hayye Yehuda*,

> since there were a large number of linguistic mistakes in the book, and in addition since there were still a few things in it which I feared might not find favor with Christians, I decided to publish a second edition here in Venice, excising some things and adding others with that in mind.[25]

In fact, despite the proscription of his manuscript in 1637, Modena somehow succeeded in obtaining a license to publish a second, thoroughly revised edition of the *Riti* in Venice in 1638, with the omission of the two passages censored a year earlier. To be sure, he was partly motivated by Gaffarel's editorial mistakes: he made literally scores of spelling, syntactical and other stylistic changes in the new edition. But it is also likely that he was provoked by Gaffarel's letter prefixed to the Paris edition. In that epistle the French mystic had expressed his dissatisfaction with the *Riti's* failure to satisfy his curiosity about many of the more "mystical" practices of Judaism.[26] Both in tone and by his examples Gaffarel reflected a traditional Christian view of Judaism as a mass of superstitions and incredulities, in other words, the very misrepresentation which Leone da Modena had set out to combat. Accordingly, Modena made about two dozen tendentious changes in the 1638 edition which served to strengthen his polemic against this prejudice.

The disparaging portrayal of inner Jewish life to which the *Riti* was a response had found renewed and vigorous expression in the sixteenth and early seventeenth centuries in a number of Christian books on Jewish rites and beliefs. These included Ortuinus Gratius' *De vita et moribus Judaeorum* (1504), François Tissard's *De Judeorum ritibus compendium* (1508), the Jewish apostate Viktor von Carben's *Opus aureum . . . in quo omnes Judaeorum errores manifestantur* (1509), and Pfefferkorn's series of diatribes against Judaism.[27] The apostate Antonius Margaritha's *Der gantz Juedisch glaub* (1530) "represented the first attempt to explain to non-Jews all the prayers of the Jews and interpret all their customs and ceremonies." This hostile treatise became a *cause célèbre* a few months after its appearance, when the Emperor Charles V summoned Josel of Rosheim before the Diet of Augsburg to defend the Jews against allegations of disloyalty which Margaritha had leveled against them in his book.[28] Lastly, following the pattern set by Margaritha, but far more comprehensive in scope, there was Johann Buxtorf the Elder's German *Synagoga Judaica,* published in 1603, less than fifteen years before Modena first penned the *Riti.* We shall soon see that the *Riti* was an apologetic response to this Christian literature, and, above all, to Buxtorf's *Synagoga Judaica.* In a letter written in 1639 or 1640 to a Christian friend, Vincenzo Noghera, Modena confessed this openly:

The judgement made by you on my work about our Rites is most correct insofar as I had indeed the intention of refuting entirely that work of Buxtorf and of giving a true account of the fundamentals [i.e., of Judaism], leaving out those items which have been considered by our own people (by the intelligent men among them) as superstitious.[29]

A brief description of Buxtorf's work is appropriate in order to establish more exactly the literary and historical context of the *Riti.* *Synagoga Judaica*[30] is an impressive manual of Jewish belief and practice

seen from a Protestant bias. Johann Buxtorf (1564–1629), the greatest
Protestant rabbinic scholar of his time,[31] had a thorough grasp of post-
Biblical Jewish literature, and when he applied this erudition against
Judaism the results were formidable. At least as early as 1600 he had
evinced interest in the conversion of the Jews, and that, indeed, is one of
the reasons he gave in 1603 for writing *Synagoga Judaica*. But it appears
that his primary orientation was towards his Christian audience. He
seems to have been disturbed by certain philo-Jewish tendencies among
Protestants who idealized the Jews for their ostensibly strict adherence
to the Bible. He voiced this concern in the "Vorrede," and explained
that he had composed the book to expose the non-Biblical foundation of
contemporary Judaism and thus demonstrate how false the contrary
assumption was. He hoped, he said, that Christians would "take to
heart" the lesson to be learned from the debased state of deviant Judaism
which had resulted from God's rejection, and thereby prevent the same
thing from happening to them.[32] His third expressed goal was to refute
Judaism. To that end he also appended, though without identifying it, a
German translation of Calvin's *Ad quaestiones et obiecta Judaei cuiusdam Responsio,* which he called on the title page, simply, a "disputation
between a Jew and a Christian in which Christianity is defended and
Jewish unbelief is refuted and knocked to the ground." In his own attack
upon Judaism, however, Buxtorf noticeably avoided the kind of rabid
vituperations so characteristic of Luther's biting treatises against the
Jews. Buxtorf confined his calumnies to the traditional "hardheartedness," "perversity," and "blindness" of the Jews. Only rarely did he slip
into abuses of a more vulgar nature. Clearly he intended his refutation
of Judaism to derive from his evidence, not from his rhetoric. Finally,
Synagoga Judaica is the only book the Protestant scholar ever wrote in
the German vernacular, which indicates that he wished to insure it as
wide a circulation and as favorable a reception as possible among both
Christians and Jews.[33]

The structure of Buxtorf's manual is simple. In a lengthy general
introductory chapter (chapter i) he applied classical Protestant categories
of thought and divided his deprecating analysis of Judaism into faith
(*Glaube,* namely the thirteen articles of Maimonides) and works (*Wercke,*
namely the history and theory of Jewish law).[34] In the remaining thirty-
five chapters he detailed Jewish practices from womb to tomb, culminating in a discussion of messianic doctrines.

While Buxtorf seems to have patterned his work on that of Margaritha,[35] he departed from his model in the arrangement of the material and, above all, in his erudite and extensive use of information drawn from Jewish sources. In addition to the Bible, he extracted material from such rabbinic and medieval books as: the Talmud (quoted about 85 times!); Alfasi's *Halakhot;* the Biblical commentaries of Rashi, Ibn Ezra and R. David Kimhi; Midrashic collections like *Pirkei De-Rabbi Eliezer* and the *Tanhuma; Sefer Hasidim;* the book *Reshit Hokhma;* Rabbi Bahyye ben Asher's *Kad ha-Kemah* and his Bible commentary; as well as some thirty other rabbinic and later compilations. In addition, he drew heavily from more recent compendia, such as Moses b. Hanokh's moralistic *Brantspiegel* (in Judeo-German);[36] a Judeo-German abridgment of Jewish law for women and children called *Orah Hayyim;*[37] and various *Minhagim* (custom) collections.[38] The result was a much longer and more diffuse handbook than Margaritha's, with lengthy, detailed excursuses on selected Jewish beliefs and practices, particularly ones Buxtorf deemed superstitious. At the same time, the sheer weight of his Jewish quotations made the book an impressive challenge to Jews and Judaism.

Leone da Modena was, of course, acquainted with the Christian antecedents of his own manual of Jewish ritual. In fact, he invoked their existence as one of his reasons for hesitating to publish the *Riti.*[39] He had read *Synagoga Judaica*[40] and, as we have seen, claimed to have compiled the *Riti* in order to confute Buxtorf's damaging, superstitious portrayal of Jewish ceremonies.[41] Though this particular fact has been known since Roth published the revealing letter to Noghera,[42] no one has addressed himself to the task of actually comparing the two books to ascertain *how* Modena went about formulating his rebuttal. As it turns out, a comparative analysis of the two works shed enormous light on the content, methods and, above all, the historical significance of the *Riti,* and discloses, even more than Modena's candid confession would suggest, that his book was a fundamental repudiation of the image of Judaism fostered by Buxtorf.

THE *RITI*—STRUCTURE AND CONTENT

The *Riti* is divided into five parts, "according to the number of the books of the Law of Moses."[43] Each part consists of an unequal number of chapters, the sum total of which is fifty-four. Each chapter, in turn, is subdivided into numbered paragraphs.[44] Modena's principle of organization is not wholly clear. Part i opens with a general statement on the classification of Jewish rites and customs, then proceeds chapter by chapter, apparently on the basis of association of ideas, to describe: Jewish houses; household utensils; sleeping and dreams; vestments, fringes and *tefillin;* modesty in the toilet; ritual washing in the morning; impurity incurred by touching unclean objects; benedictions; synagogues; daily prayers; priests, Levites, and priestly dues; agricultural laws; charity. Part ii contains a potpourri of information about Jewish education, civil law, and the preparation and eating of food, distributed in chapters as follows: languages of the Jews; academies and the Talmud; rabbinic authority; oaths and vows; trading and usury; judicial procedure; forbidden foods and ritual slaughtering; wine and its sacral uses; separation of dough *(hallah)*; customs associated with mealtime. The chapters of Part iii, describing in succession the Sabbath, New Moon, Passover, Shavuot, Rosh Hashanah, Yom Kippur, Sukkot, Fast days, Hanukkah and Purim, are the most obviously structured, for with one exception they follow the order in which these matters are taken in Caro's *Shulhan Arukh.*[45] Part iv is devoted almost entirely to laws relating to women, and, by association, to rites connected with childbirth and child rearing, arranged as follows: forbidden degrees of sanguinary relations and sexual taboos; marriage; weddings; release of a minor from prearranged marriage *(mi'un)* and punishment for rape; menstrual laws; jealousy and divorce; Levirate marriage and release therefrom *(halitsah)*; circumcision; redemption of the first-born son; education of children; respect for elders. Finally, Part v is another apparent medley, ending however, quite appropriately, with death rituals, mourning customs, and concepts of afterlife. Chapter by chapter, Part v covers: heresy in Judaism; augury, divination and magic; precepts incumbent upon women; slavery; confession and penance; sickness and death; death and burial; mourning; paradise, hell, purgatory, and resurrection.[46]

Despite its apparently loose construction, the *Riti* contains a vast amount of data on inner Jewish life. It treats many more subjects, for instance, than Buxtorf's *Synagoga Judaica,* even though the *Riti* is much smaller.[47] The reason for this is two-fold. As we have already noted, Buxtorf was prone to long digressions on single details, while Modena was extremely terse.[48] The Italian rabbi, well aware that Jewish ceremonial manuals were expected to be verbose in their detail, justified his brevity by explaining that he had decided to omit ceremonies no longer observed by Jews.[49] His conciseness was undoubtedly also motivated by the desire to avoid Buxtorf's method of giving disproportionate attention to many of the aspects of Judaism which Christians found either enigmatic or offensive.

Some of the information in the *Riti* which supplemented *Synagoga Judaica* was clearly included to satisfy the craving of Modena's Christian friends for more detailed knowledge about inner Jewish life. For instance, the itemized description of the interior of the synagogue and of its functionaries must have proved extremely useful to Christians who frequented Venetian synagogues to hear rabbis like Leone da Modena preach.[50] The clarification of the place of confession in Jewish devotion must have produced some greater awareness among Christians of the Jewish posture on this important part of their own religion.[51] But much of the "new" material in the *Riti* was plainly meant to persuade the Christian audience of the essential rationality and morality of Judaism and the Jewish people. Thus, in the short chapter devoted to slavery, Modena tersely stated that Jews in Europe no longer owned slaves.[52] In the chapter on augury, divination and magic, he vigorously asserted that Jews were forbidden to practice these or any other black art.[53] In a discussion of respect due to parents, teachers, pious men and aged persons, he tried to portray the Jews as lovers of mankind.[54] Finally, like Luzzatto and Menasseh ben Israel, he felt obliged to include in his work a forthright defense of Jewish business ethics.[55]

Besides these obvious partisan sections, the very literary character of the book betrays Modena's apologetic overtones. From occasional asides, emphases—and, above all, his selectivity—it is possible to discern the principal arguments in favor of the Jews which he built into the book. Modena's methodology and message are particularly evident in the series of tendentious changes he made when he revised the *Riti* in 1638, but they are perceivable throughout the unrevised portions as well. Three apologetic themes may be isolated: contemporary Judaism is not superstitious; Jewish (rabbinic) law is an authentic expression of the Divine will; and Jews do not hate or mistreat Christians but rather possess virtues which make them deserving of greater social toleration and acceptance. Nowhere in the book, incidentally, are these themes formulated synthetically or abstractly. They are subtly imbedded within the descriptive superstructure and in the literary nuances and techniques employed by the author. They emerge into full light only when the book is read against the background of antecedent Christian books on Jewish rites and beliefs, particularly the one singled out by Modena himself, Buxtorf's *Synagoga Judaica*.

JUDAISM—NOT SUPERSTITIOUS

Judaism and superstition were almost synonymous in *Synagoga Judaica*. Buxtorf gave special attention to scores of Jewish ceremonies and beliefs having apparent superstitious or magical content. A comparison of a selection of Buxtorf's "superstitious" customs with Modena's treatment of the same ceremonies will serve to illustrate the Italian rabbi's direct polemical rebuttal of the Protestant scholar's derisive portrayal of Judaism.

Among the numerous "superstitious" rites singled out by Buxtorf were: (1) the well-known *adam-hava-huts-lilit* prophylactic amulet placed around the bed of a woman in labor;[56] (2) the "night watch" on the eve before a circumcision;[57] (3) the order of paring the fingernails, "with particular superstition," on the eve of the Sabbath;[58] (4) the belief that the souls of the damned rest on the Sabbath and that prolonging the Sabbath benefits the souls of the damned;[59] (5) the spreading of *havdalah* wine on the eyes, face, and beds of children, "considered good for all kinds of witchcraft";[60] (6) the smelling of the *havdalah* spices to revive the body, weakened by the sudden departure of the "additional soul" at the close of the Sabbath;[61] (7) the procedure of putting on the right shoe, then the left, then tying the left and finally the right;[62] (8) the positioning of the bed North-South in order to produce male children;[63] (9) the separation of meat and fish at meals to avoid leprosy;[64] (10) the custom of casting water out of the house following the death of one of its residents, in the belief that the angel of death cleanses his knife in it;[65] (11) the belief in the torment of the dead for three days after burial, called *hibbut hakever*;[66] (12) the ceremony of *tashlikh*;[67] (13) the ceremony of *kapparot*;[68] and (14) the search for crumbs of leaven on the eve of Passover.[69]

By way of contrast, Modena deliberately minimized, qualified, or even totally suppressed such practices. In a general declaration at the end of the chapter on augury and magic he stated that "the Rabbins have also forbidden a great many other superstitions which were practised by the idolatrous Amorites and are called by them *Darch[e]i [H]aemori.*[70] More significantly, throughout the *Riti* he addressed himself specifically to Buxtorfian nuances. In describing the *adam-hava-huts-lilit* amulet, Modena added the qualifying comment that *"some* use [practice] to put little papers in the four corners of the woman's chamber" but "nobody is obliged to observe this, it being grounded upon no precept, but is rather a vanity."[71] The implication is clear: Judaism requires adherence to precepts, but not to superstitious inanities.

Modena portrayed the "night watch" as merely a social occasion.[72] In the account of pre-Sabbath preparations he carefully omitted mention of the ritualized order of paring the finger nails.[73] A passage on the prolonging of the Sabbath for the repose of the souls of the damned, which he had included in the original version, was deliberately excised by him in the 1638 edition.[74]

After describing the *havdalah* ceremonies, Modena added: "And all these things are with them of very mysterious signification. But in short it all signifies that the Sabbath is at an end and that it is now separated from the working days; and with this all is concluded."[75] He thus lightly dismissed ceremonies which Buxtorf had found magical and to which he had devoted some eight scoffing pages.[76]

Where Buxtorf had characterized the ceremonial donning of the shoes as a universal Jewish custom, Modena qualified it: *"some* of them observe in their dressing in the morning to put on the right stocking and right shoe first . . . which they account to be the most fortunate."[77] Further, he deleted the entire passage in the 1638 edition.[78] It is true, Modena admitted in another place, that the rabbis advise positioning the bed North-South instead of East-West "out of respect to Jerusalem and the Temple . . . ; but," he went on, "there are but few that regard it."[79] He said nothing, however, about the belief mentioned by Buxtorf that this will magically produce male offspring. When describing the prohibition against eating fish and meat together, Modena made no reference to leprosy, conceding only that the rabbis warn that this is unhealthy. Furthermore, he concluded, the separation of fish and meat "is not observed nowadays."[80] In his chapter on illnesses and death, Modena minimized yet another alleged superstitious custom featured in *Synagoga Judaica.* "In some places," he wrote, "it is customary . . . to throw into the street all the water which they have in their houses." Why? Not because the angel of death might have polluted the water with his knife, but simply because "they believe [it] was an ancient custom used to give notice that there was somebody dead in that quarter."[81] When discussing other beliefs Jews associated with death he carefully circumscribed the embarrassing Kabbalistic doctrine of *hibbut hakever* claiming that only "the simpler sort of people" subscribe to it.[82] Not satisfied even with this formulation, he deleted the whole section in the 1638 edition.[83]

The ceremony of *tashlikh,* which Buxtorf had depicted in all its enigmatic detail, was prudently omitted from the chapter in the *Riti* on Rosh Hashanah, even in the original printed version of 1637.[84] Modena's treatment of the related rite of *kapparot* is typical of his whole method of dealing with superstitious customs in Judaism.

They used formerly on the vigil of this [Yom Kippur] fast a ceremony with a cock, turning it about their head and giving it up in exchange for themselves. This they call Capara. But this custom is laid aside both in the Levant and in Italy as being superstitious and not built upon any foundation.[85]

Finally, Modena took cognizance of Buxtorf's lengthy account of the troublesome ritual search for leaven before Passover, a ceremony which had long evoked Christian suspicions of Jewish sorcery to the point where some rabbis had counseled its abandonment altogether.[86] In the section on pre-Passover preparations, Modena had originally not bothered to apologize for this custom. But, rethinking the passage in 1638, and perhaps mindful of how the *Riti* had backfired on Gaffarel, he judiciously edited out one short phrase depicting how the Jews "lay up and down in certain places of the house little pieces of bread," etc. He thus thoroughly denuded the search for leaven of that procedure, so enigmatic to Christians, which the rabbis had instituted to prevent the pronouncement of an unwarranted benediction *(berakhah levatalah).*[87]

Many other parallels could be adduced to corroborate what Modena wrote in that letter to Noghera; that he had composed the *Riti* to offset the superstitious image of Judaism mirrored in *Synagoga Judaica.* It is interesting, though, that both in that letter and in the *Riti* itself Modena did not deny the superstitious nature of many Jewish ceremonies. He merely argued that they were either unessential or no longer practiced. Apparently he considered this approach more realistic with a Christian audience than, for instance, explaining such rituals rationally or, as in the case of the search for leaven, in purely halakhic terms.[88]

JEWISH LAW—AUTHENTIC

Indeed, the halakhic argument would have been particularly self-defeating since most Christians deprecated rabbinic law altogether. In Christian company Modena had in fact been taunted with the slur: *"lex Judeorum lex puerorum"* (the law of the Jews is the law of children) and it is not without significance that he chose to feature this maxim at the end of the "Proemio" to the *Riti* as a kind of paradigm of erroneous Christian notions about Judaism.[89]

This stereotype of perverse Jewish law permeated Buxtorf's *Synagoga Judaica* as well, though his critique differed in emphasis from the medieval assault on the Talmud. In earlier polemics the Talmud had been either condemned as an anti-Christian document (in France), or exposed as a veiled testimony to the truth of Christianity (in Spain).[90] Disparagement of the traditional sanctions, exegetical methods, and ceremonial content of the oral law had played only a minor role in Catholic indictments, perhaps, as Baron hints, since the Catholic Church had gone far afield of early Christianity with its own massive system of ceremonial law.[91] Protestant Buxtorf, however, not bound by Catholic tradition, found it pertinent to discredit the entire rabbinic system—the authority of the oral law, rabbinic exegesis, and specific Talmudic legislation—perhaps because he saw in it the analog of Catholic "distortion" of pristine Christianity.

As pointed out earlier, Buxtorf's confutation of rabbinic Judaism had two purposes, only one of which was specifically directed at the Jews. The other, and perhaps more important one, was to debunk the notion, cherished by many Protestants, that contemporary Jews adhered to pristine Biblical faith. In this vein, in the first chapter of *Synagoga Judaica* Buxtorf had exposed Judaism as a man-made perversion of Biblical truth. Starting from the traditional view, expounded in Catholic polemics, about "blindness" inflicted upon the Jews by God on account of their obstinate refusal to accept the new Christian dispensation,[92] Buxtorf had gone on to show how that "blindness" had been compounded and protracted by the pack of "lies" perpetrated by the rabbis. He had ridiculed the Jewish claim that the oral law had Divine inspiration and derided the so-called "chain of transmission" linking the rabbis of the Talmud with Sinai.[93] Finally, he had condemned the rabbis for having invented the self-serving dogma that the Talmud was even more important than Scripture and, as it were, infallible.[94]

In addition, when describing in the rest of the book specific beliefs and practices, Buxtorf had made no real distinctions between *halakhah, aggadah,* custom, and Kabbalistic interpretation. All, to him, were part of the same godless mass of Jewish doctrine and observance. In a typical passage he grouped together: the Biblical commandment to wear fringes *(tzitzit)*; the fact that some Jews wore them under their garments all day while others wore them only while praying; an *aggadah* about fringes from the Babylonian Talmud *(Shabbat* 118b); a "good Kabbalistic computation" of the symbolic significance of the five knots and eight strands; a famous aggadic tale (see *Menahot* 44a) about a student who was saved from promiscuity by his *tzitzit;* some other Talmudic *aggadot;* the *halakhah* exempting women from the obligation to wear *tzitzit;* and finally the folk belief that "whoever wears these (fringes) all day and continuously is safe from the devil and all evil spirits."[95]

As if with Buxtorf's damaging representation of Jewish law in mind, Leone da Modena was careful, in the very first chapter of the *Riti,* to draw a line of demarcation between the written and oral laws, incumbent upon all Jews everywhere, and those "minhaghim" *[sic]* or customs, not universally obligatory. Customs had originated, he explained, "upon account of the Jews being scattered into several countries and taking the names and customs of the inhabitants." Consequently, customary law was not essential to Judaism and did not share equal authority with the Bible and Talmud.[96] In this way he attempted to refute the allegation, leveled by Buxtorf and others, that everything Jews believed in and observed was part of the same immutable perverted rabbinic tradition.

Secondly, he drew an important distinction between the Kabbalah and the Talmud:

Some few of them [the Jews] study the Cabala, that is the secret divinity of the Scripture; some few others study philosophy and other sciences, both natural and moral. . . . But the most common study among them is that of the Gemara or Talmud, where it is permitted them; and where they have it not, they read the writings of the Rabbins' paraphrases or an abridgment of the Talmud.[97]

With this brief statement, the only time in the *Riti* the word "Kabbalah" is mentioned, Modena dismissed all those Kabbalistic interpretations and practices which Buxtorf had lumped into the same category with the Talmud in an attempt to show the absurdity and deception of Jewish law.[98]

Moreover, the very form of the *Riti* seems to have served as a vindication of the oral law. Modena's division of the book into "five parts, according to the number of the books of the Law of Moses,"[99] may well have been a symbolic gesture designed to remind the Christian reader that while a large number of the rites described in the book were rabbinic in origin, all of them derived ultimately from Divinely revealed Scripture—a claim which Buxtorf, of course, had vigorously denied. The subdivision into fifty-four chapters, corresponding to the number of pericopes *(parshiyyot)* in the Pentateuch, may have had a similar purpose.[100] More concretely, the whole work is singularly free of Talmudic quotations. In fact, whenever Modena referred to the Talmud he almost invariably employed some circumlocution like "the rabbis say," etc. On the other hand he used Biblical citations copiously; in fact he quoted virtually no other Jewish work but the Bible. This is hardly fortuitous. The intended message seems clear: rabbinic Judaism, the Judaism practiced in his day, was true religion because it was grounded in Scripture.

But more even than simply stressing the Divine basis of Talmudic law, Leone da Modena attempted to prove its superiority by demonstrating that many rabbinic enactments had actually improved Jewish life. Thus, for instance, where Buxtorf had scoffed at some of the rituals associated with the toilet,[101] the Venetian rabbi declared:

The Rabbins deliver many things to be observed in evacuation or easing the body, the place and manner how they are to order themselves on this occasion, all which tend to health, civility, and modesty.[102]

Where the Protestant scholar had ridiculed the extreme care which Jews took in washing their hands and in other acts before and during meals,[103] Modena commented:

Before they sit down to table, they [the Jews] are obliged to wash their hands with a great deal of circumspection concerning which the Rabbins have delivered a great many circumstances. . . . The Rabbins have laid down a great many rules relating to civility and modesty to be observed in eating.[104]

In similar fashion, Modena countered Buxtorf's disparagement of Jewish divorce. Echoing the New Testament (Matthew 5:31–32; 19:2–9), Buxtorf had explained the Biblical divorce dispensation as a concession to Jewish "hardheartedness" ("von wegen der Haertigkeit jhres Herzens"). That is why Moses had permitted the Jews to dismiss their wives for any cause, no matter how trifling (see Deuteronomy 24:1–4). Notwithstanding the Talmudic limitation of the acceptable grounds for divorce, Buxtorf went on, even today "a person can easily find grounds for divorcing his wife." [105] Leone da Modena, by way of contrast, went out of his way to picture the divorce laws as a "progressive" institution. First of all, the Biblical injunction was a vast improvement over the ancient ordeal (sotah) by which a wife was tested for infidelity. "Nowadays . . . ," he emphasized, "the Rabbins will constrain the man to divorce his wife for good and all, whether he will or not." [106] It is true, he went on to concede, that according to "the strict letter of the Law" a man may divorce his wife "upon any, though never so little disgust."

However a man ought not to do it . . . unless upon the account of jealousy or for some notorious wickedness. And to prevent men's putting away their wives for nothing but some sudden displeasure . . . the Rabbins have made it very difficult by annexing a great many formalities to be observed, both in writing and delivering a bill of divorce, on purpose, that before they can have it done, they may come to themselves and be reconciled. [107]

Finally, in his account of Simhat Torah, a festival particularly susceptible to Christian ridicule, Modena subtly turned the tables on Buxtorf. The Protestant scholar had stressed the non-Biblical origins of Simhat Torah by adeptly isolating it in a separate chapter (chapter xxii) from his description of the Biblically ordained eight-day Sukkot celebration (chapter xvi). "One can find nothing about this festival [i.e., Simhat Torah] in the Law; their rabbis ordained it . . . " [108] Here was one more proof that the rabbis had deviated from the true Torah. As if directly responding to this explicit indictment of the oral law, Modena wrote in the *Riti* in the chapter on Sukkot:

This feast lasts nine days, seven of which are commanded *and one more is kept by ancient custom* as there is also in the Passover . . . ; and one day commanded Numb. xxix for the convocation [i.e., Shemini Atseret]. . . . The two first and the two last days are kept as a solemn feast and those five intermediate days are not so strict. [109]

By thus subsuming the ninth day of Sukkot under the rubric of that "ancient custom," namely the extra day added because of uncertainty in the calendar, Leone da Modena neatly avoided having to mention that the joyous celebration of the annual completion of the reading of the law on Simhat Torah was very late in origin, in fact post-Talmudic. [110]

Leone da Modena's defense of the oral law, which represented, incidentally, the counterpart of those seventeenth-century Jewish apologies for rabbinic tradition written in response to Jewish and Marrano skeptics,[111] was motivated, as seems fairly clear, by Buxtorf's Protestant analysis and critique of Jewish law. However, Modena's argument, with its insistence upon what amounted to little more than the standard orthodox posture on the authority and significance of the Talmud, would hardly have evoked much sympathy in Protestant readers. His presentation affirmed rather than denied the gap between Biblical and post-Biblical legislation and made no attempt to apologize for rabbinic exegesis. Indeed had Buxtorf lived long enough and wanted to revise *Synagoga Judaica* he could very easily have quoted the *Riti*, as he had so many other Jewish compendia, to reinforce his contention that contemporary Judaism was a gross deviation from the Bible.

Whom then among his Christian readers did Leone da Modena hope to persuade? How did he intend to promote Christian toleration of the Jews by such a traditional portrayal of the Talmud? A possible answer lies in an understanding of his social context. Modena's immediate milieu was an Italian Catholic society, whose apostolic tradition and ecclesiastical ritual, as he and other Jews well knew, were analogous to rabbinic institutions. Simone Luzzatto, for instance, exploited this similarity in the *Discorso* to imply that Jews could be relied upon to be loyal to Catholic regimes in the counter-reformational conflict.[112] In much the same way, by defending Jewish law in terms familiar to Catholics from their own tradition, Modena may have hoped to gain a sympathetic hearing from Catholic readers, his immediate audience. At the same time, the Italian rabbi knew that Buxtorf's critique of rabbinic institutions and laws could just as easily have been applied, *mutatis mutandis,* against the Papacy and the ritual of the Catholic Church. In a sense, Jews and Catholics in the counter reformation had a common enemy in men like Johann Buxtorf. Exploiting this unspoken bond, as Luzzatto did in the *Discorso,* Leone da Modena hoped to demonstrate Judaism's affinity with Catholicism and to reap social dividends for Jews in Italy.

It is understandable why Modena and Luzzatto might have expected fruitful results from this line of argument. The prevailing sentiments of contemporary Catholic Churchmen, locked in a struggle to uphold their own apostolic structure against the onslaught of Protestant reformers, were of course conservative and tradition-minded. In addition, it was not yet the time when Catholic skeptics would join Protestants in deprecating Jewish tradition and observance as part of their own assault upon the fabric of the medieval Church.

JEWS—NOT HOSTILE TO CHRISTIANS AND CHRISTIANITY

Christian disdain for the allegedly superstitious in Judaism and for the Talmud were only two of the components making up the predominantly negative image of the Jew and Judaism. A third, and perhaps even more deleterious stigma, was the age-old suspicion of the Jew as a misanthrope. Leone da Modena was fully aware of the lingering medieval stereotype of the Jews as the inveterate enemies of Christianity—anxiously awaiting their Messiah-Antichrist, secretly undermining Christendom by poisoning wells, desecrating Hosts, and murdering Christian children.[113] He knew too that Jews fanned the flames of this suspicion by many of their attitudes towards Christians, expressed in writing and in social intercourse.[114] Moreover, he was cognizant of the fact that in the preceding century Christians has become increasingly familiar with real or apparent anti-Christian passages in Jewish literature, whether through the malicious activities of apostates or through actual first-hand reading of the sources. By his own time, the charge of misanthropy, reinforced by the exposés of the Margarithas and the Buxtorfs, had also begun to take on threatening social implications, especially in countries like Italy and Holland where a certain class of Jews stood on the threshhold of more enduring social and intellectual contacts with Christian society.

Buxtorf's commentary on Jewish liturgy provided fuel for the old libel. Like Antonius Margaritha before him, Buxtorf warned Christian readers that when Jews prayed for the downfall of Edom they meant Christendom.[115] Like Margaritha again, Buxtorf cited the *alenu* prayer in its incriminating original version ("they bow down to vanity and to nothingness and pray to a God who cannot save them") as an anti-Christian polemic. This phrase, Buxtorf added, had been censored from Jewish prayerbooks printed in Italy "because it is a blasphemy against Christ."[116] In addition, Buxtorf extracted from the liturgy other "proofs" that the Jews hated and vilified Christianity. The passage in the morning service right after the Song of Moses emphasizing God's unity had been included, he claimed, to impugn Christian belief in the Trinity.[117] The chant "cursed be all idolators *(arurim kol ovedei elilim)*" recited on Purim, he noted in the margin, referred to Christians.[118] In a long discourse on the *birkat haminim* he traced the development of the text, characterizing it as a curse against apostates as well as all Christians.[119] Citing R. Bahyye ben Asher as his authority, he even portrayed the *hakkafot* on Sukkot as a symbolic yearning for the downfall of Christianity.[120]

Understandably, then, Leone da Modena was very circumspect when dealing with Jewish liturgy. In order to counter the charge that Jews cursed Christ and Christians, he, like Menasseh ben Israel after him, noted that Jews prayed for the welfare of the reigning prince every Sabbath and holiday.[121] When he came to the controversial *alenu*, and other prayers indicted by Buxtorf, he cautiously avoided any suggestion that they might ever have been directed against Christianity.[122]

However, more than their prayers, it was Jewish actions that Christian polemicists like Buxtorf invoked as evidence of Jewish hostility to Christendom. Buxtorf pointed out that by refusing to use kitchen utensils acquired from Christians until they "purified" them, Jews demonstrated that they considered Christians impure and unholy.[123] Jews would refrain from inviting an "uncircumcised Christian" to a wedding feast because they believed he would bring evil spirits.[124] On the testimony of "every convert from Jewish unbelief" Buxtorf alleged that when selling the forbidden hindquarters of an animal to Christians, Jews purposely sullied the meat and put a curse upon it.[125] They also taught their children to hate Christians and to have nothing to do with their children; and instructed their own children to use Hebrew words in their speech with the result that "they cannot be understood by everyone."[126]

In the *Riti*, Leone da Modena attempted to offset accusations of Jewish misanthropic behavior. For instance, in the chapter "On their Drinking" he drew an invidious distinction between German and Levantine Jews on the one hand, and Italian Jews on the other, and reported that Italian Jews, at least, did not heed the prohibition against using wine touched by Christians since they did not consider Christians idolators.[127] In another passage, perhaps responding directly to Buxtorf's implication that Jews intentionally hid things from Christians with their hybrid speech, Modena explained:

the common people use in their ordinary discourse the language of the nation they dwell in, mixing *now and then a few* broken Hebrew words among it.[128]

And there is more than a hint of apologetics in his statement (in a chapter *added* in 1638) that Jews taught their children to honor every aged person "though he is no Jew."[129] Then, too, Modena may have had a tendentious reason for deleting in the second edition the chapter depicting the procedure of accepting proselytes after establishing their sincerity. One of the allegations leveled against Jews was that they seduced Christians to their religion. Menasseh ben Israel some years later would fight this charge vigorously.[130] Finally, with the thirteen Maimonidean articles excised from the *Riti* in the 1638 edition, the book was left without any reference to Jewish messianic hopes. Buxtorf, on the other hand, had devoted his entire last chapter to a detailed exposition of messianic doctrines, which Christians often cited as evidence of Jewish disloyalty.[131]

On the more controversial issue of usury and business ethics, Modena, like Luzzatto and Menasseh ben Israel, took up the cudgels of defense.[132] His explanation of the damaging Biblical verse ("Unto a foreigner thou mayest lend upon interest; but unto thy brother thou shalt not lend upon interest"—Deuteronomy 23:21) was, to be sure, slightly irregular. In place of the usual Jewish exegesis, which took the first part of the verse as a tacit sanction for interest-bearing loans to Christians, he offered the minority opinion that the word "foreigner" in the verse referred exclusively to the "Seven Nations" of ancient Canaan. Thus Christians were to be included in the prohibition against usurious lending to one's "brother." To explain why Jews, nevertheless, took interest from Christian debtors, Modena resorted to an historical explanation: "because they [the Jews] are not suffered to use the same means of getting a living as others which are brethren by nature [!], they pretend they may do it lawfully."[133] Modena's contemporary, Luzzatto, at least conceded in the *Discorso,* along with the dominant Jewish interpretation, that Deuteronomy permits Jews to take interest from Christians; he hastened to add, however, that the early rabbis had advised against it on prudential grounds. To account for the current state of affairs Luzzatto explained, much like Modena, that once the Jews had come to be excluded from all other walks of life, the rabbis had relaxed their admonition and reverted to the Deuteronomic dispensation.[134]

In the same chapter of the *Riti* in which he justified usury, Modena characterized *all* economic offenses committed by Jews as aberrations resulting from "the narrowness of the circumstances *[stretezza]* which their long captivity has reduced them to, and to their being almost everywhere prohibited to purchase lands or to use several sorts of merchandizes and other creditable and gainful employments."[135] Modena's and Luzzatto's use of history to apologize for the Jews constituted an "historical" explanation of distasteful Jewish economic behavior which in the next century would be extended by Christian proponents of Jewish emancipation like Toland, Grégoire, and Dohm to account for all kinds of Jewish deficiencies, moral and religious as well as commercial.[136]

The identity of approach by Luzzatto and Modena to the charge of Jewish mistreatment of Christians went beyond this interesting congruence. In evidence of basic Jewish benevolence, both Venetian rabbis cited Biblical commandments admonishing Jews to treat all men justly.[137] Both invoked the statement frequently quoted by medieval rabbis and going back to classical Jewish sources that it is a greater offense to God *(hillul hashem)* to defraud a non-Jew than a co-religionist.[138] And finally, both men, conceding that there were certainly some Jewish criminals, pleaded with their Christian readers not to condemn the whole nation for the misdeeds of the few.[139] This proclivity for blaming all Jews for the crimes of individuals was a hazard of Venetian Jewish existence which the two rabbis fully appreciated. According to the well-known description in Modena's journal, it had manifested itself in a quite frightening manner in 1636 when the whole ghetto stood in terror for months in the face of Christian threats to punish the entire community for the fraudulent activities of a couple of Jewish embezzlers. Apparently the scandal almost led to a general expulsion, and repercussions were still being felt as late as March of the following year. Shulvass has even argued that it was this crisis that brought Luzzatto to write the *Discorso*.[140] Modena, of course, had written the *Riti* well before 1636, and his apology for Jewish backsliding was directed more at the general Christian attitude than at some specific instance of its application. But apparently with an eye on the events of 1636, he appended a paragraph to the chapter on commerce in the 1638 edition and stressed that extortion had been permitted to the Jews only where the "Seven Nations" were involved, but "not of those people among which the Jews are now planted and suffered to dwell and are used kindly by the princes of the countries especially amongst the Christians, because this would not only be against the written, but also against the Law of Nature."[141]

To complete the amiable image of his co-religionists and acquit them of suspicion of misanthropy, Modena portrayed the Jews as non-dis-criminatory philanthropists. "It cannot be denied," he announced at the beginning of the chapter on charity, "but that the Jews are a people very charitable and compassionate towards all people in want."[142] In the 1638 edition, mindful perhaps of Jewish philanthropic efforts in Venice during the terrible plague of 1630, he added a paragraph to that chapter.

They also account it a good work to give alms and relieve all persons whatsoever in affliction, though they are not Jews; especially those who live in the same city or place with them, as an act of charity due to all mankind indifferently and particularly recommended to them by the Rabbins.[143]

Here, in the form of an abstract principle, Modena may well have been reminding Christians of the concrete contribution which the Jews of the ghetto had made to general welfare during the devastating pestilence. It will be recalled that Luzzatto exploited this same instance of Jewish charitability in the *Discorso* to prove how useful the Jews were to the Republic.[144]

By denying the hostility of Jews to Christians on the one hand, and insisting upon the benevolence of the Jews on the other, apologists like Modena, Luzzatto, and Menasseh ben Israel clearly hoped to improve or advance Jewish status. Menasseh ben Israel and Luzzatto had mainly political goals, at least as immediate objectives. Menasseh ben Israel hoped to gain readmission of the Jews to England and perhaps also ultimately to see his personal messianic expectations fulfilled. Luzzatto, it seems, was moved to defend the residential status of Venetian Jewry as a result of the threat to their security in 1636. But Leone da Modena's motives were not, so far as we know, political. His main object seems to have been to make Christians more tolerant of Jews and their religion in much the same manner, incidentally, as he had tried some years earlier to make Jews more aware of gentile culture by translating the ethical treatise *Fior di virtù* into Hebrew.[145] His vindication of Jewish commercial ethics, in reality only one chapter out of a total of fifty-four, was merely one aspect of the more general argument that Jews did not hate Christians. The apology for usury carried no more weight than the description of the prayer for the government or the portrayal of the Jews as universal philanthropists. The theme of Jewish benevolence, in turn, had the same purpose as his insistence upon the non-superstitious nature of Judaism and upon the authenticity of rabbinic law:[146] to combat anti-

Jewish stereotypes which fostered Christian suspicions of Jews and made Jews like Leone da Modena himself uncomfortable in Christian company.

The essentially social goal of the *Riti* is evident also in some of the other Jewish virtues which the author chose to emphasize. One of these was the unity of the Jewish people in spite of its dispersion. In the first chapter of the *Riti* he argued that with the exception of certain locally-acquired customs, there were no real differences between the various nations of the Jews scattered throughout the world.[147] In discussing Jewish prayers, he underscored that only in their liturgy did the major cultural Jewish groupings (Levantines, Germans, and Italians) really differ from one another.[148] What is more, Judaism in his time brooked no sectarian dissension. Modena emphatically reported that there were no longer any heretics in Judaism, except for residual elements of the Karaites. But even they were tucked away in the Levant, in Turkey, and in Russia. In other words, they had nothing to do with the European Jewish communities. Religiously, he added, Karaites were held to be *mamzerim* (bastards) and consequently could not qualify as Jews; despite Karaite claims to the contrary, the rabbis would refuse to recognize them as such, even if they were to accept orthodox rabbinism.[149] Modena seems to have invoked the issue of Karaite status in hopes of striking a responsive chord in his Catholic readers. In arguing that the Jews did not tolerate sects he may well have been preaching that Judaism was closer in spirit to Catholicism than to fragmented Protestantism, and, hence, that Jews ought to be treated by Catholics as friends rather than as enemies.[150] This nuance, if indeed the interpretation presented here is correct, dovetails with the appeal for Catholic sympathy suggested above in the discussion of Modena's defense of Jewish law.

An additional Jewish virtue which the Italian rabbi highlighted was that of self-sufficiency. In the chapter on charitable institutions he proudly asserted that the Jews took care of their own poor. Though the number of wealthy Jews was actually small, he emphasized, they happily provided for the impoverished majority. In describing the elaborate system of collections and disbursements he especially stressed its humane procedures, thus perhaps countering a notion expressed by Buxtorf that Jews were rather insensitive towards their less fortunate brethren.[151] Interestingly, Modena did not hesitate to reveal that Jews contributed alms to their brethren in the Holy Land.[152] The charge that diaspora Jews always had their eyes on Palestine was still a thing of the future.

Finally, anticipating later Jewish apologetics of the period of political emancipation, Leone da Modena claimed adaptability as one of the Jews' most meritorious qualities. Whether in revealing that, despite the Biblical prohibition against graven images, "in Italy many [Jews] take the liberty of having pictures *[ritratti]* and images *[pitture]* in their houses, especially if they be not with relief or embossed work, nor the bodies at large";[153] or in printing his own bareheaded (!) portrait on the title page of the 1638 edition, Modena argued quite forcefully that the Jews were capable of changing and adapting to Italian Christian culture.[154] As is well attested, Jews in Italy had come to accept the concession of uncovering the head in public with a notable lack of self-consciousness. In the *Riti,* Leone da Modena explained to Christians why:

The men ... have no very good opinion of going bareheaded. . . . Notwithstanding, living as they do among Christians where this custom is used in reverence to superiors, they use [practice] the same.[155]

In addition, he reported, although Jews did not generally like to dress like others, they nevertheless followed local styles when "their own make them seem very ridiculous."[156] Likewise, the dark mourning costume Jews wore was not an indigenous religious requirement, but rather patterned after that worn by the surrounding people.[157] Finally, as another demonstration of adaptability, Modena pointed to the fact that Jews inserted the dates of Christian holidays into their Jewish calendars to guide them in their dealings with Christians.[158]

CONCLUSION AND PROSPECT

It is not at all surprising to find the seeds of late eighteenth- and nineteenth-century Jewish emancipation rhetoric in Leone da Modena. Well versed in non-Jewish culture, on intimate terms with Christian intellectuals and Churchmen, he possessed many of the traits which later characterized the "enlightened" Jews of the classical era of political emancipation.[159] Living in repressive counter-reformation Venice, when civil emancipation for Jews (as well as emancipation in general for that matter) was not even a remote dream, he hoped only for greater Christian toleration of Jews on the social plane—a kind of *social emancipation.* He correctly recognized, long before his later counterparts, that age-old Christian calumnies against Jews and Judaism were impediments to such social emancipation. With this in mind he composed the *Riti* to combat damaging stereotypes. He hoped to alter the prevailing unfavorable image of the Jew and Judaism, especially as set forth in *Synagoga Judaica,* and thereby advance the social integration of Jews into Christian society.[160]

In the light of this it is appropriate to pose the question: to what extent did the book attain its author's purpose of changing Christian attitudes towards the Jews? This is a significant historical question because the *Riti* achieved enormous popularity after its publication and was read all over Europe during the seventeenth and eighteenth centuries, in the original Italian[161] and in five different European languages into which it was translated: English,[162] French,[163] Dutch,[164] Latin,[165] and German.[166] Indeed, the *Riti* achieved such popularity that the Amsterdam publisher J. F. Bernard chose the French version of Modena's book as the text on Judaism for his nine-volume *Cérémonies et coûtumes religieuses de tous les peuples du monde.* This series, which began to appear in 1723, featured beautiful detailed engravings of scenes of religious life by the famous artist Bernard Picart. Picart's *Cérémonies* appeared subsequently in many different editions and languages (Dutch, English, German, Italian[!]) and helped disseminate far and wide Modena's exposition of inner Jewish life.[167]

Amongst the many who read and reacted to the *Riti* during the seventeenth and eighteenth centuries were well-known Christian intellectuals. We have seen, for example, how apparently little it changed Jacques Gaffarel's opinion of Judaism. On the other hand the Bible critic, Richard Simon, who translated the *Riti* into French, seems to have been favorably impressed by the author's approach.[168] Others who found the *Riti* significant enough to quote included John Selden, the English jurist and Hebraist (d. 1654),[169] Jacques Basnage, the historian (d. 1772),[170] Dom Augustin Calmet, the French Bible exegete (d. 1757),[171] and the famous champion of Jewish emancipation, the Abbé Henri Grégoire (d. 1831).[172]

Did Modena's pro-Jewish exposition positively affect these thinkers' view of Judaism? Certainly the number and variety of available anti-Jewish exposés of the genre popularized by Margaritha and Buxtorf were impressive.[173] In the century and a half immediately preceding the political emancipation struggle, new works by hostile Christian and apostate writers like Eisenmenger, Kirchner, and Jungendres reinforced the age-old stereotypes and prejudices which ultimately would stand in the way of the smooth civil emancipation of the Jews. The *Riti* was, as far as I know, the only comprehensive exposition of Jewish practice by a *Jew* accessible to European Christians before political emancipation. In its many guises it could not have helped but alter Christian stereotypes of Judaism, if only by explaining rituals in such a way as to dispel Christian ignorance. Did Christians also catch the apologetic overtones elucidated here? And if so, did they modify their prejudices accordingly? Or, was Modena's polemic perhaps so subtle that it passed most readers by?[174] With these questions in mind further investigation of the attitudes of Selden, Basnage, Calmet, Grégoire, and others who read the book may shed some light on the problem.

The overtones of Modena's polemic eluded at least one Christian reader—Johann Buxtorf's own son—with a rather ironic consequence. In 1661, thirty-two years after his father's death, Johann Buxtorf the Younger republished his own Latin version of *Synagoga Judaica* (originally translated by the son in 1641).[175] In this "third" edition of the work the son broke down his father's chapters into smaller units for easier reference and added new material gleaned from other books, thus increasing the size of *Synagoga Judaica* by at least fifty percent. One of the books upon which he drew was Modena's *Riti*. Sometimes he quoted the Italian rabbi by name;[176] at other times he incorporated information from the *Riti* without acknowledging the source.[177] Thus the younger Buxtorf unwittingly codified into his father's opus some of the very things which Leone da Modena had subtly written against it!

NOTES

1. Published in Venice. I have used the Hebrew translation by Dante Lattes *Maamar Al Yehudei Venetsia* (Jerusalem 1950), hereafter cited *Maamar*.
2. Both published in London. Both were reprinted in Wolf, Lucien, *Menasseh ben Israel's Mission to Oliver Cromwell* (London 1901), which is the edition I have used throughout this chapter.
3. Although Modena wrote the book around 1616 it was not published until 1637. In that year Jacques Gaffarel, a Christian acquaintance of Modena's, printed it in Paris under the title *Historia de gli riti hebraici: Dove si hà breve e total relatione di tutta la vita, costumi, è riti & osservance de gl'Hebrei di questi tempi di Leon Modena Rabi Hebreo di Venetia* (Paris 1637). Modena, as we shall see, was not happy with this edition. Accordingly he published a revised edition in Venice in 1638 with the title *Historia*

de' riti hebraici: Vita e osservance de gl'Hebrei di questi tempi (Venice 1638). This "authoritative" 1638 edition was republished many times (see the list compiled by Nino Samaja, "Le vicende di un libro," *La rassegna mensile di Israel,* xxi [1955], pp. 79–80), and recently in *La rassegna mensile di Israel,* vii (1932–33), pp. 293–325, 383–93, 493–509, 558–77. On the origins and publishing vicissitudes of the *Riti* see below, pp. 289 ff.

4. Ettinger, Shmuel, "The Beginnings of the Change in the Attitude of European Society towards the Jews," *Scripta Hierosolymitana,* vii (1961), pp. 209 ff. It was Ettinger's reference to the letter (originally published by Roth) in which Modena stated that he had written the *Riti* to counter Buxtorf's *Synagoga Judaica* that led me to the comparative analysis underlying this chapter.

5. [Leone da Modena], *Shulhan Arukh,* trans. by Rubin, Salomon (Vienna 1867), introduction, pp. iv–v, viii, xiii, n. 1 and footnotes to text, *passim.* Kirchner's *Ceremoniale Judaicum* was first published in 1717, then republished in an expanded version by Jungendres in 1724 under the title *Juedisches Ceremoniel;* Jungendres is identified as the author of the supplementary notes in the 1726 edition of *Juedisches Ceremoniel;* cf. also Fuerst, Julius, *Bibliotheca Judaica* 3 Vols.; New edition (Leipzig 1863), ii, p. 190. True, in his short introduction Rubin listed *earlier* writers, including Buxtorf himself, among the authors he conjectured Modena was responding to. But these writers' names were lifted almost verbatim from Jungendres' own discussion of the antecedents of Kirchner's work in the preface to *Juedisches Ceremoniel.* That the Kirchner-Jungendres compendium was Rubin's only real point of comparison is clear from the notes to the text of *Shulhan Arukh;* see p. 13, nn. 10 and 11; p. 20, nn. 13 and 14; p. 21, n. 15; p. 58, n. 30; p. 61, n. 35; p. 67, n. 37; p. 75, n. 44; also, p viii (introduction).

6. Graetz, Heinrich, *Geschichte der Juden,* x (Leipzig 1868), pp. 149–50. Rabinowitz, the Hebrew translator of the *Geschichte,* tried to soften Graetz's harsh indictment of Modena. See *Divrei Yemei Yisrael,* trans. by Rabinowitz, S., viii (Warsaw [1900]), p. 181, n. 1; he also omitted (intentionally?) this sentence: "Unwillkuerlich gesellte sich der Verfasser zu den Veraechtern des Judenthums, das er doch selbst als Rabbiner geuebt und gelehrt hatte."

7. Libowitz, Nehemiah, *Rabbi Yehuda Aryeh Modena,* 2nd ed., rev. (New York 1901), pp. 59, 67–74.

8. Blau, Ludwig, *Leo Modenas Briefe und Schriftstuecke,* Jahresbericht der Landes-Rabbinerschule in Budapest, No. 28 (Budapest 1905), pp. 93–95 (German introduction). The letter (#193) appears on pp. 178–79 of the text.

9. Ottolenghi, Adolfo, "Origini e vicende dell'Historia de riti hebraici di Leon da Modena," *La rassegna mensile di Israel,* vii (1932–33), pp. 289–90; *idem,* "Leon da Modena e la vita ebraica del ghetto di Venezia nel secolo XVII," *ibid,* xxxvii (1971), pp. 754–57 (article reprinted from July, 1929 issue of *Rivista di Venezia*); Cassuto, Umberto, "Leon Modena e l'opera sua," *ibid.,* viii (1933–34), pp. 136–37.

10. Samaja, Nino, "Le vicende di un libro," *ibid.*, xxi (1955), pp. 73–84; additions and corrections to article, *ibid.*, pp. 298–99. Ettinger, too, called the *Riti* "clearly apologetic"; *op. cit.*, p. 209.

11. This chapter will not deal with the *Riti's* place in the literary history of Jewish codes, nor with its value as a source for the social history of Venetian Jewry. The book has, of course, been utilized by historians of the period like Roth, Shulvass, and Simonsohn.

12. Roth, Cecil, "Léon de Modène, ses *Riti Ebraici* et le Saint-Office à Venise," *Revue des études juives*, lxxxvii (1929), pp. 83–88; Ottolenghi: see above, n. 9 (first two sources cited); Samaja: see above, n. 10 (first source cited).

13. R. Yehuda Aryeh Mi-Modena [Leone da Modena], *Hayye Yehuda*, ed. by Kahana, A. (Kiev 1911), pp. 56–57. This passage was translated into English at least once to my knowledge, by Jacob R. Marcus in his *The Jew in the Medieval World* (Cleveland 1960, reprinted), pp. 406–08.

14. *Hayye Yehuda*, p. 56. Roth theorized that Modena's English patron was none other than Sir Henry Wotton, English Ambassador to Venice intermittently during the early years of the seventeenth century. Wotton had lived near the ghetto and had been friendly with several of its residents. In 1616, after an absence of five years, he was back at his Venice post; "Leone da Modena and England," *Transactions of the Jewish Historical Society of England*, xi (1928), pp. 206–15. Samaja, on the authority of Augustin Calmet, claims that Modena had published a Hebrew version of the *Riti* in Mantua in 1612; Samaja, *op. cit.*, p. 74; cf. p. 298. I very much doubt the accuracy of Calmet's statement. Besides the fact that this title does not appear in the standard bibliographies of Modena's works (e.g., Cassuto, *op. cit.*; Libowitz, *op. cit.*, pp. 102 ff.), Modena certainly would have mentioned a Hebrew "Riti" in *Hayye Yehuda* had it existed.

15. Roth, Cecil, "Leone da Modena and his English Correspondents," *Transactions of the Jewish Historical Society of England*, xvii (1953) pp. 39–43.

16. Modena to William Boswell, September 8, 1634; *ibid.*, p. 40 (Roth's translation); the Italian original letter is found in the Appendix to Roth's article; *ibid.*, pp. 42 f.

17. On Gaffarel see *Nouvelle biographie générale*, xix (Copenhagen 1966, reprinted), cols. 146–47. On his Kabbalistic interest see Blau, Joseph. *The Christian Interpretation of the Cabala in the Renaissance* (New York 1944), p. 106. On his relations with Leone da Modena see Roth, Cecil, "Leone da Modena and the Christian Hebraists of his Age," *Jewish Studies in Memory of Israel Abrahams* (New York 1927), p. 389.

18. *Hayye Yehuda*, pp. 56–57. Christian dates arrived at by reference to Mahler, Eduard, *Handbuch der juedischen Chronologie* (Hildesheim 1967, reprinted), pp. 580–81. A fragmentary journal notation of Modena's, appended by Kahana to the end of his edition of *Hayye Yehuda* (p.67), alludes to the Paris edition of the *Riti*.

19. Roth, "Léon de Modène, ses *Riti Ebraici* . . ." *op. cit.*, pp. 83–88. As is well known, Simone Luzzatto had intended to write an account of Jewish rites;

the fate of that essay has remained a mystery. Bacchi's suggestion, that he simply never completed it, is less than satisfying, especially in view of the fact that the title page of the first edition of the *Discorso* (1638) retains the information that the treatise on the status of Venetian Jewry is only an "appendix" to a tract on the beliefs and opinions of the Jews; see Bacchi's introduction to the Hebrew translation, *Maamar*, pp. 30–31. It is quite possible that Luzzatto did indeed finish his own "Riti," but, like Modena, encountered opposition from the censor. Or, perhaps warned off by his colleague's experience with the Holy Office, he may simply have decided at the last moment to withdraw it from publication. This may explain the enigmatic title page of the first edition, as well as the curious "Introduction to the Whole Work" preceding the "Introduction to This Essay [the *Discorso*]" at the beginning of Luzzatto's treatise.

This note was written before the publication of Yosef Hayim Yerushalmi's *From Spanish Court to Italian Ghetto: Isaac Cardoso, A Study in Seventeenth-Century Marranism and Jewish Apologetics* (New York 1971) wherein the author offers (p. 353 and n. 5 there) a similar hypothesis about the fate of the essay in question.

20. Baron, Salo W., *A Social and Religious History of the Jews*, 2nd ed. (New York and Philadelphia 1952 ff.), xiv, pp. 138–39. Modena's own reflections about the tight censorship in Venice are found in Ludwig Blau's *Leo Modenas Briefe*, pp. 178–79. Also see the series of cryptic journal notations regarding the censorial office, printed at the end of Kahana's edition of *Hayye Yehuda*, p. 67. Cf. also Yerushalmi, *op. cit.*, pp. 352 ff. On the censorship of Hebrew books in counter-reformation Italy see Popper, William, *The Censorship of Hebrew Books* (New York 1899), pp. 29–104.

21. *Riti* (Venice 1638), "Proemio." I have used two English translations, Edmund Chilmead's *The History of the Rites Customes and Manner of Life of the Present Jews throughout the World* (London 1650) and Simon Ockley's *The History of the Present Jews throughout the World* (London 1707), and the French translation of Sieur de Simonville [Richard Simon], *Cérémonies et coûtumes qui s'observent aujourd'huy parmy les Juifs*, 3rd ed. (Paris 1710; originally published 1674). Throughout, I have compared the translations with the original Italian to warn against possible flagrant violations of the author's sense, relying upon my French and the occasional advice of others with training in Italian, as well as upon the parallel reading of the three translations themselves. It is important to note that while all three translators based their versions mainly on the "authoritative" revised 1638 edition of the *Riti* (Venice), they all knew the earlier, 1637 edition (Paris) and, in fact, restored many of the passages deleted from it by Modena during his revision. Consequently their renditions comprise two layers: a foundation, consisting of the complete text of the *Riti* in the form which Modena had approved (1638); and a supplemental overlay, consisting of passages drawn from the text of the *Riti* which Modena had actually disclaimed (1637). Richard Simon and Simon Ockley (but not Edmund

Chilmead) went to the trouble of indicating most (but unfortunately not all) of the variants. Only by checking the three translations against both Italian originals was I able to sift out the two layers.

In my notes, citations from the *Riti* by part, chapter, and paragraph refer to the authoritative 1638 edition (e.g., *Riti*, i, 3, 4 = *Riti* [Venice 1638], Part i, chapter 3, paragraph 4. N.B.: chapter and paragraph numbers in the translations do not always correspond to those in the original). When the 1637 edition is cited it is so specified. English quotations are always identified as either Ockley or Chilmead, depending upon the case. While Chilmead's rendition is more literal than Ockley's, which tends to follow Simon's somewhat freer French in most places, it is terribly turgid. Thus I have generally opted for Ockley's more readable English. Ockley kept the two Italian editions in front of him, here and there improving upon the already reliable Simon version. Finally, I have taken the liberty of updating the spelling and eliminating many of the stylistic peculiarities of the English quotations, such as excessive capitalization and the use of emphasis not found in the original.

22. *Riti*, "Proemio." I have followed Graetz's rendition of this passage (see *Geschichte*, x, p. 150) since neither English translator understood it correctly, while Richard Simon omitted the "Proemio" completely in his French version.

23. I agree on this point with Ludwig Blau, *op. cit.*, p. 94 (German introduction). Luzzatto made a similar statement of objectivity in the introduction to the *Discorso; Maamar*, p. 78.

24. *Hayye Yehuda*, p. 57.

25. *Ibid.* My translation here differs from that of Marcus (*op. cit.*, p. 407, bottom) whose rendering of the passage conveys the impression that the 1638 edition was not very different from Gaffarel's, which, as explained below, is not the case.

26. *Riti* (Paris 1637) A^{vff}. In the Venice edition Modena reprinted Gaffarel's letter along with his own Latin "Responsio." Chilmead translated both the Gaffarel letter and the Modena response in his English edition of the *Riti*. At the end of the letter Gaffarel expressed his hope for Modena's eventual conversion to Christianity, a sentiment which must have irked the Italian rabbi no end. Curiously, Modena engaged in his own brand of "censorship" when he wrote in *Hayye Yehuda* (p. 57) that Gaffarel had "printed at the beginning of the book a letter praising me and it greatly!"

27. Baron, *op. cit.*, xiii, pp. 181, 185–86, 407 f., n. 28.

28. Stern, Selma, *Josel of Rosheim*, trans. by Hirschler, G. (Philadelphia 1965), pp. 97–103.

29. Letter published by Roth, Cecil, "Leone da Modena and the Christian Hebraists of his Age," *op. cit.*, p. 395; cf. Roth's discussion of this passage, *ibid.*, p. 392. English translation taken from Kobler, Franz, ed., *A Treasury of Jewish Letters*, ii (Philadelphia 1953), p. 420.

30. Full title: *Synagoga Judaica / Das ist Jueden Schul: darinnen der gantz*

Juedische Glaub und Glaubens ubung / mit allen Ceremonien / Satzungen / Sitten und Gebraeuchen / wie sie bei jhnen offentlich und heimlich in Brauche: Auss jhren eigenen Buecheren und Schrifften / so den Christen mehrtheils unbekandt unnd verborgen sind / mint vermeldungjedes Buchs ort und blat / grundlich erklaeret (Basel [1603]).

31. On his biography see Bertheau, E., "Johannes Buxtorf I," in *Realencyklopaedie fuer protestantische Theologie und Kirche,* 3rd ed., iii, pp. 612–14, and Kautzsch, Emil, *Johannes Buxtorf der Aeltere* (Basel 1879).

32. See also the very last paragraph in the book: "Es wird aber der Christliche Leser genugsam auss disem allem vernommen und verstanden haben / dass der juedisch Glaub und jhre gantze Religion / nicht auff Mosen / sonder auff eitel Luegen / falsche und ungegruendte Satzungen und Fabeln jhrer Rabbinen und weitverfuehrten Schrifftgelehrten gegruendet sei / *und desshalben under den Christen nicht mehr soll geredt werden / dass die Jueden starck auff dem Gesatz Mosis halten* . . . ; *Synagoga,* ch. xxxvi, p. 663 (my emphasis).

33. Buxtorf's reasons for writing *Synagoga Judaica* are spelled out by him in the "Vorrede"; see also Kautzsch, *op. cit.,* pp. 42–43; Ettinger, *op. cit.,* p. 206. On the identification of Buxtorf's appendix with Calvin's treatise see Baron, *op. cit.,* xiii, p. 461, fn. 97, suggesting that Buxtorf included the tract in order to stave off criticism that he had been too lenient towards the Jews. One of the very few anti-Jewish vituperations I was able to find in *Synagoga Judaica* is a parenthetical curse in the first chapter: "O du armer Jud / wo wird man ein gute Ader oder einigen guten tropffen bluts in dir finden"; *Synagoga,* ch. i, p. 47. On the other hand it should be added that in the "objectivity" of Buxtorf noted by Baron as well as by Joseph Kalir ("The Jewish Service in the Eyes of Christians and Baptized Jews in the 17th and 18th Centuries," *Jewish Quarterly Review,* n.s., lvi [1965–66], esp. pp. 5 f., n. 26, 58, 62) is only relative to the more disparaging treatments of Judaism by subsequent writers (see below, n. 173). Most important for our purposes, to Leone da Modena, Buxtorf's presentation was anything but "objective"!

34. Cf. his castigating summary in chapter i: "Also sind die armen / blinden unnd unsinnigen Jueden dahin gegeben / dz sie nicht verstehen koennen noch woellen / was Glaube oder gute Werck sind / sonder lauffen immerdar jhren lauff und verharren in jhrem unsinnigen wesen"; *Synagoga,* ch. i, p. 48.

35. Buxtorf quoted Margaritha frequently: *Synagoga,* ch. ix, p. 298; ch. xi, p. 361; ch. xii, p. 398; ch. xx, p. 510; ch. xxvii, p. 573; ch. xxxiii, p. 599. The topics dealt with by Buxtorf correspond in large measure to those taken up by Margaritha. Even the *title* of Buxtorf's manual (see above, n. 31) is reminiscent of Margaritha's *Der gantz Juedisch glaub Mit sampt ainer gruendtlichen und warhafften Anzaygunge / aller Satzungen / Ceremonien / Gebetten / Haymliche und offentliche Gebraeuch / deren sich dye Juden halten / durch das gantz Jar / mit schoenem und gegruendten Argumenten wyder ihren Glauben.*

36. References to *Brantspiegel:* ch. i, pp. 42, 43, 45, 83; ch. ii, p. 103; ch. iv, pp. 159, 167, 169, 172, 176; ch. v, pp. 199, 233; ch. vi, p. 238; ch. viii, p. 289; ch. x, p. 317; ch. xxxv, p. 611. On the book *Brantspiegel* see Trachtenberg, Joshua, *Jewish Magic and Superstition* (Cleveland 1961), pp. 44, 316.

37. Quoted about 75 times in *Synagoga Judaica* and almost always indicated by Buxtorf in the margin. The book, which I have not seen, is probably identifical with the Judeo-German *Orah Hayyim* (Basel 1602) described by Steinschneider, Moritz, *Catalogus Librorum Hebraeorum in Bibliotheca Bodleiana,* i (2nd ed.; Berlin 1931), col. 518, no. 3391.

38. Quoted about seventeen times as *Minhagim* with no further identification; once, however, the *Minhagim* collection of Rabbi Isaac Tyrnau is identified explicitly; *Synagoga,* ch. xxiv, p. 548. On the *Minhagim* compendia see Benjacob, I. A., *Otsar Hasefarim* (Wilna 1880), p. 336, nos. 1403–14 and Trachtenberg's bibliographical note, *op. cit.,* p. 316.

39. *Riti,* "Proemio" (Ockley, Introduction).

40. Modena probably read *Synagoga Judaica* in the Latin translation of Germbergi which appeared in 1604 and was republished at least once more (1614) before 1616.

41. See above p. 433.

42. In fact Roth published the letter twice, once in the *Israel Abrahams Jubilee Volume* (1927), and a second time in an Italian version of the same article, in *La rassegna mensile di Israel,* xi (1936–37), pp. 409–23.

43. *Riti,* "Proemio" (Ockley, Introduction).

44. The chapters are distributed as follows: 1638 edition—14, 10, 10, 11, 9; 1637 edition—14, 9, 10, 10, 11. The chapter-by-chapter outline of the contents of the *Riti* which follows refers to the authoritative 1638 edition.

45. The only difference is that in Caro's *Shulhan Arukh* the section of Fast days comes immediately before the one on Rosh Hashanah.

46. In the first printed edition (Paris) the passage on the transmigration of souls and the chapter on the thirteen articles of Maimonides had come here, at the end. Modena, of course, omitted these items in the Venice edition in accordance with the ruling of the Holy Office.

47. The octavo 1638 edition of the *Riti* contains 111 pages of text; the slightly larger octavo German edition (1603) of Buxtorf's *Synagoga Judaica* has 665 pages of text, excluding the appendix taken from Calvin.

48. The French translator of the *Riti,* Richard Simon, was the first to comment on the quantitative disparity between the two manuals and on what was, in his opinion, the qualitative superiority of the smaller: "Tout ce que Buxtorf donc a donné de bon dans un gros volume, se trouve icy dans un petit Livre, où il n'y a rien de superflu parce que l'Auteur ne s'écarte jamais de son sujet, qu'il ne dit précisément que ce qu'il faut pour se faire entendre"; Léon de Modène, *Cérémonies et coûtumes,* trans. by Sieur de Simonville [Richard Simon], A^{va} (Preface). The judgment of another French writer was quite the opposite. In the first volume of Bernard Picart's illustrated *Cérémonies et coûtumes religieuses de tous les peuples du monde* (Amsterdam 1723),

which incorporated Simon's translation of the *Riti* and the translator's supplement on the Karaites and Samaritans, an anonymous author felt compelled to add his own "Supplement" because he felt Modena's work was terse and incomplete; for this supplement he drew material primarily from Buxtorf (!) and Basnage. Basnage himself, a few years earlier, had rendered the same judgment of the *Riti* in the introduction to his *L'histoire et la religion des Juifs depuis Jésus-Christ jusqu'à présent* (5 Vols.; Rotterdam 1706–07), i, p. 5b: ". . . le traité de Léon de Modène, qui avec son Supplement a été rimprimé plusieurs fois, nous a paru trop court."

49. *Riti*, "Proemio": Take here, therefore, courteous reader, a short abridgment of the rites and customs of the Jews, wherein notwithstanding there is not any the least circumstance omitted, unless it be such as are not at all observed now or regarded by them" (Chilmead, Author's Preface).

50. *Riti*, i, 10; cf. also ii, 1, 5–7. *See* Modena's self-adulatory testimony about Christian attendance at his sermons in *Hayye Yehuda*, pp. 39, 46, 47. Also Roth, Cecil, *Venice* [Jewish Communities Series] (Philadelphia 1930), p. 217.

Christians from abroad attended Venetian synagogues too, for example the inquisitive English traveler Thomas Coryat, who visited Venice and its synagogues in 1608; a few years later Coryat attended a synagogue in Constantinople; see Yardeni, Miriam, "Descriptions of Voyages and a Changed Attitude towards the Jews: the Case of Thomas Coryate" [Hebrew], *Tarbiz*, xl (1970–71), pp. 84–104, esp. pp. 91–94. Cecil Roth had earlier suggested that the "certaine learned Jewish Rabbin that spake good Latin" with whom Coryat held a rather tumultuous disputation in the middle of the Venetian ghetto, was none other than Leone da Modena himself; see his "Leone da Modena and England," pp. 216–22. Attendance at synagogue became popular among Christians in England too, beginning immediately after readmission; see Roth, Cecil, *Anglo-Jewish Letters* (London 1938), pp. 54–65 and the same author's *A History of the Jews in England* 3rd ed. (Oxford 1964), p. 174.

51. *Riti*, v, 5.
52. *Ibid.*, v, 4.
53. *Ibid.*, v, 2 (this chapter was added in 1638).
54. *Ibid.*, iv, 11 (this chapter was added in 1638).
55. *Ibid.*, ii, 5.
56. *Synagoga*, ch. ii, pp. 97–104. Cf. Trachtenberg, *op. cit.*, pp. 36–37, 169.
57. *Synagoga*, ch. ii, pp. 105–06. Cf. Trachtenberg, *op. cit.*, pp. 170–71.
58. *Synagoga*, ch. x, pp. 311–12. Cf. Trachtenberg, *op. cit.*, p. 191.
59. *Synagoga*, ch. x, pp. 320–21. Cf. Trachtenberg, *op. cit.*, pp. 66–67, 285, n. 11.
60. *Synagoga*, ch. xi, pp. 360–61. Cf. Trachtenberg, *op. cit.*, p. 195.
61. *Synagoga*, ch. xi, pp. 361–66, also quoting a passage from Margaritha. Cf. Trachtenberg, *op. cit.*, p. 67.
62. *Synagoga*, ch. iv, p. 168.

63. *Ibid.*, ch. viii, p. 288.
64. *Ibid.*, ch. xxvi, p. 563.
65. *Ibid.*, ch. xxxv, pp. 606, 613. Cf. Trachtenberg, *op. cit.*, pp. 176f.
66. *Synagoga*, ch. xxxv, pp. 615–17. Cf. Trachtenberg, *op. cit.*, p.74.
67. *Synagoga*, ch. xix, pp. 504–05. Cf. Trachtenberg, *op. cit.*, pp. 165–66. Also see Lauterbach, Jacob, "Tashlik: A Study in Jewish Ceremonies," *Hebrew Union College Annual,* xi (1936), pp. 207–340, summoning Buxtorf, as well as Margaritha and Pfefferkorn, as contemporary witnesses of the form *tashlikh* assumed in the sixteenth century; *ibid.*, pp. 304–05, 296–97.
68. *Synagoga*, ch. xx, pp. 507–16. Cf. Trachtenberg, *op. cit.*, pp. 163–64. On the *kapparot* ceremony, particularly as it relates to *tashlikh*, see Lauterbach, *op. cit.*, pp. 262 ff. and *passim* as well as the same author's preliminary discussion of "The Ritual for the Kapparot-Ceremony," in *Jewish Studies in Memory of George A. Kohut,* ed. Baron, Salo W. and Marx, Alexander (New York 1935), pp. 413–22.
69. *Synagoga*, ch. xii, pp. 405–08. Cf. Trachtenberg, *op. cit.*, pp. 2–3.
70. *Riti*, v, 2, 4 (Ockley, p. 214) (chapter 2 was added in 1638).
71. *Ibid.*, iv, 8, 1 (Ockley, pp. 191–92; my emphasis) (the words "ma più tosto vanità" were added in 1638; Ockley's words: "and superstition" are not in the original).
72. *Ibid.*, iv, 8, 3.
73. *Ibid.*, iii, 1, 11–[12].
74. *Riti* (Paris 1637), iii, 1, 23, p. 58. *Cf. Riti* (Venice 1638), p. 61.
75. *Riti*, iii, 1, 25 (Ockley, p. 117).
76. *Synagoga*, ch. xi, pp. 360–68.
77. *Riti* (Paris 1637), i, 5, 11, p. 15 (Ockley, pp. 19–20; my emphasis).
78. *Riti* (Venice 1638), p. 20.
79. *Riti*, i, 4, 1 (Ockley, pp. 10–11).
80. *Ibid.*, ii, 7, 16 (Ockley, p. 95, where paragraph "xvi" is mistakenly printed "xiv").
81. *Ibid.*, v, 6, 5 (Ockley, pp. 223–24).
82. *Riti* (Paris 1637), v, 9, 1 (Chilmead, p. 243; Ockley, adhering here to the 1638 edition, omitted this passage).
83. *Riti* (Venice 1638), p. 111.
84. *Riti* (both editions) iii, 5, 7. Cf. Rubin's note to the Hebrew translation of the *Riti, Shulhan Arukh,* p. 73, n. 42.
85. *Riti*, iii, 6, 2 (Ockley, p. 141).
86. Trachtenberg, *op. cit.*, pp. 2–3.
87. *Riti* (Paris 1637), iii, 3, 4 (Chilmead, pp. 126–27). The "expurgated" passage reads: ". . . the evening before the vigil of the feast the master of the house goes and searches all about the house to see if he can find anywhere any leavened bread. About the fifth hour of the next day they burn some bread . . ." etc; *Riti* (Venice 1638), iii, 3, 4 (Ockley, p. 125).
88. As is well known, in his private life, Modena, like so many other educated renaissance Jews (and Christians) was quite attached to beliefs and practices

which smacked of superstition and magic; see *Hayye Yehuda, passim* and Shulvass, Moses, *Jewish Life in Renaissance Italy* [Hebrew] (New York 1955), pp. 319–23.

89. "It is a remarkable saying of a very great person, yet rightly understood by very few (though agreeable to that of the Prophet Hosea, chap. 11) *Lex Judaeorum, Lex Puerorum"; Riti,* "Proemio" (end) (Ockley, Introduction). *Cf.* Modena's *Ari Nohem,* ed. by Libowitz, Nehemiah (Jerusalem 1929), p. 22 where he quotes this calumny again *(torat hayehudim torat naarim).* The statement in the *Riti* is enigmatic and has caused some readers to suspect Modena of having rendered a pejorative gibe at his own fellow Jews; see Graetz, *op. cit.,* x, p. 149 and Libowitz, *op. cit.,* p. 58, n. 68. However this is hardly likely given the apologetic purpose of the *Riti* elucidated here. In the light of the reference to Hosea (added, incidentally, in the 1638 edition), it appears that Modena was simply alluding to the idea that God loves (chooses) His *children,* Israel, in spite of their many sins. This is the theme of a number of Midrashic interpretations of the first verse of Hosea chapter 11; see, for instance, *Sifre Deuteronomy* 31.14 (ed. Finkelstein), pp. 324 f.; *Pesikta Rabbati* 26 (ed. M. Friedmann), p. 129a; and *Exodus Rabba* 43 (end). Reggio turned the "lex Judeorum lex puerorum" aphorism into one of the stylistic cornerstones of his case for Leone da Modena's authorship of the *Kol Sakhal;* Reggio, Isaac Samuel, *Behinat Hakabbalah* (Gorizia 1852), pp. 75–76. Cf. Ellis Rivkin's criticism of Reggio's reasoning in his *Leon da Modena and the Kol Sakhal* (Cincinnati 1952), p. 100.

90. Baron, *op. cit.,* ix, pp. 79–94 on the disputations of Paris (1240), Barcelona (1263), and Tortosa (1413–14).

91. *Ibid.,* v, pp. 122–25. Of the thirty-five accusations leveled against the Talmud at the Paris disputation of 1240, nine dealt with the authority of the Talmud among the Jews; the remaining twenty-six with alleged blasphemies against Jesus, God, and Christians, and various assumed errors and stupidities. Specific post-Biblical practices did not figure into the indictment at all; see Loeb, Isidore, "La controverse de 1240 sur le Talmud," *Revue des études juives,* i (1880), pp. 252–54; ii (1881), pp. 253–70; iii (1881), pp. 39–54.

92. See Matthew 23:16 ff. On the well-known medieval Christian iconographic representation of "blindfolded Synagoga" see Seiferth, Wolfgang, *Synagogue and Church in the Middle Ages: Two Symbols in Art and Literature,* trans. by Chadeayne, Lee and Gottwald, Paul (New York 1970), pp. 95 ff. and Blumenkranz, Bernhard, *Le Juif médiéval au miroir de l'art chétien* (Paris 1966), pp. 105 ff.

93. For two medieval Jewish versions of the "chain of transmission" see Maimonides' Introduction to the *Mishneh Torah,* ed. and trans. by Hyamson, Moses, i (Jerusalem 1965, reprinted), pp. 1b–5a, and Abraham ibn Daud's *Sefer ha-Qabbalah,* ed. and trans. by Cohen, Gerson D. (Philadelphia 1967).

94. *Synagoga,* ch. i, pp. 1–94. These views are reiterated by Buxtorf here and there throughout the book, for instance in the summary at the end of ch.

xxv, pp. 559 f.: "Diss sei auch gnug geredt von den Ceremonien / welche die Jueden an jhren Feir und Festtagen / in jres jeudischen Glaubens ubung gebrauchen / darauss gnugsam zu erkennen ist / dz jhr Religion nit mehr auff Mosis und den Propheten fundament / sonder auff eitel luegen und falsche Satzungen der Rabbiner und Schrifftgelehrten / wie ich im anfang dises Buches zu beweisen mir fuergenommen / gebawet und gegruendet ist." See Maimonides' formulation of the doctrine of the immutability of the written and oral laws in his eighth and ninth articles of faith, in the Commentary on the Mishnah, Introduction to tractate Sanhedrin chapter 10 (ed. Kafih), pp. 214–16.

95. *Synagoga*, ch. iv, 176–85.
96. *Riti*, i, 1 (Ockley, p. 3). Luzzatto echoed the same idea in a different context when he explained that "the Jews take on different customs from the various nations among whom they dwell. That is why the manners of the Jew in Venice are so different from those of the Jew in Constantinople, Damascus, or Cairo and why, in turn, all of these (Jews) are so different from the German and Polish Jews"; *Maamar*, p. 106.
97. *Riti*, ii, 2, 2 (Ockley, p. 70). Cf. Luzzatto's description of the "three classes of Jewish scholars" (*Maamar*, pp. 139–47), especially his characterization of the Kabbalists: "The Jews are not obliged to agree with their doctrines, although it is popular with certain members of the (Jewish) nation, especially in the Eastern lands and in Poland"; *ibid.*, p. 143. On the censorship of the Talmud in Italy see Popper, *op. cit.*, pp. 29–104.
98. Other places where Buxtorf invoked Kabbalistic interpretations include: *Synagoga*, ch. ii, pp. 110, 124–25; ch. iv, pp. 161, 164 f.; ch. v, pp. 234–36; ch. vi, p. 248; ch. vii, pp. 277–79; ch. xxviii, p. 585. Modena's well-known refutation of the Kabbalah, despite his personal attachment to many of its practical aspects, is contained in his *Ari Nohem* and his *Ben David*. On the Kabbalah as seen by Christians see Blau, Joseph, *The Christian Interpretation of the Cabala*.
99. *Riti*, "Proemio" (Ockley, Introduction).
100. I am grateful to Professor Ismar Schorsch for suggesting that a count of the number of chapters might also yield a significant figure. In the revised edition of 1638 Modena *added* three chapters to the 54, but at the same time he *subtracted* three, thus maintaining the original total. This fact lends some credence to the conjecture that he chose 54 as the number of chapters on purpose. I would have been even more convinced had it turned out that the distribution of the chapters among the five Parts correspond to the distribution of pericopes in the Pentateuch; see above, n. 44.
101. *Synagoga*, ch. iv, pp. 169–72.
102. *Riti*, i, 6, 1 (Ockley, p. 20).
103. *Synagoga*, ch. vi, pp. 242–45; ch. vii, pp. 255–67.
104. *Riti*, ii, 10, 1 and 3 (Ockley, p. 179).
105. *Synagoga*, ch. xxix, pp. 586–87.
106. *Riti*, iv, 6, 1 (Ockley, pp. 98–100).

107. *Riti*, iv, 6, 2 (Ockley, pp. 180–81). Cf. Buxtorf's scoffing remark about the rabbinic divorce laws; *Synagoga*, ch. xxix, p. 588. See the discussion of the ordinance of R. Gershom (c. 960–1028) against compulsory divorce in Finkelstein, Louis, *Jewish Self-Government in the Middle Ages* (New York 1964, reprinted), pp. 29–30.

108. *Synagoga*, ch. xxii, p. 535. Buxtorf went on in the same chapter to deride many of the customs associated with this holiday, particularly the "enmity, jealousy, strife" and even "blasphemy" which, he scorned, often resulted from the practice of auctioning off synagogue prerogatives on Simhat Torah; *ibid.*, pp. 539 f.

109. *Riti*, iii, 7, 2 (Ockley, p. 146; my emphasis).

110. On the history of Simhat Torah see Yaari, Abraham, *Toledot Hag Simhat Torah* (Jerusalem 1964).

An interesting, although relatively insignificant contemporaneous parallel to Buxtorf's indictment of Simhat Torah, comes from the ubiquitous traveler Thomas Coryat. In September, 1613, Coryat, himself a zealous English Protestant, witnessed the Sukkot celebration in Constantinople. In his description of that holiday, preserved in Samuel Purchas' anthology of wayfarers, Coryat chastised the Jews for deviating from the Bible: ". . . their Feast of Tabernacles . . . lasted . . . nine dayes in which they differ from the ancient Jewes who were commanded by Almightie God to spend only eight dayes in the celebration of their Feast"; Purchas, Samuel, *His Pilgrimes*, x (Glasgow 1905, reprinted), p. 431. Cf. Yardeni, *op. cit.*, pp. 99–100.

111. Including, among others, Imanuel Aboab's *Nomologia* (completed 1625; published posthumously, 1629); Saul Levi Morteira's *Tractato da verdade da ley, e providencia de Dios com seu povo* (not published; see Kayserling, Meyer, *Biblioteca Española-Portugueza-Judaica* [Strasbourg 1890], pp. 74–75); and Modena's own *Magen Vetsinah* and *Shaagat Aryeh*. Saul Levi Morteira also wrote a defense of the oral law against the calumnies of the apostate Sixtus Senensis called *Repuesta à las objeciones con que el Sinense injustamente calumnia al Talmud* (1646; see Kayserling, *op. cit.*, p. 75). Professor Gerson D. Cohen kindly drew my attention to the works of Morteira. See also Rivkin, *op. cit.*, pp. 1–17, and Yerushalmi, *op. cit.*, on Isaac Cardoso.

112. *Maamar*, p. 153: "By and large, Jews do not live in lands which have broken off from the Roman Church. It is a known fact that the Jewish nation leans in some of its principles more towards the Church of Rome than to the beliefs [of the sects in the lands which have broken off from her]. The Jews maintain that many places in Scripture cannot be understood properly except in the light of the tradition, and accordingly they place great value upon it, as I have shown." Luzzatto went on in the same passage to elucidate other similarities (the belief in justification by good works; free will, etc.) and concluded by stressing that despite their differences with Protestantism, Jews were well treated in the (Protestant) Low

Countries. Catholic readers, evidently, were supposed to take an object lesson from this! Ben-Sasson has cited this passage as a late counterpart of earlier Jewish pro-Catholic and anti-Protestant sentiments (in particular, that of R. Yehiel b. Samuel de Pisa, writing in 1539) expressing Judaism's affinity with Catholicism and, at the same time, disapproval of the Lutheran reform movement; Ben-Sasson, Hayyim Hillel, "The Reformation in Contemporary Jewish Eyes," Israel Academy of Sciences and Humanities, *Proceedings*, iv, no. 12 (Jerusalem 1970), p. 294, n. 158.

113. On this see Trachtenberg, Joshua, *The Devil and the Jews* (Philadelphia 1961).

114. For medieval Jewish attitudes towards Christians and Christianity see Katz, Jacob, *Exclusiveness and Tolerance* (New York 1961), esp. chapters 1–5.

115. *Synagoga*, ch. v, pp. 213–14, 222; ch. xi, p. 392. Cf. Margaritha's allegation, quoted in Stern, *op. cit.*, p. 99. On the Jewish Christian polemic on Esau-Edom see Cohen, Gerson D., "Esau as Symbol in Early Medieval Thought," in *Jewish Medieval and Renaissance Studies*, ed. by Altmann, Alexander (Cambridge, Mass. 1967), pp. 19–48.

116. *Synagoga*, ch. v, pp. 226–28. Cf. Margaritha, quoted in Stern, *op. cit.*, p. 99. See also Kalir, *op. cit.*, pp. 78–79. Buxtorf had found the uncensored version in a prayerbook printed in Augsburg in 1534. See Menasseh ben Israel's refutation of Buxtorf's and Margaritha's allegations concerning the *alenu*; *Vindiciae Judaeorum*, pp. 28–31. On the self-censorship of the *alenu* prayer see Popper, *op. cit.*, p. 29; cf. also pp 17–18.

117. *Synagoga*, ch. v, p. 214.

118. *Ibid.*, ch. xxiv, p. 547.

119. *Ibid.*, ch. v, pp. 219–24, quoting his favorite, Rabbi Bahyye ben Asher, to prove his point. Cf. Kalir, *op. cit.*, pp. 76 f. On the text of the *birkat haminim* see Finkelstein, Louis, "The Development of the Amidah," *Jewish Quarterly Review*, n. s., xvi (1925–26), pp. 156–57.

120. *Synagoga*, ch. xvi, pp. 458–59. Cf. *Kad Hakemah* in *Kitvei Rabbenu Bahyye*, ed. by Sheval, Hayyim Dov (Jerusalem 1969), p. 289. Other examples cited by Buxtorf include the *shefokh hamatkha* prayer recited at the Passover seder; *Synagoga*, ch. xiii, p. 424.

121. *Riti*, iii, 1, 19; iii, 4, 4; iii, 5, 6; iii, 7, 3. Cf. Menasseh ben Israel, *Humble Addresses*, pp. 11–13. Menasseh ben Israel devoted fully one-third of the *Vindiciae Judaeorum* (pp. 19–31) to vindicating the Jews of the age-old charge that they cursed Christians.

122. *Riti*, i, 11, 7 and 10.

123. *Synagoga*, ch. xxvi, pp. 564–65. Cf. Modena's explanation of the purification of household utensils; *Riti*, i, 3, 1.

124. *Synagoga*, ch. xxviii, pp. 584–85. Cf. Trachtenberg, *Jewish Magic*, pp. 172–73. On the folk belief that evil spirits strive to harm newlyweds at their wedding, and the significance of the breaking of a glass as a prophylactic measure against this, see Lauterbach, Jacob, "The Ceremony of

Breaking a Glass at Weddings," *Hebrew Union College Annual,* ii (1925), pp. 351–80.

125. *Synagoga,* ch. xxvii, pp. 572–73.

126. *Ibid.,* ch. iii, pp. 151–52.

127. *Riti,* ii, 8, 1. Cf. the translator Ockley's demurrer, *ad. loc.,* p. 96. On the prohibition against partaking of wine touched by gentiles see Katz, *op. cit.,* pp. 27, 34, 40–41, 46–47, 162–63. On the dominant medieval rabbinic view that Christianity is idolatrous, and particularly on the dissenting "tolerationist" approach of the thirteenth-century Provençal Rabbi Menahem Hameiri, see Katz, Jacob, "Religious Tolerance in the Halakhic and Philosophical System of Rabbi Menahem Hameiri" [Hebrew], *Zion,* xviii (1953), pp. 15–30.

128. *Riti,* ii, 1, 1 (Ockley, p. 65; my emphasis). Of course there is a great deal of difference between combining Hebraisms with Italian, and speaking deeply Hebraized Yiddish, which is what Buxtorf had in mind.

129. *Riti,* iv, 11, 3 (Ockley, p. 207).

130. *Riti* (Paris 1637), v, 2, pp. [105–06] (the pages after page 99 in the copy of the 1637 edition I used are mistakenly numbered in the 200's). Cf. *Riti* (Venice 1638), p. 102. See Menasseh ben Israel, *Humble Addresses,* pp. 22–23; *idem., Vindiciae Judaeorum,* pp. 31–32. Also Luzzatto, *Maamar,* pp. 118 ff.

131. *Synagoga,* ch. xxxvi.

132. Buxtorf barely mentioned Jewish economic activity, save for a passing reference to cheating of Christians; *Synagoga,* ch. iii, p. 159. Margaritha, on the other hand, had devoted a whole chapter to usury in *Der gantz Juedisch glaub,* J^(ia–iib).

133. *Riti,* ii, 5, 4 (Ockley, p. 84). Modena was taken to task for this forced interpretation of the word *nokhri* (foreigner) by Rabbi Ishmael of Modena in 1806, in his "Responsa" to the twelve questions presented by Napoleon to the Paris Assembly of Jewish Notables; see Rosenthal, Judah, "The Answers to the Twelve Questions of the Emperor Napoleon by R. Ishmael of Modena, Italy" [Hebrew], *Talpioth,* iv (1949), pp. 582–83. My identification of Modena as the unnamed author of the "little book written in Italian" castigated by R. Ishmael seems certain, given the fact that the page number in that book referred to by Rabbi Ishmael (p. 47) corresponds to the page in the 1638 edition of the *Riti* where Modena outlined his views on the Deuteronomic verse. The Paris Assembly itself, apparently disregarding Rabbi Ishmael's *own* advice on how to handle the exegetical difficulty, adopted an equally forced interpretation; see Tama, Diogene, *Transactions of the Parisian Sanhedrim [sic],* trans. by Kirwan, F. D. (London 1807), pp. 197–207.

134. *Maamar,* pp. 109–10, 121–22. Cf. Menasseh ben Israel, *Humble Addresses,* pp. 20–21, echoing Luzzatto's other argument, about the relatively low interest rates Jews were allowed to exact; see *Maamar,* pp. 101–02. On the historical evolution of the theory and practice of taking interest

from non-Jews see Rosenthal, Judah, *"Ribbit Min Hanokhri,"* reprinted in his *Mehkarim Umekorot,* i (Jerusalem 1967), pp. 253–323 and esp. pp. 315–17 where he discusses Modena's and Luzzatto's views on the subject. Rosenthal traces Modena's interpretation of the crucial Deuteronomic verse back to Joseph Albo and Isaac Abravanel, both of whom Rosenthal claims accepted the Christian explanation that *nokhri* refers to the pagan nations of Canaan; *ibid.,* pp. 306–08, 315. However the use of the argument of economic discrimination to justify the taking of interest from Christians appears to be a Jewish apologetic nuance introduced to the Christian public in the seventeenth century by Modena and Luzzatto. Josel of Rosheim, writing in Hebrew for a *Jewish* audience, had adumbrated this line of reasoning in the sixteenth century; *ibid.,* pp. 311–12.

135. *Riti,* ii, 5, 3 (Ockley, p. 83).
136. Toland, John, *Reasons for Naturalizing the Jews in Great Britain and Ireland, etc.* (London 1714); Dohm, Christian Wilhelm, *Ueber die buergerliche Verbesserung der Juden* (Berlin 1781); Grégoire, Henri, *Essai sur la régénération physique, morale, et politique des Juifs* (Metz 1789). For "John Toland's Borrowings from Simone Luzzattto" see the article by Isaac Barzilay in *Jewish Social Studies,* vol. xxxi (1969), pp. 75–81.
137. *Riti,* ii, 5, 1; *Maamar,* pp. 113–14.
138. *Riti,* ii, 5, 2; *Maamar,* p. 114. Cf. Tosefta *Baba Kamma* 10.15 (ed. Zuckermandel), p. 368; also Katz, *Exclusiveness and Tolerance,* pp. 60–61, 158–62, and art. "Gezel Hagoy" in *Entsyklopedia Talmudit,* v, cols. 487–88. Modena cited this view in the name of Rabbi Bahyye ben Asher whom Buxtorf had been so fond of exploiting for anti-Christian statements in Jewish literature; cf. *Kad Hakemah* (ed. Sheval), pp. 102–03. On the possible sources of Luzzatto's similar formulation of the *hillul hashem* principle see *Maamar,* p. 162, n. 78 (referring also to the parallel in the *Riti).*
139. *Riti,* ii, 5, 2 (end); *Maamar,* pp. 78–79, 107–08.
140. *Hayye Yehuda,* pp. 54–56; Shulvass' introduction to *Maamar,* pp. 22–23. Leone da Modena divulged that his own son-in-law had been implicated by association in the scandal of 1636, and had had to flee to Ferrara. Other echoes in *Hayye Yehuda* of Jewish criminal activity in Venice include the author's vivid description of his son Zebulun's murder in 1627 by a gang of Jewish ruffians; *Hayye Yehuda,* pp. 40–41. On the political purpose of the *Discorso* see also Baer, Yitzhak, *Galut,* trans. Warshow, Robert (New York 1947), pp. 83–92.
141. *Riti,* ii, 5, 5 (Ockley, pp. 84 f.). Cf. *Riti* (Paris 1637), p. 45. For a similar assertion by Luzzatto, see *Maamar,* p. 117 (bottom).
142. *Riti,* i, 14, 1 (Ockley, p. 56).
143. *Ibid.,* i, 14, 9 (Ockley, p. 61). Cf. *Riti* (Paris 1637), p. 34. Cf. Mishnah *Gittin* 5.8 (end) for a classical formulation of the duty of charitability towards non-Jews.

144. *Maamar,* pp. 100–01. See Modena's account of the plague, in *Hayye Yehuda,* pp. 49–51, and also, Roth, *Venice,* pp. 95 ff., 332.

145. *Tsemah Tsaddik* (Venice 1600; reprinted New York 1899). Professor Gerson D. Cohen pointed out to me this interesting relationship between *Tsemah Tsaddik* and the *Riti.*

146. Luzzatto, it should be added, also dealt with the issue of superstition, in response to Tacitus' charge that the Jews were "prone to superstition, but hating all religious rites" (*History* 5.13 [*The Complete Works of Tacitus,* trans. by Church, A. J. and Brodribb, W. J., ed. Hadas, Moses (New York 1942), p. 665]). However Luzzatto's treatment of the allegation was quite different from Modena's and occupied a relatively minor place in the *Discorso* compared with the economic arguments; see *Maamar,* pp. 130 ff.

147. *Riti,* i, 1.

148. *Ibid.,* i, 10, 8. Cf. Luzzatto's comments in *Maamar,* pp. 106, 153.

149. *Riti,* v, 1. On the rabbinic debate in the sixteenth and seventeenth centuries over the status of the Karaites see Assaf, Simah, *Beohalei Yaakov* (Jerusalem 1943), pp. 185–89.

150. It is characteristic of his Protestant outlook that Buxtorf, in a passing reference to the Karaites, should have expressed his preference for them over the rabbinic Jews; *Synagoga,* ch. ii, pp. 128–29.

151. *Riti,* i, 14. Cf. *Synagoga,* ch. xxxii, pp. 595–97: "Gemeinlich sagt man / die Jueden lassen keinen bettlen under jhnen. Dagegen aber gibt die Erfahrung / dz die Armen Jueden sehr ubel bei jhnen gehalten werden" (pp. 595 f.). Further on in the same chapter Buxtorf disparaged the institution of the "begging letter" in which one Jewish community testified to the sincere need of a terribly destitute individual and thereby enabled him to collect charity from other Jewish communities. Buxtorf felt it was particularly inhumane to submit an indigent father to this indignity in order to amass a dowry for his daughter: "Wenn ein armer Jud ein mannbare Tochter hat / und kan jhr keine Ehestewr mit geben / so muss der Vatter auch mit eim Brieff so lang herumb ziehen biss er etwas zusammen bringet / dass er sie aussstewren kan / sonsten uberkompt sie nicht bald einen Man" (. 597). Contrast Leone da Modena on this: "But if a poor man has occasion for extraordinary charity, as if he has a daughter to marry, or would redeem any of his family that are slaves, whether he is one that lives with them in the same city or a stranger, 'tis all one: the overseers of the synagogue procure him a promise from every one which they call Nedava . . . ; and when they have gathered it they give it to the poor man"; *Riti,* 1, 14, 4 (Ockley, pp. 58–59). Luzzatto also cited self-help as a Jewish virtue; *Maamar,* p. 101.

152. *Riti,* i, 14, 7 (this paragraph was added [!] in the 1638 edition).

153. *Ibid.,* i, 2, 3 (Chilmead, p. 7).

154. On this portrait see Libowitz, *op. cit.,* pp. 1–2 and *Hayye Yehuda,* p. 54.

155. *Riti,* i, 5, 6 (Ockley, p. 16). Cf. Modena's famous responsum on uncover-

ing the head, published and annotated by Isaac Rivkind in the *Louis Ginzberg Jubilee Volume* (Hebrew section) (New York 1946), pp. 401–23.

156. *Riti*, i, 5, 4 (Ockley, p. 15); cf. i, 5, 9. On Jewish dress habits in Renaissance Italy see Shulvass *op. cit.*, pp. 170–73.

157. *Riti*, v, 8, 4.

158. *Ibid.*, iii, 2, 2.

159. On the sixteenth- and seventeenth-century "Italian and Dutch Haskalah" as adumbration and precursor of the "classical" period of Jewish enlightenment and emancipation, see Baron, Salo W., *A Social and Religious History of the Jews,* 3 vols. (New York 1937), ii, pp. 205–12 and iii, pp. 139–41, n. 13.

160. Even in his letter to Noghera Modena had written, immediately after the passage quoted above (p. 293): "One thing is sure, that in all my learned efforts I had no other intention than that of serving the public, and of defending my poor much oppressed nation"; translation in Kobler, *op. cit.*, p. 420.

161. The Italian version, specifically, that of 1638, was reprinted at least a half-dozen times in Italy; see the bibliographical list compiled by Samaja, *op. cit.*, pp. 79–80. There was at least one important attempt to answer the *Riti* in Italian. That was Paolo Medici's *Riti e costumi degli Ebrei confutati*, a refutation of Judaism taking Modena's *Riti* as the object of attack. It was first published in 1737, and appeared in many subsequent editions. I have seen a fourth edition from 1752; see also Libowitz, *op. cit.*, p. 121.

162. Three different English translations were made. The first, entitled *The History of the Rites Customes and Manner of Life of the Present Jews throughout the World,* was done by Edmund Chilmead in 1650. On this translation and its possible role in setting the stage for the readmission of the Jews to England see Roth, "Leone da Modena and England," *loc. cit.*, p. 225; Wilensky, Mordecai, *Shivat Hayehudim Le-anglia* (Jerusalem 1943), pp. 56–57. On Chilmead, who also published a translation of Gaffarel's *Curiositez inouyes* in 1650, see *Dictionary of National Biography*, iv (Oxford 1921–22, reprinted), pp. 257–58. The second English version, entitled *The History of the Present Jews throughout the World,* was translated by Simon Ockley in 1707. This translation was republished again in 1753 according to Libowitz, *op. cit.*, p. 120; I have not seen this edition. On Ockley, an orientalist and Anglican clergyman, see *Dictionary of National Biography*, xiv, pp. 807–11. The third English version was that contained in volume i (London 1733) of the English edition of Picart's *Cérémonies.*

163. *Cérémonies et coustumes qui s'observent aujourd'huy parmi les juifs . . . avec un supplement touchant les sectes des Caraites et des Samaritans de nostre temps,* translated by Don Recared Scimeon [Richard Simon] (Paris 1674); in the second edition (1681), and in all subsequent printings, Simon

appended an essay of his own entitled *Comparison des Juifs et de la discipline de l'Eglise*. In all, the French *Riti* underwent at least six editions before 1710 and another as recently even as 1929; see the bibliographical list of Szajkowski, Zosa, *Franco-Judaica* (New York 1962), p. 132, no. 1587 and that of Samaja, *op. cit.*, p. 80. On Richard Simon, the famous Bible critic, see *Nouvelle biographie générale*, xliv, cols. 8–11 and Hertzberg, Arthur, *The French Enlightenment and the Jews* (New York 1968), pp. 40–41.

164. *Kerk-Zeeden en de Gewoonten die huiden in gebruik zyn onder de Jooden*, translated by A. Godart (Amsterdam 1693) from the French version of Richard Simon. A new Dutch translation, again based on Simon's French, was prepared for the Dutch edition of Picart's *Cérémonies* in 1726.

165. *Deceremoniis et consuetudinibus hodie Judeos interreceptis*, trans. by Joh. Valentino Grossgebauer (Frankfurt a. M. 1693) from the French version of Simon.

166. In the German edition (Basel 1746–58) of Picart's *Cérémonies*.

167. On the history of this major publishing feat see Rubens, Alfred, *A Jewish Iconography* (London 1954), p. 6.

168. See above, n. 49.

169. A contemporary of Modena's, Selden was the recipient of one of the *Riti* manuscripts circulating in England. See *Hayye Yehuda*, p. 68; Roth, "Leone da Modena and England," *loc. cit.*, pp. 211 f.; *idem*, "Leone da Modena and his English Correspondents." On Selden's scholarship on Judaism see *Dictionary of National Biography*, xvii, pp. 1157–58; also Ettinger, *op. cit.*, p. 204.

170. Basnage quoted the *Riti* extensively in the fifth part of his *Histoire*, vol. iii (Rotterdam 1707), pp. 497–912. Most of the citations were indicated in his footnotes. For Basnage's criticism of the terseness of the *Riti* see above, n. 48 (end). On the other hand, Basnage *did* incorporate into his work a number of the partisan passages in the *Riti;* for instance, the statement about the discontinuation of the *kapparot* ceremony because of its superstitious nature (Basnage, *op. cit.*, iii, p. 722; cf. *Riti*, iii, 6, 2); the remark about how the Jews abandon their "ridiculous" clothing to suit the gentiles (Basnage, *op. cit.*, iii, p. 751, cf. *Riti*, i, 5, 4 and 9); and the passage extolling Jewish charitability (Basnage, *op. cit.*, iii, p. 767; cf. *Riti*, i, 14). However, Basnage was hardly convinced by Modena's exposition that Judaism was not superstitious!

171. Hertzberg, *op. cit.*, pp. 252–53. Hertzberg refers to Calmet's sympathetic use of material from the *Riti* in his *Dictionnaire historique critique, chronologique géographique et littéral de la Bible* (1722). Arnold Ages analyzed Calmet's earlier *Lettres de l'auteur du Commentaire littéral sur la Genèse* (Paris 1710) in an article on "Calmet and the Rabbis" (*Jewish Quarterly Review*, n.s., lv [1964–65], pp. 340–49), but without reference to the *Riti*. The *Lettres* contained a rejoinder to critics of Calmet's alleged neglect of the rabbis' positive contribution to Judaism in his *Commentaire littéral sur*

tous les livres de l'ancien et du Nouveau Testament (published in 1707). In the *Lettres*, according to Ages, Calmet defended his original position by roundly condemning the rabbis for their insistence on the divinely-inspired continuity of rabbinic tradition (contrasted by Calmet with the unbroken apostolic tradition of the Church), for their alleged preference of the Talmud over Scripture, and for their "blasphemous" and "ridiculous" theological doctrines, among other charges. In the light of these extremely disparaging views, expressed in 1710, one is struck by the "attitude of fairness to Jews, not only of the biblical era but even of the medieval and contemporary ages" that Hertzberg notes in Calmet's *Dictionnaire*, published some twelve years later. Hertzberg partly attributes this moderation to the influence of the *Riti*. Indeed, Calmet may well have come across Leone da Modena's book sometime after 1710 and been impressed enough to radically alter his attitude towards the Jews and Judaism. The problem merits further investigation. In connection with Calmet's earlier, critical appraisal of the rabbis, see also Ages' discussion of Diderot's similarly disparaging comments about " 'Rabbins' and 'Rabbinisme' in the Encyclopédie," *Jewish Quarterly Review*, n.s., lvi (1965–66), pp. 302–14.

172. See his *Essai sur la régénération physique, morale, et politique des Juifs* (Metz 1789; reprinted 1968), pp. 72–74, 118, 215 (note), all quoting the *Riti* by name. Grégoire apparently also derived from the *Riti* (i, 2, 3) his information about Jews collecting paintings; *op. cit.*, p. 101. My friend Ivan George Marcus kindly pointed out these references to me.

173. Joseph Kalir has analyzed, though without reference to the *Riti*, some twenty such seventeenth- and eighteenth-century Jewish-ceremony "manuals" and kindred works, nearly all of them written in German, in order to describe "The Jewish Service in the Eyes of Christians and Baptized Jews in the 17th and 18th Centuries" (*Jewish Quarterly Review*, n. s., lvi [1965–66], pp. 51–80; the article is signed "to be continued" but I have not seen any follow up). As Kalir points out, most of the works drew heavily upon Buxtorf's *Synagoga Judaica*. In the passages Kalir collected, most of which disparage synagogue rituals, there is no evidence of the kind of sympathetic portrayal of Judaism which Leone da Modena's *Riti* was expected by the author to produce.

174. Characteristically, Jewish "enlightened" figures (Graetz excluded) rediscovered the *Riti* in the nineteenth century, immediately recognizing its apologetic value in the struggle for intellectual and political emancipation. That is apparently what prompted Salamon Rubin, the Spinoza scholar, to publish a Hebrew translation of the work in 1867 (with some appended notes by Adolf Jellinek). Isaac Reggio planned, but never completed, a new annotated Italian edition of the *Riti*. He felt the book was of value because it "tended to burn away the thorns and nettles from the field of belief and practice" (quoted by Libowitz, *op. cit.*, pp. 120–21). The poet Yehuda Leib Gordon toyed with the prospect of rendering the *Riti* into Russian since it was "appropriate for the times, because our situation today is just

like the situation during the author's lifetime in his native land" (quoted from Gordon's letters by Libowitz, *op. cit.*, p. 65, n. 75).

175. Johann Buxtorf, *Synagoga Judaica*, 3rd ed., revised by his son (Basel 1661).

176. For instance, *ibid.*, p. 3 (a paragraph on the Karaites, taken from the *Riti*, v, 1); p. 113 (a paragraph on the Jewish customs celebrating the birth of a daughter, taken from the *Riti*, iv, 8, 11); p. 609 (a paragraph on wine touched by Gentiles, taken from *Riti*, ii, 8, 1).

177. For instance, *Synagoga* (Basel 1661), pp. 186 ff. (a section on synagogues, apparently taken from *Riti*, i, 10).

17

Tradition and Innovation in Jewish Music of the Later Renaissance

Don Harrán

In memory of Elaine Brody Silverberg

The title of this chapter bristles with as many uncertainties as derive from the fluctuating terms of its formulation. Tradition and innovation imply a process of change. Jewish music is an evasive notion, depending for its validity on an a-priori differentiation between seeming Jewish and non-Jewish musical types; such a differentiation is obviously difficult to sustain. Mention of the later Renaissance presupposes a division into early, middle and late phases of a period whose typology is actually as indefinite as the term Renaissance itself, with its varying historical, cultural and aesthetic connotations. If I enter this morass of uncertainties, I do so, as anyone would, with no little trepidation. The inscription on the gates would seem to read "Lasciate ogni speranza, voi ch'entrate."[1] Without presuming to remove the uncertainties, I shall at least attempt, and that is my only *speranza,* to explain the reasons for them.

In 1622/23 the publishing firm of Bragadini in Venice brought out a collection of music, entitled the "Songs of Solomon," by the Mantuan Jewish composer Salamone Rossi.[2] That in itself means little, for until

Originally delivered as a lecture at the Center for Jewish Studies, Harvard University (March 1988). The writer benefitted from the discussion with colleagues and students in preparing the final redaction.

then Rossi had at least nine printed collections to his name.[3] The difference is that where the previous collections consisted of secular instrumental or Italian vocal works, usually for three to five voices, his latest
one consisted of thirty-three Hebrew works for three to eight voices, set
to Biblical and post-Biblical texts and intended, in part, for use on
certain occasions in the synagogue. Since we read, in the Foreward to
the collection, that "nothing like this first step has ever been taken
before,"[4] and since we know, from historical hindsight, that no further
steps were taken until the nineteenth century,[5] we can safely conclude
that with Rossi's collection, we confront a problem of not only musical,
but also historical, social, cultural and religious dimensions. It is with
this problem, or at least certain aspects of it, that I, in all diffidence, will
be concerned here, continuing a dialogue with others in their writings[6]
and renewing a discussion of my own in a recent study on Rossi as a
"Jewish musician in Renaissance Italy."[7]

    With Rossi's collection at the center of this report,[8] it is now possible
to erect some sort of frame for the ambiguous wording of the title. By
"tradition and innovation," I mean the relation of Rossi's novel Hebrew
pieces to older and other musical practices. By the later Renaissance, I
mean the period covered by Rossi's dates, namely, c. 1570 to c. 1630,
corresponding to the concluding years of Mantuan history under the
main line of the Gonzaga dukes[9] and, from a Jewish standpoint, to the
years that preceded the sack of the ghetto and the expulsion of its
residents by the Imperial armies.[10] By "Jewish music," I mean, basically,
music made "by Jews, for Jews and as Jews," to adopt an aphoristic
definition by Curt Sachs.[11] Which brings us to the heart of the matter:
one of the difficulties with this definition is that for whatever it says, it
leaves as much unsaid. It tells us who "made" the music, but does not
specify whether making means composing or performing; it tells us who
"heard" the music, but does not specify where and when it was heard:
in the synagogue, in a study hall, in a confraternity, in a home? on which
sacred or secular occasions? We do not know the kind of music that was
heard: for one voice or a combination of voices? in a simple or an ornate
style? with instruments or without? Nor do we know what "as Jews"
means, though it vaguely indicates music experienced in relation to
Jewish culture or tradition. Clearly the open formulation of the definition does not help to dispel the obscurities of the title. The reason I abide
by it is that it seems to reinforce an initial lexical uncertainty in the title

by a parallel semantical uncertainty in the topic, which, in itself, suggests that "uncertainty" may be of the essence in defining Jewish music, whether Rossi's or any other's; the point is one to which I will return below.

Rossi's collection forces questions of identity in Jewish music; of change and continuity in the Jewish music tradition; of the forms and purposes of Jewish ceremonial song; of the connections between Jewish and Christian music. These and cognate questions will be considered, following the guidelines implicit in the title and its problematical exposition. Thus the discussion proceeds from the innovations of Rossi's collection (section I) to their incorporation into a broader Jewish heritage (section II) as well as their relationship with the traditions of Christian art music (section III).[12] The collection will be described as an example of cultural fusion, after parallel examples of a syncretistic tendency from the later fifteenth and sixteenth centuries.[13] Such a description forces a reappraisal of the "innovative" component in Rossi's synagogue music, to account for the possibility of ethnic interchanges in its constitution (section IV). I will conclude by venturing some remarks, of an ontological order, on the principles that seem to underlie the music as a prototypical case of cultural mediation within the Judeo-Christian tradition (section V).

I

The chief innovation of Rossi's collection is its polyphonic treatment of Hebrew texts, breaking with established traditions of musical song in the synagogue as music for a single voice patterned after the accents for cantillating various portions of the Bible *(ta'amei ha-miqra)* or the modal or melodic formulae for performing other prayer readings.[14] Elsewhere I have discussed the origins of the collection as a concerted enterprise between Rossi and his "spiritual mentor," the Venetian rabbi Leone da Modena, who seems to have originated the idea, then implanted it in the composer's mind.[15] "They have been sown, they have been planted" were Modena's words.[16] I shall not review, as I did there, the successive stages of the realization, from seed to flower. Rather I shall concentrate, for present purposes, on the innovations of the collection as conceived by Rossi and Modena in their prefaces to the music.

How "new" the collection was may be sensed from the title, where it is proclaimed as "a new thing in the land" (ḥadasha ba-areẓ). Rossi refers, for the origins of his works, to divine inspiration ("the Lord . . . has put new songs into my mouth").[17] Divine in their initial impulse, perhaps, but quite human in their elaboration: the composer insists that he worked hard at shaping the material "into a proper musical form." Thus through a combination of insight and industry he managed to "weave" his ideas "into an arrangement of sweet sounds, yes pleasantness is at their right hand." They were not the songs, then, revealed to Moses through his Sinaitic encounter with God and inscribed, as the rabbis opined, in the masoretic signs for reading the Bible. Salamone Rossi developed his ideas according to the conventions of sixteenth-century polyphonic composition. Unlike Moses who received, yet did not revise, Rossi intervened in the process of transmission, choosing as his guide the Gentile ars contrapuncti that regulated not the movement of one voice, as customarily heard in the synagogue, but the combination of several voices according to rules of voice leading aimed at producing "consonance," or what Rossi called "sweetness" or "pleasantness."

Thus the collection is new in having its contents composed "according to the science of music" (be-ḥokhmat ha-nigun we-ha-musiqa).[18] The implication is that whatever existed until then was practice, not science. Through scientia musicae, one established "an orderly relationship of the voices,"[19] whereby they became delightful to perceive. "Order," "sweetness," "beauty," "elegance" (seder, ne'imut, yofi, 'arevut): these are rhetorical terms, adopted from the ancient treatises on the ars bene dicendi by fifteenth- and sixteenth-century literary, art and music critics.[20] Gioseffo Zarlino, the leading music theorist of the mid-sixteenth century, aimed at teaching musicians "to compose with beauty, learning and elegance."[21] The terms entered the writings of Hebrew rhetoricians, as for example Judah Messer Leon, who applied them to the analysis of Biblical style.[22] Rossi directed his "ordered" songs to listeners educated on Renaissance counterpoint, hence able, with their "discriminating ears," to appreciate the finesses of his own songs.[23] Apparently they did appreciate them, for when the "Songs" were performed, those who heard them "were radiant, finding them sweet to the ear and wanting to hear more."[24]

The notions of order and sweetness apply to two dimensions of music making: composition and performance. It was Rossi's intention that the collection not only be well composed but also be well performed. Modena conceived an orderly and beautiful mode of performance as a complement to an analogous mode of composition. He wrote that "as pleasing to God as the offering of Abel will be the singing of his melodies when you offer them to Him with great sweetness."[25] Thus the sweet offering must be enhanced by its sweet presentation. Modena enjoins "the singer to intone his prayers in a pleasant voice,"[26] referring to a passage in Midrash: "If thy voice is sweet, go before the Ark [to pray]."[27] These and other comments were approved by the Mantuan rabbi Ezra da Fano, who noted that "the sweeter the voice, the more acceptable it is before the Blessed One."[28]

These then were Rossi's innovations. But was the collection really new? Is there any evidence of polyphonic Hebrew settings prior to Rossi's? On the basis of Modena's and other rabbis' statements from the early years of the seventeenth century, my colleague Israel Adler has assumed the existence of a tradition of polyphonic synagogue song antedating Rossi's "Songs of Solomon" by fifteen or more years.[29] The assumption is reasonable,[30] yet hard to sustain: except for one other musical document which may or may not have preceded Rossi's collection,[31] the references to part music, by one or another rabbinical commentator, are too evasively worded to know exactly what is meant.[32] At the most, the tradition may have consisted of a few sporadic attempts at introducing art music into the synagogue. Nothing remains of them though, and indeed, Rossi's collection is the first substantial document of its kind. Whether it inaugurated a tradition or represented an early highpoint in its unfolding cannot be determined. The tradition may even have been created practically *ex nihilo* by Rossi himself, who appears, from his own and Modena's statements, to have labored over his "Songs" for an extended period, gradually adding "a psalm or a hymn of praise or thanksgiving until he had succeeded in gathering many of them into one collection."[33] Modena emphasized that Rossi "made a beginning which will not cease, the like of which has never been known in Israel."[34] At the composer's behest, he supervised the publication, complaining that his editorial work on the contents was all the more demanding because of their being unprecedented.[35] It is clear that whatever previous attempts there were at forging a Hebrew polyphonic tradition, they were surpassed in quality and quantity by Rossi's "Songs of Solomon."

II

The collection seems to have divided the Jewish community into two camps (note the word *seems*).[36] On the one side stood the orthodox who, on principle, rejected any changes in tradition as tantamount to its contamination. On the other stood the more liberally minded members of the community who, as we know, found the songs "sweet to the ear and wanted to hear more."[37] Rossi could count on his friends to lend him support;[38] but without the approbation of the authorities there was little chance of his "Songs" being regularly performed in the synagogue.[39] Rossi and Modena directed their attention to silencing the voices of dissent, real or anticipated. Their strategy was built on the tactic of adjusting the new to the old, of bringing polyphony within the confines of Hebrew tradition. The effort to accord two different kinds of synagogue song may be regarded as analogous to those, among the Jewish exegetes, to accord Halakhah and Kabbalah,[40] or to those, in the Gentile world, to accord Neoplatonism and Christianity, or mythology and theology, or Platonism and Aristotelianism, and so on. Be that as it may, Rossi's and Modena's arguments to justify Rossi's innovations ran as follows: (1) The composer did not create his songs as an instance of personal hubris. Rather he acted under divine influence.[41] Thus Rossi absolves himself of all blame, pretending to operate as a medium for revelation. In effect, he is saying that should anyone wish to lodge a complaint, he had best do so not at his but at the Lord's doorstep. Such an argument is, of course, a piece of rhetorical fluff; and it had to be supported by more substantial ones, as it was, in fact, in the assertion that (2) synagogue music, as practiced in the Diaspora, had fallen from the heights of the older Biblical music. Modena criticized it for its shallowness, its boorishness. The reason for the decline is that "when it became the lot [of the Hebrews] to dwell among strangers and to wander to distant lands where they were dispersed among alien peoples, these vicissitudes caused them to forget all their knowledge and to be devoid of all wisdom. They became confused and went astray into a pit empty of all understanding. Thus when they came into a land which was not theirs, the wisdom of their sages was lost."[42] It follows, then, that not synagogue music, but (3) music of the ancient Temple should be praised. Its practioners, we are told, were men of learning, they possessed music in its perfection.[43] It is no wonder that other nations "honored them and held them in high esteem so that they soared as if on eagles' wings."[44]

(4) Rossi's "Songs of Solomon" are described by Modena as marking a renascence of Hebrew music after Biblical example. By glorifying music of the ancient liturgy and treating Rossi's "Songs" as its worthy successor, Modena hoped to dismantle whatever opposition to them did or might arise. How could anyone dispute the wonders of ancient song? How could anyone deprecate Salamone Rossi for wishing to restore music "to its ancient estate as in the days of the Levites on their dais [in the Temple]"?[45] Like the wise men of old, Rossi has "reached great heights in this science." Among his coreligionists, he is, in matters of music, "wiser than any other man," so much so as to compare advantageously with Christian musicians.[46] Music as *scientia;* the composer as an erudite musician. How lucky we are, Modena exclaims, to "be favored . . . with so auspicious a beginning: a rainbow has appeared in our days in this man of knowledge." His songs should be taught to our children "so that they may understand the art of making music. Let the learned man teach the student as did the [elder] Levites."[47] (5) Rossi's "Songs" not only display a new form, but, in their emphasis on rejoicing, they exude a new spirit. Rossi tells us that man has been given his voice in order to honor his Maker.[48] He warns anyone suspecting him of effrontery that the songs were composed "not for [his] own glory but for the glory of [his] Father in heaven." They are designated "for the times of rejoicing and the goodly seasons." It follows that we should "rejoice in the depths of [our] heart and find gladness in them."[49] From now on, Modena predicts, "the public will glorify, men of Israel will sing joyfully on the festivals and at the cyclical recurrence of the religious rites."[50]

In his *responsum* on the legitimacy of polyphony in the synagogue service, Modena maintains that the rabbinical authorities concur on the essential role played by music in creating "a joyous mood for the Torah."[51] Modena sought to accord polyphonic composition with rabbinical views on music. By a selective reading of the Talmudic and Midrashic literature, he showed that there was nothing there specifically to prevent the polyphonic rendition of Hebrew texts. He does not specify the differences between cantillation, prayer melodies, improvisation and polyphony. Rather he refers to music in general, implying that it is relatively immaterial which kind of music one uses provided one does so "for His glory."[52] Two kinds of rejoicing are distinguished: music for secular entertainments (feasting, carousing, royal diversions), music for religious observances. Modena rejects the first kind, asking how it is possible "to rejoice when our sanctuary is in ruins and we are in exile."[53] But he accepts the second, concluding that "Rashi, *Tosafot* [i.e., additions to Talmud], Maimonides and all the great authorities forbade music solely in connection with feasting and regal luxury while they permitted it in all other situations."[54] The only rejoicing allowed is that in connection with worship. "No intelligent person, no scholar ever thought of forbidding the use of the greatest possible beauty of voice in praising the Lord."[55]

III

So far I have considered the efforts to reconcile polyphony with the Jewish tradition. But Rossi and Leone da Modena seem to have had an additional end in mind: to integrate Jewish music, in its refurbished form, into a non-Jewish world. Leone's remark that Rossi took from the profane (e.g., Italian madrigals) to add to the sacred[56] suggests that, potentially, the "Songs of Solomon" could have been heard by two audiences, one Jewish, another Gentile. His other remark to the effect that the Jews will no longer be vilified for their crude music[57] suggests that, stylistically, the "Songs" were so designed as to meet the approval of any discriminating Gentiles who happened to hear them. Thus Rossi and Modena appear to be playing to two different groups of listeners, and from this standpoint the "Songs" can be treated as an attempt at cultural mediation.[58]

Neither audience could be counted on for its support. The Jews had to be won over to a new variety of Jewish music, which meant breaking down any resistance to change. The Gentiles had to be won over to Jewish music itself, which meant revising their impressions of it, from their occasional visits to the synagogue,[59] as a "braying of asses" (Modena's words).[60] Thus where innovation had to be justified for the Jewish audience, it had to be demonstrated to the Gentile one; justified, for the first, as a renewal of ancient music, demonstrated, for the second, as an example of art music. The whole point was for the Jews to recuperate their ancient skills in order for the Gentiles not to fault them for lack of learning. "No longer will arrogant opponents heap scorn on the Hebrew folk," Modena writes. "They will see that it too possesses understanding, the equal of the best endowed. Though it may be weak when it comes to dealing blows, yet it is mighty as the oak in wisdom."[61]

Where, for the Jewish audience, the appeal to ancient tradition was intended to enhance their pride in the past, for the Gentile one it was intended to emphasize the primacy of Jewish culture over all others. Hebrew music is presented as the original music; other nations learned music from the Hebrews, we are informed.[62] The implication is that the Gentiles are musically inferior to the Hebrews, for where the Hebrews were originators the Gentiles were imitators.

The "Songs of Solomon" stand between two cultures, as did their composer Salamone Rossi. They are based on Hebrew texts, yet are made palatable to Gentiles by being written as part music. Or from an opposite viewpoint, they are written as part music, yet are made palatable to Jews by being based on Hebrew texts. What I am describing might sound like a classic case of Jewish assimilation, but it is not so easily described. Actually, it falls into the category of cultural fusions, whereby disparate styles come together on common ground, losing some of their particularity in the course of their mutual accommodation. Perhaps the chief disparity between Jewish and Gentile forms of music, then and now, resides in their languages, meaning Hebrew on the one hand and Italian or Latin on the other. I am not referring to the substantive differences between texts of Jewish and those of non-Jewish content. Rather I mean morphological differences in grammar and syntax as a determinant for pitches, their durations, their groupings. No matter how advanced the process of acculturation, it cannot erase the initial linguistic discrepancies that, musically, reflect in subtle, though significant discrepancies in melody, rhythm and phrasing. A Latin motet owes as much to the peculiarities of its language as a Hebrew song of Rossi's to those of its own, or so it would seem; the question of what makes the one musically Latin and the other musically Hebrew remains to be answered, but that is a subject for another study.[63]

Where the gap between Hebrew and non-Hebrew songs can be narrowed is not in language but in certain areas of musical style. To accommodate his works to two audiences, Rossi simplified the style of Gentile music, of his own madrigals, for example, by reducing it to its basic lineaments. The general tendency in his Hebrew works is toward moderation. It may be heard in their melodic plainness, their chordal progressions, their declamatory rhythms; they are unassuming works, without ornament, without affectation. Moderation in music corresponds to the general socio-behavioral tendency, in the Jewish Diaspora, to neutralize such signs of individuality as might make the Jews an object of criticism. Mantuan Jews were subject to the constraints enforced in their sumptuary laws, first published in 1599.[64] These laws were meant to strengthen the moral and religious fiber of Jewish life and to protect the Jews in their contacts with Gentiles. Their general thrust is, in either direction, toward an elimination of extravagance. Rossi's moderation was similarly double-edged. It was meant to show the Jews that his "Songs" were not clothed in the advanced harmonic, rhythmic and melodic idioms of secular music, but in a reserved, undemanding, hence relatively innocuous style designed to serve one purpose: that of emphasizing the words, in their sacred content, in their ritual functions. It was meant to show the Gentiles that the "Songs" need not be feared as possible competition with Christian works; rather in their simplicity they could be accepted as modest examples of Jewish craftsmanship, posing no threat, proving no arrogance. Just as Rossi must have behaved discreetly in his life style, so he did in his musical style. Discretion as "the better part of valor" preserved Rossi from awakening the antagonism of opponents, real or imagined, within the Jewish and Christian communities.

IV

By signalling Rossi's "Songs of Solomon" as an instance of stylistic accommodation, it is imperative at this point to return to the question of Rossi's innovations and reassess them. So far the "Songs" have been discussed for their historical and cultural import, namely, for being the first printed collection of Hebrew polyphonic works and for being a collection whose contents can be read in the double sense of a Christianization of Jewish music and a Hebraization of Christian music. Musically speaking, though, there is a problem: can the moderate style chosen by Rossi as a means of effecting his cultural merger be related to stylistic innovation? Would it not seem rather to indicate paucity of invention? Or said otherwise: would not the simple, chordal, unaffected writing of the "Songs" characterize them as conservative?

I propose that precisely because they are conservative, they are novel.

In an era where it was the fashion, in choral music, to be madrigalistic, to be melodically and rhythmically diversified, we find a collection that is purposely plain, purposely restrained. This in itself is unusual.[65] Actually, there is a corresponding trend in Renaissance literary and music criticism: the slogan "imitazione della natura" had many meanings, but one of them was a call for simplicity, for intelligibility.[66] Straightforward, declamatory music was on the upswing in the sixteenth century, in conformity with humanistic ideas on the character of ancient melos.[67] Rossi's "Songs" form a complement to the strikingly chordal, oratorical innovations of the sixteenth and early seventeenth centuries: they include the German humanistic ode, the Protestant chorale, the *vers mesurés à l'antique,* the stark choruses of Andrea Gabrieli for the presentation of Sophocles' tragedy *Oedipus rex* in 1585 or the effective chordal writing in various madrigals by Marenzio and Monteverdi. All of them strike a new note in the otherwise prevailingly contrapuntal practice of their time.

Another point that might seem to militate against considering the "Songs" for their novelty is their musical eclecticism: that is, the mixture of Hebrew speech, implying certain intrinsic kinds of rhythm and phrasing, with a variety of stylistic *maniere* drawn from Italian secular and sacred composition. Here and there we have reminiscences of the madrigal, of the light canzonetta, of the double choruses *(cori spezzati)* of Venetian ecclesiastical music, of choral monody, of echo writing, of psalmodic recitation. But, again, I propose that in its very eclecticism the collection is novel. It is no less novel than the manneristic poetry of that most eclectic of early Baroque poets, Giambattista Marino, with its hybrid fusion of old and new, cliché and *bon mot,* ordinary and surprising, bland and brilliant.[68] Nor is it any less novel than the theatrical works of that most eclectic of early Baroque dramatists Giovanni Battista Andreini, who, in his *favole,* his comedies and his tragedies, mingled genres, styles, character types, places, times and actions to create an effective spectacle.[69]

Perhaps what is particularly novel about the collection is that, in its mixed Hebrew-Italian components, it creates an aura of ambiguity about its contents. By relating to different sources and styles, the contents can thus be differently construed. The ambiguities of the music connect with the ambiguities in the intentions and inclinations of its composer (Rossi) and its commentator (Modena). It is uncertain what they expected to gain by forming Hebrew music after an Italian model: to improve the image of Jewish song in the eyes of the Christian majority? to protect the Jews from becoming a laughingstock for their whining and wailing in synagogue music? to "revive" Hebrew music after centuries of stagnation, thus providing a solid basis for further development? And what exactly is meant by revival? A resuscitation of ancient Temple music? A reinvigoration of a developmentally dormant synagogue music? On the one hand, Rossi is described as having "restored music" to its ancient estate as in the days of the Levites;[70] on the other, as having "made a beginning which will not cease, the like of which has never been known in Israel."[71]

If Rossi "revived" ancient music, it is not clear whether he did so in status, that is, in the importance accorded to music in the Temple, or in style. By style, I mean the vague notions of Biblical music spread by commentators like Abraham Portaleone, who, in his treatise glorifying the ancient Temple, described the polyphonic use of voices and instruments in its ritual.[72] As to instruments, they would seem to be of no relevance to the "Songs of Solomon." But just because the "Songs" are written for voices only does not rule out the possibility of their having been furnished, on various occasions, with an instrumental accompaniment. True, Leone da Modena, in his *responsum*, summarized rabbinical authorities to the effect that instrumental music is prohibited.[73] Yet he allows the use of voices and instruments for wedding festivities.[74] As we know from a letter of his about a "musical academy" he founded in Venice in the later 'twenties, some Hebrew texts were, in fact, performed to the sound of voices and instruments.[75]

Another uncertainty concerns the relation of the new repertoire of polyphonic Hebrew songs to the traditional synagogue music. Were the "Songs" meant to replace the older tradition or merely supplement it at certain times, particularly feast days or holidays *(mo'adei śimḥa, yamim tovim)?* One reads that the "Songs" are available to anyone who so desires to use them,[76] but the wording implies freedom of choice, not constraint. In one passage we learn that the "Songs" were designated for joyous singing on joyous occasions;[77] in another that they were designated for joyous singing "on all sacred occasions."[78]

On the subject of joyful song, it is not clear whether the "Songs" express true joy or only a simulated joy. Rossi asserted that he composed them to rejoice in his Maker.[79] Modena continued in this vein, noting that the "Songs" will put sighs and grief to flight.[80] But then he altered his tune, conceding that there can be little joy in a state of exile ("today . . . each of us sings with a bitter heart because of the shortness of spirit and the heavy bondage of our heavy exile, when only the mouth sings while the heart is full of pain").[81] All this will change, though, with the advent of the Messiah, who, by restoring the Hebrews to their home, will inaugurate a new era of joyful song ("singing will arise in the House of the Lord and in all the Congregation with joy and exultation over all His goodness"). Modena wavers, then, between the traditional view of music, upheld by the rabbis, who treated it as joyless so long as there is mourning over the destruction of the Temple, and another, more auspicious view, according to which music is as natural a vehicle for rejoicing in God as words themselves. What danger can there be in music if the words provide its content? "Are those individuals on whom the Lord has bestowed the ability to master the technique of music to be condemned if they use it for His glory?"[82]

V

The picture that emerges is one of a collection of "Songs" whose novelty resides in their moderation, their eclecticism, their ambiguity. These three characteristics confer multiple significances on the collection, which, phenomenologically speaking, builds on the neutrality and semantical inconclusiveness of its contents to impart different meanings to different audiences. How is it that this collection of Hebrew songs speaks in many tongues? How can it be related to such disparate tendencies as traditional synagogue music, ancient Temple music, Gentile music of the court, of the church? I will not hide behind the pat formulation of Hebrew music as the original music, hence the prototype for, and link between, later developments.[83] Rather I will look for connections and continuities, for those so-called "higher verities" that might, on a conceptual level, explain how the "Songs of Solomon" relate to their varying frames of reference.

It should be clear, from the outset, that we are dealing with a syncretistic collection that, as other products of Renaissance syncretism, resolves conflicts, harmonizes differences.[84] The basic tenor of the collection is compromise. Since the composer could not, hence would not introduce into the synagogue a totally extraneous conception of musical composition, such as writing for many voices in the excessively manner-istic style of the Italian madrigal, he was forced to strike a compromise —polyphony, yes, but so toned down as to accord, at least in its empha-sis on verbal intelligibility,with synagogue monophony. What makes the "Songs" particularly complex, and for that reason all the more commu-nicative, is that they not only effect a merger between two different styles of synagogue song, but also reduce the distance between two different repertories: the Jewish and the Gentile.

Indeed, the compromising tendency cannot be limited to Jewish music alone or in connection with other musical types. The Hebrew "Songs" assume additional meanings when one realizes that the process of com-promise seems to have been very much under way in music of the Church. In the latter two conceptions of song were in conflict: the polyphonic one, with its intricacies of voice handling, and the homo-phonic one, with its intentional simplicity and straightforwardness. The two were debated at the Council of Trent, and the Catholic church opted for homophony, even though in practice composers still cultivated poly-phony along with various shades of homophony, often combining the two in their works.[85] But the main point is that the Church, in principle, threw its weight behind a kind of music, viz., homophony, which, in its opinion, could be accorded with the venerable medieval tradition of Christian chant in its clarity, in its moderation. The Christian compro-mise seems to parallel the Jewish one in intent (reconciliation) and in content (chordal writing). Thus the "Songs of Solomon" can be viewed, from another angle, as reflecting a form of accommodation already achieved, in the later sixteenth century, within the Christian church.

We are still no closer to explaining the meaning of these conflations and concordances. The basic question was, and still remains, how does the collection of "Songs" mediate between divergencies to become a *concordia discors* or a *discordia concors?* I will consider it first from a Jewish, then from a Christian standpoint.

Three points might be mentioned as relevant to the linking process in Jewish music. The first is that, in introducing the collection, the com-poser and his commentator develop a broader conception of Jewish song than that traditionally known as prayer melody or cantillation. Jewish song is presented by them as a generic category of music, standing above a specific mode of realization. It subsumes monophonic and polyphonic song, in their many varieties, as parts of a whole. Jewish music thus becomes neutralized of any particularity to become a kind of musical meta-concept as variable in its denotation as the so-called Jewish culture to which it applies.

The second point follows as a corollary to the first: by conceiving Jewish song as a genus inclusive of its varying species, the composer and his commentator deny absolute value to traditional synagogue music. They treat the latter as relative to a certain cultural-historical framework, namely, the period of Jewish wanderings in the Diaspora. Yet in longing for a renewal of ancient Hebrew culture, and in setting their sights on a Messianic era, they acknowledge other historical kinds of song that range on an extended time scale from songs of old to new songs and songs forthcoming. Thus synagogue music is divested of its seemingly universal validity, or as much as was ascribed to it by rabbinical custom, to become one of various kinds of Jewish song. The polyphonic song that succeeded it, in the "Songs of Solomon," is not regarded as the ultimate song. Though it may be referred to or compared with ancient music in its learning, i.e., its compositional literacy and artistic refinement, it does not mark the end of a development. Rather it is designated a "beginning,"[86] and hence by definition it cannot be an end.

The third point is that Jewish music may be described not by style, but by spirit. Rossi and Leone da Modena emphasize its ritual importance. Central to Jewish worship, according to them, is the act of thanking and praising the Lord, of rejoicing in his omniscience, his omnipotence. Rossi tells us that he wrote the "Songs" to give thanks to Him . . . with a sound of gladsome thanksgiving . . . , to honor the Lord."[87] It was Rossi's intention, according to Modena, to provide us with "songs and hymns of praise . . . to honor the Lord of the universe as do the angels expressing praise."[88] Though we obviously know nothing about angels' songs, and unless Modena was privy to some secret information he was no better instructed than we, it is clear that they were as far removed from Rossi's music as Rossi's from traditional synagogue song. Yet, again, form is of no consequence here. What all three share is their reverent content, their reverent presentation.[89] Attention is directed away from the shapes of music to its purposes. Religious piety, like synagogue song itself, constitutes a category above the specific modes of its expression.

With regard to possible connections between Jewish and Gentile music, two points might be mentioned. The first is that, by and large, both kinds comply with the principle of verbal superiority. Words first, music next: the principle stands at the root of the Judeo-Christian musical experience; it forms the crux of humanistic trends in music of the Renaissance.[90] Thus, in theory, one can speak of a certain congruity among the widest varieties of musical expression, from cantillation to polyphonic Hebrew songs, madrigals, chansons, Masses, motets and more. I am, basically, talking about a logogenic versus a melogenic approach to music; the composer and the performer proceed by accommodating themselves to the structural and substantive demands of the words. Thus synagogue song and sundry kinds of Gentile music meet on the common ground of verbal primacy.

The second point is that, practically, the idea of verbal primacy reflects in a declamatory approach to music. The cantor intones his text with attention to the accentual and syntactical structure of its components; recitation is as much a part of traditional synagogue song, in its different varieties, as it is of the "Songs of Solomon," which have sometimes been described as choral monody.[91] Yet declamation is equally relevant to Protestant hymns, to large portions of chordal music for the Catholic church, to certain types of madrigals, to music in the secular theater, to choruses in the early opera, and last but not least to some of the most striking and innovative developments of the later sixteenth and early seventeenth centuries, namely, the solo monody and, in opera, the recitative.[92] Declamation has many forms then, from synagogue cantillation to dramatic recitative.

Going beyond these two points, that is, a word-oriented approach to music and its declamatory realization, and looking for an even broader principle to tie the most disparate pieces of musical experience into some sort of conflated whole, I would venture to say that the one item common to the Jewish and Christian musical traditions from their beginnings is the Psalm. Eric Werner's magisterial book of the late 'fifties, entitled "The Sacred Bridge," rests on the thesis of the psalmodic origins of Jewish and Christian song.[93] I should like to carry this argument one step further by premising the continuity of the psalmodic principle for large parts of Renaissance music. What do the "Songs of Solomon" share with Protestant chorales, with large portions of the motet and hymn repertories of the Christian composers? If anything, it is their emphasis on the "psalm." By "psalm," I mean both the literary canon of

150 psalms and psalms as songs of praise, of glorification, the psalm, that is, in the most elemental sense, as a paradigm for hymnody. Rossi described his collection as a mixture of "praises, hymns, and songs."[94] His intention was to "enhance the Psalms of David, King of Israel, and glorify them."[95] As his model, he could refer to the singing of psalms in the ancient Temple. Luther, in the preface to his *Wittemberg Gesangbuch* (1524), wrote that "the special custom of singing psalms has been known to everyone and to universal Christianity from the beginning."[96] The desire to honor and glorify the Lord is as intrinsic to Hebrew psalms and post-Biblical hymns as it is to Christian songs of praise. It forms the motivating impulse behind Rossi's "Songs of Solomon," which, as we already know, were composed "for the glory of [his] Father in Heaven."[97]

It should not be forgotten that one of the many themes in the Psalms is that of composing a New Song. It appears in several variations. As an instruction to others: "Sing unto the Lord a new song; play skillfully with a loud noise" (Psalm 33:3). As an instance of revelation: "And he hath put a new song into my mouth, even praise unto our God" (40:3). As a statement of purpose: "I will sing a new song unto thee, o God: upon a psaltery and instrument of ten strings will I sing praises unto thee" (144:9). The Renaissance was full of *cantica nova* in religious and secular spheres. Novelty became a desideratum that led composers to search for untried varieties of musical expression. There was a fashion for collections entitled "Musica nova" or "Nuove musiche."[98] And returning to Rossi, he, too, sought to renew, though staying within the traditional categories of religious hymnody. Rossi's *canticum novum* was his "Songs of Solomon," as impressive an achievement in Jewish music as were any new-styled sacred and secular compositions in Gentile music.

By trying to impose a single larger principle on a heterogeneous repertory of musical styles and forms, there is always the danger of slipping into circular argumentation and of turning a *reductio ad limitem* into a *reductio ad absurdum*. In some ways, the notion of the "psalm" helps to explicate the unity of diverse, often contradictory phenomena; in others, it does not. Yet for the notion to be confirmed or confuted, it obviously needs to be considered. I hope, in another study, to explore the broader implications of the "psalm" for an understanding of certain homologies between Jewish and Christian music. For the time being, I might mention that in the book of Daniel (5:16–17), the king approached the prophet with the words, "I am told that you are able to give interpretations and to unravel difficult problems." Though I cannot answer, along with Daniel, that I can read the handwriting on the wall, I am at least trying, and so should we all.

NOTES

1. *Inferno* III, 9.
2. *Ha-shirim asher li-shlomo* (Venice: Pietro & Lorenzo Bragadini, 5383 [according to Hebrew calendar]). The collection is available in two editions: the older one by Samuel Naumbourg, *Cantiques de Salomon Rossi hebreo* (Paris, 1877, repr. New York, 1954)—lacks three numbers, supplied by Eric Werner in his edition of *Three Hebrew Compositions for Mixed Chorus* (New York, 1956); and the more recent one by Fritz Rikko (New York, 1967–73), 3 vols.
3. *Canzonette*, 1589; four, perhaps even five books of madrigals for five voices (1600, 1602, 1603, 1610, 1622); one book of four-voice madrigals (1614); three, perhaps even four books of instrumental works (1607, 1608, 1613 [no longer extant; available in two later editions, as below], 1622). (The only collection to follow the *Shirim* is a book of *madrigaletti* for two-three voices, 1628.) Several collections were reprinted: Book I of five-voice madrigals, 1603, 1607, 1612 (lost), 1618; Book II of same, 1605 (lost), 1610; Book III of same, 1620 (lost); Book IV of same, 1613; Book III of instrumental works, 1623, 1638; Book IV of same, 1642. The number of reprints preceding the *Shirim* is eight, possibly nine, which means that anywhere from seventeen to twenty collections of Rossi's music were issued before 1622/23 (there may have been others, for up to ten further editions mentioned in the sources either have been lost or cannot be authenticated).
4. All translations of texts from the introductory matter to the "Songs of Solomon" are quoted from Rikko's edition, Vol. III, hereafter *Shirim* (see, for present quotation, p. 19). For a critical reading of the Hebrew originals, see Israel Adler, ed., *Hebrew Writings Concerning Music in Manuscripts and Printed Books from Geonic Times up to 1800* (Munich, 1975), pp. 212–21, 285–88.
5. Salomon Sulzer, *Shir zion* ("Song of Zion"), a collection of four-voice works for the reformed synagogue service (Vienna, 1840/66), 2 vols. See Avraham Zvi Idelsohn, *Jewish Music in its Historical Development* (New York, 1929, repr. 1967), pp. 246–60, also Eric Mandell, "Salomon Sulzer 1804–1890," *The Jews of Austria* (London, 1967), pp. 221–29.
6. In particular, Shlomo Simonsohn, *Toledot ha-yehudim be-dukasut mantova* (Tel Aviv, 1962/64), 2 vols.; Engl. tr. "The History of the Jews in the Duchy of Mantua," (Jerusalem, 1977), Chap. 7; Israel Adler, "The Rise of Art

Music in the Italian Ghetto," *Jewish Medieval and Renaissance Studies*, ed. Alexander Altmann (Cambridge, Mass., 1967), pp. 321–64, esp. 340–47; idem, "La pénétration de la musique savante dans les synagogues italiennes au XVIIe siècle: le cas particulier de Venise," *Gli ebrei e Venezia: secoli XIV–XVIII*, ed. Gaetano Cozzi (Milan, 1987), pp. 527–35; and Massimo Torrefranca, " 'I Canti di Salamone' di Salamone Rossi: un caso di confluenza fra tradizioni italiane ed ebraiche nel primo Seicento" (unpubl. *tesi di laurea*, University of Rome, 1986); Torrefranca is now preparing a doctoral dissertation on Rossi's *Shirim* at Hebrew University.

7. Don Harrán, "Salamone Rossi, Jewish Musician in Renaissance Italy," *Acta musicologica* LIX (1987), 46–64, esp. 53–64. Though the title ends with a period (here comma), it might, for present purposes, be imagined as ending with a question mark. For another study, treating Rossi's and Modena's prefaces in a broader conceptual context, see idem,"Cultural Fusions in Jewish Musical Thought of the Later Renaissance," in a volume of essays for Nino Pirrotta on his eightieth birthday (1988, forthcoming).

8. Beyond the items mentioned above, the major studies of Rossi's life and works are Eduard Birnbaum, *Jüdische Musiker am Hofe von Mantua von 1542–1628* (Vienna, 1893; rev. and tr. into Ital. 1967, into Hebr. 1975), esp. pp. 16–35; Joel Newman, "The Madrigals of Salamon de' Rossi" (Ph.D. dissertation, Columbia University, 1962); Franco Piperno, "I quattro libri di musica strumentale di Salamone Rossi," *Nuova rivista musicale italiana* XIII (1979), 337–57; Don Harrán, "Salamone Rossi as a Composer of Theater Music," *Studi musicali* XVI (1987), 95–131. For fuller bibliography, see the listings at the end of Newman's dissertation and of his and Fritz Rikko's *Thematic Index to the Works of Salamon Rossi* (Hackensack, New Jersey, 1972). The writer is preparing a critical edition of Rossi's Collected Works (to be published, in twelve volumes, by the American Institute of Musicology); in this connection, he thanks the Israel National Academy of Sciences for continued support, over the past several years, toward its realization.

9. For general writings on the Gonzagas in Mantuan history, see, among others, Maria Bellonci, *Segreti dei Gonzaga*, 2nd rev. ed. (Venice, 1974); Selwyn Brinton, *The Gonzaga—Lords of Mantua* (London, 1927); Giuseppe Coniglio, *I Gonzaga* (Milan, 1967); also variously in *Mantova: la storia, le lettere, le arti*, ed. Giuseppe Coniglio, Emilio Faccioli & Giovanni Paccagnini (Mantua, 1958–65), 9 vols. in 11; *Mantua e i Gonzaga nella civiltà del Rinascimento* (Mantua, 1977).

10. For studies on the status of the Jews in sixteenth- and seventeenth-century Italy, see, beyond the major work on Mantua by Shlomo Simonsohn, cited above, Salo Wittmayer Baron, *A Social and Religious History of the Jews* (New York, 1952–83), 18 vols. esp. Vols. IX–XIV; Attilio Milano, *Storia degli ebrei in Italia* (Turin, 1963), esp. pp. 212–337, 459–551; Cecil Roth, *A History of the Jews in Italy* (Philadelphia, 1946), esp. Chap. 5; idem, *The Jews in the Renaissance* (Philadelphia, 1959), esp. Chaps. 1–3; Moses A.

Shulvass, *Ḥayei ha-yehudim be-iṭalya bi-tqufat ha-renesans* (New York, 1955); Engl. tr. "The Jews in the World of the Renaissance" (Leiden, 1973). (Further writings could be listed for separate cities: Florence, Milan, Padua, Venice, and so on.) For a contemporary account of the sad events of the years 1627–31, see Abramo Massarani, *Sefer ha-galut we-ha-padut* (Venice, 1634); facs. ed. plus Ital. tr. as *L'esilio e il riscatto: le vicende degli ebrei mantovani tra il 1627 e il 1631* (Bologna, 1977).

11. Proposed by him at the First International Congress of Jewish Music in Paris, 1957.

12. For general writings on music in Mantua, including that of Rossi's Christian contemporaries (e.g., Gastoldi, Pallavicino, Wert), see Stefano Davari, "Musica a Mantova" (orig. 1885; repr. Mantua, 1975); Antonio Bertolotti, *Musici alla corte dei Gonzaga in Mantova dal secolo XV al XVIII* (Milan, 1890; repr. Geneva, 1978); and Iain Fenlon, *Music and Patronage in Sixteenth-Century Mantua* (Cambridge, 1980/82), 2 vols.

13. Two examples will suffice: the Christianization of pagan myths (Marsilio Ficino; see n. 84 below) and, from the Jewish sphere, the classicization of Biblical literary analysis (Judah Messer Leon). For syncretistic operations in Christian Hebraic thought, with particular regard to Kabbalah, see François Secret, "Pico della Mirandola e gli inizi della cabala cristiana," *Convivium* XXV (1957), 31–47; idem, *Les cabbalistes chrétiens de la Renaissance* (Paris, 1964); Chaim Wirszubski, *Shelosha peraqim be-toledot ha-qabala ha-noẓrit* ("Three Studies in Christian Kabbalah" [Jerusalem, 1975]); and Gershom Scholem et al., *Kabbalistes chrétiens* (Paris, 1979). On the same from a Jewish point of view, see Roberto Bonfil, "Cultura e mistica a Venezia," *Gli ebrei e Venezia*, pp. 472–74, 478–79, and on a broader scale, Moshe Idel, "The Magical and Neoplatonic Interpretations of the Kabbalah in the Renaissance," *Jewish Thought in the Sixteenth Century*, ed. Bernard D. Cooperman (Cambridge, Mass., 1986), pp. 186–242. For its application to Jewish musical thought, see Moshe Idel, "The Magical and Theurgic Interpretation of Music in Jewish Sources from the Renaissance to Hassidism," *Yuval, Studies of the Jewish Music Research Center* IV (1982), 33–62 (in Hebrew).

14. The chief writings on synagogue song are Idelsohn, *Jewish Music in its Historical Development* (see n. 5 above); Hyman Harris, *Toledot ha-negina we-ha-hazanut be-yisra'el* ("History of 'Negina' and Cantorial Singing in Israel" [New York, 1950]). On Italy, see, for a quick orientation, Leo Levi, "Italy: Musical Tradition," *Encyclopaedia Judaica* (Jerusalem, 1971), 18 vols., IX, 1142–47. For an anthology of Hebrew songs, of recent vintage, from the Roman synagogue, see Elio Piattelli, ed., *Canti liturgici ebraici di rito italiano, trascritti e commentati* (Rome, 1967).

15. See "Salamone Rossi, Jewish Musician in Renaissance Italy," esp. pp. 53–64. On Modena, see, among numerous writings, Adolfo Ottolenghi, "Leon da Modena e la vita ebraica del ghetto di Venezia nel secolo XVII," *La Rassegna Mensile di Israel* XXX–VII (1971), 739–63 (orig. publ. in *Rivista*

di Venezia, 1929); Cecil Roth, "La vita travagliata di Leone da Modena," *Gli ebrei in Venezia* (Rome, 1933), pp. 243–60; and most recently, Howard E. Adelman, "Success and Failure in the Seventeenth-Century Ghetto of Venice: The Life and Thought of Leon Modena, 1571–1648" (Ph.D. dissertation, Brandeis University, 1985).

16. From first dedicatory poem; *Shirim,* 11.

17. *Shirim,* 7. The next two quotations are drawn from the same.

18. From title. In the second dedicatory poem (by Modena), we read that the composer "set the words of [David's] psalms organized [into parts] . . ." (*Shirim,* 21).

19. Modena's expression (from his *responsum* on polyphonic music, written in 1604, yet also appended to Rossi's collection); *Shirim,* 23.

20. On their application to music, see Don Harrán, "The Concept of Elegance in Sixteenth-Century Music Theory," *Renaissance Quarterly* XLI/3 (1988), forthcoming.

21. *Le istitutioni harmoniche* (Venice, 1558; facs. repr. New York, 1965), from Proem, p. 2 (". . . a mostrar la via del componer musicalmente con ordine bello, dotto et elegante"). On Zarlino as a musical rhetorician, see Don Harrán, *Word-Tone Relations in Musical Thought from Antiquity to the Seventeenth Century* (Stuttgart, 1986), esp. pp. 189–217; and idem, *In Search of Harmony: Hebrew and Humanist Elements in Sixteenth-Century Musical Thought* (Stuttgart, 1988), pp. 137–73, esp. Chap. 9 on "music and rhetoric."

22. *Sefer nofet ẓufim* (Mantua, 1475/76; facs. repr. Jerusalem, 1981), or in its recent critical edition and translation by Isaac Rabinowitz, "The Book of the Honeycomb's Flow" (Ithaca, 1983).

23. From his Dedication; *Shirim,* 7.

24. From Leone's Foreward; *Shirim,* 18.

25. From first dedicatory poem; *Shirim,* 11.

26. In his *responsum; Shirim,* 28.

27. *Yalqut shim'oni, 1* Kings *remez* 221; quoted by Modena in same (*Shirim,* 29).

28. In his approbation of Modena's *responsum; Shirim,* 33.

29. Cf. "The Rise of Art Music in the Italian Ghetto," pp. 342–43.

30. As I already noted elsewhere: cf. "Salamone Rossi, Jewish Musician in Renaissance Italy," pp. 58–59.

31. A single voice *(canto secondo)* from a handwritten miscellany of twenty-one prayers and *piyutim,* originally composed for an eight-voice double choir; in the Eduard Birnbaum Collection, Hebrew Union College (Cincinnati, Ohio), Ms. 4 F 71. Cf. Eric Werner, "The Eduard Birnbaum Collection of Jewish Music," *Hebrew Union College Annual* XVIII (1943–44), 397–428, esp. 407–17 (Werner ascribed them to Leone da Modena, who, he believed, could have composed them from 1630 on). The collection appears as no. 133 in Israel Adler's inventory of *Hebrew Notated Sources in Manuscripts up to 1840,* pp. 395–401 (forthcoming), where it is dated anywhere from

1605 to 1639 (I wish to thank Professor Adler for allowing me to consult proofs of the relevant pages prior to publication).

32. Modena mentions six to eight musicians who, in Ferrara, around 1605, "raised their voices in songs ... to the glory of the Lord in an orderly relationship of the voices in accordance with the science of music" (in the "question" to which he provided his *responsum; Shirim*, 23). In a letter from the same period to the Venetian rabbi Judah Saltaro da Fano, he confirms that after he moved to Ferrara (in 1604), a group was formed for cultivating "the science of music" (*Igrot rabi yehuda arye mi-modena* ["Letters of Rabbi Leon Modena"], ed. Yacob Boksenboim [Tel Aviv, 1984], pp. 110–11).

33. Modena's words; *Shirim*, 18. In the Dedication, Rossi thanks his patron Moses Sullam for encouraging him to work hard at finding "the proper form for the utterance of songful lips" (*Shirim*, 8). The process of "sowing" and "planting" a new kind of Hebrew song (cf. n. 16 above) is not likely to have been completed overnight.

34. In his Foreword (*Shirim*, 19).

35. Not to speak of personal difficulties: Modena lost his son, and was not particularly inclined to "listen to the voice of singers" (loc. cit.). On the topos of fathers mourning sons in writings from fifteenth-century Italy, see George W. McClure, "The Art of Mourning: Autobiographical Writings on the Loss of a Son in Italian Humanist Thought (1400–1461)," *Renaissance Quarterly* XXXIX (1986), 440–75 (it may be traced back, in a literary tradition, to Quintilian; see p. 444n. for relevant bibliography).

36. Otherwise it is hard to explain why Rossi and Modena mobilized such heavy artillery as appears in the extensive introductory matter (two prefaces, two dedicatory poems, an early plea for polyphony [Leone's *responsum*], five rabbinical statements of approbation, a copyright declaration).

37. See above, n. 24.

38. Rossi, speaking of Moses Sullam and his parents: "I have chosen to take shelter under the shade of your distinction, and you have spread the protection of your glory over me and over the work of my hands. I am bound by the cords of the kindness and goodness which you and your noble parents (may they rest in peace) have bestowed on me" (*Shirim*, 8); Modena, speaking of the new enthusiasm for Rossi's works: "Then some individuals and especially the generous and ever praiseworthy, honored Master Moses Sullam (may God on high preserve him) pressed him and he agreed to have them printed" (ibid., 18). Modena himself, from the time he became Rossi's friend, "urged him strongly with many words of persuasion . . ." (ibid., 19).

39. For information on Mantuan synagogues, see Simonsohn, *Toledot ha-yehudim be-dukasut mantova*, II, 412–15. Though the Jewish community was relatively small (in 1612, some 2,325 Jews were resident in the city of Mantua, out of a total population of 50,000; after ibid., I, 140–41), it had not one, but several synagogues, some of them were maintained in private homes. The story of Mantua's synagogues in the later sixteenth and early

seventeenth centuries is yet to be written. It will have to take into account differences in ethnic rites (particularly Ashkenazic and Italian), with their concomitant differences in musical practices. Until such data are available, we cannot be certain how Rossi's works fit into the prayer services or how they were received.

40. For recent studies on this point, see Jacob Katz, "Post-Zoharic Relations between Halakhah and Kabbalah," *Jewish Thought in the Sixteenth Century* (as in n. 13 above), pp. 283–307; Isadore Twersky, "Talmudists, Philosophers, Kabbalists: The Quest for Spirituality in the Sixteenth Century," ibid., pp. 431–59; and Robert Bonfil, "Halakhah, Kabbalah and Society: Some Insights into Rabbi Menaḥem Azariah da Fano's Inner World," *Jewish Thought in the Seventeenth Century*, ed. Isadore Twersky & Bernard Septimus (Cambridge, Mass., 1987), pp. 39–61.

41. See above, n. 17. On divine inspiration as a topos in Renaissance literature, see this writer's "Salamone Rossi, Jewish Musician in Renaissance Italy," p. 56 (and n. 47).

42. Modena's Foreward; *Shirim*, 18.

43. "For wise men in all fields of learning flourished in Israel in former times. All noble sciences sprang from them. . . . Music was not lacking among these sciences. They [the wise men] possessed it in all its perfection" (ibid.; *Shirim*, 17).

44. From the portion indicated by dots of omission in previous footnote.

45. From second dedicatory poem; *Shirim*, 21.

46. "For he has been compared with, and considered the equal of, many of the famous men of yesterday among the families of the earth" (Modena's Foreward; *Shirim*, famous men of yesterday among the families of the earth" (Modena's Foreword; *Shirim*, 18).

47. Ibid.; *Shirim*, 20.

48. Rossi's Dedication, *Shirim*, 7; see there for next two quotations as well.

49. Second dedicatory poem; *Shirim*, 21.

50. Modena's Foreword; *Shirim*, 19.

51. *Shirim*, 27.

52. Ibid., 29.

53. Ibid., 27.

54. Ibid., 30.

55. Ibid., 29.

56. His Foreword; *Shirim*, 18.

57. Second dedicatory poem; *Shirim*, 22.

58. I have pursued this theme at length in another study ("Cultural Fusions in Jewish Musical Thought of the Later Renaissance"; see n. 7 above).

59. The synagogues were open to curious passers-by. Duke Vincenzo usually visited the Great Synagogue during Carnival, and his successors continued the custom on this and other occasions. Cf. Simonsohn. *Toledot ha-yehudim*, II, 483, 486–87n.

60. From his *responsum; Shirim*, 29. Modena continues: "Shall they [the Gen-

tiles] say that ... we cry out to the God of our fathers like dogs and ravens?" Pietro Cerone, in his *El melopeo y maestro* (Naples, 1613; facs. repr. Bologna, 1969), said of singers who try to improvise embellishments simultaneously that they sound like a "synagogue of Hebrews" (p. 550). Parodies of Hebrew song may be found in works by Andrea Banchieri, for example, his *Barca di Venetia per Padova* (1605), p. 18 ("La trainana. Ste su a sentì ol noster Samuel. Sinagoga di Hebrei"); his *Canzonette* (1597), p. 20 ("Samuel, Samuel. Mascherata di Hebrei"); or his *Studio dilettevole* (1600), p. 32 ("Tich tach tich tach. O Hebreorum gentibus. Sinagoga di hebrei"). Orazio Vecchi was no less caustic in his own works, for example, his *L'Amfiparnaso* (1597), p. 33 ("Tich tach, tich tach"); or his *Veglie di Siena* (1604), from the section *Chiusa del gioco* ("Corrit, corrit, messer Aron, che gli Goi. Imitatione delli hebrei"). Here and there, in the literature, one finds a piece entitled *ebraica*, as in Filippo Azzaiolo's *Villotte del fiore alla padoana*, Book III (1569), p. 4 ("Adonai con voi, lieta brigada").

61. Second dedicatory poem, p. 22. For a similar passage in the Prologue to Leone de' Sommi's Hebrew play "A Comedy of Betrothal" *(Ẓaḥut bediḥuta de-qidushin)*, from the 1550s, see Chaim Schirmann's edition of same (Jerusalem, 1965), p. 29: "They believed the sons of the Hebrews to be deprived and deficient because until now no pleasure or profit could be derived from their stories or books. ... The Hebrew language falls behind no other language of the Gentiles in any of their works of art" (spoken by *Hokhma*, "Wisdom"); my translation. On Sommi in relation to Rossi, and vice versa, see Don Harrán, "Jewish Artists in the Renaissance: Separate Activities, Common Questions," (forthcoming in proceedings of the conference, "Leone de' Sommi and the Performing Arts in Mantua," June, 1988).

62. Modena refers to the statement of the fourteenth-century poet and friend of Dante's, Imanuel of Rome, from his "Notebooks" (VI, 172), as to the primacy of Hebrew music: "What does the science of music say to the other peoples? 'Indeed, I was stolen out of the Land of the Hebrews' " (after Genesis 40:15); cf. *Shirim*, 17. On the motif of Hebrew singularity, see Reuven Bonfil, "Biṭuyim li-yeḥud 'am yisra'el be-iṭalya bi-tqufat ha-renesans" ("Expressions of the Uniqueness of the Hebrew People in [Writings of] the Italian Renaissance"), *Sinai* LXXVI (1974), 36–46, with references to further literature. For the process of idealization in the political sphere, see the chapter entitled "The Biblical Hebrew State as an Example of Ideal Government in the Writings of Political Thinkers in the Seventeenth and Eighteenth Centuries," in Saul B. Robinson, *Ḥinukh bein hemshekhiut li-ftihut* ("Education between Continuity and Openness"; Jerusalem, 1975), pp. 13–69.

63. No work has been done on this crucial subject, though it belongs to an area of research with considerable potential for illuminating basic discrepancies between national song repertories. Any analysis of Hebrew song would have to take into account the morphological, accentual and intonational particularities of Hebrew, testing their effect on the various parameters of musical

construction. The results would then have to be compared with those obtained for other linguistic song types, in a suitable sampling for the period in question.

64. On *pragmatica* as they regulate Jewish life in Mantua, see Simonsohn, *Toledot ha-yehudim*, II, 386–95.

65. On the Italian madrigal, see Alfred Einstein, *The Italian Madrigal* (Princeton, 1949; repr. 1971), 3 vols; on music in Mantua, see Fenlon, *Music and Patronage in Sixteenth-Century Mantua* (as in n. 12 above), and for neighboring Ferrara, Anthony Newcomb, *The Madrigal at Ferrara, 1579–1597* (Princeton, 1980), 2 vols.; on music in the Italian theater, see Wolfgang Osthoff, *Theatergesang und darstellende Musik in der italienischen Renaissance (15. und 16. Jahrhundert)* (Tutzing, 1969), also Nino Pirrotta, *Li due Orfei: da Poliziano a Monteverdi* (Turin, 1969; rev. ed. 1975).

66. On the doctrine of imitation in Renaissance literature, see, from an extensive bibliography, Hermann Gmelin, "Das Prinzip der Imitatio in den romanischen Literaturen der Renaissance," *Romanische Forschungen* XLVI (1932), 83–360; Ferruccio Ulivi, *L'imitazione nella poetica del Rinascimento* (Milan, 1959), esp. Chap. 4 ("L'imitazione nel pensiero del pieno Rinascimento," pp. 79–109); Eugenio Battisti, 'Il concetto d'imitazione nel cinquecento italiano," in "his *Rinascimento e Barocco* (Turin, 1960), pp. 175–215; G. W. Pigman III, "Versions of Imitation in the Renaissance," *Renaissance Quarterly* XXXIII (1980), 1–32; and with reference to Pietro Bembo, Giorgio Santangelo, *Il Bemo critico e il principio d'imitazione* (Florence, 1950). On the doctrine of imitation in music, see Armen Carapetyan, "The Concept of *Imitazione della natura* in the Sixteenth Century," *Journal of Renaissance and Baroque Music* I (1946), 47–67, and on a broader scale, Tibor Kneif, "Die Idee der Natur in der Musikgeschichte," *Archiv für Musikwissenschaft* XXVII (1971), 302–14; Howard Brown, "Emulation, Competition, and Homage: Imitation and Theories of Imitation in the Renaissance," *Journal of the American Musicological Society* XXXV (1982), 1–48; Don Harrán, *In Search of Harmony* (see n. 21 above), esp. Chap. 8 ("General Concepts: Imitation, *Melopoeia, Musica poetica"*); and for a later period, Walter Serauky, *Die musikalische Nachahmungsästhetik im Zeitraum von 1700 bis 1850* (Münster, 1929).

67. On the impact of humanism on sixteenth-century music, see Edward Lowinsky, "Humanism in the Music of the Renaissance," *Medieval and Renaissance Studies,* ed. Frank Tirro (Durham, North Carolina, 1982), pp. 87–200; Claude Palisca, *Humanism in Italian Renaissance Musical Thought* (New Haven, 1985); Don Harrán, *Word-Tone Relations in Musical Thought* (as in n. 21 above), Chap. 4 and passim, also *In Search of Harmony,* particularly Part II ("The Humanist Conception of Music"); and most influential of all, perhaps, as the first of its kind, Daniel Pickering Walker, *Der musikalische Humanismus im 16. und 17. Jahrhundert* (Kassel, 1949).

68. Marino appears with increasing frequency in Rossi's works, starting from his third book of five-voice madrigals (1603). The composer set thirty-seven

poems by him, drawn largely from his *Rime* (Venice, 1602), later entitled *La lira*. For Marino's impact on seventeenth-century vocal music, see R. Simon & D. Gidrol, "Appunti sulle relazioni tra l'opera poetica di G. B. Marino e la musica del suo tempo," *Studi secenteschi* XIV (1973), 81–187. The booklet *Doctoral Dissertations in Musicology* (Dec. 1985–Nov. 1986), ed. Cecil Adkins & Alis Dickinson (American Musicological Society, 1987), p. 11, lists the following work in progress: Peter G. Laki, "Marinist Poetry and Vocal Music in Italy, 1600–1640" (Ph.D. dissertation, University of Pennsylvania).

69. For Rossi's connections with Andreini, see Don Harrán, "Salamone Rossi as a Composer of Theater Music," *Studi musicali* XVI (1987), 95–131, esp. 102–09 (with relevant bibliographical citations).

70. Second poem of dedication; *Shirim*, 21.

71. From Modena's Foreword; *Shirim*, 19.

72. *Shiltei ha-giborim* ("Shields of Heroes"; Mantua 1611/12), with musical portions reprinted as *Ha-shir she-ba-miqdash* ("The Song in the Temple"; Jerusalem, 1964/65) and in *Hebrew Writings Concerning Music* (as in n. 4 above), pp. 246–83. For an extended study, see Daniel Sandler, "Pirqei ha-musiqa be-sefer 'Shiltei ha-giborim' " ("The Musical Chapters in the Book 'Shields of Heroes' ") (Ph.D. dissertation, Tel Aviv University, 1980).

73. *Shirim*, 25 ("the first category, instrumental music, is the most stringently prohibited").

74. *Shirim*, 27 ("for even instrumental music and music-making while feasting, the two categories [ordinarily] most to be avoided, are permitted at a wedding").

75. The letter is quoted by Cecil Roth in his study "L'Accademia musicale del ghetto veneziano," *La Rassegna Mensile di Israel* III (1927–28), 152–62, at 160–61. Modena refers obliquely to "musici e di voci e di mano" ("vocal and instrumental musicians"). Giulio Morosini, a convert to Christianity, though originally Modena's student (as Samuel Naḥmias), describes the influx of Mantuan musicians, including instumentalists, after 1628, to Venice; with their arrival "si formò nel Gheto, che ivi stà, un'Accademia di Musica" (*Via della fede* [Rome, 1683], p. 793).

76. From second poem of dedication; *Shirim*, 22.

77. Rossi's Dedication; *Shirim*, 7 ("for times of rejoicing and the goodly seasons").

78. Second dedicatory poem; *Shirim*, 22 ("u-le-khol davar miẓwa"). Modena spoke, in his Foreword, of using the "Songs" on "the cyclical recurrence of the religious rites" ("ba-hidushim shel miẓwa"); *Shirim*, 19.

79. Dedication; *Shirim*, 7. Rossi is said, moreover, to have instructed the singers "with great gladness" (first dedicatory poem; *Shirim*, 12).

80. First dedicatory poem; *Shirim*, 11.

81. Modena's Foreword; *Shirim*, 20, for this and next quotation.

82. From Modena's *responsum; Shirim*, 29.

83. See above, notes 43–44, 62.

84. Syncretistic tendencies underlie many of the cultural mergings to be noted in Renaissance allegorical, mythological and philosophical commentaries. See, for example, Don Cameron Allen, *Mysteriously Meant: The Rediscovery of Pagan Symbolism and Allegorical Interpretation in the Renaissance* (Baltimore, 1970), also the by-now classic studies by Jean Seznec, *The Survival of the Pagan Gods: The Mythological Tradition and its Place in Renaissance Humanism and Art* (New York, 1953), and Edgar Wind, *Pagan Mysteries in the Renaissance* (London, 1956). One should not forget Daniel Pickering Walker's various writings on Neoplatonism, e.g., *Spiritual and Demonic Magic from Ficino to Campanella* (London, 1958), and *The Ancient Theology: Studies in Christian Platonism from the Fifteenth to the Eighteenth Century* (London, 1972). For literature on Kabbalah in Christian Hebraic and Jewish writings, see n. 13 above. On Moses as a member of the *prisca theologia* and his relevance to Renaissance musical thought, see Don Harrán, "Moses as Poet and Musician in the Ancient Theology,"*La musique et le rite, sacré et profane* (Strasbourg, 1986), 2 vols., II, 233–51. On Biblical narratives allegorically conceived, see idem, "Stories from the Hebrew Bible in the Music of the Renaissance," *Musica disciplina* XXXVII (1983), 235–88, esp. 252–56.

85. On the Council of Trent, and the effect of its decisions on Church music, see Raphael Molitor, *Die nach-Tridentinische Choral-Reform zu Rom: ein Beitrag zur Musikgeschichte des XVI. und XVII. Jahrhunderts* (Leipzig, 1901/02, 2 vols.; repr. 1967); Karl Weinmann, *Das Konzil von Trent und die Kirchenmusik* (Leipzig, 1919); and Karl Gustav Fellerer, "Church Music and the Council of Trent," *Musical Quarterly* XXXIX (1953), 576–94.

86. See n. 71 above.

87. From his Dedication; *Shirim*, 7.

88. From second poem of Dedication; *Shirim*, 22.

89. On reverence in an entirely different framework, namely, as a basic criterion for performing the Christian liturgy, see Don Harrán, *In Defense of Music: The Case for Music as Argued by a Singer and Scholar of the Late Fifteenth Century* (Lincoln, Nebraska, forthcoming), Chap. 4 and Appendix (concerning regulations of the Council of Basel, 1435).

90. The principle has been developed at great length in this writer's Word-Tone Relations in Musical Thought and *In Search of Harmony*. It may be subsumed under the general theme of humanism in music (see n. 67 above).

91. After the initial use of the term, for many of Rossi's madrigals, by Joel Newman ("The Madrigals of Salamon de' Rossi" [see n. 8 above], p. 127).

92. For the declamatory principle in Renaissance composition, see this writer's remarks in "The Concept of Battle in Music of the Renaissance," *The Journal of Medieval and Renaissance Studies* XVII (1987), 175–94, esp. 192–93.

93. Eric Werner, *The Sacred Bridge: Liturgical Parallels in Synagogue and Early Church* (New York, 1959; repr. of Part I, 1970).

94. After title ("mizmorim we-shirot we-tishbaḥot").

95. Rossi's Dedication; *Shirim*, 7. On the centrality of the Psalms in the Hebrew tradition, see Sigmund Mowinckel, *The Psalms in Israel's Worship*, tr. D.R. AP-Thomas (Oxford, 1962), and for their hymnal functions, pp. 81–105.

96. For English translation of Foreword, see Oliver Strunk, ed., *Source Readings in Music History* (New York, 1950; repr. 1965), pp. 341–42.

97. See n. 48 above.

98. For example, Adriano Willaert's *Musica nova* (Venice, 1559) or Giulio Caccini's *Nuove musiche* (Florence, 1601/02), followed by a second collection entitled *Nuove musiche e nuova maniera di scriverle* (Florence, 1614).

18

Baroque Trends in Italian Hebrew Poetry as Reflected in an Unknown Genre

Dan Pagis

Hebrew poetry flourished in Italy for more than a thousand years, longer than in any other country[1]. From the 10th to the 12th century it followed the classical Palestinian *piyyut* of the Byzantine period; from the middle of the 12th to the end of the 13th century it came under the influence of the famed Hebrew literary school of Spain; and from about 1300 to 1850 or even later it combined Hebrew-Spanish traditions with new elements which it adapted from Italian literature at its various stages. Thus the third period of Hebrew poetry in Italy also was the longest and most varied. However, since Immanuel of Rome, Dante's contemporary, was the first and probably the most famous author who combined Hebrew literary traditions and Italian literary innovations, scholars have often tended to oversimplify the subsequent history of this synthesis and considered all Italian elements in Hebrew poetry as belonging to the early Renaissance. This fallacy has been pointed out by Jefim Haim Schirmann and Joseph Sermoneta, who rightly claimed that this poetry reflected consecutive trends and schools in Italian literature: the early and high Renaissance, the Baroque period and the Arcadia.[2] Hebrew sonnets written in about 1300 by Immanuel of Rome differ from those written around 1640 by the brothers Frances just as any Italian sonnets of the "dolce stil novo" differed from those of the Marinismo.

Reprinted by permission of Istituto Polligrafico e Zeccia dello Stato from *Italia Judaica 2: Gli Ebrei in Italia Tra Rinascimento Ed Eta Barocca*, Atti del II Convegno internazionale, Genova 1984 (Rome 1986).

Evidently such differences were general and affected the very choice of forms, genres, style and ideas, as well as poetic theory, though the theory did not always keep pace with the practice. Hebrew treatises on prosody and poetics preceding Šamuel Archivolti's *Arugat ha-Bossem* (Venice 1602) did not yet acknowledge Renaissance Italian forms which at the time had already been used in Hebrew poetry[3]; but Immanuel Frances, in his treatise *Metek Sefatayim* (1678) not only presented these forms by their Italian names (*sonetto, ottava, canzone,* etc.) but gave them Hebrew names in order to fully integrate them. Moreover he encouraged his fellow-poets to use various post-biblical layers of Hebrew, in direct opposition to the medieval norm of biblical purism, and advocated the Baroque concept of 'acutezza', wit (which he termed 'ḥarifut') as the very essence of poetry[4]. Indeed 'ḥarifut' was the mainspring of ingenious conceits which abound in his own poetry, that of his brother Jacob, their friend Moses Zacut and others. Less than fifty years after Frances' book, Moses Haim Luzzatto (Ramḥa 1) in his treatise *Lešon Limmudim* (1724 and 1727)[5] already advocated neo-classical concepts, balance, harmony and decorum, which he realized in his own poems and plays.

Yet periodization is more complex than that, each stage being affected by both diachronic and synchronic factors. A strictly parallel development between the two literatures was anyway precluded by the inherent differences not only in language, but also in the stylistic traditions, religious life and social standing of the respective audiences. Hebrew poets who followed Italian models (and in the 17th century also Spanish models of the *siglo de oro*) produced adaptations, not imitations, and always blended influence with their own tradition. They were fully aware of this synthesis and quite early acclaimed it as an important literary and social end[6]. However, they did not always follow the latest trends and occasionally adapted earlier Italian forms or genres which were already considered obsolete in their original sphere. Conversely, Hebrew Renaissance and Baroque poets, though inspired by both innovation and tradition, occasionally produced genres or sub-genres with completely new patterns which nevertheless reflected the general trend of their period. Such an innovation could subsequently establish a tradition of its own and prolong its existence unchanged, though not unchallenged, after it had become an anachronism.

This chapter deals with a striking (though hitherto unknown) example of such complexities: a peculiar sub-genre of literary Hebrew riddles which first appeared around 1645 in Italy (probably Venice) and shortly afterwards in Spanish-Jewish circles in Amsterdam, and soon became a literary fashion in those two prominent centres of Baroque Hebrew poetry. These riddles had a peculiar pattern, headed by an enigmatic picture and comprising a long and intricate Hebrew poem with concealed Italian or Spanish key-words and many other encoding devices. By their complex structure and ingenious conceits, the emblem-riddles at their emergence were a typically Baroque or even mannerist product, yet they were still in vogue during the Arcadia period and even later. It was only after 1850 that they disappeared from the literary scene, falling into utter oblivion. For almost two centuries, however, they enjoyed a prominent status and were the core of riddling contests held at weddings and various other occasions, some within the Jewish 'academies' in Italy and Holland. New emblematic riddles were specially composed for every contest, printed as broadsides (fogli volanti) or copied in manuscripts to be distributed before the ceremony. We shall later return to their social and cultural role; first we must deal, however, briefly, with their specific textual traits, their complex structure and style.

Each of these peculiar riddles held at least two disparate sections. The first, an enigmatic picture (or a short verbal description of it) was known by the technical term 'ṣurat ha-ḥidah' (or similarly 'ṣiur ha-ḥidah)', the riddle's picture, or image. Its graphic media varied. In broadsides it usually was an etching, woodcut or blockprint; in manuscripts, a drawing, watercolour or collage[7]. Authors who reprinted their riddles in their collected works sometimes replaced the original etching or drawing by a cheaper and simpler medium (e.g. a blockprint) or even by a verbal description of the picture[8]. For similar financial and technical constraints authors would use a description even at the outset, in the original edition, but still call it 'ṣurat ha-ḥidah'. Indeed the graphic medium, though visually effective, was of secondary importance to its specific purpose; namely to conceal the riddle's subject while presenting clues needed for the riddle's solution, such as encoded icons, symbols alluding to the shape of letters or to their numerical value, and usually a combination of several devices.

In Italian and Spanish treatises Jewish writers variously translated the term 'ṣurat ha-ḥidah' by descriptive phrases such as 'figura dell'enimma' (Sp. 'figur del enigma') and by terms borrowed from other genres which were not proper riddles: 'emblema', 'impresa', or the Spanish 'jeroglyfico'[9]. In English Philip Sarchi, an apostate Italian Jew, wrote that in the these Hebrew riddles '... the object ... ought to be pointed out by an emblem, and accompanied by a motto alluding to it'[10]. Others, like Anania Hai Coen, though writing in Italian, simply referred to the 'ṣurat ha-ḥidah' by its Hebrew name, even in Hebrew script[11]. The absence of a fixed foreign term for this device seems to suggest that the 'ṣurah' had no counterpart in riddles written in other languages, although it had indirect sources, as we shall see.

The second main section of the emblem-riddles (as we shall call this sub-genre) was the 'body', an enigmatic poem in strict metre and rhyme, occasionally in the medieval monorhymed pattern of Hebrew-Spanish provenance, and more often in an Italian form adapted to Hebrew: *terza rima, ottava rima, sonetto, quartina* etc. This section, whose length varied but could expand to some 200 lines, was a dramatic monologue in which the riddle's subject, personified, cryptically described itself in paradoxical imagery and other devices. In most cases the structure comprised not only the obligatory 'ṣurah' and 'body' but additional sections as well. Those had their own technical terms: 'motto', 'mafteaḥ' (= key), 'pitron ha-ḥidah' (= the riddle's solution, in fact also an enigmatic part which had to be decoded, resulting in 'the solution to the riddle's solution', 'pitron le-pitron ha-ḥidah')[12]. Since each of these sections could be written in a different rhyme-scheme, structures of mammoth proportions sometimes emerged, for example, sestines, octaves, sonnets, quatrains and passages in rhymed or simple prose, headed by a picture, all in one riddle. The structural complexity was further exphasized by the typographical lay-out of the broadside; thus, the various sections would be headed by sub-titles in bold print stating their technical names.[13]

But it was of course the semantic complexity which presented the main challenge to the participants of the riddling contests. While the riddle's subject was often simple and traditional (silk, wheat, honour, love) and occasionally more learned or esoteric (the parabola, white as a mystical colour, the air as 'element'), the encoding technique was always highly sophisticated. The clues referred to virtually unlimited frames of reference: the Bible, Talmudic literature, classical mythology, baroque heraldry, music, alchemy, astrology, later also astronomy, chemistry, meteorology and other sciences, and at most times the Cabbala; several authors (including the first, Moses Zacut, to whom we shall return) were noted Cabbalists. Even more striking than the vast body of knowledge alluded to were the encoding techniques. Many of the devices were traditional and had individually been used in earlier Hebrew riddles: paradoxical imagery, meta-linguistic puns, letter combinations (anagrams, logogryphs, palindromes, 'notarikon') or the numerical value of letters ('gimatria' and its special variations such as 'kolél' or 'millui'). But whereas older Hebrew riddles relied on a single device or on very few, each emblem-riddle combined many if not most of such devices into unexpected patterns; moreover, it added novel devices, structural (and in themselves complex) like the ṣurah, as well as semantic. The most conspicuous among the novel semantic devices was called 'ha-lo'ez' (= the foreign language word). This was a pun based on bi-lingual homonyms and synonyms: the key-word denoting the riddle's solution was inserted in the Hebrew text of the 'body' in Italian (or Spanish) translation, but disguised as *another* Hebrew word which happened to sound like it. For example, the solution *Ahvah* (love) could be alluded to by the Hebrew phrase *Amor amarti* kan (literally: indeed here I said . . .), with the pun on AMOR. The 'lo'ez' could also be split and its syllables dispersed among several Hebrew words: *Nes po zoreaḥ* (literally: a miracle here shines), alludes to '. . s . . po . . so', *sposo*, bridegroom; or *kallah al hammittah* (literally: a bride on the bed) alludes to *calamíta*, magnet; and there were even stranger combinations. To further complicate matters the 'lo'ez' keyword could be omitted from the text and only alluded to by means of an additional pun. On the other hand, a sense of fair play obliged the authors to assist the reader (but also to tease him even more) by revealing to him the approximate hiding place of this device; within the relevant passage they would insert the technical term 'lo'ez' as a referential word; for example, *Amor amarti le-' am lo'ez* (= indeed I said to a foreign people) would imply that the foreign 'lo'ez' keyword should be looked for in that passage. Some emblem-riddles contained several such keywords, in different languages, and accordingly polyglot clues. For example, an 18th century Venetian author used Italian, Spanish, French, German and Aramaic keywords, all in one and the same Hebrew emblem-riddle[14].

Paradoxically, as it were, the 'lo'ez', the non-Hebrew keyword as a riddling device, was probably a specifically Hebrew invention. It had a general European background in the polyglot editions of sacred and secular writings, and the various macaronic mannerist works of that period (sonnets composed in three languages, etc.). Hebrew literature, too, had known various kinds of macaronic poetry since the Middle Ages, and later even developed a most ingenious device of simultaneous bi-lingual texts, i.e. a poem whose sound-combinations could be understood both in Hebrew and in Italian (though in each language in a different sense), like Leone Modena's dirge beginning "Qinnah shemor ..." with the paralleled sound pattern in Italian: "Chi nasce, muor ..."[15] Such mannerisms were used in other literatures, too. And yet the 'lo'ez' as an encoding device appears in Hebrew emblem-riddles only (except for three, in Italian, Spanish, and Portuguese respectively, all by Jewish authors who used *Hebrew* keywords, a sort of inverted 'lo'ez')[16]. The device seems to have had no counterpart in Italian, Spanish, or other European enigmas. Jewish Italian writers referred to it not by a technical term but by descriptive phrases such 'paronomasia maccheronica'; or 'la parola ebrea che espresso il soggetto con voce italiana'[17]; Sarchi described it in English thus: "the object of the riddle ... is ... to be named somewhere in the body of the poem both in Hebrew and in Italian; yet the writer is allowed to conceal these words as artfully as he can or pleases"[18]. Again, as with the ṣurah, the absence of a fixed Italian, Spanish or English term of the 'lo'ez' may suggest that it was an original encoding device.

What, then, was the origin of this sub-genre? In its genre affiliations, it had several direct and indirect sources:

a) Hebrew literary riddles preceding it, and written during the Middle Ages or the Renaissance (in Spain, 11th to 14th century, in Italy, between the 12th and the early 17th century)[19], yet these were usually shorter and always simpler and had no disparate sections, and of course no 'ṣurah' or 'lo'ez'.

b) the great number of Italian and Spanish literary riddles during the Baroque period, yet these usually were uniform poems (enigmatic sonnets, octaves, etc.) without complex structure, and, as far as I could ascertain, did not use enigmatic pictures such as the ṣurah-section; the pictorial riddles of the period, mainly the rebus, included no poem or scarcely any other text, except the sentence they encoded.

c) several genres of the late Renaissance and the Baroque which combined symbolic pictures and short texts, sometimes in poetic form, such as the emblems, then in vogue, the imprese and the Spanish jeroglyficos. All could have inspired the ṣurah-section, yet they were not themselves riddles and posed no challenge of decoding; their text (besides being short, unlike the 'body' of emblem-riddles) served to elucidate the emblematic picture, rather than obscure it further.

d) polyglot trends in Baroque literature and in Hebrew poetry of the time, including special devices such as simultaneous bi-lingual texts, which could have inspired the 'lo'ez'; yet these served to enhance the effect of a continuous correspondence between languages, openly and ingeniously represented, whereas the 'lo'ez' was an encoding device that concealed the keyword, the riddle's solution, somewhere in the Hebrew text.

All these possible sources, then, could explain only the *separate* elements in this peculiar sub-genre, not its overall structure and encoding techniques. For these I could find no close parallels.

It is then most probable that the emblem-riddles were an original novel composition which, though using several sources, selected only a few elements from each and combined them into a novel pattern. The first emblem-riddles emerged between 1645 and 1650 in Venice and Amsterdam and seemed to have been invented by a prominent man who was active in both these centres: Moses Zacut, the scholar, Cabbalist, poet and playwright. Born in Amsterdam in a Jewish-Spanish milieu, Zacut studied Cabbala in Poland and around 1645 settled in Italy. He served as rabbi in Venice and then Mantua where he died in 1698. Although he was influential in many fields including poetry, only part of his literary work has been published: the play *Yesod 'Olam*, the long dramatic poem in *Tofté Arukh*[20] and a collection of his devotional poems. Most of his secular and occasional poems are still in manuscript only; among them are 17 long poetic riddles, all headed by a ṣurah-section and some with 'lo'ez' (in Spanish keywords which were close to the Italian)[21]. Zacut probably invented the main novel devices ('ṣurah' and 'lo'ez'), and others.

He was also the first to give them their technical terms[22]. It was only after he had settled in Italy, around 1645, that emblem-riddles first appeared. In 1650 Jacob Frances already emulated Zacut as a prominent author of contrived riddles[23]. The fashion soon spread. In 1678 Immanuel Frances, Jacob's brother, while discussing the literary riddle in general, gave only two examples, both emblem-riddles of his own[24]. From

1652 onwards, Salomon de Oliveyra in Amsterdam composed typical emblem-riddles some of which he included in his Biblical story *Ayelet Ahavim* (Amsterdam 1667) making special mention of their ṣurah device[25]. Shortly after that Miguel (Daniel Levi) de Barrios composed several such riddles in Spanish; one, with Hebrew keywords (a sort of inverted 'lo'ez'), in honour of a 'ḥatan Bereshit' in 1684, was posed and solved in the Jewish-Spanish *Academia de los floridos*[26]. In 1724 Moses Ḥaim Luzzatto (Ramḥal) in his *Leshon Limmudim* described the Hebrew riddle as a genre (in more detail than any other genre, including drama!) but focused on that particular sub-genre which contained 'Ṣurah' and 'lo'ez'[27]). In Holland, where the 'ṣurah' was obligatory but the 'lo'ez' was rarely used, the fashion was reinvigorated by Hebrew poets from Italy who composed, for Jewish notables in Amsterdam, emblem riddles with 'lo'ez' keywords valid in both Italian and Spanish. David Franco Mendes in 1734 collected some of these and others in a special volume, adding beautiful graphic 'ṣurot' of his own making, mainly coloured collages[28]. In fact, many prominent Hebrew poets in Italy and Holland from 1650 onwards tried their hand at emblem-riddles with complex patterns. Among these were in the 17th century, apart from Zacut himself, Bondì Valvason (as early as 1647)[29], Salomon de Oliveyra and Immanuel Frances; in the 18th century, Moses Ḥaim Luzzatto and others of his family (his brother Leon Vita, later the poets Ephraim and Yiṣḥak), Moses David Valle, Mattitia Nissim (Donato) Terni, Simon Calimani, Isaia Romanin, Immanuel Ricchi, Samson Pincherle, Jacob (Dattilo) Almagià, Menahem Navarra, David Franco Mendes; in the 19th century, poets from the Almanzi family, Abraham Shalom, S. D. Luzzatto, Rahel Morpurgo, Giuseppe Tivoli, and since the beginning of the vogue, also lesser-known poets as well as scores of occasional versifiers.

Indeed the literary quality of emblem-riddles was very uneven and could not have been the mainspring for this fashion. It was rather their social function which ensured their long-lived popularity. Thus this obscure sub-genre, long forgotten, acquires some importance in both literary history and literary theory, and obliges us to make a short digression.

It has not always been made clear that the essence of the riddle as a literary *genre* (comprising several sub-genres) lies in the reciprocal affinity of two conditions, each obligatory but none in itself sufficient: one condition is the partial obscurity of the riddle's text (partial since the text must contain clues for a logical solution); the other condition is the specific social function of this obscurity: the 'riddler' (in 'learned' literature he is often the author himself; in folk-literature he is a tradent or adapter) poses a direct challenge to the 'ridlee', i.e. that reader or listener who accepts the challenge. They enter a game with set rules. The 'riddler' is obliged to be fair, i.e. to pose a true and appropriate riddle, balanced between obscurity and lucidity to enable both the challenge and a reasonable solution. The 'ridlee' is required not only to solve the riddle, but also to proclaim its solution and explicate its clue according to the author's intention[30]. This proclamation, the proof of his understanding, is essential. Whenever a reader or listener accepts the challenge and thus becomes a 'ridlee', there evolves a 'riddling situation'. This may take several forms, such as a public contest, in which the author (as riddler) may be present, or a seemingly private situation, where a solitary reader enters a battle of wits with an author who is physically absent (and perhaps long dead) but is still present *qua* riddler. It is the riddling situation, the game of this particular challenge, which essentially distinguishes a true riddle from other genres. These may also be phrased obscurely like riddles; but only the riddle requires the active participation of the reader; he must prove his understanding and supply the keyword which resolves the tension by completing and elucidating the riddler's text.

The social implications of riddling have mainly been studied in the realm of the folk riddle, not in that of the 'learned' literary enigma, which has usually been described as just an obscure text. But it turns out, that here, too, riddling is an essential condition of the genre, although in different circumstances which demand special attention.

This fact, which has been largely overlooked, is particularly clear in the long-forgotten emblem-riddles. They most certainly belong to 'learned' literature, yet their social function and riddling situation are clear and moreover well documented in dedications, sets of rules, memoirs, theoretical treatises, critiques, and apologetics, as well as in the 'body' of the riddles themselves. In this as in other respects they are unique among Hebrew literary riddles and (at least as a large group) quite prominent even among literary riddles in other languages. Each and every emblem-riddle was composed for a special occasion in honour of the author's friends or sponsors. Most were for weddings (allegedly in the tradition of Samson's riddle which he posed at his wedding, *Judges* 14:12), others for the 'Brit Millah', for feasts such as Simḥat Torah (for example in honour of 'ḥatan Torah' or 'ḥatan Bereshit'), and for sheer enjoyment in private circles, such as the 'academies'. But all these riddles had detailed dedications and other laudatory sections which explicitly mentioned the friend's or sponsor's name.

From this point of view the emblem-riddles reflected a general trend: the Hebrew poets in Italy and Holland during the 17th and 18th centuries tended more and more to produce occasional pieces, epithalamiums, dirges, eulogies and others that centered on personal or social events. Indeed, emblem-riddles and individually addressed wedding poems were often presented together[31]. But among all other incidental pieces, the emblem-riddles enjoyed a special status as a genre, since as we saw before, they presented a challenge involving a public competition held in the sponsor's honour. Copies of the riddle would be handed out a week or so before the contest, to allow the participants to prepare a detailed explication, which they would submit in writing or read out loud at the ceremony. The author (called *autore* in the rules written in Italian, and in Hebrew *meḥid*, the riddler) would then read his own explication, which was binding[32], and the judges would then decide the winner (*spiegatore, maggid*, the solver, the Hebrew term derived from the story of Samson's riddle) and allot him a prize (*perás*, premio), namely an elegant hat, a set of silver spoons and such, and of course the prestige that went with it[33]. The explications of the author and some of the participants were sometimes presented in metre and rhyme; thus there developed an additional genre, the 'explication poem', often presented as a witty bi-lingual text[34]. A wealth of evidence concerning the riddling situation is to be found in the detailed dedication to the riddles, as well as the explications, the 'explication poems' and other auxiliary texts. Several manuscripts and printed broadsides contain specific rules for the ceremony, sometimes written in both Italian and Hebrew (*Avvisi alli spiegatori dell'enimma; Azharot el meggide ha-ḥidah*) and stating, for example, that the explanation must include the 'ṣurah', the 'lo'ez' and some other devices, that it must conform to the intention of the author, and that it must be submitted before the first explanation is being read aloud, somewhat in the manner of the 'rien ne va plus' at roulette[35].

The social function of Hebrew emblem-riddles, as well as their structure, was also discussed in two or three theoretical treatises, as late as 1824 in English, by Philip Sarchi, and 1827, in greater detail, in Italian by Anania Coen[36]; both described the riddling competitions at Jewish weddings in Italy as a still living tradition, whose cultural importance Coen extolled. He also wryly remarked that the antagonism the emblem-riddles occasionally aroused was mainly due to the fact that many readers were unable to solve them[37].

This matter, however, went deeper; the fashion as a whole was by then rapidly declining. It had become an anachronism even before. During the 18th century, while other Hebrew literary genres in Italy acquired a Neo-Classical character compatible with the Arcadia school, the emblem-riddles retained their Baroque complexity and even increased it. In about 1760 Rabbi Menahem Navarra (Noveira) of Verona, an enthusiastic author and solver of emblem-riddles, complained of a growing indifference to this genre, which he ardently defended; he considered it as eminently suited to the 'mitzvah' of bringing joy to the wedding feast, and in addition sharpening the wits of the audience[38]. Navarra and other authors (among them the graceful Joab Dattilo Almagià) pledged to curb the excesses of obscurity and artificiality[39]. Such 'Apologies of Enigmas' could no longer appease Neo-Classical critics. Later in the 18th century the learned Benedetto Frizzi, though praising the (mainly Neo-Classical) poems of Simone Calimani, took exception at his emblem-riddles as being full of 'confused ideas'[40]. The impact of such criticism was not immediate, and the fashion continued into the early 19th century, witnessed, as we saw, by Coen and Sarchi, and documented by broadsides and manuscripts.

Samuel David Luzzatto (Šadal) gave a detailed personal account of its late stage in his Hebrew memoirs and his Italian autobiography. In 1818, when he was a timid youth of eighteen, his father urged him to enter society by participating in a riddling contest at a local wedding, and brought him a copy of the enigma, which as usual had been handed out in advance. Šadal who at first refused, considering the matter 'a waste of time', later yielded, and solved the enigma. He explicated it in three languages, a sonnet in Hebrew and sestines in Italian and French, in which he acclaimed the author, Lustro Sabsone Pincherle, as the New Samson, and himself as the new Oedipus ('novello Edipo'). The trilingual explication-poem impressed the learned audience and in his own opinion paved Šadal's literary career[41].

The last dated emblem-riddler I could find also happened to be related to Šadal; it was composed for his second wedding in 1852 by his cousin, the well-known poetess Raḥel Morpurgo[42]. But by then the fashion had already declined in the wake of new trends, especially Haskala poetry from other centres. The Hebrew emblem-riddles vanished from the literary scene.

They were also ignored or misunderstood in literary research. At the turn of the century, Steinschneider chanced upon some broadsides with the sub-title 'ṣurat ha-ḥidah', but apparently thought this a reference to the poem's form (rather than the enigma's picture) and wondered whether this 'form' was of Italian origin[43]. It was not until 1930 that J. Schirmann in a short note explained the terms 'ṣurat ha-ḥidah' and 'lo'ez', relying on Ramḥal's description in the early (and then still unpublished) version of his poetics[44]. Benhamin Klar later used the relevant passage in this poetics to solve two difficult emblem-riddles written by Ramḥal himself[45]. J. Tishby and M. Benayahu, each in a separate study dealing with a third emblem-riddle by Ramḥal, also took recourse to this passage[46]. Other scholars who overlooked it and misunderstood terms like 'lo'ez' went astray and arrived at some strange conclusions. As for the origin of riddles with 'ṣurah' and 'lo'ez', next to nothing was known; the invention was attributed to Ramḥal. All in all, only Ramḥal's three extant emblem-riddles have been closely studied.

Research in various libraries has made it possible for me to collect some three hundred emblem-riddles and 'solution-poems'—thousands of lines, the work of dozen of authors—apart from commentaries, apologetics, sets of rules, theoretical descriptions and other writings pertaining to this peculiar sub-genre between 1650 and 1850. They had gathered dust in manuscripts, broadsides and neglected books[47].

The oblivion into which the emblem-riddles had fallen could serve as an illustration of conflicting elements: the relative tenacity of Baroque trends within a confined area, as opposed to, and finally conquered by, the changes in literary taste. As we saw, the emblem-riddles are still of some importance for both the history and the theory of literature. But in their own right, too, they are an interesting, at times even fascinating, phenomenon whose literary implcations have yet to be studied[48].

NOTES

Abbreviations:
Bodl.   = *The Bodleian Library*, Oxford.

BM	= *British Museum* (= *British Library*), London
EH	= *Portugees Israëlietisch Seminarium Ets Haim*, Amsterdam.
Ginzburg	= *The Ginzburg Collection, Lenin Library*, Moscow.
Isr. Mus.	= *The Israel Museum*, Jerusalem.
JNL	= *Jewish National and University Library*, Jerusalem.
JTS	= *Jewish Theological Seminary*, New York [unless otherwise stated, *Italian Broadsides, Occasional Poems*, vols. 1–5; Mic 9027].
Kaufmann	= *David Kaufmann Collection, Bibliotheca Academiae Hungaricae Scientiarum*, Budapest.
Mantova	= *Comunità Israelitica*, Mantova.
Nahon	= *S. Umberto Nahon Collection, Tempio Italiano*, Jerusalem.
Ros.	= *Bibliotheca Rosenthaliana, Universiteits-Bibliotheek*, Amsterdam.
Roth	= *Cecil Roth Collection, The Brotherton Library*, Leeds University.
Strasb.	= *Bibliothèque Nationale et Universitaire*, Strasbourg.
Verona	= *Biblioteca Comunale*, Verona.

1. J. Schirmann's *Mivḥar haš-širah ha-'ivrit be-Italia*, Berlin 1935, still the best and most comprehensive anthology of Hebrew poetry in Italy, begins with a famous 'seliḥa' by Šefatya bar Amittai (died 886) and concludes with two sonnets on Herzl's death in 1904 and the Russian-Japanese war in 1905 by Yitzḥaq Vittorio Castiglioni (died 1911).

2. J. Schirmann, *Mivḥar haš-širah ha-'ivrit be-Italia*, Berlin 1935, introduction as well as in various lectures; more explicitly. J. B. Sermoneta, *Šne Širei Ḥatunah le-Ribbi Ya'acov Yosef Caivano*, in *Scritti in Memoria de Enzo Sereni*, Jerusalem 1970, Parte Ebraica, pp. 182–212 (see especially pp. 193–195, notes 18–21).

3. S. Archivolti, *'Arugat ha-Bossem*, Venice 1602, f. 119a was probably the first to include a Hebrew sonnet (his own) in a theoretical treatise. The form had been known long before in Hebrew: Immanuel of Rome, around 1300, introduced 38 Hebrew sonnets into his Maḥbarot (thus Hebrew was the first language, after Italian in which sonnets were written). Archivolti did not mention other Italian forms which had been adapted by 1600.

4. The book survived in manuscript and was first edited by H. Brody, Cracow 1892. The various Italian forms, on pp. 48–53; the 'ḥarifut' principle, p. 53. See also J. B. Sermoneta, *Šne Širei . . .* cit.; D. Pagis, *Ḥidduš u-Massoret*, Jerusalem 1976, pp. 251 ff., 276 ff.

5. M. H. Luzzatto, *Lešon Limmudim* ('Version A'), first printed 1727, latest edition by A. M. Habermann, Tel Aviv 1950. *Lešon Limmudum* ('Version B'), in manuscript written 1724 and suppressed; ed. A. M. Habermann, Tel Aviv 1951.

6. For example Moses Rieti, in the opening verses to his *Miqdaš Me'aṭ* (written 1415–1416), ed. J. Goldenthal, Wien 1851.

7. Examples of graphic media used for the 'ṣurah' in riddles. *Pen and ink drawings*, e.g. *JNL*, ARC 4° 1537, 2: 18; *Roth*, Ms. 103, f. 45b; *Roth*, Ms. 115, f. 3B, f. C4 and more in this and other collections. *Watercolours, coloured collages, mixed media*, e.g. *NJL*, L 904; *EH*, Ms. 47 B, 26 f. 129 ff. (coloured collages by David Franco Mendes), *Isr. Mus.*, Ms. 177/64 watercolour on parchment). *Etchings, blockprints, woodcuts* in dozens of broadsides for riddling contests, for example *JTS*, Mic 9027, vols. 1–5; later collected in books, e.g. I. Ricchi, *Adderet Eliyahu*, Livorno 1742, ff. 49b–59b. Yosef Ya'acov = Giuseppe Tivoli, *Divre Šir, Carmi Ebraico-Italiani*, Padova 1831, pp. 22–36.

8. Three examples: 1) Immanuel Ricchi, *Hen hi ke-met;* in the first edition (1734, a broadside, *JNL*, L 904, coloured, and elsewhere) the ṣurah is a delicate etching; in the second edition (1742, in Ricchi's book *Adderet Eliyahu*, Livorno 1742, f. 53 b) it is a simpler woodcut depicting the same enigmatic scene. 2) Avraham Šalom, *Mispar šemi:* first edition (single manuscript sheets for the contest) pen-and-ink (*JNL*, ARC 4° 1537, 2: 7); second edition, in print, a verbal description of the picture (in Šalom's book *Ya'ar Avšalom*, Padova 1855, p. 10). 3) Yosef Haim Hak-kohen = Giuseppe Vita Sacerdote, *Aḥim šelošah:* in manuscripts, the ṣurah is a description in Hebrew and Italian (e.g., 'due navi in burrasca di mare'; *Verona*, Ms. Ebr. 1682 busta 48/8); in the broadside printed for the contest, it is a detailed etching of the scene (*JTS*, vol. 2, no. 32). There are many other instances of such changes.

9. Examples of non-Hebrew terms for the 'ṣurah' used by Jewish writers. 'Figura del-l'enigma': Leon Vita Luzzatto, in a tri-lingual booklet, *Debil Fatiga*, Amsterdam 1734, p. 6 [in Italian], p. 15 [in Spanish]. Giuseppe Sacerdote, *Verona*, Ms. Ebr. 68/8; Anania Coen, *Saggio di eloquenza ebrea*, Parte I, Firenze 1827, pp. 86–87. 'Impresa dell'enimma': Azaria Levi, *JTS*, vol. 2, no. 40. 'Hieroglyphico': Miguel de Barrios, *Enigma del Principio, Academia de los Floridos, Memoria* [booklet bound in several of his compilations, e.g. *Estrella de Jacob*, Amsterdam 1686, p. 161].

10. P. Sarchi, *An Essay on Hebrew Poetry, Ancient and Modern*, London 1824, p. 132.

11. A. Coen, *Saggio . . .* cit., p. 87 (note 9 above): '. . . un Emblema o distico e talvolta l'uno e l'altro, e chiamasi ṣurat ha-ḥidah ossia figura dell'Enimma'.

12. Examples:: Motto (Italian sub-title of the encoded Hebrew Section), Yešayah, 'Yeš li korvah' (*Isr. Mus.*, Ms 177/64). 'Pitron ha-ḥidah', 'Peruš le-pitron ha-ḥidah' (both titles for encoded Hebrew sections; the actual 'pitron', i.e. solution, is given separately): Yosef Šiprut de Gabbay, 'Af ki ani' (broadside bound in *EH*, Ms 47 B 26, p. 163). 'Mafteaḥ' is a very frequent term for an encoded section attached to the ṣurah.

13. Examples of complex structures: Moses Zacut, *Illemet anokhi*, written in Venice, April 1650: motto, first 'ṣurah' and body, second 'ṣurah' and body, enigmatic epilogue—in couplets, quatrains and sestines (*Kaufmann*, Ms. 459, p. 207). Yoav Dattilo Almagia, *Ani domem*, with author's explication

poem, Pesaro, approx. 1750: several sections—in prose, couplets and *terza rima* (*Roth*, Ms. 119, f. 37b–41a). Ašer Viterbo, *Ma lakh dod:* introduction, double 'mafteaḥ', triple motto, triple 'ṣurah', body and encoded epilogue—in rhymed prose, simple prose, quatrains, and a *sonetto caudato* with unusual rhymes (in his *Minḥa Ḥadashah,* Venice 1748, pp. 10–14). Yosef Šiprut de Gabbay, *Haskel ba-amarai,* written in Amsterdam for David Franco Mendes' wedding: opening poem concerning the riddle, 'ṣurah', body comprising three dramatic monologues, encoded 'pitron', and poetic reply (not solution) by 'a group of poets'—in quatrains, prose, sonnets, with distinctive sub-titles (*JTS,* uncatalogued broadside).

14. Rafael Yeḥiel Sanguinetti, in his emblem-riddle *Qore yedidi,* before 1750, included in a manuscript collection of his poems (*Osef Hakkesil,* BM, Add. 27, 178, f. 52a). The solution *(water)* is suggested by Hebrew words or syllables suggesting the sound of: *acqua, agua, Wasser, eau, maya* (Aramaic) as well as the Hebrew *mayim* in disguise. This example is the more remarkable since Sanguinetti, after having completed the riddle on 'water', attempted to change the solution, while preserving the entire given text, in order to confuse the participants at the contest. The new solution ('heart') was now suggested by other clues among which were Hebrew words which happened to be included in the text, and were now elevated into lo'ez words, because they sounded like: *cuore, cor, Herz, coeur.* In other emblem-riddles, too, Sanguinetti used polyglot 'lo'ez' (e.g. *Avi ke-'is, ibid.,* f. 23a).

15. The latest edition in Y. A. Modena, *Leqet Ketavim,* ed. Penina Naveh, Jerusalem 1968, pp. 25–26. This poem (and similar devices, like bi-lingual echo-rhymes) inspired other simultaneously bi-lingual poems, by Moses Catalano, Šelomo Oliveyra, Ephraim Luzzatto and others. Some are still in manuscripts (e.g. *EH,* Ms. 47 D 15, *EH,* Ms. 47 B 26, etc.).

16. Bondì Valvason, "Donna infelice . . ."; in a broadside dated 9 dic. 1647, also containing a Hebrew emblem-riddle and various Hebrew and Italian poems (*JTS,* vol. 5). Miguel de Barrios, "Enigma del Principio: No via . . . Hieroglyphico, una rosa en la boca de un Hebreo", *Academia de los Floridos* (see end of note 9). Anonymous, "O Barbaro que sego sendo Hebreo" (Portuguese version of a Hebrew riddle with 'lo'ez', both on the same page: *EH,* Ms. 47 B 26, p. 141).

17. 'Paronomasia', etc., Giuseppe Tivoli, *Divre* (see end of note 7), p. 30; 'con voce' etc., A. Coen, *Saggio . . .* cit.

18. P. Sarchi, *An Essay . . .* cit., p. 132.

19. Long poetic Hebrew riddles—in medieval Spain, by Yehuda ha-Levi, Abraham Ibn Ezra and others; in Italy previous to the emblem-riddles, for example by Yerahmiel ha-Yerahmeli (12th century, *Bodl.,* Ms. 2079/9, f. 53a–55b), Giuseppe Concio (16th–early 17th century; *Strasb.,* Ms. heb 115, f. 12 ff.).

20. On the Spanish Baroque elements in his dramatic works see Professor Sierra's article in *Italia Judaica 2: Gli Ebrei in Italia Tra Rinascimento Ed*

Eta Barocca, Alti del II Convegno internazionale, Genoa 1984 (Rome 1986), pp. 279–293.
21. Zacut's emblem-riddles in autograph: *Kaufmann,* Ms. 459, pp. 200–213, and in other manuscripts, copied by Italian Jewish scribes. In his riddle about the sun (*ibid., p.* 203) he declares that the 'lo'ez' is 'Sefardi', Spanish (an allusion to *sol* by a complex pun, the fifth sound in the musical scale do-sol).
22. Such as the 'Kasdi' (an Aramaic key-word similar to the lo'ez) or the 'Ivri' (the Hebrew key-word, i.e. the solution, but disguised as a referential word, and yet alluded to by the technical term 'Ivri' which also appears in the text).
23. Ya'akov Frances, *Kol Šire,* ed. Penina Naveh, p. 267. In the editor's opinion he refers to Zacut's enigmatic style in general; it is however quite clear that he specifically refers to Zacut's peculiar riddles. The terminus *ad quem* 1650 emerges from various other sources.
24. Immanuel Frances, *Meteq Sefatayim,* ed. H. Brody, Cracow 1892, pp. 54–58 (see also note 4).
25. Fo. 15a–18b. Other, earlier emblem-riddles (dated from 1651 on) he included in his poetics *Šaršot Gavlut* (Amsterdam 1665), f. 47b–50a.
26. See end of note 9.
27. M. H. Luzzatto, *Lešon Limmudim,* 'Version B' . . . cit., pp. 146–147.
28. In his *Emeq haš-širim* (*EH,* Ms 47 B 26, calligraphy and graphics in 1734). In this manuscript he also included several printed broadsides with emblem-riddles which Italian authors (I. Ricchi, S. Calimani, Leon Vita Luzzatto) composed for weddings in Amsterdam (*ibid.,* pp. 156, 158, 164).
29. See note 16.
30. The assumption is that each literary riddle has only a single correct solution, the one intended by the author. This is not necessarily so in folk-riddles, which (being short and providing few clues) may be open to several solutions; they also have no known author and are often changed by tradents. In literary riddles, the author's intention (accepted as the only correct solution) touches upon a general and much disputed hermeneutical issue (the 'Intentional Fallacy'), which cannot be dealt with here. Concerning the obviously literary, learned emblem-riddles, the author's intention, revealed by the author himself at the ceremony, was the sole criterion for all contestants. The author's obligation to present an adequate, solvable riddle is explicitly stated by M. H. Luzzatto, *Lešon Limmudim* 'Version A' . . . cit., pp. 144–145, A Coen, *Saggio* . . . cit., pp. 87–88, and various 'Avvisi alli spiegatori' (see below, note 35).
31. Thus already in the first dated example I could find: a broadside from Venice dated 1647 (above, note 16) with five pieces by Bondì Valvason in Hebrew and Italian (including two emblem-riddles) all for the same wedding. Later such sequels were often expanded and comprised entire booklets for weddings (e.g., those by Leon Vita Luzzatto and Ašer Viterbo, above notes 9 and 13), or various celebrations at the literary academies in Livorno, Verona, Amsterdam and elsewhere.

32. See above.
33. For example, silver: *Mantova*, broadside no. 21; elegant hats: *EH*, Ms. 47 B 26, p. 140; M. de Barrios, *Enigma del Principio* . . . cit., A Coen, *Saggio* . . . cit., p. 86 and others.
34. Explication poems by the authors and solvers of emblem-riddles, e.g. I. Frances, *Meteq Sefatayim*, p. 54 (possibly the first). Yoab Dattilo Almagià, *Roth*, Ms. 119, fo. 38a–41a (long poem in *terza rima*). S. D. Luzzatto, *Autobiografia*, Padova 1882, pp. 76–77 (triple tri-lingual explication-poem). G. Tivoli, *Sonetti Maccheronici, Originale e Traduzione, in ispiegazione del precedente Enimma* . . . *Divre Šir*, pp. 30–31 (see end of note 7).
35. *Avvisi* in various formulations: *Verona*, Ms. Ebt 68/8; *JTS*, vol. 2, no. 32 and *ibid.*, several uncatalogued broadsides; *JNL*, L 2162; *Mantova*, no. 218 and others.
36. P. Sarchi, *An Essay* . . . cit.; A. Coen, *Saggio* . . . cit. In 1831, Tivoli still lavishly reprinted, as a matter of course, emblem-riddles and explication-poems in his *Divre Šir*.
37. A. Coen, *Saggio* . . . cit.
38. In *Roth*, Ms. 102, f. 22a.
39. Navarra, *ibid.*, and Almagià in his explication-poem (above, n. 34) and others.
40. B. Frizzi, *Elogio dei Rabbini Simone Calimani et Giacobbe Saravale*, in *Elogio del Rabino Abram Abenezra*, Trieste 1791, pp. 57–58.
41. In Hebrew 'Toledot Šadal', *Ha-maggid*, vol. 7 (1863), no. 4, p. 29, and no. 8, p. 61. In Italian in his *Autobiografia* (see note 34), pp. 76–77.
42. 'Al ha gaḥon' (1852) in *'Ugav Raḥel*, Cracow 1892, pp. 67–68.
43. M. Steinschneider, *Die italienische Literatur der Juden* in "Monatsschrift für Geschichte und Wissenschaft des Judentums", XLII (1898), p. 421; Id., *Rangstreitliteratur*, Wien 1908, pp. 79–80.
44. J. H. Schirmann, 'Rätsel', *Jüdisches Lexikon*, IV, 1930, col. 1252–1253.
45. In: M. H. Luzzatto, *Sefer Haš-širim*, ed. S. Ginzburg and B. Klar, Jerusalem–Tel Aviv 1945, pp. 45 ff.
46. M. Benayahu, *Šire ḥuppah ḥadashim le-Ramḥal*, in "Hasifrut", 7, no. 24 (1977), pp. 92–99; I. Tishby, *Širim u-piyyutim migginze R. Moše Ḥaim Luzzatto*, in "Molad", 7, no. 37–38 (1976), pp. 346–372.
47. I gratefully acknowledge the help of the libraries mentioned above and of other libraries and research institutes. The full list will be given elsewhere, see next note.
48. For a detailed though still preliminary report on the history and style of this sub-genre see my study *Al Sod Ḥatum* (a supplement issue of "Tarbiz", Jerusalem, due to appear during 1985). For a discussion of the theory mentioned here, see my *The Literary Riddle. A Proposed Genre Model* (a forthcoming article in "Ha-Sifrut / Literature", Tel Aviv).

19

The Impact of Science on Jewish Culture and Society in Venice (With Special Reference to Jewish Graduates of Padua's Medical School)

David B. Ruderman

In 1624, Joseph ben Judah Ḥamiẓ successfully completed his doctorate in philosophy and medicine at the University of Padua[1]. Besides the joy Ḥamiẓ and his immediate family must have felt at this achievement, the event itself hardly seemed to merit any real significance either for Padua or for its Jewish community. In the beginning of the seventeenth century, a constant trickle of Jews were among the hundreds of students annually graduating from Padua's renowned medical school[2]. Nevertheless, Ḥamiẓ's graduation appears to have elicited an unusual outpouring of favorable, even elated, response from some of the most important luminaries of Italian Jewish culture of this era. Undoubtedly, their reaction was encouraged by Ḥamiẓ's illustrious mentor, Leone Modena, who apparently undertook the responsibility of publishing an entire pamphlet of poems and approbations to honor his favorite prodigy[3]. Yet the participants' enthusiastic response appears to signal a genuine excitement over Ḥamiẓ's personal triumph, far exceeding the standardized conventions required by this literary exercise in public flattery. No less impressive is the wide spectrum of contributors, ranging from the expected—fellow classmate, Benjamin Mussafia[4]—to the less expected "wise man of secrets", Azariah Figo, Rabbi of Pisa[5]. For all of these distinguished panegyrists, Ḥamiẓ's rite of passage into the hallowed corridors of li-

Reprinted by permission of Fondazione Giorgio Cini from *Gli Ebrei e Venezia*, edited by Gaetano Cozzi, Milan, 1987.

cenced medical practice was deservedly cause for celebration and com-
mendation to both Ḥamiẓ and his own community of co-religionists.

Writing almost a hundred years later, the German orientalist Johann
Jacob Schudt also had occasion to note the phenomenon of Jewish
graduation from Padua's medical school. In contrast to the effusive
accolades lavished upon Ḥamiẓ and his accomplishment by his fellow
Jews, the German scholar could find nothing praiseworthy about Padua's indiscriminate admission of "every ignoramus and even the despised
Jews", especially those admitted from his own country. According to
Schudt, such practice was indeed unbecoming to so famous a university
whose only motivation in welcoming such unworthy degree candidates
must have been its love of lucre, following the proverb: "We take the
money and send the ass back to Germany"[6].

Two isolated notices of Jewish medical graduates from Padua almost
a century apart—the first, adulatory, the second, deprecatory—both
share, at least partially, a common insight. Padua's regularized and
unprecedented admission and subsequent graduation of hundreds of
Jews was a matter of no small consequence to the university, to its
Jewish graduates and to the communities they eventually served. Indeed
neither Ḥamiẓ's associates nor Johann Schudt were ever fully capable of
appreciating the momentous significance of Padua's admission policy,
spanning well over two centuries, for the development of Jewish culture
and society in Padua, in Venice, in Italy, and throughout the rest of
Europe.

Both historians of Venetian and Paduan Jewry and historians of
Jewish medicine have long acknowledged the presence of many Jews in
Padua's medical school[7]. No less noticed have been the large numbers
of these students originating from Central and Eastern Europe and
returning to serve as physicians in their respective communities[8]. Yet
beyond mention of the sheer number of these students, assorted biographical data about some famous graduates, and bibliographical references to their writings, the larger story of their encounter with one of
the major centers of European culture in the early modern era remains
generally untold. Padua, although not the only Italian university to
welcome Jews, was the foremost center for training Jewish physicians
from the sixteenth century well into the eighteenth, superseded only at
the end of this period by more prominent medical schools in the North,
such as the University of Leiden[9]. The Paduan experience is not distinc-

tive merely because large numbers of Jews demonstrated a conspicuous interest in and capacity for medical practice. Medical practice was already a well-established profession among Jews both in Christian and Moslem societies long before the sixteenth century[10]. Nor does the mere admission of individual Jews to a European university define the novelty of Padua's Jewish encounter. Long before Padua, Jews had earned medical degrees; they also had served as physicians to important non-Jews and they had fostered conspicuous social and cultural liaisons with the upper echelons of Moslem and Christian society because of their medical practice[11].

The Paduan experience is unique, however, because for the first time a relatively large number of Jews graduated from a major medical school, entered the medical profession and practiced medicine across the entire European continent. Padua also was unique because it afforded the opportunity for intense socialization among Jews from remarkably variegated backgrounds—former Conversos from Spain and Portugal, together with Italian, Turkish, German, Polish, and Russian Jews. Moreover, Padua's university did not allow its Jewish students to segregate themselves socially and culturally by living and working among themselves. Jewish students at Padua had no collective identity; they were considered only as individual members of the Italian, German, or Polish "nations" and integrated physically among non-Jewish student populations[12].

Above all, Padua offered hundreds of talented Jewish students an intense and prolonged exposure to the study of the liberal arts, to Latin studies, to classical scientific texts, as well as to the latest scientific advances in botany, anatomy, chemistry, and clinical medicine. During the course of their systematic formal instruction which lasted at least five years, these young and impressionable Jewish youths were introduced to a radically new social network of close and intimate encounters with non-Jews, also originating from diverse communities all over Europe, Finally, Padua was special for Jews because its graduates, despite their dispersion throughout Europe, maintained social and intellectual ties with each other and constituted a significant cultural force within their respective communities years after their graduation[13].

From the perspective of Jewish history, Padua's medical facility thus constituted more than a center for training Jewish physicians. In its broader dimensions, it represented a major vehicle for the diffusion of secular culture, especially scientific culture, within the pre-emancipatory Jewish communities of Europe[14]. It provided one of the richest opportunities for Jews to familiarize themselves intellectually and socially with the best of European civilization, an encounter generally unavailable to the overwhelming majority of their fellow co-religionists. Ultimately, so formative an experience was bound to affect profoundly the cultural priorities, the values, even the self-image of such Jews.

Since the early fifteenth century, Padua was under Venetian control, and because of its proximity to Venice, the university became an official state institution of the Veneto and the primary center for training its lawyers and doctors. Ultimately, many of Padua's graduates returned to Venice to assume leadership roles in the Venetian government while maintaining a constant interest and direct voice in university policies and appointments[15]. Thus Padua's impact on Jews also is a chapter in Venetian history. Likewise, the cultural transformations of Paduan Jewry, stemming primarily from the university training offered to growing numbers of Jews, were directly felt, first and foremost, within the cultural sphere of the Venetian Jewish community.

Between 1517 and 1721 some 250 Jews received medical diplomas from Padua, and assuredly many more attended classes without matriculating[16]. Many of this number are well known for their contributions to Jewish culture and society: individuals like Joseph Delmedigo[17], Joseph Ḥamiẓ[18], Tobias Cohen[19], David Nieto[20], Solomon and Israel Conegliano[21], or Isaac Cantarini[22]. Others are hardly familiar at all. Ultimately only an exhaustive scrutiny of their lives and literary remains will yield a penetrating appreciation of their encounter with Padua and the impact this had on them and their communities. Such a task is clearly beyond the limitations of this preliminary study. Nevertheless, from what is known about the most illustrious of Padua's Jewish graduates and from what is available about the ambience of Paduan university life in general, the overall contours of this interaction already are evident.

At the beginning of the sixteenth century, European students favoring the University of Padua had good reasons for their choice. Padua generally was regarded as the best medical school in Europe. Although it nominally was a Catholic University, Protestant and subsequently Jewish students were not prevented from studying there[23]. The high level of medical training Padua offered was related directly to the significant place a university-educated doctor held in Italian society[24]. Unlike much of the rest of Europe, Italy enjoyed the availability of relatively large numbers of university graduates serving a wide spectrum of social classes both in the large cities and in the small towns. The Venetian government's keen interest in and consistent support of the university reinforced the high social standing of Padua's medical graduates[25].

Padua's success in attracting large numbers of foreign students— Germans, Flemings, Belgians, Dutch, Silesians, Poles, Russians, Hungarians, Spanish, French, Swiss, and English—was attributable to other reasons as well. Besides its scientific reputation, its geographical proximity to Venice undoubtedly was a great asset. The excitement of so great a commercial and intellectual center surely was contagious to medical students interested in familiarizing themselves with different places, climates, diseases, and drugs. The ideal of enlarging one's cultural horizons, together with the mythology associated with *la peregrinatio medica,* undoubtedly resonated in the hearts and minds of Padua's student body. And in a university where humanities courses were integrated into the scientific curriculum, Padua certainly was no stuffy parochial environment. For outside the walls of specialized study was the romantic ambience of Renaissance architecture, art, theatre, and music augmented, no doubt, by excursions to exotic cultural treasures throughout Italy and beyond[26].

Padua's medical curriculum was based on a two-tier system of courses to be completed over a five-year period[27]. During the first two years, students acquired a basic familiarity with logic and natural philosophy, based primarily on the texts of Aristotle. During the three-year cycle, students specialized in both theoretical and practical subjects, utilizing the basic texts of Hippocrates, Galen, Avicenna, and Rhazes. The instructor of theory would treat the general explanatory principles of health and disease, while his colleague in medical practice would cover the same ground from a more pragmatic perspective. In addition, a student would enjoy an ample exposure to the rest of the liberal arts curriculum. At the beginning of the sixteenth century, for example, students were expected to master Aristotle's rhetoric, Greek epigrams and poetic, Cicero's topics, his *Tusculanae Disputationes* and his *Somnium Scipions,* Sophocles' *Oedipus Tyrannus,* some writings of Demosthenes, Horace's first book of odes, Livy's history, and so on. All of this learning hardly was passive. Each doctor reading in arts and medicine was required to hold public disputations at least twice a year; seven students took part in each disputation. Every evening, informal disputation took place in the presence of instructors whose attendance was required at least one hour each day to allay student doubts. A typical graduate of the medical school accordingly received a doctorate of philosophy and medicine, a title earned upon mastering this remarkably integrated curriculum.

Padua's curriculum underwent major changes throughout the sixteenth and into the seventeenth century. By the late sixteenth century, through the collaboration of the Hospital of St. Francis at Padua, daily hospital rounds became a standard feature of Padua's clinical training[28]. Such bedside teaching still was unparalleled outside of Italy even by the end of the sixteenth century. In the same period, botany emerged as an autonomous subject in the Paduan medical curriculum and botanical gardens were established at the university. Professors of botany often included in their teaching the animal and mineral worlds as well. Herbaria often were supplemented by natural history museums. Observation and research in the natural sciences also led to experiments in alchemy and iatrochemistry[29].

This period also witnessed major developments in the teaching of anatomy and surgery. In 1594, the first permanent anatomical theatre elevated considerably the status of surgery at Padua while elsewhere in Europe its status was on the decline[30]. Finally, although inferior in the overall educational scheme, the mathematical subjects, including optics, mechanics, cosmography (astronomy and geography) and the like, were considered important adjuncts to medicine and were integrated as well into the curriculum[31]. By the end of the seventeenth century, the scientific education Paduan medical students received was radically different from that of their medieval ancestors, who had focused primarily on the classical texts of medicine.

The intellectual feast offered by Padua's curriculum provided one primary dimension of the learning experience; the social circumstances of this learning provided another. Within the university of arts and medicine, all students were organized according to their "nations". Each "nation" elected a councilor to serve the rector. Most of the non-Italian Jewish students belonged either to the German or Polish nations. As members of individual nations, they were assigned licensed lodgings in the city. Almost like religious confraternities or merchant guilds, the student "nations" constituted the primary social group for all students, providing them mutual aid and comfort and free medical care[32].

For a Jew, regardless of his origin, this environment was dramatically unlike anything he had ever encountered before. More often than not, he was unprepared linguistically, culturally, or socially for such an intense experience. With the exception of former Conversos, no group of Jews had ever lived so intimately as a tiny minority among such an international population. Few Jews arrived in Padua with the educational prerequisites to assume the rigorous course load of an entering medical student. The social and cultural shock of entering the university world, from even the most enlightened of Jewish family backgrounds, was no less formidable. No doubt, the extraordinary challenges posed to Jewish religious sensibilities and ritual practice were similarly compelling. Problems of dietary and Sabbath observance were not the only obstacles in the path of the Jewish student. The emphasis on surgery and autopsies, many of which were performed on bodies obtained illegally, even from Jewish cemeteries, also was troublesome[33].

Despite the non-threatening circumstances of Padua's relatively tolerant policy toward non-Catholics, Jews still encountered special obligations and disabilities. Jews paid higher tuition than others; at the time of their graduation, they were taxed additionally by being obliged to deliver 170 pounds of sweet meat to Christian students[34]. No doubt such formal liabilities were only a small part of the abuses Jews encountered on a day-to-day basis in trying to compete with non-Jewish students. Thus Tobias Cohen, in decrying those Jews who practiced medicine without adequate university training, points explicitly to the hardships he and other Jews undoubtedly experienced as medical students: "Why should a doctor expend his time, increase his expenses, inflict his body and endanger himself in his study at the academies of the gentiles who hate Jewish students?"[35]

Above all, the Jewish student had to resist the temptations of weakening or even losing his faith. Thus, from personal experience, Joseph Delmedigo could write: "This is a warning directed to those parents who cause their sons to sin by sending them to Padua 'to philosophize' before the light of the Torah has shined upon them so that the nature of faith would have been implanted previously in their souls in order that they not turn away from it"[36]. And elsewhere, he alludes to the problem of medical studies involving more than the limited mastery of medical texts: "How good it would be that you would request medicine from medical texts and faith from the source of Israel and not from the 'children of strangers and aliens' as the secular disciplines; therefore be faithful to the Lord your God"[37]. No doubt David Provincial had in mind the same problem when in the middle of the sixteenth century, he proposed the establishment of a Jewish institution of higher learning to train doctors, among others, insulated from the corrosive influences of general universities like Padua[38]. In similar fashion Solomon Marini wrote, at the beginning of the seventeenth century, of those he had seen who desired "to learn and understand philosophy without prior learning of our holy Torah"[39]. And certainly by the beginning of the eighteenth century the same issue remained critical for Tobias Cohen when he warned: "No one [Jew] in all the lands of Italy, Poland, Germany, and France should consider studying medicine without first filling his belly with the written and oral Torah and other subjects[40].

Tobias resolved his problem, as did many other Jewish medical students at Padua, by taking advantage of an extraordinary Jewish network of educational and social services that prepared foreign students like himself and his classmate Gabriel Felix to enter the university. Thus he continued: "As I will testify also regarding the numerous students of my wise teacher [. . .] Solomon Conegliano, those of whom become rabbis and those of whom become physicians to kings and important princes; for I am the least notable among them all"[41]. The Jewish doctor Solomon Conegliano's preparatory school for Jewish students desirous of entering the university surely arose as a necessary solution to a set of pressing problems. Under the able direction of an illustrious graduate of Padua, Jewish students could master Latin, Italian, and other propaedeutic disciplines in order to prepare themselves sufficiently for university entrance. Moreover, Solomon's home obviously offered them an appropriate social and cultural setting, a kind of transitional "half-way house" between their own homes and the university itself. Most important of all, it provided the necessary spiritual reinforcement—"A filled belly of Torah"—to ward off all "heretical" inclinations fostered by Padua's cosmopolitan setting. Conegliano trained students not only for medical careers but also to become rabbis. Clearly both professional goals, when properly implemented under his guiding hand, were most compatible. Torah and medicine still were, as they had been in the past, the most natural and complementary of disciplines. Together they provided the most beneficial training for Jews to assume leadership roles either in the Jewish community or among "kings and important princes."[42].

The absence of concrete documentation does not allow us to conclude that institutions like the Conegliano boarding school were a staple of Jewish student life at Padua in earlier periods. What seems clear, however, is that Jewish students could not have flourished, indeed, survived, without such supportive institutions. Moreover, the fact that Jewish graduates of Padua maintained lively social and intellectual liaisons with each other long after their departure from the university leads one to believe that such tangible support for future graduates was always forthcoming. The remarkable comaraderie among Jewish doctors and rabbis demonstrated by the celebration surrounding the Ḥamiẓ graduation is only one example of many. Equally telling is the special fellowship between Abraham ha-Cohen of Zante, Shabbetai Marini, and Solomon Lustro at the end of the seventeenth century[43]. Tobias Cohen's *Ma'aseh Tuviyyah* contains introductory approbations by colleagues and friends which also illustrate the social context of Jewish medical activity[44]. The life and social involvements of Isaac Vita ha-Cohen Cantarini of the seventeenth and early eighteenth centuries offer a similar and equally impressive example of support and liaison with other Jewish medical students and doctors to that of Solomon Conegliano[45].

The impression of social fellowship and mutual support among Jewish medical students before, during, and after graduation is strengthened even more by the disproportionate numbers of Jewish graduates stemming from the same family. Names like Delmedigo[46], Wallich[47], De Castro[48], Pardo[49], Cantarini[50], Cardoso[51], Morpurgo[52], Winkler[53], Maurogonato[54], Loria[55], Felix[56], and Conegliano[57] often appear among the graduates of Padua throughout the sixteenth, seventeenth, and eighteen centuries. In the cases of these individuals, educational, financial and social support was available from older family members who had undergone the same experience some years earlier. When this intricate web of social relationships is examined beyond the confines of Padua and Venice and even beyond Italy, one discovers similar bonds among Jewish graduates of Padua as colleagues, as teachers and students, as correspondents, and as cultural and intellectual allies in such cities all across Europe as Prague, Bingen, Frankfurt, Hamburg, Cracow, and Salonika[58]

What ultimately emerges out of the simple fact that some 250 Jews graduated Padua's medical school in the early modern era is the evolution of a definable social and cultural group of Jewish intellectuals, almost all of them physicians, many of them rabbis as well, sharing a common university background, a common cultural heritage, common interests and values, linguistically and culturally assimilated, maintaining close contact among themselves, with other non-Jewish colleagues, and with the upper echelons of Western and Eastern European society, maintaining in many instances an instable and itinerant lifestyle as well as a cosmopolitan and often restless spirit. Indeed, the term "scientific society", having a particular connotation and significance for seventeenth-century European culture, also might convey an approximate description of this emerging fraternity of Jewish medical graduates from Padua with other graduates of Spanish and Northern European universities[59]. Perhaps this Jewish network's membership ties were less formal than those of actual scientific societies, but they existed nevertheless. They were nurtured by an enthusiasm and commitment to science and enlightenment, along with a growing antipathy and impatience for obscurantism and parochialism; they were reinforced also by a swelling resentment and antagonism among non-Jews throughout Europe towards the "ubiquitous" Jewish doctor[60]. For such disparaging recognition could easily be taken by Jews as an ethnic badge of honor. Had not Jews always been associated with a tradition of scientific and medical achievement[61]? The impressive collective accomplishments of Jewish physicians in recent times undoubtedly were a further acknowledgement of Jewish national honor. "Though scattered all over the world", writes one Jewish practitioner of the seventeenth century, referring to Jewish physicians, "they manage to maintain the unity and purity of their nationality [. . .] Since the time when the world was created, no other nation has thus preserved its strength and integrity"[62].

The impact of Padua's scientific ambience on Jewish culture is evident from the actual writings of the more prolific and illustrious of her Jewish graduates. That many of these compositions were published by Venetian presses—either in Hebrew or in Western languages—indicates a substantial cross-fertilization of culture between Paduan and Venetian Jewish societies. Most of these writings have yet to be studied systematically and in the wider context of general cultural developments. In the confines of this presentation, no full-scale treatment of all the major issues or most of the writers is possible. Utilizing, instead, a more limited sampling of the works of some of Padua's Jewish graduates, some preliminary observations are forthcoming.

The most striking feature about Jewish writers on scientific or medical subjects among Paduan graduates is that they demonstrate an impressive familiarity with scientific literature, both ancient and modern. This fact seems hardly unexpected in view of the greater availability of printed scientific texts by the sixteenth and seventeenth centuries[63], and because of the coherent and exhaustive course of scientific study these writers undertook at Padua. Nevertheless, this knowledge explosion is vividly impressive when one observes the overwhelming number of cited sources in contrast to those of previous generations, the diversity of considered fields, the contemporaneity of cited authors, and the universality of interests discussed.

No doubt the most dramatic advances in early modern science are to be found in such physical sciences as mechanics, pneumatics, or astronomy. While references to the most outstanding of these achievements, particularly with respect to the heliocentric theories of the Copernican school, can be located in contemporary Jewish writing, they fail to convey the full impact of science on Jewish writing. For the most part, scientific experiments in these fields were undertaken outside the universities and were inaccessible to most Jews, with occasional exceptions. Yet most advances in medicine and its related fields were carried on primarily within the framework of universities like Padua. When viewed exclusively from the perspective of the physical sciences, the scientific culture of the university appears almost retrograde; seen however, from the perspective of life sciences, the university's role in fostering scientific knowledge is in fact pivotal[64]. It is precisely in those same areas of science that the university fostered—medicine, botany, zoology, and mineralogy—that the Jews' overwhelming interest and accomplishment are to be located. A catalogue of reactions to Copernicus in contemporary Hebrew literature is thus a misleading guide for evaluating the degree of Jewish receptivity to the new science in the sixteenth and seventeenth centuries[65].

A more significant area in which such receptivity is readily apparent is that of the new chemical philosophy, that is, the new chemical and medical procedures associated with the Paracelsian school[66]. A number of the Jewish graduates of this period were markedly influenced by the chemical medicine of these Paracelsians or iatrochemists, apparently a vital stand of Padua's medical training by the end of the seventeenth century. The latter school was characterized by the union of chemistry and medicine; a contempt for ancient medical authority (particularly that of Galen and Aristotle); a new theory of disease which denied the Galenic system based on humours and cure by "contraries", which it replaced with a doctrine of cure by "similitude"; and most importantly, a search for chemical analogies in the biological realm. By regarding chemical processes such as decomposition or distillation as keys for understanding nature as a whole, the Paracelsians offered a revolutionary perspective for understanding pathology and physiology, as well as a flood of new medical remedies, chemically derived from minerals and plants. Despite the rapid acceptance of the mechanical philosophy by the second half of the seventeenth century, the chemical philosophers never lost their enthusiastic adherents.

Of all the Jewish students at Padua, Tobias Cohen seems to have been the most attuned to the new chemical philosophy. Almost in revelatory terms, he announces in his *Ma'aseh Tuviyyah* the flowering "of a new medicine which dwells in the bosom of the physicians of our time"[67]. He regularly quotes the major exponents of this philosophy: Sylvius, Van Helmont, Sennert, Willis, Ertmuller, and more[68]. He often casts aspersions on Galenic medicine and presents the new chemists as a preferable alternative[69]. Like the seventeenth-century iatrochemists, he strongly opposes Galenic bloodletting and the Galenic explanation of fevers[70]. He is indebted especially to the Englishman Thomas Willis (1621–75), who ascribed the most frequent changes in nature to the process of fermentation. He even accepts the latter's rejection of the four elements in favor of five "principles", three active ones (spirit, sulfur, and salt) and two passive ones (water and earth)[71].

In addition to Tobias, other Jews display the definite influence of the iatrochemists. David Nieto, in a long passage where he presents the conflicting philosophies of Descartes and Gassendi, also describes accurately the chemical philosophers, and even more revealingly, describes the same five principles of Willis[72]. Abraham Wallich quotes Sylvius, Willis, and Ertmuller[73]. Among Jewish physicians elsewhere in Italy and in the North, these Paduan graduates hardly were unique.[74] Similar Paracelsian influences are found earlier in the sixteenth-century writings of Abraham Portaleone[75] and Abraham Yagel[76], and, among contemporary Jewish physicians, Isaac Cardoso[77] and Jacob Zahalon[78], to name only a few.

Such an abiding commitment to a philosophy of medicine whose founder had once vilified Jewish doctors might strike the modern reader with considerable irony. For in fact, Paracelsus had sought emphatically to overturn the idea that the Jews possessed a medical tradition superior to that of the Christians:

As regards medicine the Jews of old boasted greatly, and they still do, and they are not ashamed of the falsehood [involved], they claim that they are the oldest and first physicians. And indeed they are the foremost among all the other nations, the foremost rascals, that is [...] He [God] also put a curse on those who protect the Jews and who mix with their affairs, and yet they vindicate for themselves all praise of medicine. Let us pay no attention to all that, for if the Jews achieve anything in medicine they have not inherited it from their forefathers but have stolen it away from others, from strangers by robbery as it were [...] medicine has been given to the Gentiles and the Gentiles therefore we revere and praise, as the most ancient physicians[79].

Although the medical field at first may appear an odd setting to do battle with Jews, in the case of Paracelsus and his followers, it is more understandable, given the deeply religious overtones of the chemical philosophy. Paracelsus' search for natural knowledge was colored throughout by a religious quest for God. For Paracelsus more than others, the search for divine "signatures" in nature, the quest for analogies and correspondences was connected intimately with understanding the Divine mystery. Indeed Paracelsus, Van Helmont, and other iatrochemists had promoted the notion that the physician's office was divine. Had not Ecclesiastes spoken of the Paracelsian *magus* and physician when he proclaimed: "Honor the physician for the need thou hast of him; for the Most High has created him"[80]? For such a researcher, his chemical search throughout the natural realm performed the pious duty of showing to mankind the infinite love of the Creator. Although so elevated a ministry was conceived for only pious Christians, the fusion of medicine, scientific inquiry, and theology no doubt was an appealing proposition to sixteenth- and seventeenth-century Jewish physicians as well[81]. They could ignore or repudiate Paracelsus' calumnies regarding Jewish medicine while soundly approving of so satisfying a rationale for their own professional and personal vocation. Could Solomon Conegliano have understood his calling any differently than that of Paracelsus and his followers when the physician-rabbi casually shifted from a medical text to a Talmudic tome in the classroom of his heralded academy?

Besides the chemical philosophy, the new atomistic theories of seven-

teenth-century science found their Jewish adherents as well. Joseph Delmedigo displays considerable familiarity with atomism, even identifying
atoms with the kabbalist theory of "points" in the system of Isaac Luria,
as understood by Israel Sarug[82]. David Nieto presents Gassendi's atomism as a viable alternative to either the iatrochemists or Descartes,
although he ultimately rejects all three theories for the more reliable
truths of the Torah[83]. Of all seventeenth-century Jewish writers, Isaac
Cardoso, trained in medicine at Salamanca but also the father of the
Paduan medical graduate, Jacob Cardoso, reveals the most intimate
knowledge of recent atomistic theories, quoting a long list of contemporary atomists as well as Gassendi. While approving of the atomists who
free themselves of "peripatetic slavery", he is careful to steer clear of
their mechanistic implications by strongly defending the concept of divine providence[84].

In the allied fields of botany and zoology, mineralogy and geography,
these same writers also clearly demonstrate their competence and wide
erudition. In the fifteenth and sixteenth centuries, Jewish scientific writers such as Yohanan Alemanno, Abraham Farissol, Abraham Yagel,
Abraham Portaleone, David de Pomis, and others had evinced particular
interest in the spectacular, the peculiar, the irregularities of nature[85].
Their writings abound with descriptions of strange beasts and monsters,
rare stones, and exotic plants. The seventeenth-century writers display
similar proclivities, yet if there is any shift of emphasis, it lies in their
growing analytic concern for describing the known rather than the
mysterious. No doubt Isaac Cardoso still amuses his readers with digressions on monsters and unicorns just as David de Pomis earlier had
relished the opportunity of discoursing on buffalo eggs[86]. Yet the later
Paduan graduates seem to display more immediate and pragmatic concerns. Tobias Cohen is more inclined to focus on practical medical
subjects—anatomy, embryology, pediatrics, pathology[87]. He has at his
command a wealth of practical and theoretical knowledge which limited
considerably any fanciful digressions from his primary goal—a coherent
presentation of a medical textbook for the educated layman. A similarly
pragmatic agenda, albeit more constricted in scope, is found in Abraham
Wallich's *Harmonia Wallichia Medica*[88]. Jacob Zahalon's *Ozar ha-
Hayyim,* published in Venice in 1683, is designed along similar practical
lines—to provide a useful medical encyclopedia for Jews who live in
small towns where trained physicians are not always available[89]. Like

Cohen's work, massive sections of Cardoso's *Philosophia libera* are practically orientated, leading the reader through informed discourses on biology, human anatomy, and medicine. Although less imposing, the knowledge of these Jewish savants in other scientific disciplines is hardly negligible. Cohen, Nieto, and Cardoso are quite informed and indeed persuaded by the heliocentric theory, even though they ultimately reject it on theological grounds [90]. Delmedigo's relationship with Galileo and subsequent positive views of Copernicus already are well known [91]. Nieto accurately describes Descartes' mechanical philosophy [92]; Tobias Cohen also refers to Cartesian mechanics as well as Mersenne's experiments with air pressure [93]. Numerous other examples of scientific knowledge among Jewish writers, Paduan and non-Paduan graduates alike, are forthcoming but unnecessary to substantiate the indisputable fact that by the seventeenth century Jewish writers on science were conversant with all the major trends of contemporary science. Their scientific learning focused especially on the practicable, utilitarian areas of medicine and its related fields. They were conscious of an explosion in knowledge and a radical improvement in medical treatment as a result, and they sought to convey their enthusiasm for these newly found techniques in both their Hebrew and Latin writings.

No doubt such unwavering commitment to the study of the new medicine and new science was bound to stir up longstanding anxieties within the Jewish community about the disproportionate amount of time expended on such studies and the potential displacement of the time-honored curriculum of Jewish learning by secular pursuits. Such concerns focused not only on the quantity of scientific study but also on its quality; ultimately a Jewish student prepared to invest five or more years of his education in non-traditional learning had opted for the priority of scientific over rabbinic learning. Certainly a prior grounding in rabbinic texts along with a restrengthening of traditional values through the agency of a Jewish supplemental school were useful in bolstering Jewish loyalties. But ultimately, by entering Padua's medical school or other comparable institutions students had chosen to pursue the secular at the expense of the holy. They eventually required strategies designed to help them adjust to so radical an educational dislocation, to legitimate scientific pursuits within the context of Jewish tradition and to promote the medical scientific profession within Jewish culture and society. Additionally there remained the external need to justify the increasingly conspicuous presence of Jewish physicians before unfriendly and even hostile colleagues in the European scientific and academic community.

The new Jewish scientific virtuosi already had at their disposal two venerable devices to achieve their purpose, one explicitly and the other implicitly located within the Jewish tradition itself. The first was to argue that scientific-physical pursuits, like philosophical-metaphysical ones, were endemic to Judaism from the time of Abraham or Solomon. According to this argument, science, with the emphasis either on medicine or astronomy, always was a Jewish discipline. The Hebrews had it first; they only lost it because of the trials and tribulations of their long exile[94]. If such sophistry appeared forced in light of the historical record, the major heroes of ancient science could be easily Judaised. Had not Aristotle or Plato studied with Jewish teachers[95]? Was not Moschus the Phoenician, the first atomist, indebted to a Jew for his knowledge[96]?

The second device was to legitimate the pursuit of scientific knowledge in religious terms, to construct a Jewish theology of medicine and science. Unquestionably the sources for such a theology were diffused richly throughout Jewish sources from the Psalmist to the rabbis and to the philosophers[97]. They also were available in even more comprehensive form among contemporary Christian practitioners of science[98]. By highlighting the religious dimensions of studying nature, by arguing that the signs of nature lead ultimately to a better knowledge of God, and by insisting that medical and scientific study are no less than a religious duty, the growing breed of Jewish doctor-scientists not only vindicated themselves before their fellow co-religionists: they staked out a claim to a dominant leadership role within the Jewish community.

The first strategem of appealing to a Jewish tradition of science was no more than a contemporary variation on the primary defense mechanism of Jewish cultural history[99]. Particularly in the era of the Renaissance, contemporary Jews, undoubtedly flattered by the new-found Christian interest in their cultural heritage, were quick to point out that Israel was the font of all learning; the "Renaissance" was a return to their own national treasures no less than those of Greece or Rome[100]. If Neoplatonism, Hermetic magic, or Ciceronian rhetoric could be Judaised by Renaissance Jewish writers, why not science as well? In fact, the latter task was made easier by the prominence of so many outstanding scientists among the luminaries of the Jewish cultural past, from Maimonides to Gersonides to Ibn Ezra and Zacuto. By the prominent place these earlier giants had given to science, they already had validated its pursuit for their eventual successors. Prior to them, both the rabbis and even earlier heroes of the Biblical past supposedly had paved the way for a Jewish appreciation of scientific endeavor. Thus David Nieto argued that "the source of the sciences went out from us and our holy Torah includes them all"[101]. Abraham, Job, and Solomon all were knowledgeable about nature; the rabbis demonstrated expertise in geography, engineering, medicine, and surgery as well[102]: "Behold our sages certainly have an advantage of some 1500 years in their knowing [science] what the moderns still do not know at present"[103]. Nieto qualifies this generalization by conceding that the rabbis' knowledge was imperfect because they mastered only what was critical to understand the Torah[104]. Similarly in the field of astronomy "it already is known" writes Tobias Cohen "that our sages tried harder than the Gentile scholars to know and understand the wisdom of astronomy [. . .] And thus the words of the Torah and sciences were mixed and diffused among Israel throughout the duration of the first and second Temples and then arose the spirit of the Babylonians, Persians, Greeks, and Romans to learn from them, to exchange [knowledge] about the science of the spheres as well as other sciences"[105]. Even Joseph Delmedigo, who laments the inferior status of science in the conventional curriculum of contemporary Jews, acknowledges, at the very least, the existence of a Jewish scientific tradition, "one in a city, two in a state, who represented a powerful support for the house of Israel", men like Saadia Gaon, Abraham Bar Hiyya, Abraham Ibn Ezra, Isaac Israeli, Moses Almosnino, David Gans, and others[106].

The argument for a tradition of Jewish science also is unequivocal in the apologetic literature of contemporary Jewish doctors writing in Latin. Isaac Cardoso argues that Abraham and Joseph taught the Egyptians mathematics, that Solomon's scientific knowledge was second to none, and even that atomism was of Jewish origin[107]. Both David de Pomis and Benedict de Castro would have concurred fully with Paracelsus' remark regarding the Jewish claim that they are the first physicians. De Pomis unabashedly declares in his *De Medico Hebraeo*, published in Venice in 1588, that medicine was first discovered among the Jews and only later was revealed to the Gentiles. His list of illustrious Jewish physicians includes both the medieval doctors, Ibn Ezra, Gersonides, and Maimonides, as well as contemporaries, Abraham de Balmes and Joseph Delmedigo. To this he adds additional lists of distinguished Jewish physicians in France and Turkey[108]. For de Castro, it was God who conceded to the Jews the privilege of medical practice as their hereditary right:

Moses, the most famous of all legislators [...] was the one who laid the foundation of medicine as the most conspicuous of all arts [...] Solomon the wise [...] left an exhaustive history of healing plants [...] But why need I dwell on that when there is virtually no part of medicine which cannot be traced to the Hebrew forefathers[109]?

For him, the crowning achievements in Jewish medicine, however, are reserved for his own time—those of the Converso physicians "scattered all over the world" as well as the "numerous Jews engaged in medicine all over Holland, Brabant, Gaul, Italy and Germany"[110].

A theological claim accompanied the historical rationale for legitimizing scientific endeavor among contemporary Jews. The materials for constructing such a theology were readily available within Biblical and post-Biblical writing; Christian writers on science regularly had employed similar arguments in affirming their religious motives for scientific pursuit[111]. Thus Jewish writers declared that the acquisition of scientific knowledge constituted a kind of natural revelation. The more the scientist discovered the natural world around him, the more he confirmed his religious beliefs. It became, accordingly, a religious duty to study nature since by ignoring the manifestations of God's glory in nature, one robs the Creator of some of His glory. Of course, such pious demands for scientific involvement unconsciously assumed that nature was no more than an extension of God's providence. When decoded, the multifarious forms of nature would reveal, in their magnificent splendor, a total pattern of divine harmony, and that nature only would divulge its benevolent side. These Jews based such prior convictions on the unshakable belief in God's infinite goodness[112]. Nevertheless, whatever its logical inconsistencies, such an argument functioned more than adequately as a satisfying rationalization for Jewish doctor-scientists to view their medical pursuits within the safe confines of Jewish tradition itself. Thus Jacob Zahalon set the proper tone in authenticating his professional activity through his well-known physician's prayer: "I pray [...] that I may discover the secrets of thy wonderful deeds and that I may know the peculiar curative powers which Thou hast placed in herbs and minerals [. . .] and that through them I shall tell of Thy might to all generations to whom Thy greatness shall come"[113]. Similarly David Nieto proclaimed: "There is not a single creature, even among the least of them, that does not show in some form of its constitution the impress of God"[114]. Even Joseph Ḥamiẓ who eventually turned from scientific to mystical study, could still acknowledge: "One must understand natural things in order to know what is beyond nature [. . .] for one must look at heaven to see what is considerably higher than nature, that there exists a leader and organizer of nature regarding every particular thing"[115]. In like fashion, Joseph Delmedigo extols the purposefulness of natural phenomena, the wonders, of such seemingly insignificant oddities as roots, seeds, or spiders[116]. Elsewhere, he concludes: "Contemplating every one of [God's] creatures leads man to recognize his exalted Creator and to praise the Master and Cause of everything good, since 'from our flesh, we shall see God' (Job 19:26) our Maker and glorify him since all of 'His judgments are like the great deep' (Psalms 36:7)"[117]. Perhaps the most felicitous description of the Jewish doctor-scientist's calling was penned by Isaac Cardoso: "We shall investigate nature and its founder, so that from the world and its multitude of things, as if by a ladder, with enlightened and instructed mind, we may be lifted to God its maker; for his creatures are the ladder by which we ascend to God, the organ with which we praise God, and the school in which we learn God"[118].

The reassuring coincidence that so many physicians were also rabbis no doubt was confirmation of the underlying spirituality of the doctor's role. Thus Ẓahalon would remind his readers that "most of the doctors in Israel are masters of the Torah and Godfearers"[119]. The curriculum of Solomon Conegliano's preparatory academy assuredly confirmed this observation. Moreover for Isaac Cardoso, the integration of the physician's "truths" with those of the theologian was not fortuitous; on the contrary, it was deliberate and constituted the ultimate objective of the Jewish physician: "For it behooves the philosopher to handle both, that is, the human things, and the divine, so from the visible to the invisible, from the perishable to the immortal, from the temporal to the eternal, we may train, uplift and kindle the mind"[120].

Here then lay the most compelling argument in favor of the medical profession: to contemplate the visible world or to ruminate over a rabbinic text were essentially equivalent activities. Deciphering the signs of God's marvelous presence in the pages of a sacred literary document or in the operations of natural processes were extensions of the same Jewish imperative: to celebrate God's majesty and to sing praises of his manifold works. Cardoso and his colleagues presumably had succeeded, as Paracelsus and his disciples before them, in suppressing any apparent strains between the demands of their mundane and divine vocations. What greater assurance could a Jewish student be offered in choosing a medical and scientific career than to be told that the dramatic discoveries in his anatomy class were substantively no less uplifting from a religious point of view than the most ingenious subtleties of a Talmudic discourse [121]!

Such historical or theological apologia could not conceal for long the inevitable incongruity between scientific research and conventional modes of Jewish study. Unquestionably the Jewish anatomy student eventually came to appreciate the qualitative difference between scientific and traditional methodologies of learning. No doubt Joseph Delmedigo's preference for engineers and builders over "academicians with their endless disputations, which only distract people from their useful pursuits", was symptomatic of a change of heart in more than one Jewish graduate of a medical school [122]. So too was his unqualified resentment for those rabbis of his day who failed to understand anything "on the subject of the sphere and its construction just as the goat or ass fail to understand" [123]. Such religious leaders, in Delmedigo's estimation, were culpable of breaking an eternal covenant and rebelling against the prophet's word: "Look at the Heavens and see who created these" [124].

Delmedigo's sarcasm stands in sharp contrast with the pious affirmations of those who naively believed that the methods of the rabbis and those of the scientists were indeed the same. As Delmedigo transparently acknowledged, they were not only the same; the latter was often superior to the former. The education of non-Jewish children in the natural sciences was far better than that of Jewish children. "Is this the Torah which Moses placed at the head of the nations [. . .] which is the tree of life to those who grasp it [. . .] ?", Delmedigo tauntingly asks [125]. His scornful question undoubtedly discloses the shattering consequences intense scientific study could hold for at least one Jewish university graduate on the threshold of the modern era.

Delmedigo's Jewish inferiority complex was perhaps the most palpable among his Jewish contemporaries but hardly an isolated case of

Jewish cultural insecurity. David Nieto, notwithstanding his arsenal of arguments to demonstrate the credibility of rabbinic over scientific truths, is forced ultimately to admit that the rabbis' knowledge was incomplete since there was no necessity for them to be "learned or surgeons or astronomers or doctors [...] It was sufficient that they master these disciplines [only] as completely as required in order to understand our holy Torah"[126]. Tobias Cohen's motivation in writing his Hebrew medical compendium is inextricably bound up with a deep-seated feeling of cultural inferiority, nurtured especially by the unpleasant experiences of his student days in Germany prior to coming to Padua. He writes in order to respond to the Gentiles:

who vex us, raising their voices without restraint, speaking haughtily with arrogance and scorn, telling us we have no mouth to respond, nor a forehead to raise our heads in matters of faith and that our knowledge and ancient intelligence have been lost, as I heard the slander of many from the surrounding den during the days of my youth. The truth of the matter is that because of our many sins men of learning are lost and we have no one who knows how to answer the doubters who abuse us with an appropriate winning response [. . .][127].

When David de Pomis earlier called for the study of science among his co-religionists ("for it raises the lowly, frees those despised and in bondage, and secures respect and honor"), he assuredly shared his colleague's lack of confidence in the enduring vitality and integrity of traditional Jewish culture[128]. Regardless of both Cohen's and de Pomis' pious affirmations of a proud and time-honored scientific tradition with Judaism, they reveal at the same time unmistakable feelings of inadequacy. The contest between science and Jewish tradition had left its shattering mark on the cultural sensibilities of Jews like Cohen, Nieto, Delmedigo, and many others in Padua and elsewhere. The demonstrative assurance of earlier Italian Jews regarding the adequacy of their own cultural legacy was no longer self-evident to their successors[129]. The results of the new scientific explosion were imposing, and they no longer could be explained away solely by appeals to the grandiose cultural achievements of an ancient past. The emerging sense of Jewish inferiority among such impressionable Jewish observers of enlightened Christian society would become a propensity for an increasing number of university-educated Jews in subsequent years[130].

A diminished confidence in the modes of Jewish education was one thing; an uncertainty regarding some of the cardinal principles of Jewish faith was quite another. The basic compatibility between science and Judaism had appeared axiomatic to the early Jewish practitioners of science; to their successors, it increasingly was fraught with difficulties. No less immune than their Christian counterparts to the formidable challenges science ultimately presented to religious faith, Jewish scientific writers soon learned to appreciate that their naive belief in the congruence of the two systems of truth was often unreliable[131].

Jewish writers on medicine and science had proposed most often arguments from the design and order of the universe to demonstrate the supposed affinity between science and belief in one God. As we have seen, such arguments could bolster, on the one hand, their prior convictions that the more they knew of the universe, the more they were capable of glorifying God. On the other hand, these claims also tended to obscure the potential complication that when God is seen exclusively as a reflection of nature, He might easily be mistaken for nature itself. With such emphasis on arguments from design, proof of God's existence based on the subjective historical experience of the Jewish people often assumes a minor or even negligible role[132]. Moreover, the idea of divine providence over all individual creatures is passed over in favor of an immanent and natural causality.

This is not the place to examine in detail the theological implications of this more than subtle shift in emphasis in speaking about God among these same Jewish writers. Suffice it to say they are quite sensitive to the serious obstacles these new formulations might pose for the Jewish faith. Tobias Cohen, for example, writes:

there exist weak minded men of deficient intelligence and understanding not only from among the Gentile nations who never observed the light of the Torah but also among the members of our people, the nation that walks in the darkness of the exile and the light of the Torah [. . .] and they think that the world has no originator or creator or leader but only that everything is determined by nature and its custom. Some of them are skeptical of this matter and doubt it, among them believers and non-believers [. . .][133].

Joseph Delmedigo, in discussing the issue of divine providence, is no less explicit: "Some philosophers thought that nature is equivalent to God Himself because His works were wondrous in their eyes"[134]. Isaac Cardoso speaks more innocently about God being "a universal axiom of nature"[135]. However David Nieto has no illusion about the pitfalls of such formulations. Because of his own attempt to define the Jewish concept of God as identical with nature, he finds himself embroiled in a heated theological controversy, even accused of pantheistic proclivities. No doubt he composed his entire treatise, *On Divine Providence,* in the context of similar English and continental theological discussions regarding the dangerous implications of the new science.[136].

No less troubling for these men were the apparent points of friction between the authority of scientific hypotheses and that of sacred tradition[137]. The Copernican theory was the most obvious and dramatic case in point. Here the sheer logic and rationality of the heliocentric position was pitted against the utter weight of Biblical authority. Among Jewish discussants of Copernicus, Tobias Cohen and David Nieto disclose most transparently their personal dilemma in assuming a stance that violates neither their rational nor their religious sensibilities. While both writers eventually opt for a conservative Biblicist position, there is more to their convoluted discussions than initially meets the eye. Neither of them is overly impressed by the weight of the Aristotelian position[138]. Nieto openly disparages those who blindly adhere to the Peripatetic teachings[139]. Both are noticeably swayed by the refreshing consistency and utterly simple arguments against the Ptolemaic universe which they present to their readers with little or no refutation at all. Tobias may caustically label Copernicus "the first born of Satan", but more revealingly, he offers no resistance to six cogently argued Copernican demonstrations other than limply stating: "These are the proofs that the teachers, according to Copernicus' view, would teach; however the counterarguments are easily proven for one who understands [them]: thus I will not dwell on them anymore"[140].

Additional theological hurdles arose not only regarding the position of the Earth but also its unique status in a universe of seemingly infinite scope. The idea of a divinely ordered world, its harmony and proportion, had been traditionally tied to a finite universe. This proposition naturally led to the unique status of the Earth, the centrality and unique moral purpose of the Earth's creation, and the image of man as the master of that creation[141]. For Jews, the special vocation of their chosen status and the singular revelation of the Torah seemed considerably undermined if not debilitated altogether by the notion of infinitely inhabited worlds. Fully aware of the various strands of the seventeenth-century debate, Cohen, Nieto, and Delmedigo surprisingly offer no serious opposition to this revolutionary concept. Nieto is unoffended by the notion of the plurality of worlds since it fails to contradict any Biblical verse[142]. Cohen remains comfortably neutral, offering his readers five arguments in favor and five against plurality[143]. Delmedigo waxes eloquent about his personal delight in realizing that the world's plurality leads ineluctably to a heightened appreciation of the Creator Himself[144]. Cardoso alone firmly objects to the concept of many worlds. Many worlds imply many creators while "unus Deus unum mundum creavit"[145].

Not one of the encomiasts who participated in Joseph Ḥamiẓ's celebrated college graduation could have fully anticipated the rich symbolism of so seemingly modest an occasion. For Padua offered Jews like Ḥamiẓ more than the limited opportunity of acquiring technical knowledge. It afforded them a radically novel learning experience, a new basis for sociability with non-Jews, and a unique environment for cultivating different, often conflicting, values. It provided them a stage, a forum for wrestling with the inevitable tensions of living a Jewish life in a dramatically changing social and intellectual universe. They had entered merely to study medicine; they came out thoroughly transformed human beings. The story, sketched here of Ḥamiẓ and his contemporaries, only in preliminary fashion on the basis of limited data, requires considerably more attention. More graduates deserve their own biographers—studies of their life experiences, their tribulations, and their attitudes shaped in the formative years of their education and professional careers. Such a nuanced investigation of Jewish scientific figures, emerging, to a great extent, at Padua under the aegis of the government of the Veneto, undoubtedly will contribute to a greater appreciation of the process of intellectual and social integration of early-modern Jews in Western and Eastern Europe[146].

Meir Benayahu perceptively reminds us to examine carefully the actual portraits of the Jewish doctors he has studied—Abraham Cohen of Zante, Shabbetai Marini, and Solomon Lustro[147]. They, like their illustrious contemporaries Tobias Cohen and Joseph Delmedigo, flattered themselves by having their own images printed on the opening leaf of their published writings. How stately, how solemn, how pretentious, and how "non-Jewish" they appear in their formal medical attire! Who would doubt that underneath the composed external appearance of each of these gentlemen lies an inner world of variegated and edifying life experiences, of intellectual ferment, of cultural strains and agitations, and perhaps even of psychological turmoil, a world not unlike that of subsequent generations of Jews striving to enter modern European society?

NOTES

1. A. Modena and E. Morpurgo, *Medici e chirughi ebrei dottorati e licenziati nell'Università di Padova dal 1617 al 1816,* ed. A. Luzzato, L. Münster, and V. Colorni, Bologna 1967, p. 8.

2. On Padua's medical school in the sixteenth and seventeenth centuries, see G. Whitteridge, *William Harvey and the Circulation of the Blood,* London-New York 1917; C. B. Schmitt, *Science in the Italian Universities in the 16th and Early 17th Centuries,* in M. Crosland (ed.), *The Emergence of Science in Western Europe,* New York 1976, pp. 35–56; Id., *Philosophy and Science in 16th Century Universities: Some Preliminary Comments,* in J. E. Murdoch and E. D. Sylla (eds.), *The Cultural Context of Medieval Learning,* Dordrecht 1975, pp. 485–537; J. Bylebyl, *The School of Padua: Humanistic Medicine in the Sixteenth Century,* in C. Webster (ed.), *Health, Medicine and Mortality in the Sixteenth Century,* Cambridge 1979, pp. 335–70; C. Fichtner, *Padova e Tubingen: la formazione medica nei secoli XVI e XVII,* "Acta Medicae Historiae Patavina", XIX (1972–73), pp. 43–62. See also the articles of F. D. Derroussiles, G. Ongaro, and C. Maccagni in G. Arnaldi and M. Pastore Stocchi (eds.), *Storia della cultura veneta: dal primo Quattrocento al Concilio di Trento,* III, Vicenza 1980, sections 2 and 3. References to the earlier standard works on Padua's university are found in these articles. On Jewish students at Padua, see C. Roth, *Venice,* Philadelphia 1930, pp. 285–93; V. Colorni, *Sull'ammissibilità degli ebrei alla laurea anteriormente al secolo XIX,* in *Scritti in onore di Riccardo Bachi,* Città di Castello 1950; G. Kisch, *Cervo Conigliano: A Jewish Graduate of Padua in 1743,* "Journal of the History of Medicine", 4 (1949), pp. 450–59; J. Shatzky, *On Jewish Medical Students of Padua,* "Journal of the History of Medicine", 5 (1950), pp. 444–47; H. Friedenwald, *The Jews and Medicine,* 2 vols., Baltimore 1955, I, pp. 221–40, 253–58; A. Ciscato, *Gli ebrei in Padova (1300–1800),* Padua 1901; D. Kaufmann, *Trois docteurs de Padoue,* "REJ", 18 (1889), pp. 293–98; M. Soave, *Medici ebrei laureati nell'Università di Padova nel 1600 e 1700,* "Il Vessillo Israelitico", 24 (1876), pp. 189–92. I was unable to consult J. Warchal, *Jan. Zidzi polscy na Universytecie padevskim,* "Kwartalnik poświecony badaniu przeszłości Żidóm w Polsce", Warsaw 1913, I, n. 3, pp. 37–72. Beside the list of Jewish students located in Modena and Morpurgo, *Medici e chirughi ebrei,* cit., see now, for the sixteenth century, E. Veronese Ceseracciu, *Ebrei laureati a Padova nel Cinquecento,* "Quaderni per la storia dell'Università di Padova", 13 (1980), pp. 151–68. Additional bibliography is mentioned in the works above and see also below.

3. The collection is entitled *Belil Ḥamiẓ* and was printed in Venice in 1624. It is reprinted in N. S. Leibowitz, *Seridim Mikītve ha-Pilosof ha-Rofe ve-ha-Mekubbal R. Yosef Ḥamiẓ*, Jerusalem 1937, pp. 35 ff.

4. Benjamin Mussafia graduated from Padua a year later in 1625 (Modena and Morpurgo, *Medici e chirughi ebrei*, cit., p. 10). On Mussafia, see D. Margalit, *Ḥokhme Yisra'el Ke-Rofim*, Jerusalem 1962, pp. 142–51.

5. On Azariah Figo, see A. Apfelbaum, *R. Azariah Figo*, Drohobycz 1907. Compare Figo's critique of "gentile" learning discussed by Y. Yerushalmi, *From Spanish Court to Italian Ghetto*, New York 1971, pp. 373–74.

6. J. Schudt, *Jüdische Merekwürdigkeiten*, Frankfort on the Main 1714–18, II, p. 404, described in Friedenwald, *The Jews and Medicine*, cit., I, pp. 227–28.

7. See the bibliography in note 2 above.

8. See Warchal's article mentioned in note 2 as well as N. M. Gelber, *On the History of Jewish Doctors in Poland in the 18th Century* in *Shai le-Yishayahu (Jubilee Volume in Honor of Isaiah Wolfsberg)*, Tel Aviv 1956, pp. 347–71; G. Kisch, *Die Prager Universität und die Juden 1348–1848*, Mährisch-Ostrau 1935.

9. On Jewish medical students at the University of Leiden, see J. Kaplan, *Jewish Students from Amsterdam at the University of Leiden in the 17th Century*, in *Meḥkarim al Toledoth Yahadut Holland*, Jerusalem 1979, pp. 65–75 (in Hebrew).

10. The standard works on the history of Jewish physicians include the aforementioned writings of Friedenwald and Margalit; M. Steinschneider, *Jüdische Aerzte*, "ZHB", 17 (1914), pp. 63–96, 121–68; 18 (1918), pp. 25–57; I. Münz, *Die Jüdische Ärzte in Mittelalter*, Frankfort on Main 1922; E. Carmoly, *Histoire des médecins juifs anciens et modernes*, Brussels 1844; R. Landau, *Geschichte der Jüdischen Ärzte*, Berlin 1895; S. Krauss, *Geschichte der Jüdischen Ärzte*, Vienna 1930; and S. R. Kagan, *Jewish Medicine*, Boston 1952. See also S. Goitein, *The Medical Profession in the Light of the Cairo Genizah Documents*, "HUCA" 34 (1963), pp. 177–94.

11. See the works listed in the previous note, as well as Colorni, *Sull'ammissibilità*, cit.; C. Roth, *The Qualification of Jewish Physicians in the Middle Ages*, "Speculum", 28 (1953), pp. 834–43; D. Carpi, *R. Judah Messer Leon and His Activity as a Doctor*, "Michael", I (1973), pp. 277–301 (in Hebrew).

12. Cf. Shatzky, *On Jewish Medical Students*, cit., p. 446; on the "nations", see P. Kibre, *The Nations in the Medieval Universities*, Cambridge (Mass.) 1948.

13. For documentation regarding these conclusions, see below.

14. Cr. Shatzky, *On Jewish Medical Students*, cit., p. 444; Gelber, *On the History of Jewish Doctors*, cit., p. 351; N. Shapiro, *The Natural Sciences and Mathematics as Pathfinders for the Haskala Movement*, "Koroth", 2 (1958), pp. 319–44 (in Hebrew).

15. Bylebyl, *The School of Padua*, cit., pp. 342–43; O. Logan, *Culture and Society in Venice 1470–1790*, London 1972, pp. 20–21, 46–47.

16. From 1617 to 1816, the names of all Jewish graduates are listed in Modena and Morpurgo. *Medici e chirurghi ebrei*, cit.; L. A. Schiavi, *Gli ebrei in Venezia e nelle sue colonie. Appunti storici su documenti editi ed inediti*, "Nuova antologia", s. III, 47 (1893), p. 333 was the first to maintain that 80 Jews graduated the university between 1517–1619 and he was followed by all subsequent authors. For further clarifications regarding this number see the article of Veronese Ceseracciu mentioned in note 2 above.

17. On Delmedigo, see I. Barzilay, *Yoseph Shlomo Delmedigo, Yashar of Candia: His Life, Works, and Times*, Leiden 1974.

18. On Ḥamiẓ, see *Encyclopedia Judaica*, VII, coll. 1239–40 and the bibliography listed there and see note 3 above.

19. On Cohen, see Carmoly, Histoire des médecins juifs, cit., pp. 247–51; A. Levinson, *Tuviyyah ha-Rofe ve-Sifro Ma'aseh Tuviyyah*, Berlin 1924, and see below.

20. On Nieto, see J. L. Petuchowski, *The Theology of Haham David Nieto: An Eighteenth-Century Defense of the Jewish Tradition*, New York 1954, reprint 1970; I. Solomons, *David Nieto and Some of His Contemporaries*, "JHSET", 12 (1931), pp. 1–101, and see below.

21. On the Coneglianos, see D. Kaufmann, *Dr. Israel Conegliano und seine Verdienste um die Republik Venedig bis nach dem Frieden von Carlowitz*, Budapest 1895; on Solomon, see T. Cohen, *Ma'aseh Tuviyyah*, Venice 1707, pp. 5a–b, 93a.

22. On Isaac Cantarini, see M. Osimo, *Narrazione della strage compiuta nel 1547 contro gli ebrei d'Asolo e cenni biografici della famiglia Koen-Contarini*, Casale Monferrato, 1875, pp. 67–93; H. A. Savitz, *Dr. Isaac Hayyim ha-Cohen Contarini*, "The Jewish Forum", 43 (1960), pp. 80–82, 99–101, 107–8.

23. See the references in note 2 above.

24. See C. M. Cipolla, *Public Health and the Medical Profession in the Renaissance*, Cambridge 1976, pp. 67–116; Bylebyl, *The School of Padua*, cit., p. 336.

25. See note 15 above.

26. See especially Fichtner, *Padova e Tubingen*, cit., who refers to Thomas Bartholin's work, *De peregrinatione medica*, Hafniae 1674.

27. The description of Padua's curriculum and social setting that follows is based on the works of Bylebyl, Whitteridge, and Schmitt cited in note 2 above. See also, J. P. Tomasini, *Gymanisum Patavinum*, Udine 1645; J. Facciolati, *Fasti Gymnasii Patavini*, 3 parts in 1, Padua 1757; A. Favaro, *Atti della nazione germanica artista nello Studio di Padova*, 2 vols., Venice 1911–12; S. de Renzi, *Storia della medicina in Italia*, 5 vols., Naples 1845–48; H. F. Rashdall, *The Universities of Europe in the Middle Ages*, 3 vols., 2nd ed., ed. by M. Powicke and A. B. Emden, Oxford 1936; P. O. Kristeller, *Philosophy and Medicine in Medieval and Renaissance Italy*, in S. F. Spicker (ed.), *Organism, Medicine and Metaphysics*, Dordrecht 1978, pp. 29–40;

A. Favaro, *Saggio di bibliografia dello Studio di Padova*, Venice 1922, and "Quaderni per la storia dell'Università di Padova", Padua 1968 ff.

28. L. Münster, *Die Anfänge eines klinischen Unterrichts an der Universität Padua in 16. Jahrhundert*, "Medizinische Monatsschrift", 32 (1969), pp. 171 ff.; F. Pellegrini, *La clinica medica padovana attraverso i secoli*, Verona 1939.

29. On the latter, see below.

30. E. H. Underwood, *The Early Teaching of Anatomy at Padua with Special Reference to a Model of the Padua Anatomical Theatre*, "Annals of Science", 19 (1963), pp. 1–26.

31. A. Favaro, *I lettori di matematiche nell'Università di Padova dal principio del secolo XIV alla fine del XVI*, "Memorie e documenti per la storia dell'Università di Padova", I (1922), pp. 1–70.

32. Kibre, *The Nations*, cit., pp. 43, 116 ff.; Favaro, *Atti della nazione germanica*, cit.; Cipolla, *Public Health and the Medical Profession*, cit., pp. 6–7; *Omaggio dell'Accademia polacca all'Università di Padova*, Cracow 1922.

33. Ciscato, *Gli Ebrei in Padova*, cit., p. 209; Moses Vital Cantarini composed a treatise on the problem of using Jewish corpses for dissections. See "Hebraische Bibliographie", 16 (1874), p. 37.

34. On this, see B. Kisch, *Cervo Conigliano*, cit., pp. 457–59; Ciscato, *Gli ebrei in Padova*, cit., pp. 213 ff.; Friedenwald, *The Jews and Medicine*, cit., I, pp. 226–27.

35. Cohen, *Ma'aseh Tuviyyah*, cit., p. 93a.

36. J. Delmedigo, *Sefer Elim*, Odessa 1864–67, p. 63. Compare this remark with a similar traditional concern discussed in M. Idel, *On the history of the Inderdiction Against the Study of the Kabbalah Before the Age of Forty*, "AJSR", V (1980), pp. 15–20 (in Hebrew).

37. Delmedigo, *Sefer Elim*, cit., p. 92.

38. Provincial's proposal is found in S. Assaf, *Toledot ha-Ḥinukh be-Yisra'el*, 4 vols., Jerusalem 1939–43, II, p. 118. Also quoted in R. Bonfil, *Ha-Rabbanut be-Italya bi-Tekufat ha-Renasans*, Jerusalem 1979, p. 124.

39. Leibowitz, *Seridim*, cit., pp. 44–45.

40. Cohen, *Ma'aseh Tuviyyah*, cit., p. 93a.

41. *Ibid.*

42. On Conegliano and his school, see note 21 and Kaufmann, *Trois docteurs*, cit.

43. See M. Benayahu, *R. Abraham ha-Cohen of Zante and the Group of Doctor-Poets in Padua*, "Ha-Sifrut", 26 (1978), pp. 108–40 (in Hebrew).

44. Cohen, *Ma'aseh Tuviyyah*, Introductions.

45. He is discussed by M. Benayahu (note 43 above) as well as in the works cited in note 22 above. See also his correspondence with Christian Theophil Unger published by S. D. Luzzato in "Oẓar Neḥmad", 3 (1860), pp. 128–50 as well as his other books and letters discussed by Osimo and Savitz.

46. Abba di Elia Delmedigo (graduated 1625, and brother of Joseph); David Vita di Donato Delmedigo (1655); Joseph Isaiah di Jacob Delmedigo de

Dattolis (1677); Abramo Delmedigo (1683); Emmanuel di Jacob Delmedigo de Dattolis (1686). On Joseph, see note 17 above.

47. Lazzaro Wallich (1626); Abram Wallich (1655); Isaac Wallich (1683); Leone di Abram Wallich (1692); Hirsch di Abram Wallich (1692); Jacob Wallich (1722).

48. Daniel di Rodrigo De Castro (1633); Ezekiel alias Pietro di Isacco alias Lodovico De Castro (1645); David di Abram De Castro (1700). See also Friedenwald, *The Jews and Medicine*, cit., II, pp. 452–53.

49. Daniel di Abram Pardo (1624); Abram di Daniel Pardo (1646). See also L. Della Torre, *La famiglia Pardo*, in *Scritti sparsi*, Padova 1908, II, pp. 251–56.

50. Clemente di Simone Cantarini (1623); Leon di Simone Cantarini (1623); Simon Cantarini (1654); Isaac Vita di Jacob Isacco Cantarini (1664); Vidal Moise di Angelo Cantarini (1686); Angelo di Vidal Moise Cantarini (1697); Grassin di Samuel Vita Cantarini (1703); Angelo di Grassin Cantarini (1705); Joseph di Simon Cantarini (1718); Angelo di Simon Cantarini (1722); Simon di Grassin Cantarini (1730); Vidal Cantarini (1748). See also note 22 above.

51. Jacob Cardoso, son of the distinguished Isaac Cardoso, graduated in Padua in 1658. See Yerushalmi, *From Spanish Court to Italian Ghetto*, cit., on Isaac.

52. David di Shemaria Morpurgo (1623); Aron Morpurgo (1671); Marco Morpurgo (1694); Samson di Salvador Moise Morpurgo (1700); Mario Morpurgo (1747); Moise Raffael di Jacob Morpurgo (1768); Joseph Morpurgo (1805). See also E. Morpurgo, *La famiglia Morpurgo di Gradisca sull-'Isonzo (1585–1885)*, Padua 1909.

53. Leo di Isacco Winkler (1629); Jacob di Leo Winkler (1669); Isacco di Leo Winkler (1699); Wolff di Jacob Winkler (1701). See D. Kaufmann, *Hundert Jahre aus einer Familie Jüdischer Aerzte—Dr. Leo, dr. Jakob, dr. Isak, dr. Wolf Winkler*, "Allegemeine Zeitung des Judentums", 52 (1890), pp. 468–71 (reprinted in *Gesammelte Schriften*, Frankfort on the Main 1915, III, pp. 286–95).

54. Eleazoro di Sabbato Maurogonato (1620); Elia di Sabbato Maurogonato (1620); Jacob di Sabbato Maurogonato (1629); Geremia Maurogonato (1633); Sabbato Maurogonato (1678); Geremia di Sabbato Maurogonato (1708); Samuel di Sabbato Maurogonato (1708).

55. David Loria (1623); Isacco di David Loria (1563); David Vita di Isacco Loria (1696); Constantino di Josue Loria (1740).

56. Vitale di Moise Felix (1658); Gabriel di Moise Felix (1683). On the latter's relationship to Tobias Cohen, see Kaufmann, *Trois Docteurs*, cit.; on his relationship to Yair Bachrach, see D. Kaufmann, *R. Jair Chajim Bachrach (1637–1702) und seine Ahnen in Worms*, Treviri 1894.

57. Salomon di Giuseppe Conegliano (1660); Israel di Giuseppe Conegliano (1673); Abramo Joel di Israel Conegliano (1686); Joseph di Leon Conegliano (1688); Joseph di Israel Conegliano (1703); Aron Conegliano (1707);

Issachar di Israel Conegliano (1710); Zevulun di Israel Conegliano (1716); Naftali di Giuseppe Conegliano (1743); Beniamino di Moise Conegliano (1766); Giuseppe Conegliano (1774); Salomon di Naftali Conegliano (1775); Amadeo Conegliano (1783). See also note 21 above.

58. This is not the place to document fully so broad a generalization. Yet merely a study of the origins and points of return of graduates listed by Modena and Morpurgo will yield numerous cross-references to each of these places, among others. See also Gelber, *On the History of Jewish Doctors in Poland,* cit.; G. Kisch, *Die Prager Universität,* cit.; D. Kaufmann, *Ein Jahrhundert einer frankfurter Aerzte-familie,* "Monatschrift für Geschichte und Wissenschaft des Judentums", 41 (1897), pp. 128–33 (reprinted in *Gesammelte Schriften,* cit., III, pp. 296–301); J. Elbaum, *Zeramim u-Magamot be-Sifrut ha-Mahshavah ve-ha-Musar be-Ashkenaz u-ve Polin be-Ma'ah ha-16,* unpublished Ph.D. dissertation, Hebrew University, 1977, ch. 9; J. Leibowitz, *On the History of Jewish Doctors in Salonika, Sefer Yavan,* I (= *Sefunot* 11), Jerusalem 1971–77, pp. 341–51 (in Hebrew); J. Nehama, *Les médecins juifs à Salonique,* "RHMH", 8 (1931), pp. 27–50.

59. Cf. M. Ornstein, *The Role of Scientific Societies in the Seventeenth Century,* Chicago 1938; R. Westfall, *The Construction of Modern Science: Mechanisms and Mechanics,* Cambridge-London-New York-Melbourne 1977, ch. 6.

60. See Friedenwald, *The Jews and Medicine,* cit., I, pp. 31–68; S. Muntner, *Allilot al Rofim Yehudi'im be-Aspaklariyah shel Toledot ha-Refu'ah,* Jerusalem 1953.

61. On this theme, see below.

62. Benedict de Castro, *Flagellum Calumniantium seu Apologia,* Hamburg 1631, quoted in Friedenwald, *The Jews and Medicine,* cit., I, p. 65.

63. On this, see E. Eisenstein, *The Printing Press as an Agent of Change,* Cambridge 1979, II.

64. This point is made by Schmitt, *Science in the Italian Universities,* cit., p. 38.

65. Cf. A. Neher, *Copernicus in the Hebraic Literature From the Sixteenth to the Eighteenth Century,* "Journal of the History of Ideas", 38 (1977), pp. 211–26.

66. On this school, see especially the writings of A. G. Debus, especially *The English Paracelsians,* London 1965, and *The Chemical Philosophy: Paracelsian Science and Medicine in the Sixteenth and Seventeenth Centuries,* 2 vols., New York 1977; J. R. Partington, *A History of Chemistry,* 4 vols., London-New York 1961–70; W. Pagel, *Paracelsus, An Introduction to Philosophical Medicine in the Era of the Renaissance,* Basel-New York 1958, and Id., *The Religious and Philosophical Aspects of van Helmont's Science and Medicine,* Baltimore 1944.

67. Cohen, *Ma'aseh Tuviyyah,* cit., p. 93a.

68. See, for example, *ibid.,* pp. 79b, 107a, 118b, 120a, 121a, 123b, 126b, 126a, 127b, 138b, 141a, 141b, etc. On these chemical philosophers, consult the works cited in note 66 above.

69. See, for example, Cohen, *Ma'aseh Tuviyyah*, cit., pp. 93b, 120a, 125b, 127b, 139b.
70. *Ibid.*, pp. 125b, 127b.
71. On Thomas Willis, see Debus, *The Chemical Philosophy*, cit., II, ch. 7; L. R. Rather, *Pathology at Mid-Century: A Reassessment of Thomas Willis and Thomas Sydenham*, in A. G. Debus (ed.), *Medicine in Seventeenth Century England*, Berkeley-Los Angeles-London 1974, pp. 72–112; K. Dewhurst, *Thomas Willis as Physician*, Los Angeles 1964. On the five principles, see R. Hooykaas, *Die Elementenlehre der Iatrochemiker*, "Janus", 41 (1937), pp. 26–28.
72. D. Nieto, *Ha-Kuzari ha-Sheni-Mateh Dan*, ed. by J. L. Maimon, Jerusalem 1958, p. 143.
73. A. Wallich, *Harmonia Wallichia Medica (Sefer Dimayon ha-Refu'ot)*, Frankfurt on Main 1700, pp. 47, 48, 73.
74. Osimo, *Narrazione*, cit., p. 74.
75. A. Portaleone, *De auro dialogi tres*, Venice 1584, p. 1–2, where he cites Sylvius among other chemical philosophers.
76. Cf. D. Ruderman, *Unicorns, Great Beasts and the Marvellous Variety of Things in Nature in the Thinking of Abraham b. Hananiah Yagel*, in I. Twersky (ed.), *Jewish Thought in the Seventeenth Century*, Cambridge (Mass.), 1986; D. Ruderman, *Kabbalah, Magic and Science: The Cultural Universe of a Sixteenth-Century Jewish Physician* (Cambridge, Ma., 1988).
77. I. Cardoso, *Philosophia libera*, Venice 1673, pp. 261 (where he mentions Paracelsus), 262–64, and elsewhere. For his later deprecation of "fallicious chemistry", see below, note 120.
78. Jacob Zahalon, *Ozar ha-Ḥayyim*, Venice 1693, p. 38b, refers to Joseph Duchesne (Quercetanus) among others. For a negative view of the chemical philosophers, see Y. Kaplan, *Mi-Naẓrut le-Yahadut: Ḥayyav u-Fo'alo Shel ha-Anus Yizḥak Orobio de Castro*, Jerusalem 1982, p. 279.
79. Quoted by Friedenwald, *The Jews and Medicine*, cit., I, p. 55, from Paracelsus *Labyrinthus medicorum Errantium*, 1553. Cf. F. Kudlien, *Some Interpretative Remarks on the Antisemitism of Paracelsus*, in A. G. Debus (ed.), *Science, Medicine and Society in the Renaissance: Essays in Honor of Walter Pagel*, New York 1972, I, pp. 121–26.
80. Ecclesiastes 38:1.
81. On this see my earlier formulation of the "ministry" of the doctor in Ruderman, *Unicorns*, cit., and see below. Cf. Debus, *The Chemical Philosophy*, cit., II, pp. 357 ff., and W. Pagel, *Religious Motives in the Medical Biology of the Seventeenth Century*, "IHM", 3 (1935), pp. 97–128, 213–31, 265–312.
82. M. Idel, *Differing Conceptions of Kabbalah in the Early Seventeenth Century*, in Twersky (ed.), *Jewish Thought*, cit.; see also Barzilay, *Yoseph Shlomo Delmedigo*, cit., p. 295.
83. Nieto, *Ha-Kuzari ha-Sheni*, cit., pp. 141 ff.
84. See especially Cardoso, *Philosophia libera*, cit., pp. 1b–4a, 9 ff. (Quaestio

II, "De atomis & illarum natura"); Yerushalmi, *From Spanish Court to Italian Ghetto*, cit., pp. 225–28, 233–35.

85. On Alemanno's interest in the spectacular in nature, see especially *Ḥayyai Olamin* (Ms. Mantua Jewish Community-21), fols 141b ff., the section entitled "Olam ha-Muḥash". See also E. J. F. Rosenthal, *Yohanan Alemanno and Occult Science*, in *Prismato . . . Festschrift für Willy Hartner*, Wiesbaden 1977, pp. 349–61. On Farissol, see D. Ruderman, *The World of a Renaissance Jew: The Life and Thought of Abraham b. Mordecai Farissol*, Cincinnati 1981, chs. 10 and 11; on Yagel, see Ruderman, *Unicorns*, cit.; on Portaleone, see the previous reference. Numerous other examples are found throughout his *Shilte Gibborim* and his *De auro dialogi tres*. On de Pomis, see, for example, his discussion in *Ẓemah David*, Venice 1587, pp. 62b, 86b, 100a, 150a, 181b, 232a, etc.

86. Cardoso, *Philosophia libera*, cit., pp. 473 ff.; de Pomis, *Ẓemah David*, cit., p. 62b.

87. Each of these fields is covered comprehensively in Cohen, *Ma'aseh Tuviyyah*, cit.

88. See note 73 above.

89. Ẓahalon, *Oẓar ha-Ḥayyim*, introduction; Friedenwald, *The Jews and Medicine*, cit., I, p. 271.

90. Cohen and Nieto are discussed by Neher, *Copernicus*, cit. Cardoso discusses Copernicus in *Philosophia libera*, pp. 20 ff.; Yerushalmi, *From Spanish Court to Italian Ghetto*, cit., pp. 236–27. See also below.

91. See Neher, *Copernicus* cit., and Barzilay, *Yoseph Shlomo Delmedigo*, cit.

92. Nieto, *Ha-Kuzari ha-Sheni*, cit., pp. 142 ff.

93. Cohen, *Ma'aseh Tuviyyah*, pp. 65a–b, 84b.

94. On this strategy, see Shapiro, *The Natural Sciences and Mathematics as Pathfinders*, cit., pp. 319–20; I. Zinberg, *Toledot Sifrut Yisra'el*, Tel Aviv 1960, II, appendix 2, pp. 395 ff.; cf. also J. Elbaum, *Editions of the Book "Ẓel Olam"*, "Kiryat Sefer", 47 (1971–72), p. 167, note 44 (in Hebrew); Yehudah ha-Levi, *Sefer ha-Kuzari*, 2:66; Maimonides, *Mishneh Torah*, Hilkhot Kiddush ha-Ḥodesh, 17:24; *Moreh Nevukhim*, 1:71.

95. On this theme in Jewish literature, see E. Adler, *Aristotle and the Jews*, "REJ", 82 (1926), pp. 91–102; cf. also R. Bonfil, *Expressions of the Uniqueness of the Jewish People during the Period of the Renaissance*, "Sinai", 76 (1975), pp. 36–46 (in Hebrew).

96. On Isaac Cardoso's reference to Moschus and his sources, see Yerushalmi, *From Spanish Court to Italian Ghetto*, cit., p. 235; cf. also J. E. McGuire and P. M. Rattansi, *Newton and the "Pipes of Pan"*, "Notes and Records of the Royal Society of London", 21 (1966), pp. 108–43.

97. A sampling of these sources is found in Ruderman, *Unicorns*, cit., note 84.

98. For a discussion of the Christian theology of nature in this period, see especially R. S. Westfall, *Science and Religion in Seventeenth-Century England*, Ann Arbor (Mich.) 1973); M. Foucault, *The Order of Things: An Archeology of the Human Sciences* (English translation of *Les Mots et*

les Choses, Paris 1966), New York 1970, pp. 17–50; H. Kocher, *Science and Religion in Elizabethan England,* New York 1953; J. W. Evans, *Rudolf II and His World: A Study in Intellectual History (1576–1622),* Oxford 1973, ch. 6; see also the works cited in note 66 above and those cited in Ruderman, *Unicorns,* cit., note 68.

99. See note 94 above.
100. See note 95 above.
101. Nieto, *Ha-Kuzari ha-Sheni,* cit., p. 100.
102. *Ibid.,* pp. 101 ff.
103. *Ibid.,* p. 105.
104. *Ibid.*
105. Cohen, *Ma'aseh Tuviyyah,* cit., p. 32a.
106. A. Geiger, *Melo Ḥofnayim,* Berlin 1840, Hebrew section. J. Delmedigo *Mikhtav Aḥuz,* (ed. A. Geiger), p. 11; see also pp. 12–13.
107. Cardoso, *Philosophia libera,* cit., p. 1a (Yerushalmi, *From Spanish Court to Italian Ghetto,* cit., p. 221).
108. *De Medico Hebraeo Enarratio Apologica,* Venice 1588, chap. 11, translated in Friedenwald, *The Jews and Medicine,* cit., I, pp. 31–53.
109. De Castro, *Flagellum Calumniantium seu Apologia,* cit. (translated by Friedenwald, *The Jews and Medicine,* cit., I, p. 60).
110. *Ibid.,* I, p. 65.
111. See the references listed in notes 97 and 98.
112. Cf. Westfall, *Science and Religion,* cit., p. 50.
113. Translated by Friedenwald, *The Jews and Medicine,* cit., I, p. 277.
114. *Esh Dat,* London 1715, p. 36b (in Petuchowski, *The Theology of Haham David Nieto,* cit., p. 107).
115. *Sefer Or Nogah,* in Leibowitz, *Seridim,* cit., p. 15.
116. *Novlot Ḥokhmah,* pp. 94 a ff. (cf. Barzilay, *Yoseph Shlomo Delmedigo,* cit., pp. 203–4).
117. Delmedigo, *Sefer Elim,* cit., p. 130.
118. Cardoso, *Philosophia libera,* cit., p. 46 (translated by Yerushalmi, *From Spanish Court to Italian Ghetto,* cit., p. 231).
119. *Ozar ha-Ḥayyim,* introduction.
120. Cardoso, *Philosophia libera,* cit., p. 4b (translated by Yerushalmi, *From Spanish Court to Italian Ghetto,* cit., p. 232). However, Cardoso, in his *Las Excelencias de los Hebreos,* Amsterdam 1679, p. 135, seems to have shifted his position. He writes (Yerushalmi's translation, p. 370): "And, in truth, Israel does not cultivate human sciences, nor treat of uncertain philosophy nor of doubtful medicine, nor of false astrology, nor of fallacious chemistry, nor of secret magic. It does not care to know the histories of the nations, nor the chronologies of the times, nor the politics of the rulers. All of its intent and desire is to study the law, and to meditate on its precepts, in order to keep and to do them". Yerushalmi attempts to explain this shift as a reflection of the intellectual milieu of sixteenth- and seventeenth-century Italian Jews who oscillated between attraction and

resistance to "Gentile" wisdom. He links Cardoso's change of heart to those of his contemporaries—Judah Moscato, Azariah Figo, and Abraham Portaleone. See Yerushalmi, *op. cit.*, pp. 370–73.

Yosef Kaplan, on the other hand (*Mi-Nazrut le-Yahadut*, cit., pp. 276–81), compares Cardoso's later view with a similar position of Isaac Orobio de Castro and relates both to the diffusion of sceptical currents in sixteenth- and seventeenth-century Europe, especially prevalent among such Converso writers as Francisco Sanchez and Michel de Montaigne. On these currents, see R. Popkin, *The History of Scepticism from Erasmus to Descartes*, Assen 1960 (revised edition, Berkeley-Los Angeles-London 1979) and his *Scepticism, Theology and the Scientific Revolution in the Seventeenth Century*, in J. Lakotos and A. Musgrave (eds.), *Problems in the Philosophy of Science*, Amsterdam 1968, pp. 1–39; C. Nauert, *Agrippa and the Crisis of Renaissance Thought*, Urbana 1965; P. Grendler, *The Rejection of Learning in Mid-Cinquecento Italy*, "Studies in the Renaissance", 13 (1966), pp. 130–49; H. Haydn, *The Counter-Renaissance*, New York 1950.

The extent to which scepticism, and especially Pyrrhonism (associated with the revival of interest in the writings of Sextus Empiricus), influenced Jewish and Converso thinkers like Cardoso and de Castro in the sixteenth and seventeenth centuries is yet to be determined. Clearly a sceptical or fideistic reaction to rational knowledge can be located in the thought of some writers of the period. Yet a negative reaction to scholasticism need not be synonymous with scepticism in general nor with a sceptical attitude toward the new scientific discoveries in particular. It also is necessary to distinguish between a total scepticism and what Popkin calls a "constructive or mitigated scepticism", the latter employed by such thinkers as Marin Mersenne and Petrus Gassendi, both important scientific writers. I hope to consider more fully the question of scepticism in Jewish thought of the period at a later time. For the present, cf. Bonfil, *Ha-Rabbanut be-Italya bi-Tekufat ha-Renesans*, cit., pp. 188 ff.; I. Barzilay, *Between Reason and Faith*, The Hague-Paris 1967; and Idel, *Differing Conceptions*, cit., pp. 31 ff. who discussed Agrippa's influences on Jewish thought and on Jacob Zemah in particular. Among the writers considered in this paper who appear to be influenced by sceptical and fideistic tendencies, Joseph Hamiz and David Nieto especially should be mentioned.

121. Compare my earlier formulation regarding Yagel in Ruderman, *Unicorns*, cit.

122. Delmedigo, *Sefer Elim*, cit., p. 92. Cf. Barzilay, *Yoseph Shlomo Delmedigo*, cit., p. 139–40.

123. Delmedigo, *Mikhtav Ahuz* (ed. A. Geiger), p. 13.

124. *Ibid.*

125. *Ta'alumot Hokhmah*, II, p. 80b. See Barzilay, *Yoseph Shlomo Delmedigo*, cit., pp. 316–17.

126. Nieto, *Ha-Kuzari ha-Sheni*, cit., p. 107.

127. Cohen, *Ma'aseh Tuviyyah*, cit., p. 11a.

128. De Pomis, *De Medico Hebraeo*, cit., I, p. 34.

129. Compare R. Bonfil's remark in his, *Some Reflections on the Place of Azariah de Rossi's "Meor Enayim" in the Cultural Milieu of Italian Renaissance Jewry*, in *Jewish Thought in the Sixteenth Century*, Cambridge (Mass.), 1983, pp. 34–37.

130. Compare, for example, the reactions found in the letter of Naphtali, in S. R. Hirsch's *The Nineteen Letters of Ben Uziel*, translated by B. Drachman, New York 1942, from the beginning of the nineteenth century.

131. This theme among Christian writers is developed by Westfall in the last chapters of *Science and Religion*, cit.

132. Cf. Petuchowski, *The Theology of Haham David Nieto*, cit., p. 114.

133. Cohen, *Ma'aseh Tuviyyah*, cit. p. 9a.

134. *Ta'alumot Hokhmah*, II, p. 94b.

135. Cardoso, *Philosophia libera*, cit., p. 726: "esse non tantum est propositio de fide, sed universale nature axioma luminea, naturali impressum".

136. See Petuchowski, *The Theology of Haham David Nieto*, cit., ch. 8.

137. Compare the remarks of Popkin in *Scepticism, Theology and the Scientific Revolution*, cit., on this point.

138. Cohen's discussion of Copernicus is found in *Ma'aseh Tuviyyah*, cit., pp. 49b–52b; Nieto's discussion is in *Ha-Kuzari ha-Sheni*, cit., pp. 126–28. Compare with Neher, *Copernicus*, cit., who notes only their rejection of Copernicus.

139. Nieto, *Ha-Kuzari ha-Sheni*, cit., pp. 129–30.

140. Cohen, *Ma'aseh Tuviyyah*, cit., p. 53a.

141. On the debate over a plurality of inhabitable worlds in this period and earlier, see especially S. J. Dick, *Plurality of Worlds: The Origins of the Extraterrestrial Life Debate from Democrites to Kant*, Cambridge 1982; G. McColley, *The Seventeenth Century Doctrine of a Plurality of Worlds*, "Annals of Science", 1 (1936), pp. 385–430; P. Rossi, *Nobility of Man and Plurality of Worlds*, in Debus (ed.), *Science, Medicine and Society in the Renaissance*, cit., II, pp. 131–62. Hasdai Crescas's view of infinite worlds is discussed by H. A. Wolfson, *Crescas's Critique of Aristotle*, Cambridge 1929, pp. 215–17.

142. Nieto, *Ha-Kuzari ha-Sheni*, cit., pp. 126–28.

143. Cohen, *Ma'aseh Tuviyyah*, cit., pp. 67a–68a.

144. Delmedigo, *Sefer Elim*, cit., pp. 292–93.

145. Cardoso, *Philosophia libera*, cit. pp. 124–25. Cf. a later critique of plurality in E. Ph. Hurwitz, *Sefer ha-Berit*, Brunn 1797; *Ma'amar*, 3, ch. 2, pp. 15a–17a.

146. Cf. J. Katz, *Out of the Ghetto*, Cambridge (Mass.), 1973, pp. 43–44, who minimizes the significance of this encounter.

147. Benayahu, *R. Abraham ha-Cohen of Zante*, cit., p. 119.

20

The Eve of the Circumcision: A Chapter in the History of Jewish Nightlife

Elliott Horowitz

I

The study of history, it is well known, thrives upon the utilization of new perspectives which sometimes invert our habitual modes of thinking about the past. We have learned in recent years, for example, how much can be gained from looking at social realities from below as well as from above, from the perspectives of women as well as those of men, and through the eyes of minorities as well as from the majority point of view. The study of death, similarly, has taught us a great deal about perceptions of life, and the study of crime a great deal about the meaning of law. Likewise, paradoxically, can the night be used to illuminate the day. Although the daylight hours clearly enjoyed paramount importance in pre-industrial Europe (the time and place which shall concern us in this essay), those of nocturnal darkness were hardly removed from the historical process. If the night was the realm of fear, associated both with evil and the unknown,[1] it was also a time, for Christians and Jews alike, of relative freedom from conventional restraints and responsibilities in which such diverse activities as storytelling, lovemaking, study, and gossip could be pursued.[2] How the night hours were filled, and to what extent they were controlled, had much to do with the thoughts, values, fears, and fantasies harbored during the day. The historian who succeeds in piercing the veil of darkness thus paves for himself a path into the hearts and minds of the people of the past.[3]

The contrast between day and night which exercised the "troubled

Reprinted by permission of the author and the *Journal of Social History* 23 (1989).

imagination"[4] of late medieval and early modern Europe paralleled another which it found increasingly problematic—that between the sacred and the profane. These realms had intermingled with relative freedom during the Middle Ages, often amid the chiarascuristic scenes created by the night's flickering lights. Popular behavior at the vigils held on the eve of a notable feast or parish festival prompted complaints from the clergy that "some dance in the very churches with obscene songs, others play at dice, with oaths denying God and cursing of the saints."[5] It has been persuasively argued that whereas medieval attempts to curb such abuses seem to have been rather halfhearted,[6] the post-Tridentine Church was both more persistent and more successful in its efforts to control popular amusements. Although they were not always suppressed, great care was taken to sever their profane elements from the realm of the sacred. By the late seventeenth century, John Bossy has observed, "eating and drinking, like dancing, gaming, and ritual obscenity had everywhere been expelled from the churches."[7]

What, however, of the synagogues? There, too, and in Jewish ceremonial life in general (much of which took place inside the home) the domains of the sacred and the profane had defied neat separation during the Middle Ages. In early modern times, by contrast, the intermingling of these two domains seems to have become increasingly problematic as the dominant religious sensibility turned increasingly austere. This, of course, is a wider topic than can be treated properly within the confines of a single essay and one, moreover, which has received remarkably little attention in scholarship. Historians of popular culture and popular religion have neglected to look into the Jewish dimension of this transformation in the social and spiritual life of Europe between late medieval and early modern times whereas Jewish historians, for their part, have not concerned themselves much with these themes. Natalie Davis has called recently for a more broadly comparative approach to the study of religious cultures in early modern Europe, pointing especially to the need to ask "the same questions about Jewish communities in Italy and central Europe that we have been asking about 'popular religion' in Christian societies, and trying to use the Jewish case to verify our conclusions about the Protestant and Catholic cases."[8] This essay shall move in a similar direction. Its primary emphasis, however, shall be upon the reconstruction of the social history of a Jewish observance—that held on the night or nights preceding a boy's circumcision and known as the "veglia" in Italy and as the "wachnacht" in central Europe.[9] The changes it underwent suggest certain striking lines of continuity across the boundaries of the religious cultures of Jews and Christians in early modern Europe.

In that observance, as we shall see, the twin themes of nocturnal fear and nocturnal freedom intermingled, as did, to differing degrees over time, elements of the sacred and the profane. It thus provides a valuable opportunity to gauge both the vitality of Jewish popular culture and the extent to which (Jewish) institutional tolerance for some of its more exuberant manifestations declined. This decline occurred precisely during a period in which such a shift in sensibilities occurred in Europe as a whole, but particular attention shall here be paid to the similar efforts among Jews and Catholics in post-Tridentine Italy to tone down popular celebrations by means of sacralizing them. In central Europe, too, a process of sacralization may be discerned, although in both instances the Jewish populace successfully resisted efforts from above to totally transform the character of its traditional celebrations.

Emerging in the Middle Ages as a night of largely profane festivity in which women, too, played a prominent (and in some cases dominant) role, the pre-circumcision vigil began, during the seventeenth century, to take on a more sober and sacred character, as well as becoming an increasingly masculine affair. This was due to the intervention of rabbinical or communal authorities, who came to regard as problematic forms of festivity which had previously been tacitly tolerated if not explicitly endorsed. Their initiatives would appear to be rooted in the fundamental shift in European sensibilities discussed above no less than in internal developments in Jewish society. After the seventeenth century the vigil was to retain considerably less of the free and easy atmosphere which had characterized its earlier history, but perhaps not as little as we might imagine. The accounts of actual observances sometimes contrast strikingly with the prescriptions of the normative sources. So, too, is it necessary to utilize the testimonies of both "insiders" and "outsiders" in reconstructing a total picture of such observances. The former, though ostensibly more familiar with the details of their own culture, are sometimes less willing to divulge its excesses of failures, and may even, as Peter Burke has suggested, be blind to its particular codes. "Outsiders," by contrast, he has furthermore noted, often take less for granted of what the historian most wants to discover, and there is a strong case, therefore, for inverting the normal order of things and beginning with their testimony.[10]

II

In his *Synagoga Judaica,* first published in 1603, the Swiss Hebraist Johannes Buxtorf (the elder) described the night of "festival jollity and facetious merriment" observed by the Jews on the seventh night after the birth of a boy, that is, on the eve of his circumcision.[11] It was, he explained, an extended visit with the mother in order to allay her fears considering the possible harm that might come to her child at the circumcision or, following popular belief, during the night preceding it.[12] The visit, however, is described by Buxtorf as an all-night affair, involving, besides abundant food, such amusements as cards, dice, singing, and storytelling, all accompanied, especially among the men, by rather heavy drinking, in which the circumcisor must be warned against overindulging. The account, however, does not neglect to mention, though it does so as a kind of afterthought, that the most learned and pious among the guests also recite several devout prayers.[13] The overall picture which emerges from his description is that of a practice combining both raucous amusements and pious recitation, with the emphasis clearly upon the former.

Was this emphasis the author's own or did it honestly reflect Jewish practice? Although the Protestant Buxtorf was not, to be sure, a wholly disinterested informant concerning the Judaism of his own day,[14] his obvious pleasure in recording its less spiritual aspects does not necessarily undermine his reliability. In fact, his tendency, as an "outsider" to emphasize the coarse and superstitious elements in Jewish life may sometimes provide a useful counterbalance to the reticence of "insiders" less willing to come to grips with them. Such a stance may be encountered not only in the distant past, but among an earlier generation of Jewish scholars as well. Thus two eminent Victorians writing at the end of the last century, Solomon Schechter and Israel Abrahams, were both content, after noting that a pre-circumcision vigil was known to Jewish authors of the thirteenth century, to drop the subject by adding that "it is considered by the best authorities ... to be of foreign origin."[15] Whatever its origins, however, the social historian (rather than the historian of religion) must ask what forms the practice took after its incorporation into Jewish society and what such changes can tell us about that society, beginning his inquiry at the very point at which nineteenth-century scholars terminated theirs.

One thirteenth-century source to which Schechter and Abrahams may well have been alluding is the *Zohar,* which modern scholarship regards as having been written in Spain late in that century, though most late medieval Jews saw it as a much earlier work. In that "mystical novel," to use an expression of the late Gershom Scholem, the custom is mentioned of remaining awake all night in Torah study on the eve of the circumcision ceremony.[16] Like most Zoharic customs, however, it is mentioned descriptively, almost in passing, and seems to have remained dormant, not having been translated into practice until much later.[17]. On the other hand, it is likely that the author was acquainted with some sort of pre-circumcision night ritual, to which he may have sought to present a more pious alternative.

Such an observance is reported in the early fourteenth century by R. Aaron of Lunel in neighboring Provence, though it undoubtedly predated the author's time. He mentions the custom of men, women, and children gathering in the mother's home not only on the Friday night after her giving birth but on the night of the eighth day as well, at which point she would be given gifts by those present. Furthermore, he adds, "in some places the members of the mother's household remain awake for the first seven nights after her giving birth to a boy or girl . . . and on the eighth night [i.e. the eve of the eighth day] this is practiced everywhere, with singing and dancing. . . ."[18] R. Aaron, significantly, saw no reason to criticize either version of the custom. His words were written less than half a century after the composition of the *Zohar,* in an area which for Jews was essentially part of the same cultural orbit as northern Spain, and would appear to reflect a practice which had been known for some time in both regions.

Moreover, the festive observance, or a version thereof, seems to have been fairly widespread among Marrano circles in late fifteenth-century Spain, where it was known as the "hadas." Inquisition testimonies, it has been noted, report that it was customary for young women and female relatives to gather in the mother's room on the night preceding the eighth day after birth "singing and dancing to the accompaniment of cymbals and feasting to their hearts' content," especially on fruits.[19] Although Inquisition scholars have not detected the lines of continuity between this practice and that described by R. Aaron in the previous century, there would appear to be little doubt that both stem from the same vigorous tradition of Jewish popular culture associated with the eve of the circumcision. Traditions of this sort were able to withstand the pressures of Catholic conformism just as they were able, a generation earlier, to withstand those of Zoharic reformism.[20]

It is not only among crypto-Jews that we know of the custom in the fifteenth century. At around the same time that the inquisitorial testimonies were given in Spain R. Joseph Colon in Italy mentioned in one of his responsa the custom of gathering at the mother's home on the eve of the circumcision and feasting there on fruits.[21] From the fifteenth century has also been preserved a priest's account of the all-night vigil observed at the mother's home among the Jews of Vienna which was intended, he reports, to protect both the child and his mother from demons.[22] In the following century this anti-demonological practice makes its appearance in Jewish sources of both West and East European provenance, suggesting that it had become rather widespread.[23] These sources, however, mention neither the *Zohar* nor the importance of Torah study on the night before a circumcision. In fact, they seem less concerned with the content of the vigil than with the fact of its observance, implying that it was essentially the wakefulness of the participants which kept the demons away. Thus the eve of the circumcision was a night of fear, but it was also a night of freedom, a rare opportunity for the members of a community to spend the nocturnal hours together in a manner of their own choosing.

III

What actually did go on then during these long nights? Buxtorf, as we have noted, mentioned gambling, singing, and storytelling in addition to the consumption of much food and drink. Sixteenth-century evidence from south of the Alps points in a similar direction, with, however, the significant addition of dancing. In 1530 the Jewish community of Padua decided to ban dance celebrations among its members except at specifically stated occasions. One of the exceptions was for "the nights of the 'veglia,' these being the nights preceding the circumcision of a male child, and only in the mother's home."[24] The inclusion of dancing in the "veglia" was undoubtedly part of the Renaissance heritage of Italian Jewry, yet like Renaissance dance in general its actual practice among Jews of the Padua region in the early sixteenth century was sometimes far from chaste, as Robert Bonfil has demonstrated.[25] Seven successive nights of dancing undoubtedly created a rather free and heady atmosphere among those same Jews, conducive to the sorts of amusements not normally engaged in on a regular basis. Gambling, too, seems to have figured prominently in the night's festivities. When, in nearby Cremona, word arrived in 1575 of the impending arrival of the plague, the "health officers" appointed by the Jewish community decided, as a penitential gesture, to ban games of chance. One of the exceptions made, however, was for "the night of the 'veglia' and the day of the circumcision ... and only in the home of the child's father."[26] Significantly, dancing in Padua was associated with the mother's home, whereas gambling in Cremona was mentioned in connection with the home of the father, suggesting parallel male and female amusements.

The Paduan statute was reconfirmed in 1580, indicating that the communal authorities still regarded dancing as an acceptable form of celebration at the "veglia."[27] In contrast, however, to that statute and the aforementioned one in Cremona, both of which treated the festive vigil as an event outside the customary sphere of control, a decade later sumptuary legislation was passed among the communities of the Monferrato which did seek to impose certain limitations on the pre-circumcision celebration. Articles of clothing which women were not to wear in public, it was decreed, were also not to be worn in their homes during the "veglia" festivities (when their homes, presumably, became public domain) and the number of local guests who could be invited to the meal held on that evening was limited to six.[28] A more striking form of control was exerted some three decades later in Ancona where, in 1619, the council of the "Italian" (as opposed to Levantine) Jewish community decreed that on the night before a circumcision "no refreshments, whether food or drink, may be served to the men coming to celebrate with the father but only to the women, as is the custom."[29] The prohibition, however, proved easier to legislate than to enforce, and less than five years later the community decided to nullify it, citing the Talmudic policy against promulgating a decree by which the majority cannot abide.[30]

The Ancona ordinances point, therefore, to two kinds of celebrations on the eve of a circumcision, one in the women's sphere and the other among the men. Only the former was officially sanctioned, which would suggest that it was there the more traditional of the two observances. The men, however, seem to have had a hard time staying away, perhaps enjoying then a night of gambling with the father as had been customary in Cremona. In Venice, too, gambling had been one of the activities associated with the "veglia" until it was banned by the sumptuary regulations issued by the local community in 1616–17 in the interest of maintaining order and avoiding scandal on such occasions.[31]

It is not surprising, therefore, that the Venetian Rabbi Leone Modena omitted any reference to gambling, of which he was personally quite fond, in the description of the "veglia" provided in his work on the rites and ceremonies of the Jews (the *Riti*), which he composed around the same time.[32] There he explained that "the night before the circumcision is called the *watching night,* because those that belong to the house watch all night, to look after the child; and that evening, the father's friends come and visit him, and the women go to the mother, and spend the evening in merriment and making good cheer."[33] Modena's failure to mention gambling should also be seen, however, in the context of his implicit polemic with Buxtorf's *Synagoga Judaica* throughout that work, the first of its sort written by a Jew for a non-Jewish audience. The *Riti,* as one scholar has described it, "was a fundamental repudiation of the image of Judaism fostered by Buxtorf" who, Modena felt, had unfairly stressed its superstitious and otherwise offensive elements.[34] This polemical concern clearly shaped the latter's depiction of the pre-circumcision rite. Like Buxtorf he presented it as an all-night affair, yet he was careful to describe its intent as being "to look after the child," rather than to protect him from demons. Moreover, the merriments in which outsiders of both sexes participated are presented as merely the initial stage of the rite, to be followed by the vigil kept by members of the household. Although Modena, unlike Buxtorf, understandably made no mention of such amusements as drinking or gambling, it is significant that he failed to include either prayer or study among the activities pursued at the "veglia." Both had been mentioned, albeit marginally, by the latter, and Modena's silence on this score would seem to stem not from polemical motives but from the fact that these pietistic touches had not yet been added to the Italian version of the rite. It was still a rather gay and festive affair in which formal "religious" observances had not yet found their place.

A similar picture emerges from the *Via dalla fede* penned by Modena's former student, the apostate Giulio Morosini, who was baptized in 1649. Morosini, who was familiar both with Buxtorf's *Synagoga* and his own teacher's *Riti,* presents in that work a description of the "veglia" which conforms strictly with neither of their treatments and would seem to have been based largely on his own experiences as a Jew. Like the former he notes the superstitious element in the night watch ("per guardia del puttino, e per assicurarlo dall'offese, che pottrebon farsegli dalle streghe . . .") which was characteristically underplayed by Modena. The sorts of amusements engaged in by the (male and female) guests in order to drive away sleep, while lively ("si fà strepito continuamente con balli, e con far girare per tutto regali secondo la possibilità d'ogni uno, e rinfreschi di cose dolci, di frutti, e di vino il megliore che possa haversi") are neither quite as raucous as those described by Buxtorf nor as tame as suggested in the *Riti*.[35] Dancing appears but not dicing (in line with sumptuary legislation in the Venetian ghetto), drinking but no drunkenness. Yet in that surprisingly straightforward account, which seems to reflect more accurately than his teacher's the actual character of the "veglia" in early seventeenth-century Italy,[36] no mention is made of either prayer or study.

The silence of both Modena and Morosini, coupled with the testimony from Padua, Cremona, and Ancona cited above, strongly suggests that through the mid-seventeenth century the rite as observed among Italian Jewry consisted of a social gathering on the eve of a circumcision in which the participants enjoyed considerable freedom to pursue a wide variety of amusements. It was a rite essentially profane in content but perceptibly linked, nonetheless, with the spiritual domain through its association with the holy act of circumcision and through its battle, by means of wakefulness, with the threatening spirits. In this respect it was typical of the popular religious culture of late medieval Europe, which saw no reason to sever the sacred from the profane. It maintained itself as a popular tradition, untouched by the religious authorities, and hence an authentic expression of the religion of the people.

IV

One person, however, with whom this tradition did not sit well was Leone Modena's cousin, the kabbalist R. Aaron Berechia of Modena. If the former attempted to present a tame version of the "veglia" in his *Riti,* the latter sought to create one. In his 1626 work *Ma'avar Yabok,* devoted albeit to the subject of death and its related rituals, the latter proposed a radical reform in the accepted practice. There, while discussing the salutary effects of reciting "pareshat ha-ketoret," the Biblical and Talmudic passages describing the offering of incense in the Temple, R. Aaron added the following suggestion:

And also on the night before a circumcision how beneficial it would be to recite it before the Chair of Elijah, together with the Psalms of David . . . as against those who spend that night in merrymaking, men and women . . . young and old. Go and observe what the custom was among those of earlier generations who did not interrupt their study for a moment on the night before a circumcision . . . as may be seen from the *Zohar* . . .[37]

R. Aaron Berechia's statement would seem to throw cold water on the entire festive tradition of the "veglia" which had developed in Italy, with local variations, over the previous centuries. It is linked, of course, to the general rediscovery of the *Zohar* as a source for religious practice, in the aftermath of the efflorescence of Lurianic spirituality in sixteenth-century Safed; a process whose major contours have been described by the late Gershom Scholem but which still remains to be fleshed out in detail.[38] The statement's significance, however, would seem to extend beyond the Jewish sphere alone. Its criticism of the popular observance of the "veglia" and its attempt to transform it, with the aid of the Kabbalah, into a more sober and mystical ceremony cannot be seen in isolation from an important trend then gaining force throughout Western Europe. This trend, which Peter Burke has described in terms of the triumph of Lent over Carnival, had as its aim the reform of popular culture, whether by means of suppressing traditional practices or of purifying them.[39] The latter, Burke has argued, was the path favored by Catholic reformers as opposed to their Protestant counterparts, and would typically take the form of replacing a raucous parade at a parish festival with a solemn procession rather than attempting to abolish the festival itself.[40] R. Aaron Berechia of Modena's proposed innovation, which sought to purify a popular observance from its more offensive elements, thus joined a chorus of similar initiatives advanced by the Catholic clergy of his native Counter-Reformation Italy.[41] His efforts, and others which followed in their wake, suggest that the campaign against popular culture during this period may be seen as a process whose contours extend beyond the confines of Christian society.

This campaign, as both Burke and Robert Muchembled have stressed, drew its force from the increasing tendency, especially on the part of the post-Tridentine Church, to clearly demarcate the boundaries between the sacred and the profane in an attempt to keep these two domains far more separate than they had been in medieval times.[42] A tendency of this sort has been noted, as an internal development, by Robert Bonfil, who has sensitively discussed the impact of resurgent Kabbalah in Italy during the late sixteenth and seventeenth centuries. Its particular pious orientation, he has argued, "contributed to distancing the sacred from the profane in Jewish life."[43] The stance taken towards the traditional "veglia" by R. Aaron Berechia, himself a leading kabbalist, provides an ideal example of this internal shift, but it would also appear to be part of a wider one. His criticisms of the observance and proposal for its reform came during the period which Burke has seen as the first phase in the campaign against popular culture, that between 1550 and 1650, in which the initiative came primarily from the clergy. In the next century and a half followed another phase, as Burke has shown, in which the laity took over the struggle.[44] Such a phenomenon may also be encountered in Italian Jewish society, where from the late seventeenth century the battle against the traditional "veglia" and its characteristic forms of festivity was waged by the communal authorities rather than by the rabbinate. The former used the means at its disposal, primarily sumptuary legislation, to delegitimize the more profane elements of the observance and to lend support to some of the more pious practices which had begun to emerge. Their efforts to exercise tight control over festive celebration, however, in contrast to those of the rabbis, would seem to have been less rooted in internal pietistic trends than in the wider campaign then being waged outside the ghetto walls to curb the excesses of popular culture.

V

Despite R. Aaron Berechia's call, in 1626, for a "return" to the Zoharic custom, no more trace of any sort of ritual study may be found in the description of the "veglia" provided by the apostate Morosini than in the *Riti* of his former teacher, Leone Modena. The latter's grandson, however, does allude, just after mid-century, to the incorporation of this pious element in the Venetian ceremony, although it seems to have been intended to complement the traditional festivities rather than to displace them.[45]

Yet by century's end the communal authorities of the Venetian ghetto stepped in to insure that this aspect of the pre-circumcision vigil became its main feature rather than a mere appendage. The sumptuary regulations of 1697 stated firmly that on the nights before a circumcision a "veglia was absolutely prohibited." By this was meant that no guests could attend the household celebration other than immediate relatives of the mother and father. Exception was made, however, for "the rabbis, to give a lesson."[46] By admitting them and excluding others the lay communal authorities not only lent their support to the new pious manner of observing the vigil, but also stepped up their campaign to tone down the more traditional observance.

It is thus significant that the very term "veglia," which had earlier been associated (like "carnival" among the Christians) with freedom from restraint, underwent a shift in connotation—to the realm of the prohibited. Whereas the Venetian sumptuary regulations of the mid-sixteenth century had sidestepped the issue of the "veglia" and those of the early seventeenth had sought only to eliminate specific abuses such as gambling, by the end of that century efforts were made to impose more total control upon the event, and, in effect, to delegitimize its traditional character.

The process of tightening control may also be observed in the Roman community whose 1661 sumptuary regulations permitted dancing at the "veglia" only between members of the same sex.[47] Those of 1702 went a step further, stating that it was prohibited for "men quite as much for women, of any age, to dance alone as well as with a partner." They did, however, permit some "public festivities" on such occasions, provided that only Jewish musicians were to perform and that no comedies involving the use of costumes were to be staged.[48] The increasing trend to tone down the event is clear, but no less evident through the efforts to contain them are the vital and diverse forms of Jewish popular amusement which thrived in the Italian Ghetto. An inevitable tension thus emerged between the intensifying thrust of control from above and the tenacity of popular traditions.

In Ancona, where the "veglia" had still, in the early seventeenth century, possessed something of the character of a women's festival, the community's statutes of 1716 paid considerable attention to the event. One paragraph stipulated that on such nights, as on other occasions when many men or women gathered together, it was incumbent upon the host to see to it that the pillars of his home were properly reinforced.[49] Another prohibited married or engaged women from dancing except in the course of their lessons, at weddings and on the nights of the "veglia," where they presumably did so unaccompanied by men. A third dealt with the problem of masquerade, forbidding women from attending the pre-circumcision observance while wearing masks or any kind of costume.[50] This paragraph followed directly after one generally prohibiting masks (especially small ones of black silk) for married or engaged women. Its somewhat redundant character, coupled with the absence of a parallel restriction for men, would seem to suggest that it had been especially common, if not customary, for Jewish women in Ancona to attend the "veglia" in masquerade as a sign both of its free and festive character and of the special place they occupied in it. Yet, as in Rome, amusements which had previously been acceptable on such occasions were, in the early eighteenth century, no longer tolerated.

In Jewish as well as in Catholic society the reform of popular traditions had become by this point a lay rather than clerical affair. However, there were local differences in the intensification of the process. The leaders of the Rome and Ancona communities refrained, at this stage, from the blanket prohibition upon the "veglia" which had been imposed in Venice in 1697. In neither case, moreover, was rabbinical study presented as the community-sanctioned alternative to profane festivity, as it had been there. Rather, the main concern was with toning down the popular observance.

Yet study as a ritualized form of "veglia" observance was gaining momentum among Italian Jewry. In 1702 the kabbalist R. Abraham Rovigo (who, like R. Aaron Berechia in the previous century, came from Modena) led a group of his disciples on a pilgrimage to the land of Israel, where a grandson was born to him. A member of his entourage relates that a quorum of ten scholars remained awake studying during the night preceding the circumcision, and furthermore, that only those who had stayed up all night were invited to participate in the meal following the rite itself.[51] Less rigorous forms of the practice were also gaining ground. In Modena itself a pious confraternity which had been founded in 1702 primarily for the purpose of study decided nine years later that if a son were born to one of its members the others would be obliged to attend the "veglia" in his home on the eve of the circumcision. There they would read the *Zohar* together for an hour after the rabbis had completed their study for the evening.[52]

The members of the Modenese society were thus adding a further layer of pious practice to that which had been instituted by the local rabbis. In Venice, where the 1697 sumptuary regulations had also referred to rabbinical study on the night of the "veglia," there was published a decade later a handbook of selections from Biblical and rabbinic texts entitled *Divrei ha-Berit* (Words of the Covenant), which was clearly designed for use on that occasion by a wider audience. Moses Venturin, who sponsored the work, explained in his foreword that he was motivated to do so upon seeing that at the vigil "people were leafing through books in confusion in order to find texts appropriate to the matter of circumcision." Its editor, R. David Altaras, praised those who, preferring the eternal to the ephemeral, chose to spend the night before a circumcision reading holy texts but he found "no order to their study, this one stands and the other sits, though their hearts are directed to heaven."[53] The publication of their volume undoubtedly served not only to standardize the practice of ritualized reading at the "veglia" but to popularize it even further.[54]

As the pious rite became more widespread so was the popular rite further repressed by the communal authorities. The Roman sumptuary regulations which had, in 1702, permitted Jewish musicians to perform at the "veglia" prohibited even these in 1726, stipulating further that only Hebrew songs (unaccompanied by music) could be sung on the night before the circumcision or at the ceremony itself.[55] In addition to filtering out its profane elements, the community took a further step towards sacralizing the observance by specifying that only the members of the confraternity who had come to recite prayers (perhaps from the *Divrei ha-Berit* published in the interim) could be offered coffee and biscuits. Thus coffee, which could be used to extend the night and prolong the traditional festivities, was carefully limited to the practitioners of the pious rite.[56] Theirs was treated as the main event while whatever remained of the popular festivity was banished thereby to the sidelines.

VI

More seems to have remained, however, than would appear from the strict sumptuary regulations. In 1727, the year after those discussed above were promulgated, a confraternity dedicated to the prophet Elijah (who was believed to attend all circumcisions) was founded in Rome by the rabbi of its Jewish community, Tranquillo Vita (Manoah Haim) Corcos. Its stated purpose was to recite passages from holy texts in the home of the newborn on the night before his circumcision[57] but its founder hardly sought to conceal the fact that by promoting one nocturnal rite he hoped to displace another. The introduction to the confraternity's statutes, which he seems to have written, bears the following testimony:

The custom is that when a man has a male child born to him . . . tumultuous sounds rise forth from his home throughout the night before the circumcision. For the father gathers together his friends and relatives . . . to display the pomp and splendor of his majesty . . . and with a joyous heart they partake of delicacies . . . in accord with their desires, [and] in a manner worse than their fathers. They drink fine wine from elegant vessels . . . and instead of reciting prayers of praise and thanksgiving to God, all sing lusty songs with their faces ablaze. They engage in vain and ridiculous activities, young and old, women and children. Some dance, young men and maidens together, mouthing obscenities and devising sins in their hearts, while others give utterance to the evil desires of their souls, drinking to forget their abject poverty . . .[58]

The author attributed this sorry situation to the absence from the "veglia" of those who could provide guidance to its participants in the conduct appropriate to the occasion—this, despite the appearance of a printed handbook in Venice some two decades earlier. The aim of confraternal study, it is implied, was to be the spiritual benefit of the guests no less than that of the infant. Although the passage, which was written in rhymed prose, undoubtedly contains some poetic exaggeration, it is nonetheless striking that the Roman celebration as described by Corcos (or his confraternity's scribe) in 1727, featuring mixed dancing, drunkenness, and obscene song, was hardly less earthy in character than that described more than a century earlier by the Protestant Buxtorf. In fact, it considerably exceeded in this respect the description provided somewhat later in the seventeenth century by the apostate Morosini! Yet the Roman rabbi could hardly be accused of harboring a bias against the Jewish religion or its practitioners. Rather, it would appear that both critical observers outside the Jewish community and reformers from within shared a similar interest in faithfully portraying some of its embarrassing flaws. The value of combining the accounts of "insiders" and "outsiders" in reconstructing the popular dimensions of Jewish life is therefore quite evident. The contrast, moreover, between Corcos's testimony and the sumptuary legislation which preceded it suggests that Jewish popular culture, like its non-Jewish counterpart, possessed no small measure of resiliency in the face of efforts to reform it.[59]

The rabbi's description of the "veglia," in fact, bears particular comparison with that provided by yet another apostate, Paolo Sebastiano Medici, in his *Riti e Costumi degli Ebrei*. This work, written during the late seventeenth century, had aroused the fears of the Roman community even before its publication, on account of the negative views concerning Jews and Judaism expressed orally by its author. The Jews of Rome attempted, therefore, to have its publication blocked, and to this end sent a formal representative in 1697 with a lengthy petition to the Congregation of the Holy Office at the Vatican. The representative was none other than Tranquillo Corcos who succeeded in delaying the book's publication for almost four decades.[60] How ironic then, and yet how telling, that Medici's portrayal of the "veglia" in that work did not differ substantially in content, though it did somewhat in tone, from that of his rabbinical antagonist!

Medici reports that on the night before the circumcision a good number of men and women gather in the home where the ceremony will occur. There a lecture is given by "some youth, and sometimes by a rabbi," praising the commandment of circumcision and exhorting the parents to have courage during the performance. Afterwards, he continues, follow music, dancing, eating, and drinking as well as general merrymaking, at the conclusion of which some return home and others remain the entire night in order to protect the child from the sorceress Lilith. These, it is reported, pass the time in various amusements, songs, games (of chance?), useless talk, and idle pursuits.[61] Medici, therefore, like Corcos, saw the "veglia" as a celebration in which the pleasures and amusements of the flesh predominated over affairs of the spirit. Yet unlike the earlier account by his fellow apostate Morosini, and before him by Modena in his *Riti,* his description does mention a religious discourse delivered at the beginning. This is the sort of detail he would have been least likely to fabricate, and it suggests that if communal efforts to suppress the profane elements in the "veglia" were less than successful, the parallel campaign to introduce more explicitly sacral observances seems to have enjoyed a measure of success. Rather than replacing the traditional rites, however, as had been intended, in many cases they simply took their place alongside them in a decidedly subordinate manner. This phenomenon, which testifies to the vigor and tenacity of the popular tradition, is to be encountered in the course of the eighteenth century not only in Italy, but in central Europe as well. It was part of the ongoing tension between official religion and that of the people.

In Germany, R. Jacob Reischer (d. 1733) informs us that it had been customary in his day to enjoy meat and wine on the night before a circumcision even when the latter fell during the customary days of mourning before the Ninth of Ab. The perceived threat of the Sabbatian heresy, which tended to minimize mourning for the Temple's destruction, forced him to alter his tolerant stance toward this custom. Yet he could do no more than require his congregants to forego *either* meat or wine. A modus vivendi had to be found between the powerful popular tradition and his anti-Sabbatian fervor.[62]

A more detailed picture of the actual goings-on at the "wachnacht" in Germany may be gained from some of Reischer's non-Jewish contemporaries. We learn from the Orientalist Johann Schudt, who had a firsthand knowledge of Jewish life, that it was customary on the eve of the circumcision for many men and women to gather in the mother's room where the "most pious" would study and pray so as to protect the mother and child from demons. Afterwards, however, there would be drinking and gaming until dawn. Unlike Buxtorf, whose work he knew well, Schudt mentioned prayer and study towards the beginning rather than end of his account, evidently reflecting the increasing sacralization of the observance during the course of the seventeenth century. Yet in his account also festivity predominates over ritual. This impression is reinforced by an engraving in which five men are shown seated at a table, four of whom are eating and drinking while in the corner one sits somewhat sullenly before an open book.[63]

A similar illustration was included by the apostate Paul Christian Kirchner some years later in his *Jüdisches Ceremoniel,* although it adhered less closely to his description of the rite.[64] The latter, unlike Schudt, mentioned neither women nor gambling in his account, yet the accompanying plate to both their descriptions shows the lying-in woman at the opposite side of the room from the men holding a hand of cards closely to her breast, engrossed in a game with two female companions. None of the men, by contrast, is shown gambling. Perhaps this activity was shifted to the women's sphere as the men's event became more central to the observance and more sacral in status. The recognition of gambling as an appropriate form of post-partum recreation among central European Jewry is confirmed by the 1708 statutes of Kremsier (now Kromeriz) in Moravia. These prohibited gambling at all times except to women visiting a mother recovering after childbirth.[65]

Like the policy in Ancona of limiting dancing at the "veglia" only to women, this would seem to imply a certain recognition also north of the Alps of the night or nights before the circumcision as constituting a kind of women's festival. Such a notion, which has escaped the attention of modern writers on the subject, appears to have been relatively widespread among world Jewry at the time. Lancelot Addison, in describing the customs of late-seventeenth century North-African Jewry, noted that "Upon the Eve of the Circumcision, the Women visit their Gossip, with whom they usually pass the whole night in mirth and freedom."[66] Early in the eighteenth century the traveller J. E. van Egmont found that the Jews of Rhodes "have a very friendly but not the most frugal custom. At the birth of the child, in any family of note, all the Jews . . . are continually visiting the house, the men in the evening, after business . . . but some women continue there day and night and this lasts eight days . . ."[67] Despite the differences in their accounts, both authors stress the feminine element in the observance.

In Italy, however, as a result of the efforts to repress profane elements in the "veglia" and the increasing emphasis upon the masculine activity of Torah study, the feminine element in the rite was de-emphasized. Whereas, for example, sixteenth- and seventeenth-century sources described the observance primarily in terms of a visit with the mother, Rabbi Corcos of Rome saw it (unhappily) in the early eighteenth as a party given by the father. In Ancona, where women were first prohibited in 1716 from attending the "veglia" in masquerade, they were, in 1739, effectively prohibited from participating at all, since the sumptuary regulations promulgated in that year limited attendance to officials of the community and first-order relatives of the parents.[68] Although men were obviously excluded as well, it had previously been members of the female sex who were the dominant presence at the event and it was they who were therefore most affected by the new regulation.

Beginning with the Venetian regulation of 1697, then, a policy emerged in the Italian communities of transforming the pre-circumcision vigil from an open observance into a relatively closed one. This, of course, went hand in hand with the weeding out of its more profane elements, for controlling who goes in has much to do with controlling what goes on. In some instances this took the form of limiting admission to relatives and other privileged individuals, thus toning down the affair considerably. A year after this was done in Ancona, a similar regulation was enacted in Mantua.[69] Both communities, however, eventually abandoned this form of control in favor of that introduced earlier in the community of Rome—the limitation of access to stimulants. By retreating from their earlier position they seem to have recognized that a modus vivendi had to be found in which more tolerance was shown for the popular dimensions of the pre-circumcision observance. Neighbors and well-wishers could not be turned away, but the duration of their revelry could be held in check. In Mantua the sumptuary laws of 1771 imposed no limit on who could attend the "veglia," but stipulated that coffee could be served that night only to the learned men engaged in study around the table.[70] These, rather than the dancing women in Ancona a century and a half earlier, had become the evening's main performers. And if the popular observance could not be abolished entirely, it could be transformed into a prelude to the main event. In an era in which coffeehouses had become perhaps the dominant form of nocturnal entertainment throughout Europe[71] it was understood that only those given access to coffee were given the wherewithal to get through the night. In Ancona itself the sumptuary regulations of 1766 formally divided the "veglia" for the first time into two shifts, at the first of which only sweets could be served and at the second coffee and other refreshments.[72] It is clear that the first of these "mishmarot" was devoted to the traditional festivities whereas the latter consisted of a study vigil. By limiting the use of stimulants to those involved in the more "sacred" of the two ceremonies, these communities seem to have found an effective, if not necessarily subtle, means of placing the new ritual at center stage while at the same time allowing some vestiges of the old rite to survive.

VII

In the nineteenth century, however, a combination of new forces succeeded in stifling the traditional rite more effectively than did the sumptuary regulations of the previous centuries. The editors who in 1806 founded the *Sulamith,* the first Jewish periodical in the German language and whose avowed purpose was mediation between tradition and assimilation, devoted a regular column in their journal to "pernicious abuses, unseemly customs, and absurd ceremonies among the Jews."[73] One of the earliest of these dealt with the "Knabenschmause" (boy's banquet) held in the parents' home on the night before a circumcision. One contributor criticized the barbarity of the custom, especially towards the convalescent mother who needed her rest, and reported that "enlightened Jews" no longer practiced it. An editorial note added that "in many places in northern Germany our coreligionists have either abolished the 'knabenschmause' or have sought to make it more tolerable to the mother."[74]

Such steps were taken not only by avowed reformers. In the middle of the nineteenth century one of the changes introduced by the Rabbi of Rome after the Ghetto walls had come down was to terminate the pre-circumcision vigils of the "Elijah" society for fear of antagonizing the gentile neighbors. One suspects that it was not merely the sound of their *Zohar* recitations that posed the problem, but that the forms of festivity against which Rabbi Corcos had inveighed during the previous century had not entirely subsided.[75]

At around the same time the Jewish traveller Israel Joseph Benjamin (better known as Benjamin II) reported on the customs among the Jews of North Africa. Unlike his predecessor Addison in the seventeenth century who noted the "mirth and freedom" enjoyed by the women on the night before the circumcision, he reported that it was customary for the *father* to hold a feast for his friends and relatives on each of the eight nights preceding the ceremony. On the last night the scholars of the community would study for about two hours and then partake of the feast, after which they would engage in study and song until morning.[76]

The night-long vigil which had been discontinued in Rome survived in Reggio in a curious form. During the 1870's it was still customary for friends and relatives to visit the parents of the newborn on the evening before the circumcision, where prayers would be recited and sweets distributed. During the remainder of the night, however, a single "persona religiosa" would maintain a prayer vigil in the infant's home. When the proposal was raised to abolish the "veglia" entirely one of the community's members was moved to bring the matter to public attention, publishing a short notice on the subject in the *Vessilo Israelitico.*

Besides the practical benefits of the "veglia," he argued, permitting well wishers to greet the mother and child and to comfort the anxious parents before the circumcision, it also made the gaiety and festivity of the occasion complete.[77] The image of the pre-circumcision observance he presented was precisely that which had existed before the efforts of kabbalistic pietists and communal authorities had begun, two and a half centuries earlier, to reform it.

The tradition of gaiety and festivity was not entirely lost upon some rabbinical authorities of the twentieth century, who, while recommending prayer and study on the night before the circumcision, nonetheless sat fit to inform their readers that "in times past it had been customary to dance and to rejoice."[78] If they had any explanation for why this was no longer the case they kept it to themselves. What, however, were their readers to conclude?

NOTES

The earliest draft of this chapter was prepared with the assistance of a fellowship from the American Council of Learned Societies and was delivered as part of a lecture at Indiana University in February, 1986. Subsequent versions were presented before audiences at the Institute for Advanced Studies of the Hebrew University in Jerusalem, at Bar-Ilan University, and Ben-Gurion University of the Negev, whose Research Authority made possible the completion of the final draft.

1. See Robert Mandrou, *Introduction to Modern France, 1500–1640*, trans. R. E. Hallmark (London, 1975) pp. 55–75.
2. The association of the night with freedom has been stressed by Elisabeth Pavan, "Recherches sur la nuit vénitienne à la fin du moyen âge," *Journal of Medieval History* 7 (1981): 339–56. On groups of young men roaming the streets at night see *ibid*. p. 351 and Jacques Rossiaud, "Fraternités de jeunesse et niveaux de culture dans les villes du Sud-Est à la fin du Moyen Age," *Cahiers d'histoire* 21 (1976): 69 ff. On the village institution known as the veillée in France and veglia in Italy which featured storytelling and gossip see N. Z. Davis, *Society and Culture in Early Modern France* (Stanford, 1975), p. 201 (and the sources cited there p. 329 n.31) and the anthropological study by Alessandro Falassi, *Folklore by the Fireside: Text and Context of the Tuscan Veglia* (Austin, 1980). On the Jewish tradition of nocturnal study see S. W. Baron, *The Jewish Community* v. 2 pp. 176–77, and the sources cited there v. 3 p. 162, to which might be added *Shulkhan Arukh* "Orah Hayyim," #238. In that standard code of Jewish law, the laws of sexual intercourse follow closely upon those relating to

evening prayer and study, thus reinforcing the explicit instruction *(ibid.* #240: 11) to limit sex to the hours of darkness. On the Christian tradition of abstinence from daytime sex see Georges Duby, *The Knight, the Lady and the Priest: The Making of Modern Marriage in Medieval France,* trans. Barbara Bray (New York, 1983) p. 29. Needless to say, there were deviations from both these norms, but they undoubtedly shaped the general perception of the night.

3. See Piero Bargellini, "La vita notturna," in P. Bargellini et al. eds. *Vita privata a Firenze nei secoli xiv e xv* (Florence, 1966) pp. 75–89.

4. The phrase is Mandrou's (above, n. 1). On night and darkness see also Robert Muchembled, *Popular Culture and Elite Culture in France 1400– 1750,* trans. Lydia Cochrane (Baton Rouge, 1985) pp. 25, 53, 85–86, 111, 117.

5. The passage, from the fourteenth-century preacher Nicholas of Clemanges, together with some contemporary parallels, is quoted by J. Huizinga, *The Waning of the Middle Ages* (New York, 1985) p. 160 and by John Bossy, "The Counter-Reformation and the People of Catholic Europe," *Past and Present* 47 (1970): 61. On wakes and church ales, which "would drag on for days and even weeks" see Keith Thomas, "Work and Leisure in Pre-Industrial Society," *Past and Present* 29 (1964): 54 and David Underdown, *Revel, Riot, and Rebellion: Popular Politics and Culture in England 1603– 1660* (Oxford, 1985) passim.

6. See Bossy, "Counter-Reformation," p. 61 who points to the evidence from visitation reports. See also Peter Burke, *Popular Culture in Early Modern Europe* (London, 1978) pp. 109, 217 and idem, "Le domande del vescovo e la religione del popolo," *Quaderni Storici* 41 (1979): 549.

7. Bossy, "Counter-Reformation," pp. 61–62. The implications of this shift for attitudes towards popular culture are discussed at greater length below. For a survey of some recent studies related to this theme see the review article by E. M. Peters, "Religion and Culture, Popular and Unpopular, 1500–1800," *Journal of Modern History* (1987): 317–30.

8. N. Z. Davis, "From 'Popular Religion' to Religious Cultures," in Steven Ozment ed. *Reformation Europe: A Guide to Research* (St. Louis, 1982) p. 335. By contrast, it is worth noting that not one of the seventeen essays in Kaspar von Greyerz ed. *Religion and Society in Early Modern Europe, 1500–1800* (London, 1984) (discussed also by Peters in his essay cited in the previous note) deals with Jewish society, nor is there any mention of Jews or Judaism in the index, though almost fifty Christian saints are listed there.

9. For some discussion of this practice see Moritz Güdemann, *Geschichte des Erziehungswesens und der Cultur der abendländichen Juden* (Vienna, 1880– 88) v. 3, p. 103; Jacob Glassberg, *Zikhron Berit la-Rishonim* (Berlin, 1892) p. 148; Joshua Trachtenberg, *Jewish Magic and Superstition* (New York, 1939) pp. 170–71; Hayyim Schauss, *The Lifetime of a Jew* (New York, 1950) pp. 32–33, 60–61; Herman Pollack, *Jewish Folkways in Germanic*

Lands (1648–1806) (Cambridge, Mass., 1971) pp. 19–22. The latter's treatment is the most ambitious but it is also marred by inaccuracies. Of particular value are his bibliographical references as well as the illustration of an eighteenth-century "wachnacht" scene which he reproduces.

10. On inside vs. outside sources see Peter Burke, *The Historical Anthropology of Early Modern Italy: Essays on Perception and Communication* (Cambridge, 1987) ch. 2, esp. pp. 15, 23–24.

11. The work was originally published in German under the title *Synagoga Judaica/Das ist Jüden Schul* (Basel, 1603), and appeared the following year in Latin translation. Both versions were frequently republished but the original German will be utilized here. On Buxtorf see the entry in *Encyclopedia Judaica* (Jerusalem, 1972) [hereafter *EJ*], v. 4 p. 1543, and the bibliography cited there. See also n. 13 below.

12. Popular belief held that the child was especially susceptible to the influence of demons before his circumcision, which broke their power. Güdemann (above n. 9) called attention to the parallel belief among medieval German Christians concerning the period before baptism and to the related ceremonies practiced on the night preceding it. See also Joseph Gutmann, "Christian Influences on Jewish Customs," in L. Klenicki and G. Huck eds. *Spirituality and Prayer: Jewish and Christian Understandings* (New York, 1983) pp. 130–31.

13. Buxtorf, *Synagoga* ch. 2, pp. 105–6: "Un der siebenden Nacht kommen etliche der geladenen Gästen, auch wohl andere zu der Kindbetherin, halten ein gut Mahl mit einander, wachen die ganze Nacht bei ihr, treiben viel kurzweilige Sachen, spielen mit Karten, Würffein, singen, sagen Mährlein, die Männer sauffen sich blind voll, die Kindbetherin damit zu trösten, und zu ergötzen, dass sie sich wegen der Beschneidung des kindleins nicht zu sehr besümmere, wie sie dann auch wöhnen es geschehe ihnen leichtliche dieselbe Nacht etwas Ubels." I have followed, in part, the English translation in A[lexander] R[oss], *A View of the Jewish Religion* (London, 1656) (p. 61), which, though somewhat free, is more precise than the translation of the passage which appeared the following year in *The Jewish Synagogue, or an Historical Narration of the State of the Jews* (London, 1657) p. 45. The latter work, in contrast to Ross's, was an acknowledged translation of Buxtorf's *Synagoga* by two individuals who identified themselves merely as "A:B." The relevant passage in that work begins "The night following the woman's delivery, seven of them which were invited . . ." (!) In a forthcoming study I shall discuss the relationship between these two translations as well as some of the uses to which Buxtorf's book was put in seventeenth-century England.

14. Although the *Encyclopedia Judaica* entry (above n. 11) bluntly informs us that "Buxtorf's attitude toward the Jews, as voiced in his work *Juden Schül* . . . was negative," this view should be contrasted with the more positive one expressed by Rudolph Hallo, who found that in that work "Buxtorf describes the systematic completeness and exact breadth the customs and

mores of the contemporary Jews . . . on the whole with greatest familiarity, with astonishing erudition and with complete respect" (quoted by Joseph Kalir "The Jewish Service in the Eyes of Christians and Baptized Jews in the 17th and 18th Centuries," *Jewish Quarterly Review* n. s. 56 [1965–66]: 56 n. 26). S. W. Baron has also pointed to "the fairly objective treatment" of Jews and Judaism in Buxtorf's work, an evaluation which the latter's description of the "wachnacht" would appear to support. See his *Social and Religious History of the Jews* v. 13 (New York and Philadelphia, 1969) p. 462. Note also the balanced discussion by M. R. Cohen, "Leon da Modena's *Riti*: A Seventeenth-Century Plea for Toleration of Jews," *Jewish Social Studies* 34 (1972): 293 ff. (see chapter 16 of the present volume).

15. Solomon Schechter, "The Child in Jewish Literature," *Jewish Quarterly Review* o.s. 2 (1890): 6 [=*Studies in Judaism* (Phil., 1896) pp. 288–89]; Israel Abrahams, *Jewish Life in the Middle Ages* (London, 1896) p. 143 n. 2. Both found the visit paid to the boy on the Sabbath eve before his circumcision "more Jewish" than the pre-circumcision vigil. For Schechter's influence upon Abrahams, who was later to succeed him at Cambridge, see the latter's preface to *Jewish Life* p. viii. For more modern "scholarly" attempts to deny the authenticity of the festive rite see below n. 75.

16. *Zohar* I:93a–b. On the work and its author see Gershom Scholem, *Major Trends in Jewish Mysticism* (New York, 1985) ch. 5, and the latter's more recent summary in *EJ* s.v. "Zohar" [=*Kabbalah* (New York, 1974): 213–43]. It is possible that the author may have been influenced by the Talmudic "Shavu'a ha-ben" concerning which see Schechter, "The Child," p. 6.

17. On the process whereby customs alluded to by the *Zohar* were, from the sixteenth century, translated into practice see Gershom Scholem, "Tradition and New Creation in the Ritual of the Kabbalists," *On the Kabbalah and its Symbolism*, trans. Ralph Manheim, (New York, 1965) p. 118–57.

18. Aaron b. Jacob ha-Kohen of Lunel, *Sefer Orhot Hayyim*, ed. M. Schlesinger (Berlin, 1902) pt. 2 v. 1 p. 14. The passage, though absent in the Moscow-Guenzberg ms. (#107) which represents the preliminary version of the work, does appear in the London-Montefiore ms. (#131) in addition to the one used by Schlesinger in his edition. There, however, the night before the circumcision is referred to by the curious term "Shemini Azeret," and the custom is mentioned of distributing fruits to the guests who arrive. Furthermore, it is reported that "in one place it is customary to recite liturgical poems ("piyyutim") on the eighth night."

19. See Haim Beinart, *Conversos on Trial: The Inquisition in Ciudad Real* (Jerusalem, 1981) pp. 279–80. On this subject see more recently R. Levine Melamed "Women in Spanish Crypto-Judaism, 1492–1520" (Dissertation, Brandeis, 1983) pp. 179–86. I thank Dr. Levine Melamed for making her work available to me. On the infrequent practice of infant circumcision among Marranos see Cecil Roth, *History of the Marranos* (Philadelphia, 1932) p. 174.

20. On the latter phenomenon see Yitzhak Baer, *A History of the Jews in*

Christian Spain v. 1, trans. L. Schoffman (Philadelphia, 1971) ch. 6 "Mysticism and Social Reform," esp. pp. 261–70.

21. Joseph Colon, *Responsa* (reprint, Jerusalem, 1973) #178 (also quoted by Joseph Karo, *Bet Yosef* "Orah Hayyim" #640). The serving of fruit, which is also mentioned in the London ms. of *Orhot Hayyim* (see above n. 18) suggests that the Spanish and Italian customs were of common origin. It would seem that the fruits were chosen on account of their association with fertility and not, as has been suggested, on account of their satisfying Jewish dietary laws. Cf. Levine Melamed p. 181 n. 8. A festive meal on the night before the circumcision is mentioned in a much earlier source, the *Mahzor Vitry* (ed. S. Hurwitz, Berlin 1889–93, p. 624), yet there is no explicit reference there to visiting with the mother, nor of remaining awake.

22. The account was published by Arthur Goldman, "The Wachnacht among Vienna's Jews," [Yiddish] *Filologishe Shriften* 1 (Vilna, 1926): 91–94. "So haben die juden die gewohnheit, wann sie ain chind besneyden wellent sam morgen, so chomment als heut alle seine freunt zu der müter in daz haus, da die müter und daz kind inne ligent, und wachent die gancz nacht, daz der teufel icht chom und toett daz kind und dez teufels müter, die da haysset Lylles, daz die dew müter nicht würg" (p. 93). On Lilith see most recently Joseph Dan "Samael, Lilith, and the Concept of Evil in Early Kabbalah," *AJS Review* (1980): 17–40.

23. Naphtali Hertz b. Eliezer Treves in his *Naftulei Elohim* (Heddernheim, 1546) quoted by Nehemiah Brüll, "Das Geschlecht der Treves," *Jahrbuch für Jüdische Geschichte und Literatur* I (1874): 103 n. 71 [and from there by Joseph Perles "Die Berner Handschrift des kleinen Arukh," *Jubelschrift ... H. Graetz* (Breslau, 1887) p. 23] reports that this was the practice among Jews in Alsace and Germany. Later in the sixteenth century the Galician rabbi Moses b. Abraham Mat, in a work completed in 1584, mentioned the custom of remaining awake all night before the circumcision, adding "I have found it written that this is because Satan seeks to prevent the child from [fulfilling] the commandment of circumcision ..." See his *Mateh Moshe* (London, 1958) p. 383a. This source, in turn, was cited by the eighteenth-century Italian R. Isaac Lampronti in his *Pahad Yizhak* (reprint, Benei-Berak, 1981) v. 4 s.v. "milah."

24. Daniel Carpi ed. *Minutes Book of ... the Jewish Community of Padua* v. 1 (Jerusalem, 1973) p. 97. It is worthy of note that the location is also defined as "the mother's home" in sources as diverse as Rabbi Colon's responsum and the Viennese priest's account in the fifteenth century and Buxtorf's work in the early seventeenth.

25. On Jews and the dance during the Italian Renaissance see Otto Kinkeldey, "A Jewish Dancing Master of the Renaissance (Gugliemo Ebreo)," *Studies in Jewish Bibliography ... in Memory of A. S. Freidus* (New York, 1929) pp. 329–72 and the survey by Cecil Roth, *The Jews in the Renaissance* (Philadelphia, 1959) pp. 274–81. On problems of prurience in connection with dance see Robert Bonfil "Aspects of the Social and Spiritual Life of the

Jews in the Venetian Territories at the Beginning of the Sixteenth Century"
[Hebrew] *Zion* 41 (1976) 71, 84–86, and my own comments in "The Way
We Were: Jewish Life in the Middle Ages" *Jewish History* 1 (1986): 89
n.62.

26. Meir Benayahu and Giuseppe Laras "The Appointment of 'Health Officers'
in Cremona in 1575" [Hebrew] *Michael* 1 (1973): 98–99. These regulations
were paraphrased by Leone Modena in one of his responsa. See *Ziknei
Yehudah* ed. Shlomo Simonsohn (Jerusalem, 1956) p. 105, but cf. there n.
23 where the meaning of "veglia" is misconstrued.

27. Carpi, *Minutes Book* 1 pp. 97, 115.

28. The Monferrato regulations were published in broadside form in 1598 but
actually date from 1590. On these and others like them see Cecil Roth,
"Sumptuary Laws of the Community of Carpentras," *Jewish Quarterly
Review* n.s. 18 (1927–28): 357–83. The sumptuary regulations of the Jews
of Venice issued in 1543–48, by contrast, made no effort to subject the
"veglia" to such controls. They were published by Isaiah Sonne "Sources
for the History of the Jews in Verona" [Hebrew] pt. 2, *Kobez 'al Yad* 3 (13)
v.2 (1940) pp. 159–65. On sumptuary legislation see also D. O. Hughes,
"Sumptuary Law and Social Relations in Renaissance Italy," in John Bossy
ed. *Disputes and Settlements: Law and Human Relations in the West* (Cambridge, 1983): 69–99.

29. Minute Book of the Jewish Community of Ancona, ms. Rosenberg-UCLA
no. 44 (779b×.13.1) I have used microfilm #32468 at the Institute for
Microfilmed Hebrew Manuscripts of the Jewish National and University
Library in Jerusalem. The manuscript's pagination is inconsistent but the
entry is dated 24 Tishri, 1619.

30. *Ibid.*, 24 Iyyar, 1624. The source of the Talmudic phrase is *Baba Kama*
79b.

31. ". . . per ovviar molti scandoli et disordini che nelle Vigilie intervengono."
See Carla Boccato, "Ordinanze contro il lusso e sul 'suonatore del sabato'
nel Ghetto di Venezia nel secolo XVII," in *Rassegna Mensile di Israel* 45
(1979): 253. As in the case of the Monferrato regulations, the "veglia" was
considered a public occasion insofar as women's clothing was concerned
(*ibid.* p. 249). The Venetian "Pragmatica" thus continued and intensified
the emerging tendency to control the "veglia" and limit the freedom associated with it.

32. The book was originally written around 1616 and published for the first
time in Paris in 1637. See Cohen, "Leone da Modena's *Riti*," pp. 287–89
and the sources cited there. On English translations of the work see *ibid.* p.
291 n. 21. Modena's penchant for gambling is referred to repeatedly in his
autobiography *Hayyei Yehuda* (Tel-Aviv, 1985). Cohen's English translation of this work, with notes by Benjamin Ravid and Howard Adelman and
an introduction by N. Z. Davis has appeared under the title: *The Autobiography of a Seventeenth-Century Venetian Rabbi* (Princeton, 1988).

33. Leone Modena, *Historia de' riti hebraici* (rev. ed. Venice, 1638) IV, 8:3. I

have quoted from the English translation by Simon Ockley, *The History of the Present Jews throughout the World* (London, 1707) p. 193. The original reads "La notte precedente al giorno della circoncisione, si chiama della Vegghia, poiche quelli di casa vigilano tutta la notte à far guardia alla creatura nata, e vanno la sera gl'amici a visitar il padre del nato, e donne alla madre e si fa allegrezze quella sera, e ricevimenti." Although Modena introduced both additions and deletions between the first edition (Paris, 1637) and the second (see Cohen, "Leone da Modena's *Riti,*" pp. 291–92, 320–21) this passage remained substantially unchanged.

34. See Cohen, "Leone da Modena's *Riti,*" pp. 292 ff. who discusses the relationship between the two works in great detail.

35. Giulio Morosini, *Via della fede mostrata a'gli Ebrei* (Rome, 1683) v. 1 ch. 2 pp. 113–14. On the author see most recently Benjamin Ravid, "Contra Judaeos in Seventeenth-Century Italy: Two Responses to the *Discorso* of Simone Luzzatto by Melchiore Palontrotti and Giulio Morosini," *AJS Review* 7–8 (1982–83): 328–48, and the literature cited there p. 328 n. 57.

36. Cecil Roth noted over half a century ago that Morosini's work is "extraordinarily replete with information for the reconstruction of the social history of the Ghetto." See his *History of the Jews in Venice* (Philadelphia, 1930) p. 118. More recently Benjamin Ravid has observed that the work still awaits systematic examination, especially from the perspective of its relationship to those of Buxtorf and Modena ("Contra Judaeos," p. 339). The use made of *Via della fede* in this study illustrates the appropriateness of his observation and should, it is hoped, stimulate further research along these lines.

37. Aaron Berechia da Modena, *Ma'avar Yabok* (Mantua, 1626) 4:5, p. 121a. (In the more commonly available reprint of the Vilna, 1896 edition the passage appears on p. 255.) On the chair of Elijah see Trachtenberg, *Jewish Magic* p. 171, and most recently, Daniel Lasker, "Transubstantiation, Elijah's Chair, Plato, and the Jewish-Christian Debate," *Revue des Etudes Juives* 143 (1984): 31–58. For the Zoharic passage alluded to see above n. 16. On R. Aaron Berechia see Isaiah Tishby, "The Confrontation between Lurianic and Cordoverian Kabbalah in the Writings and Life of R. Aaron Berechia of Modena" [Hebrew] *Zion* 39 (1974): 8–85.
   At around the same time that R. Aaron penned his words R. Isaiah Horowitz (d. 1630) wrote "A newborn child should be watched over carefully in order to protect him from Lilith . . . and the primary protection is to remain awake on the *nights* before the circumcision studying Torah and engaging in good deeds . . ." See his *Shne Luhot ha-Berit* (Amsterdam, 1648–49) p. 113b. The latter work underwent final revision in Palestine during the 1620's and although it is unlikely that it drew upon *Ma'avar Yabok,* the two may have been influenced by a common source. Compare below n. 41.

38. Scholem, "Tradition and New Creation" pp. 118–57. See, more recently, Jacob Katz "Post-Zoharic Relations between Halakha and Kabbalah," in B. D. Cooperman ed. *Jewish Thought in the Sixteenth Century* (Cambridge,

Mass., 1983): 283–308 for a different perspective on this process. On the impact of Kabbalah in Italy see most recently Robert Bonfil, "Cultura e mistica a Venezia nel Cinquecento," in Gaetano Cozzi ed., *Gli Ebrei e Venezia* (Milan, 1987): 469–506.

39. It is interesting in this connection to note the complaints of parish priests in the *doyenné* of Baudemont in the late seventeenth century concerning the "disorderly conduct" at *veilleries*. As one of them wrote "One of the greatest abuses found in this parish and which we have always attempted to destroy are certain nighttime gatherings and assemblies of girls and women in the cellars during the winter to spin until nearly three hours after midnight, and boys and young men ... join in these public gatherings [and] spend the entire night in marauding, quarreling, and committing a hundred insolent acts." See Muchembled, *Popular Culture and Elite Culture* p. 217. As in the case of the pre-circumcision vigil, the object of criticism is a traditionally female rite which has been "invaded" by males.

40. Burke, *Popular Culture in Early Modern Europe* ch. 8 "The Triumph of Lent: the Reform of Popular Culture," esp. pp. 207–8, 215–16, 230–33. For an evaluation of his work see the review by Robert Muchembled in *Journal of Modern History* 51 (1979): 548–51. The subject has also been sensitively dealt with by P. T. Hoffman, *Church and Community in the Diocese of Lyon, 1500–1789* (New Haven, 1984) pp. 88–97. Note especially pp. 89–90 on the campaign "to replace traditional practices with sober ritual" such as Sunday vespers in place of tavern gatherings. Muchembled, too, notes the transformation of secular into religious celebrations (*Popular Culture and Elite Culture* pp. 127, 174) yet unlike Burke who stresses "reform" he speaks of a "great, systematic, repression" of popular culture in the seventeenth and eighteenth centuries (*ibid.* pp. 153, 159). For a penetrating critique, Arthur Mitzman, "The Civilizing Offensive: Mentalities, High Culture and Individual Psyches," *Journal of Social History* 20 (1987): 663–88, which came to my attention after this essay was written.

41. The European flavor of R. Aaron's remarks stands out especially when they are compared with those of his Palestinian contemporary R. Meir Poppers. The latter reported in his *Or Zaddikim* (Hamburg, 1690), which he completed in 1643, that it was customary in the land of Israel to remain awake in study for seven nights prior to the circumcision in the mother's home, and to dance and rejoice there on the eve of the ceremony (*ibid.* 19b). His support for the former custom, however, gave him no reason to condemn the latter.

42. Burke, *Popular Culture* pp. 211–12; Hoffman, *Church and Community* pp. 89–91. Note also Muchembled, *Popular Culture and Elite Culture* p. 138 who asserts that "before the Counter-Reformation men in Western Europe made no clear distinction between the sacred and the secular." See also *ibid.* p. 174 and n. 7 above.

43. Robert Bonfil, "Change in Cultural Patterns of Jewish Society in Crisis: The Case of Italian Jewry at the Close of the Sixteenth Century, *Jewish History*

3(1988): 24 (see chapter 15 of the present volume). See also his article cited above n. 38. On the sacral status of study in post-Biblical Judaism note the important comments of Jacob Katz, "Halakha and Kabbalah as Competing Subjects of Study," in Arthur Green ed. *Jewish Spirituality* v. 2 (New York, 1987) p. 34, especially n. 1.

44. Burke, *Popular Culture* pp. 222, 240. On similarities between the status of the rabbi and the priest in Italy see Robert Bonfil, *The Rabbinate in Renaissance Italy* [Hebrew], (Jerusalem, 1979) pp. 47–49. Note also *Medabber* (cited in the following note) p. 102 on the privilege of confidentiality.

45. He tells, in his autobiography, of having been snubbed when several advanced students were selected by the head of the "academy," R. Simha (Simone) Luzzatto, to accompany him, after they had completed their evening session, to a "veglia" held at the home of one of the community's prominent members. See Isaac Min-Halleviyyim, *Medabber Tahpuchoth*, ed. Daniel Carpi (Tel Aviv, 1985) p. 79. R. Isaac relates the incident as having taken place shortly after his thirtieth birthday, which occurred in 1651. The procession of the yeshiva members to which he alludes would seem to be of the type mentioned in the "Pragmatica" of 1616–17 (above n. 31) "né si possa andar con torchio a levar la gente alla vigilia." I have discussed the matter of torch processions among the Jews of the Veneto in a paper on "Confraternal Processions and Social Tensions in the Jewish Communities of the Veneto" presented at the conference cited above n. 43.

46. Leone Luzzatto, "Norme suntuarie risguardanti gli Ebrei: 29 Febbrajo 1697," *Archivio Veneto* 33 (1887): 159–60. The family members permitted to attend were the parents, siblings, grandparents, aunts, uncles, nieces, and nephews of the newborn's parents together with their spouses. Thus, despite the formal prohibition to observe the "veglia," the pre-circumcision observance must have remained a rather festive affair. Nonetheless, the official effort to control it is what here interests us. The resiliency of popular culture in the face of such efforts shall be discussed at greater length below.

47. These were summarized by Emmanuel Rodocanachi, *Le Saint-Siège et les Juifs: Le Ghetto à Rome* (Paris, 1891) pp. 86–87. On the control of dancing compare Burke pp. 208–9 and infra.

48. See Attilio Milano, "La 'Pragmatica' degli Ebrei Romani del secolo XVII," *Rassegna Mensile di Israel* 7 (1932–33): 179 and the English translation of these regulations in the appendix to Herman Vogelstein, *[History of the Jews in Rome,]* trans. Moses Hadas (Philadelphia, 1940) pp. 382–83. Note there also the stipulation that the celebration take place only in the home of the parents, and the limitations on the kinds of food and drink that might be served.

49. Ghetto houses were, of necessity, unusually high and collapses were hardly rare. See Cecil Roth, *History of the Jews in Italy* (Philadelphia, 1946) p. 356.

50. On changing attitudes towards masquerade during the seventeenth and eighteenth centuries note Shlomo Simonsohn, *History of the Jews in the*

Duchy of Mantua (Tel Aviv, 1977) pp. 536–37 as well as the sources published by Milano "La 'Pragmatica'," p. 179; J. R. Marcus, *The Jew in the Medieval World, A Source Book: 1315–1791* (Cincinnati, 1938) p. 220 and the statutes from mid-18th century Ferrara published by Simha Assaf in his *Mekorot le-Toledot ha-Hinnukh be-Yisrael* v. 2 (Tel Aviv, 1930) p. 200 (prohibiting both men and women from attending weddings or circumcisions in masquerade, and prohibiting any householder from admitting masked guests into his home). Simonsohn *(op. cit.)* has asserted that this diminishing tolerance for masquerade was due to "the influence of the ghetto spirit . . . as it conquered and repressed the simple joys of life." The interpretation offered here, however, would link this shift to fundamental changes that went beyond the confines of the ghetto. On this matter see also Hermann Pollack, "An Historical Inquiry Concerning Purim Masquerade-Attire," *Proceedings of the Seventh World Congress of Jewish Studies* (History of the Jews in Europe) (Jerusalem, 1981) pp. 228–31, where the period 1500–1700 is seen as that of the custom's duration. The entire matter, however, requires further investigation. See my forthcoming article in *Poetics Today*.

51. Abraham Ya'ari ed. *Iggerot Erez Yisrael* (Ramat Gan, 1971) p. 240. The decision to limit the number of participants in the meal seems to have been related to the exigencies of Passover eve, on which it took place. R. Meir Poppers, as early as 1643, testified that "it was the custom throughout the kingdom of the land of Israel to remain awake on each of the seven nights before a circumcision studying Torah in the mother's home." See above n. 41. For a later reference to the custom there, see Zevi Hirsch b. Azriel of Vilna, "Bet Lehem Yehuda," Yoreh De'ah #265. The latter may, however, have received his information from Poppers' work.

52. Pinkas Hevrat Mishmeret Boker, Ms. Modena, Communità Israelitica #4, [Institute for Microfilmed Hebrew Manuscripts #2908] unpaginated. The decision appears in the statutes dated R. H. Heshvan, 1711, par. 15. There, too, as in the case of Abraham Rovigo's entourage, stress was placed on the presence of a quorum of ten, in keeping with the sacral perception of the event. Later in the century the Tikkun Hazot Laila society of Modena decided that when a son would be born to one of its members they would hold an all-night vigil in his home, and in 1765 they published their own handbook of readings for that purpose. See *Seder Mishmeret ha-Ben* (Livorno, 1765). This may have been the source for Jacob Glassberg's assertion that "in Italy it is customary that [the members of] a confraternity called Hazot Laila study in the infant's home on the night before the circumcision, and this is a proper custom." *Zikhron Berit la-Rishonim* p. 148. On earlier editions of such handbooks see below. A manuscript copy of prayers recited by a confraternity in early eighteenth-century Siena on the night before a circumcision exists in the collection of Mr. William Gross of Ramat Aviv who graciously permitted me to examine it.

53. *Divrei ha-Berit* (Venice, 1707) 1b, 93b. On this work see Moritz Steinschneider, *Catalogus Librorum Hebraeorum in Bibliotheca Bodleiana* (Ber-

lin, 1931) #3224. Moses may have been the son of Joseph b. David Venturin who had been instrumental in the publication of Nathan Shapira's *Tuv Ha-aretz* (Venice, 1655), which contained the first printed version of the rite of midnight lamentation (Tikkun Hazot). Thus a concern with ritualization of the night would run in the family. On David Altaras, who was then serving as one of the rabbis of the Venice ghetto, see *EJ* v. 1 p. 776 and the sources cited there.

54. A shorter handbook for study on this night, based on the custom of Jerusalem, was published in Amsterdam, 1719, under the title *Shomer ha-Berit*. In his letter of approbation the rabbi of the Portuguese community, Solomon Ayylon, referred to the practice as recently having spread among the dispersion of Israel. See also *Berit Yizḥak* (Amsterdam, 1729). Thus within the first third of the eighteenth century three editions appeared whereas previously there had been none. The last was reprinted in 1768 and was used in the brief veglia service attended in Amsterdam a decade later by H. Y. D. Azulai. See his *Ma'agal Tov ha-Shalem* ed. Aron Freiman (Berlin-Jerusalem, 1921–34) p. 149.

55. See Abraham Berliner, *Geschichte der Juden in Rom* (Frankfurt, 1893) v. 2 p. 196, who gives a German summary of the 1726 regulations. On vernacular songs at the "veglia" cf. Roth, "Sumptuary Laws," p. 366.

56. On the impact of coffee, which came to Italy from the East at the beginning of the seventeenth century see, most generally, H. E. Jacob, *Coffee: Epic of a Commodity* (New York, 1935) and the sources cited below n. 71. For its impact on Jewish nocturnal rituals see my study "Coffee, Coffeehouses and the Nocturnal Rituals of Early Modern Jewry," in the *AJS Review* vol. 14 (1989).

57. Berliner, *Rom* p. 195; idem, "Sarid Me-'Ir," *Kobez 'al Yad* 5 (Cracow, 1893) pp. 11–12. On Corcos see *EJ* v. 5 p. 963 and the 1723 caricature reproduced in Attilio Milano, *Ghetto di Roma* (Rome, 1964) fig. 83. On Elijah's presence at the ceremony see above n. 34. The custom of dedicating a confraternity to a "patron saint" is remarkably similar to Catholic practice at the time and somewhat unusual in Jewish society. On Catholic confraternities in Rome see Vincenzo Paglia, *La pietà dei carcerati: confraternite e società a Roma nei secoli xvi-xviii* (Rome, 1980) and, on those of the Jews, Hermann Vogelstein and Paul Rieger, *Geschichte der Juden in Rom* (Berlin, 1895–96) v. 2 pp. 316–18, and Milano's more extensive survey "Le confraternite pie del Ghetto di Roma," *Rassegna Mensile di Israel* 24 (1958): 107–20, 166–80.

58. Quoted by Berliner, "Sarid Me-'Ir," pp. 11–12. On eighteenth-century confraternities sponsoring pious exercises of devotion "which were actually designed to supplant popular celebrations" compare Hoffman, *Church and Community* p. 133.

59. On this subject compare the general observations of Burke, *Popular Culture* pp. 217–18, 242, as well as the more specific ones of R. W. Malcolmson, *Popular Recreations in English Society 1700–1850* (Cambridge, 1973) pp.

13, 150, and Underdown, *Revel, Riot, and Rebellion: Popular Politics and Culture in England 1603–1660* pp. 261–62, 280, 283. The latter asserts that "throughout the eighteenth century popular culture continued to express, often in disorderly and violent ways, vigorous traditions of popular independence" (*ibid.* 283).

60. See Vogelstein-Rieger, *Geschichte* v. 2 pp. 228–29, 275 and the sources cited there.

61. Paolo Medici, *Riti Costumi degli Ebrei* (Florence, 1736) ch. 3 pp. 9–10. "Iva da qualche fanciullo, e tavolta eziandio dal Rabbino della Sinagoga si suol fare un discorso in lode di essa Circoncisione, col quale si esortano i Genitori ad aver coraglio ... Terminato il ragionamento, suonano, ballano, mangiano, bevono, e danno segni di allegrezza ... e altri rimangono tutta la notte, per custodire il bambino dalle insidie dela strega Lilit. Passano il tempo in varj trattinamenti, in canti, in giuochi, e in discorsi inutili, e oziosi." The reliability of Medici's account was also sensed by Paul Rieger who relied on it exclusively, quoting it verbatim, in his discussion of the "veglia" custom in the Roman ghetto. See Vogelstein-Rieger, *Geschichte* v. 2 pp. 298–99. For other instances of his reliance on Medici see *ibid.* pp. 308–11. Thus Medici's work should, like Morosini's (see above n. 36), be treated as a valuable source for the social history of Italian Ghetto life, and should be compared more systematically than has been possible in this study with Buxtorf and Modena.

62. "But now that the heretics and sectarians who believe falsely in ... Shabbetai Zevi ... have multiplied, and these treat the mourning associated with the Ninth of Ab very lightly ... now permit (in those places where it is customary) only one, whether meat or wine with a dairy meal, in order to memorialize the [Temple's] destruction and to negate the view of these heretics ..." Responsa *Shevut Ya'akov* pt. 3 (Metz, 1789) #36, 19b-c. On the Sabbatian heresy see Gershom Scholem, *Sabbetai Sevi: The Mystical Messiah*, trans. R. J. Z. Werblowsky (Princeton, 1973) and on Reischer's own contacts with the Sabbatian sympathizer R. Hayyim Lipschuetz (before 1710) see Isaiah Tishby, *Netivei Emunah u-Minut* (Ramat Gan, 1964) pp. 43–44, 206–7, 333 n. 25. Reischer's comments on Sabbatianism in this responsum, however, are not mentioned there nor in Scholem's discussion of the movement in the 18th century (*EJ* v. 14 pp. 1247–53 [= *Kabbalah* (New York, 1974) pp. 277–84].)

63. Johann Schudt, *Jüdische Merkwürdigkeiten* (Frankfurt, 1714–18) v. 4 pp. 74, 90. "Die Nacht/so vor dem Beschneidungs Tag hergeht/kommen viele Juden und Judinnen im Zimmer der Kindbetterin zusammen/die frömmste lesen und beten ... Da isset/trincket und spielet man dann die ganze Nacht hindurch ..." On Schudt's treatment of Judaism see *EJ* v. 14 pp. 1003–4 and the more positive evaluation by Kalir, "The Jewish Service" p. 56 n. 31, following Rudolph Hallo.

64. Paul Christian Kirchner, *Jüdisches Ceremoniel* (Nuremberg, 1730, reprint Hildesheim-New York, 1974) pp. 149, 156–57. "Wird eine gute lustige

Mahlzeit gemacht mit gedachten zehen Männern, und nach vollendeter Mahlzeit betet der Rabbiner oder der genannte Beschneider mit lauter Stimme ein Gebet, und stellen sich darauf alle mit einander um die Kindbetterin herum und beten ihren Abend Seegen auf Ebraisch, nach dessen Erfolg begiebt sich ein jedweder nach Hause." For earlier editions of this work (which I have been unable to consult) see Julius Fürst, *Bibliotheca Judaica* (Leipzig, 1863) v. 2 p. 190 and Cohen "Leon da Modena's *Rita*" p. 28 n. 5. For other scenes depicting the lying-in woman at the "wachnacht" playing cards see Johann Bodenschatz, *Kirchliche Verfassung der heutigen Juden* (Erlangen and Coburg, 1748–49) v. 4, illustration facing p. 60 [reproduced in *Jüdisches Lexicon* s.v. "kindbett"]. The exact relation between these plates remains to be determined. On Bodenschatz's illustration see Israel Abrahams, *By-Paths in Hebrew Bookland* (Philadelphia, 1920) pp. 160–65. On the link between childbirth and women's gambling see also Isaac Rivkind, *The Fight Against Gambling Among Jews* [Yiddish] (New York, 1946) p. 122.

65. See Israel Halpern, *Constitutiones Congressus Generalis Judaeorum Moraviensium* [Hebrew and Yiddish] (Jerusalem, 1951) p. 92 n. 6 and the sources cited there. This special exception was also noted by Jacob Katz, *Tradition and Crisis: Jewish Society at the End of the Middle Ages* (Glencoe, 1961) p. 163. The latter, in describing Ashkenazic Jewry during the sixteenth–eighteenth centuries notes that "amusements and other neutral manifestations of sociability were never entirely eliminated. For the most part, there was no clear and definite wish to do so" *(ibid.)*. The evidence marshalled in the present essay, however, points to a somewhat different picture.

66. *The Present State of the Jews* (London, 1675) p. 59. His stress upon the freedom associated with the night dovetails with some of the observations made at the beginning of this essay. Addison, who was the father of the better-known Joseph, explained that the purpose of this custom was "to console and recreate the Mother, that she may not be over-troubled for the pains of her son's circumcision, as also to prevent those mischiefs to which they imagine child-bed women are very liable the seventh night after their Delivery" *(ibid.)*. Addison's explanation for the practice, seems, however, to be taken not from his informants but from Buxtorf's *Synagoga Judaica* (ch. 2). I hope to devote a more detailed study to Addison's book, and especially to this problematic aspect of it. (See above n. 12) For the present see the brief essay by Israel Abrahams, *By-Paths* pp. 153–59.

67. J. Aegidius van Egmont and John Heyman, *Travels through Part of Europe, Asia Minor*, trans. from the Dutch (London, 1759) p. 276. The book is based upon travel impressions during the period 1700–1723. See Michael Ish-Shalom, *Christian Travels in the Holy Land* [Hebrew] (2nd edition, Tel Aviv, 1979) pp. 30–31. This account is not cited in a recent monograph on the Jews of Rhodes where it is reported that on the night before the circumcision "those who spent the night with the baby read selections from the Bible, Mishnah, Midrash and Zohar." This evidently became the practice in

the nineteenth and twentieth centuries. See M.D. Angel, *The Jews of Rhodes: The History of a Sephardic Community* (New York, 1978) pp. 117–18. A more systematic survey of travel literature from this period would undoubtedly uncover equally rich accounts of the various practices.

68. Attilio Milano, "Documents pour l'histoire de la communauté juive d'Ancone," *Revue des Etudes Juives* 88 (1929): 56. ("che la Visita solita farsi al Bambino prima della Circoncisione . . . non possa intervenirvi solo che Uffiziali e Parenti de' Genitori in primo grado . . ."). See also Roth, "Sumptuary Laws," pp. 366–67.

69. Copy in the Jewish National and University Library in Jerusalem, L38. The regulations were to be in effect for the period 1741–47. See Simonsohn, *Mantua* p. 541 n. 108.

70. Copy in same collection. See there par. 34. On the link between coffee and study at the "veglia" note also Azulai's comments (cited above n. 54) as well as the following note.

71. On the increase of coffee consumption in Europe from the mid-eighteenth century see Fernand Braudel, *Capitalism and Material Life 1400–1800*, trans. Miriam Kochan (London, 1973) pp. 186–88. On coffeehouses see Jean Leclant, "Coffee and Cafés in Paris," trans. P. M. Ranum in R. Forster and O. Ranum eds. *Food and Drink in History, Selections from the "Annales"* (Baltimore, 1979) pp. 86–97, and, for Italy, Antonio Pilot, *La bottega da caffè* (Venice, 1916). On Jewish coffeehouses in eighteenth-century Mantua see Simonsohn, *Mantua* pp. 530, 548; for Venice see Giacomo Carletto, *Il Ghetto veneziano nel settecento* (Rome, 1981) pp. 146, 191, 251. I have dealt with the subject at greater length in my article cited above n. 56.

72. *Pragmatica da osservarsi dalli singoli dell' Università degli Ebrei d'Ancona* (Ancona, 1766) pp. 12–13.

73. On the *Sulamith* I have relied primarily upon M. A. Meyer, *The Origins of the Modern Jew: Jewish Identity and European Culture in Germany, 1749–1824* (Detroit, 1967), pp. 119–20.

74. *Sulamith* 2 (1807) pp. 129–30. Both are quoted in full by Leopold Löw, *Die Lebensalter in der jüdischen Literatur* (Szegedin, 1875) pp. 90–91.

75. R. Moses Israel Hazzan, *Kerakh shel Romi* (Livorno, 1876) #11 (30b), and see Roberto Bonfil, "Mutamente nelle usanze religiose degli ebrei di Roma durante il ministero del rabbino Israel Mosé Hazan" [Hebrew], in *Scritti in Memoria di Enzo Sereni* (Jerusalem, 1970) pp. 228–51.

76. *Masa'ei Yisrael*, trans. David Gordon (Lyck, 1859) pp. 127–28. An English edition appeared the same year. *Eight Years in Asia and Africa: From 1846 to 1855* (Hanover, 1859) p. 285. Compare also Schauss, *The Lifetime of a Jew* pp. 60–66, and the account provided by J. Mattieu, "Notes sur l'enfance juive de Casablanca," *Bulletin de l'Institut d'Hygiène du Maroc* n. s. 7 (1947) pp. 29–30, quoted (in English) by A. N. Chouraqui, *Between East and West: A History of the Jews of North Africa*, trans. M. M. Bernet, (Philadelphia, 1968) pp. 69–70.

77. Alfredo Soliani, "Sulla Veglia precedente la Circoncisione," *Il Vessilo Israe-litico* 26 (1878): 23.
78. Asher Greenwald, *Sefer Zokher ha-Berit* (Uzhgorod, 1931) 22a; Sheftel Davidson, *Ateret Paz* (Tel Aviv, 1945) p. 35. Jacob Verdiger, in his *'Edut be-Yisrael* (Benei Berak, 1963) quoted from Meir Poppers (above n. 41) the custom of studying on the eve of the circumcision but deleted from the same author's testimony his reference to the custom of dancing and rejoicing on the same night!

Index

Aaron [= Aharon] Barachia [= Berakhiah] of Modena, 31, 352, 562–64, 566
Aaron of Lunel, 558
Abraham, 46, 58, 123, 133, 534, 535
Abraham ben Meshullam of San Angelo, 347–48
Abraham of Montalcino, 95
Abraham of Perugia, 328
Abravanel [= Abrabanel], Isaac, 46, 147, 181, 184, 196, 203, 255, 259, 261, 284, 303, 336; and magic, 134–36
Abravanel [= Abrabanel], Judah ben Isaac. See Leone Ebreo
Abudiente, Moses, 310
Abulafia, Abraham, 109–10, 118, 119, 137, 143, 310, 325, 326, 327, 332, 359
Accessus ad auctores, 56–57, 233
Addison, Lancelot, 571, 573
Adrutiel, Abraham, 336
Aggadah, 213
Agricola, Rudolph, 72, 77, 78
Agrippa, Henry Cornelius of Nettesheim, 15, 112, 144–47, 258, 329, 355, 357
Alashkar, Joseph, 336
Al-Batalyusi, 136
Albert of Trent, 303
Alberti, Leon Battista, 1
Albertus Magnus, 116, 133, 357
Albo, Joseph, 131
Albotini, Yehudah [= Judah], 290. 332
Alcastiel, Joseph, 335
Al-Constantini, Solomon, 130
Alemanno, Yohanan, 15–16, 17, 23, 24, 57–59, 109, 111, 112, 114, 115, 116,

303, 304, 327, 328, 332, 336, 337, 345–46, 348–49, 355, 357, 360, 532; on magic, 118–36; on Neoplatonism, 136–44
Alfarabi, 65, 66
Al-Ghazzali, 58, 136
Alkabetz, Solomon Ha-Levi, 291, 349, 350, 351
Almosnino, Moses, 535
Altmann, Alexander, 12–13, 63–84
Anatoli, Jacob, 68
Ancient theology, 14, 140. *See also* Poetic theology
Ancona, 7, 24, 560, 562, 565, 566, 571, 572
Annius of Viterbo, 20, 252, 256–69
Antonino of Florence, 8
Apologetics, Jewish, 27–28, 429–73
Appolonius, 115–16, 357
Aquinas, Thomas, 11, 356
Arama, Isaac, 80, 336
Archivolti, Samuel, 89, 503
Aristotle, 10–11, 30, 52, 55, 63, 64–66, 68, 71, 73, 74, 75, 80, 120, 121, 170, 173, 178, 180, 183, 325, 333, 479, 523, 530, 534, 541
Ashkenazi, Joseph, 334
Ashkenazi, Saul Cohen, 17
Assisi, 5
Astrology, 122–23, 126, 130, 131, 133, 325; and messianic prognostication, 302–3. *See also* Magic
Atomism, 531–32, 534, 535
Augustine, St., 69, 252, 306, 311

Averroes, 11, 17, 52, 65–66, 67, 68, 132, 139, 171, 173, 174, 177, 178, 181, 184, 327
Avicenna, 65, 131, 171, 327, 523
Azriel, Rabbi, 324
Azulai, Abraham, 305

Baer, Yitzhak [= Yizhak], 283, 286, 301, 311
Babel, 264
Bacon, Francis, 30
Bacon, Roger, 357
Bahyye ben Asher, 435, 447
Bar Hiyyah, Abraham, 307, 535
Baron, Salo W., 219–20, 221, 241, 242, 244, 253, 441
Baroque, 26, 484; and Jewish culture, 27, 29, 411–13, 502–18
Barukh ben Barukh, 356
Barzilay, Isaac, 4, 361
Basnage, Jacques, 453, 454
Basola, Moses, 414–15
Behinat ha-Dat. See Delmedigo, Elijah
Benivieni, Domenico, 183
Benjamin, Israel Joseph (Benjamin II), 573
Ben Sheshet, Jacob, 324
Bernardino of Feltre, 8, 87
Bernardino of Siena, 8, 87
Berosus, 256, 257, 258, 259, 262, 263, 265, 267, 268
Bettan, Israel, 94
Biography, Hebrew, 57–59
Biondi, Albano, 257
Biondo, Flavio, 243
Bodin, Jean, 253, 258
Bologna, 7, 8, 116; medical school of, 30
Bonfil, Robert, 5, 18–20, 25–27, 29, 219–51, 253–54, 401–25, 559, 564
Book of Beliefs and Opinions. See Saadia Gaon
Book of the Honeycomb's Flow. See Messer Leon, Judah
Botticelli, Sandro, 303
Bracciolini, Poggio, 69
Brant, Sebastian, 303
Bruni, Leonardo, 72
Bruno, Giordano, 112, 258, 354
Burke, Peter, 556, 563, 654

Burkhardt, Jacob, 1, 2, 3; and his influence on Jewish historiography, 2–3
Buxtorf, Johann the Elder, 433–35, 436–48, 454, 557, 559, 561, 568, 570

Calmet, Dom Augustin, 453, 454
Calvin, John, 314, 434
Camillo, Guilio, 357
Campanella, Tomasso, 112
Cano, Melchor, 258, 259, 268
Cantarini, Isaac Hayyim (Vita ha-Cohen), 87–88, 91, 522, 527
Capistrano, John, 87
Capsali [= Kapsali], Elijah [= Eliyahu], 19, 20, 192, 202, 206, 207, 227, 228, 232, 233, 236–37, 239, 241, 284
Cardozo [= Cardoso], Abraham, 310–11
Cardozo [= Cardoso], Isaac, 527, 530, 532, 533, 535, 537, 538, 540, 542
Cassuto, Umberto, 87
Castiglione, Balassare, 1
Charles VIII, King, 304–5, 307
Choral music, 28–29, 474–501
Christianity. *See* Christian kabbalah; Conversion: to Chritianity; Counter-Reformation; Jesus Christ; New Christians; Papacy
Christian kabbalah, 13–17, 22, 110–11, 182, 183, 305, 309–10, 328–30, 358–59. *See also Kabbalah*
Cicero, 12, 13, 19, 50, 63, 67–69, 70, 71, 72, 73, 74, 76, 77, 78, 226, 233, 236, 411, 523, 534
Coen, Anania Hai, 505, 511–12
Cohen, Mark R., 27–28, 429–73
Cohen, Tobias, 522, 525, 526, 527, 530, 532, 533, 535, 539, 540, 541, 542
Colon, Joseph, 559
Comedy of Bethrothal. See Portaleone, Yehudah Sommo
Condotta, 7, 47
Condottieri, 1
Conegliano, Solomon and Israel, 522, 526, 527, 531, 537
Confraternities, 26, 31, 416–17, 566–68
Consolations for the Tribulations of Israel. See Usque, Samuel
Conversion: to Christianity, 24
Conversos. See New Christians

Copernicus, Nicolaus, 529, 541
Corcos, Tranquillo Via (Manoaḥ Ḥaim), 568–69, 571, 573
Correggio, Giovanni Mercurio da, 303
Coryat, Thomas, 382
Counter-Reformation, 24–25, 254, 377, 383, 393, 432, 445, 563
Cremona, 402, 560, 561, 562
Crescas, Hasdai, 108, 131
Crescas, Meir, 125
Crusade chronicles, 196, 198, 200
Cum Nimus Absurdum. *See* Paul IV, Pope

D'Ailley, Pierre, 307
Dante, 90
Da Pisa family, 8
Da Pisa, Isaac ben Yehi'el, 110, 126–27, 134, 176, 345–46, 347, 349
Da Pisa, Yehi'el Nissim, 346, 349
Da Rieti, Antonio, 393
Dato, Mordecai, 91, 351, 418
David, 48, 53, 58, 490, 563
David ben Judah he-Ḥasid, 334
De Balmes, Abraham, 327, 345, 536
Delaqrot [= Delacrut], Matitiahu [= Mattitiahu], 287, 335, 347
De Barrios, Miguel (Daniel Levi), 509
De Castro, Benedict, 527, 535, 536
De Lattes, Bonet, 303, 308
De Lattes, Isaac Joshua, 305, 347–48, 349
Del Bene, Yehudah [= Judah], 359, 411, 412
De Leon, Isaac, 331
De Leon, Moses, 325
Delmedigo, Elijah, 11, 15, 17, 63–64, 67, 122, 132, 137, 139, 141, 174–76, 178, 180, 183, 184, 185, 186, 328, 332
Delmedigo, Joseph Solomon (Yashar of Candia), 148, 327, 354, 355, 361, 522, 525, 527, 532, 533, 535, 536, 537, 538, 539, 540, 541, 542
Del Rio, Bathazar, 308
De' Medici, Cosimo, 266
De' Medici family, 1
De' Medici, Lorenzo, 132, 181
De Occulta Philosophia, 144–47. *See also* Agrippa, Henry Cornelius of Nettesheim

De Oliveyra, Salomon, 509
De Pomis, David, 28, 532, 535, 539
De' Rossi, Azariah, 13, 18, 20–21, 54, 64, 75–77, 78, 81, 91, 147, 192, 202, 203, 211–15, 226, 239–43, 252–79, 361
De' Rossi [= Rossi], Salamone, 28, 474–501
De Vidas, Elijah, 351
Descartes, René, 30
Dialoghi d'amore. *See* Leone Ebreo
Di Alba, Jacob, 92
Dieulosal, Isaac, 300–301, 302
Dinur [Dinaburg], Ben Zion, 193–94
Dionisotti, Carlo, 171–72
Di Vali, Elijah ben Solomon ha-Levi, 91
Divrey ha-Yamim shel Moshe Rabbenu, 228–29
Domus cathecumenorum, 391
Drama, Hebrew, 54–55
Dubnov, Simon, 2
Duran, Profiat, 48–51, 80, 125

Efodi. *See* Duran, Profiat
Egidio [= Giles] of Viterbo, 15, 89, 107, 111, 308, 309, 314, 328, 329
Eldad the Danite [= ha-Dani], 19, 228
Elior, Rachel, 21–22, 23, 283–98
Emblem-riddles, 29, 502–18
Emmanuel of Benivenito, 349
Empedocles, 137
Enoch, 125, 133, 179, 268
Erasmus, 258
Ergas, Joseph, 357
Espina, Alonso de, 307
Estensi family, 24. *See also* Ferrara
Eusebius, 230–31, 232, 261
Ezovi, Isaac, 333
Ezra, Rabbi, 120, 324

Fano [= da Fano], Ezra, 352, 478
Fano, Menahem Azariah of, 351, 352, 356–57, 402–3, 408, 414, 415, 417, 418
Farissol, Abraham, 90, 171, 183, 303, 304, 532
Felix, Gabriel, 526
Ferrara, 7, 8, 24, 171, 239, 266, 303, 407; medical school of, 30

Ficino, Marsilio, 14, 15, 16, 58, 59, 112, 118, 136, 147, 181, 182, 183, 326, 328, 329
Figo, Azariah, 94, 98, 359, 519
Finzi, Jacob Israel of Recanati, 414
Fioravanti, Leonardo, 405–6
Florence, 5, 8, 14, 16, 87, 111, 112, 114, 132, 133, 136, 138, 176, 178, 180, 181, 378, 407
Foa, Eliezer Nahman, 408–9
Forlì, 7
Foucault, Michel, 406
France, 8, 257, 526
Frances, Jacob, 502, 508
Frances, Immanuel, 502, 503, 508, 509
Franciscans, 8, 9

Gaffarel, Jacques, 431–33, 440, 453
Gakon, Isaac, 331
Galatino, Pietro, 309
Galen, 405, 523, 530
Galia [= Gallei] Raza [= Razaya], 284, 287, 289, 291, 332, 333
Galileo, Galilei, 30
Gallico, Samuel, 351
Ganz [= Gans], David, 19, 192, 196, 202, 206, 209, 227, 232, 236, 243, 258, 308, 535
Gelli, Giambattista, 265, 266
Genazzano, Elijah, di, 142
Gerizim, Mount, 263–64
Germany, 8, 257, 380, 381, 434, 435, 447, 451, 520, 524, 525, 536, 539, 570
Gerona, 120, 324, 327
Gersonides. See Levi ben Gershon
Ghetto, 3, 4, 5, 6, 24–32, 373–85, 386–400, 407–13, 565, 573
Giambullari, Pierfrancesco, 253, 258, 265, 266
Gikatilla, Joseph, 109, 128, 142, 325, 335
Giorgio, Francesco, 15, 111, 330, 358
Gonzaga family, 24. See also Mantua
Graetz, Heinrich, 2, 430, 432
Gratius, Ortuinus, 433
Grégoire, Abbé Henri, 449, 453, 454
Grimani, Domenico, 171
Guicciardini, Francesco, 19, 223, 231
Guide of the Perplexed. See Maimonides, Moses

Habib, Levi ben, 308
Ha-Cohen [= Cohen], Abraham of Zante, 527, 542
Ha-Cohen, Jacob and Isaac, 325
Ha-Cohen [= Ha-Kohen], Joseph, 19, 192, 202, 203, 204, 205–7, 209, 227, 232–36, 239, 241, 305
Ha-Cohen, Saul [Ashkenazi], 147, 180, 184–86
Hai ben Yoktan, 137
Hakham Kolel [= Shalem], 12, 58
Halevi, Abraham ben Eliezer, 284, 293, 303, 304, 305, 330–31, 333
Halevi, Yehuda [= Judah], 48, 77, 80, 81, 108, 132, 193, 265, 349
Halevi, Zerahiah, 209–10
Halfan, Elijah Menahem, 108, 358
Hallewa, Judah, 335
Hamdan, Joseph of, 334
Hamiz, Joseph, 357, 359, 519–20, 522, 537, 542
Hamon, Ovadia, 333
Harrán, Dan, 28–29, 474–501
Hayon, Joseph, 283
Hayyat [= Hayat], Judah, 110, 141, 142, 143, 284, 287, 335, 346
Hebrew, 50–51, 80–82, 171, 253, 264–67, 410–11, 482
Heilprin, Yehiel, 197
Hermes Trismegistus, 14–15, 148–49
Hermeticism. See Magic; Kabbalah
Herrera, Abraham, 108, 148, 327, 332, 354, 355, 361
Historia de' riti hebraici. See Modena, Leon
Historical writing: among Jews in the Renaissance, 4, 17–21, 55–57, 191–279
Horace, 77
Horowitz, Elliott, 5, 31, 416, 554–88
Humanism: and Jewish culture, 4, 9–10, 11–13, 45–62, 63–84; and Jewish sermons, 13, 77–82, 89–90. See also Sermons

Ibn Basa, Moses ben Samuel of Blanes, 88
Ibn Daud, Abraham, 198, 200, 201, 232, 255, 261
Ibn Ezra, Abraham, 80, 116, 124, 131, 133, 136, 349, 435, 535, 536

Ibn Ezra, Moses, 66, 75, 136, 137, 197
Ibn Falaquera, Shem Tov, 137
Ibn Gabbai, Meir, 335, 336
Ibn Gabirol, Solomon, 136
Ibn Ḥabib, Moses, 77
Ibn Hayyan, Jabir, 134
Ibn Latif, Isaac, 136, 325, 326
Ibn Lavi, Simon, 287, 292
Ibn Malkah, Judah ben Nissim, 327
Ibn Motot, Samuel, 130, 131, 140, 349
Ibn Shraga, Joseph, 284, 303, 346
Ibn Verga, Solomon, 20, 192, 197–98,
    202, 203, 204, 205, 207–8, 210–11,
    227
Ibn [-ben] Wakar [= Waqqar], Joseph,
    130, 131, 140, 325, 327, 346
Ibn Yaḥya [= Yahia], Gedalya, 115, 192,
    202, 203, 206, 208, 226, 232
Ibn Yaḥya [= Yahia], Tam, 56–57, 199–
    200, 210
Ibn Zarza [= Sarsa], Samuel, 125, 130,
    131, 325, 346, 348
Ibn Zimra, David, 330, 336
Idel, Moshe, 6, 15, 16, 22–24, 86, 107–
    69, 303, 324–68
Iggeret Rab Sherira, 196, 198
Immanuel of Rome, 502
Israeli, Isaac, 136, 535
Isserles, Moshe, 347

Jabez, Joseph. *See* Yavets, Yosef
Janus. *See* Noah
Jesus Christ, 58, 182, 183, 242, 257, 261,
    306, 446
Jews, Italian: and apologetics, 27–28,
    429–73; and choral music, 28–29; and
    conversionary pressures, 24; and com-
    munal organization, 8; and ghettoiza-
    tion, 24–32, 373–400; and historical
    writing, 17–21, 55–57, 191–279; and
    humanism, 11–13, 45–62, 63–84; and
    their impact on Renaissance and ba-
    roque cultures, 6; and magic, 107–136;
    and medicine, 519–53; and messianism
    and mysticism, 21–24, 283–368; and
    music, 474–501; and Neoplatonism,
    131–33, 136–49; and the origins of
    their community, 6; and poetry, 502–
    18; political and legal status of, 6; and

preaching, 85–104; and Renaissance
    culture, 9–24, 45–188; and science,
    29–31, 519–53. *See also* Moneylend-
    ing, Jewish
Job, 54, 55, 535
Josel of Rosheim, 433
Joseph ben Hayyim of Benevento, 89
Josephus, Flavius, 18, 19, 55, 56, 192,
    199, 204, 259, 261, 263, 267, 268
Jugendres, Sebastian, 430, 453

Kabbalah [= *Cabala*], 4, 13, 14, 15, 17,
    21–24, 86, 88, 107–169, 175–76, 177,
    179, 181, 182, 184, 214–15, 285–95,
    324–68, 442, 506, 563–64; as a media-
    tor between medievalism and moder-
    nity, 26, 402–5, 413–19; in Spain,
    324–26. *See also* Christian kabbalah
Kafman, Berakiel ben Meshullam, 349,
    357
Karo [= Caro, Joseph], 291, 292, 312,
    436
Karo, Yitzhak, 283
Katz, Jacob, 287, 418
Katz, Zalman, 97
Katznellenbogen, Samuel Judah, 85, 92,
    93, 95–96, 97
Kimhi, David, 259, 261, 435
Kirchner, Paul Christian, 430, 453, 570
Kordovero [= Cordovero], Moses, 293,
    333, 347, 349, 350–54, 357, 402, 416
Kuzari. See Halevi, Yehuda

Lemlin [= Lamlien, Lemlein], Asher, 115,
    287, 290, 291, 303, 308, 310, 332,
    336, 337
Leone Ebreo, 11, 16–17, 108, 111, 170–
    88, 327, 360
Lesley, Arthur M., 11, 12, 13, 17, 18, 20,
    45–62, 170–88
Letter of Aristeas, 239
Levi ben Gershon [= Gersonides], 203,
    402, 535, 536
Levita, Elijah, 50, 328
Liber Clavicula Salomonis [= *Sefer Maf-
    te'ah Shlomo*], 115
Liber de Causis, 137, 141, 142–44
Lichtenberg, George, 302

Light of God (Or ha-Shem). *See* Crescas, Hasdai
Loan banking, Jewish. *See* Moneylending, Jewish
Loyola, Ignatious, 22, 313–14
Luria, Isaac, 18, 22–24, 147, 214–15, 285, 287, 295, 310, 312–15, 330, 333, 334, 335–37, 351, 352, 353, 354, 355, 356, 357, 402, 415–16, 532
Lustro, Solomon, 527, 542
Luther, Martin, 304, 314, 434, 490
Luzzatto [= Luzzato], Moses Hayyim, 357, 413, 503, 509, 513
Luzzatto [= Luzzato], Samuel David, 509, 512
Luzzatto [= Luzzato], Simone, 28, 384, 429, 437, 445, 448, 449, 450

Ma'arekhet ha-Elohut, 109–10, 119, 141, 143, 146, 149
Machiavelli, Niccolo, 1, 19, 223, 231, 258
Magic, 4, 15, 16, 23; and Jewish culture, 112–36, 417–18
Maharal of Prague [Judah Loew b. Bezalel], 196, 243, 263
Maimonides, Moses, 10–11, 30, 55, 66–67, 70, 80, 108, 173, 174, 184, 185, 252, 325, 359, 412, 431, 434, 481, 535, 536
Manasseh [-Menasseh, Menashe] ben Israel, 243, 327, 355–56, 429, 437, 447, 448, 450
Manetti, Benedetto, 299
Manetti, Gianozzo, 80
Mantua, 4, 5, 8, 18, 24, 52, 81, 97, 178, 202, 211, 213, 228, 256, 348, 349, 378, 402, 418, 474, 475, 483, 508, 572
Margaritha, Antonius, 433, 435, 446, 453
Mar Hayyim, Isaac, 110, 176, 178, 180, 346
Marini, Solomon, 526, 527, 542
Marino, Giambattista, 484, 502
Marranos. *See* New Christians
Medici, Paulo Sebastiano, 569
Medicine, 405–6. *See also* Physician, Jewish
Medieta, Geronimo de, 304, 306, 307
Meleto, Francesco da, 299–301, 302, 306, 307

Mendes, David Franco, 509
Me'or Einayim. *See* De' Rossi, Azariah
Messer Leon, David, 11, 137, 138, 139, 327, 331, 332, 345, 350
Messer Leon, Judah [Yehuda ben Yehiel], 11–12, 52–53, 57, 64, 67–75, 77, 78, 79, 137, 138, 139, 331, 346, 402, 411, 477
Messianism, 4, 21–24, 283–323; Christian influence on Jewish, 302–6; and Christian kabbalists, 309–10; in Christianity, 313–15; and New Christians, 310–12; in historical writing, 207, 255; Jewish influence on Christian, 306–9
Metasthenes, 256, 260, 261, 262, 263
Milan, 5, 7, 24
Min ha-Levi'im [= of the Levites], Isaac, 91
Min ha-Levi'im [= of the Levites], Jacob ben Kalonimus, 352
Minhat Yehudah. *See* Hayyat, Judah
Mirandola, Giovanni Pico della, 11, 13–17, 24, 58, 59, 80, 81, 90, 107, 109, 110, 111, 112, 117, 118, 120, 121, 122, 123, 132, 136, 137, 140, 147, 171, 174, 182, 183, 252, 307, 309, 326, 328, 329, 330, 358, 359
Mithridates, Flavius, 15, 111, 183, 328, 359
Modena, 8, 407, 566, 567
Modena, Leon (da) [= Yehudah Arieh], 27–29, 86, 89, 90, 91, 92, 96, 97, 98, 352, 359–60, 384, 411–12, 429–73, 476–82, 484–86, 488, 507, 519, 561, 562, 564, 569
Molkho [= Molcho], Solomon [= Shlomo], 284, 287, 290, 291, 308, 310, 312
Momigliano, Arnaldo, 230, 234, 243
Moneylending, Jewish, 1, 5, 7, 8, 375–76, 394, 407
Monti di Pieta, 8. *See also* Moneylending, Jewish
Morosini, Giulio, 561–62, 568, 569
Morpurgo, Rahel, 509, 512
Moscato, Judah, 13, 64, 77–82, 85–86, 93, 96–97, 111, 148–49, 265, 332, 349, 361
Mosconi, Judah, 199
Moses, 54, 58, 73, 81–82, 123–24, 125,

127, 129, 133, 183, 266; as magician, 123–24, 443, 446, 477
Moses ben Joab [= Yo'av], 87, 95, 132
Münster, Sebastian, 254, 258–59, 268, 308
Music, 474–501
Mussafia, Benjamin, 519
Mysticism. *See Kabbalah*

Nahmanides, Moses [= Moses ben Nahman], 81, 120, 124
Nanni, Giovanni of Viterbo, 303
Naples, 24, 52, 172, 174, 176
Narboni, Moses, 132, 178
Nathan of Gaza, 310
Navarra (Noveira), Menahem of Verona, 512
Neoplatonism: its impact on Jewish culture, 4, 10, 13–17, 80–81, 131–33, 136–49, 170–88, 325, 327, 346, 354, 355, 360, 479, 534
New Christians, 8, 22, 87, 207, 301, 309, 521, 525; and messianism, 310–12, 558
Nieto, David, 522, 530, 532, 533, 535, 537, 539, 540, 541
Nissim of Marsaille, 132
Noah, 256, 257, 264, 265, 266
Norsa family, 8

Organon. See Aristotle
Origen, 46–47
Orlandini, Paolo, 307

Padua, 5, 7, 8, 11, 52, 85, 87, 174, 178, 180, 375, 378, 407; medical school of, 30, 354, 519–53, 560, 562
Pagis, Dan, 29, 502–18
Papacy: Jewry policy of, 5–6, 377, 386–400
Paracelsianism, 529–30, 531, 535, 538
Patronage: of Jewish culture, 7
Paul of Middleberg, 302
Paul IV, Pope, 24, 25, 87, 377, 386, 388, 391, 392, 393
Pawnbroking banks. *See* Moneylending, Jewish
Perugia, 5, 7
Pesaro, 8
Petrarch, 69, 72, 90

Pfefferkorn, Johannes, 433
Philo, 82, 147, 170, 239, 253, 256, 259, 260, 261
Picart, Bernard, 453
Picatrix [= Ghayat al-Hakim], 112, 113, 114
Piedmont, 5
Pines, Shlomo, 185–86
Physician, Jewish, 29–31, 519–53
Plato. *See* Neoplatonism
Plotinus, 138, 170
Poetic theology, 14. *See also* Ancient theology
Poetry, Hebrew, 53–54, 502–18
Pompeo del Borgo, 386–87
Popular culture: among Jews, 31–32, 554–88
Porphyry, 138
Portaleone, Abraham, 19, 361, 485, 530, 532
Portaleone, Yehudah Sommo, 54–55
Postel, Guillaume, 15, 309, 330
Pratensis [= Prato], Felix, 328, 359
Preachers. *See* Sermons
Proclus, 16, 140, 141, 142, 143, 144, 148. *See also Liber de Causis*
Provence, 53, 54, 558
Provenzal [= Provençal, Provencial], David, 51, 54, 81, 86–87, 91, 264, 526

Quintilian, 12, 63, 67–69, 71, 72, 73, 74, 77, 96

Rabbinic chronology, 254–55, 260–64
Ramus, Peter, 72
Ramusio, Giambatista, 308
Ravid, Benjamin C. I., 24–25, 373–85
Raya Mehemna, 286
Recanati, Menahem, 109–10, 119
Reggio Emilia, 8, 407, 573
Reisch, Gregorius, 82
Reischer, Jacob, 570
Renaissance: and Jewish culture, 9–24, 26, 27, 45–104, 107–88
Reubeni [= Ha-Reuveni], David, 87, 193, 308, 382
Reuchlin, Johann, 15, 107, 111, 329, 330, 358
Rhetoric: *See* Humanism
Rhetorica ad Herennium, 52

Riccius [=Ricius], Paulus, 328, 330, 359
Rittangelus, S., 359
Rome, 5, 7, 19, 24, 25, 172, 256, 377, 386–400, 407, 566, 567, 568, 569, 572, 573
Rossillo, Mordekhai Raphael, 127, 346, 349
Roth, Cecil, 3, 9, 59, 93, 431, 435
Rovigo, Abraham, 566
Ruderman, David B., 1–39, 299–323, 519–53

Saadia Gaon, 108, 259, 535
Sabbatian movement. *See* Shabbetai Zevi
Safed, 21, 23, 149, 301, 327, 330, 333, 336, 349, 350, 351, 418, 563
Salutati, Coluccio, 72
Samaritans, 263–64
Sambari, Josef, 227, 228
Saperstein, Marc, 13, 85–104
Sarchi, Philip, 505, 511
Sarug, Israel, 147–48, 347, 352–54, 356, 357, 532
Saturn, 129–30
Savonarola, Girolamo, 303, 304, 307, 308
Scaliger, Joseph, 260, 268
Schmitt, Charles, 10
Scholasticism. *See* Aristotle
Scholem, Gershom, 18, 21–22, 86, 283, 286, 301, 308, 310, 335, 336, 558, 563
Schudt, Johann Jacob, 520, 570
Science: and Jewish culture, 29–31, 519–53
Seder Olam Rabbah [and] *Zuta*, 201, 228, 262
Sefer ha-Atzamim [Ha-Elyonim], 116, 131, 141, 143
Sefer ha-Levana, 115
Sefer ha-Meshiv (Answering Angel), 291, 303, 325, 331
Sefer ha-Tamar, 116
Sefer ha-Yashar, 229
Sefer Kaf ha-Ketoret, 332, 333
Sefer Ma'aseh Efod. See Duran, Profiat
Sefer Mlekhet Muskelet, 115
Sefer Nofet Zufim (Book of the Honeycomb's Flow). See Messer Leon, Judah
Sefer Pil'ot Olam, 116, 133

Sefer Razi'el, 112, 114–15
Sefer Shimushei Torah, 120
Sefer Tahlit he-Hakham, 113, 120, 121
Sefer Yezira, 119, 121, 123, 141
Sefer Yossiphon, 19, 56, 57, 196, 198, 199, 201, 204, 210, 228, 258, 259
Sefirot, 109, 116–17, 118, 119, 120, 122, 123, 124, 126, 127, 128, 129, 139, 140, 141, 142, 144, 145, 146, 147, 149, 346
Selden, John, 453, 454
Septuagint, 253, 254, 258, 261
Sermons, 13, 85–104
Sforno, Obadiah, 137, 255–56, 258
Shabbetai Zevi, 22, 88, 295, 308, 310, 333, 403, 570
Shapira, Nathan, 357
Shem Tov ben Shem Tov, 325, 326, 335
Shevet Yehudah. See Ibn Verga, Solomon
Shomerim la-Boker Society of Venice, 356, 357
Shulvass, Moses Avigdor, 3, 9, 449
Siena, 89, 378, 407
Simeon Bar Yohai. *See* Zohar
Simon of Trent, 87
Simon, Richard, 453
Simonsohn, Shlomo, 3–4
Sippur Nathan ha-Babli, 198
Sixtus V, Pope, 388–90, 391–93, 395–97
Solomon, 48, 57–58, 112, 115, 127, 129, 131, 132, 134, 135–36, 176, 534, 535, 536
Song of Solomon's Ascent (Shir ha-Ma'alot). See Alemanno, Yohanan
Songs of Solomon. See De'Rossi, Salamone
Sonne, Isaiah, 17, 171
Spain, 48, 49, 53, 54, 256, 257, 502; and the expulsion of the Jews, 8, 10, 18, 20, 21, 22, 23, 46, 110, 173, 202–4, 206, 223, 234–35, 283, 285, 300, 301, 307, 311, 324, 326, 332, 335, 336, 337, 350; and *Kabbalah*, 109–10, 286–87, 324–26
Steinschneider, Moritz, 67, 193, 513
Steuchus, Augustinus, 254
Stow, Kenneth R., 25, 306, 386–400
Studia humanitatis. See Humanism
Suetonius, 58

Sulamith, 573
Sullam, Sara Coppia, 384

Taitazak, Joseph, 312, 350
Talmud, burning of, 24
Tamari-Venturozzo controversy, 402
Terence, 50
Tikkunei Zohar, 141, 284, 286
Tishby, Isaiah, 286, 352, 513
Tissard, Francois, 107, 433
Torella, Girolamo, 303
Torquato, Antonio, 302, 303
Trattati d'amore, 17
Trent: rural murder of, 9
Treves, Yohanan, 415
Tsarfati, Reuben, 143
Turiel, Shlomo, 284, 287
Tuscany, 24

Urbino, 7
Usque, Samuel, 19–20, 171, 202, 205, 207, 226, 304
Usury. *See* Moneylending, Jewish

Valla, Lorenzo, 72
Van Egmont, J. E., 571
Venice, 5, 11, 24, 28, 92, 181, 229, 349, 353, 356, 374–82, 384, 402, 403, 407, 417, 418, 419, 431, 432, 449, 450, 452, 474, 504, 508, 519, 520, 522, 523, 528, 535, 561, 564, 565, 566, 571
Verona, 5, 407
Vesalius, 30, 405

Victorinus, Fabius Laurentius, 69, 72
Vital, Hayyim, 285–88, 290, 291, 329, 333–34, 337, 353, 356
Von Carben, Victor, 433

Wallich, Abraham, 527, 530, 532
Weinberg, Joanna, 19–20, 252–79
Widmanstat, J. A., 308

Xenophon, 58, 256, 261

Yagel, Abraham, 111, 144–48, 304, 327, 332, 348, 349, 353–55, 357, 359, 361, 412, 530, 532
Yavets [= Jabez], Yosef [= Joseph], 176–77, 180, 336
Yerushalmi, Yosef H., 18–19, 20, 191–218, 221–24, 232–33, 305, 311

Zacuto [= Zakut], Abraham, 192, 202, 203, 206, 208, 226, 228, 232, 303, 308, 535
Zacuto [= Zacut], Moses, 26, 29, 357, 412–13, 503, 505, 508
Zahalon, Jacob, 88, 530, 532, 536–37
Zinberg, Israel, 2
Zohar, 31, 89, 91, 109, 149, 284, 285, 286, 288, 290, 291, 292, 325, 326, 330, 331, 333, 334, 346, 349, 350, 351, 352, 353, 402, 418, 419, 558, 559, 563, 564, 566, 573
Zunz, Leopold, 88, 243, 252, 268

About the Editor

David B. Ruderman is Frederick P. Rose Professor of Jewish History at Yale University. He is the author of *The World of a Renaissance Jew: The Life and Thought of Abraham b. Mordecai Farissol* (Cincinnati, 1981); *Kabbalah, Magic, and Science: The Cultural Universe of a Sixteenth-Century Jewish Physician* (Cambridge, Mass., 1988); and *A Valley of Vision: The Heavenly Journey of Abraham ben Hananiah Yagel* (Philadelphia, 1990). He has also edited *Preachers of the Italian Ghetto* (Berkeley and Los Angeles, 1992), and written numerous essays on Jewish cultural history in early modern Europe.